A WAR OF SECTIONS

How Deep South Political Suppression Shaped Voting Rights in America

STEVE SUITTS

NEWSOUTH BOOKS
An imprint of
The University of Georgia Press
Athens

NSB

Published by NewSouth Books
an imprint of the University of Georgia Press
Athens, Georgia 30602
www.ugapress.org/newsouthbooks/

Designed and set by Randall Williams
Printed and bound by Sheridan Books, Inc.

The paper in this book meets the guidelines for permanence and durability of the Committee on Production Guidelines for Book Longevity of the Council on Library Resources.

Most NewSouth/University of Georgia Press titles are available from popular e-book vendors.

Printed in the United States of America
23 24 25 26 27 P 5 4 3 2 1

Library of Congress Control Number: 2023941256
ISBN 9781588384911 (hardback)
ISBN 9781588385130 (paperback)
ISBN 9781588384935 (epub)
ISBN 9781588385048 (PDF)

A War of Sections

Also by Steve Suitts

Hugo Black of Alabama: How His Roots and Early Career Shaped the Great Champion of the Constitution

Hugo Black's Pocket U.S. Constitution: 'Keep One on You All the Time'

Overturning Brown: The Segregationist Legacy of the Modern School Choice Movement

To Elizabeth McDonald ("Miz Mac"),
Jean Ball, Bertha Godfrey, Gracia Culver

The teachers of Coffee High School
who helped me discover the joy and skills of learning
and the possibilities, perhaps the responsibility,
of working for a South beyond poverty and racism

". . . the climactic conflicts always were fought and won on Alabama soil."

— Martin Luther King Jr.
March 25, 1965

Contents

Acknowledgments

Writing a book of nonfiction accumulates more debts than an author can ever repay. In my case, it includes unpayable obligations over several decades to the activists who risked so much in doing the deeds that kept the ideals and practices of democracy alive and to scholars and archivists who preserve the history and records of our democratic struggles. Several of those activists, although certainly not all, are mentioned in the text and endnotes of this book as it relates to Alabama, and I hope readers will pause over their names to give the considerable respect they are due.

I also should express my particular appreciation for the men and women of the Alabama Department of Archives and History, Emory University Libraries, and the HathiTrust Digital Library. Their commitment to preserving and making accessible historical records, documents, and images enabled me to undertake essential research during a period when much of the world was in shutdown.

Many friends have been vital to my understanding of voting rights and their perspectives helped me develop the arc of this book. Among these who have departed this earth are Ralph I. Knowles, Lynn Walker Huntley, Peter Buttenwieser, Gwen Cherry, Julius Chambers, Ginny Montes, Bob Moses, Mary Frances Derfner, John Lewis, Chuck Morgan, Estelle and Eugene Witherspoon, Leslie Dunbar, Donald Strong, Johndelle Johnson, and, foremost among the equals, my late wife, Ginny. Those remaining are too numerous to mention by name, but I hope they know they are valued dear friends who have enriched my life and expanded my outlook about the past and the present.

I want to acknowledge my debts to my publisher, Suzanne La Rosa, and my editor, Randall Williams. They are a remarkable pair, who faithfully supported and improved my writing and share my devotion to uncovering the hidden meanings of our common places. Also I want to mention Allen Tullos, editor of the online journal, *Southern Spaces,* who has given me the opportunity to write deeply about the politics of voting and the place I have always called home.

My first involvement in politics was in 1954 in Bear Creek, Alabama, where on the cab of my maternal grandfather's pick-up truck, I yelled "Y'all Come!" in the high-pitched accent of a rural, four-and-a-half-year-old white boy, as James E. "Big Jim" Folsom arrived to give a campaign speech. He had adopted the phrase as his campaign slogan and would make it famous. I remembered that episode more than fifteen years later when as a college student I helped a sixty-nine-year-old Black woman in Greene County, Alabama, joyfully vote for the first time in her life. And, of course, I recalled it while writing this book. An old staple in the South's bluegrass and country music canon, "Y'all Come" begins with the line, "When you live in the country, everybody is your neighbor," signifying communities where there were no greater bonds of respect and belonging. This book is dedicated to all who have made and will make this simple Southern term the powerful, unqualified expression of their own democratic politics.

— Steve Suitts

A War of Sections

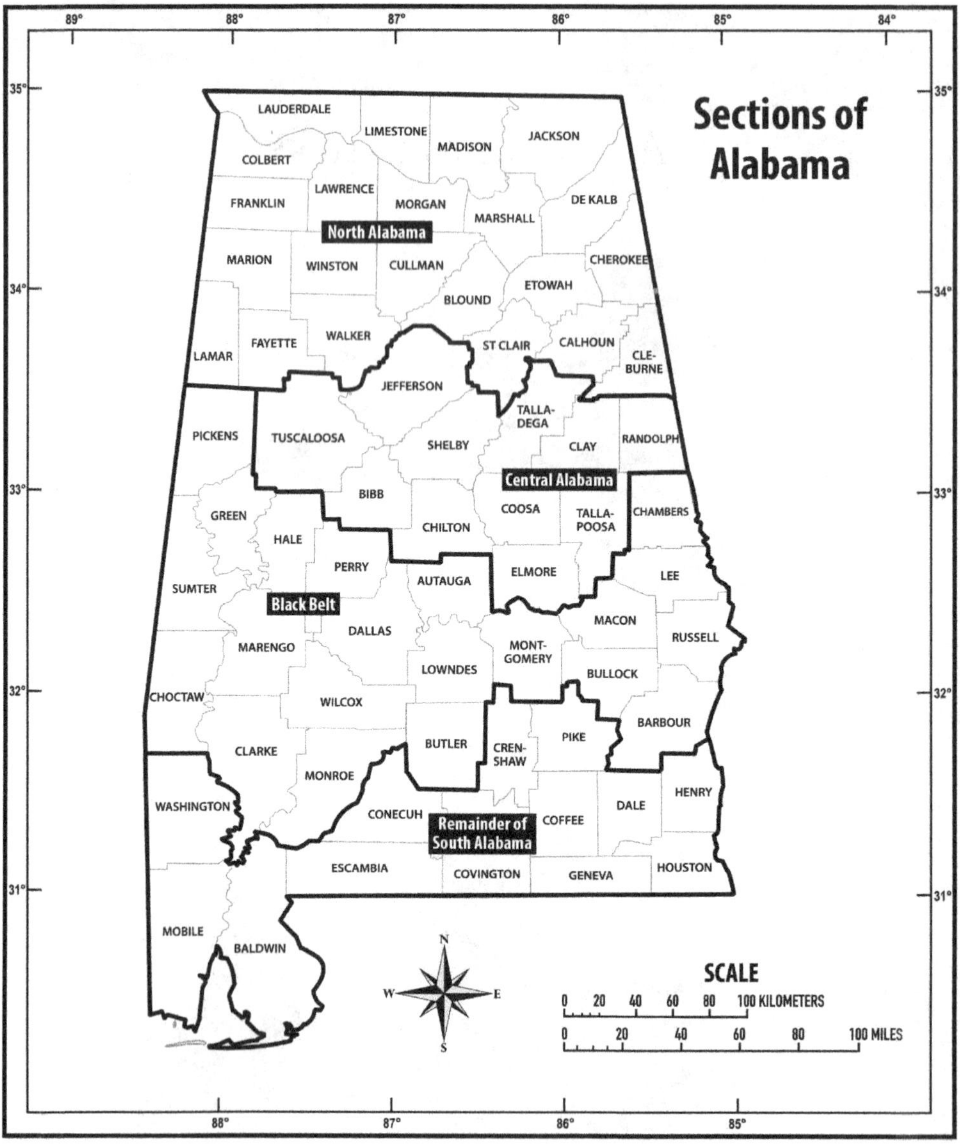

Sections of Alabama
North Alabama
Central Alabama
Black Belt
Remainder of South Alabama
LAUDERDALE
LIMESTONE
MADISON
JACKSON
COLBERT
LAWRENCE
MORGAN
MARSHALL
DE KALB
FRANKLIN
MARION
WINSTON
CULLMAN
CHEROKEE
BLOUND
ETOWAH
LAMAR
FAYETTE
WALKER
ST CLAIR
CALHOUN
CLE-BURNE
JEFFERSON
TALLA-DEGA
PICKENS
TUSCALOOSA
SHELBY
CLAY
RANDOLPH
BIBB
COOSA
TALLA-POOSA
CHAMBERS
GREEN
HALE
CHILTON
PERRY
AUTAUGA
ELMORE
LEE
SUMTER
MACON
DALLAS
RUSSELL
MARENGO
MONT-GOMERY
LOWNDES
BULLOCK
CHOCTAW
WILCOX
BARBOUR
CLARKE
BUTLER
CREN-SHAW
PIKE
MONROE
HENRY
WASHINGTON
CONECUH
COFFEE
DALE
ESCAMBIA
COVINGTON
GENEVA
HOUSTON
MOBILE
BALDWIN
N
S
E
W
SCALE
0 20 40 60 80 100 KILOMETERS
0 20 40 60 80 100 MILES
89° 88° 87° 86° 85° 84°
35° 34° 33° 32° 31°

Introduction—Alabama's Political Geography in Voting Rights History

'If the politics of the South revolves around any single theme, it is . . . the Black Belt'

Since passage of the Fifteenth Amendment to the U.S. Constitution in 1870, perhaps the most persistent theme of Deep South political history has been the state governments' undying resistance to the voting rights of African Americans. From Reconstruction into the twenty-first century, Southern politics has often been a battleground over the right of all citizens to vote and the powers of the federal government to enforce that right.[1]

Beginning in the 1870s, the South's Democratic "Redeemers" wrested control of state governments from biracial coalitions of Republicans, often as a result of campaigns of raw racial invective, violence, and illegal vote-counting. Afterwards, Mississippi led the region in holding a state constitutional convention to erect permanent electoral structures and standards for the avowed purpose of keeping "the negroes out of politics" and preventing "negro domination" through means that did not expressly violate the Fifteenth Amendment.[2] As V. O. Key, dean of Southern political science, observed in 1949: "The disfranchisement movement of the 'nineties gave southern states the most impressive systems of obstacles between the voter and the ballot box known to the democratic world."[3]

The South's turn-of-the-century era of disfranchisement was "one of the most dramatic and decisive episodes in American history," according to historian Michael Perman.[4] Even more far-reaching was how the Deep South states maintained their profoundly undemocratic societies for almost three-quarters of a century, as the politics of Jim Crow disfranchisement continued for decades into and well beyond the 1940s when Gunnar Myrdal observed that the South remained "the only region where Negro suffrage is a problem."[5]

Only the Deep South states, with the nation's largest Black populations, engaged regularly in fraudulent and violent methods of voter suppression as the means to enshrine in their state constitutions the political structures and rules that would enable a small number of white elites to maintain white supremacy for their own social and economic enrichment for generations. To accomplish the incredible feat—consolidating and sustaining undemocratic political control of an entire society over such a long period, the southern-most states did much more than adopt of an authoritarian constitution. They put in place and carried out laws, strategies, machinations, and acts of violence that also were unmatched in any other part of the country.

The Deep South states shared several common methods and maneuvers for establishing and maintaining a severely restricted franchise. Together they also constituted the bedrock of a Solid South in which the Democratic Party became the states' exclusive political machinery for advancing white supremacy and segregation. Although these states had their own differing white leaders and individual political dynamics, each's Jim Crow politics followed a similar basic narrative. Disfranchisement was preserved by an elite coalition amid challenges often from competing white interests within the states' differing sections and always by the unyielding efforts of the states' own Black citizens claiming their federal constitutional right to vote and to have each vote count equally in a fair, democratic process.[6]

As the Heart of Dixie, Alabama was not the first nor the last Southern state to hold such a constitutional convention, nor has its history of rebellion against inclusive democratic rights been unique in the South.[7] But it was the only state where voters were asked to ratify the work of a disfranchising convention and where over a period of five decades voters were required to decide whether to fortify or enlarge a state constitution's voting restrictions.[8] These elections and their campaigns provide a unique opportunity to examine the history of popular politics in Southern disfranchisement. They also have a living legacy. Today Alabama continues to operate under the constitution first adopted more than 120 years ago at its disfranchising convention and that, due to its unique, antiquated terms, is the nation's longest constitution, arguably the world's longest, with more than 900 amendments and 400,000 words.[9]

Before authorizing a state convention to establish constitutional impediments, the Alabama legislature passed in 1893 the Sayre Act, named after its author, an attorney who later became a leading justice of the Alabama Supreme Court (and was Zelda Sayre Fitzgerald's father). This initial legislative effort took place during the state's Populist era, when a loose alliance of Black and white interests joined to threaten the Redeemers' political rule. In effect, the Act indirectly restricted voting only to those who could read or write.[10] Less than a decade later, Alabama voters authorized a state constitutional convention and ratified the 1901 Constitution with a wider range of disfranchising provisions developed from prior Southern state conventions and other sources.[11]

"Throughout the next four decades," observed Steven F. Lawson, a careful scholar of the Southern struggles for Black voting, "the fear of mass Negro suffrage . . . perpetuated Alabama's passion to disfranchise its black citizenry."[12] Enforcement of the new constitution eliminated all but a token number of Black voters across the state within a few years. Decades later, in 1946, Alabama voters approved the Boswell Amendment (named after its sponsor, Representative E. C. "Bud" Boswell of south Alabama's Geneva County), requiring would-be Alabama voters to demonstrate an ability to understand and explain the state and federal constitutions and exhibit "good character" and "good citizenship"—all to the satisfaction of a local white registrar—before becoming eligible.[13] Even after qualifying, citizens had to pay a poll tax to vote. V. O. Key observed that in Alabama after adoption of the Boswell Amendment, any "proposal for white supremacy gains great support or at least people are fearful to dissent."[14]

These developments and their consequences are well known to historians and writers of Alabama history.[15] The state's leading historian, Wayne Flynt, has written that the adoption of barriers to voting meant "in Alabama, the constitution did not empower the people; it empowered the legislature. . . . Democracy was forfeited . . ."[16] Behind this simple, undisputed observation, often merely a preamble or afterthought to other considerations, lies the story this book tells—the untold saga of how over three generations a relatively small group of white men maintained political control of much of Alabama's government and its laws by controlling the state legislature and keeping democracy hostage by preserving the state's disfranchising constitution. As such, it captures the elemental political history of the Deep South.

This story begins in recalling an oft-forgotten primary conclusion that V. O. Key reached in his seminal study, *Southern Politics: In State and Nation*:

> It is the whites of the black belt who have the deepest and most immediate concern about the maintenance of white supremacy. Those whites who live in counties with populations 40, 50, 60 and even 80 per cent Negro share a common attitude . . .
>
> The black belts make up only a small part of the area of the South and—depending on how one defines black belt—account for an even smaller part of the white population of the South. Yet, *if the politics of the South revolves around any single theme, it is that of the role of the black belt.* Although the whites of the black belt are few in number, their unity and their political skill have enabled them to run a shoestring into decisive power at critical junctures in southern political history.[17]

Key and other scholars of this internal, sectional history illuminated how during moments of political upheaval—the Civil War, Reconstruction, the Populist era, and the Great Depression—Black Belt leaders found enough allies and means to block efforts at disturbing their dominant political rule. This book includes those historical periods in Alabama but is more focused on how Black Belt planters kept control of the state legislature and the state's politics with few interruptions across most of six decades, always making suppression of voting their first order of political business. It encompasses their alliances with the cities' Big Mules[18]—Alabama's historical term for large industrial and business interests—and how they found ways to shut down Black activists and to divide, conquer, or silence their white opponents, often from north Alabama[19] and occasionally from south Alabama's Wiregrass counties[20] bordering the Florida-Alabama line. This book also investigates how the Black Belt's rule of the Alabama legislature not only protected the section's economic and social systems that originated in slavery and continued through subordinating Black citizenship and Black labor but also brought home disproportionate, unearned appropriations and rewards that further enriched white planters and their families across generations.

Alabama's history of voter suppression was largely a war of sections within the state, involving what noted Southern historian Barbara Fields has persistently illuminated—the fact that "white supremacy held one meaning for the back-country whites and another for the planters."[21] But, of course, it involved more than Black Belt planters, their allies, and their white political opponents. It is also the story of those men and women, mostly African Americans, who attempted over the decades to overcome the barriers and systems of white supremacy, to beat the odds and even to change them in heroic struggles for full American citizenship, especially for its most powerful, equalizing right—a universal right to vote.

In bringing together the people who built and sustained disfranchisement as the linchpin of white supremacy in the era of Jim Crow, those who opposed Black Belt/Big Mules control, and those who pushed and pulled to expand a right to vote, this book offers a more complicated perspective than the one usually told in describing Alabama's "passion to disfranchise its black citizenry" during the last century. Details about the people, strategies, and chronology of events that shaped outcomes are essential in understanding this history, but a few simple statistical facts that unfold in this story introduce the foundation for this more complex, different view of Alabama disfranchisement.

Across six decades, Alabama's Black Belt-controlled legislature authorized eight statewide referenda among existing voters, the vast majority of whom were white, to establish or ratify constitutional provisions expressly offered to deny or limit African American voting. Two of the eight were passed through election fraud. One passed with 53.7 percent of the white vote; another passed by a margin of fewer than 400 white votes among more than 120,000 statewide votes; three referenda failed to pass among white voters; and the final amendment that passed had no legal effect. This tally suggests that while no one should doubt the Black Belt's passion for disfranchisement, there is ample reason to question such a sweeping, unqualified conclusion about all of Alabama's white citizens over three generations.

Another tally argues for the same caution. In the first six decades of the last century, the legislature permitted Alabama voters, a virtually all-white or majority-white electorate, to decide seven times on whether to limit the state's poll tax—established in the 1901 disfranchising Constitution and opposed over the years on occasion by labor leaders and north Alabama white political leaders and consistently opposed by the state's Black leaders. All were passed. Five statewide votes approved exemptions from the poll tax for war veterans, including Black ex-soldiers. Each veterans' exemption passed with overwhelming voter support. The 1953 referendum cut the maximum poll tax from $36 to $3, and the measure passed with 57 percent of the predominantly white electorate. Alabama voters were never allowed to vote on whether to eliminate the entire poll tax.

A final tally adds even more weight to why a renewed reckoning with Alabama's political history on voting rights is in order. Among the state's 67 counties, 17 voted against at least six of the seven constitutional amendments proposing to restrict voting and voted in favor of all seven proposals to limit the state's poll tax. Most of these predominantly white-populated counties are in north Alabama.

There is no doubt that direct, racist appeals in support of segregating the state's Black citizens from full citizenship always helped to produce votes among the white population to restrict Black suffrage in Alabama, and the "infamous Boswell Amendment" rightly became "synonymous with southern intransigence" in voting rights after 1946. Although overturned by federal courts, Boswell cast a long shadow as a blatant act of disfranchisement and arguably may be the starting point for the resurgence of the South's states' rights movement that at times offered nonracial reasons in opposition to the right of Blacks to vote. In her sweeping, Pulitzer-winning chronicle of Birmingham's modern civil rights movement, published 40 years after its passage, Diane McWhorter still remembered the law as "the notorious Boswell Amendment."[22]

But the Amendment was only one part of a longer, more nuanced story. Less well-known and largely unexamined was the adoption of the so-called "Boswell Amendment Jr.," the amendment ratified by Alabama voters in 1951 after the Boswell Amendment was declared unconstitutional. The new amendment aimed to preserve and expand those elements of Boswell that the federal courts had not found expressly unconstitutional.[23] It passed by only 369 votes among a mostly white statewide electorate.

Entirely forgotten is an earlier disfranchising state constitutional amendment that was put before Alabama's white voters in the aftermath of World War I. This 1921 referendum proposed to achieve the same purpose with much the same language as what passed 25 years later in Boswell. The "Evins Amendment" was sponsored by Black Belt state senator Robert Evins of Greensboro in Hale County. The *Alabama Official and Statistical Register* never recorded the referendum's county voting returns for posterity.[24]

The Evins Amendment failed to pass. In February 1921, Alabama's white voters refused to ratify the amendment—despite hearing the same dire warnings offered in 1901, 1946, and 1951 as to how a failure to do so would lead to "Negro domination." The factors and circumstances surrounding the 1921 amendment and its campaign for ratification were arguably unique, but most Alabama elections on voting rights had some exceptional circumstances that help to explain how a proposal passed or failed. Regardless, the Evins Amendment adds an important, revealing episode to Alabama's political history on voting rights—one where common economic interests appear to have moved white voters to reject overt racial appeals and fears of Black voting.

The addition of the Evins Amendment to the history of Alabama's resistance to Black voting does not reverse the dominant theme of Alabama political history nor does it reshape the historical arc of events and developments across the twentieth century. But it warrants inclusion and adds to the importance of reappraising the depth, content, geography, and mechanics of "Alabama's passion" for racial disfranchisement.

Therefore, this book is an inquiry into *how* a small number of political leaders in the Black Belt—a relatively small section of Alabama with a quite small white population—masterfully controlled and ruled the state government in their own self-interest for decades. It chronicles the details of a political war of sections within Alabama, a complex struggle amongst white folks, mostly between the Black Belt counties and north Alabama counties, over questions intermingling race and class amid aristocratic political corruption. It encompasses moments of small, incremental democratic promise and progress that involved, among others, white women. It portrays unrecognized struggles for voting rights that many Black Alabamians, mostly unknown outside their local communities, relentlessly undertook, too often on their own. And it suggests poignant moments of lost opportunity for a different direction in state history and perhaps even a contemporary, cautionary tale for the nation.

Finally, as Alabama's internal war of sections ended and morphed into a united state of white resistance—led in the 1960s by an adroit, amoral Black Belt politician—the story emerges of how events and leaders in the Heart of Dixie catapulted Alabama into a central role for shaping the nation's renewed pursuit of the universal right to vote. No less, it foreshadows political dynamics and legal strategies that countered this freedom movement and would reappear in the early decades of the twenty-first century in renewed forms and shapes to suppress universal voting in Alabama, the South, and nation. In other words, Alabama's political past became prologue for America's continuing democratic struggle over the right to vote.

PART 1

. . . The threat of the free exercise of the ballot by the Negro and the white masses alike resulted in the establishment of a segregated society . . . That's what happened when the Negro and white masses of the South threatened to unite and build a great society: a society of justice where none would pray upon the weakness of others; a society of plenty where greed and poverty would be done away . . .

— Martin Luther King Jr.
March 25, 1965

CHAPTER 1

A Forgotten Evins Amendment—Black Belt Defeat after a Fraudulent Past

'Carpetbag Scalawaggery, Dominated by the Most Depraved Considerations for Racial Equality'

As the end of World War I approached, several Alabama Big Mules and Black Belt leaders worried that federal wage and hour regulations set for vital war industries were making "slackers" of African American workers. Corporate attorney Forney Johnston informed Alabama's pro-business Governor Charles Henderson in 1918 that he had seen "at least three hundred darkies loafing around the streets of Birmingham." Johnson drafted model local legislation adopted by towns and cities that let white police arrest any person who lingered "in idleness during any working day in any calendar week." Black Belt business leader Lloyd Hooper of Selma also worried about the aspirations of returning Black veterans. As chairman of the governor's Council of Defense—composed of Black Belt planters and urban Big Mules—Hooper authorized a survey of white businessmen to gauge if there was increased talk among African Americans in the state about social equality or the right to vote.[1]

In a meeting with the Alabama congressional delegation, hosted by Hooper's friend, U.S. Senator Oscar W. Underwood, the Council's members agreed that the biracial political insurgence of the "Reconstruction period . . . is not expected to repeat itself," but that Alabama's state government should establish a state spy agency and maintain an all-white militia as important safeguards for maintaining white supremacy after the war. They also agreed that the state's "conservative citizens" must organize "to render it impossible for citizens of less stability to administer affairs in their own way." As one Talladega merchant observed, while "the colored population . . . will respond to the best [citizens], poor white folks give more trouble along these lines and cause more trouble than the negro."[2]

By the time the Alabama legislature met in July 1919, nine months after Armistice, the state's conservative leaders faced another potentially unsettling development. Congress had sent to the states a proposed Nineteenth Amendment that would give women the vote. Most Southern congressmen, including all but one of Alabama's, had opposed passage; after a long speech against the amendment, Underwood reminded a constituent that "the very basis of our civilization in the South is the control of the suffrage by the people of our state."[3]

Governor Henderson and the legislature's Black Belt members led opposition to ratification of the amendment. Among the leaders was Senator Robert B. Evins, an attorney who represented Hale and Greene counties in Senate District 32, which had a Black population of 78 percent. Evins had grown up in adjacent Perry County, with a similarly large Black population, and had been legal advisor to Governor Emmet O'Neal, a member of the suffrage committee in the 1901 constitutional convention that developed the state's disfranchising amendments (he had also opposed women's suffrage). O'Neal was from north Alabama, where the African American population was comparatively small, but he regarded the Black Belt as the guardian of white supremacy. "We know that in every great crisis of the Democratic Party, we turn to the Black Belt with confidence," he had told the convention delegates.[4]

Early in the 1919 session, Evins joined 19 others in a caucus of mostly Black Belt senators led by J. B. Ellis of Selma, who announced the group had enough votes to block ratification. Evins was on the group's steering committee to lead the attack.[5] One of the main lobbying groups against the amendment was the Women's Anti-Ratification Committee led by Alabama's First Lady, Mrs. Charles Henderson, and the group's legislative leader, Marie Bankhead Owens, daughter of U.S. Senator John Bankhead Sr. (a suffrage opponent) and wife of the director of the Alabama Department of Archives and History. These women refused to address the legislature in person since it would not befit a Southern lady to engage in political debate. Instead, they sent a memorial that Evins was to read to the senate.

Claiming to represent more than 80 percent of Alabama's white women, the Committee stated that as homemakers and mothers their role in society was to preserve home life, not to vote and hold office. They also saw a sinister plot by outsiders to enfranchise Black women. Through Evins, they asked the legislature "to protect us from this device of Northern Abolitionists" which threatened to tear down the barriers "you and your fathers have raised between Anglo-Saxon civilization and those who would mongrelize and corrupt it."[6]

Alabama Chief Justice John Anderson assured the legislature that the 1901 Constitution would continue to bar voting by all African Americans, both women and men, even if "the Susan B. Anthony amendment" were adopted, but his dispassionate statement of law was no match for the opponents' inflamed rhetoric.

In describing the federal amendment for women's suffrage, attorney John R. Tyson bellowed that it was the "Blood brother of the Fourteenth and Fifteenth Amendments . . . conceived in inequity and born in sin based on hatred and frenzied desire of carpetbag scalawaggery, dominated by the most depraved considerations for racial equality." Tyson explained that "Susie's Amendment," as opponents called it, was the first sign of a renewed attempt by the U.S. Congress to fix the qualifications for voting to "enable every negro man and woman in Alabama, and in the South, to vote." Remember the "conditions which prevailed during the Reconstruction days," Tyson warned. "Now, the young negro men who served in the great war, both as officers and privates, regard themselves as heroes and are demanding recognition politically and socially."[7]

Tyson's speech helped to carry the day for opponents and afterwards helped him win election over an incumbent for the Second Congressional District, then Alabama's Black Belt seat in Congress. Evins proposed the state senate resolution that officially rejected the women's suffrage amendment on behalf of the State of Alabama.[8]

Black Belt planters and the state's Big Mules also were worried about emerging labor problems, especially in and around Birmingham, and about increased economic clout and political activism among union members. Due to federal regulations to assure uninterrupted fuel, weapons, and military supplies in wartime, unions had enjoyed federal protection in organizing workers. Now with enlarged membership, the unions were unwilling to revert to prewar conditions when Alabama industries refused to recognize or negotiate with them about wages or working conditions.

Marie Bankhead Owens (ADAH).

Tensions and economic conflicts mounted. In the fall of 1919, a national steel mill strike threatened to shut down United States Steel's Birmingham plants. Electrical workers and a few other local unions also threatened to strike. In November, after occasional wildcat strikes in some Alabama mines, the United Mine Workers of America (UMW) began a nationwide strike that shut down much of the mining around Birmingham for two weeks until a federal judge ordered the union and mine owners back to the bargaining table with the federal coal commission. During this period, newly elected Governor Thomas E. Kilby moved state troops (later called the National Guard) close to Birmingham, and the county sheriff, after requesting the state send him a few machine guns for his deputies, enlisted a large, new contingent of special deputies, customarily paid by the mining companies. Industrialists hired dozens of their own private, armed guards. "America is not ready for a proletariat dictatorship," the editor of the *Birmingham Age-Herald* declared on behalf of the city's business leaders.[9]

In Montgomery, Evins bolstered the industrialists' cause by introducing S. 578 and S. 579, wide-ranging bills redefining and outlawing conspiracy. They allowed a fine of one thousand dollars and up to six months of hard labor for anyone who entered into an agreement or understanding with another person that they "shall not engage in or aid in carrying on public service" or who agrees to impede anyone from engaging in or working at a public service corporation—meaning any work advancing the public or public interest.[10] Alabama already had a law sponsored in 1903 by Representative Augustus Benners, local counsel for U.S. Steel, outlawing boycotting or conspiracy to prevent any corporation from carrying on lawful business. As the *Gadsden Times* observed, the new bills went further in punishing anything and anyone that attempted "to stop the wheels of industry in the state."[11]

The bills passed both houses of a legislature rushing to adjourn shortly after the start of Birmingham's steel mill strike and on the eve of the national miners' strike. Seeking political ground between warring factions, Governor Kilby let the bills die without his signature after an influential north Alabama legislator assured him the house did not really know what the senate bill contained. Representative Thomas Orr explained that the bills denied the "right of the laboring man to agree with one another to quit the employment of any public service corporation."[12]

Kilby did permit another anti-labor bill sponsored by Benners to become law in 1919. It effectively banned Northern labor agents, who were recruiting primarily African American workers, from doing business in Alabama. Its new definition of "labor agent" expressly excluded railroads transporting workers since industrial managers would need to import strike-breakers in the event the unions ordered a work stoppage in the Birmingham area.[13]

At the same time, unions also were working to enlarge their members' political clout. The Alabama Federation of Labor president, William Harrison, a UMW official, had been elected to the state house from Jefferson County, whose seven-member delegation often included industrialists' representatives such as Benners.[14] But the unions' political activities and agenda were not limited to Birmingham. In January 1919, for example, the central labor council in Montgomery was pushing to get every union man onto the poll tax rolls, and a special union committee planned to enlist more than a thousand union voters.[15]

A year later, the unions were continuing similar political work in the Black Belt. "The union men are registering and paying poll taxes in large numbers," attorney Robert Mangum wrote to Senator Underwood, who faced a serious primary election challenge in May 1920. Underwood had become a major voice for corporate interests and had worked through Forney Johnston, his advisor and manager of his 1914 campaign, to advance the railroad industry's interests after the war. Mangum had recently been appointed as assistant to Underwood's campaign chairman, Lloyd Hooper. "There can be no doubt that this is the result of systemic work on the part of these leaders. The railroad men especially are very active," Mangum observed. Black Belt state senator J. B. Ellis, owner of an iron works, also warned Underwood about the steep political challenge ahead.[16]

The unions were, in fact, mounting an all-out challenge to the planter-corporate coalition's economic and political control of Alabama, and they were willing to breach the color line to achieve their objectives. Faced with recalcitrant operators and owners, the UMW was preparing a massive strike involving more than twenty thousand workers in the coal fields of north Alabama. At the national convention of the American Federation of Labor (AFL) in June 1919, delegates authorized hiring a full-time "colored organizer for the Southern district of Alabama." A few weeks earlier in Mobile, during the annual state AFL convention, a union local in the mining area of Tuscaloosa County proposed a resolution declaring that the "disfranchise law be repealed and the negro be allowed the use of the ballot as in other states." The resolution was sent to a committee that then reported to the national convention that the AFL would strive "in the next legislative session to make every man a legal voter in the State of Alabama."[17]

Underwood's 1920 reelection campaign became the first line of engagement in this battle between labor and Alabama's controlling powers. Following Johnston's guidance, Underwood attacked first by portraying outside union bosses as the problem and himself as a victim of his loyalty to Alabama. "A man not of this state, sitting in his office in Washington, gives orders to defeat me . . .," Underwood proclaimed. "I am blacklisted because I represent you in the Senate and not this labor leader."[18]

Using information gathered from the undercover network that Lloyd Hooper's Council of Defense had erected, Johnston guided the Underwood campaign in publicizing the unions' recruitment and recognition of Black workers' rights as clear evidence of labor's "mongrelizing" intentions. But the ad campaign was upended once members of a printers' union tipped off state AFL President William Harrison. His attorney, Hugo L. Black, secured a state court order restraining the state's newspapers from running the ads. The newspapers, however, gave substantial news coverage to the court's decision, including the content of the embargoed ads. The Black Belt's J. B Ellis told Underwood that the court injunction turned out to be a "very great asset to your campaign." And the campaign for Underwood's main opponent, "Breck" Musgrove, provided even more publicity by running its own ads repeating the senator's charges in order to refute them. In the end, Underwood lost Birmingham and other industrial areas but won the May primary due to overwhelming support from Black Belt counties. It was a troubling political defeat for both Musgrove and for labor.[19]

'TO HELL WITH THE LAWS OF THE UNITED STATES . . .'

Four months afterwards, more than twenty thousand miners walked off the job in the greater Birmingham area, starting a violent, six-month strike that occupied the entire state and led to the death of miners, operators, and state soldiers, the eviction of thousands of families from company-owned houses, the building of a tent city for strikers' and their families, and martial law in the coal fields, where all speeches and meetings were prohibited. Many assemblies in union halls and churches were broken up by armed, company-paid guards, deputies, and state soldiers, one of whom declared when reminded of the guarantees of the U.S. Constitution: "To hell with the laws of the United States . . . I am getting my orders from General Steiner!" Brigadier General R. E. Steiner was the Montgomery corporate attorney who had served in the nineteenth century as a state legislator from Butler County (51 percent Black population in 1900).

As the strike persisted, both sides abandoned all pretense of law and order. Strikers used guns and dynamite to block "scabs." There were shoot-outs. After one gunfight that killed a miner and a soldier, white miner Willie Baird was charged with the murder of the soldier. As court testimony later revealed, nine state soldiers in plain clothes without masks forcibly took Baird from his jail cell to a deserted road where they riddled his body with bullets.

Many of the state's prominent leaders and businessmen rallied behind the soldiers after they were arrested and accused of lynching Baird. Former Governor B. B. Comer, a Black Belt native and owner of Avondale Mills in the outskirts of Birmingham, contributed to the soldiers' defense fund and argued publicly that even if the accused were proven guilty "it is still evident that there was strong provocation and an element of self-defense in the conduct of these men" who shot an unarmed man 12 times at close range with Winchester rifles.[20]

The Big Mules accelerated their public campaign to discredit the strikers and their union for promoting "social equality." Businessmen claimed the strike occurred because local Black laborers were misled by an "invasion of negro and white agitators." U.S. Steel's local attorneys circulated rumors of UMW meetings where Negro men sat next to white women. The chief of the state investigative unit complained in a widely publicized court filing that a UMW African American vice president was giving orders to a white female secretary at the union's Birmingham offices. And a coal mine owner charged that the local Black workers were striking only because the "union promised them equal votes and equal marriage laws."[21]

Black Belt legislators added restrictions on voter registration. In the 1919 session, a house member from Choctaw County (55 percent Black population) sponsored a bill effectively limiting registration that year to a few days in January—almost five months before the Democratic primary and more than ten months ahead of the general election. In the 1920 special session, draconian proposals advanced by Evins and other Black Belt state senators included abolishing the requirement to publish voter registration rolls and allowing local boards of registrars to remove voters from the rolls at any time "with or without cause without giving their reasons thereof." The house refused to accept the senate version of the bill so that a conference committee could work out a bill that both houses would pass.[22]

The conference committee abandoned some of the most severe restrictions, but Black Belt leaders negotiated significant new cutbacks in voter registration. First, local boards of registrars were authorized to open their books for less than four weeks in October 1920 during a special, one-time-only period to permit registering women newly franchised by the Nineteenth Amendment. After October, however, no one in Alabama could register to vote until July 1921—and only during a ten-day period.

Second, the law severely curtailed the future opportunity across the state for both men and women to register by establishing that: a) registration could take place only every two years—not every year; b) the maximum number of days most local boards of registrars could operate was cut from 60 to 40; and c) registrars were no longer required to spend a full day in each of the county precincts during each of the annual ten days of registration—only half a day. In addition, registrants had to pay a poll tax in an entirely separate process during a different period of the year in order to be qualified to vote.[23]

E. B. Gaston, editor of the *Fairhope Courier* in Alabama's Populist-inspired single-tax town, asserted that the legislature deliberately created confusion and inconvenience for women voters by failing earlier to provide in advance for an orderly process by which women could vote in the event other states ratified the Nineteenth Amendment. But he also saw something more menacing—a legislature that was making a "studied effort to eliminate as many voters as possible and to concentrate power in the hands of the few." He complained that settling disputes between groups of citizens, "for instance the coal miners and their employers," depended on all citizens having an "equal voice" in selecting those who make and enforce the laws.[24]

It was the specter of an "equal voice" that prompted Evins to sponsor another bill in the 1920 special session, proposing a state constitutional amendment that would add new requirements to who could qualify to register as a voter:

> A person to be entitled to register or vote must in addition to the qualifications already prescribed be of good character and must understand the duties and obligations of citizenship under a republican form of government.[25]

This 1920 proposal borrowed language from the 1901 Constitution that had provided a temporary set of qualifications by which males in Alabama could register and vote if they did so before the end of 1903. This "grandfather" clause included all men who fought for the United States in wars before the Civil War or who fought in the "War between the States" for the Confederacy as well as the male descendants of those soldiers. And it included all "persons who are of good character and who understand the duties and obligations of citizenship under a republican form of government."[26] Any Alabama man 21 years or older registered under any of the three qualifications became a voter for life.

A test of character for voting at the 1901 constitutional convention came from political leaders such as the Black Belt former governors Thomas Jones and William Oates. They had argued "to make intelligence and good character the test of the right to vote" since they believed "disfranchisement of the whole negro race would be unwise and unjust."[27] After the convention convened, the suffrage committee's majority report, drafted by Greene County's Thomas Coleman and others in the Black Belt, included "good character" as one of the temporary terms for permitting white males to vote.[28]

The "good character" clause prompted vigorous objections from delegates from north Alabama, including those representing Winston and St. Clair counties, where a goodly portion of current residents and their ancestors had not fought for the Confederacy and were ineligible under the soldier provisions of "grandfather" clauses. Objectors also believed the majority report's plan for a board of registrars appointed by the governor and other state officials to assess an applicant's "good character" would be equally disqualifying.

"You can take the words 'all persons of good character' in Section 4 of the majority report and qualify whoever you desire and also disqualify whoever you desire," complained N. H. Freeman, a Republican delegate elected from Winston County. "For when this partisan Board of Registration appointed by a partisan party or composed of a partisan party, the common people of Alabama has just as well say, 'Oh, King, where is thou crown?' for it will be equal to monarchial government, and we will be

Life certificate of voter registration (Paul Pruitt).

subject at their hands for disposal."[29]

Napoleon Bonaparte Spears, an old Populist-turned-Republican from St. Clair County (northeast of Birmingham), accused the Black Belt leaders of attempting to disfranchise Black and white voters. Spears declared, "You must admit that the negro got his right to vote from the National Government, and not from the State of Alabama. Can the State of Alabama undo what the National Government has done?"

Napoleon Bonaparte Spears (ADAH).

Spears called the proposed board of registrars who would apply the "good character" clause the head of "this serpent that is about to beguile this Convention." Since the current constitution (and all prior constitutions) had allowed any male citizen of voting age in Alabama to vote, Spears charged the majority report would turn the right to vote over to county registrars appointed by Democrats elected statewide to decide which Republicans, Populists, and Negroes would be disfranchised. He also belittled the proposed process of appeal since it placed the burden of proof on the citizen denied the vote, not on the board who denied him for lack of good character.[30]

Republican delegates were not alone in challenging the "good character" clause. Birmingham's Robert J. Lowe, chairman of the State Democratic Executive Committee, condemned the notion that a board of three men appointed in Montgomery to serve for two dollars a day for a few days each year would decide whose character in a community is good enough to enjoy the right to vote. "I say the law as written here," Lowe stated, "should determine whether I have a right to vote"—not a board whose judgment will vary from county to county. Lowe also feared that the boards in the Black Belt would become local instruments for continuing the "infamous frauds" in past voting.[31]

The convention's Black Belt leaders scoffed at these charges, with shouts of "Amen" from the Big Mules. The Black Belt chair of the suffrage committee, Thomas Coleman, became livid over Spears's defense of the U.S. Constitution's Reconstruction Amendments, asserting that "not one of our fair women has ever been assaulted in this land but that the infamous act may be traced to the Fifteenth Amendment."[32]

Convention president John Knox, perhaps Alabama's leading railroad attorney, assailed critics of the majority report while defending the Black Belt. He warned delegates that a board of registrars was the only practical way to "purge the electorate and separate the fit from the unfit." In attempting to explain the racial impact of the suffrage proposals, Knox actually confirmed the fears of Freeman, Spears and others from north Alabama when he assured them that the "plan which requires the voter to be a person of good character and understanding will exclude more negroes than white men." In short, in ridding the state of "the ignorant and vicious negro," whites could become collateral damage.[33]

Black Belt delegates claimed that disfranchising Alabama's Black voters, most of whom lived in their section of the state, was a political sacrifice on the part of white planters. Sumter County's Reuben Chapman told north Alabama delegates that "the Black Belt has come to this convention bringing a gift . . . turning over to you the majorities which we have heretofore held, ranging anywhere from 25,000 to 50,000 votes"[34]—in other words, up to 50,000 Black votes who in the past were counted *however the Black Belt's white planters saw fit* in order to win a majority vote in statewide elections.

In return, the Black Belt's white leaders insisted that it was only fair that the new constitution guarantee representation in the legislature and the Congress on the basis of total population—even though the Black population was to be effectively disfranchised and unable to participate in choosing elected representatives. Greene County's Thomas Coleman, a former justice of the Alabama Supreme Court claimed, "We ask no favors. We simply want justice."[35]

Emmet O'Neal, the north Alabama lawyer who ten years later would become governor with almost unanimous support in the Black Belt, joined in pleading on its behalf. "They have always been true and loyal," he told his fellow delegates. "We do not say to you [the Black Belt section] that we intend to reduce your representation to your voting strength."[36]

Most north Alabama delegates voted against the proposition, but the convention approved providing representation on the basis of total population, and the constitution's Section 284 prohibited this basis from being changed except by amendment. It meant that, so long as Black voters were disfranchised, the Black Belt and all majority-Black counties could count all Black persons for the purpose of increasing their white representation in the legislature and in Congress while counting them out of the voting booth and the government. Ironically, the deal gifted the Black Belt counties with more political power than Southern states had gained from the infamous 1787 compromise that counted slaves only as three-fifths of a person for drawing districts in the U.S. House of Representatives.[37]

These debates and decisions from 1901 echoed across the decades, including in 1920 as Evins shepherded his proposed constitutional amendment through the Alabama legislature. As a young lawyer in Greensboro, Evins did not participate in the 1901 convention, but his senior partner, Edward deGraffenreid, was an active delegate, as was, of course, Emmet O'Neal whom Evins would later serve as legal advisor during O'Neal's term as governor from 1911–1915. In addition, Evins was a direct beneficiary of the convention's endowment of Black Belt districts with oversized political power. Evins represented Senate District 32 in the Black Belt encompassing Hale and Greene counties, which had in 1920 a combined white population of 9,471 persons. By comparison, Senate District 3 in north Alabama was comprised of Blount, Cullman, and Winston counties with a combined white population of 71,004—almost seven and a half times more persons.[38]

Evins's bill set the statewide referendum for February 8, 1921—barely more than four months away. This choice for Election Day gave the senator's proposed amendment some clear advantages. When the bill passed, Birmingham and surrounding north Alabama counties were in what the newspapers would call "the most stupendous struggle between organized labor and organized industry Alabama has ever seen." Most of those counties failed earlier in the year to vote for Senator Underwood and decades earlier had opposed the 1901 Constitution. Now their voters would likely be preoccupied by economic struggles, not political changes on Election Day. Also, it was the time of year when bad weather was likely to make impassable many of the primitive dirt roads connecting small farmers to polling places in the hills of north Alabama.[39]

Elsewhere in the state, including the Black Belt, the miners' strike had outraged many voters who found it scandalous that white workers had joined or supported a walk-out in brotherhood with Black workers. This was exactly the racial threat that the 1901 Constitution meant to prevent. Voters in these counties were most likely to believe in the necessity of new constitutional safeguards against the "ignorant and vicious element"—especially after unexpected developments emerged barely three months before the referendum.

A small number of Black women showed up in parts of Alabama when the county boards opened their doors in October for the special one-time-only period to register newly franchised women. In Anniston, three Black women appeared and registered on the first day. In Jefferson County, among more than 23,000 white women who registered, "100 of the leading colored women of the community . . . were allowed to register after they had shown themselves able to fulfill the qualifications." The first African American woman was Carrie Tuggle, head of Birmingham's private school for Black children.

In Gadsden, two Black women registered amid reports that local Republican leaders were assisting them in order to increase their votes in the upcoming November general election. Handpicked by Governor Kilby, the board of registrars made no pretense to be nonpartisan. In public statements, the Democratic board accused local Republicans of exerting every effort to get Black women onto the voter rolls. The stated policy was only "registering white ladies," but the board reluctantly registered two Black women as if only to report that they were recruited by the "daughter of one of the leading republican citizens." The controversy became an issue in the local congressional race with both sides accusing the other of advancing Black women's voter registration.[40]

Black women registered in a few places in south Alabama, although the numbers were also symbolic. In Montgomery, 35 Black women and 20 Black men were among the total of 4,500 new registered voters. In the Black Belt, registrars in Marengo County registered three Black women among 888 new voters. But the *Dothan Eagle* reported in Houston County that "there were no negro women to register," as was true in most counties.[41]

During this period, south Alabama newspapers reported Black women attempting to register in substantial numbers in other Southern states. "You have noticed in some Southern states," wrote a front-page letter in Elmore County's *Weekly Herald*, "negro women are registering in greater numbers than white women." In Bullock County, the newspaper reported that in Florida the ballot was being "placed in the hands of negro women indiscriminately," and the *Montgomery Times* reported that thousands of Black women were registering in Kentucky.[42]

These reports helped shape the overall political climate for Evins's strategy of a quiet, focused campaign in south Alabama for passage of his amendment. It began in earnest in January 1921, when by law the governor started advertising a proclamation about the upcoming referendum in a newspaper in every county. Apparently, Evins had not consulted closely with the leaders of the state Democratic Party in developing campaign plans, or the state's political leaders considered it unnecessary or unwise to highlight the amendment campaign. The party's state executive committee failed to adopt any resolution or allocate any funds in support of passage, although some influential Big Mules, their attorneys, and Black Belt representatives sat on the committee.[43]

'To Assure the Continuation of White Supremacy in a Legal Manner'

By mid-January, problems were evident in Evins's low-key strategy. The *Montgomery Times* described the amendment as a way to disfranchise Blacks and whites. Later, the *Union Springs Herald* suggested the amendment was necessary to keep women (not just Black women) with bad character from voting. The *Montgomery Advertiser* complained about the absence of a more organized campaign for passage, a sentiment echoed in other Black Belt papers. The Columbus, Georgia, newspaper knew more about the amendment than did the newspaper across the Chattahoochee River in Russell County (76 percent Black population), which only reprinted the former's editorial.[44]

Also, Evins failed to consult with the editor of the newspaper in Greene County, a county he represented in the state senate, about the true purpose of the amendment's requirement of "good character" before a column appeared complaining that the amendment might exclude "some Confederate Veterans," who some believed did little more than hang around the courthouse until their state pension checks arrived each month. And the editor refused to retreat even after Evins belatedly assured him that the amendment was of the "utmost importance especially for the Black Belt."[45]

Evins enlisted other Black Belt leaders and probate judges to inform voters of the amendment's true purpose. Former Congressman W. B. Craig, whose uncle was a delegate in the 1901 convention, explained the true purpose of the "good character" amendment to the Selma Kiwanis Club. In Evins's hometown, Greensboro newspaper editor William E. W. Yerby joined with 12 leading local Democrats in an open letter informing voters that the "sole purpose of the amendment is to assure the continuation of white supremacy in a legal manner." [46]

The *Abbeville Herald* editor echoed this view, assuring readers that the amendment would deny the right to vote to Blacks without disfranchising any whites. Autauga County's probate judge publicly endorsed the amendment in the *Prattville Progress,* which also printed an Evins letter explaining that women's suffrage made the amendment necessary to assure "negro elimination from Alabama politics." In Escambia, Evins's letter to the editor repeated much the same language and argument, adding that "unless this 'good character amendment' is adopted, the door is wide for negro domination in Alabama and their leaders know it."[47]

The only Alabama leaders who organized opposition to the amendment came from labor. As AFL leaders worked across the state to maintain its members' support for the miners' strike, they also spread word that the Evins amendment was attempting to allow three persons on a board of registrars to decide who are "sufficiently intelligent to vote" and who shall "pass satisfactorily an examination as to moral character." In its resolution, the local central labor council in Decatur, representing a dozen north Alabama labor crafts, condemned the amendment as the effort of "a few people controlling the elections of the state."[48]

The trial of the soldiers accused of lynching UMW member Willie Baird only exacerbated the union members' distrust about those controlling Alabama. During January, the soldiers' attorneys won a change of venue after claiming their clients could not get a fair trial in Walker County. Before and during the trial, the defense strategy involved discrediting the good character of those testifying for the prosecution while calling scores of witnesses to testify to the "good character" of the men who shot Baird in cold blood. There were rumors that coal operators had created a large slush fund to help the soldiers' case in and outside the courtroom. The defense also called as a potential witness UMW's local African American vice president, thus requiring him to sit in the courtroom where his presence reminded the jury of white farmers that Baird had belonged to an interracial union that Black men helped run.[49]

In the last days before the referendum, Evins attempted to use the statewide press to focus on "good citizenship" more than "good character," while selectively employing a crude, early twentieth-century dog whistle for disfranchising Blacks. The *Montgomery Advertiser*, the paper of record for the Black Belt, urged adoption since the measure was "protective and preventive" in nature and proposed the same language as had the 1901 Constitution's temporary sections. The *Advertiser* suggested the addition would avert "the conditions from which Alabama escaped in 1901." Two days before the election, Evins published in the *Advertiser* a lengthy defense. He argued that passage of the Nineteenth Amendment had raised the "spectre which overshadowed us from Appomattox to the adoption of the Constitution of 1901"—an electorate with a large percentage of the "vicious and ignorant." The amendment, Evins argued, was how to prevent Negro women from voting without provoking "Federal interference."[50]

In Birmingham, the newspapers ran a chorus of supporting voices from the Big Mules. Corporate attorney Jelks Cabannis urged adoption to prevent "one of the vicious element, man or woman," from meeting the qualifications to vote. Former governor Emmet O'Neal warned against the dangers of the "vicious element"—Black women who as a mass of new voters "threatened our future with peril it would be folly to ignore."[51]

Perhaps to the shock of many, especially in the Black Belt, white voters engaged in folly by defeating the Evins Amendment—28,723 "yes" or 38 percent, against 46,984 "no" votes. The Black Belt provided huge margins for the proposal. In Dallas County (Selma), the vote was 744 in support of the amendments and only 55 opposing it. In Montgomery County, 1,072 voters supported it and only 194 opposed it. But Birmingham's Jefferson County and many north Alabama counties provided large margins in opposition. Jefferson cast 1,208 vote as "yes" and 6,384 "no" votes. In Walker County, 577 votes supported the amendment but 3,523 voted "no."[52]

The amendment's supporters suggested unique circumstances explained its defeat. Some complained there had not been enough education of the voting public about the necessity for the Evins Amendment. Some blamed a low turnout. In Mobile County, for example, the amendment won with 71 percent of the vote but in an unusually small total turnout (955) due to the city simultaneously celebrating Mardi Gras. The Selma newspaper editor said election officials failed to open more than half the city's polling places. He and other Black Belt editors also blamed the "recalcitrant" counties of north Alabama that "will not stay hitched to the Democratic bandwagon."[53]

In contrast, Alabama's struggling labor movement claimed the defeat as its victory. A week after the special election, at a large rally in Birmingham's Bijou Theater, striking UMW officers and other labor officials lambasted Governor Kilby and mine owners for colluding to break the strike, but they boasted that labor was responsible for the defeat of the Evins Amendment. Voting returns generally support their claim. The largest turnout and the heaviest votes against the amendment appeared in the counties primarily affected by the strike: Jefferson, Walker, Cullman, Shelby, and Blount. There were also large "no" turnouts in Morgan and Colbert counties where labor unions were active in north Alabama, although much less so in Etowah (Gadsden) where the issue of Black voting had been injected into a close congressional race.[54]

Also, some of Alabama's newly enfranchised white women may have distrusted any new voting restrictions that were proposed by a legislature that had opposed women's right to vote. A north Alabama editor explained that his county strongly opposed the amendment because voters were "getting tired of so much 'regulating' . . . of the suffrage." At Mobile Bay, populist editor E. B. Gaston noted that, with white women casting half the votes, his town voted 95 to 13 against the amendment, "showing the almost unanimous sentiment of Fairhope against any further opportunities . . . to limit the suffrage in this state."[55]

The defeat of the amendment did not diminish Evins's own political career. Within the next two years, he was elected chairman of the state Democratic Executive Committee and president of the Alabama Bar Association. In 1924, he was appointed vice chairman of the state's Underwood for President campaign.[56]

The returns for the February election were preserved in state government files, but, unlike most other referenda, especially relating to registration and voting, the county election returns for the Evins amendment were never recorded in the *Alabama Official and Statistical Register*, compiled and published under the guidance of Marie Bankhead Owens, who had succeeded her husband as State Archivist. The 1923 *Register* referred to the referendum and only its statewide total votes in a section entitled "Miscellaneous Statistics."[57]

'ELIMINATION OF THE IGNORANT NEGRO VOTE . . . A SOURCE OF MUCH CORRUPTION'

Obscuring the defeat of the Evins Amendment in the state's official public record was a small, but an essential contribution to the intellectual project of the Black Belt planters and Big Mules: sustaining over time a public narrative that most white Alabamians supported the state's restriction on who should be allowed to vote. Preserving the idea and ideal of white unity for a limited suffrage was useful, if not at times vital, in assuring both continuity and legitimacy for disfranchisement as a political weapon, for the power and control that disfranchisement gave Black Belt planters and their allies, and for the 1901 Constitution which had enshrined both the weapons and the control through fraudulent elections.

In the decades following the adoption of the 1901 Constitution, scholarly journals and Alabama historians made no mention of the controversy that surrounded the 1901 Constitution's fraudulent referendum. Alabama historian William Garrott Brown wrote as early as 1903 simply that the constitution "was ratified by the people." Joel Campbell DuBose followed this approach in the 1908 and 1915 editions of his *Alabama History*. "After the constitution had been framed, it was submitted to the people," Dubose wrote. "The records of election returns gave a majority of votes in favor of ratifying it. By proclamation of the governor, it went into effect on Thanksgiving Day."[58]

This benign neglect of election fraud was not confined to historians from the Black Belt. In *The Southern Oligarchy* in 1924, former Jeffersonian Democrat William H. Skaggs full-throatedly condemned Alabama's history of election corruption and subterfuge, especially in the Black Belt. He lambasted those who had argued that the adoption of the 1901 Constitution and its disfranchising clause was the best means for eliminating dishonest elections and preserving white supremacy. But he wrote not a word about the questionable nature of the 1901 referendum.[59]

In the first edition of his influential history, Albert B. Moore, head of the University of Alabama's history department, made no mention of the vote to ratify the 1901 Constitution but wrote that "the United States Supreme Court held that the suffrage clauses of the new constitution were not repugnant to the Federal constitution. This was the last straw for the negro. He was disfranchised, and the drama of political Reconstruction was over."[60] In later editions, Moore acknowledged vocal opposition to ratification but afterwards wrote that the "leaders for the constitution conducted a vigorous campaign of 'education' upon its merits and secured its adoption by a majority of 26,879 votes." Perhaps to vouch for the uprightness of the election, a footnote also observed that Oscar W. Underwood was chairman of the ratification campaign. Moore wrote: "By the elimination of the ignorant Negro vote, which was a source of much corruption, the constitution contributed a great deal to the improvement of elections in Alabama."[61]

Emerging later in the century to lead a new generation of Southern historians, C. Vann Woodward both documented and exposed the glaring facts surrounding the vote to ratify. Writing at mid-century, Woodward pointed out that Alabama's white counties flatly turned down the constitution while "the black counties carried it by majorities often exceeding the white voting population." Malcolm C. McMillan, in his seminal study of Alabama constitutional development, perceived the reality of a fraudulent election, but he qualified his findings with softer language and an apparent assumption that in 1955 he would need a smoking gun to prove swindling of votes in 1901. "Although one cannot prove that the large Negro vote in the black counties in favor of the constitution was fictitious," McMillan wrote, "a study of the election returns, contemporary sources, and Black Belt voting practices has convinced the author that in some counties almost every eligible Negro was 'voted' although thousands never appeared at the polls."[62]

In 1958, a young Black scholar finished his dissertation on "Negro Suffrage and Politics in Alabama since 1870" at Indiana University. Joseph Brittain's research led him to conclude that in the 1901 election "most Negroes stayed away from the polls, but where they did vote, they cast their ballots against the constitution." Yet, even after reviewing the far-fetched voting returns in the Black Belt, Brittain avoided calling the election fraudulent although he quoted the charges of constitution's opponents that "it had been 'counted in' by the fraudulent counting of the Negro vote whether he appeared at the polls or not."[63]

Sheldon Hackney, in his 1969 study of this period of Alabama history, rehearsed the same basic facts about the voting patterns used to ratify the constitution, but added nothing to the interpretation except an exclamation point and this benediction: "Again the Black Belt provided the margin of victory." In 1974, in his study using quantitative methods to examine the history of suffrage restrictions, J. Morgan Kousser cited basically the same election returns and contemporaneous statements of intent that others had recorded from the Black Belt. But his conclusion conveyed a clear indictment: "the Negro vote was not merely suppressed; it was counted for suffrage restriction."[64]

In his 1985 book on the Tuskegee civil rights movement, Robert J. Norrell did not shy away from a similar conclusion about the 1901 election: "In Macon County the constitution was ratified by a large majority, a result in all likelihood of vote fraud." A decade later, most Alabama historians abandoned reluctance to declare the election for what it was. "The contest was a repetitive story in Alabama's history of 'stolen' elections, fabricated returns, and a perjured black vote," wrote Leah Rawls Atkins in 1994. In the same year, Bailey Thomson wrote a public essay entitled "Conceived in Fraud," concluding that supporters of the 1901 Constitution had "imposed their will through a criminal act." More recently, Wayne Flynt left no doubt as to his scholarly judgment. After writing that Black Belt voting "fraudulently gave Alabama a new constitution," he concluded: "The organic law that governed Alabama in the twentieth century was, like the political process that created it, stained with racism and corruption. And the progenitors of this political bastardy were Alabama's finest, wealthiest, and self-proclaimed 'best' citizens."[65]

This recent scholarly assessment is based on both clear statements of intent by those white leaders who were involved in 1901 and overwhelming evidence of manipulated, fraudulent vote-counting. In the 1901 convention, Black Belt leaders made it plain that they would resort to fraud if necessary to adopt the governing document they desired. A delegate from majority-Black Russell County admitted that the white "men of the Black Belt . . . are to be sent home to perpetuate the most outrageous fraud in all the history of fraud"[66] in order to get the constitution ratified. And the evidence is unmistakable that they did exactly that. In Talladega, for instance, the city precinct reported 849 votes for and 0 votes against the amendment in a town with 692 white men and 622 Black men of voting age, including several African American faculty and students at the private, historically Black Talladega College. The statistical data and contemporaneous accounts from Black Belt leaders and newspapers leave no doubt about the certainty of present-day conclusions.[67]

Today's prevailing judgment concerning election fraud carries over to the earlier statewide vote that authorized white leaders to convene Alabama's disfranchising convention. The same problems of fraud in votes for the adoption of the constitution are found in the April 1901 referendum enabling the convention—a conclusion that earlier scholars were more willing to express without deflecting qualifications. "The 'greatest steal' in Alabama's history took place," according to Joseph Brittain, who examined the "warped, deceptive returns" from majority-Black counties in an election where the margin of victory was less than 25,000 votes[68] (a smaller margin than in the later ratification vote).

Malcolm McMillan recorded similar voting patterns and wrote that "it is safe to conclude that even on an issue so vital to the Negro as his franchise, the Black Belt leaders could still manipulate the Negro vote." McMillan's confidence in his own published assessment seemed bolstered by his discovery in the minutes of the State Democratic Executive Committee clear admissions of an intent by members in majority Black counties to commit fraud. For example, a member from Sumter County reported that his county had "four negro voters to one white vote," no white Republican, and "buried the last Populite about a month ago. All we want is a small vote and a large count."[69] In Sumter, 1,440 voted for holding the convention, with 69 against it, in a county with 1,419 white men and 5,304 Black men of voting age.

In six other Black Belt counties, votes for the convention exceeded the total number of white men who were old enough to vote. In Dallas County, for example, for the voting to be honest and accurate, every one of the 2,525 white males 21 years and older in the county had to have voted for a convention and 3,143 Black males 21 years and older in the county also must have voted for the disfranchising convention. There were only 200 "no" recorded votes in Dallas. In other words, the election returns in Dallas could have been non-fraudulent only if every eligible white man showed up and voted for the convention and almost 15 times more African Americans voted to hold a convention to disfranchise themselves than those voting to keep the right to vote.

In Greene County, the election could have been honest and accurate only if every eligible white man showed up and voted for the convention and almost 32 times more African Americans in the county voted for a disfranchising convention than voted against it. When computed for all of Alabama's majority-Black counties, the number of "yes" votes exceeded "no" votes by an accumulated margin of more than 28,000 votes in a statewide election decided by a margin of less than 25,000 votes.[70]

Amid this background, the defeat of the Evins amendment in 1921 ran counter to the widely accepted idea that the state's passion for disfranchisement had been shared by most of Alabama's white voters for generations, including those who ratified the 1901 disfranchising convention and the 1901 Constitution it produced. Without Black votes to fraudulently count, however, the Black Belt had little choice in 1921 but to accept the outcome of the referendum. It could not be overturned by old means. But it could be hidden in obscurity so that in future years the idea that most white voters in Alabama were always united as one body for restricting the franchise in the name of white supremacy would continue largely unexamined and unchallenged as a proven fact and a unifying force. Such an idea helped build a common perception of the present and of the future, but no less it could erase from common memory a past that involved as much sectional rivalry as statewide unity, especially over the notions of voting and representation.

This strategy seems to have worked. Twenty five years after the Evins Amendment's defeat, virtually the same language would become a part of the infamous Boswell Amendment, and not one word can be found in the raw, bitter public discussion during the 1946 campaign about the Evins Amendment, its language, or its rejection by Alabama's white voters.

CHAPTER 2

Boswell, Boswell Jr., and Big Jim

'The Negro Will Never Be Fit for the Ballot'

Forty-five years after the fraudulent passage of the 1901 Constitution, Alabama voters approved the Boswell Amendment, whose voting restrictions included some rejected in 1921 as the Evins Amendment. There is no evidence that the Boswell measure was enacted through election fraud, although there is no doubt that truth-telling was a rare commodity and gross racism was the standard message during the campaign for its passage.

The Amendment essentially added new provisions requiring a voter to "understand and explain any article of the Constitution of the United States in the English language" and empowered a local board of registrars to do what Senator Evins had proposed—register only persons "who are of good character and who understand the duties and obligations of good citizenship under a republican form of government."[1]

V. O. Key described the 1946 campaign for the Amendment as a steady, loud beating of the "drums for white supremacy"—a conclusion joined by virtually all scholars.[2] But earlier campaigns for erecting constitutional voting restrictions also were advanced with the drumbeat of white supremacy, and they failed to attract a legitimate, honest count of a majority of voters. Thus the Boswell Amendment was only the first constitutional proposal restricting voting to win the approval of a majority of Alabama voters. That fact alone warrants a fresh, more nuanced examination of the campaign and the referendum returns.

The U.S. Supreme Court's 1944 decision in *Smith v. Allwright,* outlawing the all-white Democratic primaries, confronted one of the major bulwarks of white control of Southern politics. Naturally, it was condemned as a federal intrusion and compelled segregationists to fortify white supremacy.[3] A year later, World War II concluded while the Alabama legislature considered the Boswell Amendment. Both white and Black Alabamians had fought for the global survival of democracy against fascism and imperialism, and leading Alabama Democrats feared that the returning Black soldiers would become more assertive at home about their democratic rights, including voting.[4]

The strategies and messages of Boswell proponents shared much with prior efforts to suppress voting, but their campaign differed from the past in one distinct respect: it was not spearheaded publicly by Black Belt leaders. Instead, the Amendment's sponsor and one of its chief public advocates was Edward Calhoun (E. C.) Boswell from Geneva County in south Alabama's Wiregrass section. Boswell led his county's Democratic Party and was a longtime member of the state Democratic Executive Committee; he had served as a page at the 1901 convention and by 1946 was hailed

E. C. Boswell (ADAH: Robert Adams, Birmingham News*)*

as a leading constitutional lawyer. As a state representative, Boswell chaired the interim joint committee on constitutional reforms and actively supported reapportioning the state legislature to reduce Black Belt political power. Boswell also was not a corporate lawyer, though he was certainly a conservative who preached "a gospel to save white supremacy."[5]

As chairman of the joint committee, Boswell proposed the Amendment in the summer of 1945 and later was virtually the only legislator who spoke on the floor of the house or senate concerning its necessity (the senate met as a committee of the whole to allow Representative Boswell to speak on the senate floor). After the bill setting up the referendum passed, Boswell campaigned for adoption of the Amendment, especially in and around the Wiregrass section and across parts of north Alabama. The references to "Representative E. C. Boswell of Geneva" as sponsor were so frequent that the Amendment took on his name, offering evidence that this effort was not the machination of Black Belt politicians.[6]

Statewide, perhaps the most prominent proponent of the Amendment was Gessner McCorvey, a Mobile attorney and chair of the state Democratic Party Executive Committee who had defeated Boswell and others for the post in 1939. McCorvey was from Hale County in the heart of the Black Belt, but after graduating law school in 1903 he moved to Mobile where he came to represent important local politicians such as Congressman Frank Boykin and large shipping and railroad companies. McCorvey was involved from the beginning in helping to fashion the Amendment's language and support.

Throughout the campaign, however, the chairman spoke only as a representative of the statewide Democratic Party, not as an attorney and certainly not as a corporate attorney. He orchestrated a unanimous resolution within the party's state executive committee urging adoption of the Amendment and authorizing the party to spend $3,500 placing large ads in practically every weekly newspaper in the state, which rarely had such significant out-of-town ad revenue.[7]

In his role as spokesman for the party of white supremacy and state executive committee members from throughout the state, McCorvey largely escaped criticism as a corporate attorney doing the bidding of the

Big Mules. In the paid ads that McCorvey placed, he referred to criticism from unnamed sources aimed at "our State Democratic Executive Committee," which he noted unanimously favored the Boswell Amendment. In counties where the local Democratic executive committee also publicly endorsed the Amendment, McCorvey positioned his role as a spokesman for the local party, not for Big Mules and Black Belt planters.[8]

A third visible proponent of the Amendment, especially in the Birmingham area, was Horace Wilkinson, an enduring demagogue of the state's bare-knuckled politics who over the years had been both for and against almost every major political group and many statewide officials. Now a devout member of the Democratic Party of white supremacy, Wilkinson had been a state leader of the 1928 movement to defeat the Democratic presidential nominee, Al Smith, and elect Republican Herbert Hoover. In recent years, however, Wilkinson allied with some of the state's New Deal Democrats, and in 1945 and 1946 he burnished his reputation as advisor and reputed "master mind" behind the progressive governor-elect, James E. "Big Jim" Folsom.[9]

In arguing for the Amendment, Wilkinson was both brutal and brutish in his public attacks about Black Alabamians. His speeches and writings attacked all African Americans as unfit for full citizenship. In a well-publicized debate, he claimed, "Equality means that the white race is asked to dilute its strength by swapping some of its white blood for the blood that runs in the Negro. A superior breed is thus to be contaminated by interbreeding with an inferior one . . . The Negro's racial constitution cannot be educated out of him any more than the pigment in his skin can be educated out of him. Education will not remake a racial constitution. The Negro will never be fit for the ballot under our form of government."[10]

Governor Chauncey Sparks, a Black Belt conservative, joined the gallery of pro-amendment leaders. Sparks had won election in 1942 primarily because the largely popular Bibb Graves died during the campaign. Sparks did little more than issue a statement supporting the Amendment, but his predecessor, Frank Dixon, a war hero and lawyer for Birmingham's Big Mules, actively campaigned for adoption, including broadcasting a statewide radio address the night before Election Day.[11]

Opposing the Boswell measure was a similarly eclectic group. Its most active, visible leader was Montgomery attorney Richard Rives, a major political operative for the late former Governor Graves and a close advisor to Lister Hill, who had followed Hugo Black into the U.S. Senate as a New Deal Democrat. Rives's recent role in state politics and law was more complicated. He supported conservative Sparks in 1942 and a Graves ally in the May 1946 primary—instead of the upstart, progressive Folsom. Also, as an attorney, Rives had recently represented south Alabama counties hauled into court by the National Association for the Advancement of Colored People (NAACP) for obstructing Black voter registration and voting. But as a public citizen, Rives argued for the defeat of the Boswell Amendment.[12]

Other state leaders on record opposing Boswell included the New Deal Democrats: U.S. Senator Lister Hill, U.S. Senator-Elect John Sparkman, Alabama Attorney General-Elect Albert H. Carmichael, and most importantly Big Jim Folsom, who had won a runoff in a landslide victory in June. But, only Rives and Carmichael actively and publicly campaigned against the Amendment, and Rives mostly in the Montgomery area. Both Hill and Sparkman issued public statements opposing Boswell but did no more.[13]

The most vocal, visible opponents of the Amendment were daily newspaper editors. For example, Charles G. Dobbins, editor of the *Montgomery Advertiser*, did far more than express his view on the editorial pages. Dobbins traveled the state speaking against the Amendment, debated Governor Dixon at perhaps the most widely covered event during the Amendment campaign, and appeared on radio programs, including a paid broadcast heard in parts of the state on election eve. Other daily newspapers whose editors opposed the Amendment included the *Birmingham News* and the *Anniston Star*.[14]

These newspapers had savagely opposed Folsom's election a few months earlier and were often associated with his named opponents—the Big Mules and Black Belt planters. The *Advertiser*, a longtime voice of Black Belt power and interests, had ridiculed Folsom as the state's best entertainer who believed "when you have good music and big feet the problems of State

James E. Folsom Sr. (ADAH).

Government will disappear." A *Birmingham News* editorial, "The Desire Is Not Enough," condemned a "shallowness and expediency that would mark his administration if, unhappily, Mr. Folsom should be elected." Folsom supporters were so upset with the *News* that they ran ads asking "WHY? Does the *Birmingham News* Refuse to Print the TRUTH about 'BIG JIM' FOLSOM" and warned "The Big Mules and The Big Press have decreed the political death of ex-GI 'Big Jim' Folsom." In its editorial, the *Anniston Star* called Folsom "mentally dishonest" and proclaimed that his election would be "the greatest calamity that has befallen Alabama since the days of Reconstruction after the Northern invasion."[15]

The "lying newspapers," as Folsom famously pegged Alabama's daily press in late 1946, were far more prevalent and visible than the Governor-elect in the campaign opposing the Amendment. Folsom stated his opposition during his June runoff campaign and later announced he would "take the stump to defeat the measure." But he did not mount a campaign against Boswell and did not provide "political direction" for the coalition opposing it.[16]

In fact, after securing the Democratic nomination, Folsom was out of Alabama for most of the summer of 1946. In the fall, after announcing in September that he would speak against the Amendment which would appear on the November 6 ballot, Folsom departed for the national American Legion convention in California where he stayed for weeks visiting Hollywood and other attractions. He returned home close to the second week of October and embarked on a series of rallies, but they were events to raise funds in Alabama for the national Democratic Party—with no reported mention of the Boswell Amendment. In mid-October, Folsom's office announced that he would make a statewide radio address opposing Boswell, and two weeks before the referendum his office issued a statement of Folsom's position on all nine proposed constitutional amendments. But a week from Election Day he was in Washington, D.C.[17]

On the eve of the referendum, short news articles and paid ads in the daily newspapers reported that Big Jim would make an address of fifteen minutes at 6:45 p.m. on several of the state's radio stations. There were no news reports of what Folsom said during his broadcast, but farmers in north Alabama—the stronghold of Folsom's runoff votes—were probably the least likely to listen. They would not have seen the ads in the cities' daily newspapers before the broadcast; daily newspapers traveled slowly by mail to the rural areas, and few north Alabama farmers subscribed. Also, urban radio stations' signals in 1946 were weakest in the hilly terrains of north Alabama. And, while radios were widespread by the mid-1940s, the fewest radio owners were in rural areas in the South—perhaps only 50 percent of households.[18]

The Boswell Amendment passed on November 5 by a margin of 12,320 votes. Voting by county followed the general pattern of prior referenda: Black Belt counties provided the most support and north Alabama counties had the largest percentages against. For example, 94 percent of voters in Sumter and Wilcox supported the Amendment, while 83 percent in Jackson and 77 percent in Winston voted against it. The outliers in historical voting patterns were Montgomery, where 57 percent of voters followed Rives and the *Advertiser*'s Dobbins in opposing the proposed voting restrictions and, on the other side of the scale, 69 percent in Shelby and 55 percent in Jefferson favored adoption. It was somewhat surprising that 53 percent of Mobile County voters opposed adoption in light of McCorvey's prominent role and of increasing Black activism for voter registration in the city.[19]

The support for Boswell in Shelby County was probably related to the steady, decades-long decline of the local Republican Party, midwifed earlier by the 1890s' Populist revolt. In both Shelby and Jefferson, the numbers and strength of labor unions, especially those supporting interracial solidarity, had also fallen over the years. In Shelby, union jobs relating to mining and coal production had almost vanished, and by 1946 in the Birmingham area, as Robert J. Norrell writes, "strong support for black voting existed among some white leaders of labor, not the white rank and file."[20]

Perhaps the most striking, decisive development in the Boswell referendum related not to voter preferences but to voter participation. Referenda on constitutional amendments in Alabama always garnered fewer votes than the candidates for major offices on the same ballots, in large measure because the 1901 Constitution vested control in the legislature, requiring local questions to be approved statewide. Perhaps as many as 5,000 proposed constitutional changes have been on Alabama ballots over the decades. In 1946, these differences existed, but most voters who abstained from casting a ballot on the Boswell Amendment were in north Alabama counties where most voters opposed Boswell and Folsom was overwhelmingly their favorite candidate.

The numbers on turnout for the 1946 referendum tell a story. Across Alabama at least 12,480 more votes (7.5 percent) were cast for congressional candidates in the general election of November 5 than were cast for or against the Boswell Amendment. However, among north Alabama counties (north of Jefferson), 21.4 percent more votes were cast in congressional races than in the referendum. Five months earlier, Folsom had carried all but one of these counties, and in most he received at least two of every three votes. In these counties, 58 percent of those voting on the Boswell Amendment said "No."[21]

In contrast, among the south Alabama counties with 45 percent or more Black population, only 1.7 percent more votes were cast in congressional races than on the Boswell measure. Folsom lost the majority of these counties in June, and 69 percent of their voters cast a "Yes" ballot for the Boswell Amendment. If Montgomery County is taken from the group, the vote for Boswell was 80 percent.

The disparities between the two regions are extravagant when comparing votes cast on the same ballot for the Amendment and for governor in the general election. In the north Alabama counties, 41.4 percent more votes were cast in the governor's race than for or against the Boswell Amendment. In the south Alabama counties, only 3.5 percent more voters marked their ballots in the governor's race than in the referendum. In raw numbers, the Boswell Amendment was added to the state constitution by a margin of 12,320 votes in an election where 24,217 north Alabama voters went to the polls but did not vote on the question of Boswell. Only 1,106 voters in south Alabama counties were undecided or failed to vote on the question.

These numbers cannot easily be dismissed or explained by a lack of interest or lack of knowledge about the Boswell Amendment as a proposal for new voting restrictions. This was no ordinary referendum. Along with Folsom's surprise victory, the referendum was the political story of the year. In 1946, the Boswell Amendment appears to have been mentioned in Alabama's daily and county newspapers almost as often as Big Jim, who frequently did not like what the papers wrote but did seek newspaper coverage.

The most likely explanation involves the confusion and indecision that thousands of north Alabama white voters had when trying to understand whether the Amendment was or was not another attempt by the Black Belt and Big Mules to serve their own interests by waving the flag of white supremacy "to disfranchise thousands."[22]

Many of Folsom's north Alabama supporters distrusted the city newspapers as much as their favorite candidate did. And those newspapers, often considered the voices of Big Mules and Black Belt planters, were the most vocal, visible, and opponents of the Amendment. At the same time, the weekly newspapers in north Alabama were generally neutral, and some supported the Amendment. Several county Democratic committees outside south Alabama also endorsed the Amendment. The opposition of Senator Hill and Senator-elect Sparkman was a one-day news story amid a four-month campaign. Big Jim issued more than one statement condemning the Amendment, but despite his promises he did not stump against it. He made only one speech against it—his radio address on election eve. It may have been a stem-winder like many of his speeches, but it is doubtful that a large number of voters in rural north Alabama heard it.[23]

Marshall County, part of the Sand Mountain area of northeast Alabama, is an illuminating example of the peculiar circumstances of uncertainty and confusion that probably explain the north Alabama abstainers on the Boswell Amendment. Marshall County was Big Jim country. A decade earlier in the New Deal, Folsom had been the county's work relief director for 18 months. In the May 1946 primary Folsom received statewide only 30 percent of the total vote among five candidates, but in Marshall County he pulled 54 percent. In the June runoff, Folsom received 82 percent of the county's votes. In November, Marshall gave Folsom 89 percent of its votes but approved the Amendment that Big Jim opposed by a margin of 166 votes, while 904 voters casting ballots that day skipped the Boswell Amendment.[24]

As the Democratic nominee, Folsom was in Marshall County during the run-up to the November election. At the start of August he traveled to the Guntersville lakes to attend a boat race, to crown (and kiss) beauty contestants seeking to be "Queen of the Boat Race," and to enjoy a fishing trip with his local drinking buddies, including one politico who became his executive assistant in the governor's office. Folsom also returned in mid-September to attend the Marshall County Democratic Executive Committee meeting. Dressed in overalls for another fishing trip, Folsom spoke about the importance of Alabama contributing to the national Democratic campaign fund to improve the chances that there would be a Democratic Congress willing to provide federal aid for better roads and schools in Alabama.

But there were no reports of the governor-elect making any remarks about the Boswell Amendment. According to the local newspaper, after Folsom left, the county's Democratic executive committee voted unanimously to support the "'white supremacy' amendment sponsored by the state Democratic committee." Within a week, a large ad appeared in one of the local weekly newspapers sponsored by the state Democratic committee and "other friends of the Boswell Amendment" (a likely euphemism for the Big Mules whose deep pockets could finance a statewide advertising campaign). The ad warned of "negro domination" by "negro Legislators and negro Law Enforcement Officers" and dismissed opponents of the Boswell Amendment as out-of-state "radical reformer elements," communists, and Republicans.[25]

Nothing else appeared in the local newspapers about the Amendment until two and a half weeks before the election when the *Albertville Herald* ran a small story headlined "Sparks, Poole, and Frank Dixon Are for Boswell Bill." The three-inch story noted: "Opposition to the amendment has been strengthened by the announcement of Governor-elect James E. Folsom that he is against it and will make speeches against it." It was the only indication in the local press until after Election Day that Big Jim opposed the Amendment. During the week leading up to the election, local papers ran large ads urging adoption of the Boswell measure from the self-appointed statewide committee, the Marshall County Democratic Executive Committee, and a little-known Black Belt planter. There was also a short article reporting that the Guntersville American Legion post had voted to support the Amendment, in a county where as many as one in four of the qualified voters in 1946 were World War II veterans.[26]

Some Republicans in north Alabama counties claimed that the Democrats who controlled the polling places ran short of the ballots that included the Boswell Amendment, and in Marshall County the local newspaper reported a large discrepancy between the numbers of voters reported by precinct officials and those announced as final by local Democratic officials—a discrepancy where "official figures showed a vote more favorable to the amendment."[27]

In examining the fall-off of voting on the Boswell Amendment, *Birmingham News* reporter Hugh Sparrow recognized that, unlike north Alabama counties, the vote in pro-amendment south Alabama counties rarely had significant discrepancies between the amendment totals and the general election tally. His explanation was succinct. "Maybe that's what the Black Belters means when they crack: 'North Alabama has the votes and we have the brains'"[28]—and, in this case, with experienced, well-financed leaders who knew how to turn out their south Alabama votes as many north Alabama white voters apparently remained flummoxed.

'That Which Is Built upon Prejudice or Ill Will Cannot Survive in a Democracy'

Richard Rives argued in 1946 that the Boswell Amendment would fail to pass the federal courts' scrutiny; he proved prophetic. After the Amendment's passage, African American groups, especially in Birmingham, Mobile, and Tuskegee, persisted in attempting to register to vote. W. C. Patton, John LeFlore, C. G. Gomillion and Birmingham attorney Arthur Shores—all associated with the NAACP—were among those who led much of the ongoing local work to challenge the new powers of registrars to discriminate on the basis of race. In early 1948, African Americans sued in federal district court in both Birmingham and Mobile attacking the Boswell Amendment as unconstitutional. The cases were consolidated and tried before a three-judge panel. One of Governor Folsom's appointees to the Mobile Board of Registrars provided key testimony when he admitted under oath that his fellow board members discriminated against Black applicants, and he described how his colleagues used the Amendment to enforce a double standard for white and Black applicants.[29]

In January 1949, the federal court (composed of three Alabamians appointed by President Roosevelt) unanimously held that the Boswell Amendment violated both the Fourteenth and Fifteenth amendments of the U.S. Constitution. The court found that the words "understand and explain" in the Boswell Amendment were so ambiguous that they conferred the boards of registrars with arbitrary power to register or to refuse whomever they pleased. The judges also held that the Amendment's clear purpose and recent application were to discriminate on the basis of race.[30]

Alabama's attorney general had argued that the Amendment's language made no mention of race and therefore could not contain a racial purpose; however, the court cited a long string of overt appeals for protecting white supremacy during the Amendment campaign and how the new law in fact was being used to disqualify many Black applicants—but not whites. "We cannot ignore the impact of the Boswell Amendment upon Negro citizens because it avoids mention of race or color," the court concluded. "'To do this would be to shut our eyes to what all others than we can see and understand.'"[31]

Shortly after the U.S. Supreme Court affirmed the three-judge court's decision, state Democratic Party chairman Gessner McCorvey met with Black Belt legislators. He proposed a new amendment that included a section found in the Mississippi state constitution requiring persons to read and write as well as understand any section of the constitution, while keeping the sections from Boswell requiring good character and good citizenship. In light of the court's findings of racial intent, McCorvey carefully parsed his arguments in nonracial terms. "Unless something is done to amend this section of our constitution," he warned, "it will mean the registration of a vast horde of countless thousands of people who are totally unfitted to cast an intelligent ballot."[32]

In early May 1949, after more than two years in the governor's chair, Folsom was no longer slap-happy about his election nor coy about the need for reforms in voting and democracy. "I think the Supreme Court decided right," he had observed earlier about Boswell.[33] Now, in his opening address to a joint legislative session, Folsom called for a constitutional convention to rewrite the 1901 Constitution because it "adopted favored outside ownership and disfranchised a large segment of our population . . . It did not, even then, reflect the thinking of the people. It reflected prejudices and accumulated Wall Street wealth."

"I recommend the abolition of the Poll Tax . . ." he continued. "Our election laws are not consistent with Democratic Government . . . This body should give its earnest consideration to improving present voting qualifications . . . This study should not be approached with the idea of disfranchising any of our population. Restrictions imposed by prejudice and intolerance have been declared unconstitutional. The privilege of citizenship should not be abused . . . It is inherent in a democracy that a person who exercises the full rights of citizenship should be allowed to vote . . .

"Our population is 60 percent white and 40 percent Negro. We are gradually affording the Negro the opportunity to make substantial contribution for the benefit of the total population. We must strengthen the cornerstone of opportunity for them. We must remember—that which is built upon prejudice or ill will cannot survive in a democracy."[34]

Folsom also asked the legislature do something it had failed to do for almost five decades—fulfill "the constitutional mandate to reapportion every ten years on the basis of total population . . . I recommend that each county have a resident Senator. I recommend that representation in the House should be distributed on the basis of current population."[35]

In response, Representative Walter Coats Givhan, a Dallas County planter and businessman whose family had lived in the area for generations, introduced a substitute for the outlawed Boswell along the lines that McCorvey outlined. Givhan had become the Black Belt's chief spokesman on voting matters. In 1947, for example, he sponsored a resolution creating a legislative study committee to review and advise the work of local boards of registrars and to prepare the state for court challenges to the Boswell Amendment. Folsom pocket-vetoed his bill, and Givhan attacked the governor and his advisors for deserting white supremacy. "Every Negro in Alabama voted for Folsom," he told the Alabama Farm Bureau convention. "The extreme leftists or reds are going about trying to dominate us . . ." In a political twist, the Folsom-backed speaker of the house from north Alabama agreed with Givhan, but Grover Hall Jr., the new editor of the *Montgomery Advertiser,* scoffed, "White Supremacy in Alabama is threatened to the same extent today as the United States is threatened by the atomic weapons of the Republic of Liberia." [36]

Givhan's bill had enough support to pass both houses: 67 sponsors in the house, and a similar bill introduced by Black Belt senators had 24 sponsors. Richard Rives nonetheless appeared before a house committee and delayed action on the bill by advising legislators that it would be struck down by the federal courts for the same reasons Boswell had been declared unconstitutional. Rives offered a substitute that would establish educational qualifications for voting similar to requirements in New York state.[37]

With McCorvey's assistance, the House Constitution and Elections Committee developed a substitute bill only requiring voters to read and write, be of good character, and "embrace the duties and obligations of citizenship." The bill classified local registrars as judicial officers who would administer a written questionnaire prescribed by the Alabama Supreme

Court to provide information "necessary or proper to aid them to pass upon the qualifications of each applicant." The applicant also had to swear a loyalty oath and disavow any belief in the overthrow of the government by unlawful means (the press later called this the "anti-communist pledge"). Already registered persons were exempt from the requirements.[38]

C. G. Gomillion (Tuskegee University).

Dr. C. G. Gomillion, a Tuskegee Institute political scientist and community leader, read a petition on behalf of a coalition of Black organizations opposing voter restrictions. He called the proposal a mockery of democracy and argued it would involve the state in costly litigation. Rives reiterated that the amended bill violated the national constitution in several ways, but Horace Wilkinson was there to challenge every legal objection Rives raised. McCorvey stated the purpose of the substitute bill was to deny the vote to some people but not to discriminate against anyone. He contended that only those "who would tear down our government" would lose their right to vote. Looking ahead to the referendum, McCorvey also advised the bill's sponsor and its allies on the best sloganeering for the proposal developed by Big Mule and Black Belt leaders: "Don't call it my amendment, or your amendment. It should be called the voters qualification amendment."[39]

The Committee sought an advisory opinion from the Alabama Supreme Court as to whether any provision of the substitute bill violated the Fourteenth or Fifteenth amendments. The court issued a split opinion. Four justices found no violations; Justice Thomas S. Lawson's one-paragraph opinion stated that the proposed amendment failed to meet the *Davis* test that struck down Boswell; and a sixth justice said that the Alabama high court had no warrant to issue advisory opinions about whether a bill meets the standards of the federal constitution, although he assured the legislature that the bill violated no section of the Alabama Constitution.[40]

Despite scores of cosponsors, the substitute bill became ensnarled with struggles over Governor Folsom's initiative to reapportion the state legislature. It was the legislature's last regular session before Folsom was to leave office (governors were then barred by the state constitution from succeeding themselves). The last three years in office had confirmed what Big Jim already understood—the Black Belt counties' over-sized legislative power was the primary obstacle to fulfilling most of his Populist-inspired agenda.[41] As the session started, Folsom's legislative leaders filed bills to reapportion the house by population and to give each of the 67 counties one seat in the senate—a compromise Folsom hoped would attract support from the legislators representing small counties outside the Black Belt. In mid-June, when the new Boswell substitute emerged from committee, north Alabama representatives tacked on an amendment that would make the proposal effective only after the legislature had reapportioned.[42]

Black Belt leaders immediately undertook legislative maneuvers to separate the two issues, block reapportionment, and pass the Boswell substitute. But their efforts were hampered by the fact that they controlled neither the speaker's chair nor as many house committees as in the past. And while several north Alabama representatives had co-sponsored Givhan's original bill, many were much more interested in increasing political power in the legislature for their counties than in obstructing Black voting across the state.[43]

In early July, the stalemate broke, and a house majority agreed to allow Givhan a vote on his substitute bill and afterwards to allow Representative Edward Buckner, a school principal from Cullman, the governor's hometown, to have a vote on his proposal to give each of Alabama's 67 counties one senator. The house voted 77 to 6 in favor of Givhan's bill, 13 votes more than necessary to pass a constitutional amendment, which the Governor could not veto. But the reapportionment bill received only 51 votes, far short of the necessary 64.

During debate on Givhan's bill, Folsom's floor leader warned Buckner and other north Alabama legislators, many in their first terms, that they were "on a snipe's hunt" if they permitted the Black Belt legislators' bill to come up for a vote before the vote on the 67-senators bill. *Birmingham News* political reporter Hugh Sparrow agreed that the "Black Belt strategy proved too much for the eager but less skilled small North Alabama county representatives." The editor of the *Selma Times-Journal,* outraged by Folsom's maneuvers against voter restrictions, wrote that "most representatives hailing from north of Tuscaloosa and Talladega counties are political clucks, instead of political slicks" who "certainly should not be trusted with powers sufficient to dictate state policy."[44]

It was a case of "skullduggery," according to Buckner, who accused Black Belt leaders of reneging on their political deal. He claimed supporters of the 67-senators bill had done their part by voting for Givhan's bill, but 20 south Alabama legislators who promised to vote "yea" for the reapportionment bill voted "nay" or failed to vote. The accusation was probably true since, without explanation, several south Alabama legislators informed reporters that they changed their vote to support Buckner's bill when it came up for reconsideration ten days later.[45]

The 67-senators bill passed with exactly the necessary majority. One amendment submitted by a south Alabama legislator, who also had voted for the bill earlier, passed without discussion on the floor. Representative George C. Wallace of Barbour County changed the word "shall" to "may" in the state constitution's article IX, which provided for reapportioning the legislature after every census. In effect, the change made reapportionment in the future optional, not mandatory, and would sanction what the Black Belt-controlled legislature had refused to permit during the last 40 years.[46]

Some Folsom supporters in the state senate recognized Wallace's amendment as a dangerous subterfuge that they would not accept, but their concerns were moot since a Black Belt/Big Mule coalition blocked passage. Folsom's supporters kept the bill alive for several days and excluded the Wallace amendment, but they could not to get the required constitutional majority. On the other hand, Walter Givhan's bill for new voter qualifications had a good chance of receiving the senate's extraordinary majority of 21 votes. As a result, when the bill reached the top of the senate calendar near the end of the session, Folsom's allies mounted a prolonged, full-throated filibuster.[47]

The Givhan bill died on the senate floor after four Folsom loyalists led a 23-hour filibuster that began at 1 a.m. on September 8 and concluded at 11:59 p.m. on September 9, the last day of the 1949 session. Black Belt leaders could not muster the necessary two-thirds of the senate to force closure. Senator Jim Allen of Gadsden, a Big Mule ally, invoked a parliamentary rule that finally shut down the four filibustering leaders, but others from north Alabama kept talking until the clock ran out. "Left unanswered was one burning question," the Associated Press reported, "that of Negro voting—which strikes fear in the hearts of lawmakers from the heavily Negro populated Black Belt counties."[48]

Governor Folsom called defeating the Boswell substitute the most important legislative achievement of his administration. "Here we are preaching the franchise all over the world," he said, "and trying to take it away from our people at home." Emory Jackson, editor of the Black-owned *Birmingham World*, and other Black leaders fully agreed, as they announced continued efforts for an "orderly qualifying of members of our race for the ballot."[49] Later, in a well-publicized Christmas Day radio address, Folsom warned Alabamians of the dangers of a controlling minority group with wealth and power and affirmed the role of government in helping those of all races in need. "Our Negroes who constitute 35 percent of the population in Alabama—are they getting 35 percent of the fair share of living? . . . Are the Negroes being given their share of democracy, the same opportunity of having a voice in the government under which they live? As long as the Negroes are being held down by deprivation and lack of opportunity, the other poor people will be held down alongside of them."[50]

Beginning in June 1950, after Democratic primary elections, Folsom redoubled efforts to force the legislature to reduce the Black Belt's bloated power by calling the body into special session five times to adopt some form of reapportionment. His efforts were predictably unsuccessful. The first special session lasted only four days during which the governor's 67-senator plan was voted down. Black Belt leaders used the special sessions to try to pass a substitute for the Boswell Amendment and almost mustered enough votes—once again more for their legislation than Folsom's own proposals could garner.

In August, the governor's plan died when the Alabama Supreme Court ruled in an advisory opinion, requested by the state senate, that the state constitution prohibited any reapportionment plan in which each county received one senator. The court cited Section 284 of the Alabama Constitution providing: "Representation in the legislature shall be *based upon population,* and such *basis of representation* shall not be changed by constitutional amendments." The court held that the legislature had no authority "to initiate amendments to the Constitution which would have the effect of changing the basis of representation in the legislature to other than a population basis."[51]

Unbowed, Folsom pledged to try harder to reapportion "for any change"[52] in the legislature, but the irony could not have been lost on him and his allies. The state's highest court was using the state constitutional commandment that legislative districts must be apportioned according to population in order prevent his plan aimed at breaking up the current, malapportioned legislature, which had refused for 40 years to reapportion itself on the basis of current population.

A second advisory opinion, issued a few days later, offered Folsom a glimmer of hope. The Alabama Supreme Court acknowledged that the legislature had a continuing constitutional duty to reapportion according to the latest available census and "we judicially know that the population of the various counties of this state has changed during the years . . . so that the representation . . . cannot be said to be on a population basis."[53] Soon afterwards, two north Alabama lawyers (including a recently elected state representative) sued in state court to bar the secretary of state from certifying the election of legislators who were nominated from counties overrepresented in the house according to population. As residents of Blount and Jackson counties, the attorneys claimed a violation of their rights to due process guaranteed in state and federal constitutions.

When the case reached the state's highest court, the justices acknowledged that the legislature had failed to reapportion properly but held that petitioners were "seeking interference by the judicial department of the state in respect to matters committed by the constitution to the legislative department . . . The grievance . . . should be made to the legislature and the people of the state, not to the court," Justice Joel Brown wrote.[54] To divine exactly how the people of north Alabama could force the Black Belt-controlled legislature to enact a law authorizing a constitutional amendment or convention that would end the Black Belt's malapportioned political power apparently was no less outside the Court's wisdom and dominion.[55]

'Black Belters . . . Are Never Outsmarted and Seldom Outvoted in the Legislature'

Prospects for a new voter qualifications law improved in 1951. Gordon Persons, a Big Mule lawyer from Birmingham, replaced Folsom as the new governor. Persons saw no need to retain a poll tax, but he thought the legislature should decide the state's standards for voting. An interim legislative sub-committee chaired by Calhoun County's Senator Elvin McCary, a Folsom ally, proposed setting up educational qualifications for voting instead of the language in the Givhan bill defeated in 1949. McCary's bill gathered support from labor unions and the *Birmingham News*, but the senate's Black Belt leaders stymied passage and in mid-May pushed through the bill that they had sponsored two years earlier. The *Montgomery Advertiser* reported, "Advocates of white supremacy finally got a rigid new voter qualification bill through the state senate," although Black Belt sponsors carefully argued that the bill's restrictions were necessary to keep "undesirables" off the voting lists without any explicit mention of race.[56]

Demanding reapportionment, house members from rural north Alabama amassed enough votes to block the bill's passage since as a proposed constitutional amendment it required an extraordinary majority. This strategy held up the senate-passed bill for weeks until Black Belt legislators surprisingly announced their support for a 67-senator bill—a new if more complicated version of the bill they had bitterly opposed across five special sessions two years earlier.

The Black Belt maneuver was risky since their most reliable allies, Big Mules in Birmingham and Mobile, opposed the 67-senator bill, which could diminish the political power of urban counties. But as *Birmingham*

News reporter Fred Taylor noted, "Black Belters . . . are never outsmarted and seldom outvoted in the legislature." This was no exception. If both urban counties and the Black Belt opposed such a proposed constitutional amendment, it had a good chance of failing in a statewide referendum. If it did pass, the Alabama Supreme Court would likely strike it down as a violation of the state constitution.[57]

At the same time, several north Alabama legislators were largely unconcerned about passage of the senate-passed voter qualification bill. They believed the federal courts would strike down the new law for the same reason the Boswell Amendment had been found unconstitutional. Also, an amendment aimed at disfranchising Black voters could have little or no effect on their districts where few African Americans lived.[58]

Amid these crosscurrents, Black Belt leaders exhibited their cunning. Senator Miller Bonner, sponsor of what was now dubbed as the "Boswell Jr. Amendment," pleaded for passage of the 67-senator bill to prevent Big Jim Folsom from exploiting the issue in an expected reelection bid in 1954. "If we don't pass it we . . . will elect the greatest demagogue in the history of the state," Bonner declared, "and I don't have to call his name. But he's six feet eight inches tall." The Wilcox County senator explained that by passing the 67-senators bill, Folsom "can't run on an issue that is in the past tense."[59]

But Bonner announced he believed the reapportionment bill was unconstitutional and would vote "no." The bill passed the senate by only a couple of votes, while Bonner and four other Black Belt senators joined Big Mule senators from Birmingham and Mobile in opposing it. In the house, both the 67-senator bill and Givhan's Boswell Jr. bill passed without discussion or debate due to a parliamentary maneuver. Therefore, the legislative record revealed not one word in either chamber about a "Negro menace" or the necessity to protect white supremacy as reasons to pass new voter qualifications, although everyone in and outside the legislature knew exactly who the "undesirables" were.[60]

In the December 1951 campaign for passage, Black Belt proponents and others also soft-pedaled the anti-Black purpose of Boswell Jr. Instead, they pitched it as a part of the war effort. The United States had entered

Gessner T. McCorvey (Doy Leale McCall Rare Book and Manuscript Library, University of South Alabama).

the Korean War in the summer of 1950, and many feared it represented the first step in a communist campaign to take over the world. Latching onto this fear, the Amendment's proponents used its "anti-communist pledge" as a way to claim that passage was necessary to protect American values from foreign influences.[61]

Throughout Alabama, newspapers ran ads declaring, "Let's Back Our Boys in Korea and Protect Our State and Nation Against Communism by Voting 'YES' on AMENDMENT No. 5." The ads warned of the impending dangers of a "horde of new voters who are utterly illiterate and have no understanding of the fundamental principles of government. Even avowed Communists can now register and vote in Alabama." Representative Givhan was listed as the sponsor for the paid ads, which helped set the tone and text of weekly newspaper editorials in counties with substantial Black population.[62]

In letters to the editors of weekly rural newspapers and in speeches in urban areas, now former Democratic state party chairman Gessner McCorvey argued that Alabama's current voting requirements were "absurd" and "utterly ridiculous" since they permitted virtually anyone, Black or white, to register. This argument was the closest proponents came in public to making a race-based plea for passage.[63]

There was no large, organized opposition to passage. The AFL and the NAACP announced their opposition, but both groups had relatively small voting constituencies in 1951. Richard Rives, who helped lead the fight against the Boswell Amendment, was appointed to the U.S. Fifth Circuit Court of Appeals in early 1951 and could not participate in public discussions of the proposal. No one else, including former Governor Big Jim Folsom, did public speaking against the Amendment. The *Anniston Star* overtly opposed passage, while editorials in the *Birmingham News* and *Montgomery Advertiser* declared only that the Amendment was probably unconstitutional. Former Governor Sparks announced shortly before the election that he too believed the federal courts would strike down Boswell Jr. Supporters, however, continued reminding voters in their ads that in the Alabama Supreme Court had advised the legislature that essentially such an amendment did not violate the U.S. Constitution.[64]

BOSWELL JR. PASSED BY a margin of only 369 votes out of more than 120,000 votes cast. As in the past, Black Belt and south Alabama counties provided the largest support. In Russell County, only 92 voters cast a "No" ballot while 1,220 voted "Yes." Particularly important was Mobile County, which gave the Amendment 70 percent of its votes and a "Yes" margin of 3,135. Jefferson and Walker counties provided the largest margins in opposition, and all north Alabama counties except for Madison and Cherokee opposed passage. The *Birmingham News* called it "A Very Dubious Victory."[65]

At the end of 1951, Associated Press reporter Rex Thomas wrote that an "ultimate court test of Alabama's new 'Boswell Amendment Jr.,' appears certain" and quoted NAACP leader W. C. Patton: "We will go into the federal courts and seek to have this undemocratic, un-Christian and immoral amendment declared unconstitutional." Tuskegee Institute's Charles Gomillion was more guarded: "If there is obvious discrimination, suits will be filed."[66]

The Alabama Supreme Court quickly adopted a four-page questionnaire with 21 questions for local boards of registrars to administer, and the test was first distributed in January 1952. But no suit was filed to strike down the new constitutional provisions that year—or in any future year.

Boswell Jr. had been drafted carefully "in the shadow of *Davis v. Schnell*," as political scientist Donald Strong observed. The vague and unconstitutional requirement to "understand and explain" the constitution required by Boswell was removed and replaced with a long questionnaire, which the new law assured was to be "uniform in all cases with no discrimination as between applicants . . ." The federal court ruling in *Davis* found statements from legislators and the state Democratic Committee chairman proving the "Amendment was intended to be and is being used for the purpose of discriminating against applicants for the franchise on the basis of race or color." In contrast, while they were virtually the same leaders of white supremacy, both the sponsors and advocates of the 1951 Amendment argued in public that it was adopted only to give Alabama an "intelligent electorate"—not to bar African Americans from voting.[67]

In addition, the Black Belt-led legislature followed an approach that had received the U.S. Supreme Court's blessing more than a year before it passed Boswell Jr. In early 1949, the Georgia General Assembly passed a voter registration law that included 30 questions relating to state and national government which an applicant had to answer in the process of becoming a qualified voter. The law was challenged in state court specifically as a violation of the holdings in the *Davis* case; however, the Georgia Supreme Court upheld all parts of the law, stating: "The mere possibility that the Board of Registrars may under this statute act arbitrarily or recklessly in administering the law and thereby violate constitutional rights is not a ground for declaring the act as a whole unconstitutional." On May 1, 1950, the U.S. Supreme Court found no "substantial federal question"[68] and in effect sustained the Georgia state court opinion.

Across the next six years, African Americans continued, as they had in the past, to challenge in court Alabama's practices of obstructing Black registration and voting. But Arthur Shores, Thurgood Marshall, and other NAACP-affiliated attorneys representing Black plaintiffs had to attack individual registrars' local discriminatory practices in the Black Belt, Birmingham, and Mobile—not Boswell Jr. itself nor its terms.[69]

CHAPTER 3

The Rise of Black Registration and White Resistance

'The Color of Alabama Politics'

In 1949 V. O. Key observed that in the Deep South states, "Every voter registration officer is a law unto himself in determining the citizen's possession of literacy, understanding, and other qualifications." Almost ten year later, in his study of Alabama voting practices, Joseph Brittain added a friendly amendment when he wrote that "registrars were accountable only to God."[1] Indeed, African Americans in the 1950s seeking to qualify to vote under the terms of Boswell Jr. were subjected to the whims, idiosyncratic standards, and prejudices of the white men and women who served as registrars in Alabama's 67 counties.

In 1953, in a report for the Alabama Coordinating Committee on Registration and Voting, a coalition of organizations established by the state NAACP, Alabama State College political scientist J. E. Pierce reviewed the catalogue of nine discriminatory barriers that had been identified by the Southern Regional Council (SRC) and "still persist according to reports from several counties in Alabama." The list included requiring Black applicants to have white property owners vouch for their good character; proving ownership of property; completing a strict literacy test; answering detailed questions on the U.S. Constitution; filling out exactly correctly all forms, including technical questions; enduring long waiting periods; writing all answers to questions without assistance from registrars; and facing evasions such as the registrars' offices closing early and running out of registration cards just as the Negro applicants arrived. These obstacles were often employed before the passage of Boswell, used during the years of the Boswell Amendment, and continued under Boswell Jr.[2]

In addition, as in past decades, other, more forceful methods prevented or discouraged Black registration. "In many counties the fear of physical violence, intimidation and reprisals loom very high among those who are willing to register and feel responsibility for voting," Pierce wrote. He reported an instance where a local Black leader's farm equipment was badly damaged and his car destroyed after he took neighbors to register. In another incident, J. B. Newman, an African American leader in south Alabama, wrote that a "white man said to me 'you long head son of A. B. if I or someone else don't kill you, four years from now us will have to ask you who will be our judge in Henry County.'" Newman also relayed that while he was helping Black veterans try to register, another white man "drew a stick on me in the courthouse." Civil rights lawyer Charles "Chuck" Morgan Jr. believed that the home of Black attorney Arthur Shores, whose name appeared on virtually every court filing challenging voting restrictions in Alabama in the 1940s and 1950s, held "the state record for being the most bombed." Instead of "one man, one vote," civil rights activist

Bombed home of Arthur Shores (Library of Congress).

Stetson Kennedy suggested, it could easily be "one vote, one life" for the Deep South's Black voters.[3]

NAACP leaders also complained of the "Let it alone" response in Black communities to attempts to encourage and organize voter registration. It was understood that after fifty years of being denied the right to vote, "Negroes have been brainwashed to believe politics is a white man's business." Leaders also recognized that the combination of learned indifference and fear of violence or reprisals was, as one recent scholar called it, a form of "calculated inaction." Professor Pierce noted that how to arouse interest and increase activism for voting was "one of the most perplexing questions" facing Alabama's Black leaders.[4]

These conditions and problems did not prevent Alabama's Black leaders from pushing forward with persistent strategies and efforts to increase registration and voting in their communities since they knew that without the ballot they were "left out of the benefits to be shared by those who possess the power." One basic strategy was data gathering—estimating Negro voter registration by county and identifying those whose local registrars were comparatively favorable or unfavorable in allowing qualified African Americans to register. Pierce's survey of local contacts suggested a more generous attitude among registrars than statistics on registration indicated, but it confirmed a clear pattern that was no surprise. Among the 48 responses, 12 counties were identified as "unfavorable" and two more counties were marked as barring any registration by African Americans. All but two of the "unfavorable" 14 boards of registrars were in the Black Belt, Jefferson County (Birmingham), Mobile, and Montgomery.[5]

The overall estimate of Alabama's Black voters in 1952 was 26,589, or 5.1 percent of the eligible Black population. Eleven Black Belt counties had a Black registration rate of 1.3 percent. In contrast, 11 counties' registration rates were 10 percent or more—essentially twice the state average. Tuscaloosa had the highest rate of 17.7 percent, slightly more than Morgan County on the Tennessee River. Eight of the 11 were in north Alabama, and with only a few exceptions north Alabama counties had higher rates than the state average.[6]

These numbers evidenced that since the passage of the Boswell

Amendment Black voter registration had grown by more than threefold, but where African Americans had the largest proportions of the voting-age population, voter registration was still prohibited or minimal. In response, NAACP leaders engaged two added strategies: a) continue to try to break the barriers in Black Belt counties, and b) rally Black voters elsewhere when and where they might have a decisive influence in the outcome of competitive races among white candidates.

The second strategy proved more productive in the short run. In May 1952, Emory Jackson wrote to national NAACP leader Walter White that "the Negro vote was a deciding factor in the election of Mr. Selden"—Armistead Selden, who in the Democratic primary defeated incumbent first-term U.S. Representative Edward deGraffenreid of Alabama's sixth congressional seat, including its largest town, Tuscaloosa. Selden was endorsed by the local African American political group and won by less than 750 votes of more than 25,000 votes cast. Jackson reported that Selden performed considerably better than expected in the sixth district, which had an estimated 4,000 Black voters. Perhaps fearing that the national NAACP might not fully appreciate how the election of one white segregationist from the Black Belt's Hale County was a "victory" over a segregationist from Tuscaloosa County, Jackson assured White that local Black leaders thought Selden "would go to bat for a better deal for all people." Jackson added:

Emory Jackson (Birmingham Public Library).

"One has to understand the color of Alabama politics at the moment to arrive at a proper analysis."[7]

The 1952 presidential election also proved that Black voting was beginning to make a difference even in Alabama's white supremacy politics. After the November returns, the editorial page editor of the *Montgomery Advertiser* declared "the Negro can be the balance of power in southern states." He concurred with the claims of Alabama NAACP leaders that African American votes kept Tuscaloosa, Montgomery, and Jefferson counties from going for Republican president-elect Dwight Eisenhower—a "claim" that should be heard in "the ears of white Democrats." Buoyed by this trend, NAACP leaders from across the state gathered in Tuscaloosa three weeks after the election to work on having a larger impact in voting. National NAACP attorney Thurgood Marshall proclaimed, "Make the Southern white politician feel your weight!"[8]

While the *Advertiser* acknowledged the enlarging importance of Black voters, it was woefully less than honest when contending that the "Negro is over the hump in his fight for the right to vote . . . it is as easy for a Negro and a white man of identical qualifications to become registered." Pierce's 1952 data debunked that assertion, as did continuing reports to the NAACP from south Alabama, including the account of U. S. Williams, a Black teacher who was informed by the local probate judge: "I will never permit a nigger to vote in Monroe County."[9]

The NAACP persisted despite the obstacles. Its 1954 survey evidenced that Alabama had almost 50,000 Black registered voters—an increase of more voters in the last eight years than had been achieved in the prior 40 years. The survey also quantified a clear difference in registration rates between north and south Alabama. In 28 counties, the rate of Black registration in 1954 was lower than the state average of 9.6 percent. Only three of those counties were in north Alabama. Nineteen counties had a Black registration rate at least twice the state average rate, and 13 were north of Jefferson County and only three were south of Tuscaloosa. In two north Alabama counties, Walker and Marion, where the numbers of African American were small, the rate of Black registration was estimated to be over 50 percent.

The lowest county rates in 1954 were located almost exclusively in the old Black Belt/Birmingham Big Mules' axis—the rural counties where African Americans were the largest percentage of the local population, and in urban Jefferson County, with the largest number of African Americans (a fourth of the state's total Black population). Jefferson actually had a small decline in the number of registered Black voters from 1952 to 1954, according to the NAACP survey.[10]

The gains were the results of work among local voter leagues affiliated with the Alabama Coordinating Committee for Registration and Voting, which the NAACP's W. C. Patton had organized. Their efforts became considerably more successful after passage of a state constitutional amendment in December 1953, eliminating the cumulative feature of the poll tax so that the maximum cost of registering to vote for the first time changed from $36 to $3. The amendment passed by a comfortable margin in a public campaign led by professional white women's organizations, such as the League of Women Voters, and labor groups and quietly supported by the Coordinating Committee.[11]

On May 4, 1954, in the formerly all-white Democratic primary, Alabama Black voters signaled their aim to develop a role beyond choosing the lesser of evils among white candidates. Alex Herman and Clarence Montgomery were elected as the first African Americans to sit on the Mobile County Democratic Executive Committee. While she didn't win, Jessie Parkhurst Guzman became the first Black woman to run for an elective office in Alabama in her race for Macon County superintendent of education, and Arthur Shores became the first African American in the twentieth century to run for the state legislature from Jefferson County. In addition, with huge margins of support from north Alabama counties and Black voters, Big Jim Folsom was elected, without a runoff, to a second term as governor, after a campaign promising to help those most in need, enact fair reapportionment, and improve race relations.[12]

Two weeks later, white supremacy was shaken to its foundation when the U.S. Supreme Court announced its unanimous decision in *Brown v. Board of Education*, declaring that segregation in public schools violated the U.S. Constitution. Soon, fledgling signs of political change were overwhelmed as white outrage and resistance mounted among most of Alabama's political leaders. Dallas County's Walter Givhan, sponsor of Boswell Jr. in the state house, and Sam Engelhardt, Macon County's new state senator and a son-in-law of longtime Black Belt leader Miller Bonner, sponsor of Boswell Jr. in the state senate, actively organized local White Citizens' Councils (WCC) across south Alabama to clamp down on Black activism, especially for school desegregation and voting.[13]

Seven months after the *Brown* decision, Givhan urged a meeting of 400 white men in Marengo County to establish a White Citizens' Council. "This is a white man's country, always has been, and always will be," he told his audience. He charged that the NAACP was a tool of the Communist Party with its primary goal "to open the bedroom doors of our white women to Negro men." Givhan also warned that the national NAACP had a political plan to elect a Black vice president. "And after that happens, what would prevent them from assassinating the president and thus making the Negro become president."

Givhan continued, "As far as integration in the schools . . . the whole U.S. Army is not big enough to force that upon us." Now admitting that the constitutional amendment he sponsored in 1951 "was designed to hold down Negro registration," he informed his white audience that Negroes can enter Alabama schools "only through the ballot box" and "it is the purpose of the WCC to see that this does not happen." Givhan quoted a member of the nearby Perry County board of registrars as saying, "If the WCC had been organized a year ago . . . no Negro would have been registered to vote."[14]

The WCC's campaign of intimidation and harassment and occasional acts of violence against Black candidates and activists slowed but did not completely stop Black voter registration. The Southern Regional Council reported that African Americans had increased their registration by about 4,000 voters from 1954 to 1956.[15] These gains were also limited by the fact that the NAACP and its attorneys were stretched thin, using their time and energy to spur change in desegregation in schools and buses as well as on voter registration. Also, even after the 1954 reduction in the maximum cumulative poll tax, many African Americans could not afford a $3 poll tax each election year.

The gains in Black registration were primarily in the urban areas of Birmingham, Mobile, and Gadsden, where both Black organizations and labor unions were actively recruiting, and in some Wiregrass counties between the Black Belt and the Florida panhandle. The data also revealed declines in Shelby and a few north Alabama counties, although Black registration remained proportionally highest in north Alabama. For example, more than 70 percent of African Americans at least 21 years old were registered in Walker County and more than 50 percent in Marion County—the state's top rates.

SRC's report showed that only 26 African Americans had been added to the voter rolls in Montgomery County since 1954, but in 1956 thousands were engaged in the year-long Montgomery Bus Boycott that challenged segregation on the city-franchised buses. Begun with the arrest of Rosa Parks in December 1955, and led by a newcomer, the 26-year-old Reverend Martin Luther King Jr., the dispute drew national attention to the Cradle of the Confederacy and divided the state capital largely along racial lines. The bombing of King's home in January 1956 was only the first of a series of bombings, shootings, and assaults against Black and white supporters of the protest.[16]

KKK and WWC leaders used the Black protests to escalate white backlash. During the bus boycott, Sam Engelhardt organized a rally of perhaps twelve thousand to shout rebel yells and listen to "blood curdling" attacks on the NAACP and Black leaders. In Birmingham, a week after the Klan physically attacked the nationally popular African American singer Nat King Cole, the WCC held a huge meeting; membership cards asked whites to pledge to "REGISTER and VOTE for officials supporting segregation . . . to help defeat the NAACP."[17]

Meanwhile, NAACP attorneys had secured a federal court order allowing Autherine Lucy to enroll as the first Black student at the University of Alabama in Tuscaloosa. But within days of her February 1956 admittance, Lucy was summarily suspended "for her own safety" and then expelled on the trumped-up charge of making false and defamatory statements against the school. More than a thousand white men had rioted, chanting, "Hey, Hey, Ho, Ho! Where the hell did the nigger go?"[18]

By the summer of 1956, the rapidly growing white resistance across the state became evident in its politics when Alabama's white voters soundly rebuked Governor Jim Folsom for his more progressive stance on racial issues. A virtually unknown first-term legislator, Charlie McKay Jr., opposed Folsom in the May 1 election for Alabama's representative on the Democratic National Committee, a minor post traditionally held by the sitting governor as the titular leader of the state's Democrats. McKay had a well-financed campaign of hundreds of newspaper ads and paid radio addresses projecting him as "Alabama's fighting champion for segregation." But his name had only appeared two months earlier among 40 state legislators who sponsored a joint resolution declaring the U.S. Supreme Court opinions "relating to separation of races in the public schools are, as a matter of right, null, void, and of no effect." Folsom could not veto the resolution, but he called it "hogwash."[19]

McKay's ads charged that Folsom had blocked the legislature's efforts to defend segregation and become a "Darling of the NAACP" who had hosted "Adam Clayton Powell, whiskey-drinking Negro Congressman from Harlem." Many McKay ads ended by proclaiming: "Do your part to end 'Folsomism.'"[20] Folsom had entertained Congressman Powell over drinks at the governor's mansion a month before the Montgomery bus boycott erupted, and Powell bragged to news reporters about the visit, quoting Big Jim as telling him, "Integration in Alabama is not only inevitable, but it is already here." When that news spread across Alabama, Folsom's political problems multiplied. The North Alabama WCC leader, Asa Carter, called for Folsom's impeachment. At a WCC rally in south Alabama, where Georgia Governor Marvin Griffin spoke about the "sorry white folks" who would not fight against desegregation, the audience engaged in what had become a responsive reading at WCC meetings: "Where's Big Jim?" "He's gone to see Lucy."[21]

Big Jim dithered, assuring white Alabamians that "Anyone with any sense knows that Negro children and white children in Alabama are not going to school together in Alabama anytime soon." But the governor would not join the segregationists. In south Alabama, Folsom told a white audience that he was governor of the Negroes just as he was governor of the whites. He accused his opponents of "mistreating the Negro, booting and saddling them . . . If there is any time we shouldn't be kicking folks around, it is now." In north Alabama he was more direct. "When the politicians start hollering "Whip the Nigger!" then you know damn well they are trying to cover up their dirty tracks."[22]

In the election for Democratic national committeeman, Alabama's sitting governor received barely more than a fifth of the votes. Big Jim received a bare majority in only three of 67 counties, all in north Alabama. Even his home county of Cullman denied him a majority. Perhaps desperate for any triumph, Folsom threw his support behind a Black Belt bill to reapportion the legislature. The proposal was at best a Trojan horse, designed to fail at the polls by offering only the façade of a fair distribution of legislative power, especially to the urban areas, while expanding the legislature's total membership to almost 210. Six months after his humiliating defeat at the polls, Folsom watched as only 37 percent of Alabama voters supported his plan. Twenty small counties, almost all in north Alabama, gave it a majority, but voters in the Black Belt, who wanted no change, and voters in the urban areas, who wanted real change, overwhelmingly rejected the Folsom-backed plan.[23]

More than one white politician understood the meaning and opportunities of Big Jim's problems. A month after Folsom's defeat at the polls, still during the Montgomery boycott, Alabama Attorney General John Patterson sued to expel the NAACP from the state and require it to disclose its membership lists. State courts speedily considered and granted Patterson's demands.[24] He would run on this record to be elected Alabama's segregationist governor two years later.

MEANWHILE, DESPITE LEGAL, PHYSICAL, and rhetorical attacks on Black leaders and the NAACP, W. C. Patton continued his work through the Alabama Coordinating Committee to orchestrate a three-pronged program—increasing "voting strength," encouraging the payment of poll taxes, and conducting "get-out-the vote" drives. Others also began to focus on voting rights. Martin Luther King Jr. and eighty-eight others had been arrested in Montgomery in February 1956 for violating a 1921 anti-boycotting law passed by the state legislature to help crush Birmingham's interracial miners' strike. The arrests did not stop the Montgomery bus boycott, which ended that December when the U.S. Supreme Court upheld a federal district court order in *Browder v. Gayle* striking down segregated seating on municipal buses. King and other ministers from across the South announced a "Prayer Pilgrimage," and 27,000 supporters converged on Washington on the third anniversary of the *Brown* decision. King gave the final, keynote address: "Give us the ballot and we will no longer worry the federal government about our basic rights . . . Give us the ballot and we will transform the salient misdeeds of blood thirty mobs into the abiding deeds of ordinary citizens . . . Give us the ballot and we will fill our legislative halls with men of good will . . . Give us the ballot and we will quickly and nonviolently, without rancor or bitterness, implement the Supreme Court's decision of May 17, 1954."[25]

The pilgrimage and King's speech at the Lincoln Memorial were timed to push Congress to enact the first federal civil rights bill of the 20th century. After agreeing to compromises that prevented a prolonged filibuster by Southern senators, Congress passed the Civil Rights Act of 1957. The law created the U.S. Civil Rights Commission (CRC) for a period of two years to study and report to the president and Congress on issues of civil rights. It also created in the Justice Department a civil rights division headed by an assistant attorney general. But the law was actually a voting rights act. Its most striking provision strengthened the powers of the Justice Department to file civil lawsuits to stop or prevent efforts to deprive persons of their right to vote.[26]

The new law was considered cautious and tentative by Black leaders, but it was condemned in Alabama by almost every public official and white-owned newspaper as an unwarranted, dangerous attack on the state and region. South Alabama's U.S. Representative George Andrews complained that the law "placed the official stamp of approval on the NAACP." In an editorial entitled "The New Anti-South Gestapo," the *Troy Messenger* (located in Andrews's district) warned that Republicans will send "Justice

Department goon squads into the South to stand over registering boards with a club." In north Alabama, the *Decatur Daily* declared the "civil rights legislation has never been anything more than a political issue of Republicans and liberal Democrats of the North and East."[27]

Standing politically alone, Governor Folsom told a reporter, "The civil rights bill is acceptable. It's nothing but a right-to-vote, and Alabama's had that law on the books for years." Next day, the *Montgomery Advertiser* ridiculed Folsom for accepting a law that gave the U.S. attorney general "as much power over voter qualification" in Alabama as the governor and creates a "commission of federal snoopers and busy bodies" that can subpoena any citizen. "All this is 'acceptable' to Big Jim," the newspaper sneered.[28]

Legislators joined the rout. They put into the hopper nearly two dozen bills and resolutions condemning any and all versions of a civil rights bill, praising resistance to federal intervention, and proposing new ways to obstruct desegregation and Black voting. State Senator Sam Engelhardt, now the leader of Alabama's White Citizens' Councils, successfully passed bills reconfiguring the majority-Black town of Tuskegee into a dragon-shaped, majority-white town and putting on the ballot a constitutional amendment for a commission to abolish majority-Black Macon County. Other proposed legislation included disfranchising illegitimate persons, their parents, and unwed couples. The only argument needed to pass some laws was for the speaker or sponsor of a bill to say, "Boys, this resolution has the word 'segregation' in it."[29]

Governor Folsom pocket-vetoed several measures, including bills to allow boards of registrars to destroy the questionnaires and records of unsuccessful voter applicants after 30 days; prohibit, in effect, Tuskegee's Black citizens from incorporating a new majority-Black town to evade Senator Engelhardt's bill gerrymandering out the town's Black majority; proclaim the right of Alabama to maintain peace and order by resisting federal encroachment; prevent Black men from sitting next to white women in public transportation; authorize the state attorney general to represent any person or unit of government resisting desegregation; and empower a legislative committee to plan a private school system.[30]

Folsom also vetoed Representative Givhan's resolution commending

Arkansas Governor Orval Faubus in the Little Rock School Crisis for opposing desegregation and condemning President Eisenhower for sending federal troops to restore order as nine African American children were desegregating Central High School. Black Belt newspapers were outraged by both Eisenhower's actions and Folsom's vetoes. In an editorial entitled "The Price of Folsomism," the Selma newspaper accused the governor of pandering to the "bloc ballot of our Negro citizenry" to win future elections as white votes splintered among segregationists. At the same time, the Black-run *Alabama Tribune* reported that Folsom failed to annul an anti-desegregation pupil placement bill that became law without the governor's signature. Even with size-sixteen shoes, Big Jim was on less than firm political footing in Alabama's hyper-charged, changing Black and white communities.[31]

'HELPLESS TO MAKE GOOD . . . THE U.S. CONSTITUTION'

Over the next three years, the Eisenhower Department of Justice failed to rein in the evasions, misdeeds, and chicanery of local white registrars. Despite the new Civil Rights Act's enhanced tools for punishing and preventing violations of the right to register and vote, the Justice Department filed only four new voting rights cases from late 1957 until the summer of 1960. Justice's new Civil Rights Division had almost 20 lawyers to litigate and numerous FBI agents in every Southern state to investigate, but its new assistant attorney general believed his division should proceed with extreme caution in building and bringing initial test cases. He also initiated an investigation only if the FBI or Justice received a written, notarized allegation of a violation of the new law. This approach was supported by U.S. Attorney General William Rogers who explained, "I think you have to gear your law enforcement pretty thoroughly in with the development of public opinion"[32]—in this case, white public opinion in Alabama and the South.

It took Justice a year to file its first voting rights case, in Terrell County, Georgia, and the second was filed in Alabama six months later against Macon County registrars. Yet, the Alabama case was filed only after the newly formed Civil Rights Commission had begun its own investigation in Tuskegee and surrounding counties. After Alabama officials, including

Circuit Judge George C. Wallace, defied subpoenas for registration records, the CRC held hearings in December 1958 in Montgomery. White officials refused to appear or produce records. The CRC did hear from Black citizens concerning their decades-long struggles to register and vote. Afterwards, the CRC requested the Justice Department to sue to require Alabama officials to turn over voter registration records and to challenge the registrars' local practices.[33]

Alabama newspapers covered the confrontations closely, reporting—and often defending—complaints about federal encroachment and invasion voiced by white officials. The Selma newspaper complained that "officials of local governments are being hauled into Federal kangaroo courts" on the word of "civil rights snoopers." The editor was certain that "no more outrageous invasion of the rights of free citizens could be imagined." The Talladega newspaper ran a banner headline, "Federal Legal Guns Being Aimed at Alabama Officials," when the U.S. Attorney confirmed he would go to federal court in support of the Commission's attempts to see public records. And, in north Alabama, the *Decatur Daily* defended Governor-elect John Patterson's position that local registrars were "judicial officers," no less than U.S. Supreme Court justices, who were not required to produce their internal decision-making. Out-going Governor Folsom sadly observed that while the Civil War was over, "a lot of people both North and South are still arguing over the poor old Negro."[34]

Among the Black community leaders who testified before the Civil Rights Commission were Selma's Amelia and S. W. Boynton, who had led efforts to register African American voters for almost two decades. The Boyntons testified that in Dallas County, with only 165 Black registered voters, and in neighboring Wilcox and Lowndes counties, with zero registered Black voters, African Americans were discouraged from attempting to register because of economic intimidation. Both stated they knew of specific instances where Black merchants had been denied service by local white wholesalers in an attempt to block registration. Selma's white-owned newspaper provided minimal coverage of the testimony but identified for its white readers the names and positions of the four local Negroes who made complaints. In this case, however, the public exposure had little

Amelia Boynton testifying at 1958 hearing (ADAH; donated by Alabama Media Group. Photo by Ed Jones, Birmingham News*).*

effect since the Boyntons and the other African Americans who testified ran Black-owned businesses or held jobs that depended on the Black community—not the white community—to survive.[35]

Unspoken at the hearings were the Boyntons' prior efforts to prompt the Justice Department to intervene in Selma. Five months after the new Civil Rights Act became law, the Justice Department received two complaints stating, "I have been denied the right to register and vote by the Board of Registrars of Dallas County, Alabama, solely because I am a Negro." The complaints were supported by affidavits notarized by the only African American notary in Selma, S. W. Boynton. In response, the Department sent white FBI agents to collect sworn, detailed statements about how the white local registrars evaded and avoided registering Blacks to vote. The statements were sent to Washington, where a Black woman sent a third, notarized complaint. FBI agents were dispatched to interview her.[36]

Afterwards, nothing happened at Justice for six months until late October 1958, when Wilson White, assistant attorney general for civil rights, wrote FBI Director J. Edgar Hoover to request his agents "re-interview the victims in order to determine whether they have received registration certificates and, if not, whether they have made any further attempts to register or to determine the reasons for their not having received registration certificates." Within a few days, White changed his mind and asked Hoover to delay the interviews until after the election in order to determine if the victims had been allowed to vote and, if not, "whether they made further attempts to register or tried to ascertain the reasons for their not having received registration certificates."[37]

The FBI reports detailing the re-interviews were sent to Washington after the election and revealed the victims' frustration with the Justice Department's lack of understanding and action. The complainants explained that they had not gone to the polls in November because they had not received a certificate to vote and they had not been back to the registrar's office because "it wouldn't do any good." Each reminded the FBI agents that they had already been back five to eight times and always were told they would be mailed a certificate, but none ever arrived. One complainant refused to sign another affidavit for the FBI but was willing to testify. A month later, the Boyntons and some of the complainants testified publicly before the Civil Rights Commission.[38]

Justice Department files about the Selma complaints were essentially ignored until early September 1959, when the CRC issued a blistering 667-page report chronicling in detail the persistent problems of African Americans in Southern states. The report focused on the testimony from the Montgomery hearings, including the gerrymandering of Tuskegee, the refusal of Alabama officials to provide access to registration records, and the inaction of the Justice Department. Reminding Congress that it had passed the Civil Rights Act of 1957 to "protect the franchise through injunction suits," the CRC found that Justice's record after the passage of the Act was "hardly more encouraging than it was before." Pointing to only three lawsuits brought by the Department in over two years, the report noted that the Department had spent far more time and effort in compiling statistics and elections laws than in enforcing civil rights laws.[39]

But the CRC saw a problem greater than simply the Justice Department's own reluctance and inaction. It understood the enormous challenge to protect voting rights "against each new evasion of the Constitution county by county, and registrar by registrar." It called for new laws and new tools, and concluded that until the Congress provided new resources and means to fight against "the prejudice of registrars and jurors, the U.S. Government appears under present laws to be helpless to make good the guarantees of the U.S. Constitution."[40]

In Alabama, the report sparked outrage and indignation. Governor Patterson called it "an outrageous slander against the integrity of the State of Alabama." Erstwhile New Deal Democrat U.S. Senator Lister Hill said it was "indefensible and irresponsible." The state's newspapers reported that Alabama had been singled out while similar problems were ignored in other parts of the country. The *Mobile Press* applauded Patterson for working to "get big government off the neck of Alabama" and the *Alabama Journal* accused the CRC of making a "mess of its investigation" in pursuit of a "pernicious scheme."[41]

One white elected official who publicly endorsed the CRC report faced a sharp backlash. Douglas Brown, mayor of Ozark in the Wiregrass section near the Florida border, expressed overall agreement with the Commission. Earlier, Brown had accepted the post of chairman of the Alabama Advisory Committee to the Civil Rights Commission because "I feel strongly that citizens qualified to vote under state laws, whether white, Negro, or Indians in southwest Alabama, should be allowed to vote." Local Alabama officials, he said, had brought trouble onto themselves and "if we're not big enough to clean up our own house, I don't see any other outcome but that someone else will give qualified citizens the right to vote."[42]

Brown's remarks received widespread coverage and condemnation. "Douglas Brown has stirred a hornet's nest of trouble," observed the *Andalusia Star-News*, after suggesting that people would find good reason to boycott his places of business. "And most of the trouble is going to be dumped right on Douglas Brown's doorstep." The Selma newspaper suggested that Ozark voters would surely put Brown in his place—out of office. Exactly that happened a few months later when, after serving as mayor for 12 years, Brown was defeated at the polls due to what he described as a "whispering campaign" about his role on the advisory committee. Some south Alabama newspapers gloated over his defeat. The *Star-News* wrote that because the South was about to endure another era of "carpetbag rule," it was important that Brown get what he deserved, as would others if they crossed the line. "Economic pressures are sure to be applied to any Southerner joining up with the Yankee do-gooders." Other newspapers reran the Andalusia editorial, and the *Opelika Daily News* added its own warning. Douglas Brown's defeat showed that any elected official in the South had to be "a 100 percent segregationist or his goose is cooked."[43]

The CRC's report included several recommendations for new federal protections that disturbed Alabama leaders and those editors predicting the return of "carpetbag rule." They found the existence of the CRC objectionable and each of its recommendations a proof of why it should be disbanded. The recommendations included requiring registration records to be preserved and available for five years; making a failure to carry out public duties (as much as active resistance) a federal offense when done to deny a person's right to vote; empowering the CRC itself to go to federal court if subpoenas were ignored for records or testimony; and establishing "the appointment of an existing Federal officer or employee in the area from which complaints are received, to act as a temporary registrar" where the president makes a finding that there has been a practice of the denial of the right to vote. All of these recommendations were informed by what the CRC had found as Alabama's primary tactics to obstruct Black voting.[44]

In Washington, the CRC's report prompted quick congressional action to extend its work and to consider new legislation based on its findings and recommendations. Also, while publicly defending its past approach to voting rights, the Justice Department's new acting assistant attorney general for civil rights reopened the Selma files. On October 23, 1959, Joseph Ryan sent a memo to the FBI director referring him to the 1958 interviews FBI agents had conducted and to the Civil Rights Commission report about Dallas County. He requested a full-scale investigation involving new interviews with the Boyntons and anyone else the Boyntons recommended as individuals who had been denied registration. He also requested re-interviewing all earlier complainants. Ryan wanted updated information and details.[45]

Apparently, FBI Director Hoover decided without consultation with Assistant Attorney General Ryan that Alabama officials should be informed of the investigation, and his agents in Mobile advised Governor Patterson's legal advisor and the chairman of the Dallas County Board of Registrars that "the FBI was conducting an investigation at the request of the Civil Rights Division." On October 30, Patterson publicly lambasted the "politically inspired" investigation for "intimidating and harassing our officials." The Associated Press sent the story across Alabama. Afterwards, echoing several newspapers, the Selma editor wrote that it was "nothing less than a crime that the FBI should be prostituted in the harassment of the South for the purpose of harvesting minority votes for unconscionable politicians."[46]

The *Birmingham News* responded to developments in what had become the moderate white position. Affirming that voter registration should be decided only by Alabama citizens, the *News* argued that the state must be "a lot smarter than thus far we have been." Yes, we bitterly resent the CRC's recommendations, the *News* assured readers, but "we must set standards which will ensure an electorate acceptable to the state's majority." The cases of "extreme unreasonableness in barring registration" will only invite federal encroachment, the *News* warned.[47] In other words, stand together for the principle that a majority of white Alabamians have a right to decide who gets to vote in our state, but avoid barring Black persons regardless of their qualifications since doing so invites federal interference.

The Selma case proceeded into February 1960. As the U.S. Senate began considering the Civil Rights Commission's proposals to revise the

1957 Act, Ryan asked Hoover to have his agents interview Dallas County's current and recent registrars about the specific reasons for rejecting Black applicants, photograph all recent registration applications, and interview recent white applicants. He also asked that agents consult with Selma's Black business leaders to locate "additional Negroes in Dallas County who have attempted, either successfully or unsuccessfully, to register in the past two years." Hoover objected to this last request as a "fishing expedition," and it was dropped.[48]

The investigation stalled. Dallas' three-person board of registrars wasn't operating. It had only one member since the terms of office of the other two had expired, and no one had been appointed in their place. In addition, the registration records had been placed in the custody of the local grand jury and, according to the local circuit solicitor, were not available for a federal "witch hunt." The local grand jury would consider making individual records available if the FBI revealed "proof of the complaints and the identities of the complainants."[49] This was exactly the tactic Circuit Judge George Wallace and others had used to evade the CRC's access to voting records in Barbour, Bullock, Macon, and Wilcox counties. In fact, the registration records in Wilcox had been shuttled among different local grand juries to evade any possible federal court order.[50]

The passage of the Civil Rights Act of 1960 (again, primarily a voting rights act) and the election of President John F. Kennedy broke open the logjam in the Selma case and several others. The new federal law was again a compromise, demanded by Southern senators and orchestrated by Senate Democratic majority leader Lyndon Johnson. Civil rights leaders were disappointed that the compromise left out any enforcement or support for school desegregation and required an elaborate procedure before the government could initiate voting right litigation. "The bill is a fraud," the NAACP's Thurgood Marshall complained. "It would take two to three years for a good lawyer to get someone registered under this bill."[51]

Despite its shortcomings, the new law took direct aim at the problems that the CRC found in Alabama. The 1960 Act required the preservation and retention of registration and voting records and the right of the Justice Department to examine them. It clarified that a state, as well as individuals, could be sued in federal court for voting rights violations—aiming to end the practice of local registrar boards being able to escape lawsuits by claiming registrars had resigned or by not filling vacancies. And, in a novel break with the past, the law provided an evidentiary process—even if cumbersome and overlaid with procedural requirements—for appointing federal registrars if a court found a local "pattern or practice" of discrimination.[52]

John Doar (ADAH).

With these added legal tools, John Doar, the new acting head of the Justice Department's Civil Rights Division, moved within two months of Kennedy's inauguration to renew several Alabama cases, including those in Tuskegee and Selma. Shortly afterwards, Montgomery's U.S. District Judge Frank M. Johnson Jr., a native of north Alabama's "Free State of Winston County," called Doar insisting the Justice Department try the Macon County case that it had filed after the 1958 CRC hearings. When Doar arrived in Tuskegee to help colleagues prepare for trial, he found on the door of the registrar's office a sign reading, "Registration Office Closed — Invasion by Department of Injustice."[53]

While in Alabama, Doar traveled to Selma where he met S. W. and Amelia Boynton, whose names he took from the Montgomery hearings. On the wall of their real estate office, the Boyntons had the names of Dallas County residents who had attempted without success to register in recent years. A few weeks later, Doar wrote to FBI Director J. Edgar Hoover providing the names of two dozen African American Selmians who had been denied the right to register and vote in the November 1960 election. He requested that FBI agents interview these individuals and any others the interviewees could identify as possible victims. Doar listed 19 questions he wanted agents to ask, including whether anyone had ever suggested they might lose their job or suffer hardships if they tried to register. Hoover considered the request to be high-handed and unreasonable, especially since Doar had already requested FBI interviews in Macon, Bullock and Jefferson counties; nonetheless, agents from Mobile and Birmingham produced a 208-page report from 85 interviews within three weeks.[54]

On April 13, 1961, the Justice Department sued in federal district court for an injunction against Dallas County registrars denying applicants the right to register on account of race. The action also sought a court order requiring local registrars to turn over registration and voting records and an order finding that a "pattern and practice" of discrimination existed in Dallas County so that the court could appoint federal referees to fairly register voters. "This is the first voting case that we have filed," U.S. Attorney General Robert Kennedy announced. "We attempted to work this out with officials in Alabama but were unable to do so."[55]

The reaction among Alabama newspapers and officials reprised earlier condemnations of federal interference. The *Alabama Journal* protested: "Taxpayers supply the money to keep our schools going but federal judges are running them. State laws define voter qualifications, but federal judges are gradually taking charge of registration lists and ballot boxes." At the same time, white leaders were realizing that outrage and blunderbuss criticism were not enough to preserve past registration practices. The "moderate" *Birmingham News* warned that the state needed a "registration situation which can be defended with something other than criticism of federal intrusion."[56]

Signs mounted that Alabama's old ways were under serious attack. Shortly after the November 1960 elections, the U.S. Supreme Court entered the "political thicket" by declaring the racial gerrymandering of the City of Tuskegee a violation of the Fifteenth Amendment of the U.S. Constitution. In February, Judge Johnson ordered the original boundaries to be restored. On the same March date that John Doar reopened the Selma case, Johnson also issued a groundbreaking opinion holding that Macon County registrars practiced racial discrimination and ordering the names of 64 African Americans immediately placed onto the voting rolls. Johnson also ruled that the standards used to register Macon County's white voters would become the standards for registering Black voters.

This remedy had far-reaching implications since Justice Department lawyers had proven in court that illiterate white persons who did not even understand the word "registration" had been put on the voting rolls. Therefore, as John Doar realized, it meant that in Macon County in the future, if "you lived there and you breathed, you voted"—since that was the recent standard for registering whites.[57]

By the end of March, Johnson had concluded the trial of Bullock County registrars. Along with an order requiring strict guidance and a short timetable for conducting a fair registration process, he struck down the Black Belt practice of limiting the number of "vouchers" anyone could make for applicants. Soon afterwards, the U.S. Supreme Court upheld Johnson's earlier decision to require Montgomery registrars to turn over registration records. As the *Birmingham News* editors observed, something profound was changing in regard to "Court Decisions and Alabama."[58] Indeed, prodded by a young federal judge sitting at the state capital, more had been done during the first four months of the Kennedy Administration in challenging and dismantling Alabama's Black Belt registration customs than had been achieved in the intervening 12 years since the federal courts struck down the Boswell Amendment.

'SO, WE'RE GOING TO MAKE YOU REGISTER ILLITERATE NEGROES TOO'

When the Alabama legislature prepared to convene in May 1961, additional crosscurrents created by the federal government were threatening to disrupt further Alabama's old ways of distributing and maintaining political power. The U.S. Supreme Court's decision to void the gross gerrymandering of Black voters in Tuskegee had set a new precedent allowing federal courts to examine the constitutionality of political decisions involving jurisdictional boundaries. In fact, the Supreme Court had heard arguments in a challenge to the apportionment of the Tennessee legislature, which like Alabama's had not changed its district boundary lines in 60 years. In addition, due to Alabama's relative decline in population according to the 1960 federal census, the state's delegation of nine members in the U.S. House of Representatives had to be cut to eight. In other words, the legislature must eliminate one congressional seat and redistribute that district's population to other districts. According to seasoned reporters, the rulings "aroused deep interest and concern at Alabama's capitol" and they expected the upcoming session would be the "most turbulent in recent years."[59]

They were not wrong. Despite pleas from Black Belt editors to get the job done to avoid the federal courts, the legislature quickly fell into disarray. The old political coalition between the Black Belt and the Big Mules and the solidarity of the north Alabama counties splintered as small groups of legislators formed and re-formed, often resorting to parliamentary maneuvers and spontaneous filibusters to delay or avoid redrawing the state legislative or congressional maps.[60]

This muddle persisted. Black Belt members wanted the legislature to take up redistricting congressional seats first, since there was a real danger that their counties, with the state's smallest populations, would lose political power in the U.S. House. But Black Belt legislators did not agree on exactly which was their best plan, although each proposed would eliminate a north Alabama congressional district. Meanwhile, many north Alabama legislators wanted to reapportion the state legislature first since they suspected the Black Belt delegation would block any bill for real change, as they had for six decades. Also, there was no agreement about the best reapportionment plan among supporters. Governor Patterson's floor leaders introduced a compromise plan that gave Jefferson County and the counties with larger populations more representation than they had ever had, but the Black Belt opposed it because it drained much of their over-sized power, and legislators from Jefferson County and other more urban areas opposed it because it was not enough change for them.

The legislature descended into chaotic invective, filibustering, and rancor, including one north Alabama legislator who pulled out a squirming garden snake at the podium to illustrate that a south Alabama colleague was nothing more than a reptile in the grass. Finally, the senate's impasse on a congressional plan broke when Roland Cooper of Wilcox County offered a Black Belt redistricting plan that Representative Walter

Givhan had advanced earlier. The substitute proposed to split Jefferson County between four congressional districts. The bill, considered almost a joke at the start of the session, passed the senate by a large margin and later passed the house with support primarily from the Black Belt and most rural south Alabama counties. In addition, close to half of the small, rural north Alabama counties joined in support. But, as predicted, once the congressional restricting plan passed, Black Belt senators denied passage for any proposed legislative reapportionment plan.

There were allegations that Big Jim Folsom had been in the background helping to gather support to break up Big Mule power in Birmingham, and state labor leaders confirmed their pleasure during the session in seeing the Black Belt/Big Mule alliance shattered. Representative Albert Brewer of Decatur was equally hopeful that the redistricting plan he opposed could forge a new alliance. "I believe Jefferson County is now convinced it is best to look to its true friends in north Alabama," he observed.[61]

On August 12, Birmingham attorney Charles "Chuck" Morgan Jr. did what the Black Belt leaders feared most. He filed a class-action lawsuit in Judge Johnson's court in Montgomery claiming the failure of the legislature to reapportion fairly was a violation of the Fourteenth Amendment. Morgan and his clients believed Birmingham's Big Mules had used the threat of a federal lawsuit as a ploy so that "when the chop-up battle died down their divorce from the Black Belt could be set aside."[62] Morgan and members of Birmingham's Young Men's Business Club thus went to federal court in hope that the U.S. Supreme Court would provide the legal authority in the Tennessee case to win their Alabama case.

After studying his limited options, Governor Patterson sent the chop-up bill back to the legislature asking for an amendment that essentially allowed Alabama voters to decide which congressional district to eliminate according to which candidate would receive the fewest votes in statewide elections after congressional district voters decided on their nominees. The house voted to reject the proposal, but, with the aid of Lieutenant Governor Albert Boutwell, the senate's presiding officer who once represented Jefferson County, Birmingham's Senator Larry Dumas led a 96-hour filibuster that ran out the clock on the legislative session. The legislature had failed to pass any plan to redraw their congressional districts, to reapportion its two houses, or even to adopt a state budget. Afterwards, with assurances from all sides that only the state budget and his congressional redistricting plan would be considered, Patterson called a special session, in which both pieces of legislation passed.[63]

Actually, one other major bill passed in the special session—a proposal for a new constitutional amendment on voter registration along with its enabling legislation. In both houses the bills had more than 20 co-sponsors, but the bills' chief sponsor and spokesman was Lawrence King "Snag" Andrews, a longtime senator representing Bullock and Macon counties and a chief political strategist for the Black Belt. In the redistricting fight, Andrews had worked to protect his brother, U.S. Representative George Andrews, whose old district included much of the Black Belt east of

Martha Witt Burleson Smith (ADAH).

Montgomery, and helped orchestrate passage of the "chop-up" bill.[64]

In the state house, Huntsville's up-and-coming Representative Roscoe Roberts, a military veteran, was the amendment's chief spokesman. Andrews had failed to pass his bills in the regular session, but, without the chaotic acrimony over redistricting and reapportionment in the special session, the senator put together a successful Black Belt-north Alabama alliance on voter qualifications—the issue which had become a confrontation in federal court with the Justice Department in his own two counties. Roberts's sponsorship in the house attracted support from other north Alabama legislators, but he was recruited for that role most likely by the person who designed and developed the proposal, Martha Witt Smith, a Huntsville member of the Madison County Board of Registrars since 1949 and a *Huntsville Times* reporter.[65]

Formerly a nationally celebrated cheerleader at the University of Alabama, Smith seemed always ambitious and interested in "newspaper work" in an era when few women in Alabama were reporters. Her father ran a small press in nearby Hartselle as a young man, and his daughter became editor of her high school's student newspaper—as well as its head cheerleader, valedictorian, and an Eagle girl scout. In college, in addition to her famed role cheering the Crimson Tide, Smith majored in journalism and history, became an occasional stringer for the *Birmingham News,* and was awarded first prize in a statewide contest by the United Daughters of the Confederacy for her essay, "Newspapers in Alabama During the Confederacy." She graduated Phi Beta Kappa in less than four years. Before joining the *Huntsville Times* staff, Smith worked as a teacher at a Morgan County high school where she also coached cheerleading and started a boy's boxing team. "I am an Alabama girl from beginning to end," Smith proclaimed in a local front-page profile that had no byline, "and I want to stay in this state."[66]

Described as "100 pounds of vitality" who is "always stirring up something wherever she goes," Smith had been busy as a reporter covering the legislature and occasionally as a registrar advising legislators on voting for eight years. In 1957, she had vouched for the claims of Sam Engelhardt and other segregationists that passage of the Civil Rights Act would force many local registrars to resign.[67] Now she was ready to defend Alabama's voting restrictions. Smith's plan was designed to address the consequences of Judge Johnson's order that Macon County's standards for registering whites also be used for Blacks. "You have disregarded your own laws by registering illiterate whites," Smith stated, mimicking Johnson's language. "So, we're going to make you register illiterate Negroes too."[68] The plan proposed to continue letting local registrars judge an applicant's qualifications as to "good character" and to establish a state board of examiners appointed by the legislature that would create tests for understanding the duties of citizenship. The state tests would be changed regularly by the state board to prevent memorization, and tests would be administered locally in a uniform manner "in all cases with no discrimination as between applicants." The completed tests would be sent by number, not by name, to the state board for grading with an IBM computer.

Andrews called his bill "perhaps the most important piece of legislation passed in Alabama in many, many, years," but it was opposed by a few north Alabama senators, including Bert Haltom of Florence who expressed concern about the bill's impact on both Black and white voters and by Larry Dumas of Jefferson County who objected to creating a single state agency for voter registration. Dumas quoted a telegram from corporate attorney Forney Johnston, who in recent years had become the chief architect of the state plan to fight school desegregation. Johnston wrote that centralizing testing of voter registration in a single state agency "would focalize federal attacks and might make possible federal court appointment of referees for the entire state."[69]

Although Johnston was well-respected among leading segregationists, current events in Montgomery probably overwhelmed his advice. In late May, the legislature was in its regular session when the interracial "Freedom Riders" challenging segregation at interstate bus terminals were brutally beaten at the Montgomery Greyhound station by a white mob, as the Montgomery police stood by. A day of more white folks' rioting followed. The legislature reacted to the incident with a joint resolution condemning the Freedom Riders for "willful incitation to violence and disorder and as a conspiracy against the public interest," which it noted was the objective and means of "Communists and others dedicated to the destruction of the United States." The resolution offered the legislature's full support to Governor Patterson, who did nothing to contain the mob until President Kennedy sent hundreds of federal marshals to the state capital.[70]

Every member of the state senate voted for the resolution, and all but two representatives, both from Mobile, sponsored it in the house. Representative John A. Murphy explained his dissent: "I do not find it sufficient to oppose the tactics of the bus riders in this case without, at the same time, denouncing the acts of violence committed by uncontrolled groups . . . and while the presence of federal marshals is distasteful to us all, the surrender of the enforcement of our laws to mobs is indefensible." Neither he nor the other dissenting Mobile representative sought reelection the following year.[71]

The senate passed Snag Andrews's bill on the same day that Judge Johnson issued his order requiring both Macon and Bullock boards of registrars to register African American voters. Johnson repeated his earlier threat to order federal referees into Macon if the board did not speed up its work, and he ordered that 84 prior Black applicants be registered immediately. In the Bullock County case, Johnson told registrars they must do what he had ordered earlier in Macon: use the "qualifications and standards which have been applied to white registrants in the past" for current and future Black applicants. Two days later, the house passed the proposed amendment and Patterson decided to let voters decide if Smith's computer-based plan—originating from the site of the emerging space program—should be adopted.[72]

The constitutional amendment was placed on the ballot for May 1, 1962, the day of the Democratic primary. The amendment was overshadowed by the governor's race, but proponents attempted to use the wizardry of a new technology as a gloss of legitimacy. For example, Andalusia's editor heralded the advantages of having an electronic device turn down wholesale numbers of Black applicants and could not wait to "see Attorney General Bobby Kennedy name an IBM machine a defendant in a Civil Rights action in Federal Court."[73]

Soon the debate mirrored the nature of that specific moment in

Alabama politics, splintering into unusual parts and partnerships over the questions of who should be allowed to vote and how effective the proposal would be for segregating a large number of African Americans from the ballot box while keeping the federal courts from interfering. "Everybody will be treated equal . . .," Snag Andrews contended, "and there couldn't be any possible discrimination because the tests will be graded at the state level by a number rather than a name." In eliminating most illiterate Blacks from registering, the plan would create collateral consequences. "Of course, in being completely impartial . . .," Andrews admitted, "some whites will be eliminated, but the ultimate conclusion rests in the relative intelligence of the two races."[74]

The *Greensboro Watchman*'s influential editor agreed. "Boiled down, this is it: if you go along with Bobby Kennedy and his crowd in advocating the weakening or abolition of the literacy tests, then vote against this amendment." If you want to do what is best against the "current federal assault," then vote "yes." But other Black Belt leaders were persuaded by Johnston's warnings. Senator Roland Cooper, Andrews's frequent partner in maintaining the Black Belt bloc, declared, "I'm doing all I can to defeat it" since the amendment would create one state board for the federal government to sue in challenging all or most counties' practices. Dallas County Circuit Judge James Hare, who had fought the Justice Department in the Selma case, agreed with Cooper: "The only protection the South has had has been a policy of decentralization."[75]

Across south Alabama, opinions diverged sharply. In the state capital, the *Montgomery Advertiser* urged voters to reject it, and the *Alabama Journal* supported it. The Montgomery County probate judge called for its adoption, but the boards of registrars in Mobile and Marengo counties opposed it. Andalusia's editor, who earlier saw the amendment's wry merits, changed his mind in the spring of 1962, declaring he was opposed to the plan since it "will hardly circumvent the vicious Federal judges."[76]

In Birmingham and north Alabama, most local political and opinion leaders opposed the proposal, although for much different reasons. Senator Dumas repeatedly cited Johnston's objections. Jefferson County registrars opposed the Amendment, vaguely suggesting it was another damaging scheme by the authors of the congressional "chop-up" bill. The *Birmingham News* wrote that the matter needed more study since the proposal raised as many questions as it answered.[77]

Alabama's progressive voices were consistently opposed. State AFL-CIO president Barney Weeks warned that Amendment One would "disenfranchise a tremendous amount of people," especially "the labor union man and Negroes." The Black-owned *Alabama Citizen* saw an "iniquitous scheme" to deny the vote to thousands of African Americans and a large number of whites. The League of Women Voters urged the proposal's defeat because it would discourage voter registration. Running for a third term, Big Jim opposed the Amendment since it would set such a high bar that many voters would be disfranchised. "I can't even pass it," Folsom speculated, "and I have served Alabama, twice as your governor."[78]

Martha Witt Smith counterattacked. From Huntsville, she persuaded her fellow Madison County registrars to endorse the proposal. Ads were published with her explanation of the Amendment. She sent messages across the state arguing that the proposed changes would do no more than "retain literacy as a provision for voting in Alabama." She wrote news articles without her byline quoting herself in the third person.

Smith and her ally, Representative Roscoe Roberts, argued that her plan had an anti-discriminatory intent—"to assure all examinations are graded in the same way without any consideration other than the test itself." But Smith also marshaled data to make certain that white Alabamians understood how her literacy tests would really work and why they were necessary. In an unsigned news article, Smith informed readers that the federal court had ordered the registration of illiterate Negroes in Bullock County. She noted the impact of such a court order could be larger in north Alabama counties, where there were more illiterate Negroes than the 2,000 in rural Bullock. Approximately 7,500 lived in Madison County, 2,500 in Morgan County, and 495 in Jackson County—all Negroes with less than a fourth-grade education whom board of registrars would be required to register to vote unless Amendment One was passed to preserve a literacy standard for voting.[79]

Amendment One lost badly on May 1. Collecting only 36 percent of

Alton Turner (ADAH, donated by Alabama Media Group / Photo by Trudy Cargile, Birmingham News*).*

the votes, the Smith plan carried only seven of 67 counties: Smith's Madison and two adjoining counties and four in south Alabama—even excluding Snag Andrews's Bullock, which rejected the Amendment by 12 votes. Because the Democratic primary for governor was on the same day, the turnout was especially large for a referendum in Alabama, almost 260,000 votes, but three of every five voters in the eight-person governor's race did not mark their ballot on the Amendment.[80] Neither the allure of an IBM machine nor claims that a strict literacy test was a necessary barrier to Black registration were persuasive.

Smith appeared undeterred. Senator Andrews retired from the legislature, but Smith enlisted two other south Alabama legislators, Wiley Salter of Conecuh County and Alton Turner of Crenshaw County, to assemble 30 sponsors for a bill to put virtually the same amendment on the ballot again in 1963. In the aftermath of the "chop-up" bill, the unity and power of the legislature's Black Belt/Big Mules coalition had dissipated, in large part because Chuck Morgan's court-ordered reapportionment plan was lessening Black Belt representation and diversifying Birmingham's now enlarged legislative delegation.[81] But the election of George Wallace as governor in a runoff with overwhelming support from south Alabama, especially from Black Belt counties, proved in short order to be a new, forceful dynamic for Smith's agenda.

'EMOTIONALISM IS STAMPEDING US . . . BY HOLLERING "NIGGER AND THE FEDERAL COURTS"'

After promising in his inaugural address in January 1963 to preserve "segregation forever," Wallace spent much of the next few months building his influence and popularity in north Alabama, where his support had lagged. As a part of this effort, Wallace designated north Alabama legislators as speaker of the house (Albert Brewer of Morgan County) and as his administration's house floor leader (Rankin Fite of Marion County and former speaker during the last Folsom administration), while enlisting in both chambers assistant floor leaders from north and south Alabama, including Representative Alton Turner.[82] At the same time, Wallace sought to animate his public support in south Alabama, and, less than three months after his inauguration, the governor used voter registration as one of the first means to signal publicly his intent to keep his campaign promises to confront federal authorities and preserve Alabama's segregation.

On April 2, Wallace issued a blistering public statement calling for the dismissal of U.S. Attorney Vernol Jansen of Mobile who had made a speech pledging to a Black group "to help you with your fight" at a voter registration rally. Wallace accused Jansen of participating in a meeting designed for "instituting additional efforts to break down our heritage of segregation" and claimed Jansen's speech could "do more to inflame the people of Alabama than any other action by a federal official."[83]

The governor also stated that he had been "personally informed by various county officials in south Alabama that Mr. Jansen has treated them in an offensive manner." As a Justice Department official, Jansen had been investigating voter registration practices in south Alabama and earlier had asked the federal district court to hold in contempt the registrars of Perry County for continuing to deny registration to qualified Black applicants

Robert Kennedy avoids the Jeff Davis star, April 1963 (ADAH, donated by Alabama Media Group / Photo by Ed Jones, Birmingham News*).*

in violation of the court's prior order. He demonstrated that only 17 of almost 300 Black applicants had been registered since the court's order to stop discriminatory practices and that federal referees should be appointed if county registrars continued to violate the court's decree.[84]

Two days later, Wallace kept the issue alive by accusing the U.S. Attorney of gross impropriety by making a financial contribution to the voter registration group. "Mr. Jansen is involved in litigation throughout south Alabama relative to voter registration," Wallace said, but had contributed to an organization "whose avowed purpose is the breakdown of the peace and order of our system of voter registration, regardless of qualifications."[85]

On the same day, Wallace blasted Birmingham's daily newspapers for hiding news about the emerging local protests launched by Martin Luther King. SCLC's Fred Shuttlesworth had kicked off a "Double the Vote Drive" in Birmingham in February and now King had initiated SCLC's "Project C," a plan to use boycotts and marching to confront a range of racial injustices, including discriminatory registration practices, in Alabama's "Magic City," where a hard-fisted hothead, Theophilus Eugene "Bull" Connor, was police commissioner. Wallace also announced he had sent his "secret service" (undercover detectives of the highway patrol, renamed by Wallace as "state troopers") to keep tabs on the situation. He issued a warning to all local officials in Alabama, including Birmingham's newly elected mayor and city council, against encouraging integrationist activity: "it behooves any public official to govern himself accordingly."[86]

The confrontations in Birmingham began to make nightly news, but Wallace realized that his biggest opportunity to fulfill his campaign promise and make a grand stand in the schoolhouse door was in Tuscaloosa, where the federal courts had ordered two Black students admitted to the University of Alabama. President John Kennedy and Attorney General Robert Kennedy worried that white violence would break out when the students appeared on campus, as it had with Autherine Lucy a decade earlier and with James Meredith only a year earlier at the University of Mississippi. On April 24, Attorney General Robert Kennedy and Assistant Attorney General for Civil Rights Burke Marshall made a much-publicized visit to Wallace in Montgomery in an effort to secure a pledge from the governor that he would protect the students and prevent violence.

Asa Carter, who had given up his WCC and Klan positions to become one of Wallace's political operatives, arranged for picketers to greet the attorney general with what was becoming the Alabama version of Southern hospitality—chants and signs reading "No Kennedy Congo Here." The Women for Constitutional Government, a group formed after the riots at the University of Mississippi, laid a wreath over the brass star embedded on the capitol portico where Jefferson Davis had taken the oath of office in 1861 as president of the Confederacy—the goal was to "keep the enemy off sacred ground." The meeting produced only more publicity for the governor's self-portrait as a leader who would stand up to the Washington bureaucrats, even if, he pledged, he had to go to jail to protect Alabama's heritage.

Wallace faces off with Nicholas Katzenbach in Tuscaloosa, June 1963 (ADAH, donated by Alabama Media Group / Photo by Ed Jones, **Birmingham News***).*

Historian Dan Carter has noted that Wallace was put on the defensive when Kennedy suggested that the Negroes Wallace called law-breakers were simply citizens trying to exercise their democratic right to vote. "I think people ought to be allowed to vote if they are qualified to vote," Wallace responded, but he had no answer for how it was that in some counties Black college professors were denied the vote by white registrars who could barely write their own names. He muttered that there was discrimination in every county in America.[87]

A month later, President Kennedy tried his own art of persuasion when he visited Tennessee and north Alabama to celebrate the 50th anniversary of the Tennessee Valley Authority. He invited Governor Wallace to share a helicopter ride to discuss recent events in Birmingham, where national news had spotlighted the arrest and jailing of Dr. King; "Bull" Connor's use of snarling dogs, fire hoses, and mass arrests to counter SCLC's "children's crusade"; and rioting on Birmingham streets after the motel where King stayed was bombed. Wallace told the president he had control of the situation and there was no need for the federal troops that Kennedy had stationed nearby. In earlier press statements, Wallace had said that the federal government was encouraging civil rights agitators to stir up hatred and trouble and the presence of federal troops was an invitation for the "resumption of street rioting by lawless Negro mobs."[88]

Before meeting Kennedy, Wallace asked the legislature for additional funds to hire more state troopers to deal with increased Negro agitation. In addition, members of the house shouted their approval of resolutions condemning the rioters and the president and voted to approve a bill sponsored by Representative Alton Turner at the request of the governor to create the Alabama Legislative Commission to Preserve the Peace. The latter was to investigate and interrogate with subpoena powers persons and groups "detrimental to the peace and dignity of the State of Alabama." Representative Ralph Slate from north Alabama's Morgan County warned that the proposed committee could investigate anyone without any restrictions and that "emotionalism is stampeding us into this by hollering 'nigger and the federal courts.'"[89]

Barely two days after meeting the president, Wallace was on "Meet the Press" telling a national audience about the good people of Alabama and how at the University of Alabama he would fulfill his promise to stand up against federal intrusion on a state's right to run its own schools. He denied there was racial discrimination in voting or other areas of life in his state. Nine days later, with considerable planning and fanfare, Wallace choreographed his nationally televised "stand in the schoolhouse door" in Tuscaloosa. In his words, the governor was standing up against the "illegal usurpation of power by the Central Government" to "preserve and maintain the peace and dignity of this state."[90]

After Wallace stepped aside and returned to Montgomery, two African American students—Vivian Malone, who as a teenage volunteer had worked for Mobile voting rights activist John LeFlore, and James Hood—settled into their campus dormitories. No rioting broke out at the University. But later that night, as President Kennedy spoke on national television about the moral and constitutional necessity to advance fair treatment of Negroes through a new civil rights bill, NAACP leader Medgar Evers was

Wallace testifies before Senate committee (ADAH).

assassinated in his own driveway in Jackson, Mississippi, 185 miles west of Tuscaloosa. Evers's murderer would write Wallace four years later that "I have personally sold over 2500 Wallace tags myself" and that "we haven't had any trouble with that nigger since they buried him."[91]

By July, Wallace had become a national celebrity in the eyes of many white Alabamians. Appearing before the U.S. Senate Commerce Committee to oppose Kennedy's civil rights bill, Wallace declared that "Negro leaders have now pressured the President into the ridiculous position of placing his stamp of approval on mob violence and rioting in the streets in this country." This "ridiculous extreme," Wallace said, was simply to "appease the minority bloc vote leaders" for Kennedy's political gain. He complained that Martin Luther King was guided by communists, accused the president of wanting to create a "police state," and called the proposed civil rights bill the "Involuntary Servitude Act," which would require federal troops to enforce.[92]

Two senators on the committee politely asked Wallace about voter registration and political participation. Both clearly had been briefed on the Civil Rights Commission reports concerning Alabama and wanted to know how in several majority Black counties not one African American was registered to vote. Wallace questioned the accuracy of the claim, suggesting "there are a hundred thousand at least Negro voters in Alabama." He added: "I know the day that I voted in the Governor's race in Alabama I lined up with members of the Negro race in the same line."[93]

Faced with added statistics from the CRC, Wallace staked out his fundamental position: "every man and woman in Alabama who is qualified under the laws of our State, regardless of color, should be allowed to vote." Asked about the Bullock County case, the governor replied that he was not familiar with the voting cases but there were "a lot of people who are not qualified to vote by the standards of the Civil Rights Commission." Wallace added that "we don't have any utopia in Alabama, but you don't have it in any other State in the Union."[94]

Wallace was, in fact, quite familiar with the voting cases in Alabama, as his testimony showed. Attempting to take the offensive, he suggested that "Negroes vote all over Alabama and in great numbers . . . I was in my county courthouse about three weeks ago and there were Negroes registering. So they do have political rights in Alabama." Again asked about Bullock County, Wallace asserted that nearly 1,100 Negroes were voting in a county of 2,000 white voters. Because of the federal courts, he continued, "the whites don't have as much chance to register in certain places of Alabama as Negroes do . . . That is a matter of public record."[95]

Wallace was challenged to explain the statistics from the 1961 CRC report showing vast disparities in south Alabama counties between Black voting age population and Black registration rate. At first he dismissed the numbers as out-of-date, but, realizing he could not claim vast improvements, he returned to what had become his fundamental argument: "we have thousands of Negroes voting in Alabama, and they are registering every day and will continue to register *as long as they are qualified under the laws of the State*."[96]

Wallace complained that the registration numbers were no justification for "the Central Government to take over the voting procedures of the State."

He also explained that the racial discrepancies were due to the fact that "the largest percentage of Negroes are not qualified under Alabama's law to register" because they could not read or write or "discern a simple questionnaire that is to be filled out . . . Of course, it applies to all people equally."

"We have a constitutional amendment now in the legislature of the State that I hope is passed that is going to give the same literacy test to people who attempt to qualify," Wallace continued. "It is given to those in the armed services, to get in the armed services. We feel that . . . if we put the same test that the Armed Forces put to a man to get in the armed services, that that ought to be a fair and good test . . . We want more people to vote who are qualified under the laws of the state."[97]

Wallace drew laughter when he initially claimed to have appointed 100 African Americans to state government but later clarified that they were notaries who only administered oaths and certified affidavits for the public. (The *Birmingham News* ignored this and most of the other testimony about voting in an article where the banner headlines read, "Wallace Tangles with Liberals: Take Look at Your Own Records North Told.") Alabama's governor concluded his testimony by complaining that the federal courts were forcing unqualified Negroes onto the voter rolls while "whites who were turned down are still turned down." [98]

Wallace spoke knowingly of Martha Witt Smith's new proposal for qualifying voters, but the actual bill for the constitutional amendment was not introduced into the Alabama legislature until the day Wallace mentioned it in his congressional testimony. When he returned to Montgomery and appeared before legislators for the first time since "standing up for Alabama" in Tuscaloosa, he received a hero's welcome. All seemed changed. Before his schoolhouse stand, parts of Wallace's legislative agenda were in trouble, but now Wallace's support for a bill was usually a guarantee of passage, including his endorsement of Smith's proposed amendment which passed the house in early August without debate and became law after the state senate passed it in much the same fashion.[99]

The quick passage of Smith's proposal was probably helped by Robert Kennedy's Justice Department, which filed suit against Jefferson County's registrars on July 31. In what was described as the nation's "largest voting discrimination suit," the Justice Department sought to bar future arbitrary denial of voting for Negroes while securing the immediate acceptance of approximately 2,000 Blacks who had attempted to register since 1960. The 82-page complaint "takes no issue with the state's voter qualification laws," the *Birmingham News* reported, "but accuses the county of administering the laws to discriminate against Negroes." The suit charged that registrars questioned Black applicants on matters not mentioned in the state-prescribed questionnaire and rejected African Americans who gave essentially the same answers as white applicants. As a result, the suit stated, 90 percent of the rejected applicants since 1959 were African Americans.[100] The lawsuit was the first legal action on voting discrimination brought by Justice outside the Black Belt.

During the following months, before the December referendum on the amendment, Wallace clamped down on anything that might interfere with his own campaign to stand up for Alabama. He instructed House Speaker Albert Brewer, floor leader Rankin Fite, and assistant floor leader Alton Turner to jointly sponsor a bill regulating who could speak on the campuses of the state's public colleges or universities. A future house speaker, Clarke County's Joe McCorquodale, introduced a bill to deny the right to vote to anyone convicted of disturbing the peace while participating in an anti-segregation sit-in or stand-in. Wallace also demanded passage of the bill to create a state Sovereignty Commission under his immediate control to work along with the legislature's Peace Commission to keep tabs on civil rights workers and supporters. The act was approved by the legislature and signed by the governor on the day after four girls were killed when Klansmen bombed Birmingham's Sixteenth Street Baptist Church.[101] It was a telling moment for Alabama's all-white state government that was being increasingly shaped by Wallace in his own image.

The low-key campaign for the new constitutional amendment immediately met the same widespread opposition that existed a year earlier. The League of Women Voters again opposed it. One League argument was that it would "likely disfranchise more whites than Negroes." In October, labor leader Barney Weeks announced the AFL-CIO's opposition. Former Governor Folsom spread the word in north Alabama that he opposed

Amendment No. 3 because it "violates the principle of state rights and self-government." The state association of county commissioners unanimously decided to ask voters to reject it, and newspapers as diverse as Emory Jackson's Black-owned *Birmingham World*, the *Birmingham News*, north Alabama's *Florence Herald*, and south Alabama's *Selma Times-Journal* urged voters to reject the proposal.[102]

Martha Witt Smith waged a one-person campaign to ratify. She wrote long articles in the Huntsville paper arguing that the amendment was the last stand to keep a literacy test for voting in Alabama. "What effect," she asked, "would a million illiterate voters have on elections in Alabama . . .?" She wrote letters to south Alabama newspaper editors seeking support and had her own board of registrars endorse the amendment. But Wallace failed to publicly support the amendment he had endorsed before Congress in July. He strongly urged passage of two other amendments on the ballot, but he issued only an analysis of Amendment No. 3. It summarized most of Smith's arguments in what reporters called a "favorable analysis"—but it was not an endorsement.[103] Wallace may have gained control of the legislature by the end of 1963, but he apparently received enough feedback on the proposed amendment from Black Belt leaders who had opposed the first Smith proposal to conclude that he could not control the popular vote. The political damage he might incur by supporting an amendment that had no strong public backing, even in the Black Belt, was not a risk worth taking.[104]

The Amendment failed miserably again—this time with only 27 percent of the vote. It carried only Smith's home county, Madison. She was unable to persuade leaders and voters in north or south Alabama, as supporters and opponents of Black voting, that she knew best how to deal with the state's problems of voter registration. She did convince one important person—by the end of the year Smith was hired as a voting rights consultant for George Wallace through his new Sovereignty Commission. Across the following decade, she would become the primary architect and advocate of Wallace's stratagems to help registrars frustrate and clamp down on Black voting in Alabama.[105]

CHAPTER 4

Voter Registration, Commie Fronts, Justice, and State Sovereignty

'A Bloc to Redeem Alabama'

In one of her earlier news stories written from Montgomery without a byline, Martha Witt Smith reported that the Madison County Board of Registrars had discovered illiterate Black applicants were memorizing the answers to numbered questions on the voter registration form. "The NAACP and the Highlander Folk School in Tennessee have reportedly been instrumental in setting up 'literacy' classes, which according to statements of Negroes to registrars, only answers to voter application forms are taught. The Madison County board has charged some applicants have apparently memorized answers to questions by the numbers," she wrote.[1]

Smith was right about the involvement of the Highlander Folk School. It began in the late 1930s working on the South's labor issues and had turned its focus to civil rights in the 1950s, often serving as an interracial meeting place for civil rights activists to discuss strategy and build alliances. In 1957, through the leadership of Septima Clark and other Black women, Highlander initiated a Citizenship School in the Sea Islands off the coasts of South Carolina and Georgia and afterwards expanded it into a regional program to help people become voting citizens. In late 1960 and early 1961, Highlander held its first schools outside the Sea Islands in Madison County where 115 adults attended and 86 reported registering afterwards. Later in Montgomery the program had 435 adults attend and 243 reported registering to vote.[2]

The schools usually held evening classes twice a week for three months and involved "teaching the fundamentals of citizenship responsibility, reading, writing, and voter registration"—a good deal more than the rote memorizing of questionnaire answers. Segregationists accused Highlander of being a dangerous communist training center. In his congressional testimony on the civil rights bill, George Wallace had presented Senator Strom Thurmond with a photograph of Dr. King sitting at Highlander with its founder, Myles Horton, and others as evidence of King's communist ties. The photo would be plastered across the Deep South on billboards entitled "Martin Luther King at Communist Training School" and paid for by the John Birch Society.

The State of Tennessee shuttered the Folk School on a technical legal issue, but Horton declared, "You can padlock a building. But you can't padlock an idea. Highlander is an idea . . . It will grow wherever people take it." To preserve the Citizenship School program, Horton transferred

Septima Clark (Bob Fitch Photography Archive, Department of Special Collections, Stanford University Libraries).

it to the King-led Southern Christian Leadership Conference where Septima Clark and new staff member Andrew Young started increasing the program's reach as part of SCLC's regional efforts to increase Black voter registration.[3]

The other major new development in Black voting was at the Atlanta-based Southern Regional Council. With the assistance of small private foundations and the Kennedy administration, SRC established the Voter Education Project (VEP) to increase voter registration among African Americans in the South, working primarily in association with five major civil rights groups. Leslie Dunbar, SRC's executive director, who more than anyone else helped create and sustain the SRC project over seven years, described the need for VEP in societal terms: "Voting is not a panacea. Yet, it is unmistakably the indispensable precondition to all other civic advance."[4] VEP provided valuable financial support and an additional measure of accountability to expand voter registration across the region.

In Alabama, VEP supported local work largely through the activities of the NAACP, SCLC, and the Student Nonviolent Coordinating Committee (SNCC), a regional group of young civil rights activists led by Alabamian John Lewis and others. Still banned in 1963 from Alabama, the NAACP worked through the Alabama State Coordinating Committee for Registration and Voting that W. C. Patton had set up years earlier. The Association had contacts in about 40 counties, but it used VEP's funds primarily in Birmingham. SCLC used VEP money to register voters in Montgomery, Anniston, and Gadsden, and SNCC's primary work was in Selma and surrounding counties.[5]

VEP also supported a local coalition including the Huntsville Voters League, which had sponsored the Citizenship Schools earlier. Madison County was chosen because it was an urban area where VEP thought it could enable an immediate increase of registered voters in large part because white resistance was "slight or non-existent." Madison County also was the state's fast-growing location due to the immigration of skilled workers for NASA's expansion. Also, VEP expected no economic or physical intimidation.

Within three months, the local groups registered 752 new Black voters—a gain of more than 50 percent over what had been achieved during the prior 20 years. The drive used VEP's $1,200 to build community awareness and involvement through innovative efforts including outdoor lighted signs, a sweepstakes for groups and individuals achieving the most registrations, sound trucks, and a mule which the group paraded through the streets with a sandwich sign reading, "I'm not registered because I'm a mule—what's your excuse?" VEP considered the voter registration effort a shining example, and the mule became momentarily famous.[6]

Smith and her registrar colleagues did nothing to assist the registration campaign. They opened registration at the courthouse annex a minimum number of days each month and rarely on the same weekday. Local law permitted the Madison and some other boards to open more frequently, but Madison registrars refused. On open days, registrars kept office hours starting at ten or eleven in the morning and closing at five or six in the evening—hours more conducive for registering merchants and clerks than laborers and farmers who often worked from sunup to sunset. Madison registrars also required the person vouching for an applicant to be a registered voter and to appear in person with the applicant.[7]

These procedures were within the general terms of Alabama law but presented difficulties for increasing Black registration especially since Huntsville, as a rapidly growing city, had an influx of new, white applicants from other counties or states who crowded the office. In October 1962, when the VEP registration drive began, Smith reported that the board accepted 284 new registered voters, 154 of whom had previously lived in other states. Thirty were from other Alabama counties. Among those registered, 258 were white and 36 were Negroes (including 27 Black women).[8]

To help Black applicants, the VEP-funded groups produced a study sheet that replicated the official document that the Alabama Supreme Court had authorized in 1952 for registrars to use. After a few Black applicants mistakenly took the replicated questionnaires to the registrar's office, Smith accused local Negro groups of helping illiterate Black applicants memorize answers. Madison County registrars started requiring applicants to spell random words from the Constitution and routinely changed the order of the questions on the official questionnaire. The Justice Department questioned

Smith about her practices, but she stood her ground as to their legality. [9]

In other areas of the state, results in VEP's first year were more modest. In Gadsden and Anniston, SCLC's local organizers met customary evasions and problems. A series of community meetings and a telephone bank in Gadsden prompted 185 applicants to go to the registrars' office but few were registered. Often the office kept erratic hours—closing for three to four hours during lunch when Black applicants were accompanied to the courthouse by a local leader whom registrars called a "professional troublemaker." In Anniston, the number of early, new registered voters was unclear, but the problems were the same: "whenever a large group [appears] for registration, the registrar is going to close his office or move to another part of the county."[10]

SNCC organizer Bernard Lafayette arrived in Selma in January 1963 and began to develop plans and strategies with guidance from Amelia Boynton and other local leaders. In Montgomery, SCLC worked through the Montgomery Improvement Association, which King had initially led. The MIA had organized a telephone committee, a carpool, and a babysitting committee to care for applicants' children while the parents were at the registrar. But the earlier court-ordered registration of more than a thousand applicants by Judge Frank M. Johnson Jr. had not made the process easier or more successful. The SCLC report showed 400 Blacks attempted to register but only 53 succeeded. In Birmingham, VEP allocated $9,000 for its drive and had close to a thousand confirmed new voters and perhaps twice that many before Dr. King was arrested and the Justice Department filed its voting rights suit.[11]

VEP and its partners understood how prospects for voter registration differed across the state. To explain the "geographic distribution of resistance" to voter registration, SRC staff members Pat Watters and Reese Cleghorn wrote: "look at a map of the South that shows the Black Belt . . . where the plantations flourished . . . and later where the harvest of sorrow continued . . . and high incidence of racial animosity." In 1963, according to an internal report written by Birmingham's Bernice C. Johnson, there was a wide range of opportunities and obstacles in registering voters in Alabama, "a state generally considered bad all over" by those not involved in the work.[12]

Later, Andrew Young's SCLC files revealed mimeographed pamphlets entitled, "Alabama Registration," and "Alabama Politics" as tutorials for young organizers coming into the South for the first time to understand the state's geography in the distribution of opportunity and resistance. Markings on one map illustrated the different counties' percentages of Negroes of voting age who were registered voters—with the highest rates in north Alabama and a few counties in central Alabama. Another map highlighted the Black Belt, describing it as "Conservative, Reactionary / Over *38%* Negro / Large Farms / Businesses owned from without Alabama, want to be left alone to deal with the government / Lowest classes are poor Negroes who DON'T VOTE." The rest of Alabama was described as "Less conservative, Moderate" with different terms, including at the end: "Lowest classes are poor whites who VOTE."

Within this political geography, the SCLC documents suggested, "We can understand what's happening in Alabama. At the top and bottom of the state the small farmers can almost all vote if they want to. Since there aren't very many Negroes [in these locations] anyway, they can be registered without fear that they will take over the government. Through the center of the state, the government is controlled by wealthy plantation owners and large company executives who must keep Negroes from voting since in these counties there are more Negroes than whites and the Negroes would control the government."

As a result, the pamphlet concluded, "when the rich white men in the center of the state want to elect a segregationist governor, or vote to keep Negroes from registering, they can always count on the poor whites to help them, but only because they have been hoodwinked into hating Negroes . . . BUT THE SCHEME CAN BE STOPPED . . . If Negroes in Alabama could take an active part in the political life of their state, they could form a bloc to redeem Alabama."[13]

Despite their lofty aspirations, civil rights organizers faced a harsh reality for registering Blacks, especially in south Alabama where it usually took mobilizing a thousand people to yield 50 or fewer registered voters, if any. Organizers calculated that at the current "rate of 490 Negroes registered every year, 30 years from now we will have about half the potential Negro vote in Montgomery County registered, that is, if the Negro population does grow."[14] Something more had to change.

'THESE PROBLEMS MUST BE RESOLVED . . . BY THE PEOPLE AND NOT BY THE COURTS'

John Doar of the U.S. Justice Department had a close knowledge of both the geography and enormity of persisting problems of voter registration in Alabama and the Deep South. By the end of 1963, Justice had identified almost 200 counties across the region where "Negroes may have been denied their voting rights." Thirty-seven counties were in Alabama. The list for Alabama roughly followed the maps of civil rights workers. It included all Black Belt counties and most of the adjacent south Alabama counties, all urban counties (Jefferson, Mobile, Montgomery, and Etowah), and three north Alabama counties, including Madison. During the prior two years, the Justice Department had sent FBI agents into several Alabama counties to photograph 50,000 voter registration records, which government lawyers and a Washington-based staff examined to discern new and continuing patterns of racial discrimination.[15]

The Justice Department did not reveal the factors used to add a county, but its Alabama list reflected accurately places of both of resistance and progress of recent years. According to a then-recent CRC report, Alabama's average Black voter registration rate (percentage of voting-age African Americans who were registered) was 13.7 percent. Randolph County and seven north Alabama counties had the highest—Black rates of over 40 percent. Only four counties north of Birmingham had rates below 20 percent, and two of those, Madison and Limestone, were on the Department's list. All but one of the counties with Black registration rates below 10 percent were in south Alabama, and most were Black Belt counties.[16]

Since 1961, when Doar filed suit in Selma against Dallas County in the Justice Department's first case under the 1960 Civil Rights Act, the Department had litigated cases against nine Alabama boards of registrars—seven in the Black Belt, including Montgomery County, and in Elmore (an extension of the Black Belt) and Jefferson counties. Each case was still active at the end of 1963, and all had involved a huge amount of paperwork and lawyering, in part because the Department often attempted to prove a "pattern and practice" that would warrant broad remedies. In the Montgomery trial before Judge Johnson, for example, the Department ultimately submitted the oral testimony of more than 175 witnesses and put approximately 13,000 exhibits into evidence. In the Macon County case, Johnson heard more than 900 pages of testimony and reviewed approximately 250 exhibits.[17]

The Dallas County case in Selma also involved a huge amount of preparation and work, but the Department's overwhelming evidence was not enough to get a federal court order for effective remedies. The Justice Department presented in excess of 5,325 exhibits and subpoenaed 124 witnesses, 33 of whom were put on the stand, but U.S. District Judge Daniel Holcombe Thomas found that the evidence proved only discrimination by a past board, not violations by the recently appointed board. "The Department of Justice should recognize the work of the present Board and not insist on litigating over past inequities," Thomas wrote in his November 1962 opinion. He refused to enjoin the local registrars from any future discriminatory actions.[18]

Thomas did more than deny the federal government lawyers the relief they sought. He praised the Selma registrars, suggesting "the present Board has fulfilled its duties in a manner which could well be emulated by all other Boards in the United States." Also, he wrote:

> Dallas County, Alabama, has problems which other sections do not have. They have problems which other sections do have but do not admit because of political expediency. These problems must be resolved and should be resolved by the people and not by the courts.[19]

The Justice Department appealed the ruling, and, writing for the majority of a three-judge panel of the Fifth Circuit Court of Appeals, Judge Richard Rives ruled that it had been an "abuse of discretion by the trial court to refuse to grant the injunction" to prevent future discrimination. In light of the evidence in the record, Rives listed seven specific practices that, at a minimum, Thomas should include in an injunctive order. Doar and his colleagues (including U.S. Attorney Vernol Jansen, whom Governor Wallace had attacked publicly by name) also argued that the appeals court should require Thomas to impose the "freezing" remedy that Johnson had ordered in the Montgomery case. But Rives demurred, leaving that decision to the district court. Afterwards, Thomas complied with the appeals court's ruling—but did nothing more.

After Thomas's initial high praise, registrars in Selma acted with a free hand. Based on records FBI agents photographed from shortly before the original opinion until shortly after the appeals court's reversal, "89 percent of the 500 Negroes who applied for registration were rejected; 24 percent of the 752 whites were rejected." [20]

Thomas's opinion settled nothing in Selma. After a long illness, S. W. Boynton died in May 1963. Responding to organizer Bernard Lafayette's suggestion, Boynton's widow transformed the funeral service into a religious remembrance and a registration rally. It was held at Selma's most prestigious and most conservative Black church, after its minister, the Reverend L. L. Anderson, threatened to preside over the event in front of the church if his reluctant deacons refused permission. The pivotal event spurred a new level of support and involvement for Black voter registration drives. The African Americans attending rallies, marching, and attempting to register to vote rose from a handful to a church-full, and the community's enthusiasm continued after Lafayette left and SNCC organizer Worth Long arrived.

Dallas County Sheriff Jim Clark agreed wholeheartedly that the federal courts should stay out of Selma's affairs so that he and other white officials could resolve Black demands for voter registration in their own way. Clark began roughing up and arresting SNCC workers on charges of vagrancy and disturbing the peace, as well as identifying and ticketing the cars of those attending meetings. The local district attorney convened an all-white grand jury to investigate how the Justice Department was assisting civil rights workers and how African Americans involved in voter registration were violating criminal laws. He also secured unusually high bail for those arrested by Clark and his deputies.[21]

In addition, the local White Citizens' Council coordinated economic intimidation and reprisals against those attending meetings or becoming involved in voter registration. The WCC sponsored a full-page ad in the Selma newspaper quoting Wallace and warning local whites of "mob marches" and "wholesale Negro voter registration efforts." Three months later, the governor appeared in Selma at a WCC rally where more than 6,000 greeted him with a five-minute standing ovation before he attacked the Kennedy administration for advancing its civil rights agenda.[22]

The Justice Department responded by filing three federal lawsuits to restrain the Dallas County sheriff, district attorney, grand jury, and the local White Citizens' Council from intimidating and harassing Black citizens seeking to register to vote. Thomas delayed hearings on all three actions for months and afterwards delayed ruling on the issues for more months.[23]

Thomas's permissive attitude extended to other Black Belt counties. In neighboring Wilcox, where not one African American was registered in a county with almost 7,000 Negro citizens of voting age, Thomas refused to issue an order allowing the FBI to inspect and photograph registration records until the Fifth Circuit's Chief Judge Elbert Tuttle ordered him to do so. Thomas's refusal delayed inspection of the public records for two years. Thomas also refused to hold a timely hearing when the Justice Department sought an injunction to restrain 27 white landowners in Wilcox County from continuing to retaliate against Lonnie Brown, a local Black insurance salesman, who risked his life in an attempt to become the county's first Black registered voter. More than a year after intimidation and threats forced Brown to leave the county, Thomas dismissed the action without an opinion, although he was later reversed by Judge Tuttle.[24]

In neighboring Perry County, Thomas employed his standard evasive approach—finding past discrimination but avoiding the actual enforcement of specific remedies for the future. Perry's registrars understood the meaning of the judge's order. In the 45 days after Thomas's original injunction, registrars met on three days when as many as 330 African Americans attempted to register. Only 17 applications were accepted, and only one Black applicant was registered. Despite the Justice Department's efforts to hold the local board in contempt, Thomas still refused any direct remedy to halt the registrars' recalcitrance, and the appointment of a couple of new registrars in Perry only increased the board's rebellion. "As of December 31, 1963," the Justice Department reported, "more than 100 Negroes had applied for registration with the new Board . . . No Negroes were known to have been registered by the new Board during this period."[25]

Thomas's delaying tactics were nothing new in the strategies of resistance to civil rights. As Martin Luther King Jr., wrote from the Birmingham jail that April, "For years now I have heard the word 'Wait!' It rings in the ear of every Negro with a piercing familiarity. This 'wait' has almost always meant 'never' . . . We must come to see with the distinguished jurist of yesterday that 'justice too long delayed is justice denied.'"[26] As a "moderate" segregationist, Thomas was among those who argued the wisdom of waiting. He congratulated himself in one of his opinions for his habitual judicial stalling, claiming that his delay in desegregating the Mobile public golf course was why there had been no related racial disturbance.

This self-image was not unusual among white leaders; over time, whenever white Southerners did not resort to violent resistance, some white leader was likely to claim his role was the reason. Decades later, George Wallace would claim his role as a segregationist leader had reduced or prevented racial violence throughout the state. In the case of Judge Thomas, whatever the sincerity of his belief, it had not one iota of proof in Black Belt voting cases. His delays only put more local Black people in harm's way and gave local white people added sanction and time to prevent Black voting.[27]

Since his confrontation over voting records as a circuit judge with the Justice Department and the federal courts five years earlier, Wallace had been rallying white Alabamians to believe that federal judge Frank Johnson embodied the enemy—overreaching, autocratic federal courts—when, in fact, Thomas was far from the rare exception. He wasn't even the most extreme of the federal court judges in the South who believed nothing in the U.S. Constitution should disturb state-sponsored white supremacy and segregation.[28]

"The U.S. Justice Department has shown a willingness to move into some of the worst southern communities . . . and to provide sanctions against registrars who discriminate against Negroes," SRC director Leslie Dunbar observed in VEP's 1963 report. "However, it is becoming increasingly clear that federal court litigation alone will not solve the problem so long as segregationist judges preside over such litigation."[29]

'VOTING IS NOT A "RIGHT" . . . ELSE WE WOULD REGISTER THE BABIES TO VOTE'

At the start of 1964, Alabama's federal courts remained a patchy venue for enforcing voting rights across the Black Belt, but the Alabama Supreme Court was establishing its own central role for obstructing the right to vote. On January 14, the Alabama Supreme Court adopted a complex set of new questions for registrars to use in determining if a person was qualified to vote. The official questionnaire was authorized by an act of the 1961 legislature, which accompanied the legislation for Martha Witt Smith's unsuccessful constitutional amendment to create a statewide board of registrars. The act permitted the state's chief justice to request that the legislature's research bureau prepare for "consideration and approval by the Supreme Court of Alabama, at least 12 sets of questions" so that a different questionnaire could be used by county boards of registrars each month.[30]

Chief Justice Ed Livingston, a staunch Black Belt segregationist, operated in politics as much as law. He grew up in Macon County and practiced law in Tuscaloosa, where he also taught at the University of Alabama law school before being elected to the Alabama Supreme Court in 1940. Governor Gordon Persons appointed him chief justice in 1951. In teaching at the law school for almost twenty years, he had won the loyalty of George Wallace and many other future Alabama lawyers and politicians—by the 1950s they were, in the words of *Montgomery Advertiser* editor Grover Hall Jr., Livingston's "invincible political machine."[31]

The chief justice was instrumental in helping Attorney General John Patterson clean up Phenix City and led the state's highest court in burnishing Patterson's credentials as a fighting segregationist by affirming decrees banning the NAACP from operating in Alabama. In 1958, Livingston did not run but had been considered a strong candidate for governor. "One of the state's staunchest segregationists, Judge Livingston had received strong offers of support," according to *Birmingham News* reporter Fred Taylor.[32] "I'm for segregation and I don't care who knows it," Livingston declared in 1959. "I'd close every school from the highest to the lowest before I would go to school with colored people."[33]

Livingston openly expressed his contempt for the nation's highest court and its school desegregation decision. He made speeches condemning the U.S. Supreme Court for misconstruing the Constitution and told Alabamians they need not consider the Court's decisions as the "law of the land" but only "the law of that particular case." On the bench, he led his own court to flatly ignore a directive from the U.S. Supreme Court in the NAACP case on the grounds that the state's highest court had the power to tell the nation's highest court that it was wrong.[34]

The Livingston family was deeply rooted in the traditions of Macon County's Notasulga community, where the judge owned thousands of acres of land, farmed mostly by Black field hands. His brother was the county chairman of the White Citizens' Council and was on the local board of registrars when the Justice Department sued it in the voting rights case. The chief justice's son was an Alabama assistant attorney general who defended the board of registrars before Judge Johnson.[35]

Ed Livingston's father had donated the land for Notasulga's white public school decades earlier, and in 1963 Johnson ordered the admission of six Black children into the school. Their entrance was temporarily blocked by the town mayor, who claimed that an addition of six children posed a fire hazard from overcrowding. Johnson had him removed. When the Black children finally entered the high school, it was abandoned and its walls were festooned with hand-painted signs saying, "Judge Johnson's and Bobby Kennedy's School—'Godfathers of All Niggers.'" On the following night, arsonists burnt the school to the ground.[36] Afterwards, Livingston bragged that he was more of a defiant defender of segregation and the South's traditions than his old student, George Wallace. "Wallace stood in the school door," the judge admitted, but Livingston's "folks in Notasulga, Alabama, burned the schoolhouse down."[37] The chief justice did more than make speeches and issue opinions to defend segregation. He advised the other two branches of government. A gregarious raconteur, known

Judge Ed Livingston on horseback (ADAH).

for wearing overalls underneath his judicial robes, Livingston was a friend and occasional advisor to Governor Patterson, Lieutenant Governor Albert Boutwell, and Black Belt legislators such as Snag Andrews. Although state law allowed the legislature to request advisory opinions from the Alabama Supreme Court, legislative committees sought the chief justice's private counsel. For example, Livingston met privately during the 1959 session with the Segregation Screening Committee while it was considering bills supported by Andrews and other Black Belt legislators to reduce, in their words, Alabama Negroes' "multiple bastardy."[38]

Wallace considered the chief justice a mentor, friend, and chief advisor. Wallace's brother, Gerald, who became deeply involved in the finances of the Wallace administration and campaigns, had clerked for Livingston only a few years before Wallace was elected governor. "I have consulted with him probably more than with any individual in the State," Wallace said of Livingston, "because his attitude and his philosophical concept of what is right happens to be in tune with mine." Asked who he would put on the U.S. Supreme Court, Wallace usually replied: "Chief Justice Ed Livingston of the Alabama Supreme Court . . . I think that in one line he would strike down many things the U.S. Court has done in the last twenty years."[39]

At the beginning of 1964, Wallace had urgent political reasons to seek Livingston's cooperation and counsel in striking down, or at least slowing, the Justice Department and Judge Johnson in voting cases. While enjoying growing popularity, Wallace needed to expand his political support to assure passage of a constitutional amendment permitting him to succeed himself in a second consecutive term as governor. A rapid increase in the number of Black voters could endanger these ambitions. Wallace had won the 1962 Democratic primary runoff by slightly less than 72,000 votes against Ryan DeGraffenreid, who was expected to run again in 1966. Twice that number of unregistered African Americans of voting age lived in Black Belt counties and close to 400,000 voting-age African Americans were unregistered across the state. The political math was clear: preventing Black voting from rapidly increasing was necessary to give Wallace time to expand his white support across the state and deepen the loyalty and support of his base of white Black Belt leaders.[40]

In addition, Wallace was about to become a candidate in the 1964 Democratic presidential primaries. The adulatory response he was receiving from across the United States as a result of his theatrical performances in Tuscaloosa and elsewhere and his growing national coverage as someone willing to stand up for white people had convinced the governor that he should become a candidate. Wallace may have understood his chance of being elected was a long shot, but at least he could build a national base for a more competitive race in future years. As a presidential candidate, Wallace needed to avoid developments in Alabama that might distract from his messages on the national stage. And Alabama's denial of Black citizens' votes was an issue on which Wallace was potentially vulnerable since, however else Black folk were treated in the North, they could at least vote. For this reason, Wallace wanted to ensure that Alabama registrars' continued denial of Black citizens' right to vote on account of their race was hidden from the general public behind a state's right to maintain race-neutral voter qualifications. That had been his position during testimony before Congress, and it remained his best bet to keep the issue out of his presidential campaign. As a result, Wallace instructed his staff to "get the state out of federal courts and keep it out" so that the race issue in Alabama voting would not get much news coverage and not many Blacks would be added to the voting rolls.[41]

Livingston gladly obliged Wallace, but Martha Witt Smith developed the new questionnaire that the Alabama Supreme Court adopted. She had become Wallace's primary strategist, advocate, and spokesperson on voter registration and voting issues. She had persuaded Wallace earlier that the lack of state standards and supervision was "the real cause of the state losing the qualifications of literacy, character, and witnesses for registration." Now, through her position at the Sovereignty Commission, Smith undertook to do what Alabama voters had twice overwhelmingly refused: establish a coordinated state operation setting high standards of literacy and civic understanding and assisting local boards to apply those standards (and any other traditional qualifications allowed by the federal courts) to disqualify most Blacks from voting.[42]

The new application form was sent across the state in February and March. It required answers about residency, employment status, criminal history, the names of local persons vouching for the applicant, and if, when, and where an applicant may have seen the application outside the registrar's office. (Smith wanted information on the citizenship schools' activities.) The main new section, Part III, had rotating material for each month and required an applicant to read correctly one or more of four excerpts from the U.S. Constitution, such as: "The Congress shall have power to lay and collect taxes on incomes, from whatever source derived, without apportionment among the several states, and without regard to any census or enumeration." It also had questions that changed monthly asking about civics—such as, "How old must a person be to vote in Alabama?" and "What is the chief executive of Alabama called?"[43]

Smith had no authority to set up a state-based IBM computer to grade questionnaires, as she had proposed earlier, but she assembled most of the county boards of registrars and formed a statewide association "to promote uniformity in procedures and to educate the public on registration laws." The Alabama Board of Registrars Association also was created to compare problems and "take an interest in legislation relating to voter registration laws." Smith was elected "public relations director" to speak publicly for the group, and the association's officers and board of directors were heavily composed of Black Belt registrars.[44]

The Justice Department quickly challenged Smith's new questionnaire. In Elmore County, on the northern border of Montgomery, the Department had a pending case involving voter registration. Earlier, after receiving an FBI request to photocopy records, county registrars took their records to the city dump and burned them in violation of federal law. When the full case went to trial in March 1964, the Justice Department lawyers included the board's recent adoption of the new questionnaire as part of the evidence of voter discrimination.

On June 17, Judge Johnson ruled that there had been a blatant pattern and practice of racial discrimination over the last five years including "the defendants' use of three new tests as voter registration qualifications . . . tests which were not applied in their approving 95 percent of the applications of white persons since November 1959. The State and the defendant registrars may not now adopt new and more stringent registration requirements or standards, the effect of which is to perpetuate past discrimination—until the prior discrimination and the effect thereof have been eliminated."[45]

Johnson's decision sent Smith into high alert. "Whatever the state can do to help in any problems will be done," she wrote to the Montgomery registrars two weeks after the Elmore County ruling. "NONE of us can consider ourselves safe from federal suit no matter how fair we may actually be conducting registrations!"[46] Three days later, the Justice Department filed a motion asking Johnson to amend his prior order to enjoin Montgomery registrars from using Smith's new questionnaire since it was a "more stringent" test than what registrars had used to register most of the county's whites. In other words, the Department sought to apply Johnson's order in Elmore County to ban the questionnaire in Montgomery County too.[47]

In response, Smith hit the road to consult with and forewarn registrars across the Black Belt. With the help of the governor's chief of staff, Smith was apparently granted status as a law enforcement officer by Al Lingo, Wallace's free-wheeling director of the state troopers, so that she could carry a concealed pistol. Cecil Jackson wrote Lingo that this "lady is traveling for us in every county in the State of Alabama and on several occasions has been followed by persons unknown."[48]

When not traveling, Smith produced handbooks and guidelines through the Sovereignty Commission to help registrars resist the federal court's interference and to justify why and how it was the state, not the federal government, that should decide who could and could not become a voter. "Voting is not a 'right' in the sense that a person is born entitled to it," a Sovereignty Commission report stated, and, with its own sense of logic, added, "else we would register the babies to vote."[49]

The Justice Department's motion in the Montgomery case was filed on the same day that President Lyndon Johnson signed into law the 1964 Civil Rights Act. The sweeping federal mandate required most private businesses and private employers to forego racial discrimination, and it regulated private conduct and transactions as no national law ever had. The new law provided Wallace the text for many fiery speeches on the overreaching federal government now ready to "destroy the union seniority system and impose racial quotas" as well as "make it impossible for a homeowner to sell his home to whomever he chooses." To thunderous applause, Wallace declared across the nation that "a vote for this little governor will let the people of Washington know that we want them to leave our homes, schools, jobs, business, and farms alone."[50]

As Wallace sought votes in the presidential primaries, his Sovereignty and Peace commissions echoed his messages and organized Alabama's white voters in support of his national ambitions. The Sovereignty Commission donated funds to national groups publishing materials condemning the Civil Rights Act, organized state groups in opposition, sent thousands of letters to residents in states where Wallace was campaigning, and formed county and regional chapters to contribute funds to Wallace's presidential campaign. In Selma, Walter Givhan, now a state senator and a member

Sovereignty Commission members, including Walter Givhan, standing, third from the right (ADAH, donated by Alabama Media Group / Photo by Pearson, Birmingham News*).*

of the Sovereignty Commission, told his Black Belt neighbors, "Governor Wallace is doing a wonderful job," and the Selma chairwoman of the local Sovereignty Committee reported that members had sent 1,500 letters to voters in other states. Conecuh County's local Sovereignty Committee advertised "Stand Up for America . . . Now Is the Time to Help Gov. George Wallace," as it sought funds for his campaign.[51]

The Peace Commission widely distributed its pamphlet claiming the Civil Rights Act was more radical than the Communist Party's own platform. It charged that the Act would destroy private property, end trial by jury, and create "a police state in frightening similarity to the course followed by the countries now in communist enslavement." Its new director also warned local officials: "The Negro movement is almost totally under Communist direction."[52]

The little-noticed Title I section of the actual 1964 Civil Rights Act codified three new tools for enforcing voting rights. They were not major shifts in existing law and escaped public condemnation in Wallace commissions' propaganda, but all three were now in the statute book in large part as a result of voting cases in Alabama. One change essentially codified

Johnson's prior orders that registrars had to apply the same "standard, practice, or procedure" to everyone. It also prohibited registrars from using a technical or immaterial error or omission in an application to disqualify a voter. A second change established that a person with a sixth-grade education should be presumed literate in federal elections in any state where a literacy test was applied.

The third change was called within the Justice Department the "Thomas amendment." It permitted the U.S. attorney general to request "a court of three judges be convened to hear and determine the entire case" where the Department sought to prove a pattern or practice of voting discrimination. The panel would be set up by the presiding circuit judge. This amendment was a direct attempt to get around Judge Daniel Thomas's custom of delaying for months or years remedial relief in cases where voting discrimination was patently evident. In the future, Justice could seek a panel of three judges to expedite new cases in the counties where Thomas had jurisdiction.[53]

Martha Smith (**Huntsville Times**).

Martha Witt Smith moved quickly behind the scenes to mount the state's two-pronged counterattack on both the new federal law's voting rights sections and Judge Johnson's recent rulings in Elmore County. Under Ed Livingston's leadership, the Alabama Supreme Court issued on August 26 a new questionnaire for voter registration applicants. Claiming passage of the Civil Rights Act required changes, the new questionnaire included 399 questions and 139 excerpts primarily from the U.S. Constitution for testing an applicant's knowledge and comprehension. Many of the questions and excerpts were challenging, even for the well-educated. For example, "Name one of the grounds on which a person who is otherwise qualified to vote cannot be denied the right to vote." Some had nothing to do with the Constitution, although perhaps with Smith's own experience: "Name the official who is allowed to give you a permit to carry a pistol." The applicant was required to open at random a notebook containing all the questions and excerpts and begin the test at that page.[54]

Also, in line with Smith's strategies, the Alabama legislature quickly passed a new law authorizing county boards of registrars to meet up to an additional 50 days in any calendar year for purging voter rolls and requiring the reregistration of all voters. The legislation also authorized funding for this extra work "with the approval of the governor." The new law was immediately sent to registrars in all 67 counties.[55]

The white press virtually ignored passage of the law, but Black leaders and the Black press put together recent events. "In Montgomery last week," the *Mobile Beacon and Alabama Citizen* reported, "the Sovereignty Commission announced the use of a new law enacted during the special session of the legislature to control Negro registration." According to the Sovereignty Commission's bulletin, county registrars would now use the new questionnaire to reregister all qualified voters in order to eliminate uneducated Negro voters. The commission's director admitted that some illiterate white voters would be removed too, but the purge of the voter rolls was necessary to protect counties with a high Negro population. Since the "practice appears . . . a direct violation of the civil rights law which provides that a sixth-grade education gives any American citizen the right to vote," the newspaper noted, Negro leaders began filing complaints with the Justice Department.[56]

It did not take long for Justice to respond to Smith's new strategies of resistance. On October 2, the Department amended its pleadings in the federal lawsuit against Jefferson County registrars in Birmingham seeking to block use of the new questionnaire and procedures. On the following Monday, Doar and his small team of government lawyers began for the second time presenting evidence against the discriminatory practices of the Dallas County registrars before Thomas. Very little had changed in registering African Americans in Selma since the first trial. Therefore, denied the right to vote in city elections, the Dallas County Voters League held its own mock election in which the Reverend L. L. Anderson was elected mayor.

In court, Doar offered thousands of pages of photographed records and 56 witnesses as evidence that registrars were refusing to qualify hundreds of otherwise qualified Black citizens in violation of Thomas's prior injunction, including registrars' use of the new questionnaire Smith devised. The Department's new attorney, Brian Landsberg, filed a 118-page brief summarizing the federal government's evidence and concluding, "Negro citizens of Dallas County have been and are effectively disfranchised. This Court's relief must finally secure to Negroes that 'most important and powerful' privilege." Thomas took the case under advisement, and, since this was not a new case in which three judges could be convened, the Department had no option except wait to see how many months it would take for Thomas to rule. [57]

A month before the case against Dallas County went to trial, the Justice Department had taken advantage of the "Thomas Amendment" and filed a new court action against Sheriff Jim Clark, the local circuit solicitor, Circuit Judge James Hare, and the Dallas County probate judge for activities occurring since July that interfered with the "right of Negroes to vote and to the equal use of public accommodations." Among other things, the burly sheriff was arresting African Americans on a whim. The prosecutor had empaneled an all-white grand jury to intimidate local citizens, and the aristocratic Hare had enjoined Black leaders and their organizations from holding public meetings of three or more persons. "If these unsanitary, unbathed ruffians think we are going to lie down and give Selma to them," he told the city's only Black attorney, J. L. Chestnut, "they have another thought coming." A three-judge panel of Thomas, Johnson, and Rives was appointed to hear the case, but the Department received no immediate action because so many other cases in Alabama on school desegregation, civil rights, and voting rights had clogged the judges' dockets. A trial date was postponed until the end of that year, and Chestnut observed that "Hare succeeded in suspending the First Amendment in Selma for six months."[58]

By the end of 1964, the Justice Department had filed against registrars in the other five Black Belt counties where it had pending voting rights litigation, seeking to have the federal courts annul the use of the state's new voter registration questionnaire and require broader remedies for getting more Blacks onto voting rolls. For example, on November 13, the Department filed a motion in the Bullock County case asking Johnson to hold the registrars in contempt "for using a different and more stringent application form than had been used during the period of discrimination prior to the court's initial order."[59]

One of the lawyers who appeared for the first time on behalf of the registrars and other defendants was Frank Mizell of Montgomery. Governor Wallace did not trust Alabama Attorney General Richmond Flowers to present a die-hard defense of the registrars' practices nor to represent the governor's political interests in voting cases. Wallace also was disgusted with the Justice Department's progress, at least in Frank Johnson's court, in forcing the registration of an increasing number of Blacks in counties with large Black populations. Wallace had told Martha Witt Smith that he wanted the state out of federal courts. As a result, the Sovereignty Commission retained Mizell to represent both local officials and the governor in voting rights cases.[60]

Mizell had been a circuit solicitor in south Alabama's Covington County before moving to the state capital after World War II. He was elected to the state Democratic executive committee shortly before the campaign for passage of the Boswell Amendment and became head of the subcommittee on voting. According to Gessner McCorvey, the state Committee chairman who led the fight for Boswell, Mizell was "of inestimable help to me."[61] Mizell was a rabid state's rights advocate who saw segregation as the safeguard of white civilization and supremacy. During the early days of the Montgomery bus boycott he called Martin Luther King Jr. and Ralph Abernathy "imported preachers who are much like the Mau Mau and voodoo preachers of South Africa."[62]

When the legislature was considering whether to eliminate or simply alter the boundaries of Macon County, Mizell advised members that any change must maintain "white supremacy." A year after, he lost by one vote the chairmanship of the state Democratic Party executive committee to Sam Engelhardt, the choice of Governor-elect John Patterson. In 1962, Mizell ran unsuccessfully for lieutenant governor solely as "Alabama's segregation leader."[63]

Also in 1962, Mizell led the state Democratic Executive Committee to number each position in the upcoming statewide elections for committee members. Without numbered posts, Mizell warned, Negroes could do single-shot voting and elect one of their own: "We have increasing federal pressure to . . . register negroes in mass regardless of the fact that many of them ordinarily cannot qualify because of their criminal records or criminal attitudes, because of the fact that they are illiterate and cannot understand or pass literacy tests." He argued that this was not simply a Black Belt problem. He knew of "one county where there are very few darkies registered, there has been probably increased 4 or 5 hundred percent already."[64]

Mizell's proposal was opposed by Big Jim Folsom's former finance director and other north Alabama committee members, but the new rule passed primarily with support from the old coalition of Black Belt and Big Mule supporters. The county Mizell mentioned with "very few darkies" was probably Madison, whose registrar, Martha Witt Smith, had lobbied earlier for passage of the single-shot voting ban in state offices.[65]

During these last months of 1964, the Sovereignty Commission through Smith and Mizell began to focus especially on Perry County as a prime location for implementing strategies in the Black Belt. Smith was attempting to get lawmakers and registrars to understand that a strict literacy test was white Alabama's best defense against the federal court's encroachment. She prepared a special report on Perry's Negro population, showing that if the county was forced to register all illiterate Negroes, it would mean as many as 4,700 Black voters. Since Perry had only 3,200 white voters (almost all the county's whites of voting age), it was headed for Black rule unless the federal courts applied strict literacy requirements to qualify to vote.[66]

Perry was a good choice for an all-out attempt to preserve white control in Black Belt politics for three reasons. First, it was a Black Belt county that had no tradition of civil rights protest. Second, its registrars regularly purged the voter list (so that white registered voters did not outnumber whites of voting age, a problem in other Black Belt counties) while keeping a small number of educated African Americans on the voter rolls—proving that a literacy test would allow qualified Black citizens to vote.

The third major reason was even more compelling: the county was located in Judge Daniel Thomas's jurisdiction. The massive trial in which the Justice Department had documented that no African American had been permitted to register to vote since 1954, despite repeated attempts by Black applicants, had prompted Thomas to do no more than issue a short opinion finding practices of past racial discrimination but no specific remedies. Thomas had refused to order the registration of specific, individual applicants identified during the trial as proven victims of past discrimination, although subsequently the U.S. Supreme Court had upheld Judge Frank Johnson's practice of ordering such relief. Thomas went along with the county's argument that he should not do "registration from the bench." He gave registrars the opportunity to correct their past mistakes.[67]

In the two years following Thomas's inadequate 1962 opinion, the registrars had done little to change, and the Justice Department had filed more than a half-dozen petitions and motions seeking Thomas's enforcement of his own order of nondiscrimination. Almost as often, the Department filed appeals to the Fifth Circuit Court seeking to force Thomas to grant relief. Thomas's delays and prevarications were responsible for the Thomas Amendment in the Civil Rights Act, but the Perry County voting case was a pending action, not a new case where a three-judge panel could be convened.

From Montgomery, Perry County certainly appeared to be an optimal place for Martha Witt Smith and Frank Mizell to launch their new strategies of resistance, but they failed to take into account the emerging leadership, unbending tenacity, and everyday courage of a young bricklayer named Albert Turner Sr. and other members of the Perry County Civic League.

CHAPTER 5

Prequel to the Voting Rights Act of 1965

'I Don't Go for This School-Teacher Registration'

Albert Turner Sr. grew up in Perry County on his father's farm in a household of 12 children who were required to attend church and school with no less devotion than working their daily chores. Albert was educated in Marion, the county seat, at the Lincoln School, established by former slaves and the American Missionary Association as one of the South's first post-Civil War schools for Black education. Other Lincoln graduates included the wives of two SCLC leaders: Jean Childs Young, whose ancestor had helped begin the school, and Coretta Scott King.

Turner was a smart, ambitious student and the president of his high school class. But at the time "there were very few things that a Black person could aspire to be. One was to be a school teacher, and I didn't want to be that. The white community and the white superintendents treated them like they were children," he remembered late in life.[1] Turner wanted to be his own boss. So, he went to Alabama A&M, a historically Black college in Huntsville, graduated with a degree in mechanical arts, became a bricklayer, started doing small construction jobs on his own, and settled into Black life in Marion.[2]

On a Friday night in 1960, sitting at his kitchen table examining his weekly pay stub showing he had paid $27.52 in taxes, Turner talked to himself and made a far-reaching decision: "If I got to pay taxes, I got at least to be able to vote." Soon after, Turner went to the Perry County Courthouse, built in 1856 by slave labor, and asked to register. After completing the application, Turner handed it to the white registrar, who did not look at it before stating, "You dun failed on two of these here questions."[3]

Turner began talking with others in the Black community about the issues of voting. He was told that no African American had been able to register in the county since 1954, the year of the U.S. Supreme Court's school desegregation decision. In her travels from Selma selling life insurance in the late 1950s, Amelia Boynton had discussed voter registration with Perry County's Black leaders, as had the NAACP, but the local board of registrars had other ideas. In 1959, its chairman publicly admitted that Negroes were rejected. He suggested they failed to answer correctly questions on the application form, quite likely in the same manner that Turner experienced. The chairman also cited examples of several Black applicants answering "yes" to the question asking if they were a member of the communist party.[4]

Not long after Turner's rejection, word spread around Marion that a Justice Department lawyer had come to town. He was accompanied by a locally well-known white Catholic priest from Selma, Father Maurice Ouilett, a member of the St. Edmund Order that uniquely served the Black poor and supported Black voting. The lawyer, John Doar, was

Albert Turner (Bob Fitch Photography Archive, Department of Special Collections, Stanford University Libraries).

The Reverend A. Edward Banks (Montgomery County Sheriff's Department).

interviewing locals about their attempts to register to vote. Turner "got interested in that," but he discovered afterwards that he was no longer hired by whites for local bricklaying jobs and had to travel elsewhere for work. "I made up my mind I'm never goin' [to] stop," he remembered.[5]

In early 1962, as the Justice Department prepared a lawsuit against Perry County's registrars, Turner joined with a dozen or so others to establish the Perry County Civic League. An elder of the Black community, the Reverend A. Edward Banks, who had recently returned to Marion, was elected as president. A graduate of Morehouse College and Northwestern University, Banks began his career in the 1920s teaching music in segregated Black public schools in Birmingham. He became choir director of a Black Baptist church in Clanton in Chilton County, halfway between the Black Belt and Birmingham, while composing and teaching music privately through the Banks Conservatory of Music and the Alabama State Music Association, a group he formed for Black church choirs and their directors. In 1949, Professor Banks was called to preach and started the all-Black Second Baptist Church in Clanton, where he pastored for more than a decade.[6]

Banks was also a longtime member of the NAACP. His first contact with the national organization in 1922 was about the anti-lynching bill before Congress, and he became involved in the Clanton NAACP chapter. He also was an old friend of Obadiah Scott, whose daughter Coretta had married Martin Luther King Jr. in Marion in 1953. And Banks was one of the 25 Black ministers among the 90 persons indicted and arrested in

February and March 1956 in Montgomery. Afterwards, when ordering copies of Dr. King's book, *Stride Toward Freedom,* he asked SCLC to ship them to Marion in a plain box without the organization's name visible. "The crackers won't let them in if they see that name," he wrote. Apparently, he also was arrested in 1959 in Chilton County for preaching too much equality on Emancipation Day.[7]

As a precaution while they prepared for the lawsuit, the Civic League members often met several miles outside Marion in the county's all-Black sections. In April 1962, Banks wrote to a Justice Department attorney working for Doar that "we are organized and awaiting your signal to fire the torch." Banks also attended the NAACP national convention in Atlanta that year and contributed $25 from the Civic League to the NAACP as an "affiliate fee," perhaps to solidify support for the upcoming lawsuit from the state's established Black leadership.[8]

The Justice Department filed its voting case in Mobile and Judge Daniel Thomas issued his original, ineffective decree in the case on November 15. Before year's end, Banks started working with Andrew Young and others at SCLC to conduct citizenship schools to prepare local Black residents to pass the registration test. Around this time, Banks decided he could handle no more than managing and teaching the county's citizenship schools. Therefore, at age 26, Albert Turner became the Civic League's president.

With his wife, Evelyn, and friends Janie and Spencer Hogue, Turner immediately initiated a massive county-wide voter registration drive. With a copy of the federal court order in hand, Turner led 330 persons to the courthouse only to find the registrars' office closed or the registrars hiding elsewhere. When the registrars did open for business, they took two hours to examine each applicant. By the end of 1962, only 17 applications had been processed and only one person had been registered.[9]

To the surprise of Justice Department lawyers, Turner kept the Black community's spirits high despite almost total rejection of applications. As one attorney reported to John Doar, "the Board has been totally unsuccessful in discouraging them."[10] On January 9, 1963, the Justice Department filed a petition with Thomas seeking to have the registrars held in civil contempt, and on the same day the Civic League submitted to the federal court's deputy clerk 173 applications from Black citizens seeking to be registered directly by Thomas. Among those letters was one from Evelyn Turner stating she was a housewife with a high school education and on December 17 had been denied by registrars the opportunity to apply to become a qualified voter.

Turner and the Civic League had met earlier with Justice Department lawyers at a Black funeral home (a location few whites visited) in Marion and were informed that, under the Civil Rights Act of 1960, individuals who were denied the right to vote could apply directly to the federal court to become a registered voter if that court had already issued a decree finding a "pattern or practice" of discrimination in their county. With Turner briefly hospitalized, Spencer Hogue and James Carter drove to Mobile and delivered the 173 applications to the court clerk "to be sure the letter reached their destination."[11]

For months Thomas refused to acknowledge the letters as applications to register to vote despite the government's lawyers attempting to force him to act. After five months he issued an order mandating the Perry County registrars to meet within 45 days to consider the 173 letters. The registrars complied by informing each applicant in a letter that they could reapply. All but a few did, but the registrars again rejected most applicants. Thirty-nine were accepted as new qualified voters—including Albert Turner.[12]

"I don't go for this schoolteacher registration," Turner declared. It was not enough that only the college-educated Black applicants, virtually all teachers, were accepted. The League supported Banks and others in holding citizenship classes so that men and women without a high school education could pass the registration test. And Turner remembered the day when he first applied and was rejected. The white registrar had so much trouble writing Turner's name on a sheet of paper that Turner "thought that pencil in his hand was going to kill him."[13]

The registrars' stubborn resistance only spurred new action. In August, with his wife and James Carter, Turner personally delivered another batch of 142 applications to Thomas's court clerk in Mobile. A month later, they delivered 33 more letters. Turner enlisted Jimmie Lee Jackson and other recent college graduates to help Black citizens write detailed letters explaining their efforts to register. Ella D. Stewart wrote Thomas that she had a high school education and was registered to vote in 1955 in Birmingham. She affirmed that she had now resided for five years in Perry County where she was a landowner and described her six attempts to register since his original court order. Although she did not tell the judge, Stewart also spent eight days attending Banks's citizenship class before her last registrars' test, which she failed, according to the registrars, because she had provided "improper answers to one or more important questions."[14]

Thomas seemed both perplexed and annoyed by Turner's tenacity—peeved enough to act quickly in dismissing all letters. "The Court is of the opinion that said writings, if intended as applications for registration . . . do not contain requisite information to qualify them as such applications and are therefore not entitled to recognition," he ruled ten days after Turner left the first batch of letters with the court clerk. The Justice Department appealed his decision.[15]

Turner began to be noticed. Soon after his trip to Mobile, the state's circuit prosecutor subpoenaed Turner to appear before an all-white grand jury in Dallas County. Turner had traveled to Selma to speak at a meeting on voter registration, and the all-white grand jury was using its secret powers to investigate alleged misconduct by the Justice Department and, whenever possible, to intimidate activists. Turner was perhaps seen talking to Justice Department lawyers in Selma. In any case, except for losing a day's work, he remained unfazed by the tactic. Instead, at the end of the year, he testified on behalf of the Justice Department in Thomas's courtroom in a federal action to shut down the circuit prosecutor's use of the grand jury and organized a continuous line of more than 100 Black folk applying regularly to vote at the Perry County courthouse.[16]

Under John Doar, the Justice Department attorneys realized the importance of pushing forward its legal challenge and appeals to force Thomas to do something meaningful for Black applicants—and to support Turner's community leadership. When it became obvious, for example, that a newly appointed board of registrars had turned down every one of the more than 100 Black applicants who applied, Doar's attorneys sought a hearing to present evidence as to why Thomas should hold registrars in contempt of court. Soon afterwards, FBI agents reappeared in Marion to photocopy registration records for an April hearing.[17]

Turner also understood how to use the Justice Department's actions to sustain community activism even when he did not get the results he sought. The arrival of FBI agents in March showed Black citizens that the court case was still alive, and local registrars had to reveal their records to federal agents. The prospect of an April hearing gave Turner a way to explain to determined, qualified Black citizens such as Ella Stewart why they should continue to apply each month to register to vote, even as they were sure to be denied. "I was just that determined to make a change in society. That drove me day in and day out," Turner remembered years later. "Whatever it took," he undertook to keep alive a quiet struggle in a small, isolated rural town.[18]

As the hearing date approached, the *Marion Times-Standard* published a list of the county's 4,300 registered voters. The list separated by precinct the names of the 300 Negroes who had insisted on registering to vote. Perhaps worse than having each Black voter easily identified by the white community, the list illustrated what Turner already knew: during the last 18 months, all of the efforts of the Perry County Civic League and the U.S. Justice Department had added only 43 Black voters to the rolls.[19]

The Perry County registrars began in March using the elaborate questionnaire that Martha Witt Smith had developed and the Alabama Supreme Court had issued. It was one more barrier in what already was a nearly insurmountable obstacle to voter registration in Perry.[20]

Turner refused to give up. In April he cooperated with the Justice Department attorneys as they prepared documents and witnesses for a contempt hearing to be held in Selma before Judge Thomas. At trial, the Justice Department called 17 African Americans who had been denied registration, including Ella Stewart and Turner's sister-in-law, Gladys, a nurse who had attended junior college. The government also called 113 white witnesses. Each described the experience of being tested by registrars. The evidence clearly showed that African Americans were turned down multiple times for technical reasons such as failing to list their precinct number or to sign all of the several forms, but white applicants who made the same mistakes were not disqualified. The testimony and registration records also showed that Black applicants often were required to have at least one white person appear in person and vouch for them in order to be considered of "good character."

The Justice Department backed up this evidence with hundreds of pages of test results that documented how differently Black and white applicants were treated since Thomas's original court order in November 1962 as well as testimony from several Black witnesses about the hundreds of other African Americans who had appeared at the courthouse to register but who were provided no opportunity to take the test.[21]

John Blackburn, a farmer who had served as one of the county registrars since 1953 (when the board stopped registering Black voters), had been appointed chairman of the board recently by Governor George Wallace. Called to the witness stand by defendants' attorney Frank Mizell, Blackburn used the occasion to express his outrage. "Those niggers lied," he insisted. "When they testified, we took one at a time, they told a straight lie." One of the African Americans whom Blackburn accused of lying was Turner's sister-in-law. In rebuttal, government lawyers submitted into evidence the registrar's own records verifying that on the three dates in question the board had processed only seven, four, and five applications respectively, even as scores of Black applicants waited to be called.[22]

Thomas adjourned the court and took the case under advisement, where so many other motions and pleadings languished. He did act quickly on his own on one matter: he ordered the Department of Justice to pay half of the extra fees that the local registrars had charged for complying with Thomas's earlier order to open their offices more often. It was a symbolic but stinging message: Justice had to help pay the bill for Perry County registrars who spent extra time working to assure that there would be no real increase in the number of Black voters.[23]

Blackburn was not satisfied. He remained outraged that local Black folks had dared in open court to challenge his conduct. In a letter to the editor, he ignored the documentary evidence contradicting his claims and informed Perry County that during the trial, "Negroes testified on oath and lied." He assured the white public that he had not discriminated against "white or colored" since Thomas's original injunction. "I hope when I die and face God for judgment I will be an innocent as I was when I faced . . . this charge by the 'so-called' Justice Department."[24]

Three month later, the U.S. Fifth Circuit Court of Appeals overturned Thomas's refusal to accept the letters of application that Turner had delivered eleven months earlier. Circuit Judge John Brown ruled that Thomas's original findings had established a pattern and practice of voting discrimination that required him to consider registering individuals who claimed they were denied the right to vote. (It was an explicit remedy stated in the 1960 Civil Rights Act.)

Brown added a pointed commentary: "Energetic, resourceful, conscientious Judges who man the United States District Courts in these areas can, and will, find a way to make certain that this law is administered in a way that is faithful to the legislative purpose of eradicating for all time racial discrimination in voter rights." Obviously, Thomas had not met that test. Almost as an afterthought, Brown suggested, "the Judge may well find it helpful to utilize the services of a Referee" to relieve Thomas of a burden he did not want—dealing directly with Black citizens pleading for their right to vote.[25]

'I AIN'T GOING TO BE NO . . . CHEAP S.O.B.'

In response to the appeals court decision, Thomas did something that the Justice Department had not requested or expected. Thomas took Brown's advice and invoked the special procedure of the 1960 Civil Rights Act for appointing a federal referee to register voters in Perry County. It was the first time any federal judge had appointed a federal referee under the Act—invoking for the first time the law's section which Alabama opponents had warned would unleash the Justice Department's "Anti-South Gestapo" into the South.[26]

Thomas appointed as federal referee Ozmus Sigler "Tigger" Burke, a white lawyer from Greensboro, the county seat of neighboring Hale County which had fewer Black voters than Perry County. Burke was a landowner and real estate attorney whose name appeared dozens of times in public notices in the *Greensboro Watchman* as lawyer for a mortgage holder, often for his own family, foreclosing on someone's home or property. He rented houses to Black families ("For Rent: Colored house on silk stock alley") and handled wills, estates, and an occasional local civil or criminal court case.[27]

Burke's qualifications as a federal referee were threefold: he was an attorney, a personal friend of a judge on the Fifth Circuit Court of Appeals, and a lifelong resident of the Black Belt, except for his college years and service in World War II. Federal Circuit Court Judge Walter Gewin had become the Burkes' family friend in the 1940s when he practiced in Greensboro. "Gewin was no racist," according to Jack Bass, noted biographer of the South's federal judges, "but it took time for him to develop a sensitivity to the injustice of racial discrimination." If so, that time had not yet arrived in 1963. Gewin knew about the Perry County case and in response to one Justice Department request for an expedited hearing to require Thomas to act, he referred to the federal lawyers' efforts as "zealous, demanding and over-enthusiastic."[28]

Burke had had a limited role in politics. He was elected to the local school board in 1950 but did not seek reelection after the 1954 *Brown* decision. In 1960 he lost a race to be a delegate to the Democratic National Convention and in 1962 lost the election for membership on the state Democratic Executive Committee. His political endorsements appear to have been based on personal friendships, although ads in 1960 show he ran as a "States Righter" along with State Senator Walter Givhan, Frank Mizell, and others. Burke also endorsed Chief Justice Ed Livingston's son in his unsuccessful bid to be Alabama's attorney general.[29]

Before his appointment, Burke insisted on the same annual salary as a federal district court judge since he argued his role as a federal referee registering Black voters could make him unpopular in white Greensboro and across the Black Belt: "I ain't going to be no . . . cheap S.O.B.," he told Thomas.[30]

Burke proceeded to ensure that his standing in white Greensboro remained unsullied. The Justice Department learned of his appointment by reading the newspapers, and afterwards Burke sought no guidance or input from federal lawyers and ignored them whenever possible. Later, when asked what legal standards he used to decide who should be registered to vote in Perry County, the federal referee told Justice Department attorneys John Doar and Brian Landsberg that Thomas gave him these instructions: "Don't register anyone who shouldn't be registered; register everyone who should be registered."[31]

Beginning in September 1964, the nation's first federal referee for voter registration started his work in Marion, the county seat of Perry, and, in the tradition of Black Belt registrars since the adoption of the 1901 Constitution, he became a law unto himself. Applying his fastidious habits as a real estate attorney, Burke set up a filing system of his own devise and gave each of the hundreds of persons who had written to Thomas a filing number. Afterwards, he had as little personal contact with prior Black applicants as possible. They were sent a letter and required to fill out a form confirming their name, race, address, and previous attempts to register to vote. His letter also stated that the form had to be signed as complete and accurate "on penalty of perjury"—a possible punishment that no state or federal law provided for.

The applicants were instructed to appear at a joint hearing where they were required to fill out another form, quite similar to the one received by mail. They were given a registration test reflecting what Burke decided the Alabama Constitution required for proving literacy to become a voter. It included four questions on citizenship, a requirement to write a provision of the Constitution that Burke read, and four questions about the provisions of the Constitution.[32]

Initially, Albert Turner seemed delighted that Perry County had obtained the nation's first federal referee for voter registration. He offered the distinction as proof of the Civic League's impact as he attempted to sustain community involvement and persistence. Remembering what was likely his message to the Black community, Turner would claim years later that the local white leaders "saw the handwriting on the wall when we got" the federal referee.[33] But Burke's conduct quickly proved that Perry's national distinction was no giant step for local Black registration.

In his first report to Thomas, Burke stated he had reviewed applications from 204 of Perry's Black citizens and found only 24 qualified to vote.

Justice Department attorney Brian Landsberg attempted to have Thomas overrule his referee by filing an objection detailing a person-by-person review of the answers of 82 applicants whom Landsberg argued met the court's criteria of valid qualifications to vote in Alabama. The state's attorney urged the judge to uphold the referee's findings and accused the Justice Department of seeking only one standard: "Take a good look at the person, and if he is a Negro register him." Thomas affirmed Burke's decisions, and the Justice Department explored grounds for an appeal.

Meanwhile, Burke continued his practices unaltered. Black men and women like Ella Stewart who had been rejected by the local board applied to the federal referee—only to be rejected again. By the end of the year, Burke had registered only two new Black voters from among 61 new applications. Most Black applicants gave up. After receiving two written notices, 50 decided not to take off from work to appear before Burke to endure a laborious process in which they would be rejected again.[34]

The local registrars also had changed—but only for the worse. Their use of Smith's new 400-part registration test now undercut the work of the local citizenship schools. "You'd walk up to the desk," Turner remembered, "and they'd tell you to open up the book, and whatever pages you opened the book on, that would be your test. . . . It was fixed where you never would be able to pass the test. You couldn't learn all the tests in the book."[35]

With stagnant Black registration now reinforced and sanctioned by a federal referee and a federal judge, the Sovereignty Commission moved forward on the last days of 1964 to advance another part of Smith's strategy. On behalf of the Perry registrars, Frank Mizell petitioned Thomas for permission to purge the county's voter rolls of all persons registered since 1959 and to require all voters to reregister. Mizell stated that the county's registrars were seeking "to eliminate the effect of the discrimination in voter registration found to exist."[36]

There was no doubt that many Alabama counties needed to purge its voting rolls—but only among white voters. The best available data from the period shows that 17 counties (ten in the Black Belt) had white registration rates above 100 percent of the white voting-age population. It was commonly acknowledged that some people had left the counties and many "had been dead for years. Others were itinerant circus performers."[37]

Regardless, it was an unusual request by the Sovereignty Commission's attorney in a county that by the end of 1964 had fewer than 325 registered Black voters among its more than 5,000 African Americans of voting age. Would not such a purge remove white "graveyard votes" and require reregistration by Perry's more than 3,500 current white voters but by only a few hundred Black voters? Yes, but Thomas had shown he would allow even a federal referee to apply a literacy test that excluded almost all Black applicants. So Perry County, under Thomas's jurisdiction, was the best place for launching the Black Belt strategy of resistance that Smith had developed for George Wallace's Alabama.

Smith had run the numbers demonstrating that literacy as a qualification for voting was an effective method for blocking large gains in future Black registration, especially in Black Belt counties. The U.S. Supreme Court had ruled as recently as 1959 that states had a constitutional right to set up literacy as a qualification for voting, and Alabama could use that state's right as its best tool to block federal courts from increasing Black voter registration. In Perry, she argued, 90 percent of the Black population was illiterate. If a literacy test could block most or all of this segment of the Black population from voting, there was no need to apply different standards for registering Black and whites.

Of course, some illiterate whites would be disqualified from voting by applying literacy tests equally to both races, but it would be a relatively small percentage of whites, at least in the Black Belt counties, and whites would retain a sizable majority of registered voters. By requiring reregistration of all voters since 1959, Smith's strategy also would undercut any basis for a federal court to disregard in the future the state's literacy qualifications, as Judge Frank M. Johnson had done in counties under his jurisdiction. Johnson applied a "freezing" standard for registering Blacks; it froze the terms and standards previously used to register illiterate whites and applied the same standards to Black voters. In effect, Johnson had eliminated the literacy tests in counties under his purview.

In other words, a purge would wipe the slate clean and permit the use of a color-blind literacy test to determine who among new applicants of any race was qualified to vote. It would then permit the use of a color-blind literacy test to determine who among new applicants of any race was qualified to reregister. Smith was certain her plan would assure continued white control at the ballot box. Accordingly, Frank Mizell asked Thomas to authorize a purge and to permit the Perry County board to re-qualify all persons "in accordance with the requirements of the court and the laws of Alabama on a nondiscriminatory basis under standards to be equally applied to all future applicants for voter registration."[38]

If implemented, Smith's two-prong strategy promised to do more than clamp down on Black voting. It also provided Wallace's newly emerged presidential candidacy with exactly the facile posturing he continued to need in speaking to national audiences when the issue of voting came up. "I have said a hundred times or more in speeches in nearly every state in this union, and I have said it in Alabama . . .," Wallace would proclaim, "any eligible citizen of this state is entitled to vote."[39]

'We were supposed to stop after the good whipping'

In an internal memorandum, the Justice Department's Brian Landsberg argued for a speedy, vigorous appeal of Judge Daniel Thomas's decision to support O. S. Burke's work as a federal referee because his conduct "undermines the local voter registration organization" and "the Negro community will be discouraged from exercising its rights." He was half right. By the end of 1964, Albert Turner realized that the referee was as hopeless as the local registrars in treating Black citizens fairly. "So, we recognized we weren't going to get registered to vote really through the normal procedure of court actions and knocking on doors and trying to pass tests and all that," Turner told a young Alabama journalist, Howell Raines, a decade later. "We recognized that . . . so we decided to go to direct action."[40]

Fortunately, in January 1965 George Bess, a 20-year-old SNCC worker, showed up in Marion to work with Turner. A native of Tallahassee, Bess had just left his work in Selma—Selma, Mississippi—after being shot at. He arrived in Perry County as part of a major voter registration drive, "One Man, One Vote," that SNCC and SCLC were jointly undertaking to focus the nation's attention on the barriers, brutalities, and injustices in

Selma, Alabama. In keeping with its philosophy, SNCC sent organizers to surrounding Black Belt counties to help communities realize the same momentum they hoped to develop in Selma through mass protests.

As hundreds of adults and students marched—and many were arrested—in Selma behind Dr. King and SNCC's young chairman, John Lewis, Turner organized a march to the Perry County courthouse on the first day of voter registration. Facing a bitter, cold wind, three hundred adults marched in an orderly column to the courthouse and stood in a long line to register. Bess, who had spent much of his early days interacting with Marion's Black high school students, joined a few deciding "to go and test the lunch counters downtown to try to get a Coke" in white-owned drug stores on the same day.[41]

Marion's first direct action protests occurred without incident. The chief of police directed traffic around the protestors, and the drug store served Black students for the first time. "I was shocked that so many were marching," observed a local white attorney who admitted that the white community thought the protest would fizzle out before it started. Turner was also surprised by the numbers and the white reaction. "Too good to be true," he told a reporter.[42]

And it was. The next day, Bess and 15 students who attempted to integrate a white-owned cafe were arrested and roughed up. When word reached the schools, Black students walked out and joined Turner and other adults marching to the county jail. SCLC organizer James Orange, a husky man with a big heart, led the students in the march to the county jail, where they sang freedom songs. "Sing one more song, and you are under arrest," a trooper stated as Orange told the students, "Sing another song." Deputies and 20 newly arrived state troopers arrested more than 500 persons for trespassing. Orange was charged with contributing to the delinquency of minors. Turner was charged with a "breach of the peace." The protestors were bused to "Camp Selma," a nearby convict work camp where they spent a cold, wet night on concrete floors with a cattle trough for water and without a working toilet.[43]

To support this emerging direct action, Dr. King returned to the town where he and Coretta Scott had married. After meeting in the Black funeral home with Turner and local leaders, King promised to help get another court order to open the courthouse more often for voter registration. "We are going to get this right to vote even if it is necessary to fill up all the jails of Alabama," he declared at a church rally.[44] Afterwards, Turner along with SCLC and SNCC organizers continued community meetings, kneel-ins at the public square, and marches to the courthouse almost daily from the nearby Zion Methodist Church. Hundreds of Black students stayed out of school in protest and often held their own gatherings or rallies chanting "We want freedom!" or "One Man, One Vote."

The Black community also boycotted Marion's white-owned businesses. When protests did not fizzle and more than three hundred Black folks turned out for every event, the local authorities called for state troopers to return. On Monday, February 15, 300 Black applicants filled the courthouse seeking to apply to vote and scores of Black youth marched around town with signs calling for an end to segregation.[45]

Three days later, SCLC speakers energized a packed crowd at Zion Methodist. Young people were especially upset by rumors that troopers would beat James Orange as he languished in the local jail. Some national reporters showed up since they heard King might speak in Marion. Ready to do something, the crowd got on its feet to march a block and a half to the county jail where Turner and minister James Dobynes were expected to lead a prayer before returning to the church to disperse.

When the march reached the jail, Dobynes knelt and began to pray only to be clubbed by a state trooper. Other troopers and deputies began wielding batons to push marchers back. They were led by Alabama Director of Public Safety Al Lingo, who had arrived with a contingent of state troopers during the church rally. Dallas County Sheriff Jim Clark and some of his deputies also showed up. Lawmen began swinging their billy clubs as young and old protesters attempted to flee. The downtown street lights went dark, and gangs of local white men joined in the riot, attacking the newsmen covering the event and destroying cameras and film. The blood-drenched melee resulted in dozens of broken bones, cracked heads, open wounds, and one death.

Jimmie Lee Jackson, 26, an ex-soldier and church deacon who had

Al Lingo (ADAH, donated by Alabama Media Group / Photo by Robert Adams, Birmingham News*).*

been involved in voter registration rallies and marches, was shot after white officers pursued protesters into a Black-owned cafe. Jackson was attempting to protect his mother who was attempting to protect her 82-year-old father, who had been clubbed. Jackson was then shot by state trooper James Fowler, who with a few other troopers had been sent into the cafe by Lingo. Decades later, Fowler identified himself as the trooper who pulled the trigger and claimed he acted in self-defense—a claim that was challenged by eyewitnesses and that begged enduring questions.[46] Who set up the attacks on marchers? Who cut off the streetlights? And who unleashed the rampant, official lawlessness in darkened streets so that peaceful protestors and any other Black person accidentally within the range of a white officer's club or a vigilante's pipe were pursued, beaten, and, in Jackson's case, shot?

Turner had an answer. "And, of course, the powers that be felt that they had to do something to stop us because they saw our determination, and, at that point, they decided that they would organize a bunch of troopers and send them into Marion to give us a good whipping. And this is what happened . . . And it was one of those systems where they would beat us up, and we were supposed to stop after the good whipping. That was the theory at that time. So, they did."[47]

Governor Wallace had his own answer after conferring with Black Belt lawmakers. At a news conference, Wallace expressed regret that anyone was hurt in Marion but praised Alabama lawmen for defending the state against "pro-communist mobsters." All in all, he concluded, "I'd say anything they did was necessary." The Alabama Legislative Commission to Preserve the Peace promised to investigate. The Black Belt's stalwart, State Senator Walter Givhan, co-sponsored a resolution defending Marion's white citizens, condemning the national media for irresponsible and false reporting, and expressing "utmost confidence" in the state troopers. During the debate, Al Lingo was also singled out for his leadership. Jimmie Lee Jackson lingered in the Selma hospital run by the St. Edmund Order two weeks before dying—but not before Lingo personally served him with an arrest warrant for assault and battery with intent to kill a police officer.[48]

On Sunday March 7, known afterwards in civil rights lore as "Bloody Sunday," hundreds of Perry County's Black residents rose before dawn, packed bags, and drove to Selma for what had been discussed as a protest march from Selma to Montgomery. Already more than a thousand African Americans in Perry County had walked three miles in the rain to bury Jackson's body in a pine box. Another huge service had been held in Selma on that same day. King and other speakers promised Perry County residents that Jackson's death would result in Black citizens getting the right to vote, and the organizers would lead people from near and far to march to Montgomery to deliver that message to George Wallace.[49]

But King was not in Selma on March 7. SCLC's Andrew Young arrived there from Atlanta that morning with instruction from King to hold a rally, but not a march. Yet march those assembled did, since they were ready to get on their feet and vindicate Jackson's sacrifice. SCLC's Hosea Williams, SNCC's John Lewis and Robert Mants, and Perry County's Albert Turner were in the front two rows leading hundreds to the Edmund Pettus Bridge where they planned to stop and return to Brown Chapel AME Church. Amelia Boynton, who continued to inspire and advise King and Selma's young organizers, was not far behind. As the procession reached the Montgomery side of the bridge, the state troopers under Al

Albert Turner, left on the second row of marchers on Bloody Sunday (ADAH, donated by Alabama Media Group / Photo by Tom Lankford, Birmingham News*).*

Lingo's command ordered the marchers to disperse. Within minutes, the troopers and sheriff's posse, some on foot and some on horseback, rushed the marchers, swinging their billy clubs and spraying canisters of tear gas. This time, the attacks were in broad daylight, and reporters and cameras captured the repeated, raw brutality that was broadcast across the nation later that night.[50]

More than half the people on that bridge were from Perry County, according to Turner. They had come to get their voting rights. Turner knew his life was in danger for a second time on the bridge, but he also knew there was a difference, "We had television in Marion that night, but the camera was burst . . . But, see the thing that happened that Sunday . . . they allowed the nation to see the brutality . . . And that was the turning point of the civil rights movement."[51]

In the famed Selma to Montgomery March that resumed two weeks later, King and other national leaders led people from across the nation in a pilgrimage to the state capitol with the intention of presenting a petition for voting rights to Governor George Wallace. This time, Turner was at the end of the procession. Described by a *New York Times* reporter as a self-possessed, moon-faced 29-year-old who appeared at least 40, Turner had a bricklayer's perspective of how to build something. "We know now that you can't change a political system from above . . . The movement has got to be rooted in the people," he said.

As for Alabama's white folks, Turner suggested they were "not as bad as they look. They don't love us, now," he observed, breaking into a wide smile, "but it is not this vicious hate the way it looks. They're trying to make us live in their system, and we're not going to do it."[52]

When the march arrived in Montgomery, still called the Cradle of the Confederacy, and twenty-five thousand assembled in front of the Alabama capitol, one speaker after another preceded King at the podium. Amelia Boynton read the petition that would be presented and mentioned the "psychotic climate" that existed in the state. Turner was also coaxed to the podium, where he briefly read the Perry County voting statistics that had changed little during the three years in which Judge Daniel Thomas and referee Tigger Burke had overseen voter registration. "We are not satisfied," Turner concluded. The crowd roared its agreement.[53]

Martin Luther King concluded the march with a lesson on Alabama political history and the challenge ahead. Citing C. Vann Woodward's *The Strange Career of Jim Crow*, King thundered that "the segregation of the races was really a political stratagem" of the South's elite "to keep the southern masses divided and southern labor the cheapest in the land. You see," he explained, "it was a simple thing to keep the poor white masses working for near-starvation wages in the years that followed the Civil War."

King recalled the South's Populist movement when its leaders "began awakening the poor white masses and the former Negro slaves to the fact that they were being fleeced" and "began uniting the Negro and white masses into a voting bloc that threatened" to dislodge elite white control of the South's political power. "To meet this threat, the southern aristocracy began immediately to engineer this development of a segregated society" that became "the roots of racism and the denial of the right to vote," King told thousands who had marched with him for voting rights. In one of his most stirring speeches, King declared:

Crowd at Alabama state capitol, March 25, 1965 (ADAH, donated by Alabama Media Group / Photo by Tom Self, Birmingham News*).*

If it may be said of the slavery era that the white man took the world and gave the Negro Jesus, then it may be said . . . that the southern aristocracy took the world and gave the poor white man Jim Crow . . . They segregated southern money from the poor whites; they segregated southern mores from the rich whites; they segregated southern churches from Christianity; they segregated southern minds from honest thinking; and they segregated the Negro from everything. . . . We are on the move now . . . Let us march on segregated schools . . . Let us march on poverty . . . Let us march on ballot boxes until the Wallaces of our nation tremble away in silence. . . . I come to say to you this afternoon, however difficult the moment, however frustrating the hour, it will not be long, because 'truth crushed to earth will rise again' . . . How long? Not long, because the arc of the moral universe is long, but it bends toward justice . . . How long? Not long, because 'Mine eyes have seen the glory of the coming of the Lord . . . He is trampling out the vintage where the grapes of wrath are stored' . . . Our God is marching on. Glory, hallelujah! Glory, hallelujah! His truth is marching on.[54]

'MOST OF THE QUALIFIED NEGROES IN ALABAMA ARE ALREADY REGISTERED TO VOTE'

In all likelihood, Martha Witt Smith and her colleagues at the Sovereignty Commission were as surprised as Perry County's white residents by the turn of events that Albert Turner and the Civic League put into motion in 1965. Both the old tools and new plans for maintaining disfranchisement were under serious attack on several fronts, and, as Wallace's point persons on voting issues, Smith and the Commission scrambled to try and derail the momentum of change.

On the day before Jimmie Lee Jackson's funeral in early March, Smith had traveled to Camden, the county seat of nearby majority-Black Wilcox County, where no Black voter had been registered since the first years of the century. More than two hundred African Americans had attempted to march into town to the courthouse but were stopped by the mayor and policemen carrying pistols, shotguns, and cattle prods. In court, the Justice Department filed papers seeking to have Judge Daniel Thomas prohibit local registrars from requiring applicants to have an existing voter vouch for them—since all the county's voters were white and no white would vouch for a Black applicant, then no Black could register. Adding insult to injury, Wilcox registrars also required Black applicants to wait in line for hours to be rejected. And those lines had to be at the town's old jail—Blacks were not permitted into the courthouse where whites registered.

Thomas had ruled a year earlier that the voucher system was constitutional. He cited a 1947 opinion of the Alabama Supreme Court, the nominal author of the state's current voter registration literacy test, that vouchers were fair, just, and reasonable. "All applicants, irrespective of race or color, have been uniformly required to produce such a person to vouch for them," Thomas decided. "This rule is not discriminatory nor oppressive as to the Negro applicants."[55] The Justice Department had appealed, and the case was pending.

Smith was in Camden explaining to state and national reporters, covering the march after Dr. King spoke there two days earlier, that vouchers were reasonable and necessary since registrars needed to verify that applicants met the state's residency requirements. It had nothing to do with race, she argued, since both Black and white applicants were required to have a voucher. She admitted there may have been some occasional abuse of the voucher system and offered a novel solution for Wilcox's Black applicants: find a registered voter in any Alabama county who would appear in person with you and sign an affidavit verifying your character and the facts about your county residence.[56] She did not estimate how many Black or white voters elsewhere in Alabama personally knew such details about Black applicants in rural, isolated Wilcox County and would travel to Camden to vouch for the local Black resident.

It is also possible that Smith was in the Black Belt to persuade registrars in Wilcox and nearby Lowndes County that their refusal to register a single Negro voter made the state's practices and Wallace's national political posturing vulnerable to increased federal scrutiny and intervention. Within two weeks of her trip, during the next period of voter registration, both Lowndes and Wilcox registrars announced that they had accepted their first Black applicants.[57]

On the day after "Bloody Sunday," Smith was in federal court in Montgomery attempting to help lawyers preserve her 400-question voter registration form and, more significant, to preserve the state's high-bar literacy test for voting. In mid-January, the Justice Department filed suit seeking a statewide court order to ban Smith's questionnaire and to register every person who had been rejected for failing to pass the questionnaire. Even more troubling to Smith, attorney John Doar was asking the court to prohibit registrars from requiring any Black applicant "who was of school age and eligible for public education at a time when the public schools were segregated according to race, to take or complete any voter qualification test" that involved "the educational achievement of the applicant."[58]

Smith was livid. The federal government was attempting to abolish literacy tests for Alabama's Black voters. Doar's line of argument appeared radical to her. The feds were arguing it was unconstitutional racial discrimination for the State of Alabama to have forced African Americans to attend inferior segregated schools for decades and, at the same time, require African Americans to pass a literacy test as a qualification to vote. Yes, the U.S. Supreme Court had ruled that a state may impose educational or literacy qualifications for voting, the Department's papers acknowledged. But, Doar argued before a three-judge panel of Frank M. Johnson Jr., Richard Rives, and Walter Gewin, all Alabama natives, a State may not "impose a qualification for voting, which contrary to its constitutional obligation, it has afforded whites a greater opportunity to meet than it has afforded Negroes." The government complaint alleged that because of "inequalities in educational facilities and opportunities for which the State of Alabama is entirely responsible, Negroes have not been afforded an equal chance to meet the requirements of the State's literacy tests."[59]

The state's attorneys contended that the U.S. Constitution gave Alabama the right to impose any voter qualification that the legislature and voters approved, and certainly a literacy test. They scoffed at the notion that education in Alabama was unequal and repeated Wallace's claim that school funding for segregated Black schools was now equal to white schools. If there existed problems with the unequal treatment of voters, the best remedy was the reregistration of all voters who would take the same test—in other words, Smith's proposed Black Belt plan.

When asked by the judges about the remedy of reregistration, Doar responded that the Civil Rights Act of 1960 established a sixth-grade education standard for any literacy test in a federal election, and only Congress had the power to change that standard. Doar also stated that the Justice Department opposed any test that Alabama elected officials would develop and administer for reregistration since they were the beneficiaries of the discriminatory registration system. Outside the courtroom, Smith attacked Doar and the Justice Department for seeking to abolish all literacy tests. She accused Doar of asking the federal courts to "hold new federally supervised elections with all Negroes voting and put . . . all elected Alabama public officials out of business."[60]

In other proceedings before Judge Johnson, the Justice Department submitted statistical evidence of the high number and percentage of Black applicants rejected in seeking to register to vote in Black Belt counties since 1961. Smith turned the courthouse hallway into a "spin alley" where she argued to state and national reporters that all federal lawsuits charging voter discrimination in Alabama since 1961 should be voided because the persons on those boards of registrars were no longer in office. All current boards across the state had been reconstituted with new members appointed under Wallace's leadership after September 1963, and all federal lawsuits were filed earlier.[61]

Smith's argument was factually incorrect since the Justice Department's statistics included data about applicants through most of 1964. Besides, the 1960 Civil Rights Act had expressly banned that strategy since officials in Alabama and other states in the 1950s had deployed the resignations of county registrars in their legal maneuvers to dismiss voting cases. Therefore, the argument could not be made by the state in Johnson's court, but outside of it the Sovereignty Commission staff was spewing false assertions for public consumption. And, not less significant, the bogus argument recast the problems of voting in Alabama as occurring before George Wallace took office.

In regard to Perry County, Smith's strategy began to fall apart. Doar announced that his Department was appealing Thomas's ruling that upheld the federal referee's work and, in pleadings before the Fifth Circuit, accused O. S. Burke of ignoring federal law as often as had the local board of registrars. Thomas apparently decided he could no longer stonewall. He ruled on the issues he had heard about Perry County registrars in April 1964—almost a year earlier. Thomas now instructed registrars to process at least 100 applicants each day and to remove Smith's questionnaire as a requirement. Surprised, Smith defended the Perry County board claiming it was already processing more applications than the judge had ordered, and she complained that Thomas had failed to give the newly appointed registrars an opportunity to show what they had done recently.

Smith seemed especially aggrieved that even Thomas had not embraced her plans for reregistration in Perry County. She reminded reporters that its registrars were leaders in the state seeking to eradicate past discrimination by reregistering all voters. Also, the Sovereignty Commission circulated a pamphlet entitled "Perry County—Facts and Distortions," in which Smith described how the campaign there was not about "songs and prayers" but "bricks, broken bottles, riots, and threats against the personal safety" of its registrars.[62]

The strategies Smith had devised for her governor were in a tail spin. On the evening of March 15, in response to events in Alabama, President Lyndon Johnson announced in a speech to Congress and the American people the submission of a new voting rights bill. "And we shall overcome," he said. In response in the Alabama legislature, State Senator George Hawkins of Etowah County, a former legal advisor to Governor Jim Folsom, proposed a state constitutional amendment to eliminate most restrictions for voter registration across the state. The bill would eliminate the poll tax and make a sixth-grade education the only qualification to vote.

"We can sit back and let the federal government take control of our registration procedures," Hawkins said, "or we can use common sense and do something about it ourselves." He pitched it to his colleagues as a way to keep Alabama from falling under the special provisions of the proposed federal law, but Hawkins was clear that he thought "voter registration has been very restrictive in Alabama . . . unfair . . . designed to keep people from voting." Senator Ed Horton, representing Lauderdale and Limestone counties near the Tennessee border, supported Hawkins's bill with less political spin. "This is a moral cause," he asserted. "We have rendered a disservice to many decent, law-abiding Negroes in Alabama who are qualified to vote."[63]

These bills interfered with Wallace's messaging. On the day Hawkins introduced his bill, Wallace announced he was authorizing added funds to increase registrars' work days in five Black Belt counties under litigation. The gesture provided Wallace the opportunity to reiterate his claim: "I favor any eligible citizens in this state having the privilege of voting. I have made this position clear throughout the nation . . . eligible citizens are entitled to vote in this state."[64] Wallace had been using every opportunity to repeat this mantra and even included the line in his earlier executive order banning the Selma March. He had used the same refrain with the American people who watched "Face the Nation" a few days earlier.[65] Now, however, two state senators had challenged his claim.

Smith appeared before the state senate committee considering Hawkins's bill. She professed she was there only to provide neutral information, not

Walter Givhan in legislature (ADAH, donated by Alabama Media Group / Photo by Ed Jones, Birmingham News*).*

to oppose the bill, although "most of her testimony was against the measure," according to the reporter covering the hearing. After Smith shared the state's existing questionnaire, Hawkins exclaimed, "Why I couldn't pass this test"—a judgment with which most committee members agreed as they sent the measure to the full senate.[66]

During the four days in which King led marchers from Selma to Montgomery, Wallace and Smith had an opportunity to regroup while the legislature spent an inordinate time making speeches and passing resolutions condemning everything and everyone involved in the march. It became a contest as to which legislator could find the most hyperbolic language and the most obscure villain to condemn or the most politically useful heroes to praise.

Black Belt Senator Walter Givhan led the stampede with a resolution proclaiming "great strides have been made in Alabama, and are continuing to be made, to enroll all qualified voters regardless of race, which policy is fair, just, and equitable," while condemning "Martin Luther King . . . outside agitators, communist sympathizers, and well meaning, but socially ignorant crusaders" for manufacturing a crisis by "stirring up strife and dissension" to justify "vicious legislation" on voting rights in Congress. In language echoing the debate during the 1901 Constitutional Convention, Givhan's resolution declared that a "policy of registering persons of limited education and little or no qualifications . . . would lead to many serious problems which might well be the beginning of another period of reconstruction resulting in a national tragedy."[67]

A house resolution sponsored by Speaker Albert Brewer praised Wallace for the "manner in which he has handled the affairs of the State during this crisis" over an "asinine and ridiculous 'march.'" Other resolutions included condemnations of "outsiders" attempting to "incite turmoil, hatred, and violence" and of the national media as well as commendations to the fair-minded Montgomery board of registrars, police and state troopers, and Alabama's clergy leaders, such as Episcopal Bishop C. C. J. Carpenter, who strongly criticized the Selma March.[68]

Confronting the possibility of unwelcomed changes in registration by both the state legislature and Congress, Wallace endorsed major revisions in the state's voting qualifications. Alabama's existing questionnaire with its 400 questions was receiving widespread criticism and ridicule across the nation. Thousands of the nation's college and high school students as well as faculty members were taking portions of the Alabama test and failing—a fact reported widely in newspapers and by influential radio and newspaper personalities such as Walter Winchell.[69]

Black newspapers also lampooned the test: "Even a Rhodes scholar would suffer a mental hernia trying to pass the literary test for voting registration in Alabama," wrote the *Pittsburgh Courier* before providing samples of some of the most obscure questions. Humorist Art Buchwald wrote about a Black scholar with a master's from Harvard and a PhD from MIT taking the exam in Bull Whip, Alabama, where initially the courthouse is shuttered but the registration office in the courthouse is open. The Black man is asked to read, among other things, the first 14 sections of the Finnish Constitution in Finnish and interpret them. "We got to keep out agitators and the like," the Alabama registrar explains. Finally, unable to read two Dead Sea Scrolls, the Black man is leaving, as a white applicant is asked to spell "cat."[70]

To stem the tide, the governor's staff in league with Black Belt legislators developed a bill introduced by Holt Rast, one of 17 representatives from Jefferson County and a former University of Alabama All-American football player. It proposed to establish an eighth-grade education or an honorable discharge from the military as the necessary qualification to vote in Alabama. It also continued payment of an annual poll tax as a requirement to vote. If approved by Alabama voters, its sponsors asserted, the state constitution would embody educational qualifications similar to those in New York State.[71]

Questioned about Alabama's literacy test earlier on "Face the Nation," Wallace defended Alabama's right to set educational qualifications. "So, let me say New York has a literacy test unless you provide an eighth-grade certificate," Wallace responded. "We need a fair and reasonable literacy test because I don't believe illiterates should be allowed to vote, whether they are white or black." In an appearance at Vanderbilt University in Nashville, he had repeated his favored refrain about supporting voting by all qualified citizens, white or Black, and had argued that any federal law should not "punish a state now for something it did in the past." Wallace also suggested he was taking a patriotic stance, as he explained first in his testimony before Congress two years earlier: "We feel that if we put the same test that the Armed Forces put to a man to get in the armed services, that that ought to be a fair and good test."[72]

The proposed bill gave Wallace all of these political talking points, and he used them effectively before national audiences. Even James Farmer, national director of CORE (Congress of Racial Equality), was fooled at one point. After the governor declared he wanted every eligible person to vote in Alabama during his "Face the Nation" appearance, Farmer stated, "Wallace is beginning to sound like a moderate . . . we are making progress."[73]

Equally important for Wallace's purposes, the Rast bill incorporated what Martha Witt Smith considered the minimal means to effectively obstruct most Black voting in the near future. Smith undertook a statistical analysis which showed that an eighth-grade education—instead of only six grades of schooling which George Hawkins's bill proposed—was the right cutline by which to block most of Alabama's African Americans from qualifying to vote in 1965 and for the next several years.

The 1960 Census reported that slightly less than 121,000 adults among Alabama's total Black population of 980,000 persons had higher than an eighth-grade education. This number did not include Black adults between the ages of 21 and 25 (the Census did not report that statistic), but Smith did not think the total statewide numbers of Black adults who could qualify to vote under an eighth-grade requirement would be any higher than 121,000 since she calculated "a conservative estimate" that 20,000 Blacks in Alabama would be "disqualified from voting for conviction of crime." Therefore, by her math, Smith estimated that Alabama's Black voter registration in 1965 was around 115,000—close to the maximum of who could be eligible to vote under an eighth-grade standard for qualifying.[74]

The fact that New York State already had a similar standard of an eighth-grade education for qualifying to vote helped to obscure what would be the different racial impact of the proposed standard in Alabama. In New York State, the median number of school years of adults among both whites (10.8) and Blacks (9.4 years) exceeded an eighth-grade education. In Alabama, the median number of school years of adults among whites was 10.2, but among Blacks it was only 6.5—well below the proposed qualifying cutoff.

Other statistics also illustrated the different racial impact of the same voting standard between the two states: the median years of schooling for Black adults in New York State in 1960 was 15 percent below that of white adults. In Alabama, Black adults' median years of schooling was 57 percent below that of white adults.[75]

Smith also had access to Census data evidencing that eighth-grade education levels in Black Belt counties were even lower than the state's overall rates. For example, in Perry County only 866 Black persons had schooling above the eighth grade. Twice as many white adults—1,656—had schooling higher than the eighth grade. Therefore, African Americans comprised 60 percent of Perry's voting age population, but they were only 34 percent of the adults with more than an eighth-grade education. As a result, under the terms of the Rast bill, they could be only about 34 percent of those who could qualify to register to vote in the county. This pattern between Black and white adult levels of education was even more pronounced in other Black Belt counties, except for Macon County with Tuskegee Institute, and it applied in large measure to the faster growing urban counties.[76]

The data meant that Smith's basic plan to use literacy to obstruct Black voting in Alabama could still achieve its purpose. If the Rast bill set the state's minimal educational qualifications to vote and if counties undertook even-handed reregistration of only those qualified to register, the new standard would assure that no biracial voting coalition would be large enough to threaten George Wallace's political future in the state and it would preserve local white rule in Black Belt counties for the foreseeable future. Given the uncertain nature and slow pace of school desegregation in Alabama for providing Black children a better education, the foreseeable future could be a long, long time.

The Rast bill moved through the legislature's lower chamber without viable opposition once Speaker Albert Brewer urged its swift passage and, more significant, the governor indicated that he wanted the bill passed. In the state senate, George Hawkins sought support for his sixth-grade bill but focused his primary effort on banning the poll tax—a fight he had begun in his first term as a legislator. Black Belt legislators, led by Roland Cooper, the "Wily Fox from Wilcox," successfully devised a maneuver that enabled passage of the Rast bill, without any change in the poll tax, while keeping alive the possibility of passage of the Hawkins bill until the last day of the session. Wallace accepted the final bill although it left out an option of qualifying to vote by receiving an honorable military discharge. The constitutional amendment was scheduled to go before the voters in November 1965.[77]

By all appearances, with the aid of Martha Witt Smith, Wallace had maneuvered Alabama law where he wanted it for advancing his political ambitions within the state and across the nation. But dealing with the proposed terms of a new Voting Rights Act in Washington would be an entirely different challenge.

CHAPTER 6

The Voting Rights Act of 1965

'The Ghost of Lincoln Is Moving Up and Down These Corridors . . .'

Despite his increased control of the state capitol that sat aptly on Goat Hill in downtown Montgomery, Governor George C. Wallace found it much more challenging to geld the proposed voting rights bill that the Lyndon Johnson administration introduced in Congress in mid-March. Alabama's congressional delegation now included five Republican representatives, elected in 1964 when Barry Goldwater swept Alabama in the presidential election in which he was trounced nationwide by President Johnson. Representative Glenn Andrews was one of the new Republicans, and his largely central Alabama district included Dallas County, which was in the spotlight during the opening testimony of U.S. Attorney General Nicholas Katzenbach in presenting the new voting rights bill to Congress and the nation.

Because he represented Selma, Andrews attended a White House briefing on the bill where he challenged the president on his handling of the Selma March and argued for the state's right to impose educational qualifications for voting. According to a veteran *New York Times* reporter, the "President replied forcefully to Mr. Andrews, strongly upholding the right of all citizens to vote and pledging uncompromising action to reach that goal." Also, to remind the newly minted, first-term Southern Republican and others of their own party's origins, the president added a bit later: "The ghost of Lincoln is moving up and down these corridors rather regularly these days."[1]

Alabama's congressional delegation, Democratic and Republican, adhered closely to Wallace's political tunes and arguments. On March 17, 1965, after receiving a telegram from Wallace, Representative George W. Andrews (the second Congressman Andrews), who represented east Alabama's Black Belt counties, led the state's house members in an extended defense of the governor, Selma, and all of Alabama. Their remarks closely followed Martha Witt Smith's briefing materials and Wallace's public style.

"The cunningly calculated torment of Selma and Dallas County is the biggest, cruelest, and most unjust publicity stunt staged in a long time," Representative George Andrews alleged, adding that "the author of the song, 'We Shall Overcome' was a Communist." (Apparently he was referring to Pete Seeger, who sang the song but did not write it.) Republican Jim Martin introduced the text of a speech by SNCC leader John Lewis to demonstrate that civil rights activists were indicting Alabama with the "same charges being leveled against the United States by the Soviet Union and every Communist-controlled satellite in the world." Republican Bill Dickinson, who represented Montgomery and southeast Alabama counties, condemned "King Martin Luther" whose "lieutenants have belonged to Communist front organizations . . . not nearly so interested in the United States as they are in the Kremlin."[2]

On the issues of voting, Representative Armistead Selden, whose district included Tuscaloosa and some Black Belt counties, attacked the news media for untruthful coverage and for ignoring that the unruly protests in his state were not a "right to vote drive" but "an 'antiliteracy' campaign being waged simultaneously with efforts of the U.S. Department of Justice to abolish literacy as a requirement in Alabama through the Federal courts." Earlier George Andrews paraphrased the Sovereignty Commission report that Smith had written, beginning with the false claim that statistics "bear out that practically every Negro called up for the draft in Alabama fails to pass the mental test if he has not gone higher than the eighth grade." Afterwards, he entered Smith's entire report into the *Congressional Record*.[3]

Republican Representative John Buchanan of Birmingham and north Alabama Congressman Bob Jones, the state's remaining New Deal

Democrat in the House, were slightly more moderate, defending the white people of Alabama. Buchanan declared: "The people of Alabama have been libeled. The people of Alabama . . . are law-abiding people, and when the tumult and the shouting have died, they will have to live with each other and work out their problems themselves." Jones said that Alabama's white people were only asking for "time, time to adjust, time to accept change." He asserted that "if left alone, I know the people of Alabama will make the right choice."[4]

This was followed weeks later by some House members from Alabama testifying before the Judiciary Committee. Selden repeated the charge that the pending legislation was an anti-literacy bill that would discriminate against only Southern states. Buchanan argued that Alabama's low levels of voting had virtually nothing to do with discrimination but was the consequence of "widespread political apathy because we have walked in the dark valley of one-party politics"—an argument that Republican Jack Edwards of Mobile echoed.[5]

These speeches had virtually no effect or notice outside the state. In Congress and across the nation, images of Al Lingo's violent troopers on the Edmund Pettus Bridge, news reports of the killings of white ministers and a white Detroit housewife working in the Black Belt to help Blacks vote, and the powerful eloquence of Dr. King as a spokesman for change—each combined to make an irrefutable public case to the nation. The pages of the *Congressional Record* were filled with expressions of outrage and disbelief, as was the media. U.S. Senator Ralph Yarborough of Texas bemoaned the "tragic events in Alabama" and put the blame on its chief executive. "Shame on you George Wallace . . . Wallace should pattern his conduct on that of real Southerners, like George Washington . . . and Alabama's own Justice Hugo Black . . . He needs to atone for the shame he has brought to Alabama, to my beloved Southland, and the injury he has brought to the Nation."[6]

Wallace had no intention of atoning for anything, but his fundamental argument about the right of Alabama as a state to maintain literacy standards for qualifying to vote was a losing proposition in Congress. Smith's analysis and the Sovereignty Commission's work in Alabama rested on the state's right to use a literacy test in deciding who was fit to vote. But only Alabama and six other states in the South used literacy tests and other devices to exclude voters. Across the nation, a majority of states (31) had no educational or literacy requirements in 1965. And the proposed act would ban literacy tests only in states or counties where voter registration or voter turnout in 1964 was less than 50 percent of the voting-age population. Only Alabama and six other states—Alaska, Mississippi, Louisiana, Georgia, South Carolina, and Virginia—fit that bill, as did a few counties in four other states with literacy tests (Arizona, Hawaii, Idaho, and North Carolina).[7]

Therefore, the analysis and arguments Smith had concocted fell flat simply because registration practices in the vast majority of states would not be changed or endangered by the federal law's ban on literacy tests and the bill proposed a ban in only a handful of locations—primarily the Deep South where most of the violations of Black voting rights had occurred, according to the Justice Department's case docket and the Civil Rights Commission's reports. There was, of course, the question of whether the U.S. Supreme Court would find such a law constitutional, but several leading constitutional scholars argued that the narrowly defined ban on literacy tests would be upheld, and congressional lawmakers were willing to let the Court decide that question.[8]

Wallace soon read the handwriting on the wall in Congress and decided there was no political gain by appearing before the Senate Judiciary Committee to oppose the bill. Instead, he sent his Sovereignty Commission lawyers, Frank Mizell and Commission director Eli Howell, to testify. Mizell informed the Committee he was only a "pick and shovel lawyer" who represented local registration boards in Alabama and was not representing the governor, even as he and Howell failed to reveal their positions with the Sovereignty Commission.

Mizell was on his best behavior. He argued that Alabama and its voter registration test had been unfairly portrayed by the national press and defended the constitutional right of Alabama to use literacy as a qualification for voting. He reprised Smith's statistics on how it was illiteracy, not race, that disqualified Alabama Negroes and repeated almost verbatim her written materials suggesting that Alabama registration laws since 1946 had helped Black voting.

In a new twist to the Sovereignty Commission's argument, Mizell asserted that the Alabama literacy test was part of the state effort to help abolish illiteracy along with its increased funding of Black and white schoolteacher salaries and its program of free textbooks during the Wallace administration. He also condemned the communist-infiltrated Negro movement whose leaders were taking Black children out of school in Alabama to march while the kids should be in school to learn so they could later in life pass the literacy tests for voting.[9] Howell's brief remarks echoed Mizell, but he also contended that the proposed bill would produce discrimination instead of reducing it since "literate persons are discriminated against in the elimination of any test."[10]

As Congress deliberated, some notable white Alabamians broke their public silence, signaling that they did not sanction all of the resistance, turmoil, and violence that had occurred in the state during the last two years. Instead of blaming out-of-state media for distorted news coverage, they registered public concern about developments in Alabama.

Perhaps the most dramatic statement was issued by business groups, including those who represented the Big Mules of Alabama industry and commerce—the Alabama Chamber of Commerce, Alabama Bankers Association, Associated Industries of Alabama, and Alabama Textile Manufacturing Association. "What we believe and where we stand" was a full-page advertisement in the *Wall Street Journal* and Alabama's daily newspapers. It asserted the state's business community's belief in obedience to the laws, even those with which people might disagree, communication between the races, economic growth, and education.

The Big Mules' statement of voting rights was equally high-sounding: "WE BELIEVE . . . IN THE RIGHT OF EVERY ELIGIBLE CITIZEN TO REGISTER AND TO CAST HIS BALLOT." But the full statement could have been written by Smith since it tracked closely Wallace's own public posturing. "We believe, however, that qualification of prospective voters, when properly and equitably administered, is a constitutional responsibility that must be preserved," the statement added.[11] Eager for any sign of white courage in the Deep South, the White House either ignored or failed to see that Alabama's business groups had endorsed Wallace's position on voting rights. President Johnson praised the business groups, suggesting no voting rights act or civil rights bill could solve racial problems without community responsibility.[12]

Winton Blount, one of the state's wealthiest businessmen, followed by publicly praising the business organizations' joint statement as a vital response to the state's critical conditions. Blount was far more direct in his speech. He called Wallace's remarks about the killing of the Detroit housewife, Viola Liuzzo, after the Selma March "callous" and unbecoming of the people of Alabama. (Wallace had said Alabama's Highway 80 where Liuzzo was shot was still safer than the New York subway.) Blount also said, "Our political leaders . . . were just dumb enough to be outsmarted by the agitators." He called for the state legislature to provide "equitable voter rights to all people."[13]

In another speech a few weeks later, Blount made it clear that while he disliked the governor's leadership, he supported the Rast bill that carefully preserved all-white political rule in the state. He urged Alabamians to "back up this sensible effort by our legislature when the referendum is held . . . not because of pressure from the federal government or from any group of agitators, but because it is the right of every eligible citizen to vote."[14]

While filibustering on the floor of the state senate, a few legislators made direct attacks on Wallace, but these men would be supporting former Governor John Patterson or Ryan DeGraffenreid, who Wallace defeated in the 1962 runoff, in the upcoming governor's race. Patterson's former revenue commissioner also spoke publicly about how Alabama was falling behind other Southern states in job growth, and AFL-CIO president Barney Weeks spoke up about how Wallace's tax "giveaways" to out-of-state industries failed to spur job growth. None criticized Wallace for his stance on voting. A group of 50 self-described "everyday people" in Huntsville did publicize their displeasure with Alabama's registration and voting laws by petitioning the Tennessee governor for assistance in helping Alabama counties north of the Tennessee River to secede and join his state.[15]

The most prominent white leader voicing opposition to Alabama's registration laws also came out of Huntsville. The state's famed German-born scientist Dr. Wernher Von Braun, director of NASA's Marshall Space Flight Center, told his city's Rotary Club that Alabama had erected "a Berlin Wall around the ballot box." He did not question who should be eligible to vote in the state, although he observed that Alabama's voting procedures "discourage the qualified as well as the unqualified from registering." He attacked the voucher system and the limited procedures and days a person could register and pointed out that it was far easier to get an automobile tag or a marriage license than to register to vote in Alabama.[16]

Von Braun's speech received perhaps more coverage out Alabama than inside the state, where the *Alabama Journal* suggested that as one of the state's "first citizens" he had a right to speak out, even if he was guilty of hyperbole and sure to be harshly criticized. He was. Martha Witt Smith was furious. Von Braun criticized not only the registration procedures she and the Sovereignty Commission were safeguarding but also the local board of registrars on which she had served since 1949. Smith demanded an apology from the scientist "who has left his safe world of space to take [up] his ill-informed role in the voter registration controversy."

She accused Von Braun of using his national prominence to "launch an unjustified blast at his adopted state" and suggested that the NASA-employed scientist was doing the bidding of President Johnson. Von Braun did not reply or issue an apology, but he did not speak publicly on the issues again. [17]

In what the Black press called a historic event, House Speaker Albert Brewer received a Negro delegation that was permitted for the first time in memory to enter the state capitol to present grievances about Alabama voting restriction and other issues. Governor Wallace was not in the building. In the past, African Americans attempting as a group to petition the legislature were stopped from entering by state troopers. Lieutenant Governor Jim Allen did not see why that tradition was broken by the speaker. He closed the senate gallery, except to white school children, and refused to meet with the group, as did other legislators, many of whom had an engagement they considered more suitable—a barbeque at the nearby state prison.[18]

Amid this environment, in a speech before Birmingham's Young Men's Business Club, Tuscaloosa banker George LeMaistre overtly condemned the Klan, but he left Wallace out in his criticism. Instead, the banker suggested that Wallace was reaching for "the middle of the road" on racial issues in Alabama.

LeMaistre was one of the state's few businessmen with moral courage for all seasons. Two years earlier, he had been almost alone in Alabama's white business community in publicly condemning "rabble-rousing hate groups and loud-mouth politicians" in his state, and in private he told Wallace to his face that he was spouting "bullshit" in justifying defiance of the federal courts. Now, in the summer of 1965, Wallace had not changed, but the middle of the road in Alabama was shifting. The political dynamics of Wallace's leadership had evoked many white Alabamians' narrowest habits of thought and deed, and Wallace's growing popularity now reflected nothing more than his saying "whatever he thought the people out there wanted to hear."[19] It was a common, mutually parasitic political relationship emerging in full because of—and now becoming greater than—a Black Belt governor with amoral, blind ambitions.

As President Johnson and congressional leaders navigated the voting rights bill toward passage, Wallace's Sovereignty Commission also persisted in diligently echoing his political messaging and searching for new ways to legitimatize the state's right to disqualify illiterate Blacks as voters. In response to the Justice Department's appeal of Judge Daniel Thomas's order in Perry County, for instance, Frank Mizell informed a panel of the federal circuit court judges that the federal government had "embarked upon a punitive judicial experiment to destroy literacy as a requirement for voting." He argued that "such debasement of voter eligibility criteria . . . will result in an illiterate body of voters with no idea nor appreciation of self-government and citizenship responsibility." By the end of June, Circuit Judge Elbert Tuttle ignored Mizell's political claims and pointedly observed that "if the Negro applicants who persisted far enough in their desire to register to vote in Perry County, thought that after the District Court appointed a Federal Referee their troubles were at an end, they were sadly mistaken." He reversed the decisions of Thomas and O. S. Burke.[20]

In late July, Smith went on the offensive by announcing that the Alabama Supreme Court had adopted a new, simpler literacy test for the state's boards of registrars. She stated that the new test had been given to 2,400 sixth-grade students in Alabama schools and 95 percent of them had passed. Smith said all of the state's registrars would begin to administer the new test, except in Perry, Dallas, and the seven other Black Belt counties where the federal courts had barred the use of any literacy test without prior court approval.[21]

Smith's announcement was reported by the Associated Press and appeared in scores of newspapers across the country, but the last-ditch maneuver was too late, too little to salvage the literacy test. Ten days earlier, the U.S. House of Representatives passed the Voting Rights Act with 23 representatives from Southern states voting for it. Five of these Southern members came from states where literacy tests would be prohibited, although none was from Alabama. On August 4, the U.S. Senate adopted the House version, and two days later, in the room where Abraham Lincoln had signed the Emancipation Proclamation, President Johnson signed into law the Voting Rights Act of 1965, which he called the "one of the most monumental laws in the entire history of American freedom."[22]

'Left-Wing Liberals . . . Open the Way for Fraudulent Practices in the South'

On the day Johnson signed the Voting Rights Act, the Sovereignty Commission went into action to delay and disrupt its impact in Alabama. "The woman who heads Alabama's voter registration system" told registrars to continue business as usual until they received a specific formal order to comply with the Act. Smith claimed compliance was not required of registrars, outside those nine counties under current federal court order, until the state legislature changed Alabama law. She repeated her standard line that this "literacy thing in Alabama is not a race issue," but she also shifted the rhetoric and rationale of continued resistance. Smith said the new Act was "an open invitation to corruption" by those who would manipulate voters who could not read a ballot.[23]

On the following Monday, U.S. Attorney General Katzenbach

authorized federal registrars to enroll voters regardless of race or literacy in four Black Belt counties, and Mizell filed motions in Alabama federal courts seeking permission to purge voter rolls and reregister all voters in the counties under court order. The Sovereignty Commission lawyer was openly challenging the Act by proposing to implement the plan originally sought in Perry County two years earlier—supposedly "to remove the effects of past discrimination." Mizell also asked the federal courts to permit registrars to reject applicants if they failed to offer two persons who could vouch for an applicant's residence in the county or who failed to pass the new state literacy test—both direct violations of the new federal law.[24]

As expected, it did not take Judge Frank Johnson even a "Mississippi minute" to turn down the motion "as completely without merit." Even Judge Daniel Thomas after some delay could not grant Mizell's motion in direct contradiction of federal law. But the filings sent a significant political message to white Alabamians. As voters read about the federal government sending outsiders to register illiterate Black voters, outsiders whom Alabama's own registrars said "don't know a thing in the world" about their state, their governor was continuing to fight for Alabama fairness—to give everyone the same chance to reregister to vote on the same terms while the feds were trying to advance only the cause of a racial minority. "The Department of Justice has become the department of colored affairs," Mizell stated outside the court.[25]

A week later, Wallace announced he was joining other Deep South states in challenging the Voting Rights Act in federal court using his own lawyers, including Mizell and a Birmingham attorney who had defended the city's school board in desegregation litigation. Mizell also filed motions in pending state circuit court cases in Selma challenging the work of federal examiners in Black Belt counties solely because they were registering illiterate applicants. Wallace called the Voting Rights Act "punitive" and "as bitter as anything enacted by the Reconstruction Congress." With the Vietnam War escalating, the governor also argued that if "a person is not literate enough to go into the armed services of this country, then he should not be considered literate enough to vote."[26]

On September 9, Wallace called the state legislature into a second special session to adopt a new reapportionment plan. The federal courts were requiring the legislature to do what the Black Belt and Big Mules had prevented for more than 60 years, but it was the federal courts and the "federal usurpation of power" that Wallace attacked in addressing a joint session. In a statewide television address that many decided was the opening of the governor's campaign for a second term, Wallace spent seven minutes on reapportionment and 23 minutes attacking the Supreme Court, Congress, and Johnson.

It was an extraordinary speech, echoing the hyperbole of his inaugural address and capturing the political mind-set of white Alabama's popular leader and many of his supporters. Wallace told Alabamians that the legislature was acting under the duress of the Supreme Court, which was imposing the dictates of its appointed members on the elected officials of Alabama and its people. He told legislators: "Even though we do not consent, the people of Alabama expect you and me to protect this state from an apportionment plan submitted by an attorney of the American Civil Liberties Union—said to be in exile—Chuck Morgan."[27]

After promising to help develop a plan, Wallace launched a broadside attack on the three branches of the federal government as well as liberals, "left-wing radicals" and "left-wing editors." He listed a catalogue of grievous encroachments that the Supreme Court had inflicted on Alabama and the nation: banning "a simple prayer in the public schools," outlawing "the saying of grace in lunchrooms" and "bedtime prayers in public orphanages," elevating "the religion of atheistic materialism," and banishing "God from recognition in public institutions."

He continued. The Court was "running the country by injunction" through "dictatorial decrees" that sanctioned and encouraged the "occupation of small communities [such as Selma] and now large ones [such as the Watts riots in Los Angeles] by thousands of out of state riffraff, communists, and fellow travelers, kooks, beatniks, prostitutes, and bums and has handcuffed local law enforcement who seek to prevent depredations against the peace and order." He concluded his attack on the Court by reminding his audience that those nine men "coddled our communist enemies," "licensed a flood of filthy literature" preventing "states the right to protect their children from this evil," and encouraged the "Russian system" and socialism.[28]

"Are we to resist this trend?" Wallace asked as he looked directly into cameras supplied by the state-owned public television network and broadcast by it and all the state's commercial television stations.

As to the Congress, Wallace declared it was also destroying "state and local self government" by passing the "abominable Civil Rights Act of 1964 which destroys more personal freedoms than any act of Congress in the long history of the nation" and the "unbelievable voting law" that "wipes out safeguards erected by the Alabama Legislature over a period of sixty-five years for *the purpose of guaranteeing honest elections*."[29]

No longer was the fight over voting a matter of Black and white in the Black Belt. The governor detailed what his Sovereignty Commission and others characterized as outrages besetting Alabama:

> Today the bureaucrats are issuing certificates to vote to people who cannot read the ballot nor even the instructions on a ballot or on a voting machine. The left wing liberals need as many illiterates as they can get to vote in order to keep them in power. *They need the fraudulent election processes of Chicago and other large cities. Now they have felt the need to open the way for fraudulent practices in the South and the need of the illiterate vote.* This federal law says that you cannot challenge at the polls anyone to whom the federals have handed out a certificate. You cannot require identification. You cannot require witnesses to an "X" mark. The certificate can be passed from hand to hand and from person to person and it entitles the holder to vote. These certificates can be bought and sold. Local election officials have no way to identify the holder or to prove that one did or did not vote.[30]

Wallace also told Alabamians that if local election officials do not allow certificate holders to vote or "if they do not count the vote, even though fraudulent," the U.S. attorney general is empowered to prosecute them. "The idea for issuing voting certificates originated with the Communist Party," Wallace stated. He went on to condemn the federal government's actions in school desegregation, as he developed his theme of law and order. "When I stood in the doorway at the University of Alabama, I stood there to uphold the law, the Constitution of the United States . . . The Constitution has been changed. It has been violated by lawbreakers in Washington, D.C." He insisted the Supreme Court broke the law in 1954:

> When a President of the United States goes on nationwide television and sings the song of the communist street marchers and their poor dupes, 'We Shall Overcome,' he should have finished by telling the people what these lawless armies intend to overcome . . . overcome local school boards, local law enforcement, state legislatures . . . overcome the law and a civilization established by the will of the people and place over the people the will of a central tyranny . . . This encouragement of street mobs to break the law is a guarantee that the anarchy of Los Angeles [Watts riots] shall come about . . . The attempted anarchy in Alabama was stopped cold in its tracks . . . Law and order prevailed. But just today the federal court has issued a subpoena . . . This federal court . . . wants the names of all troopers who upheld the law at Selma and at Marion, Alabama.[31]

Wallace concluded by reminding Alabamians that he stood up to tyranny for them. "I want to speak for you and champion what you would have me champion. I want to know you are with me in our cause . . . If you feel a need for me in the job I try to do, then I want you to know I feel a need for you. I need your support."[32]

The legislature got the message, In the field of voting and representation, it passed a reapportionment plan so that no district in either house had a majority of African Americans of voting age and only one senate district had a Black majority in total population. To prevent Black voters from having a decisive role in any house election, the plan combined most Black Belt counties with surrounding majority-white counties into multi-county districts with three or four representatives elected at-large in each district. The law also included an "anti-single shot" technique that would prevent Black voters across the whole district from voting together for only one candidate while white voters split votes among several white candidates.

In its earlier sessions, led by the Birmingham delegation, the legislature also passed an act requiring an anti-single vote provision for Jefferson County and other large counties where an enlarging number of legislators represented the same county. The new act extended the earlier anti-single shot policies that Smith and Mizell pushed into practice in 1961.[33]

The legislature also enacted a law to address the election fraud that Wallace claimed was a product of federal examiners' work. While the bill was pending, the *Alabama Journal* under managing editor Ray Jenkins investigated the governor's charges and was virtually the only news outlet in the state to report that Wallace's concern about Negroes voting more than once "apparently is without basis." A federal examiner explained that the precinct in which a newly registered voter is entitled to cast a vote is listed on the certificate slip provided to the voter and lists of certified voters and their authorized precincts were sent to a county's probate judge, board of registrars, the state government, and the U.S. attorney general. Also, applicants had to state under oath, with possible criminal penalty for making a false statement, that they met the state's residency requirements. The examiner also verified their precincts with a local map.[34]

With Wallace's support, two north Alabama legislators sponsored a bill that required stamping all voters' hands with invisible ink after they cast a ballot so that a special light could detect the stamp. The bill's sponsors had no federal examiners in their counties, and, with so few Black citizens, there was no chance they would see federal examiners sent to their districts. Regardless, their bill passed the state senate unanimously and sailed through the house to become law.[35]

Whatever the depth of knowledge among north Alabama's legislators about the working of the Voting Rights Act, white officials in the Black Belt were well aware of its provisions—and began trying to use the federal law to disqualify or discourage Black voters. Black Belt leaders demanded formal hearings, permitted by federal law, to challenge the registration of hundreds of Black persons put on the rolls by federal examiners. In Wilcox County, the probate judge, sheriff and other county officials spent five days in hearings claiming that almost 300 registered Black voters had criminal convictions or improper residences that disqualified them.

In another maneuver, on behalf of the governor, Mizell easily convinced three state circuit court judges to prohibit probate judges in six Black Belt counties from certifying the counties' official voter rolls with the names of more than 20,000 Black voters recently registered by federal examiners. "We will continue and fight by all equitable means the so-called voting rights act," Wallace announced.[36]

Wallace's unofficial reelection campaign ran into a roadblock at the end of September when he was forced to call the legislature back into special session because the state senate had refused to pass a bill for a proposed constitutional amendment allowing voters to decide if Wallace could succeed himself in office. On September 30, in another statewide broadcast, Wallace addressed the joint session of the legislature and demanded that the people be allowed to decide whether "to permit a governor and other state constitutional officers to serve two consecutive terms." Wallace told Alabamians that no other state surpassed the people of Alabama in refinement, culture and intelligence, and, as the gallery roared with approval, he told the legislature that the refined, cultured intelligent people of Alabama wanted an opportunity to vote on his succession.[37]

"No group of men in the federal judiciary, in the Congress, or in a state legislature, has the right . . . to deny the people the sovereign right and freedom to regulate their own government. The people of this State and others are now being denied the right to vote and control their own schools," Wallace insisted. "Are the people of this State to be denied also the right to vote on an amendment respecting the executive branch of their own state government?" He concluded by looking beyond the legislature into the television camera to assure Alabamians, "I shall go wherever you send me . . . whether it's back across this nation to tell of Americanism to Americans . . . or back to Barbour County." [38]

The governor had a majority of votes for the amendment in each house of legislature, but he did not have the extraordinary majority in the state senate, where 24 of 35 votes were necessary to put a constitutional amendment on the ballot. This requirement embedded in the 1901 Constitution had for almost two-thirds of a century enabled Black Belt legislators to override the will of the rest of Alabama by blocking constitutional amendments they disliked, including reapportionment. Now, there were enough state senators who opposed succession—some for noble reasons, some for purely political reasons—to keep the Black Belt's governor from running for reelection in 1966.

A couple of days after his speech, Wallace received news that a three-judge federal court had struck down Alabama's legislative reapportionment plan, which he had signed only a couple of weeks earlier. The court did not order adoption of the plan proposed by ACLU southern director Chuck Morgan, the Alabamian "in exile," but it did find racial discrimination in the legislature's use of at-large districts in the Black Belt to dilute Black voting strength. The court ordered a new plan with new lines that created five majority-Black districts.[39]

Of course, Wallace had no intention of returning to Barbour County. He held state-financed public forums, which were actually political rallies, in north Alabama districts of the state senators opposing the succession bill and invited them to appear before his supporters to explain their opposition. In south Alabama his staff and allies continued to challenge voter registration. In Selma, state circuit judge James Hare declared the Voting Rights Act unconstitutional and barred the Dallas County probate judge from accepting any voter lists from federal examiners. The Montgomery circuit solicitor filed suit seeking a state court order removing federal examiners from his county since, as Martha Witt Smith announced, more than 50 percent of the eligible Black population was now registered in the county. Smith and the solicitor claimed that the new federal law allowed federal examiners only in jurisdictions with less than 50 percent Black registration.[40]

'TO EXERCISE THEIR RIGHTS . . . IN THIS GREAT DEMOCRACY IN AMERICA'

Wallace's south Alabama supporters did more than go into court. As soon as federal examiners arrived, Women for Constitutional Government—the group that had covered Jefferson Davis's bronze star on the state capitol's portico to prevent Robert Kennedy from desecrating it—began a voter registration drive among white residents in Black Belt counties. In addition, as the number of registered Black voters increased, white landowners, bankers, and merchants began applying economic pressure and intimidation. Newly registered voters were evicted from their homes; others had their home and equipment loans foreclosed; some were required to pay immediately all credit charges with local merchants; and others were jailed for non-payment of debts that suddenly became due.[41]

Also, the ever-present possibility of violence constituted real intimidation. A report by the ACLU and SRC documented in late 1965 that during the last five years at least 26 civil rights workers had been killed in the Deep South. In the Alabama Black Belt alone, those murdered included Jimmie Lee Jackson, Unitarian minister James Reeb, Viola Gregg Liuzzo (Detroit housewife and mother), and Episcopal seminarian Jonathan Daniels. The murderer of only one of the 26 victims had been convicted—and in that case with only a ten-year sentence. The report charged that dual justice was a way of life "from birth to death" in many parts of the South where "dual justice is a standing abuse to all Negroes—the maid, the undertaker, the field hand, the schoolteacher, the minister."[42]

Amid the turmoil and confrontations, Alabamians went to the polls in late November to vote on the proposed state constitutional amendment that would set, in effect, an eighth-grade education as the literacy qualification for voting. It drew little attention or public discussion. "There was a time when such a plan would have stirred up a tempest," the *Montgomery Advertiser* observed, "but that time ended with the passage of the federal voting law. Under that law, as it applies to Alabama, a heartbeat, a faint one at that, is the only requirement beyond age and residency."[43] At the same time, the *Southern Courier*, the newspaper of the Deep South's civil rights movement, noted that "Amendment No. 2 . . . will have no effect right away. But it might some day be important" because, if the U.S. Supreme Court were to find the Voting Rights Act unconstitutional, "voters would have to meet the literacy requirements set by the state legislature."[44]

In a light turnout, the Amendment passed by almost a three to one margin. It won by lopsided margins in almost all counties. Only in Macon County, with a Black majority of registered voters, did the Amendment lose. It appears African Americans provided most votes opposed to adoption. But they were divided, perhaps for the reasons suggested by the

Southern Courier—if the federal voting rights law was voided by the federal courts, the new standard for qualifying to vote would be less restrictive than the state Constitution's old language. Also, the actual language of the Amendment was deceptive. It did not mention requiring an eighth-grade education to vote—only an ability "to read and write . . . in English" with this added, odd phrase: "and make proof of the same in such manner as may be prescribed by the legislature." The Rast bill that had already passed "prescribed" the ability to read and write at an eighth-grade education level.[45]

The night before the referendum, Wallace spoke in Selma to the annual meeting of the Dallas County Citizens Council (the councils had finally convinced editors to drop the "white" in their name). The governor had lost his succession bill in the legislature at the end of October due to opposition from mostly north Alabama legislators, but a few days later in Huntsville, the president of the Alabama educational television network introduced—to rousing applause—Wallace's wife, Lurleen, as the next governor of Alabama.

In Selma, Wallace appeared on the grounds of the National Guard armory after 2,000 white folks had paid $1.50 for barbecue and the chance to hear their governor, who was warmly introduced by State Senator Walter Givhan. The local headlines about his speech highlighted Wallace's claims that his national prominence was generating new industry and jobs for Alabama, but the governor received his loudest cheers for his new themes of attack against those "beatniks" and "slick-haired" television commentators who had disturbed the peace of Selma and the Black Belt eight months earlier.

"The voting rights bill that was aimed at people like us who will fight in Viet Nam was passed for people who say they won't fight in Viet Nam," Wallace declared. He did not need to remind his audience that since the days of the Selma March Martin Luther King Jr. and many civil rights leaders had begun to join cause with the emerging antiwar movement to protest American involvement in the Vietnam conflict. Now broadening the range of white Alabama's enemies, Wallace assured his audience that anyone attending a state-supported college campus who circulated a petition to have the United States withdraw from Vietnam would be expelled.[46]

Wallace clearly enjoyed trying out new lines of rhetorical attack before adoring crowds in the Black Belt, but with a clear eye on the upcoming Democratic primary in May 1966, he set in motion a flurry of state-financed activities to expand and energize his base of white voters across the state. He instructed Sovereignty Commission Director Eli Howell to mail letters to more than 200,000 people who had written the governor, to make sure those supporters and their family were registered to vote. The Commission also produced a multi-colored pamphlet bearing a picture of Wallace with this message: "It is a great privilege to protect our nation and freedoms by voting. Please ask members of your family 21 years and older if they are registered to vote and if they have paid their poll tax."[47]

The brochure was distributed to Alabama's 600,000 white school children, but not to any of the Black schools where almost all the state's Black schoolchildren remained 12 years after *Brown*. After news reports emerged, Howell falsely explained that the brochure went only to white students and their parents to avoid any conflict with the federal Voting Rights Act, which he argued gave Black voters more time than Alabama law allowed white voters to pay poll taxes.[48] This was apparently Howell's explanation as to why the brochure was also distributed only to white civic and veterans groups.

"The voting rights bill is not going to affect Alabama the way many people think," an official in the governor's office confided to a Memphis reporter. "What it is going to accomplish is the biggest registration of whites in our history"[49]—with, of course, the assistance of the state government's apparatus. In addition to the mailings and brochure distribution, the governor's office helped orchestrate a statewide, county-by-county effort for increasing white registration, while sending out letters under Wallace's signature explaining to supporters, "we don't want to make this a matter of racism." It was only a matter of fairness to white people since President Johnson "wants Negro voters to register and evidently not whites."[50]

To fuel that cause, Wallace's staff also began to amplify both his revised rhetoric and the old racist themes that helped elect him in 1962. In his argument on behalf of Wallace before the U.S. Supreme Court, Frank Mizell attacked the Voting Rights Act as "despotic," "punitive," and a "political crime." Alternating between a stump speech and constitutional arguments, Mizell told the justices: "The illiterate citizen, nigra or otherwise, would find himself with more rights in Alabama . . . than the great State of New York." He repeated his charge that the Act "made the Attorney General both the judge and executioner" of a state's right to maintain its own voter registration process, and he accused federal examiners of parading a "panoply of power" in the "captive states" of the Deep South where the federal government had suspended all state elections laws. Whatever his influence on the Court, Mizell made good copy and headlines in the Alabama press for his boss's cause.[51]

A few days later, Mizell joined others on the Alabama Democratic Executive Committee to set rules for the May primary. The ADEC also was to decide if the party would remove the banner of "white supremacy" which fluttered above the image of a banty rooster as its official emblem. Wallace stayed out of the fight, but Mizell and other supporters bitterly opposed the change. "I never thought I'd see the day when we would substitute white supremacy for black supremacy," complained a member.[52] The committee agreed to a secret vote, which Wallace supporters considered cowardly. "If you are not willing to take a vote on the nigger question, you are not fit to serve on this committee," bellowed Leonard Wilson, a committee member from north Alabama's Walker County who was also an officer of the statewide White Citizens Council.[53]

The change narrowly passed. Mizell also lost a vote on his Wallace-endorsed motion to permit county Democratic executive committees to hold conventions instead of primaries to nominate candidates for local offices. This change would have virtually assured that any Black Belt counties with emerging Black voters could restrict the convention delegates in ways to prevent Blacks from winning any local primary elections.[54]

After the Justice Department announced that it was sending federal examiners to Birmingham, their first non-Black Belt location to register voters, Wallace asked Ed Morgan, the local circuit solicitor and his former executive secretary, to seek an injunction removing all illiterate Black voters registered by the feds from the official voting rolls. Morgan accused U.S. Attorney General Nicholas Katzenbach of insulting the people of Jefferson County and the feds of trampling on Alabama law in a furious rush to register illiterate Black voters regardless of their residence or criminal record. In the amen corner, Smith dismissed the federal examiners' approach to registration as "ridiculous."[55]

The Sovereignty Commission also explored with Wallace's executive secretary the possibility of a proclamation declaring Alabama in "an emergency situation created by irresponsible and illegal massive registration of illiterates and others not qualified to vote under Alabama law." The declaration would have no practical effect, but it might spur additional white backlash with increased voter registration and enthusiasm for Wallace's leadership of the state.[56]

What did occur was a major crackdown on Black activists and voters in the Black Belt. At the start of 1966, white landowners in several counties evicted more Black tenants who had registered to vote while bankers and merchants continued to cut off credit for Blacks who were found on the registration rolls. In Wilcox County, both SCLC and Francis X. Walter of the newly formed Selma Inter-Religious Project collected 85 families' sworn statements about their evictions, which ACLU attorney Chuck Morgan forwarded to the Justice Department for possible legal action under the Voting Rights Act. In Lowndes County, local white leaders escalated their economic intimidation to such an extent that SNCC organizers enlisted one of the county's Black landowners to permit them to erect a "tent city" for evicted families. "It's a very frightening thing to have to accept the cold reality . . .," observed SNCC's George Green, "that in order to exercise their rights, to get what they could get in this great Democracy in America, here in 1966, people were living in tents."[57]

In Greene County, Black leaders created a community fund to help families punished for registering, and they too set up a "tent city" to rescue the evicted who had no place to live. As local Black leader Thomas Gilmore perceived, the evictions represented a growing backlash so intense that whites "really don't care what happens to the land" as it went uncultivated so long as evicted Blacks were prevented from gaining a foothold on political power.[58]

The Black Belt's white leaders used every economic means they could muster to increase the price Blacks paid to engage in local politics. In Lowndes County, for example, the all-white Democratic executive committee hiked local candidate filing fees so that the cost of running for a position such as sheriff went from $50 to $500.[59] But, violence and terrorism against local and outside agitators remained a real threat and a threatened reality in the county. The acquittal of the white man who openly murdered Episcopal seminarian Jonathan Daniels and shot Catholic priest Richard Morrisroe signaled that anyone involved in voter registration could be killed with impunity. And assaults and shootings of local civil rights leaders, organizers, and SNCC meeting places persisted. According to local SNCC leader Stokely Carmichael: "The violence kept cropping up, and federal officials did almost nothing to stop it and Alabama lawmen did even less." One Black Belt man told a reporter that if Black voters ever elected a sheriff in his county, "they'll have to elect a new sheriff every month" since no black official would live 30 days.[60]

In an internal report, W. C. Patton had no reason to exaggerate to attract Yankee sympathy when he told his NAACP colleagues about the dangers of voter registration in this section of Alabama during this era. "In the panhandle of the Black Belt counties, volunteers . . . knock on doors to the 'tune' of shotgun blasts, pitched bottles, and brickbats. Local whites heckled Negroes after a large number of prospective voters went down to register. Heightened tensions ended in a gun battle with two persons shot. Snipers made the highways of the county unsafe at night."[61]

CHAPTER 7

Sequel to the Voting Rights Act of 1965

'Socialist-Liberal-Beatnik Communist Conspiracy'

On February 24, 1966, George Wallace, with his wife, Lurleen, announced before a cheering crowd in the state house chamber that she would become his stand-in as candidate for governor in the May 4 Democratic primary election. Governor Wallace made it clear: "I will be by her side. I will dictate the policies."[1] A surrogate candidacy was an audacious, unprecedented political strategy in Alabama, but polling showed Wallace had become unbelievably popular across the state: 90 percent of respondents (presumably all whites) believed he was doing an excellent or pretty good job and more than 80 percent approved of his junkets across the country defending Alabama.[2] By all appearances, Wallace could lose a lot of voters who might respond unfavorably to his unorthodox candidacy without losing a majority of the votes.

The other well-known candidates who lined up against Mrs. Wallace included former Governor John Patterson, who had defeated Wallace in 1958; U.S. Congressman Carl Elliott, a New Deal Democrat from north Alabama; state senator Robert Gilchrist, who had led the fight against Wallace's succession bill; former Governor James E. Folsom, who had lost a runoff spot in 1962 due in large part to a drunken statewide television appearance on the eve of the election; and Attorney General Richmond Flowers, who was in a political dog fight with Wallace that had begun the day they were inaugurated in 1963.

Both Wallace and Flowers were segregationists who expressed readiness to fight the federal government, but Flowers also had proclaimed that "the people of this state must discern and distinguish between a fighting chance and a chance to fight . . . [for] to defy the same federal arm that speaks for America to Castro, Khrushchev, and Mao Tse-tung . . . can bring nothing but disgrace to our state, military law upon our people, and political demagoguery to the leaders responsible."[3] Wallace never forgot nor forgave Flowers for these remarks and did not trust the attorney general to stay in line behind the governor's rule in state politics or policy. For this reason, Wallace had hired Frank Mizell at the Sovereignty Commission to be his lawyer in all matters of state.

One person not running was Ryan DeGraffenreid, who died earlier in the month when his small plane crashed as he traveled between campaign stops in north Alabama. DeGraffenreid had been in the runoff in 1962 and was Wallace's most formidable opponent. His death enlarged Lurleen Wallace's chance to be elected as George's proxy.[4]

The Wallaces kicked off their barn-storming campaign in mid-March in Montgomery in a televised rally before more than three thousand supporters. In a routine followed throughout the campaign, Lurleen read a short speech, on this occasion welcomed by more polite applause than she received at many subsequent campaign stops. Afterwards, she introduced her husband, "the Governor of Alabama," who spoke at length to loud, indulgent crowds.

Wallace gave his usual stump speech but added a defense of the Confederate battle flag, which had flown above the state and United States flags atop the state capitol since he ordered it hoisted to welcome U.S. Attorney General Robert Kennedy in 1963. "They want to take the Confederate flag down," Wallace announced, with no need to identify for his audience who "they" were. (In deciding to seek Black votes, Richmond Flowers had suggested the flag should come down.) "Let me tell you about that flag," Wallace confided to the crowd. "Anywhere you see the Confederate flag flying you will find people willing to fight harder for the American flag than anywhere else."[5]

The Wallace campaign spent most of its first weeks in middle and south Alabama where large, adoring audiences cheered as the governor attacked big-city newspapers, federal courts, bureaucrats, dirty beatniks, and Communists—often with amused sarcasm. Wallace rarely, if ever, spoke publicly the words "segregation" and "Negroes" (or the n-word). There was no need. He had already established in the minds of white Alabama that all issues and enemies of Alabama stemmed from those concerns. Instead, employing themes he had tested earliest in Selma, Wallace's speeches usually expounded on how the agitator for change "looks down his nose at the common folk of Alabama," when he knew, as did they, that those people were no better, and probably not as good, as Alabamians. Unspoken was the assumption Wallace shared with his audience that "common folk" and the "people of Alabama" were white.[6]

After sneering at the caricatured enemies who Wallace accused of sneering at Alabamians, he married his ambitions to white Alabamians' need to vindicate who they were and what had been done in their name. "If you want us to continue, we'll continue . . . and if you elect my wife the governor of the state, we will continue to be able to stand up in places all over our country and say this: 'I come from a state where people are just as refined and cultured and intelligent and righteous as the people in any state of this union and don't you forget it.'"[7]

Wallace's campaign claims went even further. He proclaimed that the beliefs of Alabamians, those rooted in white supremacy, belligerent individualism and military patriotism, were, in fact, what made America—not just the South—great. "We are going to show the people of this country," he shouted, "that this election shows that people have not in this state repudiated the governor of Alabama in his trips throughout this country talking about these philosophies that made our country great that are under attack by the socialist-liberal-beatnik-communist conspiracy."[8]

'WE SHOULD BE ABLE TO SAY WHO WILL BE THE NEXT GOVERNOR OF ALABAMA'

Before the Democratic primary campaigns began in earnest, civil rights groups launched a major voter registration drive in Alabama to give Black voters in the South their first opportunity to make a difference in local and state politics. In mid-February, SRC's Voter Education Project announced a new effort to support voter registration and citizenship education in Southern states, including new and ongoing work in Alabama. Albert Turner had become SCLC's field director in Alabama, and, with two SCLC cars so volunteers could drive people to the courthouses, he was coordinating the local work to increase voter registration in most Black Belt counties with and without federal examiners. Going into 1966, Turner was enthusiastic. "With proper organizing we should be able to say who will be the next governor of Alabama," he wrote.[9]

He had reason to be optimistic. The number of African Americans registered to vote in the Black Belt had skyrocketed since implementation of the Voting Rights Act. In Perry County, Black voters had increased from fewer than 300 to more than 3,000 by early 1966. In Wilcox, there were no registered Black voters six month earlier, but now the voter rolls had more than 3,000. In Wilcox and a few other Black Belt counties, such as Greene, the number of Black registered voters exceeded the numbers of registered whites. According to a report by VEP director Vernon Jordan, Alabama had close to 250,000 Blacks registered to vote on May 3—a potentially significant, new influence in statewide races.[10]

For the first time since the adoption of the 1901 Constitution, a large number of African Americans—85—qualified to run for state and county offices in the Democratic primary across the Black Belt and in the state's larger cities. Twelve Black candidates, including Albert Turner, qualified to run against whites for the state legislature; six Black men ran for sheriff; and several ran for county school board and tax collector. Almost 30 Black candidates—the largest number seeking any post—sought a position on their county Democratic executive committees, which managed local elections (polling places and balloting).[11] Many of these candidates were assured of winning since members of the county Democratic committees were elected by precinct, and most of the Black candidates resided in virtually all-Black precincts.

Across the rural areas of south Alabama, the excitement in the Black communities during the campaigning period was palpable. It was the first time in the lives of most Black adults, whether they had lived in Jim Crow's Alabama for 85 long years or only 21, that they had the opportunity to vote. Also, for the first time in the twentieth century, some white political leaders such as Richmond Flowers were seeking the votes of Black folk. In addition, Dr. Martin Luther King undertook a "get-out-the vote" tour across the Alabama Black Belt, building enthusiasm and hope as he and local organizers reminded African Americans that the ballot box was the one place in Alabama where white and Black people were now equal. On the front wall of the all-Black Antioch Baptist Church in Camden the elders had scrolled this credo, "ONE LORD, ONE FAITH, ONE BAPTISM," to which a speaker loudly added: "One Man, One Vote!"[12]

SCLC and other civil rights groups held mass meetings commemorating the first anniversary of the Selma March, as the federal judiciary announced a series of opinions that sanctified the right to vote as a guarantee of the U.S. Constitution. On March 3, a day after qualifying for the primary election closed, a three-judge federal court declared that the Alabama poll tax was unconstitutional. Circuit Judge Richard Rives of Montgomery wrote, "The poll tax was born of an effort to discriminate on the basis of race or color and it has had just that narrow effect,"[13] contrary to the Fifteenth Amendment. Four days later, Chief Justice Earl Warren announced the opinion of the U.S. Supreme Court upholding the constitutionality of the Voting Rights Act of 1965 and affirming the powers of Congress to "banish the blight of racial discrimination in voting, which has infected the electoral process in parts of our country for nearly a century."[14]

Alabama-born Justice Hugo Black dissented in part, arguing vigorously that Section 5 of the Act requiring preclearance of new voting changes exceeded congressional powers, but the Court provided a rousing 8–1 vote affirming all of the Act and the changes it mandated. Soon afterwards, U.S. Attorney General Nicholas Katzenbach used his powers under the Act to designate that federal observers would be sent on Election Day to Black Belt counties to assure that Black voters were not impeded. And, on March 24, 1966, in a case from Virginia, the Supreme Court indirectly affirmed the result of Rives's opinion in a case from Virginia in which Justice William Douglas wrote that "a State violates the Equal Protection Clause of the Fourteenth Amendment whenever it makes the affluence of the voter or payment of any fee an electoral standard."[15] The poll tax was dead, and the federal courts had set in stone voting changes in Alabama that upended Jim Crow politics as it had been practiced since 1901.

Surprisingly little was said publicly in the governor's race about these federal court decisions. As candidates headed into the last weeks of campaigning, former Governor Folsom spoke philosophically about democracy and race but seldom drew much of a crowd to listen. After mortgaging his house and cashing in his congressional pension to keep his campaign alive, former U.S. Representative Carl Elliott chided Wallace for "cursing the federal government" and using "the race issue as a whipsaw for political gain."

Attorney General Flowers secured the endorsement of the state's leading Black political organizations in recognition of his willingness to put on trial the white men who murdered civil rights workers in the Black Belt and to become the first white candidate in four generations to campaign for state office in Black churches and Black communities. Once considered the favorite, former Governor Patterson indirectly accused Wallace of a style of "reckless leadership" that had helped bring about passage of the federal civil rights laws. Claiming the mantle of the governor who successfully defended states' rights, Patterson's ads pleaded, "Think! Alabama! Think!"

Wallace ignored all of them.[16]

'LOADED-DICE CONDITIONS'

On Alabama's Election Day, Albert Turner sat in an old house not far from the monument commemorating the Perry County resident who designed the "Stars and Bars" Confederate flag. He was watching at some distance—enough distance to ensure that the white police chief had no basis to arrest him for illegally electioneering near the polls—as streams of Black folks walk to the courthouse to vote. "I like what I see! The Negroes are enthused," Turner remarked.[17] Until that morning, he had been meeting in Black churches to explain to voters how to cast their ballot—and who to vote for. "They can't write their names or read them," he observed, "but they can recognize them—just like they can recognize a picture."[18]

Whites in the county were deeply worried about the effects of what many derisively called "the nigger bloc vote." One resident said, "this is a bigger change than even after the civil war." Turner understood. "They think if we get in there, we're going to do to them like they did us," he said. "But Negro people as a whole don't want to revenge no white folk. We don't want to tear down white folks to bring us up."[19]

Many of the elderly men and women Turner watched migrating to the courthouse were wearing their Sunday-best clothes. It was a day in which they were a part of history, and they considered it a sacred act, due the respect and honor as if they were going to the Lord's house of worship. Some had risen before dawn. "I didn't really expect to live to see this day," admitted Minnie Curry, a 72-year-old African American, "so I didn't want to miss it when it came, and it sure is here."[20] Also among those voting for the first time was Cager Lee, the 83-year-old grandfather of the slain Jimmie Lee Jackson.[21] Lee had attend one of the county's citizenship classes to study the state's literacy questionnaire so he could qualify as a voter. Now, he was a voter qualified and entitled by being a citizen and enrolled by a federal examiner.

The election was deeply disappointing to those who hoped that the returns would show that Alabama had arrived at a new day in politics. By way of his wife's proxy, George Wallace was reelected governor without a runoff—Lurleen Wallace had received 54 percent of the vote. She led the voting in 60 of 67 counties, trailing only in those Black Belt counties where Black voters were a majority and in Cullman, Big Jim Folsom's hometown. It appears the Wallaces received a majority of white votes in every county except Cullman, Jefferson (Birmingham), and Winston. Richmond Flowers received perhaps as much as 90 percent of the Black votes and came in second with 19 percent of the total. Finishing third, Carl Elliott's attempt to cobble together an interracial coalition failed miserably with only 8 percent.[22] All told, it was a stunning, overwhelming endorsement of George Wallace and Wallaceism by the state's white voters.

Disappointment was not confined to the top of the ballot. Not a single Black candidate was elected on May 3rd, although 26 African Americans received enough votes to get into a runoff with white candidates. Albert

George and Lurleen Wallace, victory night, May 3, 1966 (ADAH).

Turner was among the 26. He earned a runoff against white incumbent State Representative Ira Pruitt, In Greene County, where newly registered Black voters now approached double the number of white voters, Black candidates lost by less than 300 votes in four races and got into a runoff in only one race. The difficulty Turner and most of the other Black candidates faced in a May 31 runoff was simple math: they received fewer votes than those cast for the two or more white candidates who split white support and prompted a runoff.

The national press and others focused heavily on the fact that some newly franchised Black voters admitted after the election that they had cast ballots for local segregationists who were incumbents. One example was "Lummie" Jenkins, described by the *New York Times* as the folksy Wilcox County sheriff who had served for 27 years and "refuses to wear a gun, and believes he owns a pair of handcuffs but cannot remember where he put them. When he needs to arrest a Negro . . . 'I just send out word to the niggers and they generally come on in,'" the sheriff stated. The *Times* also quoted a Black house painter saying, "It was too early for us to have a colored sheriff . . . I voted for Mr. Lummie Jenkins."[23]

Most national Black leaders agreed with NAACP Executive Secretary Roy Wilkins that Black voters should not be discouraged since their impact would grow over time, and a CORE spokesman said it was the first time since Reconstruction that Blacks and whites marched "side by side" to the polls. Attorney General Nicholas Katzenbach declared the Alabama election a "great credit to all the people involved."[24]

Perhaps Katzenbach had expected the wholesale theft and brutal measures of mischief that ended Reconstruction, or considered the defeat of Al Lingo, Wallace's former director of public safety who ran for Jefferson County sheriff, as a sure sign of fundamental change. But Katzenbach's remarks reveal that he was blind or unschooled at that time on the various newer methods of voter suppression that segregationists employed from the beginning. In retrospect, it is clear that the 1966 Democratic primary in Alabama inaugurated in the South a new era of voter restrictions—moving the line of defense of white political rule from almost a singular focus on blocking voter registration to a wider, diverse range of strategies hampering voter registration, suppressing voting, and diluting Black voting strength through election procedures and redistricting.

The machinations and deceptions began before Election Day. After the deadline for filing as a candidate passed in March, the Democratic executive committees in Montgomery and Barbour counties announced they had voted to change the method of electing committee members from precinct to county-wide in the May primary. This maneuver meant the 12 Black candidates running for positions on the county committees would have to win election among voters across the county, where whites continued to be a majority of registered voters, instead of in their local precincts which in their cases were virtually all-Black. Barbour County's white Democrats shamelessly announced they made the change to comply with the federal court decisions requiring one man, one vote.[25]

A few days before the election, the Sovereignty Commission's director assured everyone that newly registered Blacks would face no difficulties in voting. "I think election officials are going to do everything they can to see that people are given a chance to vote," Eli Howell stated.[26] He did not mention that since January he had been working with his colleague, Martha Witt Smith, and the governor's office to assist local election officials on techniques to confuse illiterate Black voters and to shorten the list of down-ballot races in which they would cast a vote.

Smith prepared handbooks for probate judges, who were responsible for local election procedures, focusing on how to use the limits Alabama law set for the amount of time a person could be in the voting booth as a tool to limit the voting choices of illiterate voters. State election law permitted voters using a voting machine three minutes to mark their ballots and five minutes if using paper ballots. These laws had been passed in earlier decades to assure that voting lines could be kept to a minimum so that the local governments would not have to spend more funds on machines or staffing. Now, Smith outlined a way to use the requirements to restrict illiterate Black voters' balloting.

"ENFORCE TIME LIMITS ON MACHINES AND BOOTHS!" Smith's handbook practically shouted. She suggested election officials in each polling location use egg timers to keep strict limits and physically remove a voter from the voting booth, when advisable, or switch off voting machines. Smith also advised election officials to warn the illiterate voter that the time limit "will be enforced even if he does not have time to vote the entire ballot."

Smith also outlined a 10-step procedure for election officials to assist illiterate voters, which, if followed, virtually guaranteed that voting lines would move slowly in polling places with large numbers of illiterate voters. "Every assisted voter, however, must be taken through all of the steps . . . in order to cast his vote with assistance," the handbook insisted.

In referring to "The Problem," Smith was careful to note that illiterate voters included whites and "non-whites," and mentioned that it was an issue in all Alabama counties. But she blamed the problem on the 1965 Voting Rights Act, and she knew, as did most Alabamians, that a reference to the "illiterate voter" in 1966 in Alabama meant "illiterate Black voter" and that the surge in illiterate voters in the state had occurred only in the Black Belt and only among Black voters.[27]

Smith did not need to worry whether her unspoken message would be understood. Once the Boswell Amendment was struck down by federal courts, citing the racist language used by its supporters, most white segregationist leaders had learned to be judicious in their public language. For years, Smith had been helping Alabama officials, including most recently Governor Wallace, to use nonracial language and rationales to defend race-targeted strategies that she and others developed for restricting Black voter registration. Now, she was using the same approach to restrict Black voters' balloting.

Several county Democratic executive committees in the Black Belt also had their own plans for manhandling Black voters. The white Democrats ignored, evaded, or rejected recommendations from Black candidates and local Black civic leagues in naming the persons to act as election officials to run voting at local polling places. In Montgomery, no Negro served as an election official since it was custom for the officials to be selected by members of the all-white county Democratic committee (yes, the same committee that changed its own election from precincts to countywide), and they selected only white persons. In Choctaw County, the local Democratic committee chairman said no Blacks were selected since the recommendations came a day after the committee had chosen only whites to

Voting line in Wilcox County, 1966 (National Archives).

serve as officials. In Dallas and Greene counties, only a handful of Blacks were chosen among scores of recommendations from Black candidates, and those few chosen were a minority of elections officials even in Black precincts.[28]

On Election Day, the effects of these and similar tactics were evident in the Black Belt and in the larger towns where African Americans resided in significant numbers. Long lines of Black voters lingered throughout the day in Montgomery, Birmingham, and most Black Belt counties. In urban areas, Black voters already in line after closing were allowed to vote, but not always in Black Belt counties. Reporters in Montgomery found that election officials were keeping time limits on voting. There were widespread complaints about white election officials' conduct with Black voters, including requiring illiterate voters to go to the back of the line after completing the ten steps Smith insisted were necessary before receiving a ballot.[29]

In a telegram to both Wallace and Katzenbach, Martin Luther King Jr. detailed the "extreme inadequacy of voting machinery throughout the Negro community in Alabama." He referred to the long lines and charged that election officials had failed to prepare polling places to handle the large numbers of newly registered Black voters. "Voting locations remained in traditional places with little or no geographic accommodation to the Negro community places," King wrote. In Wilcox County, for example, a primary polling place was the office of longtime Sheriff Lummie Jenkins, who was running for reelection against a Black candidate. The sheriff was in and out of his office on Election Day.[30]

The avalanche of complaints from Black voters about the conduct of white election officials, who were carefully chosen by the local all-white Democratic committee, revealed what Alabama writer John Beecher called "loaded-dice conditions" for Black candidates. Black voters were assigned the wrong voting precincts. According to SCLC workers, white election officials told large numbers of Black voters living in rural precincts in the Black Belt to go to town to vote, and in towns they were told to go to rural polling places to vote. White women were allowed to "assist" their Black cooks and maids by instructing them on whom to vote for.

In locations where Black poll watchers worked, some were denied the right to observe how white election officials assisted illiterate voters; others were required to return to their own homes to use the bathroom since polling locations only had "white bathrooms"; and some Black poll watchers were simply ignored when they objected to white officials marking paper ballots contrary to the wishes of illiterate Black voters.[31]

Counting paper ballots was also a shared role delegated to election officials and the county Democratic committee members. In the Black Belt, most counties had more registered white voters on the voting rolls than whites of voting age living in the county. This always raised the specter among Black candidates that some white voters were living in the local white cemetery, but certainly Black Belt counties relied on significant absentee voting by whites. In Hale County, for example, white incumbents relied on absentee votes from people not in the county as a prime vote-getting strategy. In Barbour County, late-counted absentee votes prevented Black attorney Fred Gray from winning a legislative seat on May 3.[32]

In some counties, local white leaders took more drastic action. In Sumter, Greene, and Marengo, election officials (with the support of local probate judges) prohibited federal observers from watching them assist illiterate Black voters mark their ballots. At one polling place in Greene, the federal observer yielded after a deputy sheriff threatened to arrest him in an election where his boss, Sheriff William Lee, was on the ballot. Also in Greene, election officials confiscated any sample ballots that illiterate voters brought to the polls and required the voters to cast ballots without the samples at hand. In Choctaw, just enough ballots were disqualified for having an "X" on the wrong side of a Black candidate's name to deny him election without a runoff. In Dallas County, when it became clear that Sheriff Jim Clark was about to lose to Selma's somewhat moderate white police chief, the county Democratic committee disqualified all ballots from three Black precincts due to unnamed "irregularities." Afterwards, the committee declared Clark the winner—at least until Judge Frank Johnson impounded the ballot boxes for federal scrutiny.[33]

Black leaders were unable to document one added factor that surely influenced Election Day voting: unspoken and spoken intimidation. The

Black Belt's white leaders were dead serious about preventing local political change. They proved that much in how they reacted to Black voter registration. In Marion in Perry County, where Jimmie Lee Jackson's grandfather and mother were in line to vote, the retired assistant commandant of the local all-white military academy told reporter Jack Nelson: "Three-fourths of these people don't know what they are voting for. Two generations ago they were all slaves . . . We killed one on the first night of the demonstrations—that's what it takes to stop 'em."[34]

In Greensboro in Hale County, where African American Henry McCaskill led the ticket to get into a runoff with the incumbent white sheriff, white tax assessor Clarence Lawson could not celebrate his own reelection. Instead, he was openly agitated about impending doom. "If that nigger wins, we'll be selling our land for 50 cents an acre," he declared. "Ain't no nigger going to drive me off my land. I wanted to kill that McCaskill nigger so bad one day when he stood up and made a speech by [the courthouse's Confederate monument] that has my granddaddy's name carved on it."[35]

Black voters had good reason to worry about how the local white community—white election officials, white leaders, white deputies, white landowners, white bankers, and white employers—would react when they

Henry McCaskill (Bob Fitch Photography Archive, Department of Special Collections, Stanford University Libraries).

learned how each Black person had voted. And they surely knew. Many Black voters had to bring sample ballots prepared by the political organizations into the polling place. White officials could see their marked choices. Many had to have assistance to mark a paper ballot—aided usually by white election officials. They knew. And even well-schooled Black voters could not cast a paper ballot in secret. As the Chilton County probate judge, an advocate of voting machines, told the Selma newspaper after the May 3rd election: "With the old paper ballots almost anyone can tell how you voted."[36]

Despite all of these challenges and problems, voting was close in almost all Black Belt county races where a Black candidate opposed a white. In Choctaw County, the Black candidate for county commissioner came within six votes of winning without a runoff. In Bullock County, the Black candidate for sheriff needed only 131 more votes and the Black candidate for tax assessor lacked only 66 votes to win without a runoff. In Perry County, the Black candidate for sheriff came within 270 votes of winning outright.

In Hale County, challenger Henry McCaskill came within 440 votes of wining without runoff. The Black candidates in Wilcox County lost in one-on-one races against Sheriff Lummie Jenkins and other white incumbents by a difference ranging from only 260 to 365 votes. In Greene County, Thomas Gilmore and each of the other Black candidates lost by less than 300 votes. This overall pattern of small vote differences between Black and white candidates was also found in the returns for Albert Turner and other African Americans running for the state legislature across Black Belt counties.[37]

The voting returns also evidenced another pattern: the total votes cast in these local and state legislative races usually ranged from 100 to 400 votes fewer than the total votes cast in the governor's race. In other words, there was a fall-off in votes cast for local races at the bottom of the paper ballot in comparison to votes cast at the top of the ballot—exactly the result that Martha Witt Smith sought with her rule-making on time limits and 10-step procedures for assisting illiterate voters.[38] Given these and other obstacles and irregular restrictions—discriminatory selection of election officials, excluding and interfering with Black poll watchers and federal examiners, maintaining inconvenient polling places and long lines, misdirecting Black voters as to their correct polling places, collecting absentee votes, manipulating illiterate voters' choices, disqualifying Black voters' ballots, and producing an intimidating atmosphere around the polling places and voting—little wonder that King, SCLC, and local Black leaders were outraged by how the nation's first election under the new Voting Rights Act was conducted.

The Black press screamed "De Facto Denial of Right to Vote!" in its headlines concerning the Alabama elections, but King and others were unable to get meaningful coverage or investigation of these problems from the state or national white newspapers. The narrative quickly took hold that Black voters had made a valiant but unsuccessful first step into the democratic process. Or stories often rehearsed a couple of interviews with Black voters to prove that the local segregationist officials, especially long-time sheriffs, had charmed their way back into office by enticing enough Black votes. Iconic photographs of long, slow lines of Black voters were published across the country with captions about African Americans in Alabama crowding the polling places, eager to realize their right to vote after 65 years of disfranchisement. The white press failed utterly to grasp that the long voting lines were evidence of purposeful suppression of Black voting.

The white press was not alone. Katzenbach announced that "the election was conducted fairly . . . and people voted freely and comfortably."[39] Others in the Justice Department echoed the judgment. Perhaps the white federal examiners and Justice Department officials had become inured and blinded by earlier blatant rhetoric and harsh tactics used to squash Black protest and Black voter registration. Had they imagined that Al Lingo or Jim Clark would lead troopers in an attack on a long line of Black voters to repeat the tragedy of Bloody Sunday? Or perhaps they were actually expecting to see election officials shut the doors of the polling places, like the old registrars had done in their offices, when faced with a line of Black folks wanting to exercise their rights of citizenship?

Even a true hero of voting rights, the man who had done more than anyone to elevate the word 'justice" in the Department's work on voting, John Doar seemed momentarily deceived by what he was seeing and why on Election Day. In Selma, as he drove near a polling place where a line of more than two hundred Black voters stood, he reflected, "You know, there are more people in that line than there were registered Negro voters when I first came to Selma."[40]

Doar did not daydream for long. The Justice Department moved swiftly to federal court to overturn the shenanigans of Jim Clark and the three Black Belt probates judges who expelled federal observers. In response, the Sovereignty Commission's Frank Mizell, who on May 3rd won two-thirds of the votes in his own reelection to the state Democratic Executive Committee, came to their defense. Both cases were tried before U.S. District Judge Daniel Thomas.

Perhaps buoyed by his own huge electoral victory and that of the Wallaces, Mizell mounted a free-wheeling defense of his clients in the nation's first lawsuit filed over an election under the Voting Rights Act. In Jim Clark's case, Mizell argued that Thomas should declare the entire Act unconstitutional or, at minimum, annul section 12(D) that permitted the Justice Department to file the case before him. That section violated the constitutional rights of the State of Alabama to supervise its own voting and elections, Mizell claimed, and in so doing "denies the very right of statehood."

On the factual issues, Mizell suggested that Black and white election officials at the disputed Black precincts had stuffed the ballot box. Any ruling against the local all-white Democratic Executive Committee would decree that the committee was "crooked" simply because they disqualified the irregular and illegal ballots of 1,600 "niggers," Mizell stated in the courtroom.[41] He argued that no federal judge had ever overridden a state election's vote count and accused the Justice Department of a vendetta against Clark. "They want this court to forget Alabama law . . . forget the voting officials . . . were undependable to complete the count."[42] In the case concerning federal observers, Mizell mounted a similar attack, calling them federal "snoopers" who trampled on Alabama law and violated the illiterate voters' right to cast a secret ballot.[43]

In both cases, Doar and his colleagues sought quick decisions since ballots in Dallas County had to be printed (with or without Jim Clark's name) soon. For this reason, Thomas could not delay a decision for months or years, and he gave Doar what he wanted—an order to count all ballots in the disputed precincts (enabling Clark's defeat without a runoff) and an opinion sanctioning federal observers.

Thomas's opinion indirectly scolded Mizell for offering bombast instead of facts. "The Court did not hear . . . any evidence which would indicate that votes were bought or sold, that boxes were stuffed, or that there was any misconduct . . . even approaching fraud," he wrote in the Dallas County case. As to the constitutional challenge, Thomas cited the U.S. Supreme Court's recent cases upholding the Act and noted curtly what every lawyer should know—that a federal district court judge was "bound by these decisions."

In all likelihood, Thomas was pleased to enable the election of a moderate segregationist over the rash, brutal white supremacist Jim Clark. But his opinions conveyed a subtle message that he remained a faithful Black Belt native. Thomas wrote that he was providing "due protection for all the citizens of Dallas County, white as well as negro." He did not use Mizell's "nigger" (which he permitted the attorney to use in his courtroom), but he did not capitalize "Negro." Also, Thomas failed to enjoin local white officials from barring federal observers in the future since "the court sees no need for an injunction." The defendants told the judge they would abide by his decision, and while bound by the decisions of higher courts Thomas seemed equally bound by Black Belt tradition in which its white leaders take each other's word as their bond.[44]

Black leaders were more concerned about finding lawyers to challenge the conduct and outcomes in their own elections. The Reverend Linton Spears contacted the U.S. Commission on Civil Rights as well as lawyers in Mobile after he was forced into a runoff when the Choctaw County Democratic executive committee disqualified just enough votes to deny him an outright victory. Tom Gilmore in Greene County tried unsuccessfully to reach Chuck Morgan, ACLU Southern director, who was in meetings in New York City, but reached Oscar Adams, one of Birmingham's

Tom Gilmore of Greene County (Bob Fitch Photography Archive, Department of Special Collections, Stanford University Libraries).

handful of Black attorneys involved in the city's civil rights cases. Adams enlisted the assistance of the NAACP Legal Defense Fund (LDF).

Shortly before the May 31 runoff, LDF lawyers filed a federal lawsuit on behalf of Gilmore and other Black candidates in Greene County. The complaint charged that Probate Judge Dennis Herndon had refused to allow illiterate Black voters to use sample ballots while allowing white illiterate to do so; white election officials assisting illiterate Black voters had marked ballots contrary to the wishes of the voters; and a large number of white voters were dead or no longer residents of the county.[45]

In the runoff, twenty-six candidates across the state were African American but only four won. Three Black candidates won in Macon County: Lucius Amerson would become the first Black sheriff and L. A. Locklair the first Black tax collector in Alabama since Reconstruction; Harold Webb was also nominated to join the county commission as its second Black member. The fourth African American victor was Henry

Kirksey, who won a seat on the Greene County board of education.

Turnout was uneven. Albert Turner's runoff race drew more than a thousand additional votes in the district's three Black Belt counties and almost 1,500 more votes for his candidacy. But it was not enough. On the other hand, Lonnie Brown's runoff for the four-county state senate seat against Roland Cooper, the "Wily Fox from Wilcox," had almost 5,000 votes fewer votes than in the first primary. The man who risked his life registering Black voters in Wilcox County lost badly, receiving almost a thousand fewer votes in his own county than on May 3.[46]

King and SCLC leaders were furious, and their anger was aimed at the U.S. Justice Department, which they believed had permitted the Black Belt's white leaders to void real gains for Blacks in the nation's first election under the Voting Rights Act. At a White House Conference on Civil Rights two days after the runoff, Hosea Williams, who headed up SCLC's political organizing, introduced a resolution declaring that many Black candidates in Alabama would have won "had they not been cheated out of the election and the election stolen from them. The greatest atrocity was not committed by the Alabama white segregationists but by the Federal Election officials . . . The Federal Government stood idly by and watched Negroes cheated, harassed, intimidated and schemed out of the May 3 Democratic primary in Alabama." [47]

The two-page resolution adopted by the Conference participants accused the Justice Department and FBI of willfully ignoring economic reprisals against Black voters, including losing their houses, jobs, and welfare payments, and it demanded stricter enforcement of voting rights laws as well as new presidential orders to protect Black voting. The outcry received no news coverage in Alabama or in the national press, which was focusing on the emerging dispute among civil rights groups at the conference over the Vietnam War.[48]

'George Wallace Is Flunking the Whole United States'

In truth, several factors explain the miserable election results. As everyone knew, the continuing deep hostility of the Black Belt's white leaders and citizens was the cause of the problem. The support they received from Wallace, his Sovereignty Commission, and the state legislature were vital for defeating the effects of a surge in Black registration. King and others knew as much. But SCLC had stretched its limited resources to the breaking point in attempting to win big in Alabama, and after May 3rd the organization had to severely cut back staffing within the state. This retrenchment probably diminished the runoff's Black turnout in some locations.

Also, SNCC and SCLC had split over the best political strategy in 1966, and the disunion probably did not help Black turnout in the Democratic primary. SNCC believed that creating a separate freedom party—instead of participating in the primary of the party run by white men "who oppress Negroes"—was the best way to make Black votes matter. As a result, SNCC's organizers worked in the Black Belt to hold county conventions for the "freedom organization" on Election Day, as required by Alabama law to have their candidates nominated and placed on the ballot in the November general election.

SCLC's Andy Young argued afterwards that SNCC's approach was not a major problem, but Albert Turner and others in the Black Belt strongly objected to SNCC's organizing work during their campaign. According to SNCC reports, Turner openly attacked SNCC for its strategy when appearing at political rallies and church meetings, and he barred SNCC representatives from speaking for a freedom party convention in Perry County. SNCC did hold conventions involving two to three dozen voters on May 3rd in Lowndes, Dallas, Wilcox, and Greene counties, but not in Perry.[49]

In the urban areas, there were also significant structural barriers diluting Black voting strength that the Justice Department and civil rights lawyers did not challenge. Even before Election Day, the legislature and the state Democratic Executive Committee had put into place an election scheme that kept Black voters from electing the candidates of their choice. The primary obstacle was the use of numbered posts for state legislative districts and county commissions—the law Martha Witt Smith had advanced. Instead of creating different geographic districts in counties with significant Black population and allowing voters to elect candidates from those geographic districts, Alabama's legislative reapportionment plan also created numbered posts by combining counties and allowed all voters in the combined counties to vote for all numbered positions.

This method of electing state legislators was especially damaging to Black voters in large counties. In Jefferson County, for example, voters elected 20 of the state's 105 members of the House of Representatives (19 percent) since the county had about 635,000 residents and 19 percent of the state's population. This allocation reflected the "one person, one vote" concept established in Chuck Morgan's landmark case of *Reynolds v. Sims* in 1964. The county also had almost 220,000 African Americans or 35 percent of the county population. On May 3, civil rights attorney Arthur Shores and three other Black candidates for the legislature received from 33 to 38 percent of the total county votes. It put each in a runoff but, because the vast majority of white voters across the county failed to support any of them, each lost to the white candidate.[50]

The same pattern and obstacle occurred in Mobile with a Black population of 33 percent and 10 legislative seats and in Montgomery with a Black population of 38 percent and five seats. The impact was profound. These three large counties were now home to twice as many eligible African American voters as in all Black Belt counties combined. "This makes it practically certain that no Negro can possibly be elected to a seat," John Beecher explained in the aftermath of the May elections, "since in each case he will be matched with a white person in the runoff." Since few, if any, white voters would willing to vote for a Black candidate, it meant Alabama had a "reapportioned but racially gerrymandered legislature" that remained all white.[51]

The same results were achieved in the counties with heavily Black populations that elected county governing boards in at-large elections with numbered posts—in counties such as Dallas and Perry. In addition, in counties with a majority of Black registered voters, such as Wilcox and Macon, the monkeyshines of local white officials' in manipulating first-time illiterate Black voters probably would not have been decisive had the county commission members been elected by precincts or other smaller districts than countywide.[52]

Alabama's civil rights attorneys had been well aware of the problems of at-large elections and numbered posts, but for two primary reasons they did not address the issue in the case involving the legislature's court-ordered reapportionment plan used in May's elections. First, in *Reynolds v. Sims*, Alabama's precedent-setting reapportionment case, the U.S. Supreme Court stated that single-member districts were not required by the concept of "one man, one vote." In early 1965 the Court also ruled that at-large elections in Georgia's legislative reapportionment were not unconstitutional. The Court postponed considering when a multi-member at-large district scheme "would operate to minimize or cancel out the voting strength of racial or political elements of the voting population."[53]

The plaintiffs in the 1965 legislature's apportionment case had a problem of proof—proving racial effect and motive. Before May, no Alabama election for the legislature since the adoption of the 1901 state constitution had included a significant number of African American voters. There had been no "voting strength" among Black voters for white leaders to dilute or minimize with election schemes since their registration as voters had been blocked. If and when a small number of Blacks were allowed to vote in the past, their only choice was to support a white candidate whom Black voters might consider the least objectionable segregationist. In those few instances, white and Blacks voting for the same white segregationist candidate did not evidence a pattern of minimizing Black voting. In other words, until the 1966 elections, the suppression of voter registration had been the means to minimize and cancel out Black voting—not electoral schemes.

As a result, Black voters and their lawyers were at that moment in a proverbial "catch-22." They were forced in 1966 by circumstances to leave unchallenged the use of at-large elections because there had been no past elections in which there were enough Black voters with enough voting strength for at-large elections and numbered posts to annul.

The only other possibility was to demonstrate that the legislature enacted the at-large legislative districts in urban areas with a clear intent to discriminate against Black voters. That proof was not available from past elections.[54] Men like Frank Mizell might occasionally let their true motives slip out, but most had learned the political art of evasion. In his fight against "illiterate voters," not against Black voters, in his fight against "bloc voting," not Black voting, in his fight for state's rights, not for racial segregation, George Wallace had led Alabama white leaders and much of its white population to embrace a public language and perhaps even a public understanding obscuring real motives of racism—even though Wallace, only three year earlier, had made infamous his overt segregationist language in his inaugural address.

In the legislative reapportionment case, acting as a friend of the court, Justice filed a memorandum analyzing the various plans submitted to the three-judge court. It listed the Department's view of the advantages and disadvantages of splitting up large counties into several legislative districts, including an advantage that "minority interest groups within a separate district are more likely to obtain a voice." But the Department made no claim that any proposed urban district minimized Black voting strength and, in effect, advised that, while "separate districts within populous counties may be desirable, the Court may feel that, in the circumstances, it should not take this task upon itself."[55] In effect, the Department went on record leaving in doubt its own position about at-large districts in Alabama's large, populous counties.

There's no doubt, however, that the Justice Department failed in assuring an open, fair, and free election in Alabama in 1966. While the Department had fought vigorously against various schemes to obstruct voter registration, it was not prepared to monitor and challenge the local white Democratic leaders' mischief in selecting election officials and poll watchers. It failed to identify and challenge the problems of limited, inadequate polling places and the ten-step voting procedures that helped to assure disappointing turnout and long lines of Black voters. Federal observers were not trained to recognize the subtle ways in which white election officials could steer or effectively steal the illiterate Black voter's ballot.

Also, as sweeping as the 1965 Voting Rights Act was in setting up new mechanisms and new prohibitions, white leaders in the Black Belt had learned how to shield one of their most effective strategies for maintaining white political supremacy. The new Act specifically outlawed any attempt or action to "intimidate, threaten, or coerce" a voter or anyone assisting a voter.[56] But the rub came in proving in a court of law that adverse actions by white landowners, employers, merchants, and bankers constituted economic intimidation due to the Black persons' exercising their right to vote.

Protecting the people in voter registration in the Deep South was a persistent issue causing raw tension between the Justice Department and civil rights groups. More than a year before the murder of the three voting rights workers near Philadelphia, Mississippi, in June 1964, SNCC leader Bob Moses had sued Robert Kennedy, the Justice Department, and the FBI for taking no action after Moses and others were "intimidated, arrested, beaten, and prosecuted by public officials" for attempting to register Black citizens to vote. The case was summarily dismissed by a federal district court.[57]

The Department mounted a major prosecution in rural Louisiana in late 1965 alleging landowners terminated sharecropping leases and evicted Black farmers to punish them for registering to vote. After an extensive trial, the federal judge ruled in February 1966 that the evidence in the case was "completely and totally void of any proof of intimidation, threats, or coercion" for interfering with any rights under the Voting Rights Act.[58] Similarly, even Judge Frank Johnson found that no real evidence was presented in court that dispossessed tenant farmers in Lowndes County were evicted primarily due to their voter registration.[59]

In the unreported case of *Miles v. Dixon*, Johnson dismissed the suit alleging that evictions in Lowndes were acts of intimidation for registering to vote. There may have been some miscommunications between organizers and local citizens as to what would happen to their sworn statements. Some may have been encouraged to change their story due to local white pressure as the public trial approached. But the major problem was more likely that white landowners knew better than to state the real reason they were evicting tenants. There was no "smoking gun" evidencing intent in any of their communications evicting tenants. As Francis X. Walter noted during these years, eviction notices were always obtuse. [60]

A large part of the problem in such cases arose from the fact that overall sharecropping and farm employment in the rural South, especially in the Black Belt, was rapidly declining. In 1964 there were only two Black tenant farmers in the South for every 10 who were working on the land in 1950. By 1969, the number would shrink statistically to less than one of every 10, and 96 percent of all cotton in the region would be picked by machine. Several of the Black Belt's white landowners were turning to raising cattle or growing more trees.[61] So, as a much larger number of Black sharecroppers and tenants were losing their work and homes due to changes in farming, those dispossessed due to voter registration faced an almost insurmountable challenge in demonstrating under a federal court's rules of evidence that they were victims of intimidation or coercion, not of mechanization and employment shifts. They needed hard proof of motive, and white landowners were chary to reveal it.

"A cattle grower has no need for sharecroppers," Lowndes County's white sheriff told a reporter, "and the day has pretty much gone for the small sharecropper-type small farm."[62] Black Belt sheriffs, landowners, and other white community leaders were learning to invoke general truths and trends to hide the specific motive of questionable political actions. Generations of economic dependency that Black folks had endured in Alabama's Black Belt—and now the hardship of economic change that was disrupting their lives—both worked now in favor of the white community's political leverage, so long as its white leaders dared not to say out loud the true motive for their actions.

The difference between what is common knowledge and what can be commonly proven in a court of law was evident in another case from Lowndes County brought by Mobile civil rights attorney Vernon Crawford and New York attorneys William Kunstler and Arthur Kinoy, who filed an omnibus complaint to stop the 1966 elections in Lowndes due to overriding conditions which had involved the murders of clergymen, a number of shootings, and repeated official harassment and hostility toward Black voter registration. The lawyers charged that an "array of constitutional violations . . . have enabled the minority white population to seize and retain all the political power of Lowndes County, Alabama, and thereby exclude the Negro population from participation in the administration of County affairs or the selection of its government."[63]

A three-judge panel, including Frank Johnson and Richard Rives, cited several cases in which the federal courts had addressed the chicanery and misdeeds of the Black Belt's white supremacists, but it ruled in essence that, even when "the wrongs suffered are grievous" the courts can only provide specific remedies that address specific wrongs.[64]

The Black men and women who remained in the Alabama Black Belt for decades to fight for political change under the Voting Rights Act understood much of this hardened reality. After the runoff election, for instance, Albert Turner was deeply disappointed in the outcome and in the "great movement helpers" who were quick to criticize SCLC. But already he had joined others in starting a regional co-op for Black farmers to help them become entirely independent of the local white economy in the supplies, production, and sale of their products.[65]

When he attended the White House Conference on Civil Rights two days after his own defeat in the runoff election, Turner spoke at the workshop on education and training—not political participation. Turner talked about the problems of how local hostile whites blocked funds for proposed Black-managed economic development projects, but his main topic was the education of Black children. He mentioned the failures of school integration in Marion and how necessary it was in order for Black children to have access to the resources found in white schools. Using an oft-repeated, at least in civil rights circles, pronunciation of his governor's name, Turner warned, "Wall-ass" has said flatly "he won't do a thing with the money for the public school system down there, let alone these other programs and everybody sits back and laughs about it."[66]

Turner also said higher education had to improve how it educated African Americans, whether in previously all-white colleges or historically Black colleges. "Now, I went to Alabama A&M [a publicly supported HBCU in Huntsville, the nation's new space center]. They teach you how to put shoes on mules and all the mules are dead . . . Now we are going to have improve our school system . . . we going [to have] to teach . . . how to fly to the moon."

In concluding, Turner stated that Wallace's politics and policies in Alabama were accelerating the out-migration of illiterate Black families and their poorly educated children into Northern and Western urban areas such as the recently riot-torn Watts neighborhood in Los Angeles. "If you are really interested in stopping that kind of mess," Turner stated, "go to Alabama and build a house for that man down there who can't write, who can't work, who can't do nothing—and keep the man down there."

In one sentence, Turner summed up his message about the Alabama governor: "George Wallace is flunking the whole United States."[67]

PART

2

Alabama has tried to nurture and defend evil . . . the Southern aristocracy began immediately to engineer this development of a segregated society . . . follow me through here because this is very important to see the roots of racism and the denial of the right to vote. Through their control of mass media, they revised the doctrine of white supremacy. They saturated the thinking of the poor white masses with it.

— Martin Luther King Jr., March 25, 1965

CHAPTER 8

The End and the Beginning of the Disfranchising Poll Tax

'Tragic Shadows of History Following Reconstruction'

The 1966 Democratic primary was the first time in 65 years that no Alabamian was required to pay a tax in order to vote. Two months before the election, a federal court ruled on March 3rd that Alabama's poll tax was unconstitutional, The three judges, who split two to one in the decision to strike down Section 194 of the state constitution, were all Alabamians, and each wrote a different opinion about the origins and political history of the poll tax in restricting suffrage in their state.[1]

The Justice Department brought the case to the Montgomery courthouse when it sued the State of Alabama within a few days of the passage of the 1965 Voting Rights Act. The Act directed the attorney general to take legal actions against any and all states that continued to require a poll tax as a precondition to voting. There were only four such states in 1965. All were in the South,[2] and the Justice Department undertook a massive effort in each lawsuit against them.

The Department researched Alabama's prior constitutions and journals and newspaper coverage of the 1901 constitutional convention. Its attorneys deposed tax collectors in 33 counties and three probate judges to document how the poll tax was collected or administered differently in predominantly African American Black Belt counties and predominantly white north Alabama counties. The government lawyers also took testimony from two local Black leaders of the Black Belt—C. G. Gomillion of Tuskegee and Albert Turner. Dr. Gomillion discussed the findings of his study of segregation and voter registration in Alabama and the effects of unequal, segregated education on Black income.[3]

Turner testified about his work in voter registration and the how the poll tax "for a Negro is not the same as for a white person." Negroes had been prevented from registering in the past, but still had to pay back poll taxes for those past years when they were banned from registering as well as for the current year. "For a lot of Negroes it is not $1.50 but $6 this year because he and his wife both have just had the chance to get registered for the first time," Turner stated. He also explained how and why Black folks were reluctant to go to the courthouse to pay their poll taxes where many had been mistreated while being denied the right to register. Most new registrants had done so through a federal examiner—not by local officials in the courthouse.

"The poll tax barrier is greater now than it was in 1950," Turner asserted. In 1950, the only Negroes registered were teachers, doctors and lawyers and they could pay, but "now we have 3,700 Negroes in Perry County who can't buy groceries, but want to participate in the government . . . If the government fails in this suit, we will try to qualify those persons. We might tell a man to miss a meal or two if he has to do it. We don't plan to let $5 or $10 make us miss voting," Turner insisted.

Under cross-examination by Governor Wallace's attorney John Kohn, Turner admitted he had "been put under injunctions several times." In fact, Turner was also attempting to put others under injunction. He was lead plaintiff in an ACLU lawsuit that the Justice Department had joined to desegregate juries in Perry County.[4]

In response to another of Kohn's questions, Turner replied: "As to whether I get a personal boost at being able to testify at length, the answer is yes and no . . . A lot of what I have said today are my personal feelings from talking with all types of people from all walks of life. I feel like, to a certain extent, I was born with a better mental ability than some people and my environment also had something to do with my success. I lack a lot of things I shouldn't lack with the type of education I got. I know I could be brighter and smarter, but I don't have to go to school to testify like I did today. That just goes from living thirty years."[5]

Judges Richard Rives, Walter Gewin, and Frank Johnson (ADAH).

Before the three-judge panel, Doar and other Justice Department lawyers argued that the poll tax was adopted in 1901 as a part of the overall discriminatory scheme to deny voting rights to the state's African Americans. They cited statements from the 1901 constitutional convention and related news accounts and submitted evidence from depositions showing how the poll tax was administered unequally. The government lawyers also argued that, based on the evidence submitted, the state was directly responsible for the fact that Black voters were less able to pay a poll tax because Alabama had required three generations of Black children to attend inferior, segregated schools, which meant, in turn, less income as adults—exactly the point that Turner personally expressed under cross-examination.[6]

The three federal judges who heard the case were Circuit Judges Richard Rives and Walter Gewin and District Judge Frank Johnson. Each wrote a separate opinion.

Rives wrote that "from its inception the Alabama poll tax was illegal and invalid as an attempt to subvert the Fifteenth Amendment to the United States Constitution . . . The history of the poll tax leaves no doubt this was its sole purpose." Endorsing the Justice Department's primary argument, Rives quoted several delegates to the 1901 constitutional convention delegates citing the disenfranchising purpose of the poll tax. He wrote that despite changes over the years the "poll tax remains one of the last great pillars of racial discrimination. In effect, the tax still bars a large number of Negroes from the polls." Rives also reviewed and dismissed the state's argument that the poll tax had other legitimate purposes, and he cited the Justice Department's evidence that the state "has continued to administer the poll tax in a discriminatory fashion, furthering its injustice."[7]

Gewin dissented. While affirming that he would readily join in removing "every vestige of racially discriminatory application of Alabama's poll tax laws," he complained that his colleagues' decision was improper since the U.S. Supreme Court had before it a case from Virginia on the constitutionality of its poll tax and the "principle of judicial restraint dictates that we await the action of the Supreme Court." Gewin also scolded Rives that it "is not good and proper to delve into the tragic shadows of history following Reconstruction . . . and use the emotional statements of politicians uttered in public debate over a half century ago."

"It is easy to find statements from the past which do not fit the present," he continued. Gewin wrote that statements by Abraham Lincoln, "The Great Emancipator," would "make some of the statements referred to by delegates to Alabama Constitutional Convention appear temperate and mild by comparison." While admitting that some delegates possessed a motive of discrimination, he stated that amendments ratified by voters in 1953 "has completely changed the Constitution."[8]

Johnson joined Rives in holding that the poll tax had an original purpose and effect of disfranchising African Americans and that it continued to violate the Fifteenth Amendment. At the same time, he wrote that the foremost issue in the case was "the principle of a tax on the right to vote is constitutionally indefensible." Therefore, Johnson declared the poll tax was also a violation of the Fourteenth Amendment's guarantee of due process. He dismissed the state's arguments that it had legitimate reasons to put a price tag on voting, especially attacking the contention that the poll tax only "disfranchises the shiftless." Johnson wrote that "the fact that *anyone*—not just the potential voter—may pay indicates that the state does not use the tax as a standard to measure the intelligent and interested exercise of the franchise. Just as the imposition of a tax to attend church, or a tax on the right to stand up and voice one's views on the events of the day would be unconstitutional regulations . . . financial ability has no place in a test of voting."[9]

The separate opinions of these three Alabama-born judges reflected some of the major perspectives that endured across the decades within Alabama about the poll tax.

Richard T. Rives (1895–1982), reared in a Montgomery family whose proud lineage went back to the Revolutionary War, became a well-known political figure after helping elect Governor Bibb Graves in the 1930s. Rives was a white progressive who did not challenge segregation. Quite the contrary, as a young lawyer he had advised the Montgomery board of registrars on evasive ways to bar Black voter registration, and he had represented the Macon County board of registrars in the same cause. He knew from his own experience as a lawyer that the obstacles that the 1901 Constitution established to prohibit Black voting were the tools of ongoing resistance by local registrars.

As a chief opponent of the Boswell Amendment in 1946, Rives debated amendment supporters, some of whom argued that Boswell, if passed, would be such a comprehensive barrier to Black voting that a poll tax would no longer be needed to obstruct Black suffrage.[10] After Rives became a judge, and perhaps shifted his sense of duty in combating racism, he never changed the facts. He knew what the poll tax was designed to achieve and how it had been used to accomplish that design.

Walter P. Gewin (1908–1981) was a native of the Black Belt, where he returned after attending Emory College and the University of Alabama law school. His grandfather was a captain in the 20th Alabama Regiment of the Confederate Army whose "gallantry and self sacrifice" Gewin proudly memorialized in an address in Greensboro in 1938 shortly after his election to the state legislature at the age of 30. He was a loyal supporter of Frank Dixon, the Big Mules' governor, who afterwards became a major advocate for disfranchising Black voters through the Boswell Amendment. Gewin was rewarded as a freshman legislator with a seat on the powerful house rules committee, and he developed a reputation in Montgomery as a studious politician and lawyer after serving on the committee that complied the 1940 Code of Alabama.[11]

Gewin was elected to the state Democratic Executive Committee once he became Hale County's solicitor. He was on the state committee in

January 1946, when it unanimously approved a resolution recommending passage of the Boswell Amendment to preserve white supremacy.[12] He was a candidate for a federal district judgeship in 1950, but President Harry Truman appointed another moderate segregationist, Daniel Thomas. Across the decades, Gewin and O. S. Burke, Thomas's appointee as a federal registrar, were partners in a farming operation as well as family friends. When Gewin failed to receive the federal district judgeship, he moved to Tuscaloosa and entered a law partnership with two influential Democrats, Marc Ray "Foots" Clement, a major behind-the-scenes political strategist/advisor to several of Alabama's New Deal Democrats and George LeMaistre, a national Democrat who opposed the states' rights movement and later was a banker and one of the few independent voices in Alabama's white business community. In 1961, Clement could not accept an appointment to the federal 5th Circuit Court of Appeals due to illness, but on his deathbed he recommended Gewin.[13]

The editor and owner of the *Greensboro Watchman*, perhaps the most conservative voice of Black Belt newspapers, welcomed Gewin's appointment. "Here is one Alabamian," Hamner Cobbs wrote, "who would not only be a suitable and worthy successor to another Alabamian on a higher court, but one most welcome to the public."[14] Cobbs considered the Alabamian sitting on that higher court, Justice Hugo Black, "a turncoat, quisling . . . anything so long as it is an opprobrious term."[15]

Gewin received an interim appointment since the U.S. Senate was out of session and could not confirm his lifetime appointment. During this period, Gewin asked the Fifth Circuit's chief judge, Elbert Tuttle, to keep him off panels that were assigned civil rights issues since it might create problems in his confirmation hearings before the Senate Judiciary Committee chaired by Mississippi segregationist James Eastland.[16]

After confirmation, Gewin's initial decisions as a federal judge were those of a moderate segregationist,[17] and on matters of voting during his early years on the bench he stood generally in the company of Daniel Thomas. Both judges often recognized the segregationist origins and history of Alabama's voting laws and acknowledged specific, proven examples of discriminatory behavior. But both also were prone to give white leaders in the Black Belt the benefit of almost every doubt that they knew best how to move their local communities *toward* compliance—not necessarily into full compliance—with federal laws and court rulings.

At bottom, Gewin's opinion in the poll tax case reveals a defense of the Black Belt's white leaders who he believed in 1966 had changed from the days of the 1901 Constitution. With this basic perspective, Gewin was willing as a judge to recognize specific problems of racial discrimination in voting, on a case by case basis "wherever it appears," but not to use the collective words and misdeeds of the Black Belt leaders, starting from 1901, as the basis for a finding a pattern and practice that justified striking down the state's poll tax. That was not his notion of judicial restraint.

The opinion of Frank M. Johnson Jr. (1918–1999) reflected a third perspective, one shared by many in north Alabama during and after the 1901 constitutional convention. Simply, the poll tax was a financial barrier for poor folks, Black and white, in voting. In his opinion, Johnson concurred with Rives that the poll tax disfranchised Black voters, but for him the fundamental issue was the price tag for a right to vote, which he concluded was unconstitutional.

As a native of the "Free State of Winston" and son of a former Republican state legislator and probate judge, Johnson grew up in a family and white community where many had grandfathers who fought against the Confederacy or refused to fight for anyone in the Civil War. His paternal great-grandfather and family fought for the Union Army. Afterwards, much of north Alabama remained an area of poor, small farmers, most of whom rebelled at the ballot box against the Democratic leaders of south Alabama after Reconstruction. The Democrats attempted to impose a poll tax on voting in 1893 to suppress the voting of poor farmers, but the Populists and Republicans representing them in the legislature from north Alabama blocked that proposed section of the Sayre Act.[18]

More than history separated the two regions of Alabama. In 1900, Winston County residents enjoyed less than one percent of the state's total taxable income. Twelve Alabama counties stretching northeast from Winston and Walker into the Sand Mountain and Piedmont areas had less than ten percent of the taxable income in 1900, while ten Black Belt counties together represented almost 22 percent of the state's income.[19]

A poll tax "will be hard on the poor devil who hardly makes enough to live on," warned the *New Decatur Advertiser* during this period, "and it applies to both whites and blacks."[20] In Winston County only seven persons were African American in 1900, according to the census. Its "poor devils" were white folks living amid the county's hilly terrain, deprived of deep deposits of ore and coal and covered by a gravelly topsoil too stingy for profitable cultivation. North Alabama farmers at the turn of the century were economically independent, but most also were unable, as one historian of this period wrote, "to feed and clothe their children properly, much less to give them adequate educational advantages."[21]

At the 1901 convention, the Black Belt proponents of the poll tax made no excuses about its probable effects on north Alabama's white voters. Henry F. Reese Sr. of Selma demanded passage of the poll tax as the safest protection for the Black Belt's white supremacy. He referred to other proposed restrictions on Black voting as unproven. He told delegates, "I hope you won't leave us in the fire . . . to try to let in ignorant and thriftless people in other sections . . . We cannot surrender ourselves to the negroes for the purpose of allowing a few thriftless men in North Alabama to vote."[22]

This appeal suggested the true, two-part purpose behind Black disfranchisement, according to the political leaders of small farmers and laborers who fought the Black Belt/Big Mules alliance. "There were a number of people who sat in the Alabama convention in 1901 who thought it best to restrict the privilege of voting to a small group in the state," observed Justice Hugo Black less than three years after resigning from the U.S. Senate to which he had been twice elected by Alabama white voters, beginning in 1926. "The convention was ostensibly called to disfranchise the Negro, but its real purpose was to keep the white franchise restricted and to maintain the oligarchy in power."[23]

The adoption of voting restrictions, including the poll tax, was a foregone conclusion at the convention, as was the control of the convention by the Black Belt and its allies. The legislation authorizing the convention provided majority-Black counties with the largest number of delegates, although those counties made up only 43 percent of the state's total population and only 31 percent of the white population. They elected a chairman, John Knox, reputedly the richest railroad lawyer in the state, who was not from the Black Belt but who was in full support of their cause. The Committee of Suffrage and Elections appointed by Knox had 25 members, fourteen from majority-Black counties and at least another three or four who represented corporate interests in Mobile and Birmingham.[24]

During the convention, Black Belt delegates also out-maneuvered north Alabama delegates, especially on the poll tax. Twenty proposals introduced for the Suffrage Committee's consideration included a poll tax. Only one proposed to ban it, and one other would exempt members of the state militia. In committee, disagreements among delegates focused on other restrictions for voting. The Suffrage Committee's majority report included controversial property and educational qualifications and a temporary grandfather clause. It also included payment of an annual poll tax of $1.50 for any man between the ages of 21 and 45 who wished to vote. A minority report challenged the voting qualifications and the grandfather exemption, but not the poll tax.[25]

North Alabama delegates did not consider a poll tax as draconian as other proposed barriers, especially since a poll tax was already on the books as a required payment in support of local schools, although unrelated to the right to vote. Newman H. Freeman, a delegate from Winston County, attacked the section of the majority report providing property and education restrictions for the right to vote since "the poor man's freedom is all he enjoys in this world and this would deprive him of that God-given right." But he offered the poll tax as a compromise: "why may not Alabama fall back on a simple poll tax provision of $1.50 from the age of 21 to 45 and this would guarantee our freedom and it could be met with by all deserving illiterate poor white men in Alabama . . ."[26]

In response, Henry Reese insisted on the necessity of a poll tax that included males up to age 60. His position received support from other delegates, and proponents of the tax kept the discussion throughout the remaining debate focused only on the questions of increasing the age or the amount of the poll tax—not on whether there should be a poll tax as a prerequisite for voting or whether it could be a substitute for other restrictions. By the end of the convention, Reese and the other Black Belt delegates knowingly accepted as a compromise the poll tax section proposed in the original majority report. Their Trojan horse for expanding the age limit had assured that the Black Belt's white leaders got the poll tax—and, as it turned out—all of the restrictions they wanted in the first place.[27]

If Gewin actually considered this debate as shadowy artifacts, so ancient as to be immaterial, he must have forgotten that Henry Reese's son was Selma's longtime assistant circuit solicitor to Blanchard McLeod when their offices used the grand jury and state courts in 1964 to harass civil rights workers attempting to register Blacks to vote. The convention debate certainly did not contain the words of ancient ghosts to Rives, who practiced law in Montgomery when the son of at least one of Montgomery's convention delegates was also in the local bar association. Nor were they statements of politicians uttered in far-off times to Johnson, whose father was the second Republican postmaster to serve in the town of Haleyville—following the first, Newman H. Freeman, after the convention delegate moved from Winston County to Birmingham.[28]

'66,000 white men disfranchised themselves . . .'

After the 1901 Constitution was adopted in a fraudulent vote, the poll tax was implemented immediately by Governor William Jelks, who had supported adoption. With advice from Black Belt leaders who ran the convention, Jelks guided two other state officials in the process of appointing three registrars in each county. More than a thousand men from across the state applied to serve as registrars, and most were chosen by the end of January 1902. Local reports also suggest that most of the appointed registrars were well-known in their own communities.[29]

All men wishing to vote in the 1902 statewide elections, to be held in August and November, had to pay their poll tax before February 1—less than three months after the new Constitution was approved and nine months before the general election. In most counties, the poll tax was due before new boards of registrars opened their doors in March to begin accepting applications for voter registration.

This two-step process was new and deliberately confusing, especially for Black men wishing to vote. Some paid their poll taxes only to discover later that registrars disqualified them as voters. A few were qualified by local white registrars but were denied the vote because of failure to pay the poll tax on time. Registration boards in Calhoun and Jefferson apparently decided on their own that three local "prominent and reputable white citizens" had to vouch for the "good character" of any African American applicant. Most Black men understood what the new constitution meant for them and did not go to the courthouse before or after February in pursuit of their right to vote.[30]

In trumpeting local enthusiasm for the new poll tax, the *Montgomery Advertiser* reported that "the poll tax payments in Montgomery County has been practically unanimous. Very few white men had willfully disfranchised themselves." Several other newspapers and political leaders who supported the new Constitution branded a failure to pay the poll tax as a person's self-inflicted denial of one's own voting rights. The Black Belt's Marion *Times-Standard* reprinted an editorial declaring, "The new constitution disfranchises no one. Some men have disfranchised themselves . . ."[31]

The *Birmingham News* similarly claimed in both news coverage and editorial comments that voters "disfranchised themselves" in failing to pay a poll tax. In reporting on Dallas County, the newspaper wrote, "The majority of the voters who have disfranchised themselves are of the poorer classes . . ." and later wrote on its editorial page, "White men who disfranchised themselves through failure to pay their poll tax will place a higher value on the right to vote" in future years. The *News* went so far as to report that Black men had "disfranchised themselves" after they failed to pay poll taxes—when it was common knowledge that registrars would reject most, if not all, Blacks as voters regardless of their payment of poll taxes.[32]

These claims of self-inflicted disfranchisement enraged poll tax opponents. The *New Decatur Advertiser*, a populist and labor-leaning newspaper, reprinted an editorial condemning as criminal the claims of "Ratifiers" that the "poor man disfranchises himself." A letter to the editor of the *Alabamian*, a Teddy Roosevelt-Republican newspaper, suggested that failure to pay the poll tax put the poor in the same category as criminals, who were denied a vote by Alabama law. "It is no crime to fail to pay poll tax (Oh! No!) but the political penalty is the same as attaches to a long catalogue of crimes. The poor fellow who fails to pay poll tax is, politically, in the class of embezzlers, rapists, and murderers." J. C. Fonville, an erstwhile populist, concluded that the constitution makers' "main objective was to reduce the white electorate."[33]

The editor of the *Alabamian* also crunched numbers from census data and poll tax receipts to prove the poll tax was disfranchising a large number of white voters. "The ratification papers claim 66,000 white men disfranchised themselves . . . Every one of these unfortunate white men would be voters today but for the new constitution," the editor asserted. "Might as well say the water had nothing to do with drowning the fellow, it was want of air."[34]

Historian Sheldon Hackney calculated that 24 percent of the "white, male, voting age population was disfranchised by the poll tax alone." Democrats who supported ratification insisted that voters chose to disfranchise themselves, but some admitted that 20,000 white voters had not paid the poll tax in the first year.[35] What is without question is that voting by both Blacks and whites declined notably in the first elections after the poll tax was required for voting.

Voters in the Democratic primary for governor and in the general election in 1902 comprised not much more than half the number who voted in the referendum on the Alabama Constitution in late 1901. This meant the number of voters in 1902 fell by about 75,000. In majority-Black counties where African Americans were eliminated in wholesale numbers, the decline was close to 40,000. Those were essentially only Black voters. That left about 35,000 fewer voters casting a ballot in the state's other counties. Some represented a reduction in Black voters, but most were likely whites removed from the voting rolls.[36]

This decline had its immediate effects. Jelks defeated former Governor Joseph Johnston, who attempted to regain office through an insurgent coalition of disaffected Democrats, Independents, old Populists, and Republicans. The voting returns confirmed that the "ratifiers"—led by Black Belt politicians and corporation lawyers—had in place the means to win more than one election.[37] In Alabama's first elections under its new constitution, the suffrage provisions proved they would achieve what their opponents had feared—removing almost all Black voters from the polls and eliminating enough poor, insurgent white voters to put, in Hugo Black's words, "the oligarchy in power."

During the summer of 1902, Booker T. Washington, president of Tuskegee Institute, secretly financed litigation in state court by Jackson Giles and other Black postal workers in Montgomery who challenged the suffrage provisions of the new constitution. Their claims of racial discrimination had little chance when their Texas attorney first argued the case before city judge A. D. Sayre, the former legislator who had sponsored the 1893 statute restricting voting. Across the next two years, the Black plaintiffs were turned away in state and federal courts on jurisdictional and procedural grounds as the federal courts avoided the gravamen of the case. The *Birmingham News* suggested that it was "fortunate for the Negro that no elusive hope is held out to him that he may acquire political rights without deserving them." The *News* editors referred to the fact that 1,500 to 2,000 Blacks were registered voters across the entire state as proof that the Black plaintiffs were wrong on their claims. "Negroes can vote in Alabama," the *News* asserted, as it blithely identified the rare exception as proof of the rule and forecast that more Blacks would be registered in decades ahead if and when they demonstrated they deserved the privilege.[38]

The cases reached the U.S. Supreme Court, which upheld the Alabama Supreme Court's opinions that had been written with no more intellectual or factual honesty than the *Birmingham News* editorials. In the first *Giles* case, Justice Oliver Wendell Holmes wrote that the federal courts' equitable powers "cannot undertake now, any more than it has in the past, to enforce political rights" and, therefore, the Court was without jurisdiction to provide "any relief from a great political wrong, if done, as alleged."[39] The opinion, in effect, was a concession by the nation's highest court that "Jim Crow was stronger than the U.S. Constitution," as Vernon Burton and Armand Derfner have written. Holmes's opinion would remain the law of the land for almost six decades for voting cases, especially those that might involve court supervision of state officials' conduct, until another case arising from Alabama in the name of Tuskegee Institute professor C. G. Gomillion pushed the Court, with the judicial nudging of Justice Hugo Black, into the "political thicket" for good.[40]

'A HORDE OF IGNORANT AND ILLITERATE VOTERS . . .'

After 1902, Alabama established the machinery by which the poll tax became a routine requirement for voting. In 1903, the legislature ignored a bill introduced by one of its two Republican members to abolish the poll tax. That same year it passed bills providing that voters must receive a receipt as proof of payment of their poll taxes and setting an annual deadline of March 31 for the local tax collectors to deliver to probate judges an official county list of persons who had paid the taxes. Local newspapers did little more than publish remainders of the deadline for paying the poll tax, and most continued to urge readers not to "disfranchise themselves."[41] And with each passing year of nonpayment, an additional $1.50 was added to the total poll tax due before a person could vote.

A Black Belt legislator also introduced an expanded vagrancy law patterned after a recent Georgia law. The new act added new persons deemed vagrants, including any youth 16 to 21 years old not in school or working. It increased the penalty for a first offense from a maximum fine of $50 to $500 and added up to six months of hard labor. In addition, the new act required sheriffs and police officers to provide justices of the peace with information about all persons they knew or merely suspected as vagrants so that JPs in every precinct across the state could issue arrest warrants and try the suspects.[42]

The law was designed to help address the "Negro problem" in labor and in politics. "When a negro knows he is liable to be . . . sent to the mines for vagrancy, he is going to be much more careful about how he passes the time," according to one public official quoted in the Marion newspaper. The *Birmingham News* welcomed the law that would require "loafer, white and black, to go to work or move out of the state."[43] The overall effect was to increase the supply of dirt-cheap labor in cotton fields and mills and to provide more forced labor in the mines, plantation fields, and turpentine work camps where convicts were leased to private companies and land owners.

The political impact was no less far-reaching. The new constitution added vagrants and tramps to the long list of persons disqualified from voting due to a criminal conviction, a list which previously had included only those convicted of treason, embezzlement of public funds, malfeasance in office, larceny, bribery, or other serious crimes.[44] If judged by law as idle, unemployed, or landless during some time in their lives, most poor people, Black and white, could be fined more money than they would ever see in their lifetimes (and remain in debt), be forced to provide free labor for up to half a year, and be denied the right to register and vote to change the law that criminalized them.

In 1906, the poll tax reemerged as a political issue in some local elections. A few Democrats and Republicans proposed to make the tax mandatory while removing it as a precondition for voting. Another proposal would eliminate the poll tax's cumulative amount. These efforts were aided by the *Birmingham Age-Herald*, which mounted an editorial campaign for change—claiming as many as 100,000 whites were now being excluded from the ballot. "Either the poll tax should be rendered compulsory or else it should cease to be cumulative in the matter of voting. Perhaps both remedies will be found to be safe and desirable," the newspaper asserted.[45]

Democratic Congressman Sydney Bowie, a vocal advocate for ratifying the constitution, surprised his Black Belt friends and supporters when he announced that he favored eliminating a voluntary, cumulative tax. He was worried that both school funding (supported in part by the poll tax) and white voting had dropped sharply since the new voluntary poll tax was implemented. He affirmed his belief in the necessity of protecting white supremacy in Black Belt counties but suggested that Alabama's poll tax provision "went further than any state has gone and further than any necessity required."

Bowie proposed a constitutional amendment authorizing each county commission to set the amount and age limits of the poll tax in their counties as a way to advance the principle of home rule and to let Black Belt counties protect themselves as they thought necessary. "But the adequate protection of the black belt," Bowie wrote, "does not involve the perpetuation of a ruinous and indefensible policy in the white counties, which contain four-fifths of the white population of the state."[46]

Some north Alabama weeklies reprinted Bowie's call for change and the *Age-Herald*'s supportive editorials, but Black Belt leaders would have none of it. The *Marion Times-Standard* declared that the poll tax "has done more than all else to reduce the negro vote in the Black Belt." Its editor worried the Black Belt's Negroes were becoming better educated in what he described as their "good schools" and were also more prosperous. Therefore, even if the poll tax disfranchised some whites, it excluded virtually all Blacks. The editor warned Bowie: "You are stepping on dangerous ground"—a sentiment echoed by the *Montgomery Advertiser* and others.[47]

The 1906 election brought into office Governor B. B. Comer, a wealthy, land-rich merchant and mill owner who as a self-identifying progressive fought against railroads but remained loyal to old-style white supremacy. In his first address to the legislature, Comer made no mention of the poll tax except to use it as a means to attack the state's African Americans. "I was born and reared in Barbour County," Comer declared, as if his heritage as a blue-blood of the Black Belt gave him special credentials to know his subject. Comer and family members had been involved in murdering the son of an election official to help upend Reconstruction and had built their family fortune on slavery and exploited Black labor. Now he attacked the carpetbagger, scalawag, and the federal government for misleading Black voters into creating a "conglomerate of ignorance, cupidity, vice, and power" in the decades before disfranchisement. Comer also condemned Negroes for "crying against the white man" instead of "against the criminals and vagrants of their own race."

"In Alabama there is not one negro in twenty who pays any tax whatever, including poll tax," Comer complained as he indulged in the political tradition of fabricating his own facts. "The poll taxes are devoted exclusively to schools. Of the negroes of Jefferson county, the largest county in the State . . . [where] the negro is largely employed at good wages, less than fifty pay poll taxes. Nineteen-twentieths of the tuition paid to sustain the schools to which they send their children is paid by the whites;

they pay a very small part towards the support and maintenance of the government."[48]

Comer's harangue captured the evolving attitude that Alabama's white leaders had embraced only five or six years after disfranchisement. It was immaterial to them that Black men did not pay their poll taxes because doing so would not get them the right to vote. It was of no consequence to whites that Black people would pay no poll taxes to support schools because they had absolutely no role or voice in decisions about the schools or about the inferior funding of Black schools. Rather than understanding it as an act of rational self-interest or protest on the part of Black citizens, Comer and others portrayed the Black man's failure to pay poll taxes as an innate lack of good citizenship and good character. And, in so doing, they racialized the failure to pay a poll tax in Alabama and any opinion for changing the poll tax as a "Negro problem."

As a result, some local white leaders who opposed the poll tax maligned the Negro as much or more than those who supported it. For example, in Franklin County, near the state's northwest corner where Republicans continued to run for office, J. R. Brown was the party's nominee for the legislature in 1906. He supported removing the poll tax as a prerequisite for voting and making it a mandatory tax to provide more local school funding. His Democratic opponent, a young public school teacher, also supported such a change. Still, Brown campaigned by demeaning the few Black men who lived in the county as he assured white voters that even without requiring a poll tax to vote local registrars would never permit those he called "Mr. 'nig'" and "Mr. 'Coon'" to qualify to cast a ballot.[49]

'The Question Is Not the Negro Problem but the White Problem . . .'

A few others spoke up for interracial democracy. Soon after Comer's speech, Chilton County's State Representative Osmond Middleton introduced a bill to hold a statewide referendum on the poll tax. His background was unusual for an Alabama Republican after the turn of the century. A young lawyer, Middleton's family tree included a signer of the Declaration of Independence, a U.S. senator, and a vice president. His grandfather fought in the War of 1812, and his father was a captain in the Confederate Army. Middleton had become an experienced orator by speaking as a youth to Confederate veterans' reunions and Democratic clubs. Six months after graduating from the University of Alabama law school, he was elected mayor of the town of Clanton as a Democrat without opposition. A week later, in January 1904, he was appointed the county's solicitor.[50] In 1906, this young rising Democrat switched parties to run for the state house on the combined Republican-Populist ticket in Chilton County. His reasons for the switch are unclear, although he apparently thought it would not hurt his chances. In a hard-fought election, Middleton defeated his Democratic opponent by less than two hundred votes after a campaign in which Joseph Columbus Manning, longtime Populist leader and a well-known vocal opponent of Alabama's disfranchisement efforts, had traveled across the county speaking for Middleton.[51]

To no one's surprise, Middleton's poll tax bill died in committee, as did a similar bill introduced by a legislator from mountainous DeKalb County. But Middleton was a true believer in the cause—or had become one. After the legislative session, he joined Manning on a tour in northeastern states to talk about issues of disfranchisement.

Joseph Manning (Clay County Historical Society).

Manning had been a founder of the People's Party in Alabama and was elected as a Populist to the state legislature from Clay County in 1894. Only age 24, Manning was already considered a spellbinder on the stump, especially on his favorite subject, the denial of democracy in Alabama. In a Clay County speech entitled "Liberty or Death," the young Manning once declared, "An evil money power, an unrighteous band of political pirates now seek to rob freeborn Americans of the right to vote and to have that vote count . . ."[52] His vocal support for citizens' right to vote included Black Alabamians, and he opposed the fraudulent vote counting in the Black Belt that had stolen elections from Populist candidates in the 1890s and enabled the 1901 convention and the adoption of its constitution.

Unable to keep the Populist Party alive, Manning became a Republican and received a federal appointment as postmaster in Alexander City in Tallapoosa County. He continued to speak and write widely about the corruption of politics in Alabama and the South and, after 1901, about Alabama's disfranchisement of both poor Black and white citizens. The speaking tour in the northeast was an annual event in Manning's continuing strategy to advance democracy in his homeland. With no real chance for electoral reform at home, in the face of the controlling economic and political "oligarchy," Manning turned North to arouse a constituency for pushing the federal government to protect what he called "the sovereignty" of a citizen's right to vote in the South.[53]

Manning and Middleton appeared first in Boston where they spoke at a Black church to an audience primarily of African Americans. Middleton affirmed his support of Joe Manning's crusade against the oligarchy or "Democratic machine" and condemned "political slavery" in Alabama, "a slavery which denies a man the right of suffrage, a right which 200,000 white and 180,000 colored men are not allowed to exercise." According to the *Boston Post*, Middleton also declared, "There are some bad black men where I come from, but for every one I will find you two white men who are worse."[54] He also charged that the Democrats in the state legislature killed his poll tax bill because "they did not want the common people educated; they do not want them to vote."[55]

The two young white Alabamians also appeared in Baltimore a few days later at a meeting of more than 2,000 African Americans who were assembled to fight the introduction of a disfranchisement clause in the Maryland constitution. The program involved both white and Black speakers, including George White, the last African American in Congress from the South before disfranchisement. Middleton repeated his condemnation of Alabama's disfranchisement of both Black and white voters but suggested that a younger generation in his state was coming of age without "the prejudices following the Civil War." Framing the race problem in terms rarely, if ever, heard in Alabama, the young Republican proclaimed, "The question is not the negro problem, but the white problem. The question is how to get the white people to line up to the imperative requirement of the Constitution of this country."[56]

Middleton and Manning returned to Alabama to a firestorm of criticism, especially against the Chilton legislator. The state's Democrats thought Manning "ought to be ashamed of himself" for telling "ghost stories of Southern horrors,"[57] but over the years they had become accustomed to his prolific writing and speeches about "Bourbon oligarchy." (He was sometimes called by the Northern press the "William Lloyd Garrison of the South" after the well-known relentless white abolitionist of the Civil War era.) Manning had suffered financial and physical attacks over the years for his advocacy,[58] but this time it was his follower, the 25-year-old elected member of the state legislature, with whom Democrats were furious.

The *Montgomery Advertiser* reprinted the *Boston Post*'s account of the two men's speeches, which the Alabama paper called "ridiculous performances." The *Montgomery Journal* suggested Middleton had time to learn from his mistakes but condemned him for traveling to the North to "discredit the intelligence and common honesty" of his own people. Chilton's local Democratic newspaper, *The Banner*, reprinted with approval the *Journal* article. A local columnist criticized Middleton's motives as well as his speech, and another writer called the speech a "slam on white people," adding what at the time passed as accepted racist humor: "It is enough to make a kinkeyhead grunt."[59]

Middleton defended his tour, claiming the *Boston Post* misquoted him, especially in the comparison of bad Black and white men. The state's Republican newspapers ran his corrections, and Manning's newspaper promoted him. The *Montgomery Advertiser* also published his defense as a letter to the editor, but the newspaper remained skeptical, suggesting the Republican-Populist legislator must get in line with Alabama's "dominant thought." The *Banner* castigated him for "arousing hatred" of the white people who elected him. The local editor took particular issue with Middleton's explanation of the defeat of his poll tax bill. The bill "was defeated because the people of this state thought more of good and decent government than a government dominated by ignorant and vicious blacks."[60]

Middleton enlisted a Democratic legislator to vouch for him as a "citizen of the State" not "capable of such utterances" as reported by the Northern press. For several months afterwards, Middleton attracted support in the Republican press, and he ran for Congress as a Republican in the 4th District, where his party had won office before disfranchisement. He received a slim majority of votes in Chilton and Shelby, the district's two counties once strongholds for Populists, but he lost the race by a lopsided margin due to votes in the remaining district. Dallas County, for example, gave him only four out of 1,458 votes. [61]

Now gun-shy about bucking "dominant thought," Middleton claimed he made no appeal to African American voters in his congressional race and that his Democratic opponent attracted more Black votes than he did, although the number could only have been a handful. He also told a reporter that he would not be a "revenue only" Republican looking for a federal appointment, proclaiming he would rather be a justice of the peace elected by the people in an out-of-the-way precinct than hold the best appointive federal office in the state.[62]

Middleton never sought another elective office, but he did receive appointed posts when a Republican was in the White House, although not one of the best. He moved to Mobile and was appointed during a Republican administration as an assistant U.S. attorney and afterwards as a federal bankruptcy judge—posts he held during most of his 40-year career.

While remaining active in Alabama's Republican circles, Osmond Middleton apparently never spoke again publicly in Alabama or elsewhere about the South's "white problem." Joe Manning lost his appointed postmaster's job in 1909 and moved to New York City where he struggled financially for the rest of his life but continued to publish and speak against the political oligarchy.[63]

The 1910 general election gubernatorial campaign hardened the state's "dominant thought" on voting and further obscured its origins and purposes. A native of Florence, Alabama, Emmet O'Neal successfully had run in the Democratic primary against former Selma mayor Hugh Mallory. The major issue in the primary campaign was Prohibition; race and voting were not raised since both candidates were a part of the Black Belt-industrialist political alliance, although they did compete on who was qualified as the more "refined, cultured, and intellectual christian southern gentleman."[64] In the general election, however, O'Neal ran a hard-hitting campaign against the Republican nominee, making the already-disfranchised Black voter and Republican support for changing the poll tax the paramount issues.

O'Neal called his Republican opponent "a renegade to your race and an enemy of white supremacy" due to his opposition to the poll tax. "You are not so ignorant as not to know that the poll tax provision is the most important section in the whole scheme of suffrage," O'Neal charged, ". . . and its repeal would open wide the door for an alarming and dangerous increase of negro voters." As Democratic nominee, he declared "the people of Alabama" would maintain the "wall of protection they have so carefully and wisely built for the protection of our race against the dangers and menace of negro suffrage" by electing him as their governor.[65]

Governor Emmett O'Neal (ADAH).

O'Neal's landslide victory embodied how brilliantly the Black Belt–industrialist alliance was transmogrifying notions of suffrage only a decade after a fraudulent referendum had adopted disfranchisement. Once O'Neal became the Democratic nominee in June, there was no doubt that he would win the general election in November. But his racist campaign was necessary for continuing to vilify anyone who would propose to change the terms of disfranchisement and to wipe away any remembrance of how Black Belt leaders and their corporate allies manipulated the democratic process to enlarge their own political power.

And who better than a north Alabamian to help recast living memory by declaring that "the people of Alabama" (white *people*, of course) through their political wisdom had crafted the disfranchising provisions of the Alabama Constitution—not the Black Belt and corporate leaders through a fixed convention and a dishonest election. There had been recent signs of political tremors. Birmingham had experienced in 1908 a major miners' strike involving Black and white workers joining together against mine operators. Disputes over Prohibition were producing crevices between Alabama's wet and dry Democrats.[66] How better to prevent these divisions from spurring new alliances that could disturb the existing political order than to use the poll tax and the already-disfranchised Black voters as whipping boys to discredit Republicans and anyone else who dared to question voting restrictions while preserving the current terms of suffrage that disfranchised those who were the past insurgents—Black voters and a large number of poorer whites?

Finally, by repositioning the "people of Alabama" as both author and authority of the means of disfranchisement, O'Neal provided an added layer of legitimacy to the notion that some white folks, not the suffrage sections of a fraudulent constitution, were "disfranchising themselves." Little wonder that the white voters of several Black Belt counties gave a majority or near-majority of votes to north Alabama's O'Neal over one of their own.[67] For preserving their power and way of life, O'Neal was arguably better than a Black Belt governor.

'THE BALLOT, TAKEN FROM THEM WHILE . . . FIGHTING FOR WORLD DEMOCRACY'

Across the next six years, Alabama's poll tax and related voting restrictions remained a settled political question, although never without a few lonely dissenters. The Republicans and a splinter group, the Progressive Party, composed of Teddy Roosevelt supporters and a few prominent old Populists, continued to include changing the poll tax in their state platforms. A newly formed socialist party endorsed the complete abolition of the tax and equal suffrage for men and women.[68] But rarely were candidates from these groups able to advance the issue.

A small number of young Democrats also broke from their party's "dominant thought." For example, within a few weeks of O'Neal taking office, State Senator Cecil Beasley of north Alabama's Fayette County introduced a bill to limit the cumulative payment of poll taxes to only five years. Beasley was a 34-year-old lawyer who had read law in Emmet O'Neal's firm eight years earlier and was the private secretary of newly elected U.S. Senator John Bankhead Sr. From Baldwin County on the Alabama coast, State Representative Samuel Jenkins put into the hopper a bill to eliminate all cumulative back payments of the poll tax for voting (and reduce residency-in-the-state requirements from two years to one). Jenkins was a 41-year-old attorney who had support from the county's Fairhope single-tax colony, a utopian community founded in 1894 by Midwest Populists.[69]

Alabama's Black Belt newspapers ignored the positions of the minority parties but quickly challenged the Democratic legislators' "radical" proposals. The *Montgomery Advertiser* claimed the poll tax had given Alabama ten years of purified, honest elections. "The poll tax provision has done as much or more to silence the ignorant negro vote in the State as any other provision in the new constitution," its editorial avowed, while warning the young Democrats, "let it alone." The *Greensboro Watchman* editor added his journalistic "Amen!" to the *Advertiser*'s "sound and unanswerable" editorial, which he reprinted almost in full.[70] As with other past proposals, the bills died in committee.

The poll tax increasingly became a permanent barrier to voting in Alabama for both Black and white men who failed to pay it annually and saw their total price tag for voting grow. State officials did their part to enlarge and institutionalize its effects. Attorney General William Logan Martin Jr., brother of an emerging Alabama Power Company president, issued an opinion that the poll tax had to be paid for any years an Alabama resident was not in the state once they returned to Alabama and wanted to vote. Another attorney general's opinion held that anyone convicted of a disqualifying crime and later pardoned had to pay a poll tax for the years he was disqualified in order to vote again.[71]

The Alabama Supreme Court also did its part. In an election contest, the Court issued an opinion in which it laid out 27 steps relating to the payment and administration of the poll tax—how it should be recorded and evidenced, when it was due exactly and by whom, and on which birthdate an exemption might apply to which election, etc. Also, the decision affirmed as law the attorney general's opinion that men returning to Alabama had to pay a poll tax for those years they were absent. The Court opinion was an attempt to clarify a host of detailed questions cropping up over the years, and it overturned a couple of prior decisions.[72] But most of all the Court's unusual opinion signified that the poll tax and the complex methods by which it was administered to limit voting were now institutionalized across the state.

These developments over time added to the legitimacy and acceptance of the poll tax—so much so that after a decade and a half some of Alabama's Black newspapers had absorbed the notion that African Americans' failure to pay a poll tax was an irresponsible, individual act of "disfranchising themselves." *The Emancipator* in Montgomery acknowledged the registration hurdles Black men had to surmount and that only a relative few were qualified by white registrars as voters, But it scolded readers, "Don't say it is not worthwhile; make the attempt . . . Pay your poll tax. If you fail to do this, don't blame anybody but yourself for being disfranchised." The newspaper editor argued that a failure of Black men to pay their poll taxes, even though few, if any, would be found qualified to vote, showed "the world that they do not value the ballot and thereby invite further disfranchisement."[73]

As it turned out, the first World War cracked the mould on disfranchisement—ushering in new, broad-based challenges to the dominant thought that the poll tax was inviolate. Within six months of the declaration of war and passage of a military draft in 1917, Alabama tax collectors were raising questions about the application of the law. The state constitution had exempted members of Alabama's National Guard from the poll tax,[74] but guardsmen had been mustered into the regular U.S. Army. As a result, Attorney General Martin ruled that the guardsmen were no longer eligible for an exemption. To make matter worse, the guardsmen and other soldiers who were willing to pay the poll tax were away from their homes and state law required payment "in the county in which the voter legally resides."[75] Therefore, most soldiers would be disfranchised in the 1918 elections since the constitution required payment by February 1 to vote in the August Democratic primary and the November general election.

In early 1918, Martin's legal opinions were adding insult to injury to servicemen. "Unless the law is changed," reported the *Montgomery Advertiser*, "Alabama soldiers, on their return from the war, must not only pay the poll tax for the year in which they will vote, but for the years they missed while serving at the front."[76] In Wilcox County, the local editor suggested that members of the community should pay the poll taxes for returning soldiers,[77] although he surely meant only white soldiers. In any event, the idea did not catch on.

By Armistice Day in November 1918, more than 100,000 soldiers from Alabama had served in the armed forces and all would soon be home. Most were between the ages of 21 and 45. They were among the state's best educated and healthiest men of their generation.[78] And they had real grievances to air about their rights as citizens.

They had endured the hardships of war, risking life and limb for their country. Some were not coming home whole. Despite doing their patriotic duty, soldiers were returning without a right to vote unless they paid a cumulative poll tax. Some would have to pay for the years prior to their enlistment if they had not paid poll taxes earlier. At the same time, most men over the age of 45 in Alabama did not go to war and risk their lives for democracy. Yet under Alabama law, men over 45 were free to vote without a price tag, but the men under 45 who sacrificed for their country had to pay a poll tax.

State Representative Walter Burgwyn Jones of Montgomery stepped forward to address the ex-soldiers' grievances. Soon after the legislature convened in January, he proposed a referendum to change the 1901 Constitution so that ex-soldiers who served in the military during WWI would be exempt from poll tax in all future years. Other legislators from

Mobile and north Alabama submitted similar bills, and the former Populist-turned-Republican Adolphus Parker Longshore, who had served in the legislature as early as 1888, proposed to remove any payment of the poll tax as a precondition for voting. But Jones's bill was the only one to make it out of committee.[79]

Young Walter B. Jones (ADAH).

Jones was an unusual advocate for changing the state constitution's suffrage provisions. His father, Thomas Goode Jones, had been the bearer of the Confederate truce flag at Appomattox and became a well-known railroad lawyer. He had been elected governor and in 1892 won reelection against his Populist opponent in what a seasoned historian called one of Alabama's "most corrupt electoral contests"—thanks in large part to fraudulent vote-counting in the Black Belt. Governor Jones also called out the state militia to assure that his friend and Democratic successor, William Oates, would take office after Joe Manning and other Populists had convened in Montgomery to challenge the fraud and vote-stealing that enabled Oates to win the governorship.[80]

Later, the senior Jones became a member of the 1901 Constitutional Convention where he supported disfranchisement but argued against the "grandfather clause" and other provisions aimed primarily at disfranchising only African Americans. (As a teenager, Walter accompanied his father and sat with him during part of the proceedings.) Governor Jones proposed to allow any male to vote who could pay an annual poll tax of four dollars or had enough property to pay five dollars in taxes—terms that would have excluded poor men regardless of color. After the convention, through the influence of Booker T. Washington, Governor Jones was appointed by Republican President Teddy Roosevelt as a federal district judge in Montgomery, where he served until his death in 1914. [81]

Walter Jones became an attorney in 1909 and spent most of his legal career as the self-described "court crier" of the federal courthouse—a job that involved being secretary and stenographer first for his judge father and afterwards for Judge Henry D. Clayton, a friend of Jones Sr. who succeeded him on the federal bench. Walter was elected in 1918 to the legislature (a post his father had held decades earlier) on a slate of candidates who ran largely on their opposition to Prohibition.[82]

A controversy erupted in the last days of Walter Jones's campaign for the legislature, and it may explain why the poll tax exemption for ex-soldiers became one of his top legislative priorities. Jones was accused of using his privileged position in Montgomery to "dodge military service" during WWI. He was a prime candidate by education and age (29) for being drafted. He became the chairman of the county campaign to buy war bonds in support the troops, a visible post he highlighted repeatedly during his campaign, but he never served in the army during the war.

In a major story in the last weeks of his campaign, Jones answered "innuendoes" and "cowardly attacks upon my patriotism." He claimed that he sought to enlist repeatedly but was turned down "due to physical disability." He recounted how he had served "many years in the National Guard but in 1915 was honorably discharged for physical disability." Jones also mentioned that he tried to reenlist in the Guard but was disqualified again for the same reason.[83]

After publishing Jones's own defense, the *Montgomery Advertiser* treated him during the remainder of the campaign as a war hero and implied that any criticism of the young son of an important Montgomery family besmirched the entire city. The newspaper ran an editorial condemning the "slander" against Jones as well as profiles praising him for his honesty and patriotism as the worthy son of Governor Jones, a Confederate hero, whose family had been a pillar of Montgomery for more than 80 years. When the votes were counted, Jones had survived the attacks and won the election by the largest margin among the four candidates elected to serve Montgomery County in the legislature.[84]

The election put the accusations behind Jones, but he may have wanted to bury questions of patriotism even deeper in the public mind to forestall anyone unearthing the issue again. Available records suggest that his failure to serve was not as straightforward as he publicly claimed. Alabama National Guard records show that when he joined in 1914, four months before his father died, Jones was listed with "physical condition normal." During the next two years, he seemed half-hearted about his enlistment since he missed almost as many sessions as he attended, and no National Guard record indicated any physical disability. Perhaps most damning, his signed draft registration cards show that Jones requested an exemption from the army due to his status as "Officer of U.S. Court."[85]

Jones's leadership for the cause of ex-soldiers was also important for his political ambitions, which became more evident in the months following his election to the legislature. While continuing his role as a state legislator, Jones ran and was elected in May 1919 to the Montgomery city commission, a post his father also had held. The *Advertiser* continued to promote Jones as one of city's "best known young men," but he needed votes more than praise amid Alabama's unpredictable political winds. The newly formed American Legion of ex-soldiers was growing rapidly and, while operating as a nonpartisan organization that Jones could not join, its members were becoming a potentially significant political force.[86]

Jones's poll tax bill was sent to the House Committee on Elections, where Black Belt members were well represented, but it did not come to the floor for consideration until August since the legislature faced two gigantic political issues: considering proposed federal constitutional amendments establishing national Prohibition and women's right to vote. Jones actively opposed both amendments, warning that Prohibition would endanger states' rights and the Susan B. Anthony Amendment was a "monstrous effort" that would enable Black women to vote.[87]

When Jones's bill reached the house floor, it was sharply revised in an apparent compromise. The ex-soldiers eligible for an exemption had been narrowed to include only those who served until Armistice Day. The greater change eliminated a permanent exemption from the poll tax and granted one only until September 1923. But even this substitute was too much for several Black Belt representatives. Representative A. M. "Alf" Tunstall, a Greensboro attorney who began serving in the legislature in

1896, objected that the bill would put Negro soldiers onto the voting rolls in the Black Belt—a fear echoed by others. In a close vote where a third of the members avoided a recorded roll call, the house defeated the substitute and sent the original bill to the legislative graveyard.[88]

The response was almost unprecedented for this issue. Jones mounted a publicity campaign defending his bill, as war veterans publicly registered their outrage. Jones called his bill "an act of simple justice" and pointed out that Alabama's American Legion had endorsed it. He dismissed concerns about enfranchising Black soldiers. "Every thinking man knows it is the system of registration which protects Alabama from an ignorant and vicious electorate," he stated. Another son of a former governor, Captain William Oates, expressed outrage that "Alabama is now going to disfranchise these men because of their patriotism" and said it was "absurd" to argue that the bill "would jeopardize white supremacy."[89]

Several heroes from the war added their own statements demanding "the right of the ballot, taken from them while they were fighting for world democracy." An amputee from the 167th infantry said it "certainly makes a soldier feel small," and another soldier observed that among the 3,700 men who served with him in the 167th "616 are dead and the balance disfranchised."[90]

Alabama newspapers joined in the chorus of indignation. The *Montgomery Advertiser* blithely backtracked on its prior views that the state constitution's poll tax must remain unaltered forever and called for passage as "common justice." The Birmingham newspapers also urged passage of Jones's bill, and the *Birmingham News,* seemingly emboldened by the war, argued that "every negro soldier who did military service abroad should be registered and given the privilege of voting." The Selma editor ignored that provocation and expressed confidence that Walter Jones would not disrupt the "suffrage situation." He also warned that "some more political graves will be dug" if the legislature did not heed the demands of the ex-soldiers, their families and their friends.[91]

The Jones bill was put back onto the house calendar and called up for reconsideration in September. Its sponsor offered another substitute bill reducing the exemption to September 30 of the current year (1919), which meant veterans would be forgiven past poll taxes but not future taxes. It also proposed giving the governor the duty of deciding on the exact date for the statewide referendum. Thomas Orr, a reformer from north Alabama's Marshall County, offered an amendment returning the expiration date of the poll tax to 1923, and it passed with little or no debate, as did the amended bill. Despite past objections, Representative Tunstall decided to vote for it, as did all but 11 other members present.[92]

Perhaps more stunning, the "Jones soldiers' poll tax exemption" as the press called it, received a favorable recommendation from the senate's Constitutional Revisions Committee, composed almost entirely of Black Belt members, including Greensboro's Robert E. Evins, who would sponsor the "good character" constitutional amendment in the next legislative session. With the blessing of the Black Belt, the bill passed the senate without a dissenting vote.[93]

Governor Thomas Kilby set the referendum for shortly after Christmas and almost three-fourths of voters, in a very light turnout, approved the soldiers' exemption. Walter Jones called it a "fitting tribute to the young men who sacrificed all to uphold democracy,"[94] but almost as soon as the vote was officially recorded in early 1920, Alabama's soldiers met resistance as they attempted to register. Alabama Attorney General James Quinton Smith, a native of Montgomery, issued an opinion that soldiers were not exempt from all past poll taxes—only those taxes due while they were serving in the military. He followed up with another AG's opinion declaring that only ex-soldiers were eligible for the exemption. Those still serving in the military had to wait until they were discharged to claim an exemption.[95]

The Alabama Supreme Court unanimously overruled Smith, but by the end of 1920 another court action challenged the authority of the governor to set the date of elections for a constitutional amendment—an amendment that was on the ballot with Jones's poll tax amendment authorizing millions of dollars in state bonds to build roads. In early 1921, the state's highest court ruled that the Alabama Constitution required the legislature—not the governor—to set the specific date of a referendum to change the constitution. Therefore, it struck down the "good roads" amendment and doomed the soldiers' poll tax amendment, which four months later the court expressly invalidated.[96]

Yielding to the demands of the American Legion, Kilby called a special session in which the legislature unanimously passed a bill putting the same poll tax exemption up for a statewide vote but this time specifying the exact date for the referendum. Alabama voters approved it at the end of January 1922, with a much larger turnout and an even larger lopsided vote; 87 percent of more than 120,000 voters endorsed the soldiers' exemption.[97]

This change in the state constitution represented a huge departure from the state's dominant thought and Black Belt dogma about the inviolate terms of the poll tax as adopted in 1901. The overwhelming public endorsement of the change proved that American patriotism after World War I was becoming a powerful social and political force, rivaling worship of the Old Confederacy even in the Heart of Dixie. But such a rousing ratification did not necessarily explain why Black Belt legislators allowed such a proposed change in suffrage restrictions to go before voters. They had never done so in the past, and in 1919 they had the legislative votes, especially in the state senate and its key committee, to kill the bill.

An obvious answer could be that they believed white soldiers deserved the exemption. Or, perhaps, as the Selma editor suggested, they recognized that killing the bill was politically risky even in their section of Alabama since it too had many veterans with family and friends. Indeed, Black Belt counties gave the soldiers' exemption a majority of their votes in the referendum.[98] Perhaps they settled on a strategy to pass a bill so long as it was weak and temporary. They certainly had a cooperative sponsor, the son of a Black Belt icon who had advanced the poll tax as the best means to eliminate "ignorant and vicious voters." Young Representative Jones was by birth and belief one of them and not above using duplicity or a dodge to escape a political predicament.

There is some factual support for the notion that Jones and Black Belt legislators mounted a joint effort behind closed doors to neuter his own proposed amendment. For unexplained reasons, Jones abandoned his original bill that provided a lifetime exemption for WWI soldiers. His first substitute ended the exemption in 1923. Afterwards, while enjoying a groundswell of support, Jones's second substitute further reduced his own bill's exemption—making it effective only for the current year. These changes certainly made the bill far less dangerous in the eyes of Black Belt leaders who held a majority on the senate's Constitutional Revisions Committee. But why did they not remove or oppose the house's Orr amendment that restored 1923 as the deadline for the exemption when it reached them? And why did the final bill extending the exemption through 1923 receive not a single proposed amendment or dissent from the Black Belt in the unanimous vote in the state senate?

It is quite possible that another part of Jones's substitute bill provides the best clue. That substitute also changed the language about how and when the referendum would be held. In place of dictating the specific date for the election, Jones's substitute inserted the phrase it "shall be the duty of the governor to fix the date of said election"—language that later prompted the Alabama Supreme Court to void the entire amendment.

Such language was unorthodox. It departed from the wording in all other legislation setting the date of a referendum on a proposed constitutional amendment and was contrary to explicit language in the 1901 Constitution stating, the "Legislature shall order an election" for amending the Constitution.[99] For this reason, it is highly doubtful that experienced Black Belt senators, especially John Aduston Rogers, who served on the Constitutional Revisions Committee, would fail to realize the problem with the changed wording.

Quite the contrary, Senator Rogers was a shrewd master of the legislative process and as a young man had been involved in state politics when Governor Joseph F. Johnston's role in attempting to override the legislature in amending the state constitution became such a controversial issue that the Constitutional Convention of 1901 deliberately removed governors from any role in setting the date for referendums. Rogers had served as an active member of the Convention's committee on the legislature and had urged delegates to confine more carefully the powers and responsibilities of the governor and the executive branch.[100]

Perhaps most revealing is the simple fact that Senator Rogers appears to have knowingly used the same language for the good roads constitutional amendment in what appears as a high-stakes political maneuver to enable the Black Belt a better chance to receive more than its fair share of state funding for highways (see Chapter 9). Both men were sure to have consulted with each other about pending legislation. Rogers had been a strong political supporter of Governor Jones, and Walter Jones was a recent appointee to the state highway commission, whose members were working with Rogers on the road bond bill.[101] What is beyond speculation is that Walter Jones's amendments to his own bill first reduced much of its reach and impact and later inserted the same language contained in the road bond bill that Rogers shaped and shepherded—language that led to both amendments being declared unconstitutional.

In the end, whatever the exact political machinations and ploys were, the episode was a telling moment. Jones's sponsorship of the soldiers' poll tax bill won him increased political support, which he parlayed into a successful campaign to unseat William Logan Martin Jr. as Montgomery County circuit court judge, a post Jones would then hold for more than 40 years and that allowed him to defend disfranchisement and white supremacy far more than his compromised poll tax reform might harm those causes. John Rogers and other Black Belt legislative leaders would not consider the new poll tax amendment as a real victory, but they were able to flatten a large exemption into a small one which would sunset in less than two years.

Perhaps even more significant, the episode foreshadowed emerging attitudes and renewed political aspirations in a post-war era when the state's population was growing primarily in urban counties. These changes meant Black Belt leaders would need to become more adaptive and more innovative if their strategies of using undemocratic political power and the 1901 Constitution were to remain successful in enlarging the wealth of their own families and their own section of Alabama.

It was a challenge no Black Belt planter seemed better prepared and able to meet than Senator John A. Rogers of Gainesville in Sumter County.

CHAPTER 9

Black Belt Politics—Tax Dollars at Work on the Roads

'Devilish Mud Holes That Will Almost Make a Preacher Lay His Bible Down'

John A. Rogers was an extraordinary man but a rather typical example of the Black Belt leaders whose intelligence, cunning, experience, and persistence enabled them as members of the Alabama legislature and state officials to protect the privileges and prosperity of their way of life. His official biography began: "John Aduston Rogers of Gainesville, State senator from the 14th district, was born September 1, 1861, on his maternal grandfather's plantation in Sumter county." Another stated that his father was "a brave and courageous Confederate soldier" who returned to his plantation in Sumter County.[1]

When Rogers served in the state senate in 1919, he already had a long record of public service. He had entered the senate for the first time at age 32 in 1894 and held the post for two terms. He then ran unsuccessfully for Congress, but was elected as a county delegate to the 1901 Constitutional Convention, where he was an active participant. He was reelected to the state senate in 1902, to the state house in 1914, and to the state senate again in 1918. He was elected a final time in 1934 to the same senate seat, but due to illness held it in absentia until his death in 1935.[2]

Rogers's lifelong home was Gainesville, located on the banks of the meandering Tombigbee River near the Mississippi state border. The Alabama town was established in the 1830s and was touted by some as one of the nation's largest inland ports in the decade before secession. When the Civil War broke out, Sumter had some of the largest plantations and wealthiest slaveowners in Alabama and the nation. During the War, the county saw only a few skirmishes, but Gainesville's "Confederate Cemetery," the last resting place for its earliest settlers, also included the graves of more than 250 unknown Confederate and Union soldiers who died after being brought from Shiloh and other battlefields to the local women's college that had been converted into a makeshift infirmary. Gainesville also was where the last of the Confederate Army east of the Mississippi River surrendered under General Nathan Bedford Forrest, who admonished his troops to go home and "preserve your honor."[3] At the time, John Rogers was under four years old.

During Reconstruction, Sumter and neighboring Black Belt counties experienced violent, bloody conflicts between members of the biracial Republican and all-white Democratic parties, and especially between freedmen and the white planters who once owned them. A congressional committee found widespread violence by white vigilantes and others across the state, but as early as 1868 Sumter County became the battleground for an armed conflict that sustained constant terrorism during the following two years. "Sumter Republicans tallied up a dead freedman a week," observed historian Michael Fitzgerald, and by the time Reconstruction was upended, Sumter and adjoining Greene County accounted for more than a third of the murders recorded in Alabama during this period.[4] At the time, John Rogers was eleven.

With an inherited understanding of how white planters had preserved their wealth, Rogers entered Alabama politics in 1894, as the Populist movement was challenging the old order across the state. He was a lifelong Democrat but shared a few of the Populists' agrarian concerns. He favored silver, not gold, as the basis for the U.S. currency, to have more money and lower interest rates in the economy. He distrusted Northern capital and corporations, including the railroads, and he favored state government financing, convict labor, and local private investments as necessary means for developing the Black Belt's rich natural assets.[5]

When he sought election to the 1901 Constitutional Convention,

Rogers promised he would uphold the principles on which "all conservative men are agreed" in the Black Belt. In his view, these were to "protect the individual business man and laborer from the aggression of corporate greed"; limit the taxing power of future legislatures; and "above all . . . preserve for all time the autonomy of the great white family of Alabama."[6]

Rogers emerged as an innovator among Black Belt leaders. He understood that his section depended on shipping its cotton, livestock, and other agricultural products to distant markets and became an early promoter of transportation. In 1903, he convened a county conference to raise a bond for building good roads. He sought subscriptions from investors for a local quilt factory, and, after filing a complaint with the state railroad commission claiming the Southern Railroad's nearby station was inadequate, Rogers formed his own Tombigbee Railroad Company. In the same year, he also became chairman of the interstate Tombigbee River Improvement Convention, while keeping his hand in politics as a delegate to the 1904 Democratic national convention.[7]

In 1906, Rogers ran for the Alabama Railroad Commission, but then withdrew because, he announced, regulating railroads through a state commission was an impossible way to assure fair rates and fulsome growth in the Black Belt. "This county is the richest in the world in natural resources," he stated with the pride of a third-generation planter. With a delightful climate and "a soil that produces in super-abundance every variety of fruit, food, and textile fabric needed for the comfort and happiness of man, its development however is dependent upon its transportation service." Leaving his Black Belt communities at the mercy of the railroad's monopolistic power "to make or mar" their destiny was "criminal," Rogers charged, since the company "who owns the transportation of a country will dictate its policy . . . Government ownership and control of railroads is the only rational solution," he concluded as one from the section of Alabama that usually controlled state government.[8]

Across the following decade and a half, as he joined the ranks of the county's largest plantation owners, Rogers expanded his business holdings while remaining active in politics, including campaigning across the state for various Democratic candidates for governor and Congress. During this period, he returned to the state legislature, serving in the lower house, and expanding his role in promoting the Good Roads Movement across the state.[9]

In the 1919 session, Rogers was the seasoned, unofficial leader of the state senate's Black Belt delegation within a legislature with little experience. His mastery of legislative strategies and a willingness to fight until he found a way to win earned him a reputation as the "Sage of Sumter." As one capitol reporter observed, "When Senator John A. Rogers makes a real speech, know ye, it is a finished product"[10]—in other words, the legislative deal has been done.

First-term Senator John Craft introduced the bill that would authorize the state's first bonds for building good roads. Craft was a Mobile businessman, president of the Alabama Good Roads Association, and a member of the state Highway Commission created in 1911. Under the 1901 Constitution, all state bonding for internal improvements required passage of a constitutional amendment by at least a three-fifths vote of each legislative chamber and a majority of voters. It was the Black Belt's remedy for the state's past reckless debt financing of railroads. Since the legislature had no staff to help prepare bills, the veteran Rogers was likely involved in drafting Craft's bill, which proposed a $25 million state bond.[11]

The Constitutional Revisions Committee, on which Rogers and other Black Belt senators comprised a majority, reported the bill favorably in late July. On the senate floor, Rogers introduced amendments giving a newly constituted state highway commission the power to disburse the bond's revenue with the governor's approval. The chairman of the Constitutional Revisions Committee, another Black Belt senator, proposed a change guaranteeing that the

Young John A. Rogers (Julia Tutwiler Library Archives and Special Collections, University of West Alabama).

bond would finance maintenance and/or construction of no less than 30 miles of roads in each county. Both amendments passed unanimously.[12]

This allocation of funding promised rural counties with small populations but large geographical areas, including most in the Black Belt, a disproportionate share of road building far beyond its ratio of the state's population and its number of automobiles on the roads. A month later, Alf Tunstall of Hale County, dean of the state house's Black Belt delegation, introduced a similar amendment to a bill that would re-create the highway department. This change offered each county an "equal share" of bond funding, but it was opposed by Representative Thomas Orr from Marshall County, a small, sparsely populated county in north Alabama whose mountainous terrain meant a mile of road building would cost more than a mile laid down in the Black Belt's flat lands. Orr offered a substitute assuring each county a "fair and equal share of the roads" to be built—not an equal share of the funds to be spent. Orr's substitute lost by one vote, and Tunstall's amended bill for equal county funding passed by only three votes.[13]

As the end of the session approached, Tunstall proposed a conference committee with a plurality of Black Belt legislators to work out a compromise on the issue. Afterwards, Black Belt legislators in both houses abandoned their "equal share" language and accepted a substitute requiring only that the bonds be spent connecting all county seats through "equitably apportioned" expenditures of "both money and labor." In turn, Orr accepted the defeat of his bill that would have ended leasing state convicts to planters, sawmills, and mining companies and put them to work on state roads. He had proposed to have the state highway department use the bond's proceeds to pay the state convict department for the labor of the convicts and their upkeep so that the state would not need to levy new taxes to make up for lost revenue from convict leasing.[14]

This approach for the uses of bond proceeds and the state's automobile taxes might get roads built and maintained, but the plan would not provide advantages to Black Belt counties. Orr settled for a compromise bill on convict leasing that Rogers masterminded to allow the governor to explore permitting the University of Alabama to use convicts in mines owned by the school.[15] Rogers led the senate in accepting the conference committee's language ("equitably apportion") on the road-related bills before the legislature passed them without a dissenting vote.[16]

Less than a month after the passage of both laws, Rogers, Craft, and Orr were among those appointed by Governor Kilby to the new highway commission. Rogers was named chairman and became head of the highway department. The governor set the bond referendum for February 16 in the following year, and Rogers became a leader in the campaign for the amendment. It passed in a landslide of 87 percent of the vote including every county, although turnout was light. "Work Begins Within a Few Weeks," the *Birmingham News* proclaimed.[17]

It did not. None of the $25 million in state bonds was issued. The highway department attempted to sell its bonds to investors at a five percent interest rate, the top rate set by the language of the Amendment, but, as Rogers explained to voters, "no one would buy" at that rate. As a result, Senator Rogers and Representative Orr guided passage of another bill for another constitutional amendment that would increase the bond rate ceiling to six percent. The bill set the election for February 8, 1921.[18]

Two days before Christmas 1920, ten months after the statewide bond was passed, a lawsuit was filed in Judge Walter B. Jones's courtroom challenging the Craft-sponsored law authorizing the bonds. The suit charged that the legislation violated the Alabama Constitution by allowing the governor to set the election date instead of following the constitutional mandate that "the Legislature shall order an election . . . upon such proposed amendments." The Craft bill provided that the amendment was "to be submitted to the qualified electors of the State . . . at an election to be held and called by the Governor."[19]

The court action turned out to be a "friendly" lawsuit—instigated against John Rogers and the highway department by John Rogers and the highway department after the state took the unusual step of engaging a Boston law firm specializing in bonds to examine for defects in the enabling legislation of the bond amendment. A Montgomery businessman was plaintiff and his lawyers were members of the firm of Robert Steiner, one of the state's well-known corporate attorneys and the Alabama militia's adjutant general. Judge Jones expedited the appeal to the state Supreme Court.[20]

On February 3, 1921, five days before the referendum on the new bond amendment, the Alabama Supreme Court ruled that passage of the Good Roads Amendment was null and void since the legislature had failed to follow the state constitution's procedures for setting its referendum date. In an opinion denying a rehearing of the case, Justice Thomas McClellan complained that some politicians were asserting that "the will of the people has been defeated by a technicality."[21]

McClellan protested at length in his opinion. Upholding the state's supreme law relating to the proper methods for amending the Constitution was far from a technicality, he wrote. McClellan recounted the deep political divisions that erupted in the late 1890s when Governor Joseph F. Johnston attempted to force the state legislature to rescind the calling of a constitutional convention. "The memory and purposes . . . of the contest and conflict of 1899, found unmistakable expression in the Constitution" written two years later in 1901, McClellan stated, and ". . .was intended to exclude the Governors from all participation in the process of formulating proposed amendments and of appointing the time for election."[22]

The majority opinion also pointedly noted that the legislature's prior laws had the proper language for setting an election date for amending the constitution—suggesting that the legislature either carelessly or knowingly ignored proper constitutional procedures. "Delay in road construction in this state is far better, far less hurtful, than constitutional destruction," McClellan concluded.[23] A week after the court's holding, Alabama voters in a low turnout defeated the new amendment proposed by Rogers and Orr for a rate of return of six percent.[24]

Kilby called the legislature into special session to adopt a third road amendment, and Rogers announced in advance that he would not support the two prior constitutional amendments' formula for distributing road bond funds. Now he would propose language guaranteeing each county $250,000 of the bond funds, which with 67 counties meant obligating two-thirds of the bond funds equally.[25]

The new bill Craft introduced did not include Rogers's proposed language for an equal county distribution—in all likelihood because Craft represented Mobile County with five times more people and nine times more automobiles on its local roads than Rogers's Sumter County. But the senate's Black Belt-dominated Constitutional Revisions Committee, on which Rogers sat, reported an amended bill stating, "Not less than one-quarter of a million dollars of these bonds shall be set aside for each county in the State." The amended bill also raised the bond's maximum rate of return to six percent and provided that the bonds would be paid through an increased license tax on motor vehicles.

Some parliamentary maneuvering ensued when a north Alabama senator offered changes that would give each county an equal share of both state bond revenue and new federal roads funding. Nothing came of this challenge except perhaps allowing most Black Belt senators to go on record as voting to oppose an even larger guarantee for each county while they passed Craft's bill but only with Rogers's formula.[26]

In the house, an "agrarian bloc" of legislators from rural counties, led by a Black Belt representative, initially threatened to deny the Good Roads bill its three-fifths majority necessary for passage. They sought repeal of a law establishing state tax adjusters, a reform Kilby had pushed in 1919 to prevent locally elected tax assessors from undervaluing property and understating tax assessments. As a result of the new law, the assessed property values and taxes had jumped by more than one-third in most counties from 1919 to 1922.[27] Rogers apparently helped persuade members of the bloc that they were holding themselves hostage, not the governor, since his formula would provide their counties with a large windfall. Soon, the house passed the Rogers-led bill with only the bloc's single ringleader voting "nay" in the final roll call.[28]

During the subsequent amendment campaign, Rogers spoke across the state reminding voters that the bond issue was necessary if Alabama was to receive millions more in matching federal dollars. He defended the legislation's equal distribution of funding among counties as the means to assure everyone in the state received a "fair share" and argued that good roads were especially needed in rural counties like his own Sumter so that families "can get to church and Sunday school without ruining their clothes going through devilish mud holes that will almost make a preacher lay his Bible down."[29]

He also argued that the tax on motor vehicles, which would pay the bond costs and interest charges, was fair since only those using the roads would pay for the bonds. Although half of the state's automobiles were found in only 10 of the 67 counties, Rogers insisted that "women and children in the country are . . . as much entitled to the good things in life as all those who live in town." The constitutional amendment passed, carrying every county in the state (including all but 22 votes in Rogers's home county), and more than 80 percent of the total vote.[30]

In the following year, the legislature considered a new gasoline tax to help finance maintenance of the increasing number of roads that were built. As chair of the Highway Commission, Rogers was no longer in the state senate but had full-time responsibilities overseeing the expanding highway department. The bill introduced on behalf of Rogers and Alabama's newly elected governor, "Plain Bill" Brandon of Tuscaloosa, provided that each county should receive an equal share of half the revenues from a new one-cent state gas tax, while the state retained the other half to maintain federally funded roads. Jefferson and other urban counties called the proposal grossly unfair. During 1922, Jefferson accounted for one-fourth of the gas sold in the state, but equal distribution of gas tax funds meant it would receive only 1/67 of the revenue.[31]

The house committee presented the Rogers-supported bill to provide for a two-cent tax split between the state and counties, but a north-south coalition of small, rural counties emerged. The house voted to give all revenues from the two-cent tax to the counties, equally divided among the 67 so that county governments—not the state—would maintain their own roads. The coalition was led by Representative J. L. Long of Butler County, the leader of the "agrarian bloc" during the last session, and first-term Representative Finis St. John of Cullman County, north of Birmingham. The coalition out-voted the urban counties, and their amended bill went to the state senate.[32]

No similar coalition developed in the senate. It refused to accept the house version and passed a bill with the Rogers-backed terms for distributing the new revenue. This senate version was rejected by the house on the motion of Representative Long, and the two chambers established a conference committee to work out a compromise.[33] Whatever the deal, Rogers got his way, and the Black Belt-led conference committee[34] recommended passage of the Rogers-backed bill without change. Representative St. John was livid, accusing the Black Belt's Long of "giving up everything" and pleading with his colleagues to reject the senate bill again. Instead, Black Belt legislators lined up behind Rogers's bill, as members from urban counties splintered their votes, facing a Hobson's choice. They could vote for their counties to get only 1/67 of all gas tax revenues or get 1/67 of half the gas tax and hope the governor might direct a larger amount of the state's other half to their counties where most of the state's voters now resided. The senate version became law in February 1923.[35]

'A DICTATORIAL MAN . . . AN ABLE MAN'

The legislature reconvened later that summer primarily to address the state's growing budget problems. House members led by the Black Belt maneuvered again to divert all gas tax receipts to the counties for road maintenance—this time without Rogers's active opposition and with support from the Alabama Automobile Trades Association. Because Governor Brandon's multi-faceted, 48-page bill increasing state revenues was desperately needed to cover state expenses, it passed with a provision distributing *all* gas tax revenues equally to each county for road work. The house bill also passed the senate under the leadership of its president *pro tempore*, J. B. Ellis of Selma.[36]

During the same summer session, the legislature also passed a new highway department bill that reduced its commission to three members appointed by the governor. The commission chair became the salaried head of the state highway department with continued authority to appoint the highway engineer, who oversaw most of the planning and design of state roads. Brandon appointed Rogers as chair along with commissioners Hubert Scruggs, a Birmingham civil engineer, and J. Freeman Suttle, a Dallas County planter and lumberman who relied on convict labor. "So impressed was the governor by Mr. Suttle's fitness and availability for the place," observed the *Selma Times-Journal*, "that he had the legislature modify the law to allow two commissioners from the same district [Suttle and Rogers]."[37]

Within a year, the highway department's road bonds and receipt of federal highway funds made it the state's largest agency. In 1919, when Rogers became chair of the Highway Commission, the department was spending a little more than $350,000. By the end of fiscal 1924, Rogers's department was spending over $8.5 million—and would increase to more than $11.5 million by the end of 1925. Rogers considered this growth in road work only the beginning. Soon both Brandon and Rogers were calling for passage of a $75 million bond to build more roads and construct bridges over the "navigable rivers in Alabama."[38]

Rogers's statewide campaign for another bond referendum faced a more reluctant public, which seemed to want to see the benefits of the prior bond, the state's largest debt on record, before approving another debt-financing program three times larger.[39] But, Rogers's larger obstacle beginning in the fall of 1923 became a persistent string of suspicions and accusations that members of the highway department, including its chairman, were personally benefitting from the department's swollen largesse.

In late August 1923, a member of the old commission from north Alabama called for the resignation of State Highway Engineer W. S. Keller and the dismissal of two members of his staff. Keller was accused of allowing his employees to bid on the highway department's contracts in violation of the law prohibiting any commissioner or department employee from having an interest in any of the department's contracts or sales. Keller had been state highway engineer for more than ten years and was the half brother of one of Alabama's most beloved daughters, Helen Keller.[40]

The Selma Chamber of Commerce quickly came to the engineer's defense. Before arriving at the state highway department, Keller was engineer for road building in Dallas County and, according to the Chamber's resolution, was being accused by a disgruntled commissioner of nothing more than "technical non-compliance with the law."[41] At its hearing, after considering evidence, the commission exonerated Keller, according to the *Montgomery Advertiser* headlines, despite the fact that Keller admitted he had given his two employees permission to bid on the department's own contracts.

The commission found "no wrong was done either to the state or any individual" because the two employees were not the lowest bidders and did not receive the state contract. The law prohibited only their having an interest in the department's contracts or sales, but they failed to get the contract. So, there was no violation, no problem. The commission admitted the employees' actions were "indiscreet" and clarified that their bids had been done without the knowledge or sanction of the commission members. Their resolution concluded by reaffirming their confidence in the "honesty and integrity" of Keller and both employees.[42]

A constant stream of dubious practices and disputed road projects also plagued the highway department and its commission. Barely six months following Keller's hearings, another major controversy erupted alleging malfeasance in the highway department—this time involving Rogers himself. White residents of the Boligee community in Greene County charged in a lawsuit that Rogers and Suttle had approved a rerouting of road construction in each other's Black Belt county to materially increase the value of their own lands. The lawsuit was filed by Horace Wilkinson, the free-wheeling Birmingham attorney with a reputation for ruthless, often rudderless advocacy in court and in politics. He argued on behalf of his clients that the road from Eutaw, the Greene County seat, to Livingston, the Sumter County seat, should take the much more direct, less expensive route through Boligee—not through what was called the "Gainesville detour" that went in front of Rogers's home.[43]

Wilkinson secured a temporary restraining order blocking any work on the proposed roadway, but the order was dissolved by a Montgomery circuit court. Afterwards Rogers believed the matter settled, but Wilkinson appealed to the Alabama Supreme Court where he faced a battery of Black Belt attorneys representing Rogers, including Robert Evins of Greensboro and Hugh Mallory, corporate attorney, businessman, and chairman of the Selma Chamber of Commerce which earlier mounted a defense of W. S. Keller.

In June 1924, Justice A. D. Sayre ruled for a unanimous court in favor of Rogers and the highway commission. Sayre found that the "Gainesville detour" was certainly not the shortest, least expensive route connecting the county seats and that the Gainesville route could not receive matching federal funds for construction because it had been disapproved by federal engineers as meandering and too costly. He conceded Rogers had a clear self-interest in selecting the Gainesville route:

> He owns his residence in Gainesville, a small tract of land—160 acres—in that vicinity, and 7,000 or 8,000 acres of land in Sumter county, the bulk of which lies not only between Livingston and Eutaw, but 5 or 6 miles northwest of the town. It seems likely that the construction of the highway from Livingston to Gainesville has given him better access to a railroad and to a larger market for the products of his land, and this consideration, no doubt, other things remaining equal, has added to the value of his land.[44]

But Sayre held that this was an indirect private interest not prohibited by state law, which only made it a felony for a highway commissioner to be either "directly or indirectly interested in any contract or agreement for construction or maintenance of any road or bridge in this state." There was no evidence that Rogers had a direct or indirect interest in any contract with the highway department for building the road through Gainesville. His private benefit derived from where the road would be built—not from any contract involving his own department. This was, in effect, the same rationale that Rogers's commission had used to exonerate W. S. Keller and his staff.

William S. Keller (ADAH).

Sayre's opinion also found that Rogers's decisive role in approving the construction of the road through his own hometown was "beyond impeachment" because the Alabama legislature in 1915 "adopted the route now adopted by the commission as a part of a state trunk road No. 7" extending from Eutaw through Gainesville to Livingston.[45] In other words, it was the legislature, not Rogers, that established the law and the public policy that made the "Gainesville detour" a preferred, legitimate route. The highway commission was simply implementing an earlier legislative decision.

Throughout the ordeal, Rogers spoke publicly as a gracious victor assuring Alabamians that he would not sue anyone for slander or defamation of character and considered the controversy as proof that "corruption wins not more than honesty." He did accuse the "guilty newspapers" (primarily the unnamed *Birmingham Age-Herald*) of baseless attacks against him in its efforts "to control Alabama politics" but, with "the help of Him who loved all men and sinners most of all, I shall try to do as he did, 'forgive my enemies' . . ."[46]

Construction of the "Gainesville detour" moved forward, as did Rogers in proselytizing for the issuance of an additional $75 million state bond for roads and bridges. The *Montgomery Advertiser* became a convert and ran a series of articles attempting to demonstrate how each section of the state would greatly benefit from the bond proceeds. But accusations of favoritism and self-dealing remained a lingering political issue, once the 1926 campaign for governor emerged. Rogers decided to hitch his bond campaign to the candidacy of Lieutenant Governor Charles McDowell, a Black Belt politician from Barbour County who had served in the state senate with Rogers in 1919. As a north Alabama weekly newspaper put it: "If you want John Rogers for Governor, vote for McDowell. If you don't want John Rogers for Governor, vote for one of the other candidates."[47]

McDowell fully endorsed Rogers's bond proposal, and in turn Rogers told voters it was "McDowell or Mud!" In response, opposing newspapers and other candidates for governor attacked Rogers and his record. "Under the Rogers administration of twenty five million dollars," the *Montgomery Journal* charged, "we have Rogers and mud . . . Roads that run only on the routes marked out by politics do not serve the people, only politicians."[48] Bibb Graves's local campaign committee in north Alabama ran ads claiming "Cleburne County Has Never Yet Profited By Road Bonds!" adding, "and judging the future by the past—and under the Rogers-Brandon-McDowell regime—never will!"[49]

Graves won election as governor and promptly replaced Rogers and the other highway commissioners as he reorganized the agency. Also, the legislature passed Graves's proposal for a second $25 million bond for roads and bridges, and voters approved it. Before leaving office, Rogers received what the *Montgomery Advertiser* called a complete vindication of his public service when state examiners reported they had "failed to find one scintilla of evidence of GRAFT, MALADMINISTRATION or MISAPPROPRIATION of funds." They called Rogers and his fellow commissioners good citizens "whose integrity is beyond question, who have been, and are, devoting their time and energy to their work in a patriotic spirit and with the purpose of rendering their best service to the entire State. All of these gentlemen have been identified in some way with every progressive movement for the betterment of roads in Alabama."[50]

Rogers went home to Gainesville and was able to enjoy the fruits of his earlier labors, including within a few years the "Gainesville detour's" bridge that replaced the ferry that had been the only means for townspeople to cross the Tombigbee River into Greene County for more than a hundred years. But Graves named the bridge after the late Julia Tutwiler, Greensboro's much-admired educator and an opponent of the state's convict leasing, which Graves had ended—not in honor of the Gainesville man who enabled the bridge near his own home.[51]

Rogers retired from active politics although he continued to speak out from his home in Gainesville whenever he was disturbed by political developments. He joined a long line of Black Belt planters and corporate leaders in support of former governor Thomas Kilby in 1932 when Kilby attempted to unseat U.S. Senator Hugo Black. And in 1934, he was re-elected to the state senate where he was to join one of his sons elected to represent Mobile County. Rogers fell ill before the legislature convened, and the "Sage of Sumter" died in September 1936 at his home in Gainesville.[52]

The Montgomery eulogies of Rogers remembered him as a man of high integrity and honesty who was always loyal to friends and as a public servant was responsible for the state's good roads. In Alabama politics, he was remembered as a fearless "fighter" who spoke his beliefs and took positions that were not always popular across the state, although he was beloved in his own county where he never lost an election. The weekly newspaper in Pickens County, which he represented along with Sumter in the state senate, remembered him "as an outstanding citizen for half a century" and as one of the Black Belt's largest landowners who "preferred the quiet life of the village of Gainesville." The *Birmingham News* echoed that sentiment, remembering Rogers as a Southern gentleman who engaged in politics due to "blood and rearing." A rural north Alabama editor was more plain-spoken—he wrote that Rogers was a "symbol of the Black Belt aristocracy."[53]

These remembrances suggest, but do not quite illuminate, just how devoted and masterful Rogers was in developing the means and resources of state government for growing the wealth and privileges of the plantation life that he embodied. Like others before and after him, Rogers understood how to harness the oversized political power and long political tenure that disfranchisement provided Black Belt officials for the benefit of those who ruled that section of Alabama. Nothing reveals this understanding and capacity more than his work for Good Roads.

When Senator John Craft of Mobile introduced the bill to hold a referendum on the $25 million bond for roads in 1919, the original bill had a fatal flaw, which later prompted the Alabama Supreme Court to void the law and the bond election. In justifying the court's controversial decision to annul an election, Justice Thomas McClellan laid the blame on the legislature whose leaders he argued surely remembered the political controversy that led delegates at the 1901 Constitutional Convention to bar the governor from having anything to do with proposing constitutional amendments, including setting the date of the election.

Rogers must have remembered. He was involved in the political fight surrounding Governor Johnston in 1899. He was an active member of the 1901 Constitutional Convention and served on the committee drafting the powers of the legislature. In the legislature, he probably helped to draft Craft's bill and was a member of the senate committee that reviewed and revised the legislation. He shepherded the flawed bill through the senate in a session when there were other bills in the hopper proposing constitutional amendments with the correct form. In fact, in the 1919 legislative session, the only proposed amendment with a similarly improper method for setting an election date was the soldiers' voting bill, which its sponsor, Representative Walter Jones (a member of the highway commission) mysteriously added through his own amendment.[54]

Even if Senator Rogers momentarily forgot the proper form for setting the election date, he was surely reminded when the chair of the Constitutional Revisions Committee introduced on the senate floor an amendment to remove the improper form and adopt the proper method as required by the state constitution. There is no record of the discussion or debate on the motion, but the senate journal documents that Rogers voted with a large majority against correcting the error.[55]

Less certain is why Rogers would decide to leave in the bill he guided to passage a provision that would risk a legal challenge. There is no available record of his motives, but perhaps the most likely explanation is that as "one of the shrewdest Black Belt politicians"[56] Rogers wanted to preserve an option for a second chance in passing a bond referendum, hopefully one including more favorable terms for the Black Belt such as those provisions removed in the political horse trading that preserved convict leasing.

In September 1919, Rogers had no assurance that the state road bond would pass in a popular vote. Since 1876, the Alabama state government had not incurred any new debt or issued any new bonds for anything other than re-funding old debts. The road bond proposal also was considered a staggering amount. A state debt of $25 million would be three times the size of the state government's entire annual revenue. In addition, some local leaders who supported incurring such a "tremendous sum" for roads believed it should be spent by the counties and opposed giving the money to a state highway department that they feared would build roads to "serve only a small percentage of the population."[57]

If the road amendment had failed to win voter approval, the enabling legislation's defect for setting the date of the referendum would have been arguable grounds for voiding the election and providing a legitimate second chance to win approval. As it turned out, Rogers masterminded a brilliant stratagem that proved necessary and effective, even if employed for reasons the Black Belt leader failed to foresee.

The economy and the bond market, not Alabama voters, became the obstacle to Rogers's plans. After voters passed the bond amendment with a lopsided margin in a small turnout, the state could not sell the bonds at the proscribed rate of 5 percent (the maximum rate mentioned in the 1901 Constitution and in the amendment). In February 1920, when the vote was held on the first highway bonds, the yield on U.S. bonds had climbed to 5.05 percent. Five months later yields were at 5.57 percent, while local government yields were at 5.25 percent and corporate bonds were offering yields of 7.29 percent. As Rogers explained, "No one would buy" state bonds yielding only 5 percent.[58]

The stakes were high since the state government was unable to secure millions of federal dollars for roads that would go to other states if Alabama did not have the bond money to match federal funds. Jefferson County, whose voters also had approved issuing a county highway bond at a 5 percent yield, faced the same problems in the bond markets. The county tried an evasion by agreeing to pay the Alabama Bond Company a sales commission of 10 percent on the bonds the company was buying from the county, to make up for the bonds' lower yield. But the county treasurer refused to pay the commission and litigation followed. On June 30, 1920, the Alabama Supreme Court upheld a lower court ruling voiding the sales commission as an illegal payment to the bonds' purchaser.[59]

Without an option to evade the limit on the state's bond rates, Rogers and the highway department undertook two strategies: a) Rogers guided passage of another constitutional referendum through the legislature that set bond rates as high as 6 percent; and b) the department retained corporate attorneys to develop a lawsuit to annul the bond amendment that passed.[60] As developments demonstrated, Rogers's earlier mischief with the Craft bill paid off. Voters rejected the amendment raising the bond rate, but in a "friendly lawsuit" the Alabama Supreme Court overturned the road bond election on the grounds that the governor's role in setting the election date violated the 1901 Constitution.

When the legislature met in special session in September 1921, Senator Rogers inserted into the new road bond legislation a guarantee of $250,000 for each county from the $25 million bond. Rogers and his Black Belt colleagues had enough votes and options to keep it in the law. The legislation also provided for a new annual motor vehicle license to pay off the bond debt. Its "equal share" gave a big financial advantage to Black Belt counties such as Sumter which barely had 800 taxable vehicles in 1921, while Jefferson County had nearly 30,000 that would be taxed.

Rogers's legislative strategy of providing each county an equal allotment of state funds drew enough votes from other small counties to enable passage, and it set in motion the approach Black Belt legislators employed with the aid of the highway commission chairman even after he left the legislature. Both laws instituting a gas taxes for road maintenance in 1923 divided its revenue equally among the counties (first, sharing half the revenue with the state, and later diverting all revenue equally among the counties).

After Freeman Suttle of Dallas County joined Rogers on the three-person highway commission, local Black Belt planters recognized that their own sectional leaders were in a position to decide together where and how to spend millions of state and federal dollars for highways within the terms of state laws that already advantaged their section of the state. The perception that anything goes, so long as it goes to the Black Belt, could only have been elevated after the commission's exoneration of Keller and his employees. What followed was a rush of bitter disputes among white planters about the best road routes within the Black Belt[61]—routes that could enhance the value of lands, improve a planter's transportation and price for crops, and in some cases provide local construction jobs and contracts. It was as if Black Belt planters decided the state and federal road monies were theirs for the taking, and they fell into fighting among themselves for it.[62]

This free-for-all set the stage for the controversy that cast suspicions on Rogers's role in the "Gainesville detour." The Alabama Supreme Court vindicated Rogers, but Justice A. D. Sayre wittingly or unknowingly left out crucial facts. His opinion found that Rogers gained personally but that the 1915 legislature, not Rogers and Suttle, established by law that the Gainesville detour was to become a state route. Members of the highway commission were simply carrying out an earlier legislative decision.

Sayre's opinion left out the vital fact that Rogers was a member of the 1915 legislature and as a state representative maneuvered to ensure that the state trunk route from Tuscaloosa went through Gainesville. On the recommendation of its engineer, W. S. Keller, the highway department recommended a state route through Gainesville as the trunk road, and it was included in Governor Charles Henderson's original bill introduced in 1915.

Representative Martin T. Sumner of Boligee in Greene County had other ideas. He secured an amendment that revised the route "beginning at Eutaw and extending southwesterly . . . where it intersects the road herein described from Gainesville to Livingston."[63] Instead, the amended route from Tuscaloosa would go through Boligee across the Tombigbee River, bypassing Gainesville. It was about ten miles shorter and a more direct route—and exactly the alternative route in the dispute that Sayre's opinion settled.

Rogers fought the amendment on the house floor. He claimed Sumner's route would lead travelers "into a swamp about three miles from Boligee with no way out,"[64] but house members adopted the change. The two chambers established a conference committee to work out differences. There is no record of the reasons for its decision, but the joint committee recommended the house remove Sumner's amendment, and it did. The final act kept plans for a trunk road going from Eutaw through Gainesville to Livingston.[65]

When Rogers retired to Gainesville in 1926, he had established the state government's largest department, and no one was more responsible for the financing mechanisms, taxes, and distribution of funds that were creating the statewide highway system. In that role, he also built a system that financially advantaged, first and foremost, his hometown, his county, and his section of Alabama.

In 1924, Sumter contributed less than $9,800 in motor vehicle registration fees to pay off the state highway bonds. It was three-fifths of one percent of the state's total revenue paid by county residents from vehicle registrations. From the state's gas tax, equally shared among the counties, Sumter received that year more than $27,000 for maintaining roads while the county's actual expenditures for road upkeep appears to have been little more than $6,000 annually. Similarly, all Black Belt counties contributed far less in road-related taxes than the road-related revenues they annually received.[66]

From 1922 into 1926, the Alabama Highway Department spent on roads $23 million dollars from state bonds. The largest expenditure was in Sumter County, where the state highway department spent $634,000. The next largest amount was in neighboring Greene County, which received only a few thousand dollars less. Most Black Belt counties also received more than their share, despite earlier promises that the state's funds from bonds would be spent equally among the 67 counties. Most of the under-funded counties were in north Alabama.[67]

During the same four years, Jefferson County's 310,000 residents operated about 35,000 motor vehicles and paid almost $1.1 million in vehicle licenses as well as almost $4 million in gas taxes. Sumter County's 25,000 residents had barely more than 900 vehicles (owned almost exclusively by whites), paying less than $36,000 in vehicle licenses and probably less than $40,000 in gas taxes. In other words, in return for paying approximately $5.1 million in road-financing taxes, Jefferson County received about $716,000 in total state and matching federal road funds. In comparison, while paying approximately $76,000 in state road taxes, Sumter County received almost $918,000 in state and federal road funds.[68]

In December 1925, as Rogers's leadership of the state highway program became an emerging issue in the race for governor, another of Sumter County's largest landowners hosted a dinner for outgoing Governor Brandon and Rogers. The event was part of a deer hunt in which the guests—Black Belt planters, Big Mules, and other political leaders—had felled 38 buck deer and three wild turkeys before they assembled to dine on their kill. One sign of Rogers's and Brandon's falling political standing was the fact that only three legislators showed up for the event. Perhaps it prompted Governor "Plain Bill" to become openly defiant as he discussed the highway program that Rogers had developed during his term. In repeating the widening accusations that the Gainesville sage was the power behind his throne, the governor declared that "whether Brandon is governor or he (Rogers) is, Bill Brandon will stand by Rogers and his road program to the end."[69]

When that end soon arrived, even Rogers's admirers in Sumter County were willing to acknowledge the character traits that enabled his success. "John A. Rogers influences men," reported the *Southern Home* from Livingston. "He may be a dictatorial man, a dominating character, who goes hammer and tongs after what he wants. He is an honest man, an able man, a courageous man, and an influential one."[70]

The white people of Sumter County knew John A. Rogers, and they knew what it took for a Black Belt leader to succeed, although few understood exactly what he had accomplished for them or how he had done it. They knew no less that he had helped preserve their county's traditions and advanced the prosperity of its white people, and their knowing that much was enough. "Truly old Sumter is and should be proud of her gifted son."[71]

In a fitting, if unintended epitaph to his lasting influence, published in 1961 twenty-five years after Rogers's death, Birmingham newspaperman Clarke Stallworth wrote a series to expose the persisting, oversized influence of the Black Belt. It included a study showing that Birmingham residents were paying 25 percent of the state's gas taxes and receiving only 1.5 percent of the state's expenditures for roads. As Rogers intended, these funds were still being divided equally among Alabama's 67 counties.

CHAPTER 10

Black Belt Politics—Tax Dollars at Work in Education

'Just and Equitable and for the Equal Benefit of the Children'

When John Rogers died not far from the spot where he was born, the Sage of Sumter was remembered for his devotion to education at home and across the state. "Education shared first place in his career in public life with good roads," wrote the *Montgomery Advertiser*, which remembered Rogers as a legislator always "militantly supporting" bills advancing education. "He was no less interested and solicitous of the public schools" than in the state universities, the newspaper recalled.[1]

An official biography of Rogers mentions that his wife's grandfather, Robert Bradshaw, was "the principal of Gainesville Academy and Superintendent of Education of Sumter County at the time of his death."[2] Bradshaw arrived in Gainesville three years before the outbreak of the Civil War as headmaster and teacher at the local academy. He served until 1864, when he was elected school superintendent, a post he held in the Confederate state "up to the time of the 'surrender.'"

Bradshaw was reelected in 1866 only to be replaced by an African American appointed by the state superintendent after the Reconstruction state government took control in 1868, even though the Black schools in Gainesville apparently remained taught by local whites, perhaps in a compromise that might save the schools from local white terrorism. Bradshaw returned to office but was ousted in 1871 by the county's Democratic and

Conservative Party Convention despite his pleading that the school superintendent should not have a "political character." He died the following year.[3]

Bradshaw's off-and-on years as county superintendent were a by-product of "the virulent partisan strife that was going on between Conservatives and Republicans in the State"[4] over public schools, as described by Horace Mann Bond in his masterful work, *Negro Education in Alabama.* The Reconstruction Constitution of 1868 mandated free public schools for all children between the ages of five and 21. It was silent on the question of separate schools but required one-fifth of all state revenues to be exclusively used for public schools and placed a special tax on railroads and other corporations solely for the support of public schools.[5]

Between 1868 and 1875, amid ever-shifting election returns, conservative white Democrats, often led by Black Belt leaders, fought Black and white Republicans over these constitutional commandments. Republicans controlled the legislature and the state board of education until December 1870, when Democrats won most state offices, including the governor's chair, and a majority in one chamber of the legislature. But in 1872 a Republican governor was elected, only to be ousted in 1874. Throughout this time, the Republicans kept a majority of seats on the state school board, although its powers and prerogatives were often challenged by Democrats.[6]

Conservative school board members did not overtly attack constitutional mandates. They even tacitly accepted that school funds should be divided equally, although many complained that only whites were paying taxes in support of schools. Instead, they worked at keeping schools separated by race and school funding as low as possible by controlling or obstructing legislation on taxes and revenues—powers that only the legislature and the governor held.[7]

After Bradshaw was deposed, Sumter's new Democratic superintendent reported to the state superintendent that the public schools were "growing in favor" among Blacks and whites since he had convinced some "respectable old men" who had taught white children to teach in Black schools. "Many who believed it a disgrace to teach under Radical

Rule, are most efficient and faithful teachers under the Democratic."[8]

During this period, Rogers was a schoolboy living with his father, mother, and a younger brother on a plantation in a section of Sumter County where in the immediate vicinity only one other white farmer lived. There were also 35 Black persons, all over the age of 12 with an occupation of "farmer labor" (except for a Black "cook"), according to the 1870 Census. Black children had little or no schooling during most of 1873–1874 since tax revenues were inadequate for the state to pay the teachers.[9]

As Horace Mann Bond discovered, the "financing of schools in Alabama from 1868–1875 may be discussed either from the standpoint of the amount of money which, theoretically, the schools received, and the amount which was actually paid . . . There is no way to tell how much of this money was actually spent on schools."[10]

Black Belt planters' children like John Rogers's were often educated in these uncertain times by tutors or in private schools such as the Gainesville Male Academy, while their fathers and other conservative Democrats wrestled with Reconstruction Republicans for control of the government and the schools.

Some Black Belt communities had no public schools for white or Black children. In Sumter, conservatives accused Republicans of graft and mismanagement of school funds, even when there were few funds to disperse, and the local white newspaper editors echoed complaints about white taxpayers being abused by the "corn field negroes" elected in the Black Belt by the counties' African American Republican majority.[11]

After Democrats took firm control of the state government, they assembled a convention that drafted a new constitution which the state's voters overwhelmingly adopted in 1876. It reduced school funding by eliminating earmarked school revenues and taxes, replacing them with a minimal annual appropriation of $100,000 for public education. For local funding of schools, it also continued a per capita annual tax of $1.50 on all male adults between the ages of 21 and 45 (the origins of the "poll tax") and any interest generated from the state's land sales in the county. Together, the funds were less than what was previously required. As significant, the new Constitution reduced the cap on the total taxes the legislature could enact to support all public functions, including schools. "The people pay the taxes, and elect their own representatives," argued Democrats who led the constitutional convention, "and if the public schools languish and die for the want of money, it will be the fault of the people and their representatives, and not that of the new constitution."[12]

The conservatives' Constitution also deleted any guarantee of free schooling but promised that the public schools would be funded "for the equal benefit of all children between the ages of seven and 21 years; but separate schools shall be provided for the children of citizens of African descent." This provision constituted a political compromise. Democratic leaders did not wish to risk alienating north Alabama's white voters, many of whom suspected their children were often shortchanged in the state's school funding, and all of the large number of Black voters for whom public education was a paramount issue. (Democrats also could not risk disfranchising Black voters in the new constitution lest it provoke renewed federal intervention by the Republican Congress).[13]

Conservative Democrats did find ways to skirt the constitutional requirement of "equal benefits." In early 1876, the legislature enacted a school law requiring counties to segregate their local poll tax revenues so that the amount "paid by persons of the white race shall be devoted to the schools established for the white race and the amount paid the by colored race shall be devoted to the schools established for the colored race."[14]

In the next year, the legislature passed an extensive new school code including three sections, racially neutral in their language, that had a crippling effect on Black schooling. The legislature mandated that public school teachers be paid only according to the number of days each student actually attended school.[15] Because Black children were often needed by their parents to help work the fields, the proportion failing regularly to attend school, especially in the Black Belt, was considerably higher than that of white children. This meant less pay for Black teachers. This section also gave white landowners a strong incentive to keep their Black tenants' children in the fields, not in the schoolhouses.

The second change was even more devastating. Teachers would be paid only once a year and only at the end of the school year—not monthly as in the past. Few white teachers and hardly any Black teachers could survive a school year without pay. Even after the legislature relented and allowed teachers to be paid quarterly, many could teach only if patrons or parents made private contributions to the schools—a practice the legislature also authorized. Finally, the new law permitted county superintendents to keep and redistribute unused school funds. This law also authorized white superintendents to later redistribute as they saw fit leftover funds derived from the reduced number and pay of Black teachers.[16]

During the following decade, Alabama's public schools operated under these education laws, permitting if not encouraging state and local school officials to operate footloose in reporting and spending public school dollars. In Sumter County, for example, the local superintendent's report to the state superintendent did not match the local grand jury's report on public school expenses, especially on teacher pay. The grand jury, which could charge a superintendent with perjury for a false statement, reported both lower teacher pay and unspent school funds from the prior year—something the state superintendent's report failed to document.[17]

Whatever numbers were published, Black and white leaders across Alabama became deeply disturbed by the reality of their schools. A committee of Birmingham's Black leaders petitioned the governor for improved educational facilities. White leaders outside the Black Belt also found state education funds and policies sorely lacking. As white farmers began organizing into what became the Populist Movement, men like Henry Clay Simmons challenged conservative Democrats, demanding "more schools, more money, and more teachers" for their children. They called for state funding of six months of schooling.[18]

In late 1890, outgoing State Superintendent Solomon Palmer, a Confederate veteran and former north Alabama legislator, proposed empowering township officials to apportion school funds locally in accord with the desires and needs of the township and in proportion to the number of children the local officials decided would probably attend each school. "It is alleged that in portions of the State under our present law the colored race gets well nigh all the school fund . . .," Solomon Palmer wrote in his last report, "whilst that race pays a very small per cent of the taxes."

Afterwards, H.B. 504 was introduced to implement Palmer's proposal, to the delight of Black Belt legislators. Representative James A. Steele of Marengo County explained that the bill would "remedy an evil" in the Black Belt "where white people pay nine-tenths of the taxes . . . while negroes receive nine-tenths of the school fund" and insure that funding is "equitable" for schooling "between children of the two races."[19] No legislator openly challenged this outlandish assertion. Another Black Belt member called it the best bill ever introduced in any Alabama legislature, and the bill passed the house without debate or a single dissent.[20]

Senate Education Committee Chair William E. Skeggs, a young attorney representing four north Alabama counties, sought to exempt counties in his section of the state.[21] John T. Milner, a representative of Birmingham's Big Mules, supported the bill without exemptions since he was certain it would assure equal benefit to children of both races. He claimed there was "no justice in having the schools for negroes open nine months in a year and the schools for white children open only about a month." His assertion went unchallenged in the legislative record, and the exemptions were defeated.[22] In its final form H.B. 504 instructed local school officials to distribute state revenues "as they deem just and equitable and for the equal benefit of the children thereof between the ages of seven and twenty-one years."[23]

The new law also established a fail-safe guarantee that only white landowners could allocate school funds within the townships. The law provided that trustees must be both a "householder and a freeholder"—essentially that meant a male with a family who was the head of a household and a landowner. However, in the Black Belt, custom defined the terms with one added restriction. As a Selma city court judge once ruled in excluding Black voters from a jury pool: "In this law, 'householder' means a white man who is the head of a family; and 'freeholder' means a white man who is the owner of a free-hold estate in land. It has never been supposed that these terms had any other meaning."[24]

'SCHOOLS EQUALLY SUITED TO THE EDUCATIONAL WANTS OF THE CHILDREN OF EACH RACE'

John G. Harris became the state superintendent who first implemented the new state law. He was a Sumter County lawyer whose primary qualifications were his involvement in promoting Sunday schools across the state, his status as a Confederate veteran, his role as a rabid campaigner for a "white man's government," and his current need for a job after losing a federal appointment once Democratic President Grover Cleveland left office.[25]

Harris's unofficial campaign manager was John A. Rogers, who had joined his father as a Sumter County planter and merchant after graduating from the University of Alabama. At 29, Rogers was married and beginning a career as an aspiring Black Belt politician. In his first statewide political work, Rogers led Sumter's delegates to the state Democratic Convention in 1890 to elect Harris after convincing his county convention to instruct all delegates to vote for Harris "first, last, and all the time."[26]

Superintendent Harris sought an Alabama attorney general's opinion on exactly how the State should implement the terms of the new law by which appointed householders and freeholders would apportion school funds within their townships. Attorney General William Logan Martin Sr. grew up and practiced law in Scottsboro in north Alabama before he was appointed to the statewide office in 1889. (His son, Logan Martin Jr., would become attorney general more than two decades later.) Martin Sr. was credited with helping to move his county into the Democratic column to end Reconstruction rule, and that political work as much as his legal career helped him win election in 1890 on the Democratic ticket.[27]

Martin held that the words "just" and "equitable" in the law needed no explanation beyond their ordinary meaning but did state that a per capita apportionment of school funds within the townships was unnecessary "to secure equal benefits to all the children" as required by the state constitution. "The interest of the child . . . lies . . . in affording him an opportunity to attend a suitable public school for his race," Martin stated. Therefore, trustees were duty-bound "to establish schools equally suited to the educational wants of the children of each race."[28] It meant that schools would be funded according to what white landowners believed was suitable for the children and grandchildren of men and women who as enslaved persons had been considered unfit to educate. It was a rationale for developing and maintaining unequal and segregated education that echoed across the South and later seeped into the nation for more than a century.[29]

The new law and its interpretation took effect in the school year ending in 1892. It was also the first year since the start of a functioning statewide school system that a state superintendent did not publish data on how school funds were distributed according to race among the 67 counties. Instead, Superintendent Harris included how funds were supposed to be apportioned among the counties according to *all* children of school age. According to Booker T. Washington, a sharp decline in funding for Black schooling across the state was evident that first year.[30]

Data in Sumter County confirm Washington's observation. In 1890, John Rogers's father, as freeholding foreman of the Sumter grand jury, reported that the local superintendent's books evidenced that three-fourths of the state's school monies went to Black teachers to educate Black students, who comprised three-fourths of the county's school age children. In 1892, after the new law went into effect, the grand jury report showed that Black schools received only half of all state funds for teaching the county's unchanged proportion of Black children.[31]

Local planters as school trustees began funneling increasingly larger sums into white schools in the Black Belt, but the impact was much smaller for increasing funding for white schools elsewhere in the state where fewer African Americans lived. In 1892, according to Populist Joseph Manning, only about one-third of the white children of school age were attending schools in Alabama "and the country schools were of only three months duration, summer schools, where there were any in the country. In the towns and cities the cause of education fared better, except with the Colored children."[32]

The only section of the state where schools consistently expanded the racial gap in teacher pay in the years leading up to 1900 was the Black Belt—and most of those districts widened the disparity with a vengeance. Three years after Sumter's school trustees started lawfully distributing funds on the basis of what they considered "just and equitable," instead of an equal per pupil basis, the average Black teacher pay was dropped to only half that of white teachers. In Wilcox County in 1895, the pay for Black teachers fell to only 40 percent of the white pay.[33]

With so few white children to educate in the Black Belt, the largesse of local school funds gave rise to "the pernicious practice of paying parents their pro rata of the public school fund should they feel disposed to keep their children out of the school."[34] Some white families in Black Belt townships apparently received and used their children's public school funds for private schooling and even household expenses. And there were other forms of misuse. "One township in a county not only ran its public school eight months with a first-class teacher," reported one of Harris's successors as state superintendent, "but also defrayed a considerable portion of the expenses of boys and girls off at college."[35] It can be safely assumed that these abuses of public school funds involved only white parents and white students.

By the end of the century, Black Belt leaders had done extraordinary work in challenging and defeating the aims of Reconstruction. In the field of education, they could rightfully take primary responsibility for the fact that across 30 years, from 1870 to 1900, Alabama had spoiled relatively few field hands with book learning, as a former Alabama governor once stated the common refrain. During this period, the number of illiterate African Americans in Alabama grew by almost 50,000 persons and the number of illiterate whites grew by more than 10,000.[36]

'Equal as Nearly as Practicable'

When Rogers joined other conservative Democrats in Montgomery to begin the work of creating a new state constitution, they knew that disfranchisement was the first order of business since it appeared perhaps the only way to put down and keep down the recurrence of interracial political insurgences that threatened their rule. The work started with discarding Section 38 of Alabama's 1875 constitution: "No educational or property qualification for suffrage or office, nor any restraint upon the same on account of race, color, or previous condition of servitude, shall be made by law." The conservatives' challenge was how to suppress voting through various indirect means that could avoid future interference in the state's voting by the U.S. Congress or the U.S. Supreme Court.

Mississippi and other Southern states already had adopted new state constitutional provisions for disfranchising African American voters, but the challenge for Alabama's conservative Democrats was more nuanced and complex than simply collecting from others the best tools of disfranchisement. Their aim was to build a new political order that sustained the continuity of Old South values and traditions amid the growth of New South industries in such a way that only they would rule and richly benefit from their minority rule.

By necessity, strategies to meet this larger challenge made use of other state's laws and mechanisms, but Black Belt delegates and their allies also brought their own experiences of the last quarter of a century to shape policies and structures. Perhaps foremost was that portion of their recent past demonstrating that education and voting were two sides of the same political coin. Simply put, they understood how maintaining inferior Black education was a powerful tool for controlling and suppressing Black political participation and, in turn, how restricting Black voting was highly effective in maintaining white educational advantages within their section of the state. This reciprocal relationship between the denial of education and the denial of voting meant that it was imperative a new constitution achieve both.

Young and ambitious, Rogers quickly set in motion the process of disfranchisement on the third day of the Constitutional Convention by requesting that all delegates receive a compilation of the suffrage provisions of several other state constitutions that included restrictions on voting from both Northern and Southern states. Rogers's "Resolution No. 14" later produced a palette of choices for voter suppression for the convention's suffrage committee and other delegates, but Rogers was appointed to the education committee. Of its 19 members, 14 were from majority-Black counties. There were no African American delegates at the Convention.[37]

On the day Convention committees were appointed, a group of prominent Black leaders, assembled earlier by Booker T. Washington, petitioned white delegates to remember that "for more than twenty years the Negro in this State has not, as a rule, been a disturbing or offensive element." They underscored in general terms how the Black population had exhibited both loyalty and subservience since the days of slavery and, employing their best economic argument, warned that emigration agents were trying to convince the Black worker to leave the state claiming "under the new constitution the Negro's citizenship will be taken away from him and that his schools will virtually be blotted out."[38]

With Rogers participating as an active member, the Convention's education committee issued a majority report that blotted out the requirement that schools funds be spent for "equal benefit" of schoolchildren but instead promised "to provide, as nearly as practicable, school terms of equal duration" for schoolchildren in the same school district. Also, the report recommended keeping segregated schools but eliminating the segregated poll tax receipts for local schools in keeping with the suffrage committee's overall strategy.[39]

The education committee echoed the taxation committee's earlier recommendation for revising the state's tax structure. It endorsed requiring an annual set-aside of a 3-mill tax (30 cents on each $100 of taxable property) for the state's school fund. The committee estimated it would equal the same amount of funding in the following year that the legislature had appropriated in the prior year. More significant, the committee promised that the 3-mill tax "fixes the school fund permanently" by allowing the fund to grow with the state's wealth and by barring future legislatures from making deep cuts in annual appropriations.

In addition, the committee proposed to allow counties to do what school leaders in north Alabama had been seeking for years: adopt a 1-mill local school tax, so long as three-fifths of the county's voters approved. The committee did not highlight the other part of its proposal that would lower the existing ceiling for combined state taxes from 7.5 mills to 6.5 mills. Given the near-certainty that one mill of state taxes would again be set aside to support Confederate veterans and their widows, the proposal meant the State of Alabama would have no more than 2.5 mills to operate all functions of government outside of education.[40]

The report brilliantly benefited the Black Belt. It provided a steady stream of monies so that majority-Black counties could lawfully continue to distribute the majority of school funds, apportioned among counties on the basis of both Black and white school-age populations, to a relatively small number of white schoolchildren while white plantation owners were assured of low taxes in the future—perhaps even a reduction in state taxes since the Black Belt counties probably would have no need to pass a special local school tax.

When the education committee's reports were debated a month later on the convention floor, the sections on disfranchisement and taxation of the emerging constitution already were adopted. Committee chairman J. B. Graham opened the debate with an explanation that intertwined truth and fiction:

> Many propositions were introduced providing that the school fund should be divided according to the tax paid by the several races. The Committee unanimously concluded that that would conflict with the Constitution of the United States, and they have provided . . . that equal benefits of the school fund of the races shall be equal as nearly as practicable, and thereby meet all the requirements of the Constitution of the United States and of justice between the races in Alabama.[41]

The majority report's recommendation to drop "equal benefits" prompted no debate, and there was no recorded vote. The section was included in the education article of the proposed state constitution.[42]

'The burden of educating this mass of ignorance rests on the whites . . .'

After the new Constitution was ratified in a fraudulent vote in November 1901, the Alabama legislature did not meet until January 1903. Rogers had been a major proponent during the constitutional convention of limiting legislative sessions to once every four years, but he ran and was elected a state senator to represent Sumter and Pickens counties in the legislature's first session of the 20th century. He was appointed to the Constitutional

Revision Committee. Along with other Black Belt members, who comprised a majority of the committee, Roger was there to assure no legislation saw the light of day if it proposed to change the structure and rules of the new Constitution.[43]

One bill that worried Rogers did reach the senate floor. It related to reorganizing the state's public school districts. The chair of the Education Committee from Cullman County in north Alabama proposed to eliminate townships as school districts and establish county-wide redistricting boards that would form new districts so that schools would be located nearest population centers. A key section of the bill required that, if practical, public schools should be located within two and one-half miles of each school-age child, "provided that no district shall be formed which contains less than fifteen children of the same race in the school." Rogers's amendment struck the words "of the same race." It passed the senate with 20 votes and no discussion, and it later became law.[44]

On its face, Rogers's amendment removed language segregating children for the purpose of schooling, but its intent and effect were quite different. Rogers was concerned that, while maintaining segregated schools, counting students according to race would leave many Black Belt communities without enough white students to lawfully locate a school closest to where they lived. There was no better example of how such language would be a problem than Rogers's own hometown of Gainesville.

In 1903, Roger had four children, three of school age and a four-year-old. The older children were attending segregated elementary and high schools in a town that, like its county, had a majority Black population. Most of Gainesville's white population (35 percent of the town's 817 residents) were older persons. Only about 60 white children attended the two white schools, and some of them were probably from outside the town. Also, Gainesville's population was declining. From 1890 to 1900, it lost 300 residents, and, the 1900 Census identified only 12 white children of preschool age in the town. Looking ahead, Rogers could see there might not be enough white children to keep the white schools in Gainesville if the law required at least "fifteen children of the same race in the school" in the town.[45]

A school measure that neither Rogers nor any other state senator proposed to change in 1903 was the 1876 law segregating poll taxes by race for support of schools. Some delegates, such as Governor Thomas Goode Jones, had declared that segregating the payment of any tax by race was unconstitutional, but no one in the state government moved to repeal the old law. At the same time, Alabama's Black leaders had bigger issues to address as they quietly supported a federal lawsuit challenging the new constitution's disfranchising sections, including the poll tax. Perhaps, some also intuitively understood what Horace Mann Bond later concluded—that the earlier proposal to segregate all local tax revenue by race "would not have crippled the Negro schools any more than they have been" under the school funding that white leaders implemented.[46]

As disfranchisement took effect, African Americans voted with their meager pocketbooks and refused to pay a poll tax that could not get them better schools or a right to vote. In 1898, African Americans across Alabama paid more than $37,000 in poll taxes. In 1903, they barely paid $3,500, and in 1906 they paid less than $1,000. The decline was enormous in the Black Belt. In Sumter, during the same period, the poll taxes paid by Black men fell from $1,566 to $33 to $9. Blacks in Dallas County reduced their poll tax payments from $1,650 to $21 to $12. During the same years, poll tax payments among the Black Belt's white men rose dramatically.[47]

This development infuriated many of the Black Belt's white population. "The most irritating thought to our people," observed Dallas County's white superintendent, "is . . . the unwillingness of the negroes to help in the education of their own race . . . The burden of educating this mass of ignorance rests on the whites. Under the old Constitution, perhaps a thousand dollars a year, in the shape of poll tax, was collected from the negroes, and this was applied exclusively to negro education. Since the negroes have been disfranchised, however, and, the payment of this tax left optional . . . hardly a dollar of it is paid . . . The greatest need then of the public schools of Dallas is some way by which the negro may be made to assist in his own education."[48]

The Black Belt planter's stereotypical notions about a "white man's burden" and his self-pity increasingly stood unchallenged in politics and in parlors, freeing a white minority from any reckoning with hard facts—the fact that Dallas County school officials were allocating the vast majority of its state's school funds for white children who were less than 10 percent of the school-age population; the fact that they were providing white children with an average of 30 days more schooling in a well-equipped school house that planters often built for their own children; and the fact that they operated a school system in which average daily attendance at Black schools showed four out of five African American children were out of school.

More broadly, the Black Belt's white planters ignored their own glaring hypocrisy—the plain fact that, while complaining about Black folks' failure to pay the poll tax to support local schools, the planters deliberately made payment of a poll tax a pre-condition to the right to vote because they knew few Black folks in their counties could afford to pay the tax and, for that reason, would be barred from voting.

The official reports that county superintendents dutifully filed with the state department of education evidenced the vast disparities in schooling across the Black Belt and, to a lesser extent, across all sections of Alabama.[49] But, they were facts at a time and place when the means to challenge or change them through political or legal recourse were becoming merely a symbolic act of resistance in Montgomery and in Washington.[50]

Alabama continued to segregate its poll tax revenues by race until 1907, when after more than three decades the law was repealed by what can only be described as a legal sleight of hand. James J. Mayfield was appointed to develop a new code of laws that recompiled all subsequent enactments and changes in the 1897 Code, which he also assisted in developing. The legislature did not revoke the 1875 law or Section 3608 of the 1897 Code segregating poll tax revenues, but Mayfield decided to omit the law "on account of the new Constitution." In fact, nothing in the 1901 Constitution or the Alabama Supreme Court opinions interpreting the Constitution invalidated racially segregating poll tax revenues. Mayfield, in consultation with the state school superintendent, decided to void the law by editorial fiat.[51]

In 1907, when Alabama's superintendent of education stopped reporting poll tax revenues by race, he reinstituted the reporting of state funds distributed by school boards in each county between Black and white schools. The reports revealed the huge effects of disfranchisement on education funding. In 1890, when African Americans comprised 43 percent of the school age population (ages 7–21), 42 percent of the state funds went to Black schools. In 1907, when African Americans comprised 45 percent of Alabama's school age population, Black schools were receiving less than 12 percent of the state's school funds.

This radical decline meant a vastly inferior education for the Black children lucky enough to regularly attend school. In 1890, based on the average number of students in daily attendance, per pupil expenditure for Alabama's schoolchildren was virtually equal in regard to race. Two decades later, Alabama was spending an average of $8.40 more on each white student—three and a half times more than on Blacks.[52] During both eras, Alabama maintained segregated schools, but in 1907 Jim Crow had also segregated political power.

The widest education gaps in 1907 were primarily in the Black Belt counties and the smallest were in north Alabama. Lowndes County's white education officials distributed school funds so that on average $38.98 was spent on the white child and $2.55 on the Black. No other county matched Lowndes' hyper-exaggerated practice of spending fifteen times more on a white child than Black child, but all Black Belt counties had enormous differences. In Sumter County, white student funding was almost seven times higher ($20.34 and $2.98). Almost all Alabama counties in which white students received at least five times more funding than Black students were in the state's southern sections, including all but one Black Belt county. Franklin County in north Alabama, had the state's smallest gap. White children received on average $7.50 and Black children received $6.50—a difference of $1 per pupil. All but one of the counties where the difference in white-Black per student funding was smallest were in north Alabama.

No county's per pupil expenditures for Blacks even equaled the state average for white students, but huge disparities existed among white per pupil spending—a difference largely separating the state's northern and southern counties. In northwest Marion County, for instance, spending for each white student regularly attending school was less than five dollars while Wilcox spent over $17 on each white student.[53] As a result, while always doing better than Black children, white schoolchildren in north Alabama outside a few urban areas usually had far less school days and their teachers were paid considerably less than in the Black Belt. This pattern led a state superintendent to complain that the state valued a white teacher's work less than the labor of an uneducated Negro since the teacher's salary amounted to "less money than is received from a few bales of cotton, which can be produced by any negro who cannot even write his name."[54]

The reason was self-evident to anyone who could do the math. White planters of the Black Belt counties used their majority-Black school-age populations to receive a huge portion of the state school fund, while using the authority granted by the legislature to distribute the funds as they saw fit—to spend vast, lopsided amounts educating a relatively small number of white students, often their own children. Whatever was left over went to the Black schools.

"That school for colored children up yonder," remembered African American farmer Ned Cobb in Tallapoosa County, "it'd run two or three weeks, maybe a month and half on the outside, and word would come down . . . "Cut the school out; money's gone . . . We had to run around here and supplement what money came down to us . . . Mighty little we got from the state government. That money comin here through white hands and they were half-concerned with keepin colored children *out* of school."[55] In 1907, official reports showed that on average, slightly more than one in five of Tallapoosa County's school-aged Black children attended school, compared to half of all white children.[56]

In Rogers's Sumter County, an average of 55 percent of the nearly 2,000 whites of school age attended public schools in 1907, and an untold number were in private schools. But only 12 percent—fewer than one in eight—of more than 10,000 school-age Blacks were in school.[57] As starkly as the statistics depict Black Belt education, they fail to reveal how Rogers as a Black Belt planter shaped Sumter County's public education in the vicinity of his own plantation and how he controlled both local Black schooling and local Black labor to advance his own business interests and the welfare of his family and his white community, while ironically building a reputation as a progressive farmer and a philanthropist of African American education.

'TO PUT THESE NEGROES IN THE WAY OF EARNING AN HONEST DECENT LIVING'

The railroads were finally making their way to north Sumter County in 1907, and large landowners such as Rogers were prepared to take advantage. The Alabama, Tennessee & Northern Railroad (AT&N) began laying down tracks southward from Tuscaloosa where other rail lines would connect Sumter County to markets in three directions. Railroad promoters envisioned connecting the AT&N to Mobile and its port which soon would realize new worldwide business opportunities as the Panama Canal approached completion in 1914.

Ten miles north of Gainesville stood Fair Oaks, a community named for John Rogers's plantation and designated to become one of AT&N's stations. The railroad company and others were clearing forests and laying down tracks while landowners began promoting a new railroad town named Panola as a once-in-a-lifetime opportunity. They offered for sale nearby land in lots and acreage to farmers and others who might want to be on the ground when the railroad arrived. Such an enterprise meant that men were required to do the hard labor of putting down rails, cutting and hauling timber, working at the new sawmills, constructing buildings, and helping to plow and harvest new farm lands of cotton and corn.[58] In other words, it required Black laborers.

John A. Rogers (label misspelled) (ADAH).

This requirement was a substantial challenge to white planters and promoters because the Great Migration of African Americans was underway. It began in relatively small numbers in Alabama's Black Belt and continued over more than five decades, as Black Southerners looked north for a promised land. Also, both the boll weevil and new technologies forced white farmers to diversify and find mechanical replacements for the hands that once did the planting, hoeing, and picking. In 1908, Rogers and a few other Black Belt planters realized they were facing an emerging labor shortage, which the Census two years later would confirm, showing that since the legislature voted for a disfranchisement convention in 1900, Sumter County's population had dropped by more than four thousand, and all but about three hundred who departed for cities and the North were African Americans.[59]

As the new town began to take shape, Arthur W. Mitchell, a young African American educator who had operated a colored school in Greensboro, the county seat of neighboring Hale County, made plans to move to Panola after meeting with local plantation owners, including Rogers. A native of Chambers County, Mitchell attended Tuskegee Institute and graduated from Snow Hill Institute, a private colored school in Wilcox County. More than a year before he opened Panola's West Alabama Normal and Industrial Institute, Mitchell incorporated a company in Birmingham named the Afro-American Building, Loan, and Real Estate Company. The names on the hand-written application for incorporation may have been difficult to read since as company president Mitchell was listed as "Atkins W. Mitchell" and its vice president was reported as "John H. Rodgers." The company was authorized to issue up to $10,000 in stock.[60]

Mitchell's school, which began "with one teacher and three pupils" in late October 1908, was part of a plan to build and run a school on 80 acres of land that Rogers donated near his Fair Oaks plantation and to encourage Black families to borrow money to purchase lots on the lands outside of Panola. With the help of a growing number of students, Mitchell cleared land and used the timber to build a schoolhouse and other buildings, while a local Black church served as the initial classroom.

According to an unnamed correspondent, perhaps Mitchell himself, local Negroes initially did little more than "scoff and criticise" him as the new school's principal since he required children to help build the schoolhouse and grounds. The Black community did not want children to work, he wrote, but "to learn out of books." But the community quickly changed its minds, according to the local newspaper article, and were praising the school principal in order to "learn how to farm like Prof. Mitchell." The white newspaper's article was entitled "Deserving Negro."[61]

This change in attitude probably occurred when Panola's Black residents learned that the owner of Fair Oaks plantation was providing land for the school. A committee of elders in the Salem AME Zion Church signed a resolution that apparently Mitchell drafted expressing their "deep appreciation" to the "Hon. John A Rogers . . . a friend to needy and worthy people" who was a "great and good man." It was signed, "Negroes of North Sumter."[62]

Mitchell had an aptitude for knowing how to appeal to men such as Rogers. He was on record as having supported disfranchisement—at least once it was implemented. In 1905, Mitchell told an audience of white leaders, "I do not believe in manhood suffrage. I have seen that the ignorant and unconquered vote is not only a menace and drawback to the Government, but he himself is his greatest enemy . . . I hold the new Constitution is good for both races."[63]

In a long letter published in the *Gainesville Times*, Mitchell assured white readers he understood that "after the emancipation many negroes sought education for the purposes of becoming prominent in politics or evading work." He stressed that his school was involved in industrial training of "the head, hand and heart" of Black youth so that they could become better farmers who would produce more crops for planters. "We cannot hope to do anything here without the cooperation of the white people," Mitchell concluded.[64]

This outlook exactly matched Rogers's opinions, which in the context of the Black Belt after the turn of the century defined him as a progressive planter. "In the negro farmer's helpless condition," Rogers told the editor of Greene County's *Eutaw Whig and Observer*, "he is a destruction to himself and a menace to the white farmer . . . Many of the negroes engaged in agriculture are now in the hands of intelligent white men who do not take advantage of their ignorance, their helplessness, and their poverty to keep them poor and degraded, but who look after them, doing everything to better their condition."[65]

Rogers explained his own personal sense of responsibility for the Negro in a public letter to Booker T. Washington that commended Mitchell as an educator of "great benefit to the Negroes" in the Black Belt. Rogers wrote:

> I am myself an Alabamian, the descendant of slave owners since the foundation of our government, and as my fathers were largely responsible for the Negroes' presence in America, I feel it is my duty for this reason, and for the higher reason that it is the duty of the strong to help the weak to put these negroes in the way of earning an honest decent living, which must come through training of their hands, their minds, and their hearts."[66]

At the same time, Rogers made it clear to his white neighbors that his gift of land for Black education was by no means extravagant. "Mr. Rogers says this was the poorest land he owned and was abandoned as worn out and unprofitable to work . . ." the *Sumter County Sun* reported. "Mr. Rogers says he did not give the land as a philanthropist, but as a large landowner, he took this means to teach his negro tenants the value of intensive farming."[67]

What Rogers did not tell the Tuskegee leader or his white neighbors was how he was using the Negro school to turn a profit for his own business. As Mitchell's school grew in size and enrollment over three years, it became an essential part of the strategy to attract Black families to resettle near Panola where they could buy lots for housing and farming. Mitchell organized a series of large agricultural fairs, advertised as "A Gala Day for Negroes in West Alabama," and "Excursions for Colored People" on the AT&N which brought them to a picnic area near the Noxubee River where they were entertained with games, music, and fish fries and barbecues. The events were characterized by Mitchell in his fundraising brochures as community outreach program to teach improved methods to Black farmers. But the events served more as a sales promotion to attract Black families to Rogers's new town.[68]

A scholar who interviewed residents years later suggests that Rogers's

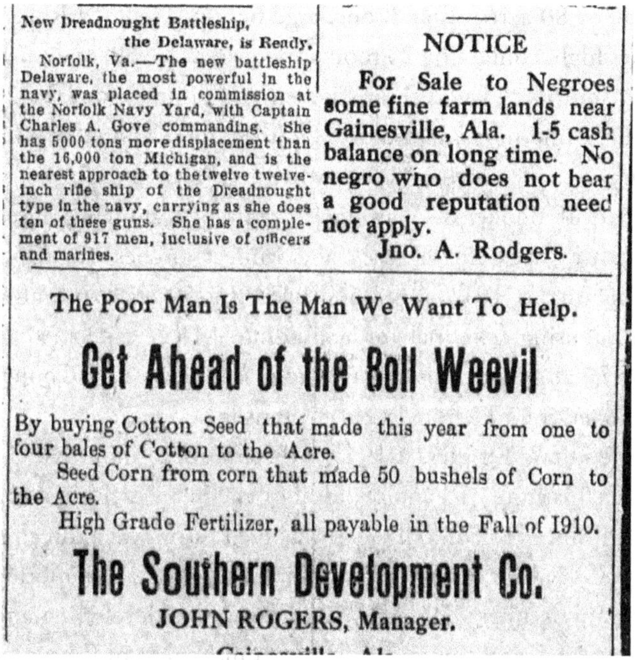

New Dreadnought Battleship, the Delaware, is Ready.

Norfolk, Va.—The new battleship Delaware, the most powerful in the navy, was placed in commission at the Norfolk Navy Yard, with Captain Charles A. Gove commanding. She has 5000 tons more displacement than the 16,000 ton Michigan, and is the nearest approach to the twelve twelve-inch rifle ship of the Dreadnought type in the navy, carrying as she does ten of these guns. She has a complement of 917 men, inclusive of officers and marines.

NOTICE

For Sale to Negroes some fine farm lands near Gainesville, Ala. 1-5 cash balance on long time. No negro who does not bear a good reputation need not apply.

Jno. A. Rodgers.

The Poor Man Is The Man We Want To Help.

Get Ahead of the Boll Weevil

By buying Cotton Seed that made this year from one to four bales of Cotton to the Acre.

Seed Corn from corn that made 50 bushels of Corn to the Acre.

High Grade Fertilizer, all payable in the Fall of 1910.

The Southern Development Co.

JOHN ROGERS, Manager.

Ads placed by John Rogers in the Sumter Enterprise, *April 7, 1910.*

scheme involved not only selling land to Black farmers but a deliberate attempt to put them into a form of peonage through debts they could never repay. "Once unsuspecting settlers were on the land and in debt, they would be trapped," observed Dennis Nordin, "unable to leave because of the binding effects of unfavorable credit terms."[69]

Whatever Rogers's motives, he began advertising and selling lots to Black farmers in the year Mitchell's school opened. The effort continued only during the years the school operated in Panola. Under the name of "Jno. A Rodgers," he advertised "For Sale to Negroes some fine farm land near Gainesville Ala." in a weekly Black newspaper published by an association of African American churches in Alabama and Mississippi. His ads offered long-term loans with little money down.[70] During this period, as manager of the Southern Development Company, Rogers also sold "improved" cotton and corn seeds to Black and white farmers and advertised as a merchant offering to provide farmers "corn, meat, and money to make your crops."[71]

Principal Mitchell claimed by 1910 to have built a "campus of 150 pupils, four teachers, 80 acres of land, one large building [named Rogers Hall], three stories high, containing 25 rooms and chapel 50x60; one small cottage, one blacksmith and wood shop, kitchen and dining room (being erected), two mules, one horse, two cows, six hogs, one 2-horse wagon, farm implements, etc., all valued at being worth ten thousand dollars."[72] Following the path of Booker T. Washington, Mitchell annually raised funds in the North by speaking at Black and white churches and white civic clubs. But in August 1911, a fire destroyed Rogers Hall and, after exploring the fundraising potential for rebuilding, Mitchell decided to relocate the school. He hitched his fortunes to a second Sumter County planter and developer, John Hendricks (J. H.) Pinson.

As Rogers's friend and business associate, Pinson knew about Mitchell's West Alabama Institute in Panola and about Mitchell's fundraising efforts in the North since the Bank of Geiger, where Pinson was a director, handled the school's funds. During the same time Rogers was promoting Panola for settlement as a new railroad town, Pinson was developing and promoting the town of Geiger, located only a few miles south of Panola, as another railroad depot and new community.[73]

Pinson had large ambitions for Geiger, primarily centered on the new town becoming a destination for a large number of white families to move into the Black Belt. Calling the area the "Valley of the Nile of the Southland," Pinson & Geiger advertised in major dailies across four states offering "Rich Lands . . . To Worthy Whites" in the "Greatest Market Spot of the South."[74] In one large Birmingham ad, Pinson enlisted testimonials from "prominent men" including Rogers who assured readers that "We are above the fever line and below that of tuberculosis . . . on the lines of latitude that have produced the great nations of antiquity."

Rogers explained, "The negro . . . is fast drifting to the lumber camps and the mineral districts of the South, leaving the farm lands to the white man, who is now growing on twenty acres of land what was formerly grown on a hundred . . . Bring many such white families among us—they are needed."[75]

Apart from building a new white community, Pinson quietly planned with Mitchell to create a Black town a couple of miles outside of Geiger in marginal lands surrounding the Noxubee River; not far, as the crow flies, from Rogers's Fair Oaks Plantation. Pinson provided Mitchell with 400 acres for his school in exchange for the 80 acres that Rogers had provided for the school's original site.

In addition, the founder of Geiger offered Mitchell a chance to buy one thousand acres of adjoining land "at a low price" for selling as lots to build "a progressive negro settlement." As an incentive, Pinson offered $15,000 to erect a new school building for Mitchell's Institute if the principal could raise $50,000 "from those interested in Negro education" in the North for the purchase of the one thousand acres. Pinson added a stipulation. The cornerstone of the school building should have the following inscription: "This building donated to the Negro race by Pinson & Geiger, Geiger, Ala., who were friends of the Negroes as slaves and who are friends to them as freedman."[76]

Mitchell was unable to raise enough funds to buy Pinson's one thousand aces, but he secured enough gifts from Northern donors to hire teachers and to build a schoolhouse, a barn, and other farming structures through the labor of his students. In pitching his school to Northern audiences, Mitchell's facts appear to varied widely on how many students he was educating—ranging often in press reports of his speeches and interviews from 100 to 360 pupils. He often stressed he had turned away hundreds of children due to lack of resources; the long distances some students walked to get to his school; the large number of pupils who worked all day but walked to school afterwards to learn at night; and "the 200,000 Negroes who live within a radius of 50 miles of our school 'scholarshiped' by the northern philanthropist."[77]

In appealing for Northern aid, Mitchell realized the importance of having prominent men from both sides of the Mason-Dixon Line to vouch for him and his school. For years, he maneuvered for Booker T. Washington's endorsement, something white Northern donors would expect. Mitchell may have manufactured such an endorsement for a while but in the end the Wizard of Tuskegee gave it to him. Northern men who served as references included white church leaders such as the Reverend William T. Holmes, a Congregational Church minister in New England who became the president of all-Black Tougaloo College in Mississippi. Holmes wrote appeals for the Geiger school after he visited the campus and met Pinson and others.

Mitchell's references also included prominent white men in Alabama. By 1914, one version of his Institute's letterhead listed J. H. Pinson, W. L. Waller (Pinson's business partner), State Superintendent of Education Henry Willingham, and even Governor Emmet O'Neal, although there is nothing in available records to indicate that Mitchell received formal endorsement from the state officials.[78]

These endorsements were useful because Mitchell wanted to portray his work and his school as an essential way for improving race relations in the South. In a brochure, entitled "White Mob Lynched Negro . . . Afterwards Converted to Cause of Negro Education," Mitchell claimed that a few years earlier a white mob lynched a Negro on "mere suspicion . . . on the same plantation and near the spot where the West Alabama Agricultural Institute is being built." Afterwards, "it was unsafe for an educated Negro to spend even one night in this section of Alabama," but the school principal told of how he persisted so that eventually even "the white men that constituted the mob and lynched a Negro three and a half years ago are now making small contributions to help the work of the school." The school's industrial education and moral training of its students would be "the only solution of the race problem and the crime of lynching," Mitchell asserted.[79]

There were lynchings in Alabama during Mitchell's years in the state, and one did occur in Sumter County in 1909. Also, Black schools across the South had been destroyed by whites who opposed Black education, and the life of an educated African American in the Deep South was always burdened by the ever-present possibility of meeting unprovoked violence.[80] But Mitchell's story of a lynching was made from the whole cloth of Southern life, not from the specific facts of Sumter County. The 1909 murder of a white woman and subsequent lynching of John Holly by the woman's white neighbors took place around Bellamy, located in the southmost part of Sumter County, almost 40 miles from Geiger.[81]

Mitchell's redemptive story was a useful tool for fundraising not only because it offered a simplistic solution to what the school's Northern donors viewed as primarily a Southern problem but also because they approved of Mitchell's type of educational program that, in the words of one benefactor, took "a little pickaninny, beginning with teaching him his letters and leads him through a course of education . . . to be good farmers and good domestic servants. It is intended for the poor classes, and plenty of work is given as a part of the course."[82]

Another essential component of Mitchell's appeal included an explanation as to the conditions that made his private school a worthy recipient of Northern philanthropy—the inadequacy of the local public schools for Black children. Often Mitchell told his Northern audiences that his Institute sat in an Alabama county where 8,000 children were "without a chance for schools or to learn the alphabet of a civilized life." He told others that until he arrived in Sumter County there was "not even one graded school, to say nothing of a high school."[83]

At other times, Mitchell described the Alabama Black Belt as a place "where there are 200,000 negroes unreached by any other school. All similar schools are crowded, and the only hope of these people is to get help from some other source." He called Sumter County the central point of eight Black Belt counties "all with large Negro populations, and all without any Negro schools, except here and there . . . a so-called public school that amounted to almost nothing."[84] On two occasions, while his Institute was in Panola, reports indicate that Mitchell's school received a small amount of state funding—$125 in 1909 and $200 in 1912.[85]

What Mitchell left unsaid in his appearances was the fact that his local benefactors, Rogers and Pinson, and other planters controlled the state funds for public schools in Sumter County's various local school districts. In their role as school trustees, these men had the power to allocate as they saw fit as much or as little of the county's state money to support Black schools. Their choice in Gainesville, Panola, and Geiger was to provide virtually all state funding to public schools educating their own children, while helping Mitchell's private school in ways that advanced their own business interests and assured the school would survive through the child labor of its students and the donations of distant Northerners—not state or county funds.

During the years Mitchell operated the West Alabama Institute in Panola with Rogers's endorsement, no private or public school for Black children existed in Gainesville. In fact, state reports fail to evidence any private Black school operating in any part of Sumter County in those years. Yet the 1910 Census reported more than one hundred African American school-age children in Gainesville, and the Census taker indicated that about half were "at school" and the other half were "day laborers."[86]

As Gainesville's school trustees, Rogers and his friends controlled the school funds that came to the town in an amount based on the number of both white and Black persons of school age in the town.[87] State law may have provided that every "minor over the age of seven years shall be entitled to admission into, and instruction in any public school of his or her own race or color,"[88] but Rogers had developed a set-up that allocated all state funds only for Gainesville's white children, including his own, and located an alternative private school that Gainesville's Black children could occasionally attend near his Fair Oaks plantation a few miles up the road.

Rogers's scheme did even more. It set up a Black school in a location he was actively promoting as a new town among both Black and white families. The school served as an important amenity for eager, ambitious Black families outside Sumter County to move to the Panola area and buy their own land—land that Rogers was selling to them on accessible, but debt-heavy terms. At the same time, the school's curriculum aimed to teach African American boys and girls the value of hard work by providing the labor to build the school campus and to develop skills for becoming more productive farmers and domestic servants.

The price tag for Rogers in this arrangement was 80 acres of land which he described as the "poorest land he owned . . . and unprofitable to work."[89] The rewards were far more substantial. According to the head of the AT&N railroad, the value of land in Panola may have jumped as much as 500 percent for enterprising planters such as Rogers who owned large tracts and could turn small landowners into tenants by foreclosing on overdue debts.[90]

The educational rewards were also considerable for Rogers and his white neighbors. In 1911, the last year in which Mitchell's school operated in the

Panola area, the all-white Gainesville public school enrolled 35 white children in grammar school and 13 white students in high school. (Some students were lodging with relatives in the town, perhaps to assure enrollment stayed above the minimum for state-funded schools.) There were three teachers, allowing a teacher-pupil ratio of one to 16, and a school term of nine months. With almost two thousand dollars in state funds and $27 of miscellaneous income, the school's per pupil expenditure for Gainesville's white children, including Rogers's own children, was $41.38. In contrast, the per pupil expenditure for white children in Sumter County's rural schools was about $18.02 and only about $2.01 for Black students.

Gainesville's per pupil expenditure was also far above those of towns with all-white schools in north Alabama. As the larger town of Republican-voting Winston County, where only three dozen Blacks lived in the entire county, Haleyville's all-white public schools spent only $11.51 per student in 1911. The difference in funding was even more stark when considering the sources of funding. Gainesville's extraordinary funding came only from state funds sent from Montgomery. In Haleyville, state funds provided $3.65 per student. The other $7.86 in the town's per-pupil expenses came from local taxes and enrolled students' fees.[91] As a result, like most others in the Black Belt, Gainesville's public school had a higher rate of expenditure for white students than north Alabama's schools, although north Alabama communities were often taxing themselves twice as much for schools as they received in state tax funds.

The role that Arthur Mitchell and his school played around Rogers's plantation was essentially repeated in Geiger for almost three years. Mitchell raised funds from Northern donors to operate the school, and his Institute served as a centerpiece for Pinson & Geiger to build their development. It appears Pinson relied chiefly on Mitchell and other African Americans as brokers to sell the marginal land to Blacks[92] while the enterprising planter concentrated on building the white town.

For white parents willing to move to find better opportunities to educate their children, Pinson's company turned Geiger's "prairie school house" into a "magnificent building which attracts so many strangers . . . This building at a cost of $17,000 was erected in 1912 and, properly equipped with patent desks, a library of about 800 volumes, and several hundred pamphlets; with a beautiful auditorium seated with opera chairs, a domestic science department," and a music department. For the white families living outside the town on land he had sold, Pinson provided two horse-drawn wagons to bring children to a school, which, like Gainesville's, was in session for a full nine months.[93]

Serving as a trustee, along with his elderly father and one of his friends and political supporters, Pinson enabled Geiger's white school to receive recognition as one of only seven to meet new state standards in 1913, and he unsuccessfully tried to have the Geiger school selected as the countywide high school, which would have brought additional state funds. The four women teaching in Geiger's white school were paid almost twice as much as the average salary for the county's female teachers. For Black education, Geiger's school trustees allocated $100 to Mitchell's school, which apparently they reported in state records as a colored public school.[94]

By the end of 1914, a worsening economy and Geiger's fortunes as a boom-or-bust railroad town meant Mitchell's school was enduring "the hardest year of our history." Even after cutting the number of his teachers, Mitchell still "was going to be taxed to the limit to stay out of debt."[95] Another fire in January 1915 rescued the school principal. As in Panola, the main school building was completely destroyed, with only a piano and some cloths salvaged, but Mitchell had an insurance policy on the building and collected two thousand dollars. When Pinson & Geiger insisted the payout belonged to the community or the company, Mitchell fled the county—with the insurance money.[96]

A few months later, Mitchell reappeared 60 miles south, where he became the principal of Choctaw County's colored school, Armstrong Agricultural Institute. He remained there until 1919, when he fled reportedly with thousands of dollars relating to land titles that school trustees considered as belonging to the Institute. Mitchell left Alabama in the cover of dark and found his way to the nation's capital where, with a bank account estimated at ten thousand dollars, he went into the real estate business in Black neighborhoods and became a lawyer. Eventually, he moved to Chicago, where was involved in politics. In 1934, Mitchell defeated

Black Republican incumbent Oscar DePriest—the first African American elected to the U.S. Congress in the 20th century—becoming the nation's first African American to serve as a Democrat in the Congress.[97]

Congressman Arthur W. Mitchell (Library of Congress).

As an educator in Alabama's Black Belt, Mitchell evidently was guilty of what scholar Dennis Nordin calls a repeated "routine of fleecing and fleeing." But at the same time his schools offered African American children a better opportunity for becoming educated and skilled than did almost any colored public school. As much as Mitchell and his primary benefactors in the Black Belt misrepresented their primary aims, misled people on the facts, used unpaid child labor under the pretext of education, and ran schools in Panola and Geiger to serve private financial interests, Mitchell's schools were nonetheless more than a one-room schoolhouse with one untrained, semi-qualified teacher attempting to educate as many as 40 or 50 students whose ages might range from seven to seventeen.

Throughout Alabama, north and south, the colored public schools were barely able to educate anyone due to an abysmal lack of community resources and public support. It became common practice for school trustees—all white landowners—to allocate only $125 from the school funds for annual support of each Black school to pay Black teachers supposedly to provide five months of schooling. Seven of every ten of the state's Black teachers had the least training for teaching, and they had the most demanding conditions. Most colored schools, especially in the rural areas, constituted a single room in a private building such as a church or lodge hall, and most of these schools were not suitable during the winter months even in the Deep South. Barely more than one of every ten schoolrooms had desks for Black students; those that did were almost all in the larger cities.[98]

Despite the duplicity and dishonesty, in comparison to what the state and local governments were willing spend to support the education of Black children, Arthur Mitchell's schools—with their four to seven Tuskegee-trained teachers, a heated schoolhouse building, some desks, a few library books, and basic teaching supplies such as chalk boards—were among the best available options for African American children actually being educated in Alabama.

'Educational Advantages Are Not Equal in Any Part of Our State'

After the United States entered World War I in April 1917, Alabamians were confronted with the fact that many of their young men were unfit soldiers because they could not read written military orders, army manuals, bulletins, or even a rifle's sight leaves. "Of all the thousands Alabama is sending to the army and navy, one out of every ten is illiterate," warned the war coordinator of the all-white Alabama Education Association. "The percentage is higher than this among the colored troops."[99]

The Alabama Department of Education abandoned its long-held aversion to illustrating and interpreting its extensive statistical tables and issued a comparative study ranking Alabama counties on key indicators of education financing and quality. Its rankings demonstrated that Black Belt counties usually led with the longest school terms, highest attendance rates, highest average per pupil expenditures, largest teacher salaries, lowest teacher-pupil ratios, highest investment in school facilities, lowest illiteracy rates, and largest percentage of well-trained teachers. Of course, all those benefits were for whites only.

When the counties were ranked on the cumulative indicators, 19 of the state's 21 majority-Black counties were in the top 20 (Clarke and Pickens were 21st and 25th) among the 67 counties. The only county in the top 20 without a majority-Black population was Elmore, located on the rim of the Black Belt, with a Black population of 47 percent.[100] In the rankings on illiteracy, the department expressly included only whites.

In 1917, the federal Bureau of Education released a report on "Negro Education," which included some 75 pages of research and analysis on Alabama's African American schools and students. Most of the Alabama section did not highlight racial disparities but the report did include a map of the racial differences in per capita expenditures for teacher pay—graphically displaying extreme disparities across the state—and especially the "wide divergencies in the 'black belt' counties."

The federal report calculated that in Sumter County expenditures in white schools were $26.16 per child and 66 cents for Black children. In Wilcox County, white schools received $27.75 per child and Black schools 54 cents, and in Lowndes white schools got $35.09 and Black schools got $1.26 per child.[101]

When the legislature reconvened in January 1919, John Rogers and other Black Belt legislators had to pick and choose what they would attempt to control and defeat amid a wide-ranging agenda of post-war reforms. In the early days of the session, the legislature passed a bill authorizing Governor Kilby to appoint a temporary education commission to study the state's system and report before the end of the session on any need for new laws. Such a rapid turnaround could happen only because the commission engaged the federal Bureau of Education, already in the middle of an extensive study of Alabama education, to undertake a "scientific study of the entire public-school system of Alabama" and make recommendations.[102]

The 522 pages of "An Educational Study of Alabama" was a comprehensive, statistical analysis which identified a host of shortcomings in Alabama law and practice while documenting how those deficiencies placed the state at or near the bottom of the 48 states in school funding, duration, and quality. The report, for example, highlighted that Alabama ranked 46th in literacy, while noting that the state's illiteracy rate among young men drafted for military service during the recent war was two and half time higher than the national rate.[103]

The report's most remarkable feature was its clear comparison of the inequalities in Black and white schools across Alabama and its spotlight on Black Belt practices. In prior years, state education reports and a few political leaders occasionally decried Black Belt methods for disadvantaging "white counties," but this report highlighted both the vast inequalities between Black and white students in the state and how those were due in large measure to practices and laws benefitting the Black Belt.

The report found that "the people of the Black Belt . . . have continued one of the retarding elements in the educational development of the State" since its white leaders effectively opposed additional school taxes as they enriched white schools for a small number of children by malapportioning funds away from Black schools. The report also suggested Black Belt planters were creating the hardships and lack of opportunity that was prompting the Great Migration, which meant in some counties the loss of a quarter of the entire Black population within a period of only 12 months.[104]

Perhaps the most unexpected and damning analysis came from the report's scrutiny of the "stock explanations" heard commonly in Black Belt counties to justify racial inequalities: "'Negroes do not pay any taxes,' and hence the county can not afford, as a matter of justice to the white people, to spend more than a small fraction of the school fund on Negro schools." The authors of the federal report found this argument put the Black Belt and others "in a bad situation if their own argument were applied to them by the State."[105] Why?—because the Black Belt counties received considerably more school funds from the state than they paid in state taxes for their own schools.

In 1918, Alabama's 21 majority-Black counties received more than $311,000 in state school funds above and beyond the amount of state school taxes they had paid in. This excess funding essentially amounted to a subsidy from other counties' taxes.[106] In five Black Belt counties—Sumter, Lowndes, Dallas, Barbour, and Bullock—local taxpayers paid not one cent in local school taxes for their schools.[107] In effect, the white schools for the families of John Rogers and other landowners in these counties were financed in large part through the taxes of other Alabamians.

In words not heard or read in Alabama in any official government report since the adoption of disfranchisement, the Bureau's report stated that the "results of this practice on the colored children . . . are wholly without defense on the grounds of the 'as nearly as practicable' clause in the constitution. For in these counties the colored population is almost wholly deprived of public school support, being obliged to depend largely on private subscriptions and donations. The thinking people of Alabama are opposed to these local practices."[108]

Former U.S. Representative Sydney Bowie, the chair of Alabama's interim education commission, issued its public report, but none of these "local practices" were included in its 20-page statement. Bowie acknowledged that the commission concurred with many of the Bureau's findings, but he stressed the two bodies' recommendations were not the same—as it turned out, especially not on Black education. "In the very important matter of negro education," the commission stated, "it is best we should proceed in a way to do justice to this large portion of our population without, at the same time, doing anything that will disturb the harmonious relations now existing between the majority of both races." Noting that conditions were materially different in different sections of the state, the commission concluded that "we must proceed with caution" since Alabama "cannot hope to solve so great and so delicate a subject with the stroke of a pen."[109]

The state commission was far more forthcoming about the problems of inequality among white children. "Surely no man can say the country child is not as entitled to as good advantages as the city child; and just as surely no man can say that the Alabama child is not entitled to as good advantages as the child of Kansas or . . . Washington," the report stated. "Surely the white children of the white counties of our state are entitled to equal advantages with the white children of the black belt of Alabama."[110]

"Educational advantages are not equal in any part of our state," the commission declared. "They are inadequate almost everywhere . . . In our opinion the crux of the situation may be stated in two words: MORE REVENUE."[111] The commission recommended that the legislature appropriate one million dollars more to the public schools than the constitutionally mandated 3-mill school tax. Also, it recommended a nine-month school term "accessible to every child in the state," an appointed state school board to divorce education from politics, better trained and better paid teachers, extending and enforcing compulsory education, and the increased supervision of schools by county boards of education.[112]

Kilby praised the commission members he had appointed, but explained: "They have written upon a sheet of white paper, not confining themselves to what under existing conditions may now reasonably be attained, but looking forward to the future"[113]—apparently, in his eyes, the very, very distant future.

Rogers and the other longtime Black Belt leaders recognized that these and related developments constituted immediate threats to their control of state politics and policies, but they already had set up some defenses against any real change. Black Belt legislators were the chair and a majority of the members in the state senate Committee on Constitutional Amendments.[114] That fact alone virtually insured the defeat of any bill proposing a referendum for a constitutional amendment to change school funding.

They also defended Kilby's unique austerity bill, passed in the early days of the 1919 session, that set up a commission with the extraordinary powers to propose a state budget which could not be increased in any amount except by a vote of "two-thirds of the members elected in both houses"—not just two-thirds of members voting.[115] This new law meant there would be no $1 million appropriation for education since the governor and the other two members of the budget commission, both born and raised in the Black Belt, had drafted a budget, under the watchful eye of Rogers's Gainesville neighbor and brother-in-law, State Representative R. H. Long, with a much smaller appropriation of general revenues for public schools.[116]

Black Belt senators also recruited more than enough votes to defeat a bill by Wyatt Brown from northeastern St. Clair County, who sought to hold a referendum to change the state's constitutional basis for distributing school funds and provide adequate funding for each county to provide equal educational opportunities to all the state's children. Brown was perhaps an unusual sponsor for such a sweeping proposal that made no mention of race since he was a Democrat whose father had been a Confederate soldier, as had been his father-in-law, who in 1919 was the only surviving member of the Alabama Secession Convention. Regardless, once the Black Belt-controlled committee had the assured votes, it reported the bill without recommendation so that the senate could vote it down.[117]

'WE MUST HAVE MONEY TO EDUCATE THE CHILDREN . . .'

Another bill endangering the planters' basic interests proposed to ban convict leasing, a social reform that almost all other states had already enacted. Alabama's state government had become grossly dependent on revenues from leasing prisoners as forced labor to private companies. During the 1919–20 fiscal year, for example, the Convict Department generated more revenues than any other source of state income—even more than from the three-mill property tax for education.[118] Therefore, ending convict leasing meant a real possibility of requiring huge increases in taxes and tax assessments.

Senator John Rogers took the lead in opposing the bill sponsored by north Alabama progressive Representative Thomas E. Orr of Marshall County. His bill called for ending private leasing of convicts and instead putting them to work under state supervision to build and maintain Alabama's roads. Twenty years earlier at the constitutional convention, Rogers supported the notion of putting convicts to work on improvements to roads, bridges, waterways, and other public infrastructures. However, he had dismissed claims that the system of convict leasing was barbaric. "Now everybody knows that the great bulk of convicts in this State are negroes," Roger stated in 1901. "Everybody who knows anything about the character of a negro knows there is no punishment in the world that can take the place of the lash with him. He must be controlled that way. He inherited that peculiarity from his ancestors when he came from the shores of Africa . . . If we take away the lash from this convict system, we will destroy the efficiency of the system."[119]

Efforts to end convict leasing had been tried during almost every legislative session in the decades preceding and following the 1901 Constitution. In 1915, with support from labor unions and civic groups, the house passed a bill banning convict leasing after a legislative committee found that life expectancy for prisoners in the state's coal mines was only seven years. But Governor Charles Henderson threatened to veto the legislation, and a senate committee kept it from reaching the floor for a vote. As a house member during this time, Rogers sponsored the compromise—proposing to end private leasing of convicts but to work them in mines on land owned by the University of Alabama. By the end of the session, nothing passed, and another interim legislative committee was established to further investigate the problem.[120]

In July 1919, the legislative committee presented a damning report on the conditions and practices of convict leasing based on its own inspection. "The convict lease system in the State of Alabama is a relic of barbarism," the committee report declared. "It is a form of human slavery . . . It has been the policy of the State to brand the convict with the dollar mark." The committee described in graphic detail what it found, including unattended men "lying on beds covered with oil cloth with secretions dripping from their burned bodies scarcely breathing"[121] in the aftermath of mining accidents. The committee recommended that convict leasing end by the first day of 1923 and that preparations begin to work convicts in the future on state roads and in state-owned cotton mills. Orr, the committee chair, introduced legislation to enact its recommendations.[122]

Joined by two other Black Belt members of the investigating committee, Rogers wrote a minority report. He claimed that they found "no general complaint from the convicts as a whole" about their treatment and stated that the dissenting members were "unalterably opposed to any disposition of the convicts that will impose additional taxes on the citizens of Alabama for their upkeep and maintenance."

"We must have money to educate the children of the State, to take care of the blind and the helpless little ones," Rogers proclaimed. The Black Belt legislators were certain that Alabamians were not "willing to pay more taxes to maintain in idleness and luxury the house-breakers, highwaymen and murderers." Instead, with the endorsement of Governor Kilby, Rogers recommended his bill proposing what he sponsored in 1915.[123]

Rogers also opposed the majority report's recommendation of transferring convicts to build and maintain roads. He suggested that Georgia's recent experience with convicts on the roads had shown that too many escaped, "endangering the property, menacing the lives, not only of the people of Georgia but of her sister states . . . To our minds the mines then are the places to which burglars, house-breakers, murderers and highwaymen should be committed for safekeeping."[124]

Rogers's moral posturing about assuring "money to educate the children of the State . . . and the helpless little ones" did not fool the state's daily newspaper editors, one of whom condemned Rogers for using the state's capstone university and needy children to sustain "man's inhumanity to man." The *Montgomery Advertiser*, however, quoted another Black Belt legislator's claim that the State would need $3 million in additional taxes to pay for ending convict leasing, and its editor suggested that taxpayers should be more concerned with having to pay extra taxes than with denouncing any profiteers of the system.[125]

Before the session ended, in a compromise, the legislature passed a Rogers bill that authorized the governor and the Convict Department to spend $250,000 to investigate working convicts in the University-owned mines. But the new law's last section also kept the Orr language that as of 1923 "it shall be unlawful for any person to lease or let for hire any state or county convict to any person firm or corporation . . . Nothing in the provisions of this act shall prevent the Highway Department from working convicts on the Public Roads."[126] It was a contradiction that served as a compromise, which kicked the issue of convict leasing down the road while allowing the possibility that the university, on whose board Rogers sat, might enjoy a windfall.

Most important, the compromise let Rogers proceed with other legislation and other high-stakes strategies to build and control the statewide roads program he sought for the benefit of his Black Belt and to make the most of a system of public education he had helped to put into law.

'The Answer Is Blowing in the Wind'

John Rogers did not serve actively in the Alabama legislature again, but the historical pattern of profound racial inequities in Alabama schools that he helped to enable had assured vast, entrenched advantages for the

Black Belt planters and their white children. From 1903 through 1924, the primary years during which Rogers was active in Alabama politics, Sumter County received $350,000 more in state school funds than it paid in state school taxes. Also, it was one of a few Alabama counties that did not enact a local school tax since the majority of its state school funds, which other taxpayers subsidized, educated only whites, a small minority of the county's children. In 2020 dollars, the subsidized portion of Sumter County's school funds during the Rogers period would have amounted to more than $7 million.

There was, of course, a pattern of subsidized white education across the Black Belt counties. Lowndes and Greene also enacted no local school taxes and along with Sumter had Alabama's highest per-pupil expenditures. These three counties received during the same 20 years what would have been in 2020 more than $27.5 million in state subsidies used primarily for schooling fewer than 7,500 privileged white children.[127] A generation of white children in planter's families enjoyed the best education that money could buy, in large measure at the expense of taxpayers in other sections of Alabama, while a generation of Black children in tenant houses received the least education that planters could manage.

Little changed even after Rogers retired to Gainesville. Other Black Belt leaders took up the section's mandate, as another generation emerged in the legislature and in statewide offices. Even in the 1930s, as Rogers approached the end of his life, honored by Black Belt voters who let him serve in absentia in the state senate, the old patterns persisted. In 1933, Sumter County spent more than $71 educating each white child, twice the state average for white students, while it spent less than three dollars for each Black child attending a Sumter County school—a white to Black ratio of funding that was more than 20:1.[128]

As in the past, Sumter and other Black Belt counties continued to enjoy far more state tax revenues for schools than they were paying to maintain such schools. In 1933, Sumter received twice as much in state school funding than it paid in state school taxes.[129]

In 1934, during the month that Rogers was elected to the state senate, Arthur W. Mitchell was elected in Chicago as the nation's first Democratic

Black member of Congress. On a return visit to Alabama, he saw his mother in Birmingham, where he was honored with a banquet, and later he visited Tuskegee Institute in Macon County. He did not visit John Rogers or Sumter County, and nothing was publicly said of Panola or Geiger, although Mitchell assured white Alabamians that, after being attacked in his Congressional campaign as a tool of white bosses, he made "no apologies for my white friends and . . . only wished I had more."[130]

After his death in 1936, Rogers was remembered fondly—and not merely by his family, Black Belt planters, Big Mules, and their allies in the press. Angie Garrett, a former slave who lived in Gainesville most of her life, had walked there from Mississippi after "the War." As an enslaved person who had been bought and sold as property and whipped at times as if she was considered an untrained animal, Garrett saw that the white planter's paternalism in Gainesville was something of an emancipation from her worst past, a life free of the constant fear of whippings, and a new experience that whenever "I be's hungry . . . along come somebody with something." Garrett remembered Rogers:

> Mr. John Rogers . . . he was what he was and wasn't deceitful . . . He was wild when he was young, but he settled down and was the best white man to the niggers I ever knowed. He'd help me right now if he was livin and seen me wearing this here rag—he sure would.[131]

Rogers willed his extensive land holdings to family members, including Barnes, his youngest son, who was in business with his brother, Max, a Mobile lawyer who served in the state house and one term in the state senate during the time his father was serving in absentia. As the succeeding member of the family in state government, C. M. A. "Max" Rogers led the fight to reinstate a runoff in primary elections in order to weaken candidates such as Bibb Graves and Hugo Black.[132] Barnes continued the family tradition of leasing plantation lands to Black tenant farmers and operating a retail and wholesale business advertised as "The Rogers Brothers—Dealers in Hereford Cattle, Horses, Mules, Turkeys, Hay, Peanuts, Corn."[133]

A small, quiet man possessing his father's physical features but none of his bravado, Barnes was elected mayor of Gainesville during World War II. He received a majority of votes among perhaps only 50 white neighbors who were registered voters in a town of a little less than 400 residents, at least 80 percent of whom were African American and disfranchised. Barnes held the post until 1961.[134]

In 1966, 30 years after his father's death, Barnes evicted 35 African American families from the Rogers' lands in Panola. Some of the families had been living there for two generations—since the time the family patriarch had promoted Panola as a railroad town. In a letter, Barnes told his tenants to "get acreage elsewhere" since he had decided to rent the Rogers land to Hammermill Paper Company for growing trees. The Rogers family could get three times more annual income from the paper company than from their tenants. "The people have gotten too old to farm and there are no younger farmers to take their places," Rogers explained.[135]

There may have been a contributing reason why Black families were evicted. Some were unwilling to sign over to Rogers the checks issued by the U.S. Department of Agriculture as subsidies to farmers who would forego growing certain crops, to create a higher market price for the nation's agricultural products. The government meant to divide subsidy payments between the landowner and the farmers working the land, but Rogers took the entire payments. In one documented instance, a Black farmer accused Rogers of evicting him because he refused to sign over his portion of the government check. Others thought they were targeted for the same reason and because of their local voting rights activities.[136]

It took more than two years before Rogers returned the money he owed Black farmers, and only after their complaints to the U.S. Department of Agriculture and the Civil Rights Commission drew publicity and a government reprimand. But all Black families were evicted from Rogers's land. Many moved away. For those remaining around Panola, SCLC's Albert Turner, activist Lewis Black, and others helped to organize a vegetable cooperative and assisted in establishing in nearby Epes the Federation of Southern Cooperatives.[137]

Despite the 1954 *Brown v. Board of Education* decision outlawing racial segregation in public education, the public schools in Sumter remained segregated and unequal across the 1960s. In 1966, all except four of the 5,082 Black students in Sumter's public schools still attended all-Black schools. Led by Governor George Wallace, the Alabama legislature passed dozens of laws to block school desegregation, and Representative Ira Pruitt, a fitting successor to John Rogers in Sumter County, sponsored a bill empowering the all-white Sumter school board to remove any teacher if the board deemed it "necessary to promote the best interest of the schools"—a clear attempt to keep Black teachers from pushing or aiding desegregation, although the bill made no mention of race.[138]

In 1970, a three-judge federal court ordered the immediate desegregation of Sumter's public schools, and every white student left the system. Many went to the all-white Sumter Academy, which was opened in the same year as the court order. Thirty-five years later, in 2005, only four white students were enrolled in the county's public schools.

That year, less than 17 percent of the school funds in Sumter County came from local taxes. The county's economy remained largely agricultural, but most large landowners grew trees instead of crops. The county's largest private employers were a wood floor company and a hazardous waste management company. On behalf of five Black public school students, civil rights attorneys in Alabama filed a federal class action lawsuit challenging Alabama's tax structure as "a vestige of discrimination inasmuch as the [State] constitutional provisions governing the taxation of property are traceable to, rooted in, and have their antecedents in an original segregative, discriminatory policy."[139] That lawsuit followed a protracted but highly successful attack in federal court challenging the racially discriminatory funding of public colleges and universities in Alabama.[140]

The case challenging Alabama's tax structure took almost five years. During that time, some of Alabama's preeminent historians gave extensive evidence through depositions and testimony, providing U.S. District Judge C. Lynwood Smith Jr., a native of north Alabama, with a doctoral seminar on the state's history of segregation and racial discrimination in public education financing and how Alabama's tax structure established in the 1901 Constitution preserved unequal, segregated education.

In 2011, Smith issued his 850-page opinion. It reviewed the long history of segregation and discrimination and cited not only experts' testimony but also more than 300 academic books and journals. It was an indulgently long, awkwardly written exposition that the professors of history involved in the case surely would have graded unacceptable in length and style, although probably not in its basic analysis.

"The evidence presented at trial illuminates Alabama's twisted racist past: a historical reality that many would like to ignore, but old sins cast long shadows," Smith wrote in perhaps his most memorable phrases after more than 750 pages of turgid prose. "Plaintiffs have shown that Alabama's governing 1901 Constitution was written with clear discriminatory intent and purposes. Its ratification was an outright fraud. Therefore, Sections 214, 215, and 216, unchanged since 1901, are infected by that racist intent."[141]

Smith understood the links between education and voting. He wrote about the origins and development of the Black Belt and documented how its white planters orchestrated and fought to maintain slavery and later disfranchisement to serve their own gains, even if his opinion failed to explicate the multiple ways in which they manipulated the state's political system with and without mention of race to reap vast, numerous economic rewards. His opinion quoted the testimony of historians Wayne Flynt and Robert J. Norrell, recounting the words of Macon County's arch-segregationist legislator Sam Engelhardt, who in 1956 made it plain that he and other large Black Belt landowners feared that "a nigger tax assessor," elected by the county's Black majority, would assess their land at its real, comparable value.[142]

However, Smith did not find racial discrimination in the two amendments to the 1901 Constitution, passed by the legislature and voters in the 1970s that reduced property tax assessments. The amendments grouped agricultural and forest property with "residential property" as one category for taxation at the lowest rate of assessment (15 percent in the 1972 amendment and 10 percent in the 1978 amendment).[143]

Smith found that large landowners in the Black Belt counties had used the 1978 amendment to reduce assessed taxes more than had other counties in the state. It found that the lowest local tax revenues for schools remained in the Black Belt and other majority-Black counties. But Smith disputed the plaintiffs' contention that the Alabama counties with the largest Black populations underutilized local property taxes for public schools, and he could find no "smoking gun"[144] for a racial purpose in the passage and use of the amendments. Black Belt legislators such as Ira Pruitt and Richard "Rick" Manley of Marengo County,[145] who were among the amendments' sponsors, had aligned with the Alabama Farm Bureau and Governor George Wallace to pass the changes. Significantly, they had learned to avoid in public any telltale language of race that Engelhardt and others had used freely before federal courts began citing their public remarks as evidence of racial intent.

These new Black Belt leaders also learned the political lessons that John Rogers and others who preceded them had pioneered in financing Alabama roads. They developed legislation giving their section of the state the lion's share of economic gains from state policies and programs, but they also shared a portion of those economic gains with other counties, especially other rural counties, when necessary to win the day. This alliance became known in Alabama politics as a rural-urban split, but it was in fact another example of the historical patterns in which Black Belt leaders often found the allies they needed, whatever the geography it involved at the time, to control Alabama politics and laws for their own advantage.

In the end, Judge Smith decided his district court could do nothing. "Like it or not, Supreme Court precedent compels a conclusion that the property tax scheme embedded in Alabama's 1901 Constitution and subsequent amendments does not offend the Fourteenth Amendment's Equal Protection Clause . . ." He bemoaned that the "Court's decisions since the early 1970s . . . have given constitutional legitimacy to separate and unequal public schools" and concluded his cathartic opus with quotations from Bob Dylan's 1962 song—"The answer my friend is blowing in the wind, the answer is blowing in the wind."[146]

Of course, there were no winds of change blowing in Sumter County, where the five public school students among the plaintiffs received no improved education or increased education funding. A faint breeze stirred in August 2018 when, after 150 years of segregated schools, Sumter County realized its first racially integrated public school. Serving 300 students, half white and half Black, in kindergarten through the eighth grade, the charter school opened its doors under the sponsorship of the University of West Alabama in Livingston. It continued to operate and grow with an integrated school population, although all other public schools in Sumter County remained 99 percent Black.[147]

An equally compelling coda for Black Belt education was preserved in a set of statistical records of Sumter County. In 2020, the Rogers family still owned more than 6,500 acres in northern Sumter County, primarily around Gainesville and Panola, at a value of more than $8.5 million, according to the state's constitutional methods of assessment.[148] And, yes, the State of Alabama continued to assess that land, as well as all other Black Belt plantations, under the basic framework and sectional advantages of a 1901 Constitution that patrician John A. Rogers helped to establish as enduring law.

John A. Rogers III, in a Civil War reenactment, Gainesville, 1965 (Julia Tutwiler Library Archives and Special Collections, University of West Alabama).

CHAPTER 11

Exceptions to the Rulers

'Women Continue to Lead in Poll Tax Race'

In the years following World War I, Alabama politics became far more uncertain and precarious for Black Belt planters and the cities' Big Mules than over the past 20 years, and much of this jeopardy emanated from changes in the poll tax. Despite their success in clamping down emerging Black aspirations for the right to vote and in blocking the state's approval of the federal amendment for women's right to vote, conservative Democrats could not easily stabilize the state's electorate or election outcomes as an increasing number of white men and women voted.

Alabama's leading conservative Democrat was the first to brush up against this new uncertainty. In April 1920, U.S. Senator Oscar Underwood won the Democratic primary by a margin of less than 8,000 votes. It was the first election when ex-soldiers who served in World War I were allowed to vote without paying a poll tax. In addition, labor unions mobilized their members in numbers never achieved before. More than 25,000 white men paid poll taxes for prior years so they could vote in the 1920 Democratic primary, and most of those new voters came from Birmingham and other labor centers where unions were organizing poll-paying among their members. Never before had so many voters restored their vote by paying back poll taxes. It was more than twice the number of any past election.[1]

Also, Underwood was probably saved from a certain defeat by the fact that ratification of the Nineteenth Amendment became effective in Alabama five months after the 1920 Democratic primary. As an ardent opponent of women's suffrage, he likely would have received few votes among the early women voters. Underwood was thus greatly aided by the legislature's earlier refusal to set up procedures for women to vote in the primary if the federal amendment became law without Alabama's ratification, as happened.

And vote white women of Alabama did when given their first chance—and only for this once—to vote without having to pay a poll tax. In the November 1920 presidential election, women pushed turnout to more than 260,000 voters, almost double the vote total in the May primary. Their huge participation had little effect on the general election's outcome since Alabama's white men and women routinely supported the Democratic candidates nominated in the May primary.[2] But the extraordinary turnout with newly enfranchised voters added an emerging element of uncertainty to Alabama elections.

The unprecedented turnout also demonstrated more clearly than in any previous election the adverse impact of the poll tax. Due to an Alabama attorney general's ruling, women between the ages of 21 and 45 could vote in the November election (and only in November) without paying a poll tax of $1.50. In addition, the state supreme court ruled in April that male war veterans did not have to pay a poll tax to vote. As a result, the 1920 presidential election had the largest voter participation in Alabama history: 145,000 white men and women were permitted to vote without paying a poll tax. The total turnout remained the state's high-water mark until Bibb Graves was reelected governor in the 1934 Democratic primary, but even then the November 1920 election had a higher percentage of voters among the state's eligible white population. Across this time, however, only a few hundred Blacks were able to vote in the state.[3]

A significant number of white women across Alabama paid their poll taxes for the right to vote in the following year and pushed up the total number of poll taxpayers by almost 27,000 in 1921, a year without a statewide election when customarily poll tax payments always dipped. The League of Women Voters campaigned for women to pay their poll taxes, reminding them of local elections in which they might vote and how poll tax stayed in the voter's county to support local schools. At least one north Alabama probate judge went out of his way to notify and assist women whose names on the poll tax rolls did not exactly match their names on the qualified voter lists to insure that the women would not be disqualified due to a lack of an exact match in the records.[4]

The women who paid the tax were able to vote on February 8, 1921, when a small turnout defeated the Black Belt's proposed state constitutional amendment requiring "good character" and an "understanding of the duties of citizenship" as precondition for voting. It is unclear if the women's vote had a major impact in the election, although Greensboro's State Senator Robert B. Evins, who helped lead the Alabama legislature in opposing women's suffrage, set the date of the referendum just late enough so that women had to pay a poll tax to participate. What is known is that Jefferson County supplied the largest number of votes against the Evins Amendment, and it was the county where the largest number of women paid their poll taxes to vote in 1921. Also, war veterans were not required to pay a poll tax to vote on the Evins Amendment since the Alabama Supreme Court did not invalidate the constitutional amendment providing the exemption until four months after the referendum.

Although several factors may have been in play in the defeat of the Evins Amendment, Black Belt and Big Mule leaders could not ignore that a measure they considered essential for political stability failed to pass after Alabama's all-white electorate expanded in unprecedented ways. After the soldiers' exemption was restored with 87 percent of the vote, including a large majority in each of the 67 counties,[5] the conservatives moved to manage the issues as best they could.

In the next legislative session, Representative William Holcombe, a former Mobile County sheriff, introduced legislation for a constitutional amendment making the poll tax exemption for war veterans permanent. Like Walter Jones, Holcombe was no veteran, but, with the support of the Black Belt's legislative leaders, he was eager to raise his profile for patriotism and his popularity back home since both he and his brother, the current county sheriff, were embroiled in political and courtroom battles that led to their federal indictment for managing a nationwide, illegal whiskey smuggling ring out of Mobile.[6]

Holcombe's bill passed unanimously without debate, although Senator

Walter Brower of Birmingham, an ex-soldier wounded in France, changed the date of the referendum so that it would join other proposed constitutional amendments on the same ballot as the 1924 presidential election.[7] Holcombe's bill would have held the referendum separately on December 31, New Year's Eve, when only a tiny fraction of voters would decide its outcome.

The voters passed the permanent exemption with 70 percent of the vote, carrying all but seven counties, and most of those were traditionally Republican-voting counties that often opposed anything the Democratic legislature wanted. An ex-soldier who wanted to vote for the exemption had to pay a poll tax since the prior constitutional exemption had expired before the vote. Perhaps quite a few veterans did pay. The poll tax rolls show that just short of 160,000 persons paid their polls taxes for 1924. It was the highest number recorded in the state in the first quarter of the century.[8]

'We Had to Kill a Few, but We Didn't Have Any Trouble'

The constitutional amendments exempting ex-soldiers from paying poll taxes did not expressly exclude the state's African American men, nearly 26,000 of whom had served in the military during World War I. Walter Jones had promised in 1919 that passage of the first military exemption would not open the way for Black voting since barriers in the "system of registration" would keep them out of the electorate and in their place. But cruder methods had often been employed.

A week after Armistice Day, the Alabama Council of Defense, speaking for leading conservatives such as John Rogers, asked the War Department to delay sending Black soldiers home until all signs of German subversion had been uprooted. The Council's leaders had already prepared local officials to crack down on "any negro soldier strutting about in uniform" and bringing home new attitudes about voting and social equality.

A large number of white Alabamians became fixated by their racialized image of Black soldiers, trained and armed by the U.S. Army, returning home with new demands for political and social rights. Some whites were alarmed by what they perceived as a lack of complete deference among

Black ex-soldiers—"the new feeling of superiority among the negroes" who "believe they have won the war." Other whites were ready to deal in the old Southern way with any Negro soldier seeking to bring an "equality of all colors" home from the War. "I would like to shoot down a few just to see them kick," wrote a white Alabama soldier, "they are getting too egotistical and important for me."[9]

Perhaps the first Black soldier of Alabama to pay the ultimate price for wearing his uniform on his way home was Charles Lewis, who was discharged the day following Armistice. After boarding a south-bound train near his Army base in Kentucky, Lewis and a few other Black soldiers were accosted by a white deputy sheriff who accused them of stealing a few possessions from other African Americans at the train station. Lewis refused to submit to a search and argued with the deputy before leaving the train and his bags. Rather than continue a search for stolen goods, the deputy pursued the ex-soldier, and the two men fought. Lewis had the better of the deputy until he was subdued and arrested by other lawmen and a posse of white citizens. The following night, Lewis was moved for his own safety to the nearby town of Hickman, but a white mob stormed the jail, removed Lewis, and hung him from a roadside tree.[10]

The recently organized NAACP, which frequently published reports of the loyalty and bravery of Black soldiers, condemned the lynching of the soldier who "was prepared, if necessary, to lay down his life to see that . . . America was free from the danger of being subjugated to German domination" but now had been murdered by a mob for conduct that would have meant only slight punishment had he been a white man.[11]

Associated Press reports in several of Alabama's white newspapers highlighted that Lewis had badly beaten the deputy, was wanted for robbery, and tried to shoot the men who captured him, while the ex-soldier was "contending that his uniform made him immune from arrest by a civil officer."[12] The Selma editor reported, "Hickman, Ky., has the distinction of hanging the first negro soldier since the close of hostilities. . . . Lewis claimed his army uniform made him immune from arrest by a civilian officer."[13]

Other Alabama's Black ex-soldiers became targets for white anger and paranoia. A few months after Lewis's hanging, Wilbur Smith, "negro and ex-soldier," was shot to death fifteen miles south of Montgomery after being accused of molesting a white girl, although the NAACP's investigation found no hard evidence of the alleged crime. In other south Alabama towns, African American ex-soldiers were met at train stations before they disembarked and forced by white vigilantes to remove their Army uniforms before setting foot on Alabama soil.

In Birmingham, in a dispute over exact change, a white streetcar conductor killed former sergeant John Green at point-blank range with three shots and badly injured another Black ex-soldier who accompanied Green. In Anniston, former sergeant Edward Caldwell was charged with the murder of a white conductor after a violent confrontation over the payment of a fare.[14] A white man in Tallapoosa County assaulted two African American ex-soldiers, including the Reverend George Thomas, former first lieutenant and military chaplain, because the Black men were still wearing "Uncle Sam's uniform."

At the end of September 1919, three African Americans, two reported as "negro ex-soldiers," were riddled with bullets by a white mob and local lawmen after the victims were accused of murdering a police officer and attacking white women in Montgomery. News stories reported that the mob released two of the Black men in a field so they could try to run for their lives as the white men killed them, apparently for sport, with repeated rifle fire. One of the murdered ex-soldiers was "dressed in the regulation uniform" of the United States Army. The Associated Press wire story provided this explanatory context: "During the past month four white women in Montgomery have been attacked, and in one case, it is alleged that a negro ex-soldier was the guilty person."[15]

Dehumanizing and murdering Black soldiers helped ignite the nation's worst year of interracial strife in modern history. More than 40 race riots took place on both sides of the Mason-Dixon Line in 1919. Less than a week after the Montgomery lynchings, the *Birmingham Age-Herald*'s front page proclaimed in a screaming banner headline: "NEGROES PLAN SLAUGHTER OF WHITES." The secondary headline read, "Wholesale Murder of White People in Arkansas May Be Part of Plot Against South."

It was a story about how poor Black tenant farmers in Arkansas, attempting to organize as a labor union, responded in kind after local white landowners violently tried to stop them.

Reacting to racial tensions in Birmingham, the Jefferson County sheriff prepared for a race war by mounting in public view two machine guns on loan from the state militia. Birmingham's Black newspaper editor Oscar Adams worried that his city "was never more filled with hysteria . . . than at this hour."[16] No one was brought before a court of law in Alabama for lynching any Black man, in or out of an Army uniform, in 1919.

In the aftermath of such a horrendous year, six of Birmingham's middle-class Black leaders demonstrated courage and dedication when they signed a public letter in the first month of 1920 making a carefully worded "appeal for the registration of colored voters." They reiterated the sacrifices and service of Black soldiers as well as the patriotism and loyalty of Birmingham's Black workers who had kept local mills and mines working overtime for the war effort.

They asked only for the "intelligent, industrious, and honest negro to register" and assured white readers of the *Birmingham News* that they were "more interested in the election of high-class white men to govern us locally than we are interested in national politics." In other words, they sought to register in order to help high-class white Democrats rule, not to support Republican presidential candidates. In an ironic phrase, the Black men concluded by asking for "equity and justice for the negro"[17]—the very terms by which the 1891 state law effectively robbed African American schoolchildren of their equal allotment of public funds.

The *Birmingham News* editor responded sympathetically, but cautiously. In a lengthy editorial he argued that recognizing a few "good negroes" as voters would lessen the city's race antagonism. But in the end, he hedged his bet: "This is a big matter, and the best brains, the strongest businessmen of Birmingham should deliberate on it."[18]

In the following weeks and months, Alabama's white business leaders and public officials offered no sign that they were ready to expand voter registration to African Americans—and certainly not to ex-soldiers. In his newspaper, Oscar Adams attempted to rally interest among Birmingham's middle-class African Americans to register and pay poll taxes, and a few Black veterans in the state tried to qualify. But they discovered that the new chapters of the NAACP and other Black groups could provide no effective challenge to their rejection, and the American Legion balked at accepting segregated Black chapters as a formal part of the organization.[19]

The white community's obsessive fear of Black soldiers did subside, but there was no basic shift in race relations, and the specter of racial violence remained commonplace. A week after the *Birmingham News* editorial, an African American ex-soldier was lynched in Florala, a small town straddling the Florida-Alabama border. Later in the year, Edward Caldwell, the ex-sergeant who had fought with a white Anniston streetcar operator, was executed by Alabama in what the national NAACP called a "legalized lynching." A few months later, Alabama daily newspapers reported a race riot in Oconee, Florida, where two white men and six Blacks were killed in a melee that started in a dispute over payment of a poll tax and ended with most African Americans leaving town.[20]

Will Alexander, the white director of the Commission on Interracial Cooperation, established in Atlanta amid the tide of racial violence, remembered years afterwards a white minister who explained how there were no lingering racial tensions after Black soldiers returned home: "No," the minister replied, "we had to kill a few of them, but we didn't have any trouble."[21]

'AN EFFORT BY INDIANA AND OHIO TO TELL ALABAMA WHAT TO DO'

Black ex-soldiers also became political scapegoats in congressional debate over providing supplemental pay and benefits to war veterans, many of whom, regardless of race, struggled in a post-war recession. Many Southern white leaders opposed direct "bonus" payments to veterans because the federal funds would go to both Blacks and whites. Southern businessmen and large farmers argued that a bonus to Black veterans would endanger the region's agriculture since Black ex-soldiers "would stop working until the money was spent." A congressional candidate's campaign manager warned a white women's club in Anniston that the bonus would leave their homes without maids, servants, and clean laundry since the Black veterans' wives also "would quit work until the last dollar was spent."[22]

At the same time, across Alabama white business leaders and local officials were falling over each other competing for the site of a new federal Veterans Bureau hospital for disabled and injured Black ex-soldiers. After Tuskegee was selected, some white-owned Alabama businesses enjoyed large federal contracts for the hospital's construction and services, while state officials insisted that only white men could serve as the hospital's administrators and doctors. The legislature already had enacted a bill to protect white womanhood by prohibiting white women from working as nurses in any hospital where Black men were treated.[23]

Despite it all, Black veterans and their families steadfastly pursued a more democratic South, especially as the state's economy emerged from the post-war recession. In Mobile and Birmingham, new groups organized to support ex-soldiers, ostensibly for job training and self-help. Ohio Bell, a young disabled veteran from Barbour County, was attending school in Birmingham when he established the Ex-Soldiers Cooperative Association. It quickly attracted an active group of men and women who were apparently ready for change. In October 1923, the Association's members, including both former soldiers and relatives, mounted a letter-writing campaign to the new Republican president, Calvin Coolidge.[24]

"I am a law abiding citizen of the U.S.A.," wrote Timothy Percy Patterson, a 23-year-old native of south Mississippi who was drafted as a student and served as an orderly at a battlefield hospital in France. "I am yet fighting for my Constitutional rights," he declared in asking Coolidge for assistance. "I am a member of the Ex-Soldiers Cooperative Association and beg that you give all petitions coming from this said organization every consideration possible."[25]

Others were more specific. Association member Lula Murry, a 55-year-old widow of a mattress maker, had two brothers who fought in the war; one died. She told the president she was "denied the constitutional rights in article XIV and XV" when she "was turn down at the Board of Registrars of Jefferson County." She also noted, "I being a woman the 19th amendment of the constitution of U.S." gave her another right to vote.[26] Another veteran, Arthur Ivey, told Coolidge that he was denied "his rights and privileges" as a citizen when the local board denied him a "voting certificate." He added: "We are segregated on account of race . . . and the Constitution forbids anyone being segregated on account of race or color."[27]

The White House stamped "Respectfully Referred for Acknowledgement and Consideration" on each letter and sent them to the Justice Department where they were dutifully filed. It remains unclear if or why the Association's members believed their letters could prompt a positive response from any branch of the federal government since each had done its part over decades in allowing Alabama and the South to establish and enforce white supremacy in law and fact. Perhaps they remembered a speech that Coolidge's predecessor, Republican President Warren G. Harding, made in Birmingham two years earlier. Before a huge segregated crowd celebrating the city's fiftieth anniversary, Harding declared, "I would say, let the black man vote when he is fit. Prohibit the white man from voting when he is unfit." According to the press reports, the proclamation received "loud and lusty cheers" from the Negro sections and stone-silent shock among whites.[28]

The 1923 letters were probably written to the White House simply because there was no better option than a new, untested president. Certainly Black Alabamians had no reason to believe they would find a sympathetic audience in Montgomery or within the county and city governments. In the months preceding Harding's speech in 1921, Governor Thomas Kilby called out the state troops who forcibly crushed a strike by the United Mine Workers, most of whom were African Americans. Afterwards, Birmingham's industrial leaders blacklisted the striking miners and prevented them from being hired in any local mine or other industry.

Probate judges across the state followed the practice, if not the public style, of Elmore County's judge who advertised that "All White Ex-Servicemen" could get a certificate exempting them from payment of the poll tax. Underscoring such practices, the State Democratic Executive Committee had also voted unanimously in 1922 that "no negro can receive a ballot" in its statewide primary election.[29]

In the summer of 1923, the Ku Klux Klan organized hundreds of cars in a caravan to Tuskegee, where Kluxers registered their opposition to hiring Black doctors to treat Black ex-soldiers at the new veterans' hospital. "White People of Ala. Won't Stand Negro Personnel," read the headline in the *Birmingham Reporter*, the city's Black newspaper. And, barely more than a month before the Association members wrote their letters, the Klan held a massive public induction ceremony in Jefferson County involving five thousand hooded members.[30]

Undeterred, the Ex-Soldiers Association's members, male and female, continued to organize. President Ohio Bell billed the organization as the Black man's American Legion and assured the white public that its primary work was to help disabled veterans. Bell and Jerry Merriweather, a former coal miner who apparently learned new skills in the Army, enlarged the Association's role to assist all Black veterans once Congress passed the Bonus Act, over a Coolidge veto, promising supplemental, long-term staggered pay to veterans, essentially in the form of an insurance policy.

The organization expanded rapidly. The *Birmingham News* began publicizing Bell's speeches, and, while he was only a private in the Army, he became a leader of Black veterans, including joining a small committee to plan African American participation in Birmingham's parade celebrating Armistice Day in 1924. By the following summer, the Association had an office on the sixth floor of the Negro Masonic Lodge Building, a hub of the city's influential Black businesses such as Atlanta Life Insurance and North Carolina Mutual Life. On the building's marquee, Merriweather was listed as the Association's "grand secretary."[31]

In June 1925, Bell announced the Ex-Soldiers Association had members in five adjoining counties and was cooperating with state and federal offices of the Veterans Bureau and was "already linked up with 28 states of the Union" to assist Black veterans. The Association now saw itself as a national organization, although Bell proudly called himself "a product of Alabama." The subject of one of his speeches, "Duty of the Cooperative Organization to Elevate Civilization," suggested that the Black Belt-born Bell and his Association had boundless ambitions.[32]

During the same year, Birmingham's Black community demonstrated a renewed interest in voting. With public support from *Birmingham*

Above, Ohio Bell, shown on a stock certificate of the Ex-Soldiers Investment Industrial Co. Right, Indiana Little, from a news clipping in the Pittsburgh Courier, *January 1926.*

Reporter editor Oscar Adams, several African Americans formed the Negro Non-Partisan Political League to promote paying poll tax, registration, and voting. Lula Murry, now a member of the Ex-Soldiers Association's national executive committee, organized renewed efforts for voter registration among the group's members and her neighbors. In accordance with Alabama law, the Jefferson County Registrar's office was closed throughout the summer, but when it reopened in early January 1926, Murry and at least a dozen others attempted unsuccessfully to qualify and register. She immediately complained to the Justice Department in Washington, which forwarded her letter to the Republican U.S. Attorney in Birmingham.[33]

Two weeks later, on the day before the Registrar's office opened, the Ex-Soldiers' Association published in the *Birmingham News* a long petition to Governor "Plain Bill" Brandon under Ohio Bell's signature complaining that Association members were denied the right to register by the Board of Registrars and "said grievances have been going on for two years or more." Bell had traveled to Montgomery earlier and presented the petition personally to the governor. It asserted that the Association now had members in practically every state and that its ex-soldiers were "exempt from poll tax." It declared, "We see no reason why the said Board of Jefferson County should deny us of our constitutional rights as a Colored American Citizen."[34]

On the following day, Monday, more than two dozen of the Association's members, mostly women, returned to the Registrar's office in the basement of the county courthouse. Indiana Little, a 29-year-old member and a sister and wife of War veterans, refused to leave unless the Registrar certified her application as a qualified voter. "I am a free born citizen of America," Little declared, according to accounts from both Black and white newspapers, "and by the Fourteenth Amendment of the U.S. Constitution I shall not be denied the right to vote because of race, color or sex, and I will not move until I have been registered."[35]

Little was arrested and taken by a deputy sheriff to the county jail where she was booked on charges of vagrancy and resisting arrest. (If convicted of vagrancy, Little would by law be disqualified from voting.) She was later released after the Association presumedly paid for a $300 peace bond that required Little "to keep the peace for twelve months" or until her case was adjudicated. The arrest made news across the nation. The headlines of Oscar Adams's newspaper told Black Birmingham that "Woman's Color Causes Assault" and its news story related how Little was "manhandled," "struck" by the jail warden, and "roughly handled at that place."[36] The *Birmingham News* and the other white newspapers made no mention of Little's mistreatment, although they did report on the group's demand for "what they called their 'rights.'"[37]

In the days that followed, the registrar issued a statement suggesting that Little and others did not understand that their applications had to be reviewed by the three members of the Board of Registrars to determine who qualified as a voter under Alabama law. "Every negro or white man must do the same," he said, noting in the public statement that the registrars had qualified African Americans in the past.[38]

The Association members sent new complaints to the Justice Department, and they included a sworn affidavit by Little in which she stated that while in jail she was "beat over the head unmercifully . . . and forced upon the officer's demands to yield to him in an unbecoming manner."[39] Bell reiterated his public call for upholding the constitutional rights of members of the Association and republished in the Birmingham and Montgomery newspapers its petition to the governor. Brandon told reporters that a Negro man had appeared in his office a week earlier with a petition about voter registration, but the governor had not read it. He also told the press that he had no authority in the matter but every assurance that local registrars would act according to state law.[40]

Bell and his associates also sent a petition to President Coolidge and to both houses of Congress. A Republican senator from North Dakota inquired about the incident with the U.S. attorney general, and the Justice Department undertook a formal investigation in which an FBI agent interviewed Murry and Merriweather at the Association's offices. Both stated that their members met the state's qualification for voting but had been turned down over the last few years.[41]

The Justice Department took no action. The Alabama-born FBI agent dismissed the Association as a bunch of "troublemakers in exciting the mass of colored people to vote." The Republican U.S. Attorney in Birmingham, Charles Kennamer, was an experienced, adroit politician who in 1920 lost a contested congressional election in north Alabama by barely more than a thousand votes. But Kennamer had decided that political patronage from a Republican president would elevate his rising star more than any attempt to expand the number of Alabama's Black voters, even if they were likely to be Republican votes. "I practically know," he wrote the attorney general, "that such power and discretion is very frequently exercised in a highly biased and unfair manner." But, realizing the nature of Alabama's white politics and the federal courts' willingness to disregard the

Reconstruction Amendments, he added, "I know of no action this office could take . . . to rectify such practices."[42]

Indiana Little's case was postponed indefinitely. The peace bond ensured she would not risk any more disturbance, else the bond money would be lost and she could be fined and charged court costs—more money than she and her husband, a janitor, could afford, especially with two children at home. At the same time, the new Negro voters league lost momentum, and no meetings were publicized in 1926. Oscar Adams continued to urge African Americans to go to the courthouse to register as a qualified voter—repeatedly suggesting, as he did after Little's arrest, that there were "numbers of Negroes in Birmingham who can qualify for registration, will be registered . . . if they would try."[43]

Bell's strategy around Little's arrest catapulted his group and himself into the public spotlight, but it also began the collapse of the Ex-Soldiers Cooperative Association. Before the end of 1926, Bell incorporated a second organization, changing the middle name from "Cooperative" to "Progressive," and in early 1927 he formed a third group. None of this legal maneuvering indicated organizational growth; more likely, it was an attempt for the association to evade the recent past—or worse. In 1928, Bell was arrested by federal authorities. He pled guilty to mail fraud for representing himself as an agent of the federal Veterans Bureau in sales pitches regarding ex-soldier's government benefits. Merriweather pled guilty to a lesser federal crime, and both were sent to federal prison.[44]

Shortly after Little's arrest, the editor of the *Gadsden Times* decided he knew what the incident meant amid Alabama's rock-solid white supremacy. "Indiana Little, negro, raised a disturbance when she sought to be registered as a voter . . . Ohio Bell, head of a negro ex-servicemen's organization took up the cry . . . Out of it all there is little to be seen except an effort by Indiana and Ohio to tell Alabama what to do."[45] Indeed, while the editor could not imagine Black folks in his own state developing a concerted strategy to spur change, he was certain that Northern politics and the federal courts would allow white Alabama to do damn well whatever it pleased in voting and politics. Or so it seemed before the Great Crash of 1929.

'THE WEAKEST AND POOREST CANNOT RULE MORE WISELY THAN THE STRONGEST . . .'

Alabama's white politics began to change even before the nation's economic collapse. After 1924, for example, the number paying poll taxes started to decline, but the number of Alabamians voting began to climb. From 1924 to 1926, the number of poll taxpayers dropped by nearly 30,000, but the number of voters jumped by almost 60,000. This pattern persisted into the 1930s and clearly indicated that the exemptions were opening up the franchise to a larger white voting constituency.[46]

This unusual phenomenon emerged in 1926 probably because larger numbers of white ex-soldiers began to use their permanent exemption from the poll tax. In preceding years, the exemption had been temporary. Also, there had been considerable confusion surrounding when and how the exemption applied within the state's often-changing, complex rules and the dates for how and when to qualify. In addition, some county officials did not always understand how certifying a white veteran as exempt from the poll tax worked. And many returned veterans had needs more important than figuring out poll taxes.

By 1926, these conditions had changed: the war veteran's exemption became permanent, the recession abated, and county officials were clear about how a white veteran could receive a certificate of permanent exemption. There also appear to have been more veterans who could use an exemption than most assumed at the time. Alabama governors and the state's newspapers often estimated that close to 50,000 white veterans from Alabama served in the World War I, but this number included only those drafted or inducted. It did not include those who enlisted or volunteered. More recent compilations suggest that the total was closer to 83,000 white veterans.[47]

In 1926 Alabama voters elected Bibb Graves as governor and Hugo Black as U.S. senator, the most progressive statewide officials since Populism. In an apparent paradox, both men also were endorsed privately by leaders of the Ku Klux Klan, which during this era reached its most visible, influential role in Alabama. Some scholars gave the Klan full credit for Graves's and Black's elections and took the historical contradictions as examples of the candidates' adroit, political expediency. But in 2004, historian Samuel L. Webb published an analysis illuminating how "the number of voters loyally supporting the Klan ticket was much smaller than we have been led to believe" and how in a ranked-choice primary election the two candidates' victories were more a result of "the existence of multiple candidates representing every major faction and interest group in state politics" than a Klan lock on the electorate.[48]

Indeed, Black referred to his supporters during his campaign as a coalition of "Dry-Protestant-Progressive Voters," in which he included veterans. Graves and Black were the only WWI veterans in their respective races, and both touted this fact as they promised to address the needs of ex-soldiers. In fact, Graves was best known across the state for his military service and had been elected by veterans as state leader of the American Legion.[49] Therefore, while it is unknown how many white veterans used their exemptions from the poll tax to vote for change in 1926, the fact remains that in the first statewide election when veterans enjoyed a permanent poll tax exemption, a coalition of Alabama voters elected two candidates who won after campaigning against Big Mules and Black Belt planters.

The poll tax became an accepted political fact of life across most of the next ten years, although the all-white League of Women Voters, with 16 local chapters, continued to include poll tax revision or repeal as a top legislative priority. Graves did little to remove it. He campaigned on wresting power from the Black Belt through reapportionment, and his administration focused on increasing school funding for all white children, ending convict leasing, and expanding the highway program. These programs required revenues, which the poll tax generated, although less than two percent of the state's education budget. "Every dollar should be made to count," Graves insisted, and apparently that meant keeping the poll tax.[50]

It remained a source of conflict and concern. Republicans in north Alabama's St. Clair County attacked the poll tax in state court after a Democratic ex-soldier challenged a local Republican officeholder for failure to pay poll taxes. But the Alabama Supreme Court unanimously dismissed the argument that the veteran's exemption created an equal protection violation by requiring only some persons to pay.[51] After the legislature reorganized the state militia, it became widely known that "every officer . . . musician and private in the Alabama National Guard" enjoyed a poll tax exemption but not Alabama men serving in the regular Army. The 1901 Constitution had grandfathered the exemption for only the state's military personnel, not members of the U.S. Army, and it fell to the Alabama attorney general to insist that probate judges enforce the rule.[52]

Naturalized citizens also were ensnared by the poll tax laws. The attorney general ruled that a naturalized citizen had to pay a poll tax for each year they had lived in Alabama after reaching the age of 21—even for all years before they became citizens and eligible to vote.[53] Of course, had this ruling been applied to Alabama women, white or Black, who became eligible to vote in 1920, they would have had to pay a cumulative $1.50 for each year since their 21st birthday.

Once the Great Depression hit Alabama and unemployment became rampant, paying the poll tax was considerably more difficult for most Alabamians, and the cumulative tax for prior years became prohibitive. In 1932, a Mobile state representative proposed a bill limiting liability for past poll taxes to only three years, but it failed to get a vote. In the next session, groups of unemployed workers and tenant farmers filed formal petitions with the legislature seeking economic and political changes, including abolition of the poll tax and "equal treatment of negroes." No such action was considered in a state government headed by Governor Benjamin Meek Miller, a native of Wilcox County and leader of the Black Belt/Big Mules political alliance, who won election in 1930.[54]

The poll tax became a major campaign issue in 1934 when Montgomery Circuit Judge Leon McCord, a vocal supporter of the Roosevelt administration's New Deal, raised it as a primary part of his platform in the race for governor. McCord called for limiting poll taxes to no more than three years regardless of how many prior years a person had failed to pay, to "make the election speak the will of our entire people."[55] The issue struck a deep chord since, five years after the stock market crash, most adults in Alabama found paying "back poll taxes was simply beyond their capacity unless they valued voting more than they did shoes, flour, or plowshares."[56] The other major gubernatorial candidates, former governor Bibb Graves and Frank M. Dixon (Birmingham's Big Mule candidate), added the reform to their platforms. It also became a frequent pledge of candidates for the state legislature.[57]

Among the first bills introduced in the Alabama House of Representatives during the 1935 session was a proposed constitutional amendment reducing payments for delinquent poll taxes. It was sponsored by a freshman, Theophilus Eugene "Bull" Connor, a sports announcer whose widespread name recognition from radio broadcasts of Birmingham Barons baseball games helped him win a seat in the legislature. The bill was quickly approved by a house committee and within a month was on the calendar for a vote.[58]

The house's Black Belt delegation, led by Representative Alf Tunstall, claimed the bill would open the way for huge gains in Black voting, "as if white supremacy in Alabama would come to an end with the passage," remarked a disbelieving Birmingham columnist.[59] Tunstall assembled enough votes to block the bill since a constitutional amendment required a three-fifths majority for passage, and 59 "yeas" were five shy of enough.[60]

Graves had been reelected as governor and decided to honor his campaign promise. He appeared before a joint session and urged legislators to pass his agenda of reforms, including the poll tax bill. He offered to accept a Black Belt amendment restricting the benefits of the bill to persons who were "qualified voters" in 1932 in order to "close the door against any possible up-set of our franchise provisions"—in essence, to keep the door closed to voting by most African Americans, only a few hundred of whom were registered to vote during the last presidential election.[61]

Black Belt representatives were joined by some north Alabama legislators in urging defeat of the Connor bill. John A. Lusk, a Gadsden attorney who often sided with the Big Mules, argued the bill would "strike down all safeguards and destroy the poll tax as a revenue measure for schools." The representative from Franklin County warned the bill would "cheapen politics in Alabama" by enfranchising white and Black Republicans in his area. But, with Graves's influence, H.B. 8 passed.[62]

The senate's Black Belt chairman of the Committee on Constitutional

Revisions had enough votes to kill the Connor bill in his committee since a majority of members were from his section's counties. But a north Alabama senator petitioned to force the committee to report the bill, and the chairman released the bill for a floor vote. That meant only one thing: Black Belt senators had the votes to defeat the poll tax reform. Wilcox County's Senator J. Miller Bonner declared, "Let's put it out now, forever and ever," and the senate killed it in a vote of 13 "yeas" and 14 "nays."[63]

Eight senators did not vote on the bill. Had they voted "yea," the bill would have passed with 21 votes, the necessary three-fifths majority of the 35-member chamber. The defeat was yet again an example of how Black Belt leaders blocked proposed suffrage changes by enlisting some members to do no more than walk, not vote, during the roll call of "yeas" and "nays." In this case, the eight included four Black Belt senators and four primarily from south Alabama's Wiregrass section.[64] They were able to have it both ways. They played their part in defeating the bill and escaped any public record revealing to voters back home that they helped kill poll tax reform.

One of the four Black Belt senators who did not vote on this occasion was actually not in Montgomery. Senator John Rogers of Sumter was gravely ill at home in Gainesville. His absence counted just the same in helping to defeat the poll tax bill, and it turned out to be his last dutiful act of public service to the Black Belt he loved and worked to preserve. Rogers died ten days after the senate vote.

In a special session the following year, another Jefferson County representative introduced the same poll tax bill with strong, vocal support from the state's labor unions. But after three roll calls the unions and north Alabama advocates fell short of the house's necessary 64 votes. Joe Poole of Butler County led the Black Belt opposition, claiming once more that the proposal would result in a huge increase in Negro registration. As in the prior session, the majority-Black counties found a handful of allies from north Alabama and the Wiregrass area—just enough to kill the bill.[65]

The *Montgomery Advertiser* also opposed any poll tax change, although two years earlier it had supported Big Mule gubernatorial candidate Frank Dixon when he joined the call for reform. The *Advertiser*'s editor wrote that eliminating the back taxes for voting would "invest the pauperized thousands of our people with the balance of power in Alabama politics." Disgusted with New Deal policies, the newspaper complained, "The dole is here to stay. The *Advertiser* is against any plan that would make the dispossessed the rulers of those who pay the cost of their maintenance . . . The weakest and poorest cannot rule more wisely than the strongest and most thrifty."[66]

The *Advertiser* had good reason to worry. In Birmingham, conservative Congressman George Huddleston lost his seat to Luther Patrick, another Birmingham radio personality, whose strong support from labor provided him the Democratic nomination despite allegations that he was nothing but a puppet for local labor leader William Mitch. The latter's union believed that "a poll tax is discrimination in favor of the rich and the denying of the vote to Negro people."[67] The 1936 elections also produced a landslide victory in Alabama and across the nation for a second term of President Franklin D. Roosevelt, who declared he was ready to address the problems of "one-third of a nation ill-housed, ill-clad, and ill-nourished." His remedy was to build a more muscular federal government governed in a democracy that "depends not on the absence of power, but lodging it with those whom the people can change or continue through an honest and free system of election."[68]

'It keeps . . . illiterate people and them that's inclined to be radical away from the polls'

At the end of 1937, the U.S. Supreme Court issued a unanimous ruling that included its newest member, Justice Hugo Black of Alabama, upholding the constitutionality of the poll tax. The American Civil Liberties Union had challenged Georgia's poll tax, which also had a cumulative feature, but Justice Pierce Butler wrote: " To make payment of poll taxes a prerequisite of voting is not to deny any privilege or immunity protected by the Fourteenth Amendment" since the tax was a long-standing privilege of voting conferred by the states.[69]

The high court's decision was hardly noticed by Alabama newspapers, but in 1938 Southern liberals in Washington and the Roosevelt administration began exploring ways to build a case and a constituency that would enable passage of federal legislation to ban the poll tax in the South. In February, Lucy Randolph Mason, Southern director of public relations for a newly created coalition of labor unions, the Congress of Industrial Organizations (CIO), informed First Lady Eleanor Roosevelt that the "only hope for progressive democracy in the South lies in the lower economic groups, particularly the wage earner. Yet this is the group so largely disfranchised by the poll-tax requirements in eight Southern states."[70]

The Women's Division of the Democratic National Committee (DNC) moved quickly to spotlight and organize Alabama. In April, the group held its Southern regional meeting in Montgomery, where speakers attempted to energize hundreds of middle-class Democratic women to increase their active support of Roosevelt's economic programs. In October, the Women's Division held another large, well-publicized meeting in Birmingham to mobilize hundreds women across the state. Several Democratic dignitaries, including the First Lady, joined speakers in urging women to expand democracy as a means of preserving the Democratic Party's control of national politics and the federal government.[71]

"People the country over are looking into the meaning of democracy in ways they have NOT done for years," declared Ellen Woodward, assistant director of the job-creating Works Progress Administration (WPA).[72] The assistant director of the Women's Division, May Thompson Evans, made a more direct case for expanding democracy in Alabama and the South. She explained that the rules of the national Democratic Party were changing, and the party would begin apportioning the number of delegates at the Democratic National Convention on the basis of the number of a state's Democratic votes cast in preceding elections. This meant Alabama Democratic women needed to work harder to "get out our votes" and to increase the number of Democrats who could and would vote.[73]

"One handicap here in Alabama," Evans ventured, "is the poll tax requirement. At the risk of touching a sore spot, I am going to say you should get rid of it. And let no one raise the race question about it. North Carolina, Louisiana, Florida, and Arkansas have abolished the poll tax . . . and there have been no disastrous results."[74]

A month later, the Southern Conference for Human Welfare (SCHW) held its organizational meeting in Birmingham. It gathered Mrs. Roosevelt and others from her husband's administration with many prominent Southern liberals, Black and white, who were ready to consolidate the president's landslide 1936 victory into an ongoing force for change across Alabama and the South. Earlier, the CIO's Lucy Mason arranged for Joseph Gelders to visit Mrs. Roosevelt in Hyde Park, where he also met the president. Gelders was a physics professor who became a full-time activist after being savagely beaten by U.S. Steel company thugs in Birmingham. In their meeting, President Roosevelt apparently suggested the young Alabama Jew "undertake a crusade to abolish the poll tax . . . in the interest of democratic government."[75]

The SCHW conference agenda was much broader and more ambitious than eliminating the poll tax and included issues such as labor rights, racial justice, education, economic security, and a federal minimum wage. Also, in addition to prominent liberals and New Deal elected officials, the hundreds who jammed into the Birmingham Municipal Auditorium included members of the communist party, the socialist party, and a string of other groups who sought far more radical change.

In speaking to local groups before the SCHW conference, Eleanor Roosevelt said, "The South's problems cannot be considered merely the South's problems. They are the nation's problems. We must get away from sectionalism."[76] Once she arrived at the SCHW conference, Mrs. Roosevelt was informed she would have to move since she was sitting in the "colored section." Earlier Birmingham police commissioner "Bull" Connor, who had given up his seat in the legislature to run for the city office, led a gaggle of policemen into the auditorium requiring the audience to segregate by race as required by local ordinance. In an act of mild defiance, Mrs. Roosevelt had her chair moved so that it was "facing the whole group."[77]

Alabama's native son, Supreme Court Justice Hugo Black, concluded the conference during an evening banquet where he was honored with the group's first award, the Jefferson Medal. He delivered an address extensively quoting the "dynamic philosophy of Thomas Jefferson" in an attempt to place SCHW's mission and future in line with the founding principles of the South and the Democratic Party. On voting, Black declared that

Jefferson "believed in the wide participation by the people in the election of public representatives" and quoted the man Southern Democrats revered as the father of their party: "I am not among those who fear the people. Let every man who fights or plays, exercise his just and equal right to vote."[78]

Many of the South's newspapers and Southern politicians begged to differ. After the meeting, they concluded that the group's attitude and resolutions on race, labor, voting and social welfare—and their willingness to allow radical groups to participate—meant the Southern Conference for Human Welfare was more in line with socialism and communism than with their Jefferson. Most Southern elected officials who attended the meeting, including those from Alabama, soon disavowed or broke off connection with the group.[79]

SCHW decided its first program of action would be a campaign to abolish the poll tax in Southern states, with a two-pronged strategy of pushing federal legislation and filing a second federal court action. Gelders considered this approach much more likely to produce "immediate success" than going state-by-state. He failed initially to find anyone in Congress from the South to sponsor a bill,[80] and SCHW's national campaign began primarily as an effort to convince representative and senators from outside the South that it was in the national interest to ban voter restrictions within the South.

Another Alabamian, Virginia Foster Durr, became the vice-chair of SCHW's anti-poll tax campaign, which in time merged into a separate coalition of national organizations called the National Committee for the Abolition of the Poll Tax. Durr also was from Birmingham and was the sister-in-law of Justice Black. She moved to Washington with her husband Clifford, who took a job in the Roosevelt administration, while she became a volunteer with the DNC's Women's Division before she met Gelders in Birmingham and became one of SCHW's founding members.[81]

Durr joined others in using both Southern charm and native intelligence to try to persuade Southern members of Congress, especially those who remained avid New Deal Democrats, to publicly support the anti-poll tax bill sponsored by Los Angeles Representative Lee Geyer, whose

Governor Frank Dixon (ADAH).

Washington office became anti-poll tax headquarters. But it soon became obvious that while Alabamians were leading the campaign, they would depend on others outside the state and region to make the federal ban happen.

In Alabama, Frank Dixon, a Birmingham attorney and longtime ally in the Black Belt/Big Mule coalition, was elected governor in 1938. Bibb Graves could not succeed himself, and Dixon, a veteran who lost a leg in World War I, ran on a progressive platform including reapportionment of the legislature, abolishing the poll tax, and "equalization" of school funds. The primary race became an oddity in which "peckerwood clubs" formed across the state in support of their "one-legged peckerwood," who was in fact a cuff-linked corporate lawyer. Chauncey Sparks, the Black Belt candidate from Barbour County, withdrew from a runoff with Dixon only a few days after his campaign manager, Emmet Hildreth of Greene County, promised voters the "fight against machine politics has just begun."[82] Apparently, the Black Belt/Big Mule machine informed Sparks to wait another four years.

As part of a seven-point plan of reform, Dixon asked the legislature to adopt a new law requiring no more than three years back payment for the poll tax to qualify to cast a ballot. But Black Belt legislators expressed confidence that they had enough allies to block both reapportionment and the poll tax. They were not wrong. Within two months, Dixon abandoned his fight against the poll tax, according to the Black press, "under pressure from Black Belt landlords." Even a bill seeking a referendum to provide a poll tax exemption to the widows and wives of war veterans could not get to a floor vote.[83]

Birmingham Age-Herald columnist John Temple Graves II, a "mildly liberal" segregationist, continued to call for changing the poll tax, as did writers in other newspapers. "Sense, not dollars, should be the prerequisite for voting in the South," Graves argued. "In other words, an educational requirement rather than a poll tax." Two Southern political scientists writing a book on Alabama government explained the politics of the issue. "It is a fight between North Alabama and South Alabama . . . The agrarian leaders fear the enfranchisement of the laborers in the cities."[84]

The *Tuscaloosa News* editor, who often defended the Black Belt, was willing to openly address the increasingly loud calls for expanding democracy, as the nation moved closer to involvement in a second world war to stop Hitler's racist totalitarianism. "This newspaper believes in white supremacy, and it believes that the poll tax is one of the essentials for the preservation of white supremacy. It does not believe in a democracy with a little 'd' because it knows this country never has had such a democracy and never will have such a democracy as long as white supremacy is preserved."[85]

Few Alabama editors were willing to disavow democracy in such blanket terms, but demands for both abolishing the poll tax and reapportioning the legislature were increasingly perceived across south Alabama—not merely in the Black Belt and majority-Black counties—as an attempt by big city politicians and devout urban New Dealers to grab political power away from the state's rural areas. At the same time, even newspaperman Graves joined a host of Alabama political leaders opposing congressional action on the poll tax, likening it to federal anti-lynching proposals.[86]

Governor Dixon led the charge against federal legislation. He continued to claim publicly that he wanted the poll tax changed, while loudly opposing any federal law attempting to override the state's right to keep the poll tax. After the country entered World War II, Dixon testified before a U.S. Senate committee, opposing a bill banning the poll tax now sponsored by a Southerner, newly elected Florida Senator Claude Pepper, a native of Alabama's Clay County. In his last year in office, Dixon claimed the federal bill was spreading "seeds of disunity and disaster" during wartime and blamed the 1938 Birmingham SCHW meeting for arousing a "tremendous storm" of "outside interference" that "prevented me from eliminating the cumulative feature of the Alabama poll tax." He assured the committee that the poll tax would be abolished if Alabama was left to govern its own affairs.[87]

In 1942, Dixon also urged Congress to defeat an amendment to the Soldiers Voting Act that would exempt all men and women in the Armed Forces from paying a poll tax when they voted by absentee ballot under procedures authorized by the Act. The governor claimed the measure would invade "state sovereignty." Congress not only passed the bill with a poll tax ban in the upcoming federal election, but a month later the House approved banning the poll taxes permanently in future federal elections.[88]

Only nine Southern House members voted for passage of the federal ban and only one from Alabama, Birmingham Congressman Luther Patrick, who was a lame duck after losing in the May primary after only one term. "We hope Luther sold out to the 'liberals' at a decent price," wrote Hamner Cobbs, who had replaced William E. W. Yerby as the hard-hitting, plain-speaking voice of the Black Belt at the *Greensboro Watchman.* "We don't like to see any man deliver himself, body and soul, without getting ample compensation for it."[89]

In 1943, Chauncey Sparks succeeded Dixon. Called by his opponents the "Bourbon of Barbour," he was elected primarily because he was the only known candidate on the ballot after former governor Bibb Graves, a virtual shoo-in, died as the primary campaign commenced. In the legislature, Sparks had been one of the few who voted in 1919 against the first war veterans' poll tax exemption—among other things. "He voted against the woman's right to vote; he voted against giving the right to vote to the soldier boys; he voted against appropriating a million dollars for free schools in Alabama," proclaimed "Big Jim" Folsom, an unknown upstart who lost to Sparks during the 1942 primary in which the Black Belt conservative seemed to have promised voters nothing but the certainty that they knew the name of the man who would win.[90]

The new governor said nothing about the poll tax in his maiden address to the state legislature, but, as soon as his speech concluded, the first bill introduced in the house was to provide for a referendum to adopt an exemption from all back poll taxes for all military personnel serving "at any time, past or present or future, when the United States was, is or shall be at war." It passed unanimously and went to the senate where Wilcox County's Bruce Henderson, chair of the Constitutional Revisions Committee, proposed his two bills, one that went further by proposing to exempt all military personnel in active service, not merely during wartime, and anyone retired after 21 years of military service. Other senators also wanted to sponsor a poll tax exemption bill. In the end, both houses adopted unanimously the house bill with Henderson and other senators named co-sponsors.[91] Supporting the troops in wartime remained highly popular politics in all sections of Alabama.

But the legislation was all but ignored by the Alabama press since during this time the U.S. House considered and passed another bill banning the poll tax in primary and general elections. The Alabama legislature's unanimous resolutions condemning the congressional bill and those supporting it received more attention than the soldiers' exemption. In Montgomery, a senate resolution castigated the legislation's attacks "on local self government in the South" and described it as "crackpot reforms" abetting the nation's wartime enemies. The state resolution's sponsor, Senator John Pinson of Sumter—the same man who tried to make it rich through land deals at Geiger—was extolled in the Black Belt for the modulated, truth-telling tone of his resolution, which also lamented how the federal bill would destroy the "lasting justice to both races" that had existed in Alabama since Reconstruction.[92]

Another unanimous Black Belt-sponsored resolution criticized national CIO president John L. Lewis, who supported the poll tax bill, for "openly rebelling against the Government of this nation in wartime." North Alabama's U.S. Representative Carter Manasco claimed communists were among the most active supporters of the federal bill since they wanted new voters to help defeat Southern members of Congress like him. Indeed, a Communist Party candidate had been on the ballot in the race against Chauncey Sparks in Alabama's 1942 general election, and he won a total of 402 votes,[93]—one-half of one percent.

The *Cullman Tribune*'s Republican editor, Henry F. Arnold, challenged his Congressman. Much like Justice Black had done a few years earlier in his Birmingham speech, the editor cited Thomas Jefferson's founding principles of "equality of citizenship of Americans." He said that in Manasco's own district "many white people, Americans, who before the depression of the thirties, were qualified voters" were now disqualified due to the cumulative poll tax. "Could it be that Carter Manasco is making a front of the American Communists," who were nowhere to be found in the Alabama hill country, the editor asked, "with the knowledge that a big electorate . . . will make his election more uncertain?"[94]

Most white editors and politicians in both north and south Alabama saw it differently. They were enraptured by Alabama's right to govern its own elections regardless of any democratic principle of an American's right to vote. In an editorial entitled "Worse Than Jackass Braying," the *Fayette County Times*, a rural north Alabama Democratic paper, lambasted the "nitwit congressmen and senators wasting precious time" on an issue about which "very few people care a 'Tinker's damn.'" Admitting that the poll tax had outlived its "usefulness," the editor nonetheless insisted "Alabama has a right to conduct her electorate any way she sees fit."[95]

Tennessee Valley's *Decatur Daily*, a strong New Deal newspaper, was less provocative but equally certain that the anti-poll tax bill was "a punitive expedition against the South." It dismissed the charge that a poll tax violated basic tenets of American democracy since the "democratic form of government, formed by our forefathers and defended through the years" gave rights and privileges to the states, including "the privilege of saying what the qualification shall be for a voter." Take away Alabama's control of its elections and, a future willy-nilly "Congress can say that only those may vote in Alabama who are on the payrolls of the WPA."[96]

In south Alabama, columnist Atticus Mullin, who often spoke for Black Belt planters, talked to several state legislators about Congress' anti-poll tax legislation as they were convening. He summed up their collective perspective: "Alabama democracy, since the days of the carpetbaggers from the North, has always placed upon its ballot in Democratic primaries the words, 'White Supremacy.' That is the slogan of Alabama democracy."[97]

A Southern filibuster in the U.S. Senate ultimately embargoed Claude Pepper's bill, but a month shy of the May 1944 Democratic primary, white Alabamians discovered that their version of democracy was threatened in

Washington by an institution other than a Democratic Congress. On April 3, the U.S. Supreme Court issued its opinion in *Smith v. Allwright*,[98] holding that a state cannot deny an African American the right to vote in primary elections since the practice violated the equal protection provision in one of the U.S. Constitution's Reconstruction Amendments.

James Simpson, a former Birmingham state senator of the Big Mules sort, was running against U.S. Senator Lister Hill, the New Deal Democrat who succeeded Hugo Black. Simpson warned that *Smith* posed the "gravest threat to white supremacy since Reconstruction." In the Black Belt, Hamner Cobbs said passage of a ban on the poll tax would have negligible effect on white supremacy compared to loss of the white primary, which "would mean the largest, final, and most important of all the barriers has been destroyed." The Selma newspaper reprinted the opinion of a mid-state Talladega editor who wrote, "The Ultimate Insanity," in which he accused the Supreme Court of carrying out "the New Deal's burning enmity against the Southern white man."[99] State Democratic Party chairman Gessner McCorvey assured Alabamians, "We are going to maintain white supremacy in Alabama," and Governor Sparks promised the white public that Alabama could adapt so long as the Supreme Court allowed the states an unfettered right to determine voter qualifications.[100]

Amid the condemnations and pledges of white solidarity, more than eight of ten Alabama voters marked their ballots in November 1944 favoring an exemption from the poll tax for all military personnel serving in wartime. In Russell County only 15 voters opposed the amendment, and most other Black Belt counties voted above the state average for the exemption.[101] Eliminating the poll tax for those who fought a war for democracy, whichever version of democracy might apply, remained one political issue on which all sections of Alabama largely agreed.

In early 1945, opponents of Alabama's poll tax thought that perhaps the political stars were aligned for change. The referendum had provided more votes for expanding the soldier's exemption than Senator Lister Hill received in his primary win against Simpson. In January, the Georgia legislature abolished the poll tax after that state's race-baiting demagogue, Eugene Talmadge, endorsed repeal, perhaps in an effort to counter young progressive Governor Ellis Arnold, who was leading the charge for a complete elimination.[102]

In early February, Hill issued a statement: "The poll tax must go." He called on the state legislature, not the Congress, to follow Georgia in ridding the state of its "most burdensome, restrictive, indefensible, and undemocratic" voting provision that disfranchises hundreds of thousands of white voters. Two other members in Alabama's congressional delegation publicly agreed with Hill, and Big Jim Folsom echoed Hill's pronouncement, promising the poll tax would become an issue in his next campaign for governor, if it was not repealed sooner.[103]

Governor Sparks responded that he too was opposed to requiring more than two years back taxes for voting but would not support such a change in the law so long "as outside agitation for poll tax abolition continues." By May, however, when state legislators convened, Sparks asked them to remove the cumulative feature of the poll tax. "The procedure through which the ballot is kept pure is registration, not the payment of poll tax," Sparks stated. "It keeps from voting many good men and women."[104]

Legislators from Jefferson and Lauderdale counties filed three bills in the house: one following the governor's recommendation, one following Georgia's example of abolishing all poll taxes, and one exempting the wives and widows of war soldiers. Despite their original optimism, the sponsors quickly discovered they had misjudged the prevailing mood in Montgomery and once again were out-maneuvered by Black Belt leaders. Both the speaker of the house, Charles Norman of Union Springs, and the chair of the committee to which he assigned the bills were seasoned Black Belt legislators. The bills could have been buried in committee, but they were reported to the house floor, where the Black Belt-controlled Rules Committee arranged the first debate on banning the cumulative poll tax bill.[105]

The committee chair, from Selma, led the offensive against the bill, claiming that any change in existing voting restrictions would be dangerous, even disastrous in the 18 counties with majority-Black populations. No one spoke on the floor in support of the sponsor's contention that the bill would not increase Black voting, and only two dozen other members, half from north Alabama and five from Birmingham, voted for the bill.

Seventy voted "nay" and 11 members denied it support by not voting. As soon the roll call was announced, the Black Belt leaders pigeonholed the other poll tax bills.[106] The pendulum had swung on Goat Hill.

Sparks's endorsement of such a bill may explain why five Black Belt Representatives broke ranks and voted for it, but that support was overwhelmed by opposition from almost every member from central and south Alabama, including Montgomery and Mobile representatives, and almost half of north Alabama's votes. The chamber's only Republican (from north Alabama's Winston County) also voted "nay."

One common theme of opposition roared across the state before and after the vote: there will be no change "so long as that crowd in Washington tries to force it down our throats"—never "as long as northern reds and Alabama CIO'ers continue their rampages." Or, as House Speaker Charles Norman's own Union Springs newspaper stated more sedately, never to happen if there is "outside agitation to force repeal of Alabama's poll tax."[107]

In Greensboro, after the bill's defeat, Hamner Cobbs used the same leitmotif, pleased that the state would abjure "principles evolved from the sidewalks of New York," while rejoicing that the vote demonstrated that the "Black Belt still has a lot of friends all over Alabama." The editor singled out Gessner McCorvey, chair of the state Democratic Executive Committee, as most responsible for the "rout of the anti-poll tax forces." McCorvey had sent a public letter to state legislators explaining his opposition to any change in the poll tax, and Cobbs was not alone in believing that McCorvey had a huge impact on the vote.[108]

McCorvey's letter did not echo whites' political anger about outsiders trying to bully Alabama but instead was a carefully crafted argument about the necessity to prevent "adding countless thousands of undesirables" to the voting rolls and the function of Alabama's current poll tax in helping to bar "large number of thriftless people." The letter made only one claim that could be construed as an aim to exclude only Black voters—how the 1901 Constitution with the cumulative poll tax had ended "Reconstruction Days ballot box stuffing." It never referred to Negroes, colored voters, or any of the more derisive white terms for African Americans. It

Gessner T. McCorvey (University of Alabama Libraries Special Collections).

mentioned "black" only once when complaining that the property qualification for voting in 1901 had been eroded by inflation. "I think it is ridiculous to permit a man, black or white, to become a qualified voter . . . merely because he might own some junky automobile assessed for taxation at $300," McCorvey complained.[109]

The letter was a smart, lawyerly approach indicating that McCorvey understood the reasoning of the Supreme Court in outlawing the white primary in Texas. *Smith v. Allwright* and the other cases leading up to that decision were based on the principle that a Democratic primary in the South was "state action," not merely a private club's activity, and the Reconstruction Amendments to the U.S. Constitution forbade state governments from practicing racial discrimination in voting. In Texas, the state had first required by statute that the primary election exclude Black voters. The Supreme Court voided that law in 1927. Texas removed it but gave its state Democratic Executive Committee the power to prescribe the primary's voting qualifications. The committee adopted a whites-only resolution for its primary, but the Supreme Court struck down that practice in 1932.[110]

In *Smith*, the Supreme Court took one logical step further by holding that whenever Texas, directly or indirectly, allowed the Democratic party to set "the essential qualification for voting in a primary to select nominees for a general election, the State makes the action of the party the action of the State." In sweeping terms that implicated any and all statements of motive and action by both state and party officials, Justice Stanley Reed of Kentucky proclaimed, "Under our Constitution the great privilege of the ballot may not be denied a man by the State because of his color."[111]

Hamner Cobbs called upon Alabamians to rally behind McCorvey as the state's wise and effective leader of "the white forces of decency." As head of the Democratic Party, McCorvey did emerge as a major public figure in advocating carefully worded proposals, including the Boswell Amendment, to suppress voting by both Blacks and some whites, although he would not be able to quiet the openly racist, inflamed rhetoric of others. Cobbs and McCorvey were part of a mutual admiration society where admission required both smart competence and a worshipful, protective affection for McCorvey's Black Belt birthplace as the citadel of elite white supremacy.[112]

Perhaps such devotion was the essence of Cobbs's definition of white decency, but for a young, perceptive white teenager in Mobile invited by McCorvey into his darkened, expansive law office in the summer of 1945, the head of the state party seemed more repugnant than exemplary of decency. The elderly lawyer laughingly shared with the boy and his friend—a grandson of Sumter's John Rogers—a crude, doctored photograph of a Black man looking like an ape. But it was not the photograph that made young Francis Walter leave the office "feeling dirty." Such sensibility about racism was still a work in progress that would mature as Walter completely unlearned the commonplace racism of Mobile. No, the boy left repulsed because he felt as if he had just been wooed by a man acting like a pederast.[113]

CHAPTER 12

It's Been a Long Time Comin'

'You and You and All My Friends Are My Campaign Managers'

Good to his word, Big Jim Folsom included the repeal of the poll tax in his 1946 campaign, although among a long list of reforms which he promised voters he would take "to the capitol and clean out the whole thing." Again considered the underdog, Folsom introduced a new style of campaigning to Alabama, including an entertaining country-hillbilly band and amusing, metaphorical language that, as old-timers might say, put the hay down where the goats could get it.[1]

Folsom also campaigned to an emerging new voting constituency. More than 200,000 men were returning home to Alabama from World War II, and they were exempt from paying a poll tax, as were perhaps 5,000 women who had served in the military or its auxiliary corps. These veterans may not have had a common political agenda, but many returned with a strong sense that the old guard needed to change. "In 1946 World War II was just over," observed an Alabama veteran who supported Folsom. "Vets saw what things were like elsewhere . . . When we got back we didn't have anything to come back to—no money, no jobs, nothin'."[2]

Some of the returning veterans were Black soldiers, who by law were also entitled to vote without payment of a poll tax so long as local boards of registrars determined they were qualified to vote. Black leaders in Alabama had renewed local efforts to increase the number of African Americans who qualified to vote. Encouraged by decisions of the U.S. Supreme Court, Arthur Shores, a young Black Birmingham attorney, began in 1939 challenging the Jefferson County registrars' habitual rejection of a large number of applicants. His work did not result in thousands becoming registered, but it enabled some additional Black voters. Similar lawsuits were filed in 1945 in places such as Mobile and Tuskegee, and in some small towns in north Alabama the numbers of Black voters began to inch upward as Black Alabamians nudged and challenged local white officials.[3]

No one thought Black voters would have any impact on the 1946 governor's race, but their small numbers did not matter to Folsom, who sought their support. A few weeks before the Democratic primary, a Birmingham Black newspaperman asked Folsom who was managing his campaign. Big Jim's reply was expansive. "You and you and you and all my friends are my campaign managers," he replied to the editor and other Black folk around him. "If elected, I will be governor of the colored people just as I will be governor of all other people of the state." Waving his long arms like a human windmill, Folsom also assured the African Americans that if elected he would "wipe out the poll tax."[4]

Folsom was unable to fulfill his campaign promise. The new governor was distracted by fame and family matters before taking office and failed to control the legislature's leadership, which remained dominated by the Black Belt and Big Mules. In addition, in 1947 an extraordinary number of house members—more than half—were new, with no prior legislative service, and most of the inexperienced were from north Alabama. The seasoned returning legislators were primarily from the Black Belt. Even the speaker of the house, a compromise candidate from north Alabama, had only one prior session's experience. In the senate, the turnover was greater. Only nine of 35 members were returning, and most of those, including key committee chairs, were masterful legislative tacticians from the Black Belt.[5]

As a result, bills to change the poll tax were never considered after they were introduced. In both houses, the committees that received the bills were controlled by Black Belt members, and the freshmen sponsoring the bills were outmatched from the opening gavel, despite Folsom's repeated calls for passage. The lower chamber officially killed its poll tax bill three days after the U.S. House of Representatives passed with almost a three-to-one margin a federal bill banning the poll tax in all federal elections, over the objections of all nine Alabama congressmen.[6]

Efforts to remove the back-taxes feature of the poll tax enjoyed no better fate in the 1949 legislative session, although the house did vote on the bill. Governor Folsom opened the session in a joint address in which he tried to recast the issue: "Alabama is the only state in the Nation having an accumulative Poll Tax . . . The issue is not whether you and I believe the Poll Tax should be abolished. The issue is whether the people will have an opportunity to vote on it."[7]

The bill's freshman sponsor, Edward Buckner, did not sit on the committee that considered the bill, but it was reported to the floor without delay—and without a recommendation from a committee whose members were almost evenly split between north and south Alabama. Black Belt leaders led the charge against the bill on the floor. Because the federal courts had recently struck down the Boswell Amendment, the section's legislators were primed to go all out.

Veteran Representative Wilbur "Doc" Martin was from Greene County, where a white population of 16 percent ruled the economy and politics. "This bill strikes at the heart of the Black Belt," he intoned. "Now with the Boswell Amendment out of the way, there is only one of three things we could do [if the bill were adopted]: One. Stay there and humiliate ourselves with an inferior race there running things. Two. Move. Three. Get our grandpa's old shotgun."[8]

The bill received only 31 "yea" votes, half of what was necessary for passage. Representatives from north Alabama and Jefferson County were 25 of the total yeas, but many of Folsom's south Alabama supporters, including Barbour County Representative George C. Wallace, voted against H.B. 24. The bill ran a gauntlet of five roll call votes before a final motion to "postpone indefinitely" was passed. These votes were designed to provide some members with political cover—to let them claim they did not vote against the bill or even against considering the bill by pointing to one vote or another among the five roll calls. "They just wanted to squeeze around and about the issue," complained Buckner, who was learning the tricks of his legislative trade the hard way.[9]

The defeat of the poll tax reform was largely overshadowed by other legislative battles—both what Buckner, a school principal, called "skull-duggery" concerning Folsom's proposed reapportionment and a filibuster by Big Jim's senate supporters to prevent passage of the bill replacing the court-annulled Boswell Amendment with a version that Democratic Party chairman McCorvey sought (*see* Chapter 2).

In the following election year, Folsom was unable to succeed himself, although some candidates for state and local offices continued to call for changing the poll tax. Birmingham's Big Mule lawyer Gordon Persons was elected governor after a 15-person race in which he declared support for changing the poll tax. It was not one of the defining issues of the campaign, although candidate "Bull" Connor, the Birmingham police commissioner, contradicted his earlier legislative support for change. Now he warned, "There are already 50,000 Negro voters in Alabama. If you repeal the poll tax, there will be 500,000."[10]

In office, Persons surprised many, especially in the Black Belt, by offering his support for eliminating the poll tax entirely as well as removing the required payment of back taxes—whichever option the legislature would enact. But the governor gave the effort little more than his endorsement. From the beginning, Persons sought to have a "business-like administration" that was, as the *Montgomery Advertiser* predicted, much more interested in the efficiency and intricacies of tax collections than poll tax reform.[11] The legislature was left largely to its own machinations on the issue.

When the legislature was gaveled to order in May 1951, almost two-thirds of the house members and 80 percent of the senators had no prior legislative experience—the second record in a row for turnover. In this session, the departures also involved some of the Black Belt's most effective, wily members, such as former Speaker Charles Newman and the section's dean, Senator Bruce Henderson, who had run poorly as an unsuccessful candidate for governor.

This vacuum of experience did not matter when the bill to expand the poll tax's veteran's exemption by including all military personnel serving when the nation is "engaged in hostilities, whether as a result of a declared war or not, with any foreign state." The undeclared Korean War had erupted in June 1950, and, while more than one-third of the legislators were war veterans, a military record was not required to rally behind the legislation. As in the past, the exemption passed unanimously in both houses without debate and later in the year every county in the state voted to ratify it.[12]

A more sweeping poll tax bill was also considered and for the first time almost passed. When a floor vote was taken on a house bill limiting payment of back poll taxes to only four years, it received a one-vote majority.[13] It was not the three-fifths of the total members necessary for passage, but it was more than twice the support for reducing back poll taxes during the last year of the Folsom administration. A bill eliminating all but two years of back taxes also passed in the senate by the necessary super-majority after J. Miller Bonner of Wilcox County secured a compromise that provided an exception from the bill's provisions for 10 Black Belt counties (two Black Belt senators had removed their counties from the exception list once Bonner's amendment was on the floor).

The house let the senate bill die quietly in committee, but the debate in the senate revealed that the Black Belt's solid opposition was cracking. In addition, the bill's sponsor focused on only one argument for passage: enactment would add as many as 100,000 women to the voter rolls. "These are the ones being hurt by the present law," argued Senator Elvin Columbus McCary, war veteran and former member of his county's board of registrars.[14]

'Half a Loaf Is Better Than No Loaf . . .'

McCary and Representative George Hawkins, the north Alabama sponsor of the house anti-poll tax bills, realized they had some powerful, needed allies. Alabama's white middle-class and professional women were organizing as never before into a growing constituency for change, and the poll tax was one of their top issues. Several women's groups, such as Democratic Women's Clubs and the League of Women Voters (LWV), had been active lobbyists in Montgomery on issues such as child labor and convict leasing, and they and other women's groups had joined labor unions in the late 1930s trying to reform or remove the poll tax.

During the past decade, the LWV had spent much of its time encouraging the payment of poll taxes by women and men, but, led by Indiana-born political scientist Hallie Farmer, a professor at Alabama College (later the University of Montevallo), and others, professional women's groups such as the Alabama Association of University Women became more energetic and outspoken in advocating for changing the poll tax. Several had surveyed their members, which confirmed that the primary obstacle to white women voting was the cumulative feature of the poll tax. Many men under the age of 45 were now exempt due to prior military service, but few women were. "Unless and until Alabama changes her poll tax law, thousands of women in this state will remain without the right to vote," Farmer declared in a 1949 speech.[15]

After the 1951 legislative session, several statewide women's groups banded together to coordinate efforts, and hundreds of other local women's groups across the state—from local parent-teacher associations to garden clubs to chapters of the Women's Christian Temperance Union—began to organize around changing the poll tax. The LWV enlisted McCary and Hawkins to develop a statewide strategy that included sending questionnaire to each legislator about their views on the poll tax, arranging for local members to meet with legislators, and providing special attention to the members on the committees that would consider the poll tax bills. The League and many other groups maintained a two-year program of public speaking about the need to abolish or change poll tax laws.

The women leaders were particularly outspoken against the defense of the poll tax as a necessary source of revenue for Alabama's chronically underfunded schools. They pointed out that the tax had never been a huge source of school revenue and in recent years had declined to less than 1 percent of state school funding.

They also were politically savvy in amplifying their message by providing a public platform for men to express their opposition to the poll tax. For example, young Montgomery attorney John Godbold, whose former law partner Richard Rives now sat on the federal appeals court, provided a well-publicized speech to the local LWV on the poll tax's history, remarking that it is "more difficult to vote today than it was in 1901." Godbold covered many facts and arguments that most League members likely already knew, but his comments gained prominent newspaper coverage that women speakers seldom received from male editors.[16]

Virtually no opposition to changing the poll tax was expressed among Alabama's daily newspapers, either in north or south Alabama. Even the *Montgomery Advertiser*, which had shilly-shallied on the question over the years, and some Black Belt weeklies wrote in support of a change. "Poll Tax Should Be Abolished," insisted the *Monroe Journal*'s editorial even as editor Bill Stewart acknowledged that the CIO labor union was one of the groups clamoring for the change. It was a total reversal of the *Journal*'s position from a few years earlier when then-editor and -owner A. C. Lee, father of young novelist Nelle Harper Lee, attacked the CIO with as much gusto as he defended the sanctity of 1901 poll tax requirements.[17]

The women's groups planned their annual statewide and local meetings to occur on the eve of the 1953 legislative session in order to assess where different legislators stood on the question, share last-minute strategies and tactics, and energize members to keep pressuring their representatives. In addition, local and state women's leaders jointly met to share plans and coordinate lobbying activities with the other groups—including an emerging organization of young Democrats who were also pushing to abolish the poll tax. In Montgomery, Farmer proclaimed the fight was for the complete abolishment of the poll tax.[18]

The white women lobbyists left nothing to chance once the legislature's men convened in May. The women were in the gallery when bills to eliminate the poll tax or to reduce back payments to two years were introduced; they were in the committee rooms when the poll tax bills were discussed; and they spoke to the committees in support of the bills. The house Committee on Constitutional Revisions quickly recommended for passage H.B. 30 abolishing all poll taxes and H.B. 64 eliminating all but two years of back poll taxes. Afterwards, Black Belt representatives attempted to have the bills recommitted to the house Taxation Committee where they and allies constituted a plurality, claiming unsuccessfully that a poll tax was a revenue bill that the Constitution required go to that committee.[19]

In the following week, Hawkins decided the house should consider the bill reducing the back poll taxes before the bill abolishing the tax. The house voted down Black Belt amendments that would require four years of back taxes instead of two and ignore Dallas County Representative Walter Givhan's warning that it was a dangerous time to remove any barrier to Black voting. In short order, a supermajority of 71 votes passed Hawkins's bill.[20]

On the next day, the Senate Committee on Constitutional Revisions met. For the first time in memory, the 1951–1953 Committee was not stacked with a majority of Black Belt members and allies who customarily would hold such bills to their death. After the LWV representative spoke, Barbour County's senator pressed her about how the state would make up for the loss of the poll tax's earmarked revenue for education since more money for education was one of the League's longstanding concerns. "Do legislators make money?" barked Senator Preston Clayton of Barbour County,[21] as if the woman required a second-grade tutorial on how a state must enact a tax to produce revenue.

The Committee released its bill reducing back payment of poll taxes, but by a one-vote margin refused to report the bill banning the poll tax after a south Alabama senator from the Dothan area changed his vote and two north Alabama senators voted to hold the bill. On the following day, in a ceremonial appearance in Tuscaloosa, without suggesting his own views, Lieutenant Governor James B. Allen, a Big Mule attorney from Gadsden whose politics were as flexible as his ambitions were limitless, indicated that the bill to repeal the poll tax was dead. [22] Apparently, senate leaders had decided that a reduction of the back poll taxes was a necessary compromise to kill the women's bill for a total ban.

Allen moved the senate to quickly consider S.B. 6, its compromise bill, and forward it to the house as a means of forestalling a total ban. Black Belt members attempted to insert an exemption for eight Black Belt counties. But such an amendment was sure to rile house members, and it lost receiving only a few votes beyond the majority-Black counties. Another floor amendment by Selma's senator did pass by one vote. It changed the date of the voters' referendum on the proposed constitutional amendment from 1953 to the first Monday of November 1954.[23]

This change in the election date was a significant rearguard action designed to increase the chances that Alabama voters might reject the proposed amendment, if developments in Washington proceeded as many Alabama politicians expected. The U.S. Supreme Court had announced that it would rehear in late 1953 arguments concerning whether racially segregated schools violated the federal Constitution, and Alabama lawmakers were already on high alert. Under a screaming headline of "Solons Face Crucial Issue of Segregation in Schools," the Associated Press reporter Rex Thomas, reviewing upcoming legislative issues including the poll tax, wrote, "Never since the hectic era following the War Between the States, when Negroes held office under protection of federal troops, has there been such a serious challenge to white supremacy."[24]

Delaying the poll tax referendum for 18 months would provide additional time in which voters could be more fully persuaded by events in Washington that it was too risky to make changes in the barriers to voting, especially if the Court decided to strike down school segregation. The senate's Black Belt legislators were mum about the rationale for this amendment, but some who publicly supported changing the poll tax argued for delay on the same terms. "As a sincere believer in the repeal of the poll tax," the *Huntsville Times* editorial stated, "we would prefer to see a state referendum on this issue after the Legislature meets in 1955."[25]

Included in the "we" of this editorial was no doubt Mrs. A. L. Smith, or Martha Witt Smith, as she would become known by her by-line once the newspaper regularly began permitting female reporters to have one. Smith was only four years into her service as a member of the Madison County Board of Registrars and had not yet joined forces with the state's leading segregationists to become a principal figure behind the scenes in fighting Black voting. She was an active member of the local LWV, although her own views about the poll tax did not square always with the League's position. For example, she reported for the local newspaper on the eve of the current legislative session that a unit of the local chapter had decided "the poll tax should not be abolished until some arrangement could be made to keep the deadwood" from remaining on the voter rolls. It so happened that Smith was the local chapter's unit expert on voting issues.[26]

When S.B. 6 reached the house floor, its committee had restored the referendum date to late 1953, but on its first vote the bill fell eight votes shy of the extraordinary majority of 63 required for passage. Nearly a third of the members failed to vote. After legislators voted to reconsider the bill (requiring only a simple majority), the sponsors and supporters rounded up missing votes and the bill passed the house with 74 "yeas" and only 16 "nays," largely from the Black Belt. Those who turned up for the final vote were mostly from south Alabama. A few Black Belt representatives also voted "yea" for the first time."[27]

Later in the session, the house defeated H.B. 30 that would have also put before voters the question of repealing the poll tax entirely. Thirty-one members who had voted for reducing back payment of poll taxes voted to defeat an outright repeal. Most of these members were from south Alabama, although some north Alabama legislators, such as Rankin Fite of Marion County, helped to reject the full repeal by taking a walk during the vote.[28]

These various votes on the different poll tax bills created a confusing political narrative, one which the capitol press corps apparently decided not to try to explain except to convey the outcomes. But the various recorded votes and changes in votes that were laid into the journals were important to many incumbent legislators, letting them have it more than one way in the future when they were called upon to answer for how they voted on changing the poll tax.

A conference committee of three members from each chamber was appointed to work out the bills' difference on the date of the poll tax referendum. Lieutenant Governor Allen and House Speaker Roberts Brown (from majority-Black Lee County) decided to stack the deck for the senate date of November 1954. Both presiding officers appointed two members who were from the Black Belt, including Representative Walter Givhan, or who had voted with the Black Belt. Of course, the committee came back with a four-to-two recommendation to accept the senate's date, but the house rebelled and refused to agree to anything but its own 1953 date. Allen and senate leaders decided it was the better part of current politics to accede, and the new law set the referendum for 90 days after the session—December 15, 1953.[29]

The election campaign to adopt the amendment was led by the state's women's organizations, young Democrats, and labor unions with a joint coordinating committee headed by the law's original sponsors, Hawkins and McCary. Most statewide elected officials supported passage, as did the state Republican Party chairman who argued that no person should be fined for the privilege to vote. Every announced candidate for governor in 1954, as well as all living former governors, endorsed the amendment, except for Frank Dixon who previously sought exactly the revised poll tax now on the ballot. Dixon explained he changed his mind because of the "tremendously increased activities of minority special interest groups" operating in Alabama.[30]

Former state Democratic Party chairman Gessner McCorvey and a few Democratic leaders in Black Belt counties echoed the former governor's concern in announcing their opposition, but Jefferson County's Democratic Executive Committee, led by the county's registrars, agreed but had no use for Dixon's language. At first it declared the amendment was the handiwork of Communists, but afterwards decided there was a better red herring.[31] "Who will Control? . . . NAACP or You? Keep Our Way of Life," screamed some of the large ads that the Committee published in Birmingham newspapers. Other Committee ads reminded voters that the NAACP was pushing for "the death of segregation in Alabama" through various actions, including the *Brown v. Board of Education* case at the U.S. Supreme Court, where oral arguments, well-publicized, concluded a week before the referendum.[32]

The Jefferson County Committee also ran ads warning the area's skilled white workers that, once the poll tax was changed, the NAACP would become the balance of power in local elections. It would mean the end of the wage differential between skilled white workers and unskilled Black workers. Union officials countered the ads in their public remarks, while the women's groups across the state maintained a steady person-to-person campaign of speeches and outreach to members and their husbands.[33]

The referendum passed with 57 percent of the vote in a light turnout of fewer than 125,000 voters ten days before Christmas.[34] The voting mostly followed the traditional patterns between north and south Alabama. All but one Black Belt county opposed the amendment and in most of these majority-Black counties the amendment received less than a third of the vote. All but two counties where the amendment received two-thirds of the vote were in north Alabama. But there were significant differences from the historical trends. Mobile County (and its neighboring Baldwin) gave the poll tax reform the state's highest level of support—over 80 percent. Also, in Montgomery County two-thirds of the voters supported the Amendment. And in Jefferson County 63 percent of the voters decided to ignore its Democratic Committee's warning about the fall of white supremacy if the Amendment passed.

Another pattern also became clear in the referendum. Demographic changes across Alabama during the last few decades had done more than empty the Black Belt of thousands of African American farm laborers. They also involved a significant increase of population and voters among the state's urban areas regardless of the section of the state. Nothing could have brought this trend home more clearly to politicians than the fact that only ten of 67 counties produced enough votes to pass the amendment. Jefferson County stood out like a smoldering volcano on an island of otherwise peaty flatlands. The county produced one-fifth of all "yes" votes in the referendum but possessed only one of 35 votes in the state senate and only seven of 105 votes in the state house for deciding what bills became law and what amendments the voters could consider on the ballot.

These trends also meant middle-class white women, most of whom lived in the urban areas, had gained a new, influential role in Alabama politics. Over the decades, both before and after women gained the right to vote, they had crafted an oversized impact on some important state policies concerning children, education, and what they considered moral issues such as Prohibition and convict leasing. But they never had occupied such a visible, leading role in Alabama politics as they did in successfully changing the poll tax. By so doing, they also unlocked the ballot box to tens of thousands of women from all walks of life for at least the potential of an even larger role for their gender to reshape the state's political future.

For their work in 1953, the male editor of the anti-poll tax *Cullman Tribune* offered "a hand to the ladies." He probably spoke for most men when he patronized the women groups' role as helpful "sideline cheering."[35] But Hallie Farmer set the record straight in her own way. As a civic leader, she had set about to abolish the entire poll tax. After losing that legislative battle, she helped lead scores of women through hundreds of meetings and speeches to pass the amendment to improve it. Farmer understood the art of politics and policymaking as well as any wily Black Belt politician. "Now . . . that our side has won . . .." she wrote matter-of-factly to newspapers across the state after the votes were counted, "I offer you . . . sincere appreciation for the cooperation . . . which gave us such unstinted support as *we* fought this battle."[36]

After more than 50 years of defeated efforts by reformers, white women were not merely cheerleaders in changing Alabama's poll tax. They had rendered real change in the state's politics and policy, But, as Farmer understood, progress came from the art of expanding the possible, and the state's history and Constitution meant such changes were usually piecemeal. "Half a loaf is better than no loaf at all," Farmer reminded her young friend Lucille Griffith at the conclusion of the poll tax campaign. In fact, reducing the back payment of the poll tax from a maximum of $36 to only $3 achieved more than a half-victory. It was, nonetheless, Farmer's last battle to expand Alabama democracy. Two years later, at the age of 65, Farmer announced she was leaving Alabama for retirement in Indiana.[37]

Hallie Farmer (Anna Crawford Milner Archives and Special Collections, University of Montevallo).

'HOW LONG WILL THE OPPRESSORS GO ON TORMENTING THEMSELVES'

Former Governor Frank Dixon and other opponents of changing Alabama's poll tax wildly exaggerated the dangers and impact of the NAACP in Alabama in 1953, yet the organization and the state's Black leaders were moving with renewed determination to take advantage of opportunities that African American attorneys and the federal courts were creating in interpreting and applying the Reconstruction Amendments of the U.S. Constitution, including especially the right to vote.

Alabama NAACP president W. C. Patton worked with a strong group of local and state leaders when he began expanding the organization's reach even before the poll tax referendum. As early as 1938, groups such as the Right to Vote Club, formed by local Black ministers and Black members of the local Communist Party, began preparing African Americans to apply as registered voters. The return of Arthur Shores to Birmingham in 1937 provided Alabama's first Black attorney ready and willing to challenge boards of registrars and voting practices in court. Two years later, from his law office in the Masonic Temple Building (reputedly the largest building owned by Blacks in the South), Shores sued the Jefferson County Board of Registrars for denying five schoolteachers the right to register because of their race.[38]

After the U.S. Supreme Court outlawed the all-white primary, NAACP national director Walter White asked Patton to take up the role of increasing Black registration and voting across Alabama. A native of Perry County and a former schoolteacher, Patton was state manager of a Black fraternal life insurance association. He agreed to travel Alabama roads to encourage African Americans to qualify as voters, attempt to register, and pay their poll taxes whenever they succeeded in registering.

Patton relied on Shores, retained by the NAACP, and national legal director Thurgood Marshall in New York to go into federal and state courts whenever practical within a very limited budget. He also had strong, steadfast support and cooperation from several other NAACP leaders, including Mobile's John LeFlore, a postal worker who was fearless and blunt in his advancement of the Black community; E. D. Nixon of Montgomery, a dedicated union activist in the Brotherhood of Sleeping Car Porters who followed Patton as state NAACP president; Dr. C. G. Gomillion of Tuskegee Institute, a brilliant strategist and political scientist; and Emory O. Jackson, editor of the *Birmingham World,* whose hard-hitting columns on Black registration and voting were often reprinted by the state's other Black editors, especially when Jackson wrote what they were hesitant to express on their own.[39]

These Black leaders usually worked in concert, although there were moments of brotherly competition, such as deciding the best location to challenge the Boswell Amendment or the best venue for investing scarce organizational resources to spark political change. But the critical, singular impetus for the NAACP's advancement in Alabama emerged when Ruby Hurley, the national organization's youth director, became its first regional director for the southeastern states.

Growing up in Washington, D.C., where she was taught by one of the sons of abolitionist Frederick Douglass, Hurley attended a teacher's college and a night law school while working at local Black-owned bank. She became involved in NAACP activities in 1939, at age 30, when she helped organize community support for opera singer Marian Anderson to perform at the Lincoln Monument after being canceled earlier at Constitution Hall by the Daughters of the American Revolution because of her race.

Hurley traveled across the country for more than ten years helping to organize scores of NAACP youth councils. In April 1951, she arrived in Birmingham for a temporary assignment to build Southern membership. Hurley was in Birmingham because Patton offered a rent-free office with some secretarial support. He was angling to locate a permanent regional NAACP office in his city and thought Hurley's presence would give Birmingham an advantage. His strategy worked, in part because the other Southern branches offered less support and because Birmingham was centrally located within the region. The Tennessee state NAACP president also admitted Birmingham was the "hot spot."[40]

Hurley operated as a Black woman in a man's world—both Black and white men. All NAACP Southern state presidents and all Southern state boards were men, as were virtually all government and business leaders in Alabama and other Southern states. In this traditional, male environment, Hurley's physical attributes—"tall, attractive, poised, elegant, and well-dressed"—probably made a good initial impression on the NAACP's Southern men. But their acceptance of her and the national office's decision to make her head of a permanent office was based on the simple fact that she did a "fine job" and proved her "worth" to the Southern branches that would help fund her office[41]—and perhaps because the appointment of a woman director from New York with 13 years of national NAACP experience permitted the organization to avoid further delays in what could have been a long, unproductive competition among Southern branches as to which of their men should get the job.

Even before her appointment, Alabamians learned that Hurley was outspoken in her dedication to the principles and work of the NAACP. Two months after arriving in Alabama, she told a citywide convocation in Montgomery, well-publicized by local white newspapers, that the NAACP was on the march to completely undo separate and unequal schools and to secure an "unhampered vote" for Black citizens. "We are going out, not for a half a loaf, but a full loaf," proclaimed an African American minister after hearing Hurley.[42]

In recalling the personal trauma of moving from New York to a rigidly segregated city, Hurley always pointed out that Birmingham's municipal ordinance in 1951 prohibited Black and white persons from playing checkers together. It was a way of life she did not accept and frequently challenged. Soon after her appointment, in a public letter to the chair of the state Democratic Executive Committee, Hurley asked the party to remove the banner of "white supremacy" from its ballots and as the party emblem. Calling it a contradiction of democratic principles, Hurley said "the time has more than come when it should be changed."[43]

Hurley freely wrote letters to the editors of Birmingham's white newspapers opposing their opinions and news coverage on issues of segregation and white supremacy. She expressed "disgust" at Birmingham's failure to considered revoking any of its segregation ordinances and said it was "pathetic" that the "handwriting on the wall cannot be seen by the blindly prejudiced." She asked Birmingham's white public: "How long will the oppressors go on tormenting themselves by a sinful and outmoded custom?"[44] When the all-white Birmingham planners proposed an urban renewal project in 1953, Hurley declared, "It is a Negro clearance rather than a slum clearance."[45]

While always ready to publicly question authorities' romance with white supremacy, Hurley spent much of her energy and time in 1953–54 working with Patton to increase Black voter participation. She held the NAACP's first southeastern training conference in Birmingham where

Ruby Hurley (Getty Images).

voting rights were the primary concern. Emboldened by a conference title of "No Compromise with Segregation or Discrimination," the meeting provided information and training on voter registration and set up a regional committee to map out campaigns for all branches to undertake "high powered registration drives."

The conference resolutions called for "complete and absolute exploitation of the ballot" as "the way to first class citizenship." They deplored those using "violence, threats or other means still try to keep the Negro disfranchised" and urged abolition of the poll tax. They condemned by name the Jefferson County Democratic Executive Committee and Police Commissioner "Bull" Connor for local bigoted actions.

Birmingham police detectives were in the audience monitoring proceedings when Walter White ended the meeting with a message for Connor and his audience. Citing the city's continued problems with police brutality and unsolved bombings in Black neighborhoods, the group's national leader said Connor's detectives should report to their boss that he "was one of the greatest allies that Joe Stalin has in America." To his NAACP members, White said simply, "register, pay the poll tax."[46]

Patton scheduled the 1953 state convention in Mobile a month before the statewide referendum on cutting back payment of the poll tax. Black registered voters had made only baby steps toward the goal of registering a half a million persons of voting age, but Patton understood that the estimated 27,000 new Black voters could make a difference in the December election with an expected low turnout. Also, African American activists were still stinging from the fact that merely a thousand more Black votes would have defeated the "Boswell Jr." constitutional amendment two years earlier. "We should begin now campaigning to get out the vote," Patton told members.[47]

After the amendment passed, Patton called it a "glorious victory for democracy" and suggested its ratification indicated that more white Alabamians were learning "to do their own thinking and are refraining from being swayed by appeals to race hatred and prejudice."[48] He began a campaign to get a large increase in the number of African Americans paying the reduced poll tax before the February 1 deadline so that Black voters could have a larger role in the 1954 statewide elections. He enlisted ministers, fraternal lodge leaders, unions, and women's clubs. He ran ads in the Black newspapers. Afterwards, he worked with local NAACP branches to turn out all three groups now eligible to vote: registered Black voters who recently paid their poll tax, African American veterans (perhaps 25,000 in number) exempt from the poll tax, and all Black persons over the age of 45, who also did not have to pay.[49]

Hurley supported and extended Patton's campaign to increase poll tax payers and registered voters, as did NAACP leaders across the state. Mobile made some notable gains in registration, but the Jefferson County board of registrars in Birmingham remained a major obstacle. An Associated Press survey found that the total of registered Black voters in Alabama was close to 40,000, although the NAACP's own numbers in 1954 pegged the total at nearly 50,000—perhaps a two-year gain of more than 25,000, who no longer had to pay a steep poll tax for past years. But NAACP officials realized they had much more work to do. Jefferson County alone had perhaps 120,000 African Americans of voting age.[50]

The increases in Black voters were attributed publicly to the change in the poll tax, but the change also remained a popular reform among white folk. More persons probably paid their poll taxes in 1954 than ever before in Alabama history, and, since white women comprised the majority of the state's gains in registered voters, politicians competed for credit in bringing about the demise of the old poll tax. In campaigning for reelection, Birmingham's Senator Albert Boutwell, for example, highlighted his role as "Co-Author of $3 Poll Tax Law" even more than he advertised his chairmanship of the legislature's segregation strategy committee. This calculated priority was especially noteworthy since Boutwell's name as sponsor was tacked onto the poll tax bill only after its passage.[51]

Big Jim Folsom's huge victory in the Democratic gubernatorial primary on May 4 did not require Black votes in a seven-man race, but strong Black support probably did add at least 10,000 votes, the margin that let Folsom avoid a runoff. Two weeks later, when the U.S. Supreme Court issued *Brown v. Board of Education*, NAACP leaders must have exhaled a sigh of relief that Black voters had saved their preferred candidate from a runoff that would have been wholly defined by segregation. Perhaps nothing proved this reality to Hurley as much as the results of a special Birmingham referendum held after Folsom's primary victory. By almost a three-to-one margin, Birmingham voters extended the ban against integrated dominos and checkers to include interracial softball, baseball, basketball, football, golf, track, and swimming.[52]

Despite vivid signs to the contrary, Hurley and former state president E. D. Nixon joined other NAACP officials in professing their public faith that the better angels of the white Southerner's nature would assure compliance with the Supreme Court's *Brown* decision. "We believe millions of Americans, Negro and white in the South, will be coming together now in a common effort for all our children," Hurley stated in a national radio program in July. She echoed her remarks made the day after the Court issued *Brown* when she reminded *Alabama Journal* readers that some had predicted "blood would flow in the streets when the Negro began to vote, but it did not happen. And neither will it happen this time."[53]

Along with Harry Ashmore and the South's few other white liberal editors, Hurley and the region's NAACP leaders expressed their private hopes in an attempt to build a climate of acceptance that would enable the Supreme Court's opinion to become a reality. Hurley was a realist whose everyday existence in Birmingham belied the notion that whites were ready to dismantle segregation. But she held to the belief stated earlier in the year in a press release condemning anti-Semitic leaflets circulating in the city: "It will not be difficult to wash away such hatemongering as more people speak out against it."[54]

Hurley had no tolerance for African Americans who defended segregation after the Supreme Court opinion. Calling the decision our "new Emancipation Proclamation," she wrote to coworkers that "many Negroes have been speaking out in favor of continuing slavery. We know that the majority of Negroes . . . throughout the South are sick and tired of wearing the badge of inferiority that goes with segregation and they want to do all that can be done to get it out of their lives altogether. . . . The NAACP will continue to lead the way."[55]

While the Alabama branch prepared to take full advantage of Folsom's upcoming term as the state's chief executive, Hurley increasingly became disturbed by developments in neighboring Mississippi. She warned that its state legislators were openly calling for violence. Shortly after Folsom's election, Patton began working with others to organize a Committee of 67 with delegates from each of the state's counties to develop a voting rights plan entitled "What We Want." In 1950, Patton had pulled together a coalition of local and state groups under the umbrella of the Alabama Coordinating Committee for Registration and Voting, which he continued to serve as chair. Some issues, such as registrars requiring Black applicants to have white property owners vouch for them, were already on the list, but the group wanted statewide input and involvement.[56]

As the school year began in the fall of 1954, Hurley helped the state's 38 local branches petition local school boards for the voluntary desegregation of schools. In November, Patton convened the state NAACP's annual conference in Selma, where two weeks later State Senator Walter Givhan would organize a rally of more than 1,200 local whites to form Alabama's first White Citizens' Council chapter. Gathering in the heart of darkness, the NAACP members passed resolutions on a variety of issues to undo segregation and Jim Crow justice but kept front and center the need to tear down barriers to increasing voter registration and paying the state's poll tax.

Selma's white newspaper relayed in detail the NAACP's political agenda: stimulate activities in counties where "registration is already easy"; develop "civic action" in the counties with barriers to registering; urge "legal prosecution of registrars and other public officials" who obstruct qualified Black applicants; call upon the governor-elect to appoint country registrars who will register qualified African Americans and remove those registrars who will not; encourage qualified Black candidates to run for local office; and continue the campaign to get the state Democratic party to remove the words "White Supremacy" as its symbol. In his keynote address, Patton assured members that the organization was having an impact in politics, including the recent referendum reducing the poll tax, and apparently claimed, perhaps for the white public's consumption, that Alabama had as many as 100,000 Black voters.[57]

'ALL MEN SHOULD HAVE THE RIGHT TO VOTE'

In January 1955, Patton called together the Alabama Coordinating Committee for Registration and Voting to build momentum for voter registration and spur local groups to get Black voters to pay their poll tax, The meeting coincided with Folsom's inauguration, an event like none Patton and other African Americans had experienced. Thousands of Black Alabamians from across the state traveled to Montgomery for the festive occasion, which included a meandering, boisterous parade of more than 70 floats and a hundred marching bands, including 12 Negro bands, "unsegregated in the line of march" and grouped with white bands by their home counties.

"I am here to be governor of all the people," Folsom announced as he began his inaugural speech, "and I am here that all might have freedom." Beamed across the state by radio and, for the first time, into black-and-white television sets, it was a message certain to carry "an impact of meaning that vibrated to the assembled audience, radio, and TV listeners everywhere," according to the Black-owned *Huntsville Mirror*'s correspondent Jo Ann Robinson, a freelancing English professor at the all-Black Alabama State College. "All men have inalienable rights as endowed by the Creator," Folsom declared afterwards, and "all men should have the right to vote as a part of their inalienable rights."[58]

More than 2,500 Blacks packed the Alabama State College gymnasium in a first-ever "Negro inaugural ball" for Folsom, who attended and spoke to the crowd. The new governor thanked them for their hospitality and told them how pleased he was by the last election's Negro vote, the largest in more than half a century and one that helped him avoid a runoff. He concluded by assuring them of the meaning of his "Y'all Come" campaign slogan: "I want every citizen of Alabama, regardless of color, to know that you have a friend in the highest place the people of Alabama can give."[59]

Folsom's words and his inclusive recognition of the Black community were unprecedented, an acknowledgment of Negroes' rights and needs as human beings not spoken by a governor since Reconstruction, and they won praise from Black leaders across the state. But Robinson captured an emerging fissure that even the extraordinary, welcoming stance of the

Governor James E. "Big Jim" Folsom, inauguration, 1955 (ADAH).

oversized governor could not easily straddle as African Americans began to insist that now was the time for setting new ways, new days for a new birth of freedom. "This writer did not condone the two balls, since another pattern of segregation was established," Robinson wrote, although she noted that "'Big Jim' meant only good in the effort and has every intention of being governor of all the people of Alabama."[60]

This fracture was beginning to develop not merely between Black and white. Robinson's Huntsville publisher let her commentary remain in the story, but he tacked on his remarks at the end of her article as those of the "publisher, Atty. Arthur A Madison." The publisher insisted that a public announcement was made at the swearing-in ceremony that the "Governor's Inaugural Ball would be held at the Alabama Coliseum with an invitation extended to all the citizens of Alabama."[61]

Madison was no stranger to segregation or voting problems in Alabama. He was the Alabama-born lawyer who in 1944 filed suit as a cooperating

Arthur A. Madison (Madison Family Collection, H. Councill Trenholm State Community College).

attorney for the NAACP on behalf of seven Black citizens in Montgomery seeking the right to register to vote. For that effort, he was disbarred in Alabama after local white officials, represented by attorney Richard Rives, accused him of unethically bringing the lawsuit without the permission of clients, who apparently had been pressured to renege. Afterwards, the elderly Black attorney became prosperous through legal work and business dealings in New York City. He also started two Alabama newspapers and a small garment factory in Montgomery, where the local NAACP secretary, Rosa L. Parks, was in charge of sewing.

In his Alabama newspapers, Madison regularly supplemented NAACP's ads with his own ads cajoling readers to pay the poll tax, register, and vote and listed his Montgomery business address as a place where Black citizens could receive voting assistance.[62] On the occasion of Folsom's inauguration, Madison insisted on the last word in his own newspaper concerning the meaning of this historic moment—when for the first time in more than three quarters of a century the emerging power of the Black ballot had a significant effect in electing a good white man to Alabama's highest office, a man not dead-set on advancing segregation but openly declaring he would serve all the people.

Hurley had her own occasional misgivings about Big Jim. His folksy, rural mannerisms and the haphazard, sometimes imprudent style in which he conducted himself and often governed were probably off-putting to someone with her Northern, urban sensibilities, self-discipline, and urbane, austere self-dignity. She was not always certain his commitment to the cause of Black freedom was genuine, but the events in neighboring Mississippi gave her and her colleagues good reason to appreciate Folsom's refusal to go along with the White Citizens' Councils and the state's rabid segregationists.[63]

By 1955, it was plain to Hurley that "Mississippi must be made to join the United States."[64] But that was easier said than done. Soon after the *Brown* opinion, Mississippi officials began trying to run roughshod over anyone who expressed support for the decision or continued efforts for voter registration, and, only four month after *Brown*, Hurley publicly accused state and local officials of trying "to run the National Association for the Advancement of Colored People out of Mississippi" through an open campaign of threats and harassment. In response, as the NAACP explored setting up a loan fund for members financially punished by local white businesses, Hurley held her annual regional meeting in December 1954 just across the Alabama state line in Columbus, Mississippi, where her newly hired state field director, Medgar Evers, was local host.[65]

When she was preparing the meeting, during a long, hot Deep South summer, Hurley had written Roy Wilkins in New York, "The heat and the politicians are driving me crazy."[66] But the Magnolia State soon went dangerously crazy. One of the founders of Belzoni's NAACP branch, the Reverend George W. Lee, was shot and killed around midnight May 7, 1955, eight hours after he was warned to stop promoting registration and voting. Hurley had worked with Lee, and she spoke at his funeral, whose organizers received death threats. The other local NAACP branch founder suffered two gunshot wounds later in the year after he ignored warnings to have a dozen Black folks remove their names from the local registration rolls.[67]

In August 1955, Lamar Smith, a WWII veteran and farmer in Brookhaven (south of Jackson) was murdered on the courthouse lawn; he had voted in that month's state primary and was coaching other Blacks to use absentee ballots to avoid intimidation at the polling place. Two weeks later, fourteen-year-old Emmett Till was kidnapped and murdered. "They took that child out and beat him, and then they tied him up with a chain from a cotton gin and dumped his body in the Tallahatchie River," Hurley remembered.[68]

Not believing that an FBI investigation would be thorough, Hurley went to Mississippi and with Evers gathered evidence in each of these cases. In the Till case, she and Evers borrowed what the well-coiffured Hurley called "cotton-picking clothes"—ragged garments—to blend into a local plantation's Black population so they could secretly interview tenant families that might have relevant information. Hurley also attended and reported on the state court trials, although in the case of Lamar Smith no one was ever arrested since everyone in town claimed they failed to see the shooter or the shooting, which took place in broad daylight on a Saturday, the town's busiest day.[69]

By the end of 1955, Hurley had clocked 40,000 miles of bus and car travel throughout the back roads of Mississippi, Alabama, and the other states of her region. (And there were no interstate highways.) She also traveled another 26,000 miles by plane, train, and car standing in for Emmett Till's mother in a national tour about his murder. Hurley also traveled to spread the word about other "cases of bestiality which resulted in a disgusting spectacle of Southern justice." The tour of Western and Northern states was grueling for a middle-aged person, although Hurley was always aided and accompanied by others. The trips across Mississippi, Alabama, and the rest of the southeast were usually taken alone.

The danger was palpable for a single Black woman traveling by bus and car often after dark as a professional staff member of the NAACP in the Jim Crow South. Hurley made the journeys even more difficult due to her own principles. "I *just could not eat* in Jim Crow places," she told Howell Raines, a young white Alabama-born reporter. All white-owned restaurants were segregated, and when she traveled often by bus, it only stopped at segregated places. "I was not going to eat in a segregated place. So, if I ran out of Hershey Bars I didn't eat . . . ofttimes twenty-four hours I didn't have anything to eat."[70]

In Alabama, while Hurley was dealing with developments in Mississippi, W. C. Patton was hired as the state's full-time field director to take on broader responsibilities, including trying to keep NAACP membership from plummeting as growing white hostility made being a NAACP member risky, if not dangerous. He continued to urge African Americans to register and pay the poll tax, support voting cases, and search for ways to enable passage of state representative George Hawkins's new bill to eliminate all poll taxes.[71]

In late 1955, Hurley told newspapermen what she considered an obvious fact to anyone of conscience: "Mississippi is the core of this new wave of oppression."[72] But it was not the only state where intimidation and violence were used to suppress the rise of Black voting and desegregated schools, as Hurley and Patton knew. "The National Assn. for the Agitation of Colored People forgets there is more ways than one to kill a snake," declared Black Belt state senator Sam Engelhardt, leader of the Alabama White Citizens' Councils.[73]

Racist Asa Carter, who found the White Citizens' Council too moderate, hosted a daily Birmingham radio show in which he branded Black and white integrationists as communists and solicited new members for a splinter group. In Selma, Senator Walter Givhan and the White Citizens' Council openly promoted retaliation for any Black who got out of line—for example, Black parents who signed a petition to the local school board seeking desegregation were fired from their jobs at a creamery.

Selma's African Americans with no white employer faced other consequences. A Black jeweler was threatened with arrest for failing to pay back taxes, a public debt the local tax collector refused to document. A Black man was kidnapped and warned against causing trouble, but then released when his white captors realized he was not the Black person they sought to intimidate. Someone fired into the shop of a Black storekeeper, wounding a Black bystander, and set fire to the home of a Black woman next door. Later it was uncovered that these were the acts of two Selma police officers, whom an all-white grand jury refused to indict.[74]

In neighboring Wilcox County, local lawmakers enacted over Governor Folsom's veto a law requiring any organization recruiting members to prove its "good character" and its benefit to the county's general welfare before soliciting anyone in the county—or else face fines and up to six months in the local jail. As Patton told the NAACP's new national director Roy Wilkins, the bill was openly promoted to "prohibit the N.A.A.C.P. and labor unions from establishing a branch." Black Belt legislators in other counties signaled they would introduce similar bills.[75]

In Birmingham, Hurley, Emory O. Jackson, and the NAACP's local cooperating attorneys were named personally along with the organization as defendants in a state court action seeking $100,000 in damages for their role in persuading the city to fire a policeman for rank misconduct involving a Black couple.

The NAACP attempted to overcome these challenges. At the request of Hurley and Patton, the Washington office pressured the U.S. Defense Department to intervene on behalf of the fired workers at the Selma creamery, which held a federal contract to supply milk to the local army base. In Selma, Black-owned insurance companies' local agents, including Amelia Boynton, offered their help to take up the mortgage of any Black property owner foreclosed in an economic reprisal.[76]

At a conference of Hurley's regional advisory board, she issued a statement: "In some areas the officials are merely ignoring the Court's mandate to proceed promptly and reasonably in good faith. In others, there is not only defiance of the law, but open and inflammatory appeals to passion, ignorance and prejudice in an effort to preserve an already outmoded way of life. . . . This has resulted in a wave of lawlessness, violence, terror, murder and has brought shame and international disgrace upon the region."[77]

If the white South felt shame and disgrace, it provided little or no deterrence. At the University of Alabama early in 1956, a white mob, including many students, rioted against the attendance of Autherine Lucy, a young Black woman whose enrollment had been required by an NAACP lawsuit that Hurley had assisted in bringing. Afterwards the university expelled Lucy from school "for her own safety." To the surprise of many of Alabama's Black leaders, Governor Folsom's office issued a statement condemning outside agitators and the NAACP for the disturbance. "The Governor has been misinformed," Hurley diplomatically replied, but in New York NAACP national director Roy Wilkins blasted Folsom for joining "the other 'hate' groups in his attempt to discredit and particularly blame the NAACP for the conditions of law and order in Alabama."[78]

In Montgomery, Rosa Parks was arrested for refusing to obey the city's regulations for segregated seating on its buses, and the Montgomery Bus Boycott emerged as a sustained, grassroots protest headed by Martin Luther King Jr. The protest was kicked off in part by a small group of Black women, including Alabama State College English professor Jo Ann Robinson. The night of Parks's arrest, Robinson composed a flyer calling for the citywide boycott; over the next couple of days, the women mimeographed an estimated 30,000 copies that were distributed across the Black community. The following Monday, the boycott began and was almost totally effective. But a month later, King's home was dynamited, and Montgomery's white leaders refused a compromise that would have addressed some Black grievances without directly challenging segregation. The situation had all the dynamics that Hurley had described only a few months earlier as the conditions for "a wave of lawlessness."[79]

'I DIDN'T GET SCARED . . . I WAS MAD'

Before Montgomery exploded in late 1956 and early 1957 with a string of bombings, beatings, and sniper fire, the state's chief law officer decided to use the force of law to put Ruby Hurley, W. C. Patton, and the NAACP out of business in Alabama. On Friday, June 1, 1956, Hurley received a phone call at home from a friendly newspaperman in Montgomery informing her that Judge Walter B. Jones was preparing to issue a temporary injunction to outlaw the NAACP in Alabama in response to court filings by the state's Attorney General John Patterson. During the call, still in her housecoat with curlers in her hair, Hurley answered a knock at her door where two deputy sheriffs served the injunction as a gaggle of news reporters and photographers recorded the moment.[80]

Hurley was livid. She was annoyed by the white deputies and white photographers ambushing her at home before she was fully dressed, but most of all she was outraged by the legal action. Hurley knew enough law to understand that the injunction was a theatrical act in the drama of white politics more than a case in law. That morning, with Judge Jones's blessings, Patterson posed for cameras in the Montgomery circuit clerk's office so that photographers could capture him filing a petition to put the NAACP out of business, when in fact Jones had already signed the order, which was being served on Hurley in Birmingham around the same time.[81]

Jones's order found that the NAACP had failed to register, as required by state law, as an out-of-state corporation doing business in Alabama. After a hearing that included only the attorney general and his assistants filing their petition, Jones mandated that the NAACP cease operations immediately since it was endangering Alabama citizens. This *ex parte* proceeding was not only one-sided but involved no evidence other than exhibits showing that the NAACP was incorporated as an organization in New York, had an office in Birmingham's Black Masonic Temple Building, and had failed to file papers as an out-of-state corporation with the Alabama Secretary of State.

Patterson told Jones that the NAACP was "causing irreparable injury to the property and civil rights of the residents and citizens of the State of Alabama." His complaint alleged, among other things, that the NAACP had paid Autherine Lucy to become its client so the group, led by Hurley and NAACP attorneys Arthur Shores and Constance Baker Motley, could sue the University of Alabama. Patterson also alleged the group had engaged in "organizing, supporting and financing an illegal boycott by Negro residents of Montgomery." No supporting evidence or testimony was presented to Jones's court before he issued the statewide order.[82] It was all self-evident to the judge.

Walter B. Jones had become an institution unto himself in Montgomery since his early days as a legislator when he parlayed his duplicitous sponsorship of the veterans' poll tax into popularity that enabled his election to the circuit court bench. He had already served as a circuit judge for three decades. He also started a night law school, wrote a weekly column in the *Montgomery Advertiser*, founded and edited the *Alabama Lawyer*, which became the official journal of the Alabama Bar Association, and wrote and spoke often extolling the virtues of the South's traditions, racial segregation, and states' rights.[83]

Jones had done his part as a state court judge to uphold these virtues. In 1942, he spoke and wrote against changing the poll tax because "the ballot should be the privilege of only the intelligent and virtuous." In 1944, he was one of the judges on the case disbarring Arthur Madison in one of the state's first voting rights cases. In 1955, when the private company operating Montgomery's buses announced it was ready to end the bus boycott and follow federal case law prohibiting segregation, Jones ordered the company to follow the city's segregation ordinance—and ignore the federal courts' opinion. Jones ruled that the power to regulate a city's passenger buses was reserved exclusively to the State of Alabama. "It has never surrendered this power to the United States Government nor given it to the Supreme Court at Washington, and this Court will not be a party to filching the power from the State," he wrote.[84]

Patterson and Jones were friends. Jones had been appointed by Alabama Chief Justice Ed Livingston to preside over the Phenix City corruption trials, prompted by the murder of Albert Patterson, who was on his way to becoming Alabama's attorney general after winning the 1954 Democratic primary. John Patterson then became the only candidate in a special election to replace his assassinated father on the general election ballot, which the son won. Jones's significant role in the trial and conviction of the men responsible for the father's murder began a close personal relationship between the young, ambitious attorney general and the courtly, aging judge.[85]

After Patterson got his well-publicized "photo op" and Hurley got her restraining order, Jones continued to advance the attorney general's political cause. NAACP attorneys Arthur Shores and Fred Gray sought a hearing to dismiss the injunction, but before the hearing Jones granted the Patterson's motion to require the organization to turn over an extensive set of documents, including bank statements, leases, deeds, and records of the names and addresses of all Alabama NAACP members and "agents." The civil rights attorneys argued the documents were not relevant and constituted a "fishing expedition," but Jones dismissed their objections, while complaining that Black lawyers took too much of his time arguing their case. After the NAACP failed to produce the records, Jones fined it for contempt of court in an amount that reached $100,000. With Ed Livingston presiding, the Alabama Supreme Court affirmed Jones's order, the contempt citation, and the amount of the fine.[86]

Hurley had closed her office the day she received the temporary restraining order, as she and Patton arranged to remove all files and records, including membership rolls, from their Birmingham offices. They understood immediately the dangers their members might face, especially since Patterson and Engelhardt were apparently cooperating in attacks on the NAACP. Hurley worked out of her home for a few days but left the final details of closing her office to her secretary as she departed for California, where the NAACP was holding its national convention.

"I've had it," Hurley decided. She was "sick of civil rights and sick of fighting the white folks, and sick of the South." For five years in Birmingham, "I could be riding down the street and white men would drive by and say, 'We goin' get you.'" She worked long hours in her office on the same floor of the Masonic building that once was headquarters of the Ex-Soldiers Cooperative Association where Indiana Little, Ohio Bell, and others fought unsuccessfully for Black voting. The NAACP office often received threatening phone calls, and, when Hurley went home to an empty house, "I never knew if there was going to be a bomb." In fact bombs were thrown at her house, located in a somewhat isolated area near two of the city's large Jewish cemeteries, and there were threatening calls at all times of the night.

Over these years, Hurley had traveled countless hours visiting community leaders and victims of racism, dodging white vigilantes or gun-toting state's righters, while surviving on chocolate bars on her way back and forth to Birmingham. "When I was out there by myself, for instance, there was no TV cameras with me to give me any protection. There were no reporters traveling with me to give me protection. . . . It played havoc physically. . . . I didn't get scared . . . I was mad. I got mad when we were put out of business."[87]

Hurley stayed in California for almost three months before returning to the South to set up shop in Atlanta, where the Georgia Bureau of Investigation began clandestinely monitoring her activities. She worked as the NAACP's regional director for another two decades. Patton moved to Memphis and transformed his state coordinating committee into a regional coalition of groups in which the NAACP was only a member. He returned to Birmingham after the ban was lifted, and his voting rights work continued into the 1970s.[88]

Jones and the Alabama Supreme Court enabled Patterson to accomplish something that no other Southern segregationist leader had achieved in attacking the NAACP—they shut it down and kept the organization out of the state for eight years. There had been a coordinated effort among Southern states to shut down the NAACP, but the other states went after the organization through legislation or legislative actions. The strategies worked, but not for so long. The NAACP went into federal courts and secured decrees voiding the other states' laws and final state court actions as discriminatory, but civil rights lawyers could not do the same in Alabama since they were bound by a state court order that remained "temporary" for five years, and a contempt citation that Jones kept revising, reinstating, and revisiting in small ways for years. Because of the constitutional rules of federalism, NAACP attorneys had to exhaust all Alabama state court remedies and could only appeal final actions of the state courts before they went to federal courts.[89]

As a result, Walter Jones and Ed Livingston deliberately engaged in years of evasion and passive resistance in which they parsed separate orders and holdings, each of which had to be appealed separately, nitpicked the meaning of the U.S. Supreme Court's words and orders, dismissed pleadings on procedural grounds, challenged the U.S. Supreme Court for misconstruing facts and law, kept a temporary order in place for more than five years, and always took their own sweet time in holding hearings and issuing orders that could be appealed.[90]

Jones seemed emboldened by his successful judicial maneuvering. In the spring of 1957, as the NAACP ban case meandered, he published in both the *Montgomery Advertiser* and the *Alabama Lawyer* an essay entitled "I Speak for the White Race." It should have been "I Speak for White Supremacy," since he catalogued across history the ways he believed Anglo Saxons had outshined the rest of humanity. "We shall never submit to the demands of integrationists," Jones concluded. "The white race shall forever remain white."[91] In a later hearing in the case, Jones refused a motion by NAACP attorney Robert Carter to desegregate his courtroom or to have Negro attorneys and witnesses referred to as "Mr.," "Mrs.," or "Miss," as were the whites.[92]

All told, the Alabama Supreme Court rendered six published opinions affirming Jones's various decisions, and the nation's highest court issued three opinions overturning each of the Alabama court's decisions. In its final decree, issued in Washington exactly eight years to the day after the deputies showed up on Ruby Hurley's doorstep, the U.S. Supreme Court ordered that the NAACP should be allowed to remedy their 1951 error by doing what Alabama law required of any "foreign corporation"—file with the secretary of state its articles of incorporation and a written statement identifying in the state its place of business and its authorized agent along with payment of a filing fee of $10.[93]

In the ensuing years, Ruby Hurley and others in the NAACP in the South developed a reputation for being overly protective of their organization's turf. In Alabama, their attitude was informed by bitter experience. The state's NAACP members and leaders had to abandon the organization in 1956 and were forced to find, create or affiliate with new civil rights groups. The eight-year banishment drained the Alabama organization of its leaders and robbed it of its past investments in the state. Also, by the time it was lifted, the ban had denied the organization much of the credit for past achievements that laid a foundation for changes in the 1960s and beyond. And no less irksome to Ruby Hurley, it put the NAACP far behind in challenging white supremacy in the Heart of Dixie, where in her years the regional director found too few white folks who could or would pronounce correctly the word "Negro"—much less accept that she or he was a full human being.[94]

Robert Carter and other NAACP lawyers before Judge Walter Jones (ADAH).

NAACP leaders Emory Jackson, W. C. Patton, Arthur Shores, and John LeFlore with Juanita Kennedy Morgan at the U.S. Supreme Court (Doy Leale McCall Rare Book and Manuscript Library, University of South Alabama).

CHAPTER 13

Ending the War of Sections

'A Fair Share for North Alabama'

In 1958, Attorney General John Patterson became a candidate for governor and was the choice of most Black Belt planters. Initially, the handsome, square-jawed Patterson was considered by political pundits as a long shot, a young, temporary officeholder whose father's death enabled only fleeting popularity and sympathy among voters, especially during a campaign with more experienced opponents, including former state representative and then current circuit court judge George Wallace of Barbour County in an overcrowded field of 14 candidates.

Patterson projected the image of an energetic young man fighting to clean up corruption, but his campaign was largely built around his recent successful attacks on the NAACP. In February, he kicked off his campaign in Phenix City, where his father was murdered, and his speech placed segregation and the NAACP front and center. "As your governor I will see to it that there is no mixing of the races in the schools," Patterson promised, just as he had waged "an all-out fight against outside agitators like the NAACP." He made other promises about increasing old-age pensions, school funding, and increased jobs, but the proof of his ability to get things done went back to the NAACP. "Now you are going to hear some people say this can't be done," the attorney general warned. "These same people said we couldn't put the NAACP out of business, but we did."[1]

In the following months, Patterson spoke across the state about how "gangsters and the NAACP" were pouring money into Alabama to defeat him, and within weeks of the primary he announced that as attorney general he was charging NAACP leaders W. C. Patton and W. P. Mitchell of

Tuskegee with doing business in the state illegally. "We have the tools to keep the NAACP out of Alabama, and I shall continue use them," Patterson declared.[2]

His campaign mounted a statewide advertising blitz during the week leading up to the primary. In most of north Alabama, ads proclaimed it was time to "clean house in Alabama" and included the fight against the NAACP as one of several examples of how Patterson was advancing "sound, clean, honest, and efficient state government." In the remainder of Alabama, he spotlighted the NAACP as if it was on the verge of an imminent invasion of the state. "NAACP Launches Negro Vote Drive Against John Patterson," the ads shouted. Why? "While other have talked segregation, John has acted" and was the only one who could stop "the integration crowd who are seeking to mongrelize our state."[3] The "integration crowd" included "the NAACP, the Northern radicals and Communists," according to Patterson backers, who cheered as their candidate closed his campaign proclaiming that the NAACP "had done more to agitate unrest and trouble in this state than any other one organization."[4]

Among the other candidates, Wallace campaigned as the most qualified and promised a range of social programs that resembled Folsom's agenda while disowning his past relationship with the outgoing governor. Another candidate was newspaper publisher Jimmy Faulkner, originally considered the frontrunner, who promised to be the governor for everyone from the day laborer to big businessman and to represent all 67 counties. Wallace promised he would uphold segregation with dignity, while all candidates avowed complete dedication to maintaining segregation, a predictable position since registered Blacks still comprised less than seven percent of the electorate.[5]

Also in the race was Laurie Battle, a former congressman who echoed the combined campaign themes of Wallace and Faulkner across much of the state, although he told Tennessee Valley residents he was the best north Alabama candidate to fight for their fair representation in Montgomery. And there was William Ralph "Shorty" Price, a five-foot-small insurance salesman from Barbour County who as the shortest candidate decided to give the longest campaign speech on the Jefferson County Courthouse steps—apparently across more than twelve hours, often delivered to one or two listeners, if any. He stopped talking after Saturday night because, as he said, a religious man never works on Sundays.

Agriculture Commissioner A. W. Todd, known as the "Fighter from Franklin" County, joined the crowd of campaigners as a self-proclaimed "north Alabama man." His campaign was largely carried out in Birmingham and the northern counties, where his ads reminded voters that "South Alabama makes fun of us." Todd attempted to project himself as the heir to Big Jim's fair treatment of north Alabama without ever mentioning the governor by name. He promised that if voters would give "Todd the Nod" they would have a "North Alabamian who will fight our battles for us."[6]

State Representative George Hawkins, the longtime advocate for abolishing the poll tax, was also a candidate. During the last years of Folsom's administration, Hawkins made no progress in getting his bills to eliminate the poll tax out of committee. The legislature did pass unanimously a bill sponsored by Jefferson County legislators exempting every deaf and blind person from paying the poll tax, and voters ratified it with 82 percent of the vote. But, despite Hawkins's pleas that the poll tax "primarily discriminates against women," he could not muster significant support in the legislature and, in fact, had to quash efforts by Black Belt Senator Roland Cooper to restore the 1901 requirements.[7]

Hawkins's campaign did not highlight the poll tax. Instead he conducted a direct attack on those who had developed and maintained the poll tax over the decades—the Black Belt. In his opening speech in his hometown at the Etowah High School gymnasium, Hawkins declared, "The Black Belt now controls the legislature and the people should not turn over the executive department to them." His platform centered on improving education, undertaking reapportionment, and improving the roads and welfare programs that Folsom had championed.[8]

A week later, Hawkins delivered from Montgomery a radio address with the same message to south Alabama. "As governor I pledge to contest Black Belt domination of Alabama's government from the day I take office," he asserted.[9] Hawkins's young campaign manager, Chuck Morgan, recalled his candidate as thoughtful, deliberate, and an excellent trial lawyer—which was a positive spin on the candidate's lack of Big Jim's magnetic charisma on the stump. So the campaign made the most of Hawkins's qualities by putting him before a radio microphone as often as their tiny campaign budget allowed and arranged a dozen or more stops each day.

This frontal challenge to the Black Belt was dismissed by south Alabama editors and Black Belt planters as the bitter, vain wailing of a labor lawyer, and the White Citizens' Council rated Hawkins as weak on states' rights and segregation. The candidate responded by trying to drive a political wedge between the Wiregrass and the Black Belt. His campaign also publicized his anti-Black Belt theme more softly as "A Fair Share for All of Alabama" in the state's northern-most section, the Tennessee Valley, where another recent University of Alabama law school graduate, Howell Heflin, was his local campaign chair.

As Election Day neared and Hawkins's candidacy failed to match the lyrics of his campaign song, "He'll set the pace . . . Movin' On," he doubled down on finding more north Alabama votes. "There won't be a road—or bridge or a single appointment for BLACK BELT POLITICIANS when I'm Governor," Hawkins exclaimed in speeches and ads, "unless and until they vote yes on a Fair Share for NORTH ALABAMA."[10]

Patterson led the primary with almost 200,000 votes, some 35,000 more than Wallace in second place. Therefore, two Black Belt candidates were in the runoff. South Alabama's Faulkner was a distant third, and Todd came in fourth with only nine percent of the vote, carrying only his own home county. Hawkins got less than four percent of the total vote—fewer than 25,000 votes, which included more than 10,000 from his home of Etowah, the only county he carried. Sending their own clear message, each of seven Black Belt counties gave Hawkins fewer than 10 votes; a few Black Belt counties gave more votes to "Shorty" Price than to Hawkins.[11]

The 1958 election is remembered in Alabama political history for the moment George Wallace, wounded by his loss to Patterson in the runoff, proclaimed in graphic terms that he would never again allow anyone to outdo him as a demagogue for white supremacy. Behind this landmark stands the simple fact that only four years after *Brown,* the NAACP as a symbol of the full citizenship for Black people had become a leading, powerful source of virile political fear that could catapult a white candidate to the lead. The name symbolically conjured a host of enemies—Black and white radicals, agitators, communists—all portrayed as not only anti-Southern but un-American because they challenged the racial traditions the state's white government had erected over decades and was preserved as a state's right by the national constitution. In short, attacking and vilifying the NAACP evoked a far more visceral response than Wallace's slogan of "Help Keep Alabama Southern."[12]

In Alabama, 1958 also signified that much was being forgiven and forgotten in the Black Belt's long history of political manipulation and economic exploitation. It had never been much of a liability for the Black Belt to use its minority rule of the legislature to disembody Black citizenship, but often it had been a real bone of political contention when the Black Belt used Black voters as a screen for enriching its own with state revenues and resources that other parts of the state produced.

When George Hawkins threatened to block any Black Belt road or bridge until north Alabama received its fair share, he understood what men like the Black Belt's John Rogers had built and set in motion across decades in the Alabama legislature. What he did not know as a certain fact until election night was that, as of 1958, Alabama's sectional conflicts no longer had significant political power among Alabama's white electorate in competition with the symbolic horrors of an NAACP operating in the state of Alabama as a free agent.

In retrospect, it seems astonishing that one smart, dedicated Black woman and her secretary sitting on the sixth floor of a Black-owned Birmingham building, often pinching pennies to keep within a meager organizational budget, and with a statewide membership of never more than 10,000 mostly low-income persons, could reshape the politics of Alabama and wipe away so completely nearly six decades of self-serving political control by a self-appointed group of aristocratic white men living in barely more than a dozen sparsely populated counties in south Alabama. It signaled more than a new political era in the state. It marked the beginning of the end of the state's political history of warring sections.

'PARLOR PATTER FOR PANTING, POSTURING LIBROOLS'

Walter B. Jones was chosen to administer the oath of office to John Patterson as Alabama's governor on January 20, 1959, in what could only be understood as an act of public gratitude for the judge's essential roles in bringing the killers of Patterson's father to justice and in enabling Patterson's winning campaign as the state's fighting segregationist. (Following custom, members of the Alabama Supreme Court swore in the other statewide elected officials.) Jones was deeply moved by this public honor, perhaps even more than when an Alabama member of the Electoral College violated his pledge by voting for Jones for President in the last presidential election. Patterson's first official act as governor was to sign the commission certifying Jones as the state's senior circuit judge and chair of the Montgomery County jury board that determined if a person had sufficient good character to serve as a juror in state courts.

Jones had been up for reelection in the prior year, and, while Patterson was campaigning, Jones faced an opponent who excavated Jones's exemption from WWI military service. The judge was apparently worried enough by his opponent's prospects that he violated judicial ethics by promising in a campaign speech that he would deliver a mortal blow to the NAACP in his courtroom. When the group's lawyers asked Jones to recuse himself for this reason in the never-ending NAACP case, he refused and continued to use his judicial discretion to slow-march the case along a circuitous, tortured route that preserved his original ban.[13]

Jones's campaign opponent failed to uncover another secret about the judge that apparently was known among some members of the local press. Jones had been arrested for molesting a boy in the YMCA, and the arrest report was buried by Montgomery police commissioner L. B. Sullivan, according to William J. MacDonald, the *Montgomery Advertiser*'s associate editor. A lifelong bachelor, Jones occasionally entertained in his study where the walls were filled with photographs of young men, some nude. He had an 800-acre country estate he called Jonesboro, which among other functions had served over the years as a retreat for convalescing young soldiers during World War II and the site of annual picnics for Boys Clubs. MacDonald also told historians after Jones's death that the judge had affixed a small photograph of a young, innocent-looking boy onto the ends of the gavel he used in court.[14]

Jones remained a close friend and advisor to Patterson throughout the governor's term and was a vital strategist of the white resistance that Patterson oversaw or enabled in the state's capital. When the U.S. Justice Department sought Montgomery's voting records, following the unfavorable Civil Rights Commission hearing in the city in December 1958, Jones declared the Civil Rights Act of 1960 unconstitutional and blocked the federal government's access to voting records in all 67 Alabama counties until federal Judge Frank Johnson overruled him.

Jones presided over the 1960 jury trial in which Montgomery police commissioner Sullivan received a $500,000 libel verdict against the *New York Times* for running an advertisement that a New York-based group had sponsored to raise funds in support of Martin Luther King Jr. The judgment was a clear attempt to punish the *Times* for giving favorable national coverage to Black activism, and Jones's rulings and one-sided charge to an all-white jury (men he had approved, as local jury board chair, as being worthy of service), helped dampen national newspaper coverage of the conflicts over civil rights in John Patterson's Alabama until the U.S. Supreme Court overturned the verdict four years later.[15]

When the libel case came to trial, Jones refused to desegregate his courtroom, declaring that the U.S. Constitution's Fourteenth Amendment "has no standing whatever in this Court, it is a pariah and an outcast." He also scolded the defendants' Black lawyers for "grandstanding" and making "loud objections to the pronouncing of the word NEGRO." Jones declared that such objections were "appeals to race prejudice" and lacked "good taste." He was so proud of himself for his public scolding of the Black attorneys that he published his remarks from the bench in the journal of the Alabama Bar Association, which he managed.[16]

Jones also attempted to do his part when Patterson and the state capital were vexed by young John Lewis and other Freedom Riders traveling to Montgomery on a Greyhound bus to test compliance with new federal regulations banning segregation in interstate transportation. One of the Riders' buses had been firebombed near Anniston, and, as Patterson came under increasing pressure from U.S. Attorney General Bobby Kennedy to protect the riders and ensure order, Jones issued a restraining order against the Riders. The injunction found that Lewis and the other civil rights activists were involved in a "breach of the peace" and should be banned from the state.

Later in life Patterson remembered that he was outraged by how the U.S. attorney general spoke to him, especially after Kennedy had learned that the Freedom Riders and one of his own aides were savagely beaten by vigilantes at the Montgomery bus terminal. Law officers had watched the bloody assault unfold and did nothing. Jones and Alabama Attorney General McDonald Gallion were also at the scene, observing the beatings with outward signs of approval. As the beaten and bruised Lewis lay on the pavement, in pain from a concussion, Gallion stood over him reading Jones's injunction. Many of the bandaged Freedom Riders subsequently traveled on to Mississippi even as Jones convened a hearing to determine if he could punish them for contempt for violating his order. Afterwards, Judge Johnson overruled Jones's injunction and found that the attacks were planned by Kluxers.[17]

From his first day in office, Patterson had no interest in Alabama's poll tax, but influential state legislators did. The legislature's interim Segregation Screening Committee recommended restoring the cumulative back payment of poll taxes, abolishing absentee voting for everyone except active military personnel and hospitalized veterans, and instituting a statewide reregistration of voters as well as an intelligence test for prospective voters. Black Belt Senator Snag Andrews introduced the proposed poll tax bill and it quickly received approval from the Constitutional Revisions Committee.

The bill failed to get a third reading and a vote in the senate due to some unexpected opposition. As expected, George Hawkins warned that north Alabama would be most hurt by restoring the old poll tax and argued that the absence of any significant number of registered Black veterans, who were already exempt from the poll tax, demonstrated that the tax had little or no effect on Black voting. Hawkins was joined by Martha Witt Smith and the League of Women Voters in opposing Andrews's bill, arguing that it would penalize white women more than anyone else. In south Alabama, the *Enterprise Ledger* editor also opposed the changes—with a different logic. Acknowledging that both Blacks and whites would be adversely affected by the bill, he thought "donations by the NAACP could keep the Negro vote heavy but where would the poor white voter be left?"[18]

By the time the legislature reconvened in 1961, Black Belt leaders had bigger fish to fry in cooking up ways to retard African American voting. Congress passed and the federal courts upheld the Civil Rights Act of 1960, and the Kennedy administration's U.S. Justice Department was moving decisively to use its new powers to unblock Black voting in Alabama and other Southern states. In a desperate attempt at renewed intimidation, Jones held another hearing in Montgomery on whether to hold W. C. Patton in contempt for operating the NAACP in Alabama. Patton had continued to work through his voters association with local groups in the state, conducting "Citizenship Sundays" at churches and speaking at other meetings where he continued to

*Above, George Hawkins; right, Grover Hall Jr. with Madera Spencer (*Advertiser* society editor) at the Montgomery Country Club (both images from ADAH).*

attack the discriminatory effects of the poll tax, especially in the Black Belt.[19]

In 1962, over the objections of Alabama's entire congressional delegation, Congress passed a proposed federal constitutional amendment to outlaw the poll tax in all federal elections. At that point, only Alabama and four other Southern states had a poll tax, and 38 states ratified the Twenty-fourth Amendment in early 1964. When the legislature was racing to pass a literacy test before Congress passed a voting rights bill in the aftermath of the Selma March, Hawkins was serving in the state senate and attempted one last time to get the legislature to ban the poll tax. He and others argued that abolishing the poll tax could help save the state from the worst of "a punitive national law." The state senate agreed and passed a ban, but the house would not go along. A voter registration bill passed that included an eighth-grade literacy test but no ban on the poll tax.[20]

One day after passage of the federal Voting Rights Act of 1965, the Justice Department sued the State of Alabama seeking to ban its poll tax. Smith, now a key staff member of the Alabama Sovereignty Commission, called the lawsuit "utterly ridiculous" since the poll tax is a "penalty to women and the absent-minded."[21] And, in a momentary reversal of rhetoric, John Kohn, Governor George Wallace's attorney, told the three federal judges hearing arguments in the poll tax case: "If this nation is going to be saved . . . It will be saved by the courts."[22]

After Judges Frank Johnson and Richard Rives held that Alabama's poll tax violated the Fourteenth and Fifteenth amendments of the U.S. Constitution, the editorial page editor of the *Montgomery Advertiser*, Grover Hall Jr., decided to write the poll tax's obituary. The son of the *Advertiser*'s prior editor, who had won a Pulitzer prize for condemning the Klan in the 1920s, Hall Jr. often opposed blatant attempts to disfranchise all Black voters, echoing the philosophy that Governor Thomas Goode Jones embodied during the 1901 Constitutional Convention. At the same time, Hall was infuriated by what he considered hypocritical sanctimony of the Northern press on Alabama's civil rights problems and from 1958 forward was an apologist for the Black Belt's most successful governor, George Wallace.[23]

"The poll tax reform today is mainly parlor patter for posturing Librools," wrote Hall in March 1966, quoting his own earlier editorial.[24] After dismissing its importance in voting, Hall defended the poll tax's "honorable original ancestry." He admitted that in the years following 1901 it "discouraged many Negroes from seeking to qualify" to vote but equally so for "poor whites and those with dim civic motivation." Over the decades, he believed the military exemptions and revocation of the cumulative back payment made the tax a "shell of itself," irrelevant to voter registration.

These observations merely introduced the editorial's primary aim—to debunk the belief that the poll tax was "the cherished weapon of the sinister Black Belt counties" and to put in print an ode to the enduring values of the Black Belt.

Hall cited a few county returns from the 1953 referendum attempting to demonstrate that some conservative counties such Mobile and Montgomery supported the referendum while some north Alabama counties, including Frank Johnson's Republican-voting Winston County, opposed the liberalizing change. Nothing is available to reveal if Johnson, sitting in the nearby federal courthouse, realized that Hall not only cherry-picked his evidence but misrepresented the vote in Winston County, where 70 percent of voters actually supported the poll tax amendment.

The editorial was also blind to other factors beginning to work in Alabama politics in the 1950s: expanding political divisions between urban and rural counties, replacing the battles between north and south Alabama counties; a lingering belief among some rural north Alabama Democrats that a poll tax suppressed white Republican voting in counties where local elections remained competitive; and, most of all, the simple fact that virtually all Black Belt counties, so long as Black folks were disfranchised, remained a solid political bloc.[25]

Also, Hall blithely disremembered that for more than half a century Black Belt legislators protected and defended the poll tax and its large back payment as a requirement to block Black voting in their counties. But Hall wrote not so much to recast Alabama political history as to give a lasting tribute to the Black Belt view of democracy. "Before the carcass is hauled off . . ., let us do it honor to recognize that voting is not a right, but a privilege of qualification," Hall insisted. "And when qualification established one's right to vote, it becomes taxable the same as the right to own property, the right to work and to eat food."

Three months later, for the first time since 1900 in an election without a poll tax, 50 of Alabama's counties did help rewrite the state's political history when they gave the wife of a Black Belt politician a majority of their votes for governor to permit her husband to continue to run the state government and run for president. At that moment, the election had the largest numbers of both Black and white voters ever to cast a ballot in Alabama. Nine Black Belt counties, where a majority of voters were now African American; four counties encompassing the state's larger cities of Birmingham, Montgomery, Decatur, and Huntsville; and four rural north Alabama counties, including Frank Johnson's Republican-voting Winston County, were the only exceptions to the Wallace landslide.

The right to vote, without a poll tax or any other qualification other than age, citizenship, and residency, had finally arrived in Alabama, but too late for any interracial, democratic formation in the state. The worm had turned and already had gnawed away so much in the Heart of Dixie that it was a fool's errand to believe that many whites in George Wallace's Alabama would un-segregate their hearts and open their minds to new possibilities.

CHAPTER 14

Alabama's Cotton Curtain

'And Who Really Is Guilty?'

"The state has woven a cotton curtain around its borders to keep out new ideas," ACLU Southern Director Chuck Morgan wrote a week after the 1965 Voting Rights Act was signed. Morgan was optimistic that change was gonna come but equally blunt about the obstacles in Alabama. "That curtain has become the shroud of isolation and ignorance . . . In no other state in the Union has dissent been so costly and society so unfree."[1] As in neighboring Mississippi, where civil rights advocates rightfully made similar claims, Alabama's closed society imposed "on all its people an acceptance of and obedience to an official orthodoxy almost identical with the one developed in the middle of the nineteenth century"—the sanctity of Black inferiority and the necessity of racial segregation.[2]

Alabama's cotton curtain was maintained tightly through overt and indirect means, as voices for change in voting discovered over the decades, but the embargo of new ideas and new ways required refortifying and whitewashing especially during the 1930s when the "left-wing advocates of racial equality" who supported President Franklin Roosevelt's New Deal programs began meddling in the state's affairs. Even though Roosevelt himself remained hugely popular among the state's white voters, by the mid-1940s a growing number of white Alabamians were estranged from the federal government. The Confederate flag-flying Dixiecrat Movement became a major response when the old ways of the Deep South were confronted by national anti-poll tax legislation—stopped only by Southern senators' filibustering—and by President Harry Truman's national civil rights platform.[3]

"I should like to see the south let alone," Alabama Governor Chauncey Sparks told a conference of ministers of the African Methodist Episcopal Church in early May 1944, a few months after the publication of *An American Dilemma*, a book that soon became the nation's bible on race relations and racism, and almost a month after the U.S. Supreme Court outlawed the all-white primary. Sparks argued that Black churchmen should advise "all who would come down here to reform the races they should stay away—that all they are doing . . . is *forcing* the white man to become more conservative and to agitate the Negro." The governor's logic was based on his simple assumption: "The interests of the two races are identical."[4]

The nation did not leave Alabama and the South alone—not even on the radio. Fred Allen's weekly radio program, perhaps the nation's most popular show during the 1940s, had a regular character, Senator Beauregard Claghorn, whose exaggerated drawl and self-important buffoonery located him in the Heart of Dixie. Claghorn's Southern jokes ("I refuse to drink water unless it's in a Dixie cup!") and catchphrases ("That's a joke, son") made the section's elected officials the brunt of his every joke.[5] "'Senator Claghorn' is holding this part of the country up to ridicule for tens of millions Americans," protested John Temple Graves, Alabama's regionally syndicated columnist.[6] At the same time, one Birmingham radio station capitalized on the parody by turning Claghorn into a symbol of sectional pride. It held a writing contest in his name on "What I like about the South."[7]

Within a few years, Klansman and White Citizens' Council leader Asa Carter was attacking radio stations and every tavern and restaurant with a jukebox in Alabama. "Rock 'n' roll is a means of pulling down the white man to the level of the 'Negro,'" he complained, announcing that his group would publish the names of those who played the music that was "mongrelizing America."[8] The Klan later tore down the radio tower of Birmingham's most popular Black station, WENN.[9]

Before white rage and resistance developed in response to the Supreme Court's *Brown* decision, Atlanta newspaperman Ralph McGill considered the 1950s "a time when 'the lie' [Black folks are the problem] seems to have so much strength, with many preferring it to the truth."[10] After the court decision, "the lie" spread in leaps and bounds with considerable assistance from Dixie's white newspapers which almost universally failed "to ask the speechmakers specifically to identify their villains, or to ask them why their statements appeared to disagree with more authoritative information on traditions, school conditions, and court decisions."[11]

As massive white resistance grew, television emerged as a source of news across Alabama in the late 1950s. Fledgling local stations had shoestring news operations, often flying by the seat of their pants instead of reporting news by independent journalistic traditions. In the early years, sophisticated political machines, such as John Patterson's 1958 gubernatorial campaign, could easily get their partisan, segregationist messaging presented as impartial news.[12]

The national TV news programs were only 15 minutes, and even shorter newsreels of national events were shown in movie theaters. The cartoon character Foghorn Leghorn, inspired by Senator Claghorn, sometimes appeared before the feature film. Despite the TV news programs' brevity, Alabama's white newspapers published complaints and suspicions of anti-Southern bias. They suggested the national media staged coverage of the region's racial issues. Also, some Alabama TV stations blocked network broadcasts that were judged out of line with Alabama's prevailing white values. A Montgomery station, for example, preempted an NBC program in which the leader of the local bus boycott, Martin Luther King Jr., debated James J. Kilpatrick, a well-known segregationist syndicated newspaper columnist.[13]

When in the early 1960s Alabama became a primary focus of major civil rights activities, beginning with sit-ins and the Freedom Rides, reporters for national news outlets became collateral targets for the white violence heaped on civil rights activists undertaking peaceful protest. In May 1961, images of dazed Freedom Riders beside their firebombed Greyhound bus in Anniston splashed onto the front pages of newspapers across the state and the nation. Freedom Riders on a second bus were attacked after they arrived at Birmingham's Trailways depot. By prior arrangement, "Bull" Connor's police stood by for 15 minutes while a mob of angry white men brutally beat the Freedom Riders inside the terminal.

During this assault, a radio reporter was roughed up and his car and equipment smashed while he was doing a live broadcast. The mob also attacked a *Birmingham Post-Herald* photographer with pipes and chains and battered his camera. The photographer was hospitalized while the local daily newspapers, outraged that one of their own was assaulted, retrieved and ran images of the beatings he had captured on film.

The violent scenario was repeated when a replacement group of Freedom Riders, including John Lewis, arrived from Birmingham at the Montgomery Greyhound terminal. The local police watched from a distance as a huge white mob savagely beat both Freedom Riders and national news reporters, including an NBC cameraman whose film and equipment were damaged, a photographer from *Life* magazine, and a Birmingham television newsman. That became perhaps the moment when many realized that militant white groups and angry white Alabamians saw the news media, especially the national media, as almost as much an enemy as were the civil right activists.[14]

Alabama leaders also employed other methods for discouraging and punishing the national news media for its civil rights coverage. L. B. Sullivan, Montgomery's police commissioner, Governor John Patterson, and others sued the *New York Times* for libel in state court because the newspaper ran an ad titled "Heed Their Rising Voices," sponsored by a national group criticizing officials in Montgomery for mistreating SCLC leaders and the local Black community. No official was identified by name. The ad referred only to "Southern violators of the Constitution." The ad misstated a couple of incidental facts, including why a group of Alabama State College's Black students were arrested. The ad stated they were arrested for refusing to move from the state capitol steps while singing. In fact, they were apprehended during a sit-in demonstration in the county courthouse grill. It is doubtful that anyone in Alabama would have noticed the ad or its message since the *Times* then distributed fewer than 400 copies across the entire state. But, with the encouragement of the *Montgomery Advertiser*'s Grover Hall Jr., local and state officials alleged libel and sued in state court.[15]

Judge Walter Jones presided over the jury trial in which Sullivan was the plaintiff. The *Times*' Alabama attorney believed that the lawsuits were actually hatched during a prior meeting in Jones's own court chambers, and the public record evidences that Jones went to extraordinary lengths to ensure that the Yankee newspaper was punished. Jones held that the *Times* could be sued in his court as a company doing business in Alabama since it distributed copies somewhere in the state and had a stringer in Montgomery who occasionally was paid for writing a *Times* article (the writer worked full-time at Grover Hall's *Advertiser*). Jones also decided a key procedural issue against the *Times,* although in doing so he had to overrule *Alabama Pleadings and Practice,* the lawyers' handbook on legal procedure that Jones himself had authored. In addition, the judge allowed Ralph Abernathy and three other local Black ministers whose names appeared in the *Times* ad to be sued along with the *Times* even though the ministers' attorneys proved conclusively in court that their clients had nothing to do with the ad's content and did not approve or know of it until after publication.

In charging the jury's 12 white men on Alabama libel law, Jones instructed them that the ad was "libelous per se"—they should assume the ad was a harmful defamation of the plaintiff's character and reputation. Jones told the jury they also should accept as fact that the ad was false and they could not decide otherwise unless the defendants had proven in court that the ad was entirely free of any and all errors. Therefore, the jury's duty in Jones's courtroom was only to decide if the *Times* had published the ad, if the ad's reference to "Southern violators of the Constitution" was "concerning" Sullivan, and how much money to award him. On those instructions, it took the jury only a few hours to award Sullivan half a million dollars (equivalent to $5.1 million in 2023).[16]

The strategy of filing libel lawsuits in state courts spread. CBS was sued for a program about the problems of voter registration in Montgomery. In Birmingham, the *Times* was sued for its local coverage, as was CBS News and its longtime reporter, Howard K. Smith, for coverage of the Freedom Rides. For more than two years, until the U.S. Supreme Court overturned the verdict in the *Times* case, libel litigation and the threat of additional lawsuits led the *Times* to permit "damn lawyers" to keep its chief Southern reporter, Claude Sitton, out of the state. Meanwhile, the corporate managers of other national and local media companies kept a close check on their reporters' dispatches from Alabama.[17]

In the months after he became governor in 1963, George Wallace transformed the state's terms of white engagement with the civil rights movement in ways that pushed virtually all Alabama news media to join him and his perspective and to part company almost entirely with the national press and its style of coverage of civil rights. Not all the state's newspapers had supported Wallace's candidacy, but almost all fell in line with his claims as to who were Alabama's enemies.

During the Freedom Rides, for example, John Patterson had blamed civil rights "agitators" for causing their own trouble, and he refused to protect them. They were "renegades who are here for the avowed purpose of stirring up trouble," Patterson complained.[18] They caused their own suffering. After his defiant inaugural speech in January 1963, Wallace changed the racial rhetoric and reframed the state's public discourse. Yes, civil rights workers were trouble-making agitators, he claimed, but they were also lawless, dangerous, and communist-inspired, and their Negro leaders had duped the Kennedy-run federal government.

Martin Luther King Jr. and his movement now had the full backing of the federal government's powers, Wallace declared, and both the movement and the federal government were attempting to embarrass and hurt Alabama by making it surrender century-old laws, traditions, and its way of life. In other words, those beaten Freedom Riders and other nonviolent protesters were not victims of hatred and violence. The real victims of current events were white Alabamians.[19]

This perspective and its impact became evident in the summer of 1963 as SCLC was challenging "Bull" Connor and Birmingham's segregation laws and practices through peaceful marches and other public demonstrations. SCLC recruited young people, including children as young as elementary students, to join the almost daily marches against segregation. Many kids skipped school to fall in line with King's style of peaceful nonviolent protests. Frustrated and angry, Connor ordered the use of fire hoses and police dogs against the demonstrators, including the children.

National news outlets reported and broadcast the images of men, women, and children being blasted by the forceful streams of water from fire hoses and attacked by barking, snarling police dogs. Graphic images were captured for print by *Birmingham News* photographers. None appeared in Birmingham newspapers. Vincent Townsend of the *Birmingham News* vetoed use of his own photographers' work in his own paper. Instead, the *News* ran a page-two story with a photograph of a small, well-dressed six-year-old Black girl standing upright waiting for a paddy wagon after her arrest.[20]

In north Alabama, the *Huntsville Times* ran a headline, "Police Squirt Negro Mob at B'ham," and the next day published a photograph with the caption, "Negro Attacks Police Dog." In south Alabama, the *Montgomery Advertiser* ran images of dogs snapping at Black adults with a caption assuring readers that the dogs were "well trained" and "disciplined" and pointing out that one Black demonstrator was holding a knife as a dog attacked him. More than one Alabama newspaper followed up its coverage with reports of how the use of dogs was now standard procedure in policing around the country.[21]

The national media images and reports had "a swift and stunning impact on the American people, all the way to the White House," according to Gene Roberts and Hank Klibanoff in their definitive book on press coverage of the modern civil right movement.[22] In the aftermath of the Birmingham demonstrations, it became clear to President John F. Kennedy that continuing events in Alabama, spurred by King on one side and Wallace on the other, would not allow his administration to avoid addressing civil rights issues.

In Alabama, the news coverage took on a different political spin. Wallace issued a statement accusing Kennedy of wanting him to "surrender this state to Martin Luther King and his group of pro-Communists." In a joint session of the legislature, Wallace warned that he would prosecute demonstrators for murder if anyone died as a result of the Birmingham agitators' disrespect for law and order. Amid lusty, repeated applause, he said it was tragic "that in Washington we have such weaklings who refuse to expose the Reds" and other "enemies of constitutional government" and states' rights.[23]

A month later, scores of state and national reporters were present in Tuscaloosa where a defiant, proud Wallace stood before Kennedy's nervous, perspiring Assistant U.S. Attorney General Nicholas Katzenbach. The governor staged his "stand in the schoolhouse door" to block the admission of Vivian Malone and James Hood, two high-performing Black students, as the melodrama was broadcast live on TV stations and carried across the state by radio. Most of the national press portrayed it as one more unsuccessful act of defiance of a Deep South segregationist governor, but journalist Diane McWhorter later understood what the theatrics really meant in Alabama and over time elsewhere. "By pitting Wallace against an ancient carpetbagging enemy rather than two young Black Alabamians, Katzenbach had sanctified anew the old racist agenda of 'states' rights,' whose currency Wallace would draw out into the next decades, and into the rest of the country."[24]

As the state's elected officials and press closed ranks behind their new governor, Wallace had a new state agency to amplify and reinforce his messaging—the Alabama Legislative Commission to Preserve the Peace. Veteran crime reporter Ed Strickland became its director and quickly began hiring freelance investigators, photographers, and paid informants to spy on civil rights groups and to keep tabs on Alabamians "known to be working with, or used by, known subversive agents." Strickland maintained a key role in publishing public reports, pamphlets, and other materials and in public speaking across the state to validate and echo Wallace's messages about the nefarious dangers of civil rights workers and their leaders. It was nothing less than a propaganda operation in which Strickland constantly emphasized "Communist Subversion in Racial Unrest,"[25] a theme that followed Wallace's rhetoric from beginning to end.

According to Strickland, the agency distributed 100,000 copies of his report attacking the 1964 Civil Rights Act while it was pending in Congress. The pamphlet claimed the Act would be worse than anything passed to punish the South during Reconstruction, since it proposed a "federal dictatorship" that would eliminate private property not only in the South but across the nation. "The Civil Rights Bill of 1964 . . . makes the Communist Party Platform seem most conservative," Strickland wrote. Never one for understatement, he concluded that the Act was the handiwork of communists and would "set in motion the feared machinery of a police state in frightening similarity to the courses followed by countries now in Communist enslavement."[26]

Nothing and no one in the Black and white struggles for democracy appeared benign to Strickland and associates. The Peace Commission charged that "the U.S. Supreme Court adopted the 'ONE MAN, ONE VOTE' policy in overthrowing long existing state legislative bodies . . . The court has made it clear in recent opinions that it is using the Communist-created slogan as a legal yardstick in its decisions." Commission publications described civil rights leader John Lewis as an "extremely radical Negro leader of SNCC . . . [who] preaches revolt, rebellion and violence . . . He espoused the line "One Man, One Vote"' and "Freedom Now," both phrases first introduced into Africa by Chinese Communist seeking to overthrow colonial rule." The Commission distributed more than 300,000 copies of these publications.[27]

In another role, the Peace Commission circulated to local law enforcement agencies so-called confidential reports that did little more than slant and reformulate news of civil rights developments across the country into an alert about supposedly coordinated, impending dangers that only involved local peaceful protest across Alabama—bulletins that reiterated themes that Governor Wallace was stating publicly. The memos stoked concerns and anxiety among sheriffs and police about the risks of local civil rights demonstrations and too often justified, if not motivated, lawmen's violent overreaction to local peaceful protests.[28]

Two months after Wallace's theatrical performance in Tuscaloosa, Martin Luther King Jr. delivered his most famous speech to a huge crowd at the Lincoln Memorial in Washington. Network television cameras captured him proclaiming, "I have a dream that one day, down in Alabama, with its vicious racists, with its governor having his lips dripping with the words of 'interposition' and 'nullification'—one day right there in Alabama little black boys and black girls will be able to join hands with little white boys and white girls as sisters and brothers."[29]

On the following night, before 6,000 admiring fans at a White

Citizens' Council rally in Selma, Wallace renewed his pledge to fight for both segregation and resegregation. He responded to King by describing the March on Washington as a "mob . . . led by a man who is a sex pervert, a convicted draft dodger, and has a Communist background."[30] Most news reporters realized the governor was smearing Bayard Rustin, a King advisor and march organizer, with words probably based on a dossier supplied by Strickland's Peace Commission.[31] It was just as likely that most of the white audience thought Wallace was referring to King himself.

Two weeks later, four Black girls were killed by a dynamite bomb at the Sixteenth Street Baptist Church in Birmingham in a tragedy that shocked the nation as images of the destruction filled newspapers and newscasts. Wallace condemned the "dastardly acts by a demented fool" but he also insinuated that it could have been a Negro who bombed the church. He called it a "crime against the people of Birmingham and Alabama." Birmingham's new Mayor Albert Boutwell, the former lieutenant governor, said, "All of us are victims, and most of us are innocent victims."[32]

It had been too much for Chuck Morgan. In a speech before Birmingham's Young Men's Business Club, he declared, "Who threw that bomb? . . . We all did it. Every last one of us is condemned for that crime and the one before it, the ones last month, last year and a decade ago." There had been more than forty race-related bombings in Birmingham's Black neighborhoods since the end of World War II. "We are a mass of intolerance and bigotry and stand indicted before our young," Morgan insisted. "And who really is guilty?" he again asked after citing a long list of common acts of complicity and omission. "Each of us. Each citizen . . . who has contributed in any way during the past several years to the popularity of hatred is at least as guilty, or more so, than the demented fool who threw that bomb." Morgan took his condemnation one step further as he insisted it was time for the city to become a part of the United States. "Birmingham is not a dying city," Morgan said. "It is dead."[33]

The speech struck a strong chord, especially among whites. A columnist for the *New York Daily News* said Morgan was "waging a vigorous, one-man campaign to bring Birmingham and Alabama back into the Union."[34] Morgan's fight would continue for decades, but less than two

Charles "Chuck" Morgan Jr. (courtesy of Charles Morgan III).

months after the YMBC speech, having endured repeated death threats and the loss of paying clients, Morgan and his family left Birmingham for good. "Alabama doesn't want him or need him," the crusty editor of the *Greensboro Watchman* intoned.[35]

In 1964, major civil rights organizations agreed to support civil rights leader Bob Moses in SNCC's proposal for a Mississippi "Freedom Summer," a statewide voter engagement and summer education drive staffed mainly by white college students from out of state. In response, the national media shifted its roving correspondents and primary focus to covering the freedom movement to the Magnolia State and Athens, Ohio, where fresh-faced college students were being hastily trained for a Deep South experience they were incapable of foreseeing.[36] The change of focus meant there would be little news coverage of civil rights activities in Alabama, and no national press to challenge or spur state coverage.

For example, on June 9, in an effort to prevent a peaceful march, the

Tuscaloosa authorities used fire hoses to push protesters into a Black church which then was tear-gassed. As occupants attempted to escape the church, they were brutally beaten and arrested by police in what locally became known in the Black community as "Bloody Tuesday." The marchers had planned to go to the new county courthouse to protest its segregation signage. The attack received spotty coverage in the state, in part because few if any newsmen were on the scene as the church was under siege. And, as often was the case in other attempted peaceful protests, headlines and reports in some Alabama newspapers referred to the Tuscaloosa attacks as a "riot."[37]

Beyond niggardly reporting and one-sided headlines, Alabama's cotton curtain was drawn tightly around all primary forms of communications in support of segregation and the state's segregationist governor. Wallace commanded favorable news coverage in virtually every newspaper and local television news program across the state and, whenever he asked for it, the state educational television network broadcast his political speeches at the legislature while also providing a free, live feed to the state's commercial TV stations.

Network programs were preempted and removed from TV schedules if they provided a platform for Black voices and alternative points of view. For example, Alabamians never saw the special public television documentary, *Lay My Burden Down*, about Alabama's Black Belt poverty and racism. Wallace ordered a network special cancelled because it included the singer Joan Baez who sang at civil rights rallies. No Alabama television station had a Black reporter or anchor, of course, although in July 1964 Montgomery's WSFA-TV began airing an all-Black television show, "TV Gospel Time," featuring African American gospel groups at 7 a.m. on Sundays.[38] That was a form of sacred Black entertainment white Southerners had found acceptable since the days of slavery.

During the Wallace years, the state-owned educational television network, with stations reaching into most Alabama counties, functioned virtually as a propaganda apparatus for white supremacy and the state's governor. Its in-school programs were all-white and designed "to shore up Jim Crow conditions in its state."[39] The network censored national adult programs with a Black perspective and whitewashed most of its remaining programming. Tony Brown's popular news program, "Black Journal," for instance, was not broadcast in Alabama. Outside of "Sesame Street," which included Black and white children and a few regular Black actors, less than three percent of the entire programming of the network involved at least one Black person appearing on screen.[40]

By the time "Bloody Sunday" and the Selma to Montgomery March occurred in 1965 under the watchful, telling eye of national reporters and network cameras, the state's cotton curtain had become an impenetrable barrier between most white Alabamians and the rest of the nation in minding what had happened and was happening within a seemingly heartless Dixie. No tragedy, no amount of bombing or bloody attacks in Montgomery, Birmingham, Tuscaloosa, Marion, Selma, or elsewhere penetrated the barriers of a mostly closed white society.

After the Selma March, Wallace led a counter-offensive to assure white Alabamians and others that the news coverage at the Edmund Pettus Bridge and the subsequent protest march to Montgomery was distorted and biased. His staff also organized a statewide tour for some fifty newspaper editors from small cities and towns across the country to hear "the other side of the story" from local white community and business leaders. This tactic not only spread Wallace's message across America but also pushed forward local leaders in Alabama to defend their state and their governor. The Sovereignty and Peace commissions jointly produced and distributed a film, *The Selma March,* to show that Communists inspired and led the demonstration. Wallace declared the film was an objective, accurate portrayal of the March. A *Montgomery Advertiser* reporter predicted the film would bore many in Alabama since most already were convinced that Communists were behind the March. The film's premiere in Montgomery attracted 1,800 people and was sponsored by the White Citizens' Council, which urged the white audience to register to vote after the showing.[41]

Dallas County Sheriff Jim Clark toured Alabama promoting his book, subtitled "I Saw Selma Raped," telling audiences how Communists used "whiskey, dope, and sex" to attract marchers and how the national news media refused to report on the mess they helped to create. A Republican public relations expert, who as a CIA agent had been involved in the failed Bay of Pigs invasion of Cuba, wrote *The True Selma Story: Sex and Civil Rights*, a 32-page booklet of photographs and short essays, including a section on how the national media distorted images in both Selma and Birmingham to fabricate the appearance of innocent Black victims and white "thug cops." The booklet was widely read in the state and distributed in the state's book shops and newsstands and by several organizations, including the National States Rights Party and the Ku Klux Klan.[42]

When asked if he worried about what the rest of the world thought of Alabama after the four girls were killed in their Birmingham church, Wallace spoke about what most white Alabamians wished for, if they did not believe: "It seems that other parts of the world ought to be worried about what we think of them instead of what they think of us."[43] And in that fateful month of "Bloody Sunday," one of Alabama's old warriors of the New Deal, Virginia Durr, wrote to her brother-in-law, Supreme Court Justice Hugo Black: "George Wallace expresses their feelings of persecution and gets stronger all the time, and I do not see any signs of repentance on his part or on the part of the white population at all so far."[44]

Later in life, John Lewis, an Alabamian who suffered more than most from his own state's brutality, reflected on the importance of the media in the successful struggles he helped to lead, including passage of the Voting Rights Act of 1965: "If it hadn't been for the media—the print media and television—the civil rights movement would have been like a bird without wings, a choir without a song."[45] Of course, he meant national media. Regrettably, in their struggles over segregation and suffrage, white Alabamians were left at home with little more than a wing and a prayer for finding a way forward beyond the past that Black Belt politicians, George Wallace foremost among them, had shaped as their current and future collective state of mind.

CHAPTER 15

Bridging the Past and the Future

'A Mass Movement . . . Brought State-Sanctioned Segregation to Its Knees'

In March 2015, on the 50th anniversary of Bloody Sunday, joined by an aging Congressman John Lewis and others, President Barack Obama spoke in Selma about the meaning of that day in Alabama when Lewis, Hosea Williams, Albert Turner, and Bob Mants led marchers across the Edmund Pettus Bridge in 1965. "The Americans who crossed this bridge . . . gave courage to millions. They held no elected office. But they led a nation," the president observed. "What they did here will reverberate through the ages."[1]

The events in Selma on March 7, 1965, have been credited with spurring then President Lyndon Johnson to introduce and the U.S. Congress to pass the Voting Rights Act. Johnson said as much to the nation when he proclaimed, "At times history and fate meet at a single time in a single place to shape a turning point in man's unending search for freedom . . . So it was a century ago at Appomattox. So it was last week in Selma, Alabama."[2]

Unquestionably, the Act has had a profound, enduring impact on the nation's democracy, stimulating "as great a change in American politics as any one law ever has," wrote David J. Garrow, a Pulitzer-winning scholar of the civil rights era.[3] At the same time, other people and other events and developments within and beyond Alabama contributed to the pivotal nature of Bloody Sunday. Albert Turner knew as much, always remembering the brutal attacks on Black marchers and the tragic death of young

Jimmie Lee Jackson in Marion. The courageous, strategic work in 1964 of SNCC leader Bob Moses and others in Mississippi's "Freedom Summer"; the clandestine murders of three young men on their way to begin voter registration; and the prophetic voice of Fannie Lou Hamer on national television asking "Is this America?" at the Democratic National Convention—they too had an impact in moving the nation toward protecting basic voting rights.[4]

In this context, Selma was not so much a singular force as it was a tipping point—when all that had happened and had been reported as happening over the years involving literally thousands of people in different Southern towns, crossroads, and plantations finally moved America's interracial, collective moral arc enough to tip its political institutions into meaningful action.

Years afterwards, some scholars and African American filmmakers have questioned the national media's coverage of Selma, Birmingham, and similar flashpoints in the South. The critics find fault in how the media cast Blacks as victims of white abuse and brutality to such a consistent extent that African Americans in Alabama and other Southern states became in the white American mind powerless in achieving their own freedom and full citizenship—often depending on a "white savior." None of the criticism doubted the importance of the national news coverage in aiding congressional action on voting rights, but some argued that the unintended consequences left the nation no less divided on race and no better equipped to comprehend structural racism.[5]

In 1993, before much of this criticism was voiced, former SNCC leader Julian Bond offered seasoned insight when he suggested that the crucial problem in both past media coverage and current national memory was the focus on a few heroes of the civil rights movement—whatever their color—as the crucial catalysts for change. "Yesterday's movement succeeded because victims became their own best champions. When Mrs. Rosa Parks refused to stand up, and when King stood up to preach, mass participation came to the movement for civil rights," Bond wrote. These individuals' actions made them heroes because many others were willing to turn their actions into a mass movement. "Three decades ago, a mass movement marched, picketed, protested and organized and brought state-sanctioned segregation to its knees," Bond asserted."[6]

In Alabama, the long struggles against segregating some citizens from a right to vote involved decades of conflicts and thousands of individuals within a far more complicated, interracial story of change than the state and national media were capable of understanding or explaining. What happened in Alabama from Reconstruction to the enactment of the Voting Rights Act almost a hundred years later was as much a part of the story of change in Alabama and the nation as were the events on the Edmund Pettus Bridge.

The Edmund Pettus Bridge, March 21, 1965 (ADAH; donated by Alabama Media Group / Photo by William McCormick, Huntsville Times*).*

In addition, while events in Selma shaped a public perception and mandate for change, Alabama's methods of white resistance to Black voter registration and voting, especially to federal intervention, shaped some of the most significant terms and tools of the Act. The Act was not developed out of thin air. Civil rights leaders and Justice Department attorneys drafted and redrafted the Act's provisions, and much of the result, after political compromises, was in response to the past struggles in Alabama.

Days before Bloody Sunday happened, the Justice Department was drafting a voting rights bill for President Johnson to consider offering to Congress at some future date. Federal officials had developed other voting rights bills, which had been discussed internally within the government in the past, and most of these drafts were aimed at addressing problems and codifying effective remedies that federal agencies had discovered in attempting to protect voting rights in the Deep South states—especially in Alabama. The federal voting rights laws passed in 1960 and 1964 had major sections largely shaped by what the Civil Rights Commission and the Justice Department found in Alabama. The refusal of Alabama registrars to open their public records to federal officials necessitated a new federal provision making such resistance a civil and criminal offense.

Judge Daniel Thomas's courtroom evasions and delays prompted passage of the "Thomas Amendment" to permit three-judge panels to decide certain voting cases. Thomas's endless support of "Tigger" Burke as the nation's first federal referee, who then blatantly refused to fairly register Black citizens in Perry County, was the reason federal law enabled federal civil service employees from other parts of the nation to act as federal registrars. The legal remedy of "freezing" was first used effectively by Judge Frank M. Johnson Jr. to prevent Black Belt counties from applying new registration standards that would unfairly disadvantage Black applicants. As veteran voting rights attorney Armand Derfner has pointed out, this concept was included in the 1960 Voting Rights Act, which authorized federal referees to use voter qualifications which had been applied to whites in their work of registering Black applicants.[7] But this standard was utterly ignored by the nation's first federal referee in Perry County. Instead, Johnson applied it in cases that came to his court in Montgomery, and his rulings led to unprecedented increases in local Black voter registration.

All of these provisions emerging out of Alabama were carried into the 1965 Act, particularly expanding the "freezing" principle into the new law's outright suspension of literacy tests and any other new test or device for qualifying to register to vote in those jurisdictions that had extreme low levels of voting in November 1964—primarily the Southern states. The "freezing" concept also gave rise to the law's novel mechanism of Section 5—requiring jurisdictions with extremely low levels of voter registration to preclear all new voting laws and practices before they could be implemented. Even with Judge Johnson in Montgomery, the Justice Department came to realize that Alabama registrars, who acted as laws unto themselves, the Sovereignty Commission's Martha Witt Smith, the Alabama Supreme Court, and the Alabama legislature—all in concert could develop new rules, laws, or practices to obstruct Black registration and voting much faster than any lawsuit in a federal court could contain, much less prevent, the damage. This was equally true in Mississippi and Louisiana, but when called upon to provide an example of a state's conduct that justified this kind of extraordinary preventive remedy, the DOJ cited the new literacy test that Smith had developed and that Black Belt registrars had required in Alabama in January 1964.[8]

Another unprecedented part of Section 5 shifted the burden of proof to the jurisdiction proposing the voting change to demonstrate that it would be nondiscriminatory. This requirement in the law also emerged from the Justice Department's experience in implementing the "freezing" principle in Johnson's Montgomery courtroom. Once Alabama registrars were blocked by Johnson's court order from using one of Smith's new literacy tests, as a practical matter it became the burden of the registrars to prove that the change was not discriminatory or else it was prohibited.[9]

Section 5 also departed from ordinary precedent by establishing an "effects" test for determining if a voting-related change could be precleared for future use. Generally, the federal law required a showing of both intent *and* effect for proving a violation of law prohibiting racial discrimination under the Fifteenth Amendment, but the 1965 Act stated that any change would be approved only if the jurisdiction showed it was not racially discriminatory in purpose or effect. In 1965, the U.S. Supreme Court had not yet decided that a voting procedure was a violation of the Fifteenth Amendment because of discriminatory effect, but if there were two cases that arguably opened the way for validating such a holding, they were Alabama cases—*Davis v. Schnell*, which struck down the Boswell Amendment, and *Gomillion v. Lightfoot*, which struck down the law describing new town boundaries that removed almost all Black citizens.[10]

In addition, Section 5 required covered jurisdictions to seek preclearance of voting changes from the U.S. attorney general or from the U.S. Court of Appeals in the District of Columbia—not from federal courts in the South. Alabama's federal district court judges were not entirely responsible for this provisions, since there were federal judges in other Southern states who were more openly hostile in handling voting cases and more dismissive of Black plaintiffs. But apart from Frank Johnson, Alabama's federal district judges had proven to be at best unreliable and at worst effectively obstructionist to protecting voting rights.

The Act also removed the South's Fifth Circuit Court of Appeals from hearing cases of preclearance even though, under the clear-minded leadership of Chief Judge Elbert Tuttle, it had been largely faithful in enforcing anti-segregation ruling and statutes. But some of the South's federal Circuit Court judges were openly sympathetic to the segregationists' arguments, and future federal judges in Alabama and other Southern states would be selected by custom by each state's U.S. senators. In the existing political climate, their choices were certain to be white men opposed to Black voting. And, as an SRC study released in April 1965 documented, federal courts in the South were also segregated institutions with no African Americans in the position of judges or law clerks, and virtually none in other professional roles.[11]

Finally, the Voting Rights Act mandated the Justice Department to file suit in federal court to have the poll tax declared unconstitutional wherever it existed. By the time the lawsuits were filed, Alabama, Mississippi, Virginia, and Texas were the only states with poll taxes. In Alabama, Judges Johnson and Rives declared the poll tax unconstitutional three weeks before the U.S. Supreme Court announced the same holding in a case challenging Virginia's poll tax. The Act did not outlaw the poll tax due to a compromise involving both politics and lawyerly doubts about the constitutional authority of Congress to do the banning,[12] but the refusal of the legislatures in Alabama and the three other Southern states to ban it necessitated the inclusion of a legal challenge in the new Act.

Former Justice Department attorney Brian K. Landsberg litigated cases in the Alabama Black Belt during the years running up to the passage of the 1965 Voting Rights Act. His careful study of the Alabama origins of the Voting Rights Act hedges in crediting events and voting cases in Alabama as the essential determinant for shaping both the Act's passage and its provisions. But, employing a literary device of double negatives to make a positive statement, Landsberg concluded, "Had there been no cases but only the official recalcitrance and violence at the Edmund Pettus Bridge, it seems unlikely that the Congress would have adopted the effects test, the "freezing" principle, or federal examiners and observers, the preclearance requirement or universal suffrage."[13] And it was these provisions of the Act, arising from the struggles in Alabama, that became the primary legal force that immobilized the white South's massive resistance to Black voting and has advanced America's interracial democracy into the 21st century.

'THE POLITICAL SYSTEM OF THE SOUTH WAS, AND IN SOME PLACES STILL IS, A TOOL OF ENSLAVEMENT'

During the congressional debate on the Act, the South's leaders in the U.S. House declared that the whole bill "drips with venom" as punishment for those states that formed the Old Confederacy,[14] as most Southern members of the House and Senate clamored about states' rights, federalism, and the Act's unconstitutionality. But their primary objection and target was the bill's provision banning all literacy tests and similar devices in jurisdictions that had an unusually low rate of voter turnout in the last presidential election. The effect of this section would ban the use of a literacy test only in Alabama and six other Southern states for a period of five years.

When President Johnson proposed the Act to Congress, these Southern states were not the only ones requiring a literacy test to qualify to vote.

Twenty-one states—more than two-fifths of all states—had some form of a literacy test to qualify to vote in 1965. The states outside the South requiring such tests as a prerequisite for voter registration included New York and New England states such as Massachusetts, Connecticut, and Maine as well as western states such as California, Arizona, and Oregon.[15]

In light of this national pattern, the South's congressmen argued that the region was being unfairly singled out so that Southern states would be overrun by illiterate voters while states in other sections of the country would continue to exclude illiterate voters. Seeking to expand his party's popularity in the South, the Republican leader of the U.S. House, Gerald Ford, floated a substitute to permit any state to use a literacy test for persons with less than a sixth-grade education.[16]

Ford's proposal—echoing the approach that Martha Witt Smith had devised—might have attracted considerable support had not Alabama's literacy test become the political pole cat that helped prompt a strong national revulsion. In the days and weeks following the events of "Bloody Sunday," Alabama's literacy tests were the subject of widespread, repeated ridicule across the nation. As the White House and Justice Department lawyers drafted the proposed Act and negotiated for support, a Gallup Poll on literary tests for voting reported that 56 percent of Americans opposed requiring a person to read or write in order to vote and almost two-thirds opposed requiring at least five years of schooling.[17]

A few weeks after the Selma March, as the attorney general sought support from the U.S. Senate's Republicans, their leader Everett Dirksen raised concerns about evasive efforts that Alabama officials might try. "What would happen . . . if the state of Alabama abolished its literacy test and substituted a provision that a high school certificate would be the proof of literacy for all voters?" Dirksen worried.[18]

At a later point, when Senate Republicans were considering if, how, and where to suspend literacy tests, including Ford's idea, Alabama's absurd multipart test reappeared in the national press. In the *New York Times*, William Van Alstyne reported that about 70 percent of the questions from the Alabama test were answered incorrectly by almost 100 law professors he surveyed. The *Los Angeles Sentinel* listed some of Smith's questions about the Constitution (such as, "If a person is indicted for a crime, name two rights he has") as proof that the test could "stump a California lawyer."[19]

It also wasn't helpful to the Act's opponents when the Alabama Supreme Court issued yet another version of its multi-layered literacy test that Smith had rebooted in July, as congressional leaders hammered out differences in the bills passed by each chamber. The *New York Times* headline read, "Alabama Using New Voter Test; Negro Sees 'Just Another Trick.'" And days before the final vote on the Act, the *Times'* Roy Reed reported on how the State Sovereignty Commission was continuing to try to circumvent the federal courts' ban of the state literacy test.[20]

This adverse publicity across the nation may have engendered resentment more than embarrassment among many white Alabamians and their political leaders, but Alabama's shenanigans became the worst-case scenario for what a state would do if permitted to use a test for literacy or education as a prerequisite for voting.[21] In this way, its practices not only aided passage of the federal ban on any literacy test for voting in Alabama and the other Southern states, but also it helped to shape public's skepticism and local activism outside the South concerning the use of education or literacy as a prerequisite for voting.

Thousands of New York citizens educated in Spanish-language schools in Puerto Rico often could not vote because they were literate in Spanish but could not pass the New York literacy test in English. After U.S. Attorney General Katzenbach admitted in congressional testimony that this form of disfranchisement was not prohibited by the proposed Act, both Democrats and Republicans sponsored amendments to address the problem. It became a bone of contention over which a majority of the House and Senate disagreed until a compromise emerged. The adopted amendment's language was aspirational, declaring that no state could condition the right to vote by "persons educated in American-flag schools" on their "ability to read, write, understand, or interpret any matter in the English language." But the actual ban was sanctioned requiring a sixth-grade education in Spanish from schools in U.S. territories and Puerto Rico as proof of literacy for purposes of voting across the nation.[22]

The attack on literacy and educational tests as a primary limitation on universal suffrage continued after 1965. The U.S. Civil Rights Commission had recommended as early as 1961 eliminating literacy tests throughout the nation, as had President Kennedy's commission on voter registration in 1963. But Southern opposition had robbed the Congress of sufficient political momentum to do more than hold hearings.[23] By 1969, however, as renewal of the temporary provisions of the 1965 Act became a subject of congressional hearings, the Civil Rights Commission joined civil rights groups in pushing for a national ban.

The Commission told a House committee that its research proved that the literacy tests in the West and North "have a negative effect on voter registration and that this impact of literacy tests falls most heavily on blacks and persons of Spanish surname." The federal agency found, for example, three-fourths of all white persons of voting age were registered to vote in the non-Southern states that had a literacy test but only 55 percent of voting-age Blacks with less than a ninth-grade education were registered in the same states.[24]

Even more significant, President Richard Nixon embraced at least the rhetoric for a national literacy ban as a part of his "Southern strategy" for winning the South. Nixon's Attorney General John Mitchell, who had served as the president's campaign manager, proposed a bill to do away with what he called "regional legislation" and make all provisions of the Act national in scope. His proposal authorized the attorney general to decide if, when, and where he should go into a federal court to seek enforcement of the Act's remedies. Mitchell claimed that this approach would wipe out literacy tests for voting throughout the nation.

Southern members of Congress applauded the Mitchell bill since Alabama and other states of the South would no longer be automatically subject to the Act's special provisions, but several Northern Republicans were chary to support it. The ranking Republican member of the House Judiciary Committee, from Ohio, said, "The administration creates a remedy for which there is no wrong and leaves grievous wrongs without adequate remedy."[25] National NAACP director Roy Wilkins understood that under Mitchell the Justice Department would leave the South to its own devices, and he accused Nixon of trying to unleash the "disfranchisers."[26]

The strategy motivating these proposals was a transparent attempt to steal the support of white Southern political leaders and voters from George Wallace, whose 1968 campaign for president had shown his deep appeal across all of Dixie. Satirist Russell Baker suggested that Mitchell and Nixon were so desperate on wooing Southern leaders away from Wallace that their secret plan was to legalize slavery. "Well," South Carolina segregationist Strom Thurmond replied in this imaginary conversation, "George Wallace is going to have trouble topping that one."[27]

Wallace did not top it, but he did run a blatantly racist campaign in a runoff for governor shortly after renewal of the Voting Rights Act was before Congress. His wife Lurleen had died of cancer, which Wallace knew she had before convincing her to run as his proxy in 1966. Upon her death in May 1968, Lieutenant Governor Albert Brewer took office as Alabama's chief executive, but Wallace needed the governor's office to support his expected 1972 presidential campaign. So, in the summer of 1970, after trailing Brewer in the Democratic primary, Wallace stoked up a racist, smear campaign against Brewer, who as an unelected north Alabama incumbent tried to figure out how to become a Southern moderate governor while appearing as much like Wallace as possible. Brewer failed on both counts, and Alabama voters awarded Wallace a narrow victory.[28]

Once again, according to the NAACP's W. C. Patton, Alabama's Dixie-style politics gave the nation renewed momentum for expanding the vote. Patton predicted that Wallace's campaign and his return to office would bolster passage of stronger civil rights and voting rights bills. Urban League President Whitney Young agreed, suggesting that Wallace had influenced Washington politics. He thought Alabama's governor-elect left no political space on his right for Republicans and the Nixon administration to occupy, if they wanted to remain electable in much of the rest of the nation.[29]

Even before Wallace's 1970 runoff, the Nixon administration recalibrated its political strategy. Northern Democrats and Republicans joined in the Congress to support renewal of the original special provisions of the 1965 Voting Rights Act for an additional five years. After having condemned literacy tests, Attorney General Mitchell acquiesced to including a new five-year national ban on them, and the Nixon White House shifted to winning Southern support on other issues, including school desegregation and the appointment of U.S. Supreme Court justices.[30]

The new 1970 Act went further. In addition to renewing the Spanish language provision, it prohibited states from requiring more than 30 days of residency to vote in presidential elections and mandated the right to vote for persons 18 years or older, although the right was also ratified by the states on July 1, 1970, as the Twenty-sixth Amendment of the U.S. Constitution.[31]

The momentum for universal suffrage in the United States continued into 1975, when Congress renewed the Voting Rights Act for a second time. During this half-decade, Nixon resigned after facing certain impeachment and conviction by the Congress for his cover-up of the Watergate scandals, and George Wallace ended his presidential ambitions after being severely crippled by an assassin's bullet in Maryland. After President Gerald Ford indicated that he did not oppose renewal, Chicano and other racial and ethnic minorities joined African American and civil rights groups in a concerted push for both renewal and additional protections.

As a result, Congress enacted a permanent national ban on literacy tests for voting, added "language" amendments that triggered Section 5 preclearance in Texas and other southwestern states and counties, allowed granting attorneys' fees to civil rights lawyers who won cases under the Voting Rights Act, and renewed the temporary provisions for another seven years.[32]

Again, Alabama did its oversized part in demonstrating that the Act remained necessary. Congress received reports revealing that, while Black voter registration had increased substantially in Alabama, Black voters continued to face obstacles that local white registrars erected so that the Black rate was still behind the white rate of voter registration by almost 25 percentage points. And ten years after the Act's original passage, Black voters had been able to elect candidates of their choice to county commissions in only four of 67 counties.

John Lewis, by then director of the Southern Regional Council's Voter Education Project, told Congress that Alabama had implemented at least 161 voting changes that were never submitted for preclearance.

"We cannot dismiss the fact that the political system of the South was, and in some places still is, a tool of enslavement," Lewis testified. "It is therefore obvious that the Voting Rights Act, which has not accomplished its intended effects over a span of 10 years, needs to be continued and strengthened."[33] U.S. Senator Jim Allen of Alabama, who while serving as lieutenant governor during Wallace's first term had helped kill the ban on the state's poll tax, mounted an unsuccessful filibuster. In August 1975 President Ford signed the Act extending its temporary provisions for another seven years.[34]

In Alabama, state and local officials did more than refuse to submit voting changes for preclearance. Along with other white officials across the South, they developed an array of methods to dilute Black voting strength[35] and continued fighting against expanding the vote to Black citizens and to whites who might become their allies at the polls. Led by Wallace's old warhorses Martha Witt Smith and Frank Mizell, the Sovereignty Commission targeted young voters, who were now able to register and cast a ballot by the age of 18 in large numbers on college campuses, and virtually all outsiders—be they military personnel and their families or businessmen and farmers moving to Alabama from out-of-state.

In addition, Peace Commission Director Ed Strickland informed state legislators as early as 1969 that left-wing "militant forces" had invaded Alabama's college campuses. He warned that the crisis would "get much worse before it gets better," claiming the radical student movement was reaching into the state's high schools that were then undergoing token desegregation. Strickland also complained that the recent decision by U.S. Circuit Judge Richard Rives striking down Alabama's turn-of-the century vagrancy law would make it more difficult to "deal with campus disorder."[36] A three-judge court ruled that police could no longer use the 1903 law to arrest students, protestors, striking laborers, and others simply for being idle and unemployed, and the decision meant they were no longer in danger of being disfranchised as vagrants.[37]

Smith echoed Strickland's dire predictions about Alabama's campuses when she told Montgomery officials that the federal constitutional amendment allowing 18-year-olds to vote would add more Blacks than whites to the state's voter rolls. She also insisted that local boards of registrars in college and university towns should require students to swear they planned to live in the county of their school after graduation or own property there in order to register to vote. *Alabama Journal* editor Ray Jenkins dubbed Smith the state's "statistical panjandrum" and quoted a state official saying the Sovereignty Commission consultant had fabricated her data. "All this is an attempt to make it more difficult for students to vote," the official admitted, "and it has the unofficial blessing of Governor Wallace."[38]

It seemed there was no place in Alabama where Strickland, Smith and Mizell could not find a radical threat they had to quell. In north Alabama, the Peace Commission stoked one community's fear and outrage when it charged that a group of Black farmers were lawless Muslims who had failed, among other things, to register with state troopers as required by a state law requiring communists and Muslims to self-report if they were in the state for more than five days.[39]

In the college towns of Tuscaloosa and Auburn, Smith and Mizell offered technical and legal assistance to the local county registrars who were following the Sovereignty Commission's guidance for fighting a lawsuit filed by students attempting to register to vote. When the new, reform-minded Alabama Attorney General Bill Baxley informed the state's boards of registrars that a decision of the U.S. Supreme Court invalidated Alabama's lengthy residency requirements for voting, Smith advised the registrars to ignore the state's top lawyer. Baxley secured a state court order restraining Smith from interfering with local registration boards, but, through the Commission's lawyer, Frank Mizell, she instigated a state court action in Montgomery to block all local boards from deviating from the state's residency requirement that was largely unchanged since the adoption of the 1901 Constitution.[40]

With the assistance of Chuck Morgan's regional ACLU office, two of Alabama's young civil rights lawyers moved during this period to shut down Wallace's neo-Confederate secret agencies. Jack Drake joined ACLU attorneys in suing state officials, including Ed Strickland and the Peace Commission, to halt the harassment of the Black Muslim farmers. He asked the federal court to enjoin the Peace Commission from operating as a state agency functioning primarily to deny the constitutional rights of "Negroes and other unpopular persons and groups, and to preserve racial segregation in Alabama."[41]

In 1972, Drake's law partner Ralph Knowles intervened in Smith's lawsuit, which Attorney General Baxley had had removed to federal court. Knowles charged that the "Alabama State Sovereignty Commission has had as a major purpose the inhibition and prohibition of certain citizens 'right to vote' in violation of the Fourteenth Amendment. The Commission and Ms. Smith have constantly used their positions and energies to hinder and prevent blacks, students and military personnel from registering and voting in the State of Alabama." On behalf of University of Alabama students and others, Knowles sought an injunction to prohibit Smith and the Sovereignty Commission from interfering with the registration of qualified voters in Alabama.[42]

Both lawsuits resulted in partial victories for the Alabamians fighting Wallace's rogue agencies. A three-judge panel ordered state officials to drop all criminal prosecutions of the Black farmers in St. Clair County and voided the state statute requiring registration of Muslims. The court also found the legislature's resolution creating the Peace Commission was "unconstitutional on its face on grounds of vagueness and overbreadth," but decided not to order the Commission to shut down.[43] In the voting suit, Judge Frank Johnson dismissed Smith's complaint against the state's other registrars but stopped short of enjoining the work of Smith and the Sovereignty Commission.[44]

Smith's decision to sue the state's other registrars was apparently enough to drain the state legislature's lingering support for the Sovereignty Commission, which was routinely criticized by a handful of Black legislators, Attorney General Baxley, and some daily newspaper editors. The legislature failed to include funding for the Sovereignty Commission in the next state budget, but Smith attempted to get through a separate appropriation to be funded as a voting consultant to the governor. Wallace was still reeling from his paralysis in the aftermath of an assassin's bullet and gave Smith no apparent support. Afterwards, Smith kept her post on the Madison County board of registrars, where she had served for nearly 25 years, and she later ran unsuccessfully as a Democrat for the state legislature. She died a year later in 1975.[45]

Ed Strickland and the Peace Commission survived with state funding until Jack Drake filed a second federal lawsuit in 1975 to shut the agency down. Drake said the spy agency had spent almost $200,000 since a three-judge court declared its authorizing legislation unconstitutional and was maintaining hundreds of dossiers on law-abiding people and organizations while working to clamp down on what Strickland considered communist-inspired activities that threatened to "disturb the peace" on college campuses. Attorney General Bill Baxley intervened in support of Drake's complaint, and Strickland recruited Frank Mizell to defend the Commission. In an unpublished opinion, Johnson ordered the Commission to cease operations and impounded its records, most of which Strickland had removed or destroyed before the court order.[46]

'If You're Too Sorry or Lazy . . . to Go Register to Vote . . . Then You Don't Deserve That Privilege'

By the 1970s, white opposition to Black voting in Alabama fundamentally changed in style and character. In Congress, Alabama's House members, who unanimously opposed the Voting Rights Act in 1965 and 1970, split their votes in 1975.[47] Segregationists such as Smith, Mizell, and Strickland were becoming relics of the bygone era when almost anything said by a white official resisting Black voter registration, no matter how outrageous or inaccurate, was accepted or acceptable in most white communities. Even George Wallace, their titular leader, toned down his public rhetoric after his racist 1970 runoff that allowed him to squeak back into office. Regardless, his three old political henchmen persisted. Smith continued to the end in conjuring facts so blatantly wrong that even Alabama reporters felt a necessity to write that her "statement is incorrect" after quoting her.[48]

By the mid-1970s, Mizell had become almost a "cartoonish racist," a Foghorn Leghorn character who did not hesitate even in 1970 to publicly declare, "I smell a nigger in the woodpile!" after his fellow white members of the state Democratic Executive Committee voted to expand its membership to include African Americans for the first time.[49] Also, Strickland seemed incapable of understanding why he was no longer publicly supported for spying on university faculty wives who privately criticized the governor or on interracial couples who in his view were "the potential cause of violence in communities."[50] Their passing into the state's obscure, uncouth political history did not represent a clear break from the past in Alabama's white resistance to the constitutional rights of Black voters. But it did signal shifts in style and loyalties amid the state's politics, some changes that no segregationist, Democrat, Populist, or Republican (Black or white) from the era of John Rogers would have imagined.

Prompted by federal litigation, the Alabama legislature was required to reapportion according to population after every census, and Black men returned to the chambers on Goat Hill for the first time since Reconstruction.[51] In 1982, something else happened in Alabama that proved how far Alabama's politics had changed in such a short period. Its Black voters helped reelect George Wallace to an unprecedented fourth term as governor when he ran against the gun-toting Republican mayor of Montgomery who most African American voters decided would be worse than their once "segregation forever" governor. By the mid-1980s, Alabama elected its first Republican governor in the 20th century, without any significant Black support, but only after a federal court overturned the earlier results of a disputed Democratic primary. Hardly more than a decade later the Republican Party in Alabama became a virtually all-white political party while African Americans comprised an extraordinary majority of the state's Democratic voters.[52] The state's political history appeared to have been turned on its head.

Amid these and other profound, often bizarre political changes, Alabama continued to help shape the nation's voting rights law, but now in ways that more often added restrictions on voting in the state and across the nation. With new appointments to the federal bench, the U.S. Supreme Court and its lower courts began adopting an interpretation of the Constitution that limited the power and reach of voting rights case law and congressional statutes. In 1982, in a case involving a challenge to the county government in Mobile, Alabama, the Supreme Court issued a sweeping opinion holding that Section 2 of the Voting Rights Act required plaintiffs to prove not only racial discrimination in voting, but also an intent to discriminate. After extensive lobbying efforts by civil rights groups and a host of allies, Congress revised the Act to make it clear that a finding of intent was not necessary for a violation of the Act under Section 2.[53]

In 1985, U.S. Attorney Jeff Sessions of Mobile led a bevy of federal attorneys and state district attorneys in issuing a 29-count indictment for voter fraud against Albert Turner, his wife, Evelyn, and Spencer Hogue Jr.—the three community activists who had fought for decades to bring universal voting rights to Perry County. Twenty years after he survived state troopers' batons and tear gas on the darkened streets of Marion and again on the Edmund Pettus Bridge, Turner faced up to 115 years in federal prison on charges that he altered the absentee ballots of some elderly Black voters.

It became clear that the Sessions-led investigation and trial in Mobile involved trumped up charges of voter fraud in an apparent attempt to intimidate African American voters and clamp down on their growing influence in the Black Belt, where Sessions grew up and retained large land holdings. During the investigation, FBI agents and state lawmen rounded up and loaded onto buses more than two dozen subpoenaed Black witnesses, many of them elderly citizens who had lived through Jim Crow injustice. They were transported more than 150 miles with an escort of Alabama state troopers to testify before a federal grand jury in Mobile, a city further away than some had ever traveled. Without explanation, the witnesses were photographed, fingerprinted, and required to give handwriting samples.[54]

At trial, a jury of seven Blacks and five whites quickly rendered a unanimous verdict of "not guilty" after testimony of witnesses for both the defendants and prosecution proved that Turner and the others had violated not a law but an outdated Black Belt custom that once endangered any Black person who helped another Black person exercise a right to vote. Nonetheless, the prosecutions of additional Black Belt voting rights activists continued in Alabama's other federal courthouses. Most of these trials resulted in hung juries or convictions on reduced charges, but, as longtime journalist Randall Williams wrote at the time, the "cases only incidentally involve voting; the real issues are power and control in the parts of the Deep South where Black majorities are wresting public offices from historically entrenched white elites."[55]

Twenty-eight years later, in a case from Shelby County, Alabama, the U.S. Supreme Court annulled the decisions of the U.S. Congress and the president to continue all sections of the 1965 Voting Rights Act. In an opinion by Chief Justice John Roberts, the Court struck down the Act's Section 5, requiring preclearance of voting changes, as a violation of the covered states' right of equal state sovereignty—a phrase and concept found nowhere in the federal Constitution. "Not only do States retain sovereignty under the Constitution, there is also a 'fundamental principle of equal sovereignty' among the States," according to Roberts, who exhumed this legal theory used earlier in the Court's infamous *Dred Scott* decision holding that no Black person, slave or free, was entitled to American citizenship.[56]

During oral arguments in the Shelby case, Justice Anthony Scalia called Section 5 a "racial entitlement" for minority groups that the other two branches of the federal government had renewed out of shameless political expediency. Chief Justice Roberts also suggested that the Obama administration's attempt to protect Section 5 was an assertion that "citizens in the South are more racist than citizens in the North."[57] These observations foretold the Court's holding, but in the context of Alabama political history they sounded hauntingly similar to the political posturing of erstwhile Black Belt politicians, including the late Governor George Wallace, as they once played politics with Black citizens' voting rights. The Shelby decision began a steady series of cases in which the highest court dismembered the Act's protections.[58]

By invoking "state sovereignty," the federal constitutional term for states' rights, Roberts gutted the Voting Rights Act and repeated arguments for voiding Section 5 that Alabama's white politicians employed for more than six decades to shield its state constitution and government from any federal intervention that would disturb the Black Belt-led practices of belittling the humanity, citizenship, and constitutional rights of Black people. These echoes ricocheted across the nation, including into Alabama where its secretary of state in 2016 suggested that voting was not a right of citizenship. "If you're too sorry or lazy to get up off of your rear and to go register to vote, or to register electronically, and then to go vote, then you don't deserve that privilege," John Merrill said, as other state and local officials in Alabama dusted off some old ways and came up with some new ones to suppress Black voting.[59]

The judicial campaign to undo the Voting Rights Act continued into the next decade. In 2021, Chief Justice Roberts assigned Justice Samuel Alito to write the Court's six-person majority opinion that weakened the basic purpose of the Act's Section 2 and the 1982 congressional amendments passed to make it easier, not more difficult, to strike down voter suppression laws resulting in racial discrimination. The Court's decision in a case from Arizona laid out five "guideposts"—Alito's judge-made version of "objective factors"—that lower courts must consider as the standards Congress intended as the "totality of circumstances" for determining if plaintiffs had proven a violation of Section 2. None of the standards Alito specified were in any official reports of the U.S. House or Senate when Congress amended the Act in 1982, but each made it more difficult to prove an unlawful voting rights infringement.[60]

Early in the following year, the Supreme Court blocked a three-judge court ruling that the Alabama legislature's congressional reapportionment plan was racially discriminatory under Section 2. After an extensive trial, the lower court ordered the adoption of a plan that would create a second House district, among the state's seven, in which Black citizens, one-fourth of the state's voting population, might elect another candidate of their choice. In their brief, Alabama's Secretary of State John Merrill and Attorney General Steve Marshall argued that the high court's action to suspend the new plan was necessary since the "district court's order would require the State to hold elections using racially segregated districts."

The case had a full hearing in October 2022. Alabama's white officials claimed that Black plaintiffs were seeking to replace the "State's policy of race-neutral redistricting" with "a race-conscious one," demanding that Section 2 "require what its text forbids: racial preferencing in redistricting."

The state officials echoed the general outlook that Roberts had expressed in his past Supreme Court opinions involving race and when in 1982, as an official in the Reagan administration's Justice Department, he opposed the Act's renewal. Merrill and Marshall insisted that Alabama's Black citizens were attempting to "replace laws that do not discriminate on account of race with laws that do," and, if the Act required as much, the law's provisions "far exceed Congress's enforcement power under the Fifteenth Amendment." In Merrill and Marshall's view, the Voting Rights Act is unconstitutional. To their disappointment, the Court failed to strike down the Act in 2023 but continued to add voting rights cases to its docket in a clear indication that the Act's forceful role in advancing universal suffrage remained in judicial jeopardy.[61]

For more than a century, from the emerging days of Jim Crow's push for disfranchisement, through the era of George Wallace's insistence on a state's right to maintain race-neutral voter qualifications, into the Robert's Court era, Alabama state officials repeated the same fundamental claim, however coarsely, benignly, or neutrally they may have phrased it. Simply stated, they consistently argued that the nation's Constitution and its courts should require all governments to be color-blind so that the law would be blind to their injustices done without mention of race although on account of race. Theirs was a bill of goods that historians failed to discredit and the courts refused to dismiss. As a result, Alabama continued to embody the never-ending democratic struggles of the South and the nation.

'UNDESERVED POLITICAL POWER AND UNEARNED, ILL-GOTTEN ECONOMIC GAINS'

The struggles in Alabama were by no measure alone over the last century in shaping the nation's fragile commitment to universal suffrage. The controversies over registration and voting in several Southern states and, in the early twenty-first century, western states also have had an oversized role in developing how the nation comes to terms with the democratic promise and constitutional mandates concerning the right to vote. While Alabama's political history of voting remains inextricably bound with all those controversies across the United States, it has had a unique, even pivotal role in shaping the national movement for equal, universal voting rights. But that role has come at a high cost for democracy within the state and with no certain outcome for the nation. The lessons America once learned and the safeguard the national government once put in place for voting too often came about only after white Alabamians and their leaders demonstrated how far a state would go—to preserve political white supremacy—in suppressing democratic rules and violating common human decency.

Of course, nothing was destined to happen. The political war of sections within the state between north and south Alabama held the potential to break out of the Black Belt/Big Mules aristocratic control and to realign political interests that in the past had led to at least a nominal political alliance involving Blacks and whites. There also were white Alabamians who did not turn a blind eye or remain publicly silent when confronted with the lack of democracy and simple injustices that virtually all Blacks and some whites suffered. But, despite heroic Black resistance, white leaders of the Black Belt often prevailed because, after stacking the deck in their favor in 1901, they were smarter, more ruthless, and more single-minded in state politics than most of their white rivals. They rarely could advance one of their own as governor, but they almost always cheated, outfoxed, or enchanted enough white legislators and governors to protect the mechanics of law that gave them undeserved political power and unearned, ill-gotten economic gains.

The ways and means were not all that complicated or arcane. Primarily, Black Belt leaders and their allies created a constitution in their own traditional image of the South and for their own privileges, and it became the law of the land by fraud. Afterwards, they controlled the legislature and the committee responsible for any and all legislation to change that Constitution, including all changes other counties had to seek from them to address communities' necessities outside the Black Belt. It was a brilliant institutional scheme of political power for the preservation of a white political oligarchy, and it worked until the nation's highest court, often prodded by Associate Justice Hugo Black of Alabama, entered the political thicket and began enforcing the Reconstruction Amendments of the U.S. Constitution.

The Black Belt's white minority rulers were doomed once federal courts began in earnest addressing unconstitutional injustices in the distribution of political power. But, in fighting to save as much power and economic privilege as possible, for as long as possible, the Black Belt leaders played a pivotal role in enabling one of their own to muster his enormous demagogic capacity and rare political skills to bring an end to the state's nearly 150-year-old war of sections. George Wallace did not restore Black Belt hegemony. That was beyond even his alchemic political powers. But as their last best hope, he bought them time by frustrating the federal government's new role in guaranteeing a right to vote and by orchestrating, as well as inspiring, local white resistance. More important and more lasting, he implanted the traditional Black Belt perspective on issues such as voting into the prevailing attitudes of voters and politicians across the state. Less than ten years after Lurleen Wallace's landslide victory in 1966, only four years after the first two Blacks since Reconstruction took seats in the state legislature, the vast majority of north Alabama house members agreed with the prevailing Black Belt belief that there was no need for continued protection of Black voting rights by the federal government.[62]

In putting an end to the state's war of sections, Wallace completely transformed Alabama politics by convincing most white voters that all parts of the state from the Tennessee River to the Gulf of Mexico were under attack by civil rights protestors, federal courts, and a federal Justice Department working together against the white people of Alabama with the gleeful, snide support of Northerners (whom Southern whites *knew* had racial problems worse than Alabama's). This was the origin of Wallaceism, and it became a major, virulent political force in Alabama and beyond. As a Black Belt politician, Wallace did not manufacture the racist sentiments and white resentments that propelled Wallaceism. He only gave his followers vitality and voice, and he adroitly stoked them into a political phenomenon that spread in conjunction with other Southern demagogues across Southern states and beyond the Mason-Dixon Line in ways that altered the direction and nature of American politics.[63]

The Southern strategy that Richard Nixon adopted and successive Republican presidents and congressional leaders adapted in response to Wallaceism realigned politics in the region and the nation, but it failed to have a consistent, prevailing impact in shaping national politics until recent decades. As Heather Cox Richardson has written, the South finally won the Civil War 150 years after Appomattox when a national war of sections reemerged—one in which most Southern and Western states joined the same political party with the same basic agenda and strategies of states' rights and voter suppression that had once been the order of the day in Alabama for Black Belt minority rule.[64]

This political movement took hold of American politics in the twenty-first century with the active constitutional blessing of the nation's highest court, whose conservative majority often abandoned their own professed judicial philosophies in order to slow down or impede expansion of voting rights. The Court's new judicial activism banned any mention or use of race to remedy past or current racial injustices, sanctified state sovereignty and states' rights as preferred constitutional values that trumped the protection of individual rights, and rewrote state and federal laws so that little or nothing could be done to expand voting or to limit the role of money in politics. In turn, the Republicans' minority control of the Congress (and occasionally minority control of the Electoral College and the presidency)[65] assured that the Court decisions in rewriting the meaning of national laws would not often be overturned.

These trends and terms in the nation's governance and politics would have appeared uncannily familiar, even heartwarming, to John Rogers of Sumter County and other Black Belt planters. For they were pioneers in strategies on how to win a war of sections to prevent the triumph of interracial political alliances. They were among the nation's masters of the politics of white supremacy. They crafted the political art of white minority rule in the Heart of Dixie and the strategies on how to preserve it within a self-avowing democracy even as wars raged to safeguard democracy elsewhere in the world. They were among the early prophets and leaders of voter suppression as the essential tool for ensuring that ill-gotten gains enrich only a few in a democratic republic. In short, unlike in 1919 or

1949, the Black Belt no longer controlled Alabama or Southern politics, but its role in the political history of Alabama, a history that molded and reflected much of the nation's struggle for a universal right to vote, was the forerunner of the conflicted American politics that appeared in the first decades of the twenty-first century.

Since that fateful day in 1965, retracing the steps of civil rights leaders across the Edmund Pettus Bridge has become both an annual remembrance of Alabama's political past and a symbol of some of the nation's best political aspirations and possibilities. But, as historian Allen Tullos has written, the Bridge's "rituals of commemoration remain vital only if the living can shift their meaning and emotional power into possibilities for an impending future."[66] In developing the character and content of that transition, as circuitous as the Alabama and Tombigbee rivers and as divergent as the country's political reversal from Obama to Trump, this nation of fifty states governed under one national constitution must decide if the nature and issues of Alabama's political past shall continue to embody the struggles of American democracy.

Page Number Guide to Notes by Chapter

Notes

Notes to Introduction

1 See W. E. B. DuBois, *Black Reconstruction in America, 1860–1880* (New York: MacMillan, 1992), 682–694; Chandler Davidson, "The Voting Rights Act: A Brief History," in Bernard Grofman and Chandler Davidson, eds., *Controversies in Minority Voting: The Voting Rights Act in Perspective,* (Washington, DC: The Brookings Institution, 1992), 7–51; Gunnar Myrdal, *An American Dilemma* (New York: Harper & Brothers, 1944), 430–439; V. O. Key Jr., *Southern Politics in State and Nation* (New York: Alfred A. Knopf, 1950), 5–12; Donald S. Strong, *Negroes, Ballots, and Judges: National Voting Rights in the Federal Courts* (University, Alabama: University of Alabama Press, 1970), 1–9, 90–94; Laughlin McDonald, *A Voting Rights Odyssey: Black Enfranchisement in Georgia* (New York: Cambridge University Press, 2003); J. Morgan Kousser, "The Voting Rights Act and the Two Reconstructions," in *Controversies in Minority Voting,* 135–176; Wayne Flynt, *Alabama in the Twentieth Century* (Tuscaloosa: University of Alabama Press, 2004), 14–15; Steve Suitts, "Voting Rights, the Supreme Court, and the Persistence of Southern History," *Southern Spaces,* June 4, 2013; Steve Suitts, "States' Rights Resurgent: The Attack on the Voting Rights Act," *Southern Spaces,* August 29, 2013.

2 C. Vann Woodward, *Origins of the New South, 1877–1913* (Baton Rouge: Louisiana State University Press, 1970) 321–333; J. Morgan Kousser, *The Shaping of Southern Politics: Suffrage Restriction and the Establishment of the One-Party South, 1880–1910* (New Haven: Yale University Press, 1975), 11–44. "The State Press," *Montgomery Advertiser,* Apr 7, 1874, 2; "Briber and the Bribed," *Montgomery Advertiser,* Apr 25, 1889, 4.

3 Key, *Southern Politics,* 555. With more modern statistical methods, Kousser persuasively challenged Key's contention that while the constitutions' disfranchising provisions were sweeping in language and techniques, their effects were a *fait accompli* due to prior informal and often illegal actions, especially on the local level. See Kousser, *The Shaping of Southern Politics,* 240–246. Earlier, Woodward also found Key's thesis overstated, if not lacking. See Woodward, *Origins of the New South,* 343–346.

4 Michael Perman, *Struggle for Mastery: Disfranchisement in the South, 1888–1908* (Chapel Hill: University of North Carolina Press, 2001), 1. Perman provides the most comprehensive analysis of the creation of disfranchisement across ten Southern states.

5 Myrdal, *An American Dilemma,* 429. The Deep South customarily includes South Carolina, Georgia, Alabama, Mississippi, and Louisiana.

6 Kousser, *The Shaping of Southern Politics,* 236; Key, *Southern Politics,* 666. See Robert Mickey, *Paths Out of Dixie: The Democratization of Authoritarian Enclaves in America's Deep South, 1944–1972* (Princeton: Princeton University Press, 2015) for an excellent

discussion of the common characteristics and supports among Deep South states for maintaining elite political hegemony (Chapter 2) and a description of both common and unique aspects of the Jim Crow politics within three Deep South states, Mississippi, Georgia, and South Carolina (Chapter 3).

7 For a scholarly study focusing primarily on the period after the end of the all-white primary in other Deep South states, see Mickey, *Paths Out of Dixie*.

8 Woodward, *Origins of the New South*, 341–342; George B. Tindall, *The Emergence of the New South 1913–1945* (Baton Rouge: Louisiana State University Press, 1970), 165–170, 556–559; Steven F. Lawson, *Black Ballots: Voting Rights in the South, 1944–1969* (New York: Columbia University Press, 1976), 89–98.

9 Flynt, *Alabama in the Twentieth Century*, 24.

10 Malcolm Cook McMillan, *Constitutional Development in Alabama, 1798–1901: A Study in Politics, the Negro, and Sectionalism* (Spartanburg: The Reprint Company, 1978), 223–225; William Warren Rogers, *The One-Gallused Rebellion: Agrarianism in Alabama, 1965–1896* (Baton Rouge: Louisiana State University Press, 1970), 237–242; Steve Suitts, *Hugo Black of Alabama: How His Roots and Early Career Shaped the Great Champion of the Constitution* (Montgomery: NewSouth Books, 2005), 64–65, 146–148.

11 McMillan, *Constitutional Development in Alabama*, 261, 350; James J. Mayfield, *Constitutions of 1875 and 1901: Paralleled, Annotated, and Indexed (*Montgomery: Brown Publishing Company, 1918), 219–225. Also, see p.83, where in contrast to the 1901 Constitution, even the Redeemers' 1875 Constitution in Article I, Section 38 provides: "No educational or property qualification for suffrage or office, nor any restraint upon the same on account of race, color, or previous condition of servitude, shall be made by law."

12 Lawson, *Black Ballots, 89.*

13 Pauli Murray, *State Laws on Race and Color* (Women's Division of Christian Service of the Methodist Church: Washington, 1951), 21; *Alabama Official and Statistical Register, 1947*, 532–533, 537–539; Lawson, *Black Ballots*, 88–96.

14 Key, *Southern Politics*, 633.

15 For example on the Boswell Amendment, see: Scotty E Kirkland, "Mobile and the Boswell Amendment," *Alabama Review*, 65, 3 (July 2012): 205–249; William D. Barnard, *Dixiecrats and Democrats: Alabama Politics 1942–1950* (University: University of Alabama Press, 1974), 59–71; Vera Chandler Foster, "'Boswellianism': A Technique in the Restriction of Negro Voting," *Phylon*, 10,1 (1949): 26–37.

16 Flynt, *Alabama in the Twentieth Century*, 15.

17 Key, *Southern Politics*, 5–6. The exact definition of the "Black Belt" in Alabama—identifying which counties are included—has varied widely depending on time and purpose. See Allen Tullos, "The Black Belt," *Southern Spaces*, Feb. 19, 2004. This book employs Booker T. Washington's political definition that, unlike the historical-geographical term referring to the section's rich, black soil, includes the 21 south Alabama counties in which a majority of the population was African American at the time of the adoption of the 1901 Constitution. (See map on page 2.) These are also the counties that had the largest slave populations in 1860. Across the six decades in

which Alabama's political war of sections raged during the 20th century, the counties' boundaries and population changed but most remained majority-Black. Only three had a decline in Black population below 40 percent by 1960, and none dropped below 35 percent. The political traditions that existed among white leaders in 1901 in these counties also lingered in these counties regardless of population changes. This political definition seems to hold up over time even by the terms of those working against Black Belt control. In 1965, the Student Nonviolent Coordinating Committee (SNCC), an activist organization of young civil rights workers, organized voter registration efforts in the Alabama Black Belt, which they defined as "counties where more than 44 percent of the population of the counties is Negro." Seventeen of SNCC's 19 Black Belt counties are encompassed in the political definition used in this book. See "The General Condition of the Alabama Negro," March 1965, Student Non-Violent Coordinating Committee (SNCC) Archives, Civil Rights Movement Archive, accessed at https://www.crmvet.org/.

18 For an overview of the alliance of Black Belt planters and the Big Mules of Alabama industries: Anne Permaloff, "Black Belt-Big Mule Coalition," Encyclopedia of Alabama, February 21, 2011.

19 There is no precise geographical boundary for defining "north Alabama." In her masterful study of the Alabama legislature, Hallie Farmer defined "north Alabama" as counties located north of the southmost tip of Jefferson County, where Birmingham is located, except for Pickens, a Black Belt County. See Hallie Farmer, *The Legislative Process in Alabam*a (University, Alabama: Bureau of Public Administration, 1949), 141. But this definition overlooks the facts that in both geography and politics Tuscaloosa County has been connected to the Black Belt more than any other section and that in 1901 Talladega County had a majority-Black population. For this study, "north Alabama" includes only those 21 counties which are entirely found north of the southmost point of Jefferson County. Therefore, Tuscaloosa County is considered "south Alabama." The five counties—Shelby, Chilton, Talladega, Clay, and Randolph counties south and east of Jefferson—are designated as "central Alabama" due to both geography and political traditions. All counties that are not Jefferson and not in north or central Alabama are "south Alabama" for purposes of this study. (See map on page 2.)

20 Martin T. Olliff, "Wiregrass Region," Encyclopedia of Alabama. As with the Black Belt, the historical-geographical definition of the Alabama Wiregrass counties does not exactly match the political definition of the section, although they are quite similar. The geographical area includes Barbour, a Black Belt county, and does not include Coffee County, which is included in the political definition of the section when referring to the Alabama "Wiregrass." The Wiregrass is also included as a part of "south Alabama" in this study. See map on page 2.

21 Barbara J. Fields, "Ideology and Race in American History," in Morgan Kousser and James M. McPherson (eds), *Region, Race, and Reconstruction: Essays in Honor of C. Vann Woodward.* (New York: Oxford University Press, 1982), 157. Historian Glenn Feldman has unsuccessfully argued, in effect, that poor whites in Alabama supported disfranchisement virtually as much Black Belt planters, but in essence he mistakenly confused widespread vulgar expressions of racism as hard evidence of white support for disfranchisement; he failed to recognize that both white supporters and white

opponents of disfranchisement often used "race-baiting" language when confronted with their opponents' "race-baiting" in political debates before other whites; and he ignored (instead of refuted) the earlier, persuasive statistical analysis by Morgan Kousser in *The Shaping of Southern Politics*. Feldman's statistics were also unpersuasive, especially since he counted some majority-Black counties and "Big Mule" counties as poor "white counties." See Glenn Feldman, *The Disfranchisement Myth: Poor Whites and Suffrage Restrictions in Alabama* (Athens: University of Georgia Press, 2004).

22 Glenn Feldman, *Politics, Society, and the Klan in Alabama 1915–1949* (Tuscaloosa: University of Alabama Press, 1999), 193; Diane McWhorter, *Carry Me Home: Birmingham, Alabama: The Climatic Battle of the Civil Rights Revolution* (New York: Simon and Schuster, 2001), 64.

23 See Lawson, *Black Ballots,* 97; Rex Thomas, "Ultimate Test of Voter Curb Is Anticipated," *Montgomery Advertiser,* Dec 30, 1951, 17.

24 See "Chapter XV: Alabama Election Statistics," *Alabama Official and Statistical Register, 1923,* 344–457. The results are summarily reported on page 505 in the section on "Miscellaneous Statistics," along with data on cotton gin production and state bonds among other things.

Notes to Chapter 1

1 Forney Johnston to Charles Henderson, Apr. 8, 1918, Charles Henderson Papers, Alabama Department of Archives and History (ADAH); Suitts, *Hugo Black of Alabama*, 235–236. For a summary of Hooper's extensive business holdings, see "Lloyd Hooper Passes Away After Brief Sick Spell," *Tuscaloosa News*, Apr. 23, 1923, 1.

2 Glenn Feldman, *From Demagogue to Dixiecrat: Horace Wilkinson and the Politics of Race* (Lanham: University Press of America, 1995), 25–27; Suitts, *Hugo Black of Alabama*, 156–158, 236–237.

3 Mary Martha Thomas, *The New Woman in Alabama: Social Reforms and Suffrage, 1890–1920* (Tuscaloosa: University of Alabama Press, 1992), 188–189; Evans C. Johnson, *Oscar W. Underwood: A Political Biography* (Baton Rouge: Louisiana State University Press, 1980), 278–280.

4 "Robert B. Evins Dies Suddenly in Greensboro," *Tuscaloosa News*, Nov 29, 1933, 1; McMillan, *Constitutional Development in Alabama*, 267, 278 n. 94, 287, 308.

5 "Antis Claim Votes Enough to Kill Suffragist Bill," *Tuscaloosa News*, Jul 11, 1919, 1.

6 "Alabama Women Opposed to Ratifying Suffrage Clause Memorialize Legislature," *Montgomery Advertiser*, Jul 17, 1919, 1; Thomas, *The New Woman in Alabama*, 195–201.

7 "Nineteen Senate Votes Are Pledged Against Measure," *Montgomery Advertiser*, Jul 17, 1919, 2; Thomas, *The New Woman in Alabama*, 197; "Anthony Amendment Vote in Senate Today," *Montgomery Advertiser*, Jul 17, 1919, 1; "Judge Jno. R. Tyson Points Danger of Enforcement Provision of Anthony Amendment," *Montgomery Times*, Apr 16, 1920, 7.

8 Tyson reprinted the news story of his speech as his campaign material. See examples: "Judge J. R. Tyson: Points Danger of Enforcement Provision of Anthony

Amendment," *Wilcox Progressive Era*, Apr 29, 1920, 3; "Judge John R. Tyson: Points Danger of Enforcement Provision of Anthony Amendment," *Andalusia Star*, Apr 27, 1920, 8; *Evergreen Courant*, Apr 28, 1920, 1; *Alabama Official and Statistical Register, 1919*, 410; "Susan B. Anthony Buried by Senate," *Montgomery Advertiser*, Sep 20, 1919, 1.

9 Henry M. McKiven Jr., *Iron and Steel: Class, Race, and Community in Birmingham, 1875–1920* (Chapel Hill: University of North Carolina Press, 1995), 105–111; Brian Kelly, *Race, Class, and Power in the Alabama Coalfields, 1908–1920* (Urbana: University of Illinois Press, 2011), 162–202; Thomas Kilby to Mitchell Palmer, U.S. Attorney General, Nov. 1, 1919, Thomas A. Kilby Papers, ADAH; "Both Sides are Confident on Eve of Steel Strike," *Birmingham Age-Herald*, Sept. 21, 1919, 5; "Little Evidence of Strike Is Apparent to Outsiders," *Birmingham Age-Herald*, Sept. 24, 1919; Jimmie Frank Gross, "Strikes in the Coal, Steel and Railroad Industries in Birmingham From 1918 to 1922," Master's thesis (Auburn University, 1952), 48.

10 *Journal of the Senate*, Special Session, 1919, 1751, 2412; "The Strike Situation," *Our Southern Home*, Feb 23, 1921, 4. Evins also unsuccessfully sponsored a bill to allow state courts to award damages against anyone who wrote an "abusive, obscene, or insulting letter" or other communications—private or public. The law could have been used to punish striking workers who "insulted" industrial managers and strikebreakers. See "Alabama Legislature to Adjourn Sine Die Today," *Montgomery Advertiser*, Sep 27, 1919, 3.

11 *Code of Alabama, 1907*, vol. III, chapter 176, sec. 6394–6399; "Anti-Strike Law Is Passed," *Gadsden Daily Times-News*, Sep 29, 1919, 5.

12 Thomas Orr to Governor Kilby, undated, Kilby Papers.

13 *Acts of Alabama, 1919*, 187–188.

14 *Alabama Official and Statistical Register, 1919*, 82, 126. When Benners was not in the legislature in 1913, his senior law partner, Walker Percy, served in that role. After 1909, their junior law partner, Borden Burr, became a forceful, frequent lobbyist on corporate and labor issues at the state legislature. See McKiven, *Iron and Steel*, 103, 163.

15 "Poll Tax Buttons," *Montgomery Advertiser*, Jan 8, 1919, 8.

16 Oscar Underwood to Norman Gunn, Feb. 24, 1920, Underwood to E. W. Barrett, Feb. 27, 1920, Oscar W. Underwood Papers, ADAH; "Proceedings of Congress and Committee in Brief: Senate," *Washington Post*, Aug 16, 1919, 6; Suitts, *Hugo Black of Alabama*, 296–300; "Underwood Campaign Launched; Hooper Opens Headquarters," *Montgomery Advertiser*, Jan 4, 1920, 1; Robert H. Mangum to Underwood, Jan. 28,1920, J. B. Ellis to Underwood, Feb. 2, 1920, Underwood Papers.

17 *Proceedings of the Twenty-Seventh Consecutive and Fourth Biennial Convention of the United Mine Workers of America*, January 5, 6, 7, 1920, 162–163; *Report of the Proceedings of the Thirty-Ninth Convention of the American Federation of Labor*, January 9 to 23, 1919, 305; "Answer: The Mobile Register, Inc. by Fredrick T. (sic) Thompson," undated, *Harrison v. Hooper* (original complaint dated May 1, 1920), Chancery Minutes and Records, Jefferson County Courthouse.

18 Suitts, *Hugo Black of Alabama*, 300.

19 Ibid., 301–305; J. B. Ellis to Oscar Underwood, May 10, 1920, Underwood Papers; "Chairman Hooper Will Discuss Decree after All Documents Served," *Montgomery Advertiser*, May 4, 1920, 1; "Underwood Executives Enjoined by Circuit Court" [ad], *Marion Times-Standard*, May 6, 1920, 9 and *Southern Democrat*, May 6, 1920, 7.

20 Suitts, *Hugo Black of Alabama*, 307–316; Kelly, *Race, Class, and Power*, 173–198.

21 Suitts, *Hugo Black of Alabama*, 317; Kelly, *Race, Class, and Power* 169–171;16; Daniel Letwin, *The Challenge of Interracial Unionism: Alabama Coal Miners, 1978–1921* (Chapel Hill: University of North Carolina Press, 1998), 182–189.

22 Rep. William Jefferson Danby of Choctaw sponsored Act 451, *Acts of Alabama*, 1919, 687–690; *Alabama Official and Statistical Register, 1919,* 80, 92; *Journal of the Senate*, Special Session of 1920, 160–169; *Journal of the House of Representatives*, Special Session of 1920, 211–220; "Suff Conferees Discuss Measure (sic)," *Montgomery Advertiser*, Sep 28, 1920, 3; "Registration Notice," *Tuscaloosa News,* Oct 10, 1920, 7; "Alabama Women Will Get to Vote," *Fairhope Courier*, Oct 8, 1920, 1; Act 78, *Acts of Alabama*, Special Session of 1920, 124–134.

23 Act 78, *Acts of Alabama*, Special Session of 1920, 124–134. Sen. Charles Teasley of Montgomery and Sen. J. B. Ellis of Dallas County led the senate in fighting for more restrictive provisions in the 1920 session. They and two others from majority Black counties (1920 census) made up four of the five Senators named to the conference committee: Senators Teasley (Montgomery, 60 percent Black population); Ellis (Dallas, 77 percent Black); B. T. Phillips (Lee, 57 percent Black); John Miller (Wilcox, 81 percent Black). The fifth member was W. P. Acker (Calhoun, 25 percent Black). Acker would be considered one of the "Little Mules" in Alabama politics since he was president of the Anniston National Bank and his wife grew up in Monroe County (55 percent Black). The Black Belt Senators apparently had the upper hand in the negotiations because they had enough votes to prevent passage of any legislation enabling women to register to vote in Alabama in the near future. Also, they adroitly included sections in the new law allowing a few urban counties to have less severe restrictions on registration and offering counties an option to pay from their own funds an annual registration period of ten days in July—albeit a busy time of the year for north Alabama's small farmers.

24 "Too Many Checks on Suffrage," *Fairhope Courier*, Oct 1, 1920, 1; "Have Demonstrated Their Unfitness," *Fairhope Courier*, Oct 22, 1920, 1.

25 Act 91, *Acts of Alabama*, Special Session of 1920, 143–144.

26 Section 180 of *Constitution of Alabama, 1901*; Mayfield, *Constitutions of 1875 and 1901,* 345.

27 "Gov. Oates's Views," *Montgomery Advertiser*, Jan 12, 1901, 4; "Opinions of the Doctors," *Weekly Advertiser*, May 31, 1901, 8.

28 "The Franchise," *Montgomery Advertiser*, Jun 4, 1901, 4; "Official Report of the Proceedings of the Constitutional Convention of Alabama," *Montgomery Advertiser*, Jun 4, 1901, 11, where Mr. Jenkins of Wilcox County proposed Ordinance No. 208; McMillan, *Constitutional Development in Alabama*, 261–281; Volney R. Riser, "Disfranchisement, the U.S. Constitution, and the Federal Courts: Alabama's 1901 Constitutional Convention Debates the Grandfather Clause." *American Journal of Legal History* 48, no. 3 (2006): 243–44, 254–256, 274–277. In 1915, the U.S. Supreme

Court upheld a literacy test for voting but found that a "grandfather clause" in the Oklahoma constitution violated the U.S. Constitution's 15th Amendment. See *Guinn v. United States*, 238 US 347 (1915).

29 "Republicans Elected," *Birmingham Times*, Apr 26, 1901, 5; *Official Proceedings of the Constitutional Convention of the State of Alabama, May 21st, 1901, to September 3rd, 1901*, vol. 3, 2808–2810. Freeman also proposed unsuccessfully that the constitution prohibit any corporation attorney from serving in the state legislature and removing the adopted language of the constitution allowing the legislature to forego publishing its proceedings when "such parts as, in its judgment, may require secrecy." *Journal of the Proceedings of the Constitutional Convention of the State of Alabama, Held in the City of Montgomery, Commencing May 21st, 1901,* 841, 907–908. The adopted language for some permissible secrecy at the legislature was carried over from the 1875 Constitution and became part of Article IV section 55 of the 1901 Constitution. *See* Mayfield, *Constitutions of 1875 and 1901,* 135. There was published both a "Proceedings" (transcript) of the convention and a "Journal" of its actions. The proceedings also were published daily in the *Montgomery Advertiser* to considerable interest. Also, see Riser, "Disfranchisement, the U.S. Constitution, and the Federal Courts," 237–239.

30 *Official Proceedings,* vol. 3, *2967–2973, 2978–2981.* For more on Spears, *see* Samuel L. Webb, *Two-Party Politics in the One-Party South: Alabama's Hill Country, 1874–1920* (Tuscaloosa: University of Alabama Press, 1997), 166–178.

31 "Official Report of the Proceedings . . ." *Montgomery Advertiser*, Jul 25, 1901, 11; McMillan, *Constitutional Development in Alabama,* 296–297.

32 *Official Proceedings,* vol. 3, 2961–2967; "Mr. Bowie on Suffrage: He Comes to the Aid of the Black Belt," *Montgomery Advertiser*, Jul 27, 1901, 5; McMillan, *Constitutional Development in Alabama*, 291–298.

33 *Address of Hon. John B. Knox, of Calhoun, on his installation as president of the Constitutional Convention of Alabama, May 22, 1901*; *also Remarks of John B. Knox, president, in support of the majority report of the committee on suffrage and elections, July 26,* 1901(Montgomery: Brown Printing Co., 1901), 23–27.

34 Michael Perman, *Struggle for Mastery: Disfranchisement in the South, 1888–1908* (Chapel Hill: University of North Carolina Press, 2001), 189.

35 Ibid., 189.

36 McMillan, *Constitutional Development in Alabama*, 307–308; *Alabama Official and Statistical Register, 1911, 284–285.* O'Neal also helped to develop the campaign strategy for ratifying the 1901 Constitution to advance the Black Belt control. See Feldman, *The Disfranchisement Myth*, 69. The Black Belt counties did not forget his support. In his race for governor, O'Neal received all but nine votes cast in Hale County and all but four votes in Greene and Wilcox counties in the 1910 Democratic primary for governor. O'Neal's father had been Alabama's governor in the 1880s.

37 *Official Proceedings,* vol. 3, *3919–3924*; See David Waldstreicher, *Slavery's Constitution: From Revolution to Ratification* (New York: Hill and Wang, 2009), 5–6. In fact, as a territory and a state, the Alabama legislature was apportioned only according to the numbers of white persons in the years before the Civil War due to the political power of north Alabama.

38 *Greensboro Watchman*, Feb 15, 1900, 3 and Mar 21, 1901, 3; *Journal of the Proceedings,* 1782, 1801–1802; "Robert B. Evins Dies Suddenly in Greensboro," *Tuscaloosa News*, Nov 29, 1933, 1; statistics computed from *Fourteenth Census of the United States, Population 1920: Composition and Characteristics of the States*, vol. 3, Alabama (Washington: Bureau of the Census, 1922), 54–65. The most extreme disparity in equal white representation in 1920 was in Senate District 13, Jefferson County, where the white population was 19 times larger than Evins's district. When considering total population, instead of only white population, Senate District 13 had more than seven times more total persons than Evins's Senate District 32 in 1920 due to changes in population since 1901.

39 Act 91, *Acts of Alabama,* Special Session of 1920, 143; "The Governor Settles the Strike," *Montgomery Advertiser*, Mar 20, 1921, 4; on road conditions, see "Better Highways Will Make Rural Farm Life More Satisfactory," *Anniston Star*, Feb 7, 1920, 4; "Bad Weather and Bad Roads," *Guntersville Democrat*, Feb 11, 1920, 1; "The Bad Roads Nearly Put A Stop to Travel . . .," *Scottsboro Citizen*, Jan 21, 1919, 1.

40 "More Than 200 Women Register on First Day," *Anniston Star*, Oct 20, 1920, 1; "23,000 Women Qualify for Participation in the General Election," *Voice of the People*, Oct 30, 1920, 4; "Herzberg Says Women Needed to Defeat GOP" *Gadsden Daily Times-News*, Oct 21, 1920, 1; "Claim Five Out of the Seven Counties," *Gadsden Daily Times-News*, Oct 28, 1920, 1; "What Republicans Are Doing Shown in This Letter to Negro Women," *Gadsden Daily Times-News*, Oct 22, 1920, 5; "What the Republican Campaign Committee of the Seventh Congressional District Say About the Negro Question," *Gadsden Daily Times-News*, Oct 23, 1920, 6. The overt partisanship of the local board of registrars is explained by the fact that the 7th Congressional District, which included the often-called rural "Republican counties" in northeast Alabama, in addition to the more industrial Gadsden, was Alabama's only district where Republicans had a good chance to win after the 1901 Constitution. See Webb, *Two-Party Politics,* 26. In the November 1920 election campaign, Democratic incumbent L. B. Rainey won by less than 750 votes over Republican Charles B. Kennamer. See *Alabama Official and Statistical Register, 1923,* 345. Kennamer was later appointed a U.S. federal judge in Alabama by President Herbert Hoover.

41 "4400 Women Ready to Wield Vote," *Montgomery Advertiser*, Oct 27, 1920, 2; "Large Percentage of Women Register," *Democrat-Reporter*, Oct 28, 1920, 1; "5,000 Voters Qualified in This County," *Dothan Eagle*, Oct 27, 1920, 1.

42 "To the Citizens of Elmore County," *Weekly Herald*, Oct 21, 1920, 1; "Go And Register Right Now," *Union Springs Herald*, Oct 21, 1920, 1; "Fifteen Million Women Will Vote Is Belief," *Montgomery Times*, Nov 2, 1920, 1. Also, see "Voting In Florida," *Selma Times-Journal*, Oct 20, 1920, 6, and "Savannah," *Selma Times-Journal*, Nov 2, 1920, 1. These reports were supported by some Northern press reports. See "Many Negro Women to Vote in the South," *Boston Daily Globe*, Oct 17, 1920, 61.

43 See *Alabama Official and Statistical Register, 1923,* 449–451.

44 "Constitutional Amendments," *Montgomery Times*, Jan 8, 1921, 4; "To Qualified Electors," *Union Springs Herald*, Feb 3, 1921, 4; "Amendments Fights Not Organized," *Clarke County Democrat*, Jan 13, 1921, 1; "Constitutional Amendments," *Russell Register*, Jan 28, 1921, 2.

45 "Your Attention Is Called to the Election Notice" and "Suffrage Amendment," *Greene County Democrat*, Jan 28, 1921, 4, and Feb 4, 1921, 1.

46 "Keller Addresses The Kiwanis Club," *Selma Times-Journal*, Feb 2, 1921, 1; for the Craig family in Selma, see O. S. Wynn, "Only Two of Dallas Born Native Sons Represented This District in Halls of National Congress," *Selma Times-Journal*, Mar 13, 1921, 11; "To the Democrats of Hale County," *Greensboro Watchman*, Feb 3, 1921, 2.

47 "Tuesday's election," *Abbeville Herald*, Feb 3, 1921, 8; "Senator Evins on the Amendment," *Prattville Progress*, Feb 3, 1921, 7; "Letter Sees Danger Ahead," *Atmore Record*, Feb 3, 1921, 8.

48 "Central Body of Labor Condemns Attack on Editor by Austin Agents," *Albany-Decatur Daily*, Jan 4, 1921, 1.

49 "Nine Members of Alabama National Guard to Be Fired," *Cullman Tribune*, Jan 27, 1921, 1; "Forty Witnesses," *Tuscaloosa News*, Jan 27, 1921, 1; "Qualifying Jury Occupies Court When Soldier Is Given A Hearing," *Albany-Decatur Daily*, Feb 1, 1921, 1; "Witness After Witness Testify Accused Soldier's Reputation in Home County Is Excellent," *Birmingham Age-Herald*, Feb 5, 1921, 1; "Who Put the For Sale Sign on Marion County?" *Marion County News*, Jul 7, 1921, 1; Suitts, *Hugo Black of Alabama*, 316.

50 "The Suffrage Amendment," *Montgomery Advertiser*, Feb. 5, 1921, 4; "The Character Amendment," *Montgomery Advertiser*, Feb 6, 1921, 4. Evins used the term "good citizens" three times and "vicious and ignorant" twice. Neither article used the term "Negro" or any more common, less proper reference to the Black race.

51 "Amendment Will Save State Grave Political Problems," *Birmingham Age-Herald*, Feb 8, 1921, 5; Suitts, *Hugo Black of Alabama*, 336.

52 "Official Count Shows Defeat of Amendments," *Montgomery Times*, Feb 24, 1921, 8; "Two Amendments to Constitution Are Defeated in State," *Montgomery Advertiser*, Feb 12, 1921, 1; "Both Amendments Lose in Jefferson," *Birmingham Age-Herald*, Feb 12, 1921, 5.

53 "Amendment Fights Not Organized," *Clarke County Democrat*, Jan 13, 1921, 1; "Two Amendments Defeated in State" *Greenville Advocate*, Feb 16, 1921, 1; "Believe Both Amendments Are Beaten," and "The 'Black Belt' Counties Voted Strongly," *Selma Times-Journal*, Feb 9, 1921, 1, and Feb 17, 1921, 4; "Election Results In Doubt Pending Official Canvass," *Birmingham Age-Herald*, Feb 10, 1921, 2.

54 Entry, February 14, 1921, Thomas D. Parke Diary and Papers, Department of Archives and Manuscripts, Birmingham Public Library.

55 "In the Amendment Election . . ." *Guntersville Advertiser*, Feb 15, 1921, 3; "For Number One Against Number Two," *Fairhope Courier*, Feb 11, 1921, 1.

56 "Ellis of Dallas Not Opposed for President Protem," *Selma Times-Journal*, Sep 10, 1922, 1; "R. B. Evins Is Elected Chairman State Democratic Committee," *Huntsville News*, Jan 16, 1923, 1; "Plans Underway Campaign of Underwood," *Montgomery Times*, Dec 3, 1923, 1; "Robert B. Evins Dies Suddenly in Greensboro," *Tuscaloosa News*, Nov 29, 1933, 1.

57 See *Alabama Official and Statistical Register, 1919, 1923.* I am indebted to the ADAH staff for finding the summary report of referendum results in the "Miscellaneous

Statistics" section. This obscure, summary placement contrasts with the report of county returns for three referenda held in November 1920 and also rejected by voters. See *Alabama Official and Statistical Register, 1923,* 356–361. Indeed, the manner of reporting on the Evins Amendment was politically convenient for the state archivist. Bankhead Owens and Evins shared political alliances beyond their mutual work in opposing women's suffrage. Evins was, for example, the lawyer representing her brother, John Bankhead Jr., in hearings before a U.S. Senate committee in 1931 after Senator "Cotton Tom" Heflin, who lost to Bankhead, contested the 1930 election. Later, Bankhead Owens was a public supporter of Gessner McCorvey, a leading advocate for the 1946 Boswell Amendment and Alabama's "Dixiecrat" movement. In fact, she headed the women's national division of the Dixiecrats while continuing to serve as ADAH director. Robert J. Jakeman, "Marie Bankhead Owens and the Alabama Department of Archives and History, 1920–1955," *Provenance, Journal of the Society of Georgia Archivists,* 21, no. 1 (2003), 36; "Bankhead Plans 'Finish' Fight on Heflin Contest," *Decatur Daily,* Apr 3, 1931. 1; "Shipeshape," *Decatur Daily,* Aug 6, 1948, 4; "Mrs. Owens to Head Dixiecrat Women," *Dothan Eagle,* Aug 18, 1948, 7.

58 "Alabama Constitutional Convention," *The Annals of the American Academy of Political and Social Science* 19 (1902): 143–45; William Garrott Brown, *A History of Alabama for Use in Schools* (New York: University Publishing Company, 1903), 333; Joel Campbell DuBose. *Alabama History* (Atlanta: B. F. Johnson Publishing Company, 1915), 300.

59 William H, Skaggs, *The Southern Oligarchy: An Appeal in Behalf of the Silent Masses of Our Country Against the Despotic Rule of the Few* (New York: Devin-Adair Company, 1924), 121–124, 131–139. Apparently, Skaggs also voted for the 1901 Constitution. See Paul M. Pruitt, "Skaggs, William H. (1861–1947), businessman, mayor, reformer, and commentator," *American National Biography,* Jun 1, 2000.

60 Albert Burton Moore, *History of Alabama and Her People* (Chicago: American Historical Society, 1927), 906.

61 Albert Burton Moore, *History of Alabama* (Nashville, Benson Printing Company, 1951), 658.

62 Woodward, *Origins of the New South,* 342; McMillan, *Constitutional Development in Alabama,* 351.

63 Joseph Matt Brittain, "Negro Suffrage and Politics in Alabama since 1870" PhD diss. (Indiana University, 1958), 140–141. Brittain did conclude that the statewide referendum authorizing a constitutional convention had voting in Black Belt counties that were "warped and deceptive returns." See, 129.

64 Sheldon Hackney, *Populism to Progressivism in Alabama* (Princeton: Princeton University Press, 1969), 229; Kousser, *The Shaping of Southern Politics,* 166–167.

65 Robert J. Norrell, *Reaping the Whirlwind: The Civil Rights Movement in Tuskegee* (New York: Alfred A. Knopf, 1985), 21; William Warren Rogers, Robert David Ward, Leah Rawls Atkins, and Wayne Flynt, *Alabama: The History of a Deep South State* (Tuscaloosa: University of Alabama Press, 1994), 353; Thomson quoted in William H. Stewart, "The Tortured History of Efforts to Revise the Alabama Constitution of 1901," *Alabama Law Review,* vol. 53:1(2001), 295; Flynt, *Alabama in the Twentieth Century,* 13. Also, see Courtney Cooper, "The Burden of Fraud on Alabama's Legacy," *Alabama*

Law Review, vol. 65:4 (2011), 1107. Also in a 2011 unpublished memorandum of opinion in *Lynch v. State of Alabama*, U.S. District Judge Lynwood Smith declared that the voting returns of 1901 "stink like rotten fish" (196) and concluded "the obvious: blacks did not vote to disfranchise themselves; and the Constitution of 1901 was not ratified by a majority of the legal, non-fraudulent votes cast" (199).

66 Perman, *Struggle for Mastery*, 187.

67 Available county precinct data confirm the irregular, trumped-up nature of the voting. See "Talladega County," *Our Mountain Home*, Nov 13, 1901, 1. Also see "Perry County" *Canebrake Herald*, Nov 20, 1901, 2. "The New Constitution Goes into Effect, and All Is Well," *Union Springs Herald*, Nov 13, 1901, 1, and "Wrong Kind of Talk," 4; "The Election," *Troy Messenger*, Nov 20, 1901, 5.

68 Brittain, "Negro Suffrage and Politics," 129.

69 McMillan, *Constitutional Development in Alabama*, 351.

70 County analysis based on the author's calculations from statistics at *U.S. Census, 1900, Statistics of Population*, Table 26, and *Alabama Official and Statistical Register*, 1903, 141–142.

NOTES TO CHAPTER 2

1 See *Alabama Official and Statistical Register, 1947*, 532–533. It is intriguing that Boswell referred to "good citizenship"—not simply "citizenship" as did the Evins Amendment. See Suitts, *Hugo Black of Alabama*, 444–447, for how "good citizenship" was used in public in the 1920s.

2 Key, *Southern Politics*, 633. Also, for example, see Barnard, *Dixiecrats and Democrats*, 59–66; Brittain, "Negro Suffrage and Politics," 190; Lawson. *Black Ballots*, 90–92.

3 *Smith v. Allwright*, 321 US 649 (1944); E. C. Boswell, "Boswell Says Texas Decision Applies But Wants Way Out," *Montgomery Advertiser*, Dec 31, 1945, 3.

4 Norrell, *Reaping the Whirlwind*, 224–231; Barnard, *Dixiecrats and Democrats*, 29–30.

5 "Edward Calhoun Boswell," *Alabama Official and Statistical Register, 1943*, 305; "Gov. Sparks Gave His Endorsement," *Birmingham News*, May 9, 1943, 10; "Constitution," *Montgomery Advertiser*, Jan 8, 1967, 2; "Sparks, Ellis, Miller Considering Recess Committees Leaders," *Birmingham News*, Aug 31, 1943, 2; "Changes Planned in Election Law," *Anniston Star*, Sep 6, 1944, 1; "Reapportioned Legislature Is Asked in Bill," *Anniston Star*, May 16, 1945, 1; John LeFlore, "Ala. Senate Oks Lily-White Vote," *Chicago Defender*, Jul 07, 1945, 2. The house unanimously passed the Amendment, and the senate had only three dissenting votes. The lopsided support may be explained in part by the wide range of legislators who had been appointed by Boswell to various interim subcommittees with several, diverse concerns for reform including poll taxes, civil defense, "Negro education," and small loans. There also were interim committees whose members may have wanted to withhold a "no" vote on a measure to be decided by voters so as not run a risk of losing support for their own interim proposals. The wide range of legislators and their interim committee assignments are found at "Legislative Group Charged with Study of White Supremacy," *Dothan Eagle*, Nov 20, 1944, 5; *Journal of the House of Representatives*, 1942–1943, 1711–1713.

6 "New Registration Rules," *Montgomery Advertiser*, Jun 28, 1945, 2; LeFlore, "Ala. Senate Oks Lily-White Vote," *Chicago Defender*, Jul 7, 1945, 2; "Measure Will Reach Voters for Adoption," *Decatur Daily*, Jun 27, 1945, 1; "Invited to Fish Fry," *Geneva County Reaper*, Apr 11, 1946, 1 "State Awaits Sparks Views in Rift Over Boswell," *Montgomery Advertiser*, September 29, 1946, 15; "Author Discusses Amendment," *Dothan Eagle*, Sep 15, 1946; *Troy Messenger*, Jul 25, 1946, 1; "State Constitution Changes to Be Decided Upon in Election," *Talladega Daily Home and Our Mountain Home*. Jul 25, 1946, 1.

7 "Gessner T. McCorvey," Encyclopedia of Alabama; "Party Picks McCorvey Over Lusk," *Montgomery Advertiser*, Jan 17, 1939, 1; Barnard, 60–62, 66; "To the Voters of Alabama," *Lamar Democrat*, Sep 18, 1946, 4. A statewide committee with hundreds of names also placed a predesigned ad in probably as many as half of Alabama's counties. See "Statewide Committee Urges Adoption of Amendment No. 4," *Lamar Democrat*, Oct 23, 1946, 4; "Statewide Committee Urges Adoption of Amendment No. 4," *Wiregrass Farmer*, Oct 24, 1946, 4.

8 "To the Voters of Alabama," *Dadeville Record*, Sep 19, 1946, 6; "Resolution Passed by County Democrats," *Shelby County Reporter*, Oct 17, 1946, 1; "Jefferson Group Is for Amendment," *Decatur Daily*, Oct 11, 1946, 2.

9 Feldman, *From Demagogue to Dixiecrat*, x–xv; Barnard, *Dixiecrats and Democrats*, 50–51; "Negro Voting," *Birmingham News*, Sep 3, 1946, 10; "Wilkinson Defends, Rivers Attacks Boswell Measure," *Birmingham News*, Sep 17, 1946, 1; "Boswell Amendment Debate," *Birmingham News*, Sep 29, 1946, 33; "Hear the Debate on the Boswell Amendment [radio program]," *Birmingham News*, Sep 30, 1946, 17; "Gov. Sparks Received an Unofficial Visit," *Birmingham News*, Jun 16, 1946, 6; "Puzzler," *Decatur Daily*, Jul 1, 1946, 4.

10 Horace C. Wilkinson, "Argument for Adoption of Boswell Amendment," *Alabama Lawyer* 7, no. 4 (October 1946): 377, 379.

11 Barnard, *Dixiecrats and Democrats*, 17–19, 64–65; "Chauncey Sparks," *Encyclopedia of Alabama*; Foster, "'Boswellianism,'" 28–29; "Democrats in Alabama Split on Boswell Plan," *Alabama Journal*, Oct 15, 1946. 12; "Hear Former Governor Frank Dixon . . ." *Anniston Star*, Nov 4, 1946, 7. Black Belt leaders also organized a committee and campaigned for the Amendment but only in Black Belt and nearby counties in south Alabama. Many speakers and advertisements favoring passage across the state referred to how Black voting could lead to "negro rule and domination" in the Black Belt but usually as only the first step in a series of developments across the state that the ads claimed would resemble the horrors of bi-racial "Reconstruction Rule." See Kirkland, "Mobile and the Boswell Amendments," 227–229; "Save Alabama from Negro Rule and Domination" [ad sponsored by Sumter County Democratic Executive Committee running in Tallapoosa County], *Alexander City Outlook*, Nov 1, 1946, 12.

12 Barnard, *Dixiecrats and Democrats*, 20, 39, 51; Foster, "'Boswellianism,'" 29; J. Mills Thornton III, *Dividing Lines: Municipal Politics and the Struggle for Civil Rights in Montgomery, Birmingham, and Selma* (Tuscaloosa: University of Alabama Press, 2002), note 15. 588–589; "U.S. Judge Hears Ala. Vote Suit," *Chicago Defender*, Sep 29, 1945, 5; "Judge Is Pondering Discrimination Suit," *Birmingham News*, Sep 20, 1945, 6. In the Macon County case, Rives was co-counsel for the county with E. C.

Boswell.

13 Kirkland, "Mobile and the Boswell Amendments," 220–222; Barnard, *Dixiecrats and Democrats,* 66–67, 69; Virginia Van der Veer Hamilton, *Lister Hill: Statesman from the South* (Chapel Hill: University of North Carolina Press, 1987), 146–148.

14 Barnard, *Dixiecrats and Democrats,* 67–69; "Money, Men, and the Boswell Amendment," *Montgomery Advertiser,* Oct 27, 1946, 4; "Dobbins and Dixon Debate Boswell Law," *Anniston Star,* Oct 18, 1946, 2; "Forum to Debate Amendments' Merits" *Montgomery Advertiser,* Sep 25, 1946, 1; "Roundup Discussion" [in ad for radio broadcast], *Anniston Star,* Nov 4, 1946, 7; "Roundup Discussion" [in ad for radio broadcast], *Dothan Eagle,* Nov 4, 1946, 2. Dobbins's stance on the Boswell Amendment was more liberal-minded than was customary for the *Montgomery Advertiser.* He left within a year and started a competing newspaper in Montgomery. See "Charles Gordon Dobbins," *Encyclopedia of Alabama.*

15 "Is Turnip Greens Enough?" *Montgomery Advertiser,* May 29, 1946, 4; "The Desire Is Not Enough," *Birmingham News,* May 31, 1946, 12; "WHY? Does the Birmingham News Refuse to Print the TRUTH about 'BIG JIM' FOLSOM," *Birmingham News,* May 4, 1946, 9; "All Right GIs" *Birmingham News,* May 31, 1946, 11; "Why 'Big Jim' Won't Do," *Anniston Star,* Jun 2, 1946. 4. Also, see George E. Sims, *The Little Man's Friend: James E. Folsom in Alabama Politics, 1946*–1958 (Tuscaloosa: University of Alabama Press, 1985), 34–38, 45.

16 "Folsom to Tell All Despite State's 'Lying' Newspapers," *Montgomery Advertiser,* Nov 16, 1946, 1; "Folsom Opposes Boswell Plan," *Dothan Eagle,* Sep 24, 1946, 1; however, see earlier summary references to Folsom's role in Barnard, *Dixiecrats and Democrats,* 66–67 and Lawson, *Black Ballots,* 91.

17 Sims, *The Little Man's Friend,* 41–44; "James Folsom Set to Oppose Boswell Plan, *Marion Times-Standard,* Sep 26, 1946; "Folsom Makes Good (Partly) on Promise," *Alabama Journal,* Oct 7, 1946, 1; "Democratic Rally at Dothan Next Wednesday Night," *Clayton Record,* Oct 11, 1946, 1; "Rally Is Moved to Auditorium," *Alabama Journal,* Oct 15, 1946, 1; "Folsom Raps Boswell Act; Favors Eight Amendments," *Alabama Journal,* Oct 25, 1946, 1; "Alabamians Confer with Truman on Cotton Crisis," *Huntsville Times,* Oct 31, 1946, 1.

18 "Hear Big Jim Folsom Speak Against Amendment Number 4," *Birmingham News,* Nov 4, 1946, 4; *Anniston Star,* Nov 4, 1946, 7; *Dothan Eagle,* Nov 4, 1946, 2; *Decatur Daily,* Nov 4, 1946, 3. It appears WMSL in Decatur was the only radio station in the Tennessee Valley area to broadcast Folsom's remarks. Some north Alabama counties such as Cherokee received radio reception from nearby, out-of-state stations. See "Listen to your favorite radio station in Rome, GA . . ." *Cherokee County Herald,* Nov 6, 1946, 1. The first radio station in Huntsville went on the air on November 10, 1946, five days after the Boswell referendum. See "Huntsville Rewound," http://www.huntsvillerewound.com. For geographical differences in radio ownership, coverage, and challenges for rural listeners during the mid-1940s in the South, see Steve Craig, "How America Adopted Radio: Demographic Differences in Set Ownership Reported in the 1930–1950 U.S. Censuses," *Journal of Broadcasting & Electronic Media,* Jun 2004, 179–195; U.S. Department of Agriculture, Bureau of Agricultural Economic, *Attitudes of Rural People Toward Radio Service: A Nationwide Survey of*

Farm and Small-Town People (Washington, DC: Jan. 1946).

19 Author's calculations from the *Alabama Official and Statistical Register, 1947,* 537–539.

20 Webb, *Two-Party Politics,* 209–210. The number of votes in Shelby County for the Republican candidate for governor, for example, dropped by 79 percent from 1926 to 1946, while the number of Democratic votes slightly increased. See *Alabama Official and Statistical Register, 1927,* 395, and *Alabama Official and Statistical Register, 1947,* 519. In the 1920s, mining and iron production were robust in west Shelby, but, hit by the Great Depression, the furnaces and mines closed. "Shelby Furnace Is Running Full Time," *Shelby County Reporter,* Mar 8, 1923, 1; "Montevallo Mines to Be Reopened," *Shelby County Reporter,* Nov 8, 1923, 1; by 1932, however, a state department of education report found "there is no industrial activity at all in this part of the county." Alabama Department of Education, *Report of the Survey of Shelby County Schools: School Year 1931–1932,* 9. Robert J. Norrell, "Labor at the Ballot Box: Alabama Politics from the New Deal to the Dixiecrat Movement," *Journal of Southern History,*" vol. LVII, no. 2 (May, 1991), 229, including note 61.

21 Author's calculations from the *Alabama Official and Statistical Register, 1947,* 537–539.

22 Word searches of 100 available on-line Alabama newspapers publishing in 1946 for the terms "Big Jim Folsom" and "Boswell Amendment" as well as similar names such as "Boswell Measure," reveal approximately 1800 items for both. See https://www.newspapers.com; "State Legislator Says He Will Vote Against Boswell Amendment," *Birmingham News,* Oct 20, 1946, 15.

23 See Sims, *The Little Man's Friend,* 45.

24 Author's computation from voting returns in the *Alabama Official and Statistical Register, 1947,* 482–483; 490–491; 517–519; 537–539.

25 Sims, *The Little Man's Friend,* 41–44; "Jim Folsom to Spend Entire Weekend Here," *Advertiser-Gleam,* Jul 31, 1946, 1. Omer Finney Jr. of Albertville who joined the fishing party had worked for Folsom when he was the county's work relief director, helped run Folsom's Cullman campaign office, and later served as Governor Folsom's executive secretary. See Sims, *The Little Man's Friend,* 13–14, 27. 52.); "Democrats Back Boswell Amendment," *Guntersville Gleam,* Sep 20, 1946, 1; "To the Voters of Alabama," *Albertville Herald,* Sep 27, 1946, 8.

26 "Sparks, Poole, and Frank Dixon Are for Boswell Bill." *Albertville Herald,* Oct 18, 1946, 1; "Statewide Committee Urges Adoption of Amendment No. 4," *Albertville Herald,* Oct 25, 1946, 5; "The Boswell Amendment," *Guntersville Gleam,* Oct 25, 1946, 2; "Turn Out and Vote," *Albertville Herald,* Nov 1, 1946, 8; "G'ville Legion Backs Boswell Amendment," Guntersville Gleam, Oct 25, 1946, 1; "County Poll List Will Be Over 10,000," *Guntersville Gleam,* Feb 15, 1946, 3.

27 "County Listed for Boswell Amendment," *Guntersville Gleam,* Nov 15, 1946, 1.

28 "Ballot Lack Claimed in Ballot Vote," *Birmingham News,* Nov 24, 1946, 22.

29 "Hearing Delayed in Vote Suit," *Alabama Journal,* Dec 4, 1946, 1; "Patton Raps Boswell Amendment," *Weekly Review,* Oct 25, 1947, 1; "Negros [sic] to Fight Registration Law," *Birmingham News,* Feb 2, 1948, 2; "State Leaders to Map Political Fight Feb. 1," *Alabama Citizen.* Jan 31, 1948, 1; Norrell, *Reaping the Whirlwind,* 66–74; Foster, "'Boswellianism,'" 33–37; Timothy Broughton and Komanduri S. Murty,

"Give Us the Ballot! Gaining Enfranchisement in Mobile, Alabama: 1944–50," in Earl Wright II and Edward V. Wallace (eds.), *Ashgate Research Companion to Black Sociology* (Abingdon: Routledge, 2016), 262–263.

30 *Davis v. Schnell*, 81 F. Supp. 872 (1949).

31 Ibid., 881. The concluding quotation in the opinion of the three New Deal appointees ironically comes from the U.S. Supreme Court opinion striking down one of the New Deal's earlier reforms, the Agricultural Adjustment Act. The *Davis* opinion was affirmed in March 1949 without comment by the U.S. Supreme Court, 336 US 933 (1949).

32 "Boswell Amendment Substitute Sought by Few Legislators," *Dothan Eagle*, Mar 18, 1949, 1; "McCorvey Asks Amendment on Qualification of Voters," *Montgomery Advertiser*, Feb 1, 1949, 2; "Demo Leaders Will Discuss New Vote Law," *Anniston Star*, May 11, 1949, 2.

33 Carl Grafton and Anne Permaloff, *Big Mules and Branchheads: James E. Folsom and Political Power in Alabama*, (Athens, Georgia: University of Georgia Press, 1985), 124.

34 *Journal of the House of Representatives*, Regular Session of 1949, vol. 1, 10–12.

35 Ibid., Regular Session of 1949, vol. 1, 11.

36 "Voter Qualification Law Passage Foreseen," *Montgomery Advertiser*, May 13, 1949, 9; *Alabama Official and Statistical Register, 1947*, 220; *Journal of the Senate*, Regular Session of 1947, 1624–1625; "Folsom Lets 13 Legislative Items Die From Signature Lack As Deadline Ends," Opelika Daily News, Oct 15, 1947, 1; "Folsom Feels Way Along Pinkish Pike," *Montgomery Advertiser*, Oct 28, 1947, 1; "Enough of That," *Montgomery Advertiser*, Oct 29, 1947, 4.

37 *Journal of the House of Representatives*, Regular Session of 1949, vol. 1, 174; *Journal of the Senate*, Regular Session of 1949, vol. 1, 215; Rives's letter to the editor, *Montgomery Advertiser*, May 19, 1949, 4; "Popular Vote Bill Readied for Senate," *Anniston Star*, May 19, 1949, 1; Solons Facing Heavy Schedule," *Alabama Journal*, May 21, 1949, 2.

38 "Legislators to Look to High Court for Advice on Voter Qualification Proposals," *Birmingham News*, May 27, 1949, 31.

39 "Legislators to Look to High Court for Advice on Voter Qualification Proposals," *Birmingham News*, May 27, 1949, 31; "2 Other Folsom," *Montgomery Advertiser*, May 27, 1949, 14.

40 *Journal of the House of Representatives*, Regular Session of 1949, vol. 1, 314–318, 356–357; *Opinion of the Justices*, 252 Ala. 351 (1949).

41 Grafton and Permaloff, *Big Mules and Branchheads*, 95–98.

42 "Reapportioning Set for Airing," *Alabama Journal*, Jun 11, 1949, 2; "Mask Ban Bill before House," *Decatur Daily*, Jun 19, 1949, 1; "House Rejects Bill to Replace Boswell Act," *Montgomery Advertiser*, Jun 22, 1949, 1.

43 While not selected by Folsom, the speaker of the house, W. M. "Bill" Beck (from DeKalb County in northeast Alabama) favored reapportionment and served as chair of the House Rules Committee. Folsom's floor leader, John Snodgrass, was vice-chair of the Committee. Two strong Folsom supporters from north Alabama, William A. Barnett of Lauderdale County and Pelham Merrill of Cleburne, were the chair and

vice-chair of the House Constitution and Elections Committee that considered and reported bills to the floor. In the past, Black Belt legislators often prevented legislation they disliked from coming out of committee.

44 "House Okehs Revised Voter Qualifications," *Montgomery Advertiser*, Jul 7, 1949, 1; "Black Belt Strategy Defeats North Alabama Group," *Birmingham News*, Jul 7, 1949, 11; "Political Clucks," *Selma Times-Journal*, Jul 1, 1949, 4. The 67-senator bill was also opposed by Mobile and Jefferson County (Birmingham) legislators since it would reduce the counties' political influence. Jefferson County, for example, had almost one in six of the state's population in 1940 but one-senator for-each-county would reduce their voting power even more—from one in 35 to one in 67. While Folsom was attempting to break Black Belt power in the senate, the Mobile and Jefferson County delegations, often divided between Big Mule and progressive representatives, were in full agreement in opposing Folsom's plan, which they considered a bogus excuse for reapportionment. See "A Time for Boldness," *Birmingham News*, Jul 8, 1949; Hugh Sparrow, "Alabama Politics," *Birmingham News*, Jul 22, 1949, 29; Fred Taylor, "He Who Laughs," *Birmingham News*, Jul 31, 1949, 24.

45 Hugh Sparrow, "Alabama Politics," *Birmingham News*, Jul 8, 1949, 2; "Reapportionment Measure Reportedly Gaining Support," *Alabama Journal*. Jul 16, 1949, 1; "House Passage of 67-Senator Bill Indicated," *Montgomery Advertiser*, Jul 17, 1949, 1; "House May Vote to Reapportion Upper Chamber," *Selma Times-Journal*, Jul 17, 1949, 1.

46 "House Passes Bill Providing 67 Senators," *Anniston Star*, Jul 19, 1949, 1; "Folsom Leader Aims Tax at Poor Man's Champagne,'" *Alabama Journal*, Jul 20, 1949, 2; Hugh W. Sparrow, "Alabama Politics," *Birmingham News*, Jul 20, 1949, 20; Sparrow, "Alabama Politics," *Birmingham News*, Jul 22, 1949, 29. Wallace remembered years later that in his first term as a legislator he worked both against and with the Folsom administration—in this case perhaps on the same issue. See Stephan Lesher, *George Wallace: American Prophet* (Reading: Addison Wesley, 1994), 82.

47 "67 Senator Bill Chance Dimmed by Single Word," *Montgomery Advertiser*, Jul 24, 1949, 23; "76-Senator and Boswell Measure Facing Fight," *Birmingham News*, Aug 1, 1949, 11; "Folsom Renews Attack as Week Recess Voted," *Montgomery Advertiser*, Aug 27, 1949, 1; *Journal of the Senate*, Regular Session, 1949, Vol. 2, 2157–2174; Hugh W. Sparrow, "Alabama Politics," *Birmingham News*, Aug 31, 1949, 29; "Filibusters Delay State Senate Work," *Birmingham News*, Sep 3, 1949, 9; "Senate Snarled by Filibuster in Final Meet," *Decatur Daily*, Sep 9, 1949, 1.

48 "Voter Curb, 67 Senator Bills Die as Filibuster Continues to Last Hour," *Montgomery Advertiser*, Sep 10, 1949, 1; Hugh W, Sparrow, "Alabama Politics," *Birmingham News*, Aug 31, 1949, 29; *Journal of the Senate*, Regular Session, 1949, Vol. 2, 2386–2501; "Legislature Goes Home," *Anniston Star*, Sep 11, 1949, 1. Even some Black Belt legislators appeared reluctant to restrict debate. Senators on both sides appear certain that the Givhan bill would pass with at least 21 votes, if a vote were taken, but the ruling in favor of Senator Allen's point of order shutting down the filibuster's four primary speakers was sustained by only one vote (15 to 14)—with two Black Belt senators voting "nay" and one failing to vote.

49 "Balloting Curb Defeat Hailed," *Decatur Daily*, Sep 18, 1949, 10; "The Franchise

All," *Alabama Citizen*, Oct 1, 1949, 2, reprinting the editorial of the *Birmingham World*; "Negroes Congratulate Senators for Blocking Voter Qualifying Law," *Birmingham News*, Sep 11, 1949, 4.

50 Grafton and Permaloff, *Big Mules and Branchheads*, 130–131. The speech was reported by both the Associated Press and United Press. See "Folsom Urges Race Hate End in Yule Speech," *Anniston Star*, Dec 26, 1949, 1; "Love Everyone, Folsom Urges in Yule Speech," *Montgomery Advertiser*, Dec 26, 1949, 1. Daily newspapers also ran large ads in advance. See for example "Hear Gov. James E. Folsom's Statewide Radio Message" [ad], *Montgomery Advertiser*, Dec 25, 1949, 7, and *Huntsville Times*, Dec 25, 1949, 10.

51 "Senator Plan Under Ban by High Tribunal," *Selma Times-Journal*, Aug 11, 1950, 2; *In re Opinion of the Justices*, 47 So. 2d 713 (1950). 714.

52 "Folsom Handed Setback by Tribunal and Senate," *Alabama Journal*, Aug 11, 1950, 3.

53 *Opinion of the Justices*, 47 So. 2d 714 (1950), 717.

54 "Suit Filed to Limit Smaller Counties' Delegation in House," *Dothan Eagle*, Aug 30, 1950, 1; *Waid v. Pool*, 51 So. 2d 869 (1951), 870.

55 The Alabama Supreme Court's advisory opinions and its opinion in *Waid* were referenced a decade later by a three-judge federal court, which included Judge Richard Rives, in holding that the failure of the Alabama legislature to reapportion on the basis of population was a violation of the equal protection clause of the 14th Amendment of the U.S. Constitution. See *Sims v. Frink*, 208 F. Supp. 431 (1962). In a landmark case affirming the lower court's opinion, the U S Supreme Court cited *Waid*, noting that "while the Alabama Supreme Court had found that the legislature had not complied with the State Constitution in failing to reapportion according to population decennially, that court had nevertheless indicated that it would not interfere with matters of legislative reapportionment." See *Reynolds v. Sims*, 377 US 533 (1964), 540–541.

56 "Explosive Registration Row Flares Anew in Legislature," *Birmingham News*, Mar 28, 1951, 30; Legislators and Governor Move in Huddle Today," *Talladega Daily Home and Our Mountain Home*, Apr 3, 1951, 3; "Tests for New Alabama Voters," *Birmingham News*, Apr 5, 1951, 14; "Rigid New Voter Curb Bill Passes Senate, Final Outcome of Measure Is Obscure," *Montgomery Advertiser*, May 26, 1951, 1; "Senate Okehs Voter Act," *Alabama Journal*, May 25, 1951, 1.

57 Fred Taylor, "Upstate Lawmakers Cry 'Snipe Hunt' on Strategy of Black Belters' 67-Senator Bill," *Birmingham News*, Jun 24, 1951, 31.

58 "Legislative Session Is at Halfway Mark with Persons and Lawmakers in Accord," *Birmingham News*, Jul 1, 1951, 12; "; "Senate Okehs Voter Act," *Alabama Journal*, May 25, 1951, 1; Pass It and Hope for the Best," *Selma Times-Journal*, May 27, 1951, 4; "Reapportionment Farce," *Montgomery Advertiser*, Jul 1, 1951, 22 (reprinting editorial of *Mobile Press*).

59 "Senate Votes 23 to 9 in Favor of Proposed 67-Senator Amendment," *Montgomery Advertiser*, Jul 27, 1951, 1.

60 Ibid.; "Reapportioning Tops Calendar," *Alabama Journal*, Aug 14, 1951; "67-Senator

Bill Steamrolled by Black Belt Group," *Birmingham News,* Aug 15, 1951, 1. The parliamentary maneuver could only have been achieved with the cooperation of the House Rules Committee, which governed the house calendar and its procedures. The committee was composed of a large majority of Black Belt members and legislators from counties that would gain political power from a 67-senator plan. It was also led by Speaker Robert Brown who represented Lee County, which recorded a majority Black population until the release of 1950 Census, and by vice-chair, Ira Pruitt, a three-term member from the Black Belt's Sumter County. See "Chapter IV: Legislative Department," *Alabama Official and Statistical Register, 1951, 238.*

61 Rex Thomas, "White Supremacy Ballot to Get Test in Voting," *Dothan Eagle*, Dec 9, 1951, 1; Act 426, *Acts of Alabama, 1950–1951,* volume 1, 760–761.

62 For examples of "Let's Back Our Boys in Korea . . ." [ads], see *Decatur Daily*, Dec 9, 1951, 24; *Fairhope Courier*, Dec 6, 1951, 3; *Monroe Journal,* Dec 6, 1951, 24; *Wilcox Progressive Era*, Dec 6, 1951, 3. "Support Urged for Amendment No. 5." *Clarke County Democrat*, Dec 6, 1951, 1; "Vote Yes on No. 5," *Talladega Daily Home* and *Our Mountain Home*, Dec 3, 1951, 2.

63 "Letters to the Editor," *LaFayette Sun*, Dec 5, 1951, 2; "Joker," *Birmingham News*, Dec 4, 1951, 8.

64 "State Conference of NAACP to Be Held Nov. 9–11," *Alabama Citizen*, Sep 29, 1951, 1; "State Federation of Labor . . ." *Mobile Journal,* Nov 23, 1951, 1; "Two Senators Back Col. Rives As Judge McCord's Successor," *Montgomery Advertiser*, Feb 27, 1951, 1; "Next Tuesday's Ballot," *Anniston Star*, Dec 6, 1951, 4; "The Voter Qualification Issue," *Birmingham News*, Dec 7, 1951, 14; *Montgomery Advertiser*, Dec 9, 1951, 34; "Sparks, Swift Oppose Bonds for Highways," *Montgomery Advertiser*, Dec 9, 1951, 1. See *Opinion of the Justices*, 252 Ala. 351 (1949).

65 *Alabama Official and Statistical Register, 1951*, 616–617; *Birmingham News*, Dec 21, 1951, 20; "Ultimate Test of Voter Curb Is Anticipated," *Montgomery Advertiser*, Dec 30, 1951, 17.

66 Rex Thomas, "Ultimate Test of Voter Curb Is Anticipated," *Montgomery Advertiser*, Dec 30, 1951, 17.

67 Donald S. Strong, *Registration of Voters in Alabama* (University, Alabama: Bureau of Public Administration, 1956), 31–33, 27–28; *Davis v. Schnell*, 81 F. Supp. 872 (1949), 877–891.

68 Act 297, *Acts and Resolutions of the General Assembly of the State of Georgia,* Regular Session, 1949, Vol. 1, 1204–1227; *Franklin v. Harper*, 55 S. E. 2d 221, appeal dismissed 339 US 946 (1950).

69 For past cases challenging local voter registration practices, see *Boswell v. Bethea*, 5 So. 2d 816 (Ala. 1942); *Hawkins* v. *Vines*, 30 So. 2d 451 (Ala. 1947); *Mitchell v. Wright*, 62 F. Supp. 580 (1945), 154 F.2d 924 (1946), 69 F. Supp. 698 (1947). For cases in the 1950s, see *Padgett v. State*, 56 So. 2d 116 (1952) and *Sellers v. Wilson*, 123 F. Supp. 917 (1954).

NOTES TO CHAPTER 3

1 Key, *Southern Politics*, 557; Brittain, "Negro Suffrage and Politics in Alabama," 176.

2 "A Report of Negro Voting in Alabama by Counties," Negro Vote-Registration: Alabama, 1952–1954, Special Subjects, 1940–1955, NAACP Papers, ProQuest/History Vault; C. G. Gomillion, "The Negro Voter in Alabama," *Journal of Negro Education*, vol. 26:3 (Summer, 1957), 283–285; Margaret Price, *The Negro and the Ballot in the South*, (Atlanta: Southern Regional Council, 1959), 15–20; *Report of the United States Commission on Civil Rights, 1959*, Washington, DC, 90–96. See also the findings of George Stoney identifying local barriers to Black voting in the 1930s and 1940 in Alabama and other Southern states in Ralph J. Bunche, *The Political Status of the Negro in the Age of FDR* (Chicago: University of Chicago Press, 1973), chapter 10, "Negro Registration."

3 "A Report of Negro Voting in Alabama by Counties," NAACP Papers; J. B. Newman to Emory Jackson, Apr 11, 1952, Negro Vote-Registration: Alabama, 1952–1954, NAACP Papers; Charles Morgan Jr., *One Man, One Voice* (New York: Holt, Rinehart and Winston: 1979), 14; Stetson Kennedy, *Jim Crow Guide: The Way It Was* (Boca Raton: Florida Atlantic University Press, 1990), 158. See also, *U.S. Commission on Civil Rights Report 1959*, 96–97. For a gripping, detailed account of the murder of a Georgia Black leader due to his involvement in voting in the late 1940s, listen to Hank Klibanoff, Buried Truths, Season 1, WABE Podcast, 2018.

4 "A Report of Negro Voting in Alabama by Counties," NAACP Papers; "The Registration Picture in Alabama," Part 04: Voting Rights Campaign, 1916–1950, Supplement, General Office Files, 1956–1965, NAACP Papers; Benjamin Houston, "Before the Bridge: Grassroots Activism in Selma in the Early 1960s," in Joe Street and Henry Knight Lozano (eds.), *The Shadow of Selma* (Tallahassee: University Press of Florida, 2018), 39.

5 "A Report of Negro Voting in Alabama by Counties," NAACP Papers.

6 Ibid.

7 Emory O. Jackson to Walter White, May 8, 1952, Part 18. Special Subjects, 1940–1955, NAACP Papers; *Alabama Official and Statistical Register, 1955*, 483; "Another Slugging Match . . ." Birmingham, May 4, 1952, 10. DeGraffenreid's father was the senior law partner of Robert Evins, who sponsored the proposed 1921 constitutional amendment.

8 "Speaking of Blocs," *Montgomery Advertiser*, Nov 30, 1952, 14; "Thurgood Marshall's Speech Climax NAACP Meet," *Huntsville Mirror*, Nov 22, 1952, 1.

9 "Speaking of Blocs," *Montgomery Advertiser*, Nov 30, 1952, 14; Memorandum from Walter White to Thurgood Marshall, Nov. 11, 1953, Part 18. Special Subjects, 1940–1955, Series C: General Office–Justice Department–White Supremacy, NAACP Papers.

10 Author computations from data found in "The Registration Picture in Alabama," Part 04: Voting Rights Campaign, 1916–1950, Supplement: Voting Rights, General Files, 1956–1965, NAACP Papers. The data is also found in Joseph Matt Brittain, "Negro Suffrage and Politics," 215–216. See *Alabama Official and Statistical Register, 1911*, 262–263 for Black registration in Alabama in 1906.

11 See Chapter 12; "Registration and Voting Campaigns" Ruby Hurley to Gloster Current, April 29, 1954, Part 25: Branch Department Files, Series A: Regional Files and Special Reports, 1941–1955, NAACP Papers.

12 "Two Negroes Win in Mobile Ballot," *Selma Times-Journal*, May 6, 1954, 1; Norrell, *Reaping the Whirlwind*, 85; *Alabama Official and Statistical Register, 1955*, 548–549; Sims, *The Little Man's Friend*, 167–169. Folsom's support among Black voters persisted through his second term. For example, see Jefferson County precinct data cited in "Eligible Voter List May Soar to 900,000," *Birmingham News*, Apr 20, 1958, 1.

13 *Brown v. Board of Education*, 347 US 483 (1954); "Three State Solons Confer with Byrnes on Racial Problems," *Selma Times-Journal*, Jun 24, 1954, 1; "Samuel Martin Engelhardt Jr." *Alabama Official and Statistical Register*, 1955, 278; "Grady Hurst Sr. to Head County Citizens Council," *Washington County News*, May 24, 1956, 1; Norrell, *Reaping the Whirlwind*, 85–88; Neil R. McMillen, *The Citizens' Council: Organized Resistance to the Second Reconstruction, 1954–64* (Urbana: University of Illinois, 1971), 42–47.

14 "Marengo Meet of WCC Draws 400 White Men," *Montgomery Advertiser*, Dec 7, 1954, 1; Bob Ingram, "WCC, Marengo," *Montgomery Advertiser*, Dec 8, 1954, 4. Ingram also quotes Givhan as recommending local bankers sit on the WCC committee: "They can play a big part in refusing credit to troublemakers, either white or black." Also, see Joseph Bagley, *The Politics of White Rights: Race Justice, and Integrating Alabama's Schools* (Athens, Georgia: University of Georgia Press, 2018), 15–19.

15 Gomillion, "The Negro Voter in Alabama," 281–282.

16 For a careful accounting of the boycott and white responses to it, see Thornton, *Dividing Lines*, 28–96. Thornton's review of the Montgomery board of registrars' records suggest numbers of Black registration that somewhat differ from SRC estimates.

17 Bagley, *The Politics of White Rights*, 21–22.

18 Charles Morgan Jr., *A Time to Speak* (Harper and Row: New York, 1964), 37–39; Grafton and Permaloff, *Big Mules and Branchhead*, 196–197. While reporting of the events suggest that the whites chanted, ""Hey, Hey, Ho, Ho! Autherine Gotta Go," Lucy corrected the record when she remembered publicly the actual chant over 50 years later in 2017 at a university ceremony dedicating a historical marker in her honor. See *Crimson White*, Sept. 18, 2017.

19 *Alabama Official and Statistical Register, 1955*, 321–323; "Delegate Candidate," *Florala News*, Apr 5, 1956, 1; "Strike a Blow Tuesday for Segregation and Honest Government" [ad], *Selma Times-Journal*, Apr 25, 1956, 7. More than 200 similar ads appeared in Alabama's weekly and daily papers shorty before Election Day. "C. W. 'Charlie' McKay Jr. . . . Speaks Tonight," *Birmingham News*, Apr 26, 1956, 60; "H.J.R. 18," *Acts of Alabama, Special Session, 1956*, 70–71; Sims, *The Little Man's Friend*, 183–184.

20 "Dictator Charge Faced by Folsom," *Selma Times-Journal*, Apr 22, 1956, 3; "Strike a Blow Tuesday for Segregation and Honest Government" [ad], *Selma Times-Journal*, Apr 25, 1956, 7. Folsom's opponents tailored the ads' headlines according to the region of the state. For central Alabama, see "Elect an Honest Man" [ad], *Clayton Record*, Apr 20, 1956, 2. For rural north Alabama, see "Strike a Blow Tuesday for Segregation and Honest Government" [ad], *Sand Mountain Reporter*, Apr 25, 1956, 3.

21 Sims, *The Little Man's Friend*, 175–176; "White Citizens Leader Asks Folsom Ousting in Segregation Failure," *Montgomery Advertiser*, Mar 10, 1956, 1; "Barbour WCC Hears Griffin Advocate Unity," *Montgomery Advertiser*, Mar 10, 1956, 1; Grafton and Permaloff, *Big Mules and Branchhead, 200.*

22 Sims, *The Little Man's Friend*, 185–186; "Governor Jim Folsom Speaks Before a Large Crowd Here," *Evergreen Courant*, Apr 5, 1956, 1; Grafton and Permaloff, *Big Mules and Branchhead*, 200–201.

23 *Alabama Official and Statistical Register, 1959*, 524–525, 338, 544–545; Sims, *The Little Man's Friend*, 157–159.

24 Warren Trest, *Nobody But the People: The Life and Times of Alabama's Youngest Governor* (NewSouth Books: Montgomery, 2008), 203–206.

25 "The Registration Picture in Alabama," NAACP Papers; *Browder v. Gayle*, 142 F. Supp. 707 (1956), affirmed at 352 U.S. 903 (1956); Thornton, *Dividing Lines*, 88–89; Lawson, *Black Ballots*, 175–176; Evan Faulkenbury, *Poll Power: The Voter Education Project and the Movement for the Ballot in the American South* (Chapel Hill: University of North Carolina Press, 2019), 16–20.

26 Charles V. Hamilton, *The Bench and the Ballot: Southern Federal Judges and Black Voters* (New York: Oxford University Press, 1973), 54–56; Strong, *Negroes, Ballots, and Judges*, 2–4.

27 Lawson, *Black Ballots*, 106–202; "Andrews Assails Civil Rights Act," *Selma Times-Journal*, Sep 1, 1957, 1; *Troy Messenger*, Aug 30, 1957, 2; "Pot Calls the Kettle Black," *Decatur Daily*, Aug 19, 1957, 4; "Folsom Says Yankees Aren't Being Christian," *Alabama Journal*, Aug 26, 1957, 1; "The Gospel According to St. James," *Montgomery Advertiser*, Aug 27, 1957, 4.

28 "Folsom Says Yankees Aren't Being Christian," *Alabama Journal*, Aug 26, 1957, 1; "The Gospel According to St. James," *Montgomery Advertiser*, Aug 27, 1957, 4.

29 "Civil Rights," *Montgomery Advertiser*, Sep 5, 1957, 2; *Acts of Alabama*, 1957, Regular Session, 185–186; Norrell, *Reaping the Whirlwind*, 96–99; Sims, *The Little Man's Friend, 187.* Engelhardt's constitutional amendment passed in December 1957, with 60 percent of the vote, carrying all but Mobile and six north Alabama counties, but a plan for abolishing Macon County was never implemented since no white leaders of surrounding counties wanted more Black residents. See voting returns, *Alabama Official and Statistical Register, 1959*, 564–566.

30 "Pocket Veto Kills Bills, Resolutions," *Montgomery Advertiser*, Sep 25, 1957, 1. Folsom found little support even in the news reporting. The Associated Press, for example, reported on the veto of the public transportation bill this way: "A bill aimed at easing racial tensions where integration is ordered in public transportation was killed by pocket veto last night." See "Folsom Lets Racial Bills Smother by Pocket Veto," *Birmingham News*, Sep 24, 1957, 2.

31 Federal Troops," *Greenville Advocate*, Sep 26, 1957, 2; *Selma Times-Journal*, Sep 29, 1957, 4; "Alabama Segregation Bill Made Law; Governor Didn't Sign," *Alabama Tribune*, Sep 6, 1957, 1. The school bill passed with a super majority and the legislature had the opportunity before adjournment to override any veto Folsom might have exercised. In general, Folsom vetoed segregation bills that did not have a veto-proof

majority or were passed late enough in a session that he could pocket-veto them. See Grafton and Permaloff, *Big Mules and Branchheads,* 189.

32 Lawson, *Black Ballots,* 205–211; David J. Garrow, *Protest at Selma: Martin Luther King and the Voting Rights Act of 1965* (New Haven: Yale University Press, 1978) 12–14; Frank E. Schwelb, "From Illusion to Reality—Relief in Civil Rights Cases," *Notre Dame Lawyer* 48, no. 1 (October 1972): note 45, 55.

33 Norrell, *Reaping the Whirlwind,* 111–118; *United States v. State of Alabama*, 171 F. Supp. 720 (1959).

34 "Discrimination Against Majority," *Selma Times-Journal*, Dec 7, 1958. 4; *Talladega Daily Home and Our Mountain Home*, Dec 11, 1958, 1; "Patterson's Ground," *Decatur Daily*, Dec 15, 1958, 4; "Folsom," *Montgomery Advertiser*, Jan 3, 1959, 8. The irony of the Selma's newspaper's complaint is that, in fact, white citizens were not a majority of Dallas County nor the other counties under investigation.

35 "Negroes Tell of Economic 'Retaliation,'" *Montgomery Advertiser*, Dec 10, 1958, 1; "Four Selma Negroes Claim Ballot Denied," *Selma Times-Journal,* Dec 10, 1958, 5. For background on the Boyntons' leadership in Black Selma, see J. L. Chestnut and Julia Cass, *Black in Selma: The Uncommon Life of J. L. Chestnut* (New York: Farrar, Straus, and Giroux: 1990), 74, 132–134; Thornton, *Dividing Lines*, 439–440.

36 Letters and affidavits to William B. Rogers, Jan 29, 1958, and Feb 1, 1958; memo from Wilson White to FBI Director, Feb 13,1958, memo to FBI Director and attachments, Feb 21, 1958; Wilson White to FBI Director, Mar 12, 1958, FBI File Number 44–12831 Election Laws, Selma/Dallas County, Alabama Voting rights and voter registration in Dallas County, Alabama, January 1958–April 1961, The Black Freedom Struggle in the 20th Century, Federal Government Records, FBI Files, ProQuest/HistoryVault; It was no small matter for Boynton, who was a registered voter, to act as a notary for a complainant. Earlier the founder of the Dallas County Voters League had been sent to prison for notarizing false documents because, in the opinion of Black Selma, "the white man didn't like him." Chestnut and Cass, *Black in Selma*, 53.

37 Wilson White to FBI Director, Oct 27, 1958; FBI Director to Wilson White, Nov 4, 1958, Election Laws, Selma/Dallas County, Alabama, FBI Files.

38 SAC Mobile to FBI Director and attachments, Nov 12, 1958, Selma/Dallas County, Alabama, FBI Files.

39 *Report of the United States Commission on Civil Rights, 1959*, 131–132 for assessment of the Justice Department.

40 Ibid., 133.

41 "Report on Probe of Rights Ruled Alabama Slander," *Selma Times-Journal,* Sep 9, 1959, 1; "State Gets Top Billing in Civil Rights Report," *Birmingham News*, Sep 8, 1959, 1; "The Rights Commission Could Do A Job," *Birmingham News*, Sep 20, 1959, 14; Trest, *Nobody But the People*, 255; "The Civil Rights Commission," *Alabama Journal,* Sep 7, 1959, 4.

42 "State Civil Rights Data Held Correct," *Montgomery Advertiser*, Sep 10, 1959, 1.

43 "Parker Elected Mayor, Carroll, Williams, Head Win Council Seats," *Southern Star*, Mar 10, 1960, 1; "Carpet-bags to Return," *Andalusia Star-News*, Mar 24, 1960, 6; reprinted in "Carpet-bags to Return," *Dothan Eagle*, Mar 30, 1960, 4, and

"Carpetbaggers Return," *Montgomery Advertiser*, Mar 30, 1960, 4; "Either 100 Percent or You're Out," *Opelika Daily News*, Mar 11, 1960, 2. Brown was elected Ozark mayor again in 1964 and continued a real estate business and other enterprises in the town until his death in 1979. His obituaries included a long list of accomplishments and public service, but none mentioned his service as chair of Alabama's first advisory committee to the U.S. Commission on Civil Rights. See "Former Ozark Mayor Dies After Long Illness," and "Brown, James Douglas," *Montgomery Advertiser*, Oct 1, 1979, 2, 15.

44 *Report of the U.S. Commission on Civil Rights, 1959*, 136–142.

45 "Justice Department's Rights Division Is Vigorously Defended," *Alabama Tribune*, Oct 30, 1959. 4; memo of Joseph M. F. Ryan Jr. to FBI Director, Oct 22, 1959, FBI Files. Available FBI records block out the names of persons to be interviewed, but it is clear that the Boyntons were the persons identified from the Montgomery hearings who "are apparently well acquainted with the facts concerning efforts of Negroes in Dallas County to register and vote."

46 Memo of FBI Director to Attorney General, Oct 30, 1959, Election Laws, Selma/Dallas County, Alabama, FBI Files; "New Dallas Vote Probe Reported by Governor," *Montgomery Advertiser*, Oct 30, 1959, 1; Teletype of SAC Mobile to FBI Director, Oct 30, 1959, FBI Files; "Resistance to Probe Promised by Patterson," *Anniston Star*, Oct 30, 1959, 1; "Prostitution," *Selma Times-Journal*, Nov 1, 1959, 4. Hoover may have alerted Patterson to prevent further estranging a sitting Governor whom he had snubbed when Patterson he was attempting to get FBI assistance to investigate the death of his father, who was murdered while serving as Alabama Attorney General. See Trest, *Nobody But the People*, 142–143.

47 "Dallas Registration Our Problem," *Birmingham News*, Nov 1, 1959, 16.

48 Memo of Joseph M. F. Ryan Jr. to FBI Director, Feb 19, 1960, memo of FBI Director to Joseph M. F. Ryan Jr., Mar 2, 1960, FBI Files.

49 Memo of FBI Director to Joseph M. F. Ryan Jr., March 10, 1960, FBI Files.

50 *Report of the U.S. Commission on Civil Rights, 1959*, 69–95; Dan T. Carter, *The Politics of Rage* (Simon and Shuster: New York, 1995), 99–103. "Wilcox Registrars Denies Negroes Seeking Votes," *Selma Times-Journal*, May 10, 1960, 1.

51 Lawson, *Black Ballots*, 238–247.

52 Garrow, *Protest at Selma*, 14–15; C. W. H. III, "Federal Legislation to Safeguard Voting Rights: The Civil Rights Act of 1960," *Virginia Law Review*, Vol. 46, No. 5 (Jun. 1960), 945–949.971–974.

53 *An Oral History of John Doar: Recorded for the United States District Court for the Middle District of Alabama*, May 20, 2011, accessed on www.youtube.com; John Doar, "The Work of the Civil Rights Division in Enforcing Voting Rights Under the Civil Rights Acts of 1957 and 1960," 25 Fla. St. U. L. Rev. 1 (1997), 2–3; John Doar and Dorothy Landsberg, "The Performance of the FBI in Investigating Violations of Federal Laws Protecting the Right to Vote — 1960–1967," *Hearings Before the Select Committee to Study Governmental Operations with Respect to Intelligence Activities*, United State Senate, Ninety-fourth Congress, First Session, Vol. 6, Federal Bureau of Investigation, 897–899. Taylor Branch, *Parting the Waters: America in the King Years,*

1954–63 (New York: Simon and Shuster, 1988), 410–411.

54 Branch, *Parting the Waters,* 410–411; Memo of John Doar to FBI Director, Mar 17, 1961; handwritten note on memo of A. Rosen to Mr. Parsons; memo of John Doar to Courtney A. Evans, Assistant FBI Director, Apr 6, 1961; Doar and Landsberg, "The Performance of the FBI . . ." 895, FBI Files.

55 "For Immediate Release, April 13, 1961," news release, U.S. Justice Department, Newspaper clippings and related memoranda pertaining to the voter registration campaign in Selma, Alabama, November 1959–June 1965, FBI Files; "First Kennedy Act Hits Alabama," *Dothan Eagle*, Apr 14, 1961, 1.

56 "Taking Charge," *Alabama Journal*, Jan 7, 1961, 4; "Some Registration Realism," *Birmingham News*, May 19, 1960, 14.

57 *Gomillion v. Lightfoot*, 364 US 339 (1960); Norrell, *Reaping the Whirlwind,* 124; *United States v. State of Alabama*, 192 F. Supp. 677 (1961); "Johnson Sets Blueprint for Negro Voting Hike," *Montgomery Advertiser*, Mar 18, 1961, 1; Doar and Landsberg, "The Performance of the FBI . . ." 900; "Oral History of Mr. John Doar," May 20, 2011.

58 "Judge Strikes Down Bullock Voting Rule, *Birmingham News*, Mar 30, 1961, 1; Hamilton, *The Bench and the Ballot.* 94–95; *1961 Commission on Civil Rights Report, 1961, Voting, Book 1,* note 88, 234–237; *Alabama ex. Rel. Gallion v. Rogers*, 187 F. Supp. 848 (1960), aff'd per curiam sub. nom. *Dinkens v. Rogers*, 285 F.2d 430 (5th Cir.), cert. denied, 366 U.S. 913. (1961); *Birmingham News*, May 2, 1961, 6.

59 Forrest Castleberry, "Two New Rulings by Supreme Court Arouse Concern," *Alabama Journal*, Dec 3, 1960, 9; Rex Thomas, "Black Belters Primed for Do-or-Die Battle," *Decatur Daily*, Apr 16, 1961, 11.

60 My summary of events is taken primarily from the excellent account of the breakup of political alliances in the legislature's 1961 session in Anne Permaloff and Carl Grafton, *Political Power in Alabama, The More Things Change* (Athens: University of Georgia Press, 1995), 119–135.

61 Hugh Sparrow, "State Attention Turns to Patterson," and "Jefferson May Cut Ties with Black Belt," *Birmingham News,* Aug 13, 1961, 32; "Most Solons regret Vote for Chop Bill," *Birmingham News*, Aug 13, 1961, 84; Permaloff and Grafton, *Political Power in Alabama*, 133,139.

62 Morgan, *A Time to Speak,* 104; Permaloff and Grafton, *Political Power in Alabama,*135–136.

63 Permaloff and Grafton, *Political Power in Alabama*, 134–135.

64 *Acts of Alabama, 1961*, 1816–1817, 2380–2384; "Snag Andrews May Quit," *Montgomery Advertiser*, Sep 2, 1961, 4.

65 *Alabama Official and Statistical Register, 1959*, 322; "County Solons Guide Their Bills to Okay," *Huntsville Times*, Sep 17, 1961, 7; "Senate Unit OKs Change in Vote Law," *Montgomery Advertiser*, May 18, 1961, 1; "North Alabama Woman Comes Up With Plan for Battered Voter Registration Bill," *Montgomery Advertiser*, Sep 17, 1961, 15. Smith regularly covered Roberts's role in the legislature during the 1961 session. See "Even Break on Congress Vote Sought by County," *Huntsville Times*, Sep 10, 1961, 16.

66 "Dream of Rose Bowl Trip Becomes True for Dixie Girl," *Los Angeles Times*, Dec 31, 1937, 25; "H. L. Burleson Died August 20," *Hartselle Enterprise*, Aug 27, 1970, 1; "Miss Burleson Will Study at the University," *Decatur Daily*, Jun 7, 1935, 1; "What's Happening in Alabama," *Birmingham News,* Nov 19, 1934, 3; "Golden Eaglets to Hartselle Girls," *Decatur Daily,* Mar 22, 1935, 1; Martha Witt Burleson, "'Sunny Jim' Will Attend Big Event Set at Capstone," *Birmingham News*, Apr 10, 1938, 21; "Ace Cheerleader Wins Award for Historical Work," *Birmingham News,* May 9, 1938, 3; "All American Cheerleaders Thinks Jinx Number 13 Is Lucky for Her," *Decatur Daily.* Nov 13, 1939, 1; "Ex-Yell Queen Has Ring Team," *Huntsville Times*, May 20, 1941, 6; "Hartselle," *Decatur Daily*, Jul 8, 1941, 3.

67 "Ex-Yell Queen Has Ring team," *Huntsville Times*, May 20, 1941, 6; "Voter," *Huntsville Times*, Jul 28, 1957, 2.

68 "North Alabama Woman Comes Up with Plan for Battered Voter Registration Bill," *Montgomery Advertiser*, Sep 17, 1961, 15.

69 "Patterson Signs Bill OKing Voter Registration Changes," *Montgomery Advertiser*, Sep 26, 1961, 17; "Dumas Loses Fight Against Voter Bills," *Birmingham News*, Sep 15, 1961, 7.

70 *Acts of Alabama, 1961*, H.J.R. 24, 44–46.

71 "Solons Denounce 'Freedom Riders,'" *Alabama Journal*, May 24, 1961, 11. A graduate of the Naval Academy, Murphy had become an accidental representative in 1956 after older brother at 30 died in office and he was the only candidate who qualified to fill the vacancy. The other dissenting Representative, Reverend Charles Trimmier, had arrived in Alabama only 12 years earlier to lead the Fairhope Christian Church and had become an officer of the state American Legion. Trimmier resigned from the legislature after he narrowly won in September a post on the Mobile City Commission in a race where he campaigned that his opponent had sought and received the endorsement and support of the "Negro vote." See "Murphy Is Named as Mobile Solon," *Huntsville Times*, Aug 14, 1956, 11; "Mobile," *Alabama Journal*, Jan 19, 1959, 28; "Trimmier, McNally Win in Port City Runoff," *Montgomery Advertiser*, Sep 24, 1961, 1.

72 "U.S. Referees May Watch Macon Rolls," *Huntsville Times*, Sep 9, 1961, 2; "Johnson Orders Registrar Boards for Macon, Bullock," *Montgomery Advertiser*, Sep 15, 1961, 1; Findings of Fact, Conclusions of Law, and Decree, *United States v. State of Alabama*, Civil Action No. 1677-N, VR-AL-0244–0003, September 13, 1961, Civil Rights Litigation Clearinghouse, University of Michigan Law School, accessed at http://clearinghouse.net; *Acts of Alabama, 1961*, 1816–1817; "Patterson Signs Bill OKing Voter Registration Changes," *Montgomery Advertiser*, Sep 26, 1961, 17.

73 "Indicting an IBM Machine," *Andalusia Star-News,* Sep 28, 1961, 6. Even sports columnists were writing about how a main-frame IBM computer at the push of a button would tell baseball managers who to pinch hit or send in as a relief pitcher. See "Nine Coaches and IBM Machine to Do Thinking and Coaching for 1961 Cubs," *Opelika Daily News*, Apr 4, 1961, 6.

74 "Patterson Signs Bill OKing Voter Registration Changes," *Montgomery Advertiser*, Sep 26, 1961, 17.

75 "Vote a Thundering 'Yes' on Amendment One," *Greensboro Watchman*, Apr 26, 1962,

4; "Opinions Sharply Divided on Centralized Grading of Voters," *Birmingham News*, Apr 1, 1962, 35.

76 "Amendment 1—Bad," *Montgomery Advertiser*, Apr 29, 1962, 18; "Defend Amendment One," *Alabama Journal*, Apr 21, 1962, 4; "Number 1 Is Essential," *Montgomery Advertiser*, Apr 27, 1962, 4; "Against Amendment No. 1," *Democrat-Reporter*, Apr 26, 1962, 8; "Registration Plan Meets Opposition," *Birmingham News*, Apr 5, 1962, 65; "On the Amendments," *Andalusia Star-News*, Apr 19, 1962, 4.

77 "Opinions Sharply Divided on Centralized Grading of Voters," *Birmingham News*, Apr 1, 1962, 35; "Registration Plan Meets Opposition," *Birmingham News*, Apr 5, 1962, 65; "Against Amendment One," *Birmingham News*, Apr 23, 1962, 12.

78 "Labor Chief Says No to Amendment 1," *Birmingham News*, Mar 20, 1962, 2; "the Alabama Democratic Primary," *Alabama Citizen*, Apr 28, 1962, 5; "Folsom Plans Talk Against Amendment," *Alabama Journal*, Mar 26, 1962. 9.

79 "Vote Yes — Amendment No. 1," *Huntsville Times*, Apr 29, 1962, 8; "Registrar Clarifies Proposed Amendment," *Huntsville Times*, Apr 1, 1962, 8; "Defend Amendment One," *Alabama Journal*, Apr 21, 1962, 4; "Opinions Sharply Divided on Centralized Grading of Voters," *Birmingham News*, Apr 1, 1962, 35; "Patterson May Veto Voter Literacy Acts," *Huntsville Times*, Sep 21, 1961, 5. Smith ignored the number of illiterate Blacks as a percentage of each county's total population.

80 *Alabama Official and Statistical Register, 1963*, 756–757, 736–737.

81 H. 727, *Acts of Alabama, 1963*, 921–923; Morgan, *A Time to Speak*, 108–109; *Sims v. Frink*, 208 F. Supp. 431 (1962).

82 See "Governor to Visit Area Cities," *Huntsville Times*, Feb 19, 1963, 1; "Wallace Lauds Fruehauf Move," *Huntsville Times*, Feb 20, 1963, 1; "Bills Offered to Create University of South Alabama," *Birmingham News*, Mar 27, 1963, 30; "Kicking the Traces," *Luverne Journal and News*, Mar 13, 1963, 2; "Wallace Huddles with Legislators," *Birmingham News*. Jan 2, 1963, 19.

83 "Wallace Seeks Officer Firing," *Huntsville Times*, Apr 2, 1963, 2.

84 "Wallace Rips U.S. Lawyer for Mix Aid," *Montgomery Advertiser*, Apr 2, 1963, 1; "Dismissal Request Is Timely," *Clarke County Democrat*, Apr 4, 1963, 4; "Contempt Citation Sought Against Registrars in Perry," *Montgomery Advertiser*, Jan 9, 1963, 1. For a detailed chronology of the Perry County case, see *United States v. Mayton*, 335 F. 2d 153 (1964).

85 "Jansen Donated to Negroes—Wallace," *Birmingham* News, Apr 4, 1963, 42.

86 "Wallace Raps Big City Papers for Hiding News," *Daily Northwest Alabamian*, Apr 5, 1963, 1; Andrew M. Manis, *A Fire You Can't Put Out: The Civil Rights Life of Birmingham's Reverend Fred Shuttlesworth* (Tuscaloosa: University of Alabama Press, 1999), 163–164; "Unions Join Birmingham Boycotting," *Montgomery Advertiser*, Apr 18, 1963, 1; David J. Garrow, *Bearing the Cross: Martin Luther King, Jr., and the Southern Christian Leadership Conference* (New York: William Morrow and Company, 1986), 236–240.

87 Carter, *The Politics of Rage*, 118–122.

88 Ibid., 128–129;

89 "Court," *Birmingham News*, May 15, 1963, 2; *Acts of Alabama, 1963*, 380–381;

"Spotlight on Racial Group," *Birmingham News*, May 21, 1963, 1; "Legislature," *Daily Northwest Alabamian*, May 22, 1963, 4.

90 Carter, *The Politics of Rage*, 135–138, 142–149.

91 E. Culpepper Clark, *The Schoolhouse Door: Segregation's Last Stand at the University of Alabama (Oxford: Oxford University Press*, 1995), 175; Carter, *The Politics of Rage*, 150–154; Jeffrey Frederick, *Stand Up for Alabama: Governor George Wallace* (Tuscaloosa: University of Alabama Press, 2007), 206–207.

92 "Wallace Charges JFK Has Nation on the Brink of Civil War on Race Issue," *Birmingham News*, Jul 15, 1963, 1; "King Target of Alabamian," *Baltimore Sun*, Jul 16, 1963, 1; *Hearings before the Committee on Commerce,* United States Senate, Eighty-eighth Congress, First Session, on S. 1732, A Bill to Eliminate Discrimination in Public Accommodations Affecting Interstate Commerce, July 1963, 434–436.

93 *Hearings before the Committee on Commerce,* 451.

94 Ibid., 452.

95 Ibid., 453–454.

96 Ibid., 478–479. Emphasis added in the quotation.

97 Ibid., 479–485.

98 Ibid., 506–509; "Wallace Tangles with Liberals," *Birmingham News*, Jul 16, 1963, 1.

99 "158 Bills Introduced in House; 31 in Senate," *Montgomery Advertiser*, Jul 17, 1963, 8; "Governor Addresses Legislature," *Montgomery Advertiser*, Jul 17, 1963, 1; "Wallace Has Had Legislative Troubles But Has Made Gains," *Decatur Daily*, Jun 23, 1963, 10; *Acts of Alabama, 1963*, 921–923.

100 "U.S. Sues Jefferson Registrars, Claims Bias," *Birmingham News*, Jul 31, 1963, 1; "Jefferson Registrars Deny U S Discrimination Charge," *Montgomery Advertiser*, Aug 1, 1963, 2; "Biggest Vote Suit Filed in Alabama," *New York Times*, Aug 1, 1963, 1.

101 "Administration Bill Would Halt Talks by Reds, Amendment-Takers," *Montgomery Advertiser*, Jul 28, 1963, 13; "Bill to Bar Demonstrators From Voting Before House," *Montgomery Advertiser*, Jul 19, 1963, 1; *Acts of Alabama, 1963*, 1098–1100. On the same day the Sovereignty Commission was established, attorney Chuck Morgan told a white Birmingham audience: "We are cursed by the failure of each of us to accept responsibility, by our defense of an already dead institution." Morgan, *A Time to Speak,* 13.

102 "Women Vote Group Urges 'No' for Amendment 3," (photo caption), *Alabama Journal*, Dec 4, 1963. 3; "Why the League of Women Voters Oppose Amendment No. 3," *Decatur Daily*, Dec 4, 1963, 34; "Communications Workers Speaker Opposes Congressional Measure on Labor Unions," *Montgomery Advertiser*, Oct 26, 1963, 6; Folsom letter to the Editor, *Daily Northwest Alabamian*, Dec 8, 1963, 4; "Folsom Opposes Amendment Three," *Decatur Daily*, Dec 6, 1963, 2; "County Officials Dodge Districting," *Dothan Eagle*, Nov 22, 1963, 5; "Those 13 Proposed Amendments," *Mobile Beacon and Alabama Citizen*, Nov 23, 1963, 4; "The Amendments," *Birmingham News*, Dec 9, 1963, 18; "Kill Amendment No. 3," *Florence Herald*, Nov 21, 1963, 2; "We're for Amendment No. 1; Against Amendments 3 and 4," *Selma Times-Journal*, Dec 8, 1963, 4.

103 Martha Witt Smith, "Amendment No. 3 Would Standardize Registration," *Huntsville*

Times, Nov 28, 1963, 22; "Urges Support for Proposed Amendment 3," *Opelika Daily News*, Dec 6, 1963, 2; "Registrars Back Amendment No. 3," *Huntsville Times*, Dec 8, 1963, 6; Hugh W. Sparrow, "Wallace Backs Corporate Tax Jump, Docks Measure," *Birmingham News*, Dec 8, 1963, 4.

104 See excerpt from Selma banker Aubrey Allen's letter to Wallace in Susan Youngblood Ashmore, *Carry It On: The War on Poverty and the Civil Rights Movement in Alabama, 1964–1972* (Athens: University of Georgia Press, 2008), 90.

105 *Alabama Official and Statistical Register, 1967*, 664, 675–677; Frederick, *Stand Up for Alabama*, 120–121; "Voting Consultant Ordered to Cease Board Interference," *Anniston Star*, Apr 7, 1972, 8; "Secret Agency Deleted in Bill," *Anniston Star*, Aug 10, 1973, 16.

Notes to Chapter 4

1 "Judge Bars Negro Voter Reading Test," *Huntsville Times*, Nov 18, 1961, 2. Also, see an earlier article likely written by Smith: "Madison Negro Vote Plan Aired," *Huntsville Times*, Apr 5, 1961, 1.

2 Frank Adams, *Unearthing Seeds of Fire: The Idea of Highlander* (Chapel Hill: John F. Blair, 1975), 110–120; Carl Tjerandsen, *Education for Citizenship: A Foundation's Experience* (web version, 1980), accessed at https://comm-org.wisc.edu/papers2003/tjerandsen/contentsd.htm; "The Citizenship School Program: A Proposal for South Wide Voter Education," Myles Horton to Patrick Murphy Malin, August 25,1961, Box 1115, Folder 21, Item 1025. American Civil Liberties Union Papers, Mudd Library, Princeton University.

3 Stephen A. Schneider, *You Can't Padlock an Idea: Rhetorical Education at the Highlander Folk School, 1932–1961* (Columbia, SC: University of South Carolina Press, 2014), 127–137; *Hearings before the Committee on Commerce*, 471; Carter, *The Politics of Rage*, 158–159; Adams, *Unearthing Seeds of Fire*, 133; Branch, *Parting the Waters*, 380–381.

4 Faulkenbury, *Poll Power*, chapter 2, 34–56, 79.

5 Leslie W. Dunbar and Wiley A. Branton, "First Annual Report of the Voter Education Project of the Southern Regional Council, Inc. for Fiscal Year April 1, 1962 through March 31, 1963," Table II, Voter Education Project Papers, Woodruff Library, Atlanta University Center.

6 "First Annual Report of the Voter Education Project," Table II, 24–27, 20, VEP Papers; see "I'm Not Voting, But I'm Mule; What's Your Excuse?" *Dayton Daily News* (Dayton, Ohio), Aug 1, 1963, 7; "Negro Registration Drive Producing Election Lever," *Cincinnati Enquirer*, Aug 2, 1963, 36.

7 "Voter Registration Laws Are Explained," *Huntsville Times*, Nov 22, 1962, 2; "First Annual Report of the Voter Education Project," 7, VEP Papers; "Registrars Set Monday Meets," *Huntsville Times*, Feb 15, 1963, 5; "Registering Set for Limestone," *Huntsville Times*, Jan 16, 1963, 11.

8 "80 Percent of New Voters From Other Counties, States," *Huntsville Times*, Oct 16, 1962, 8.

9 "PLEASE DO NOT TAKE THIS APPLICATION TO THE COURTHOUSE /Application for Registration, Questionnaire, and Oath," in Alabama, 1964, Part 4: Records of the Program Department, Records of the Southern Christian Leadership Conference, 1954–1970, ProQuest/History Vault; "Madison Negro Vote Plan Aired," *Huntsville Times*, Apr 5, 1961, 1; "Judge Bars Negro Voter Reading Test," *Huntsville Times*, Nov 18, 1961, 2.

10 Bernard S. Lee to Andrew Young, Jan 18,1963, Jan 22, 1963; Gadsden, Alabama, Voter Registration Report, undated; Memorandum—Alabama, undated, Monthly Field Report, undated; all in Alabama—Jan-Mar. 1963, SCLC Papers; "First Annual Report of the Voter Education Project," Table II, VEP Papers.

11 Bernard Lafayette Jr. and Kathryn Lee Johnson, *In Peace and Freedom* (Lexington: University Press of Kentucky, 2013), 25–32; Montgomery Report, undated, SCLC Papers; "First Annual Report of the Voter Education Project," Table II, VEP Papers.

12 Pat Watters and Reese Cleghorn, *Climbing Jacob's Ladder: The Arrival of Negroes in Southern Politics* (New York: Harcourt, Brace and World, 1967), 114.

13 "Voter Registration" and "Alabama Politics," 8–01-64, Alabama, 1964, Part 4: Program Department, SCLC Papers.

14 "Voter Registration," SCLC Papers. It appears that the organizers did not include in their calculations the one-time registration of approximately 1,000 African Americans whom Judge Johnson specifically ordered onto the rolls.

15 *Hearings Before a Subcommittee of the Committee on Appropriations*, House of Representatives, Eighty-Eighth Congress, Second Session, Jan 30, 1964, 152, 137; *Hearings Before a Subcommittee of the Committee on Appropriations*, House of Representatives, Eighty-Eighth Congress, First Session, Jan 28, 1963, 121.

16 *Voting: 1961 Commission on Civil Rights Report*, Book 1, 252–255.

17 "1964 Status Report," Burke Marshall Papers, The Black Freedom Struggle in the 20th Century, Federal Government Records, Civil Rights Division, ProQuest/History Vault; *U.S. v. Parker*, 236 F. Supp. 511 (1964), 512; *U.S. v. State of Alabama*, 192 F. Supp. 677 (1961), 678; *State of Alabama v. United States*, 304 F. 2d 583 (1962), 584.

18 *United States v. Atkins*, 210 F. Supp. 441 (1962), 444, 442.

19 Ibid., 443.

20 *United States v. Atkins*, 323 F. 2d 733 (1963), 739, 745; "1964 Status Report," Burke Marshall Papers, 17–19.

21 Thornton, *Dividing Lines*, 446–458; Lafayette and Johnson, *In Peace and Freedom*, 50–61.

22 Garrow, *Protest at Selma*, 31–32; "Ask Yourself This Important Question: What Have I Done Personally to Maintain Segregation," (ad), *Selma Times-Journal*, Jun 9, 1963, 3; "Integration Acceptance Flouted by Governor Before Large Crowd," *Selma Times-Journal*, Aug 30, 1963, 1.

23 "1964 Status Report," Burke Marshall Papers, 151–155.

24 *Kennedy v. Bruce*, 298 F. 2d 860 (1962); "1964 Status Report," Burke Marshall Papers, 156; *United States v. Bruce*, 353 F. 2d 474 (1965).

25 "1964 Status Report," Burke Marshall Papers, 65–67; *United States v. Mayton*, 335 F. 2d 153 (1964).

26 "Letter from Birmingham Jail," in Martin Luther King Jr., *I Have a Dream: Writings and Speeches that Changed the World*, ed. James M. Washington, (New York: HarperSanFrancisco, 1992), 88–89.

27 See *Davis v. Board of School Commissioners of Mobile County*, 219 F. Supp. 542 (1963). In his careful, detailed book on politics and civil rights in Alabama cities, Mills Thornton chronicles Thomas's misdeeds but disagrees with the description of Thomas as a segregationist. Instead, he suggests Thomas was a "moderate." See Thornton, *Dividing Lines*, 444–446. I combine the terms to accurately describe Thomas in a historical context. See Steve Suitts, *Overturning Brown: The Segregationist Legacy of the Modern School Choice Movement* (Montgomery: NewSouth Books, 2020), 8–11, 85–86. In surveying the South's segregationist federal judges' opinions in voting rights cases, Alabama's most knowledgeable political scientist of this era, Donald Strong, includes Judge Thomas as a segregationist who on occasion "shows signs of doubt and confusion." See Strong, *Negroes, Ballots, and Judges*, 85. When Thomas was appointed in 1951, Gessner McCorvey vouched for him as a lawyer with the "right character" for the job. See "Judge Thomas Takes Oath of Office," *Alabama Lawyer*, 12, no. 3 (July 1951), 300.

28 Strong, *Negroes, Ballots, and Judges*, 68–89; Hamilton, *The Bench and the Ballot*, 120–156. For another example of Harold Cox as an extreme segregationist federal judge, see Gerald M. Stern, "Judge William Harold Cox and the Right to Vote in Clarke County, Mississippi," in Leon Friedman (ed.), *Southern Justice*, (Random House: New York 1965), 195–186.

29 "First Annual Report of the Voter Education Project," 11, VEP Papers.

30 "Appendix A," *United States v. Parker*, 236 F. Supp. 511 (1964), 519–529; Act 92, *Acts of Alabama, 1961*, 107.

31 "Chief Justice J. Ed Livingston," *Alabama Lawyer*, 30, no. 2 (April 1969): 202–203; "Chief Justice J. Ed Livingston—Chief Justice in an Era of Change and Expansion," *Alabama Lawyer*, 33, no. 1, (January 1972): 11–12; "Ex-State Court Chief Dies Here," *Montgomery Advertiser*, Oct 16, 1971, 1; "Livingston C. J.—74," *Montgomery Advertiser*, Mar 18, 1966, 4.

32 Trest, *Nobody But the People*, 144–145; Michael Meltsner, "Southern Appellate Courts: A Dead End," 141–145; "Livingston, Hardwick Out Of Alabama Governor's Race," *Atlanta Journal and the Atlanta Constitution*, Jan 26, 1958, 5-E.

33 "Boutwell, Livingston Slam Power Driving Integration," *Montgomery Advertiser*, Mar 6, 1959, 1; Frank Sikora, *The Judge: The Life and Opinions of Alabama's Frank M. Johnson, Jr.* (Montgomery: NewSouth Books, 2007), 176.

34 "Jurist Foresees More Loss of States Rights," *Alabama Journal*, Sep 9, 1958, 1; "U.S. Attacked in Intervention," *Dothan Eagle*, Oct 24, 1958, 1; *Ex Parte National Association for the Advancement of Colored People*, 109 So. 2d 138 (1959); *NAACP v. Alabama ex rel. Flowers*, 377 US 288 (1964); Michael Meltsner, "Southern Appellate Courts: A Dead End,"143.

35 Joe Azbell, "Most Extraordinary Judge, A," *Alabama Lawyer*, 33, no. 1 (January

1972), 13–14; Thornton, *Dividing Lines,* 650, n.135; "Shut records to Rights Snoopers, Patterson Urges," *Selma Times-Journal,* Oct 21, 1958, 1; *United States v. State of Alabama,* 192 F. Supp. 677 (1961), 678–679.

36 *Lee v. Macon County Board of Education,* 221 F. Supp. 297 (1963); Sikora, *The Judge,* 170–172; "Desegregated Notasluga School Walls Painted," *Alabama Journal,* Apr 17, 1964, 13; "Fire Marshall Says Macon Blaze Arson," *Montgomery Advertiser,* Apr 21, 1964, 1.

37 Hugo L. Black and Elizabeth Black *Mr. Justice and Mrs. Black* (New York: Random House, 1986), 199–200: Author's unrecorded interview with Jerome "Buddy" Cooper, Birmingham, Alabama, April 1983.

38 Steve Flowers, *Of Goats and Governors: Six Decades of Colorful Alabama Political Stories* (Montgomery: NewSouth Books, 2015), 29–31; "Screening Committee Endorses Bill to Limit Illegitimate Children Aid," *Montgomery Advertiser,* Apr 8, 1959, 2; "Solons Study Negro Births for New Laws," *Dothan Eagle,* Apr 8, 1959, 1.

39 "Gerald O. Wallace," *Alabama Journal,* Dec 21, 1961, 35; Carter, *The Politics of Rage,* 364–365, 370; George C. Wallace, "Tributes," *Alabama Lawyer,* 32, no. 2 (April 1971), 204.

40 Frederick, *Stand Up for Alabama,* 132–133; "Governor Succession Bill Given Approval," *Piedmont Journal,* Jun 28, 1963, 1; "Filibuster Erupts Over Redistricting," *Daily Mountain Eagle,* Sep 6, 1963, 6; "Succession Bill Special Session Is Torrid Rumor," *Montgomery Advertiser,* Apr 12, 1964, 1.

41 Carter, *The Politics of Rage,* 200–204; Ashmore, *Carry It On,* 90.

42 Thornton, *Dividing Lines,* 684, no. 135; "Petition of Intervention/ Complaint," *Nance v. Jackson* Pleadings, Emily Carssow Files, 1972, Southern Regional Office Files, 1945–1990, American Civil Liberties Union Papers, Mudd Library, Princeton University; Ashmore, *Carry It On,* 90.

43 "Registrars Now Using New Plan," *Montgomery Advertiser,* Mar 12, 1964,1. The questionnaire is reproduced in Appendix A of *U.S. v. Parker,* 236 F. Supp. 511 (1964), 519–529.

44 "Organizational Meeting Called by Registrars," *Montgomery Advertiser,* Jul 24, 1964, 23; "Registration Uniform Law Group's Aimed," *Montgomery Advertiser,* Jul 25, 1964, 8.

45 "1964 Status Report," Burke Marshall Papers, 85–87; *United States v. Cartwright,* 230 F. Supp. 873 (1964), 880 no. 2, 877.

46 Ashmore, *Carry It On,* 90.

47 "1964 Status Report," Burke Marshall Papers, 36.

48 Ashmore, *Carry It On,* no. 9 313. Only county sheriffs could issue permits to carry a pistol to anyone other than military personnel, law enforcement officers, and persons involved in the manufacturing or repair of the firearms. See Title 14, sec. 175–176, *Code of Alabama, 1940.*

49 Ashmore, *Carry It On,* 91.

50 Carter, *The Politics of Rage,* 207.

51 "Commission Organized to Kill Rights Bill," *Cherokee County Herald,* Mar 18, 1964,

1; "Givhan See Bill as Most Vicious Legislation," *Selma Times-Journal*, Apr 3, 1964, 1; "Stand Up for America [ad]." Evergreen Courant, Apr 2, 1964, 6.

52 "Communist Ideas, Rights Bill Linked," *Montgomery Advertiser*, Apr 8, 1964, 1; Jordan R. Bauer, "Domestic Anti-Communism in Alabama and the Resurgence of American Conservatism," Master's thesis (University of Alabama, Birmingham, 2007), 65–66.

53 Transcript of Civil Rights Act (1964) at https://www.ourdocuments.gov/; Garrow, *Protest at Selma*, 25–26; Brian K. Landsberg, *Free at Last to Vote: The Alabama Origins of the 1965 Voting Rights Act* (Lawrence, KS: University Press of Kansas, 2007), 118; Charles E. Fager, *Selma 1965: The March that Changed the South* (New York: Scribner, 1974), 42.

54 "Affidavit of John Doar," VR-AL-0244–0002, Brian Landsberg Papers, Civil Rights Litigation Clearinghouse.

55 Act 523, *Acts of Alabama, Special Session 1964*, 350; "Purging of Illiterates Is Planned," *Choctaw Advocate*, Sep 24, 1964, 12.

56 "Negro Leaders Express Concern Over Registration Tactics," *Mobile Beacon and Alabama Citizen*, Sep 19, 1964, 1. On the same day as passage of the statewide reregistration law, legislators enacted a local law sponsored by Tuscaloosa representatives that prescribed a simple questionnaire seeking a voter's address and signature for reregistration. In effect, it prevented the questionnaire booklet that Smith developed from being to reregister voters in Tuscaloosa County. See Act 257, *Acts of Alabama, Special Session 1964*, 353–355.

57 "Dallas Voter Registration Hearing Begins," *Alabama Journal*, Oct 5, 1964, 11; "1964 Status Report," Burke Marshall Papers, 19; "Report on Mock Negro Election," *Selma Times-Journal*, Mar 19, 1964, 19; "Brief in Support of Plaintiff's Motion for Supplemental Relief," *U.S. v. Atkins*, Landsberg Papers.

58 "1964 Status Report," Burke Marshall Papers, 160–161; Chestnut and Cass, *Black in Selma*, 172–176, 175.

59 "1964 Status Report," Burke Marshall Papers, 64, 67–68, 87, 100, 15.

60 Landsberg, *Free at Last to Vote*, 141; Ashmore, *Carry It On*, 90; "Sovereignty Commission Secretary Resigns Post," *Montgomery Advertiser*, Nov 27, 1968, 1.

61 "Opens Office / Frank Mizell Jr.," *Montgomery Advertiser*, Aug 11, 1946, 8; "Mr. McCorvey Writes to Mr. Patterson," *Alabama Journal*, Dec 24, 1958, 4.

62 "Demos Slam Door," *Montgomery Advertiser*, Jan 29, 1956, 2.

63 "Macon Abolition Hearing," *Montgomery Advertiser*, Feb 28, 1958, 2; "Engelhardt Elected Democratic Chairman," *Montgomery Advertiser*, Jan 20, 1959, 1; "Elect Alabama's Segregation Leader" [ad], *Troy Messenger*, Apr 30, 1962, 7.

64 Robert J. Norrell, "Law in a White Man's Democracy: A History of the Alabama State Judiciary," *Cumberland Law Review*, 32, no. 1 (2001–2002), 158.

65 "Rule Change to Bar Negro Committeemen," *Birmingham News*, Jan 20, 1962, 1; "8th District Party Battle Told," *Huntsville Times*, Jan 22, 1962, 6. The only known registrar whose county had a relatively small Black voting population and who was experiencing a spike in Black voter registration in 1961–1962 was Madison County. In the 1961 session when Smith was advancing passage of the proposed constitutional

on voter registration which she authored, the legislature also passed senate bill S. 26, mandating numbered posts in most elections across the state. The sponsor of the bill was the state senator from Madison County. Smith testified and lobbied for the anti-single shot voting bill, which she may have helped to develop. See Act 221, *Acts of Alabama, Special Session, 1961*, 2233–2234; "Archer Fights Congress Bill," *Huntsville Times*, Sep 13, 1961, 2; "County Solons Guide Their Bills to OK," *Huntsville Times*, Sep 17, 1961, 7. Neither article in Smith's newspaper reporting on her own role and opinions on the bill has a byline, but she was the *Times* reporter covering the legislature for that session.

66 "Adjourning Becomes Legislature Problem," *Alabama Journal*, Aug 22, 1964, 9.

67 "1964 Status Report," Burke Marshall Papers, 65–66; *United States v. Mayton* 9 Race Rel. L. Rep. 1136–37 (1962); Landsberg. *Free at Last to Vote*, 120–122.

NOTES TO CHAPTER 5

1 Tom Dent, *Southern Journey: A Return to the Civil rights Movement* (New York: William Morrow and Company.1997), 284; Andrew Young, *An Easy Burden: The Civil Rights Movement and the Transformation of America* (Waco, TX: Baylor University Press, 2008), 66,135.

2 Allen Tullos, "Rebel with a Cause: Albert Turner Sr. (1936–2000)," *Southern Changes*, Vol. 22, No. 2, 2000, 24.

3 Jimmy Breslin, "At End of Line—One Man's Story," *Boston Globe*, Mar 23, 1965, 1.

4 "A Fighter for the Vote, Albert Turner," *New York Times,* Mar 26, 1965, 23; "Hale Negroes Face Tax Status Question," *Birmingham* News, Feb 25, 1959, 10.

5 Jimmy Breslin, "At End of Line—One Man's Story," *Boston Globe*, Mar 23, 1965, 1. Father Ouellett and his Order members were among only a handful of whites in Selma supporting Black voting, see Fager, *Selma 1965, 113.*

6 Landsberg, *Free at Last to Vote*, 114; "Dr. Moton to Address Teachers Here Friday Night," *Birmingham Reporter*, Mar 23, 1929, 1; "Negro Chorus to Present Musicale," *Albany-Decatur Daily*, Aug 8, 1925, 4; "15th Anniversary of Rev. A. W. [sic] Banks at Union B. Church," *Union-Banner*, Jul 11, 1946, 5; "Negro Baptists Map Songfest," *Andalusia Star-News*, Jun 14, 1951, 1; "A Musical Pity," *Alabama Citizen*, May 16, 1953, 5; "New Colored Church," *Union-Banner*, Feb 3, 1949, 9.

7 A. Edward Banks to Joseph W, Johnson, Nov 11, 1922, Part 07: The Anti-Lynching Campaign, 1912–1955; Gloster B. Current to Rev. A. Edward Banks, Feb 3, 1947, Part 26: Selected Branch Files, 1940–1955, NAACP Papers; A. Edward Banks to A. J. Young, December 20, 1962, SCLC Papers; "Boycott Trials Start Monday," *Alabama Journal*, Mar 17, 1956, 1; A Edward Banks to Rev. John L. Tilley, Sep 29, 1958, SCLC Records; "Speaker Claims He Was Jailed," *Pittsburgh Courier*, Jan 24, 1959, 30.

8 "A Fighter for the Vote, Albert Turner," *New York Times,* Mar 26, 1965, 23; Landsberg, *Free at Last to Vote*, 114; "What! No Vote Again?" *Dothan Eagle*, Jul 8, 1962, 1; "Monies Received by the Treasurer at the Annual meeting in Birmingham, Ala., September 25–28, 1962," NAACP Papers.

9 "1964 Status Report," Burke Marshall Papers, 65; A. Edward Banks to A. J. Young,

December 20, 1962, SCLC Records; "A Fighter for the Vote, Albert Turner," *New York Times,* Mar 26, 1965, 23.

10 Landsberg, *Free at Last to Vote*, 123.

11 "1964 Status Report," Burke Marshall Papers, 66; "Hospital List," *Marion Times-Standard,* Jan 17, 1963, 5; Landsberg, *Free at Last to Vote*, 123–124.

12 Landsberg, *Free at Last to Vote*, 125.

13 "A Fighter for the Vote, Albert Turner," *New York Times,* Mar 26, 1965, 23; "A. Edward Eubanks Citizenship School Monthly Attendance Sheet" [dated Dec. 4, 1962, March, April 13, 1963, May 6], SCLC Papers; Jimmy Breslin, "At End of Line—One Man's Story," *Boston Globe*, Mar 23, 1965, 1.

14 Landsberg, *Free at Last to Vote,* 125–126; "Ella D. Stewart listed on "A. Edward Eubanks Citizenship School Monthly Attendance Sheet" [dated April 13, 1963, May 6], SCLC Papers.

15 "District Court Order of August 15, 1963," 9 Race Rel. L. Rep. 1340; "1964 Status Report," Burke Marshall Papers, 66–67.

16 "Grand Jury," *Selma Times-Journal,* Dec 6, 1963, 2; "U.S. vs McLeod and Others Death to Grand Juries, Claim," *Birmingham News*, Dec 6, 1963, 38; "1964 Status Report," Burke Marshall Papers, 151–152. Thomas acted relatively quickly in dismissing the Justice Department's complaint in an opinion in which he ruled that "there has been a complete absence of any showing that the Grand Jury was not acting in good faith. *United States v. McLeod,* 229 F. Supp. 383 (1964), 387. When in 1967 the Circuit Court of Appeals reached the issue of the grand jury's investigation, Judge John Minor Wisdom wrote, "the record makes clear that the defendants' assertion that the investigation was to deal with violations of state law is a patent sham . . . We hold that the trial court's finding to the contrary that the investigation was initiated and carried out in good faith was clearly erroneous." *United States v. McLeod,* 385 F. 2d 734 (1967), 751–752.

17 "1964 Status Report," Burke Marshall Papers, 67; Landsberg, *Free at Last to Vote,* 124; Memo of Mar 19, 1964 from Burke Marshall to Director, Federal Bureau of Investigation, Intimidation of the Black population by Dallas County Officials, U.S. v. Atkins, and voter registration activities, July 1963–September 1964, FBI Files.

18 Tullos, "Rebel with a Cause," 24.

19 "List of Qualified Voters of Perry County, Alabama for 1964," *Marion Times-Standard,* Mar 26, 1964, 8–11; "1964 Status Report," Burke Marshall Papers, 65; The number of Black voters in the published list of March 26, 1964 differed by 15 persons from the numbers in Justice Department pleadings in the April hearing. The difference may be explained by a different, exact ending date in March.

20 Brief in Support of Application for an Order . . ., United States v. Blackburn, Civil Actin No, 2881, Landsberg Papers.

21 See Brief in Support of Plaintiff's Application for an Order . . ., Tables for Brief in Support of Plaintiff's Application . . ., Plaintiff's Proposed Findings of Fact and Proposed Conclusions of Law, United States v. Blackburn, Landsberg Papers.

22 Brief in Support of Plaintiff's Application for an Order . . ., 100–101,116, United States v. Blackburn, Landsberg Papers.

23 Landsberg, *Free at Last to Vote*, 122–127; *United States v. Mayton*, 9 Race Rel. L. Rep. 1337–1350 (1964); "1964 Status Report," Burke Marshall Papers, 65–67.

24 Burke Marshall Papers, 67; "Letters to the Editor," *Marion Times-Standard*, Apr 30, 1964, 4.

25 *United States v. Mayton*, 335 F. 2d 153 (1964), 165.

26 Ibid.; "Appointment of Referee," 9 Race Rel. L. Rep. 1350; Landsberg, *Free at Last to Vote*, 131–134.

27 Landsberg, *Free at Last to Vote*, 134, 224 n.154; for examples of the scores of foreclosure notices, see "Legal Notices," *Greensboro Watchman*, Apr 27, 1961, 7, Nov 23, 1961, 7, Dec 14, 1961, 7; "For Rent," *Greensboro Watchman*, Jan 26, 1956, 7; "For Sale," *Greensboro Watchman*, May 25, 1950, 5.

28 Landsberg, *Free at Last to Vote*, 134; "Mrs. Burke Hostess," *Greensboro Watchman*, Oct 16, 1941, 5; "Lem Morrison Named Commander of Legion Post," Jun 27, 1946, 1; Jack Bass, *Unlikely Heroes* (New York: Simon and Shuster, 1981), 159; *United States v. Mayton*, 325 F. 2d 433 (1963), 434.

29 "Ramey and Wilson to Be in Runoff May 30 for Other Place in House," *Greensboro Watchman*, May 4, 1950, 1; "Vote for O. S. 'Tigger" Burke" [ad], *Greene County Democrat*, Apr 19, 1962, 9; *Alabama Official and Statistical Register*, 1963, 751; "Vote for These State Righters" [ad], *Sumter County Journal*, Apr 28, 1960, 17; "To the Voters of Hale County [ad]." *Greensboro* Watchman, Apr 19, 1962, 2.

30 Landsberg, *Free at Last to Vote*, n. 148 224–225.

31 Ibid., 134; "Voting Referee Appointed to Take Perry Applications," *Alabama Journal*, Sep 4, 1964, 11.

32 Landsberg, *Free at Last to Vote*, 136–137. Burke procedures are also restated by Chief Judge Elbert Tuttle of the Fifth Circuit in his opinion in reviewing the case in response to the Justice Department's appeal; see *United States v. Scarborough*, 348 F. 2d 168 (1965), 170–171.

33 Tom Dent, Interview of Albert Turner, Part 1, Aug 7, 1991, Southern Journey Oral History Collection, Tulane University Digital Library. Also see Fager, *Selma 1965*, 42.

34 Landsberg, *Free at Last to Vote*, 137–139; "1964 Status Report," Burke Marshall Papers, 68.

35 Howell Raines, *My Soul Is Rested: Movement Days in the Deep South Remembered* (New York: Bantam Books, 1978), 205.

36 "Few Perry Negroes Return to Register," *Selma Times-Journal*, Dec 18, 1964, 1; "Registrars Ask Purge of Rolls," *Selma Times-Journal*, Dec 30, 1964, 1.

37 "Table 4—Alabama." *Political Participation*, United States Commission on Civil Rights, May 1968, 224–227; "Voter Figures Hard to Get Due to Varying Registrars," *Montgomery Advertiser*, Jan 26, 1964, 34.

38 *Guinn v. United States*, 238 US 347 (1915); *Lassiter v. Northampton County Bd. of Elections*, 360 US 45 (1959); "Registrars Ask Purge of Rolls," *Selma Times-Journal*, Dec 30, 1964, 1.

39 "Partial Text of Wallace Interview," *Minneapolis Star*, Mar 15, 1965, 3.

40 Landsberg, *Free at Last to Vote*, 140; Raines, *My Soul Is Rested*, 206.

41 Raines, *My Soul Is Rested*, 206; "2 Vote-Drive Workers Shot at in Mississippi," *The Militant*, Dec 28, 1964,6; "Perry County Report," undated, SNCC Archives; Taylor Branch, *Parting the Waters*, 553–560; Tom Brown, "Fact Sheet," undated [covering dates of Jan. 17-Feb. 5, 1965], SNCC Archives; Interview with Albert Turner, conducted by Blackside, Inc. in 1979, *Eyes on the Prize: America's Civil Rights Years (1954–1965)*, Henry Hampton Collection, Film and Media Archive, Washington University Libraries.

42 "Perry's Eating Places Tested," *Alabama Journal*, Feb 1, 1965, 1; "No Trouble at Marion Registration," *Montgomery Advertiser*, Feb 2, 1965, 1; "Marion, Ala., Integrates," *Christian Science Monitor*, Feb 3, 1965, 3.

43 Tom Brown, "Fact Sheet," undated, SNCC Archives; "Selma," *Montgomery Advertiser*, Feb 4, 1965, 2; John Herbers, "Negroes Step Up Drive in Alabama; 1,000 More Seized," *New York Times*, Feb 4, 1965, 1; "Albert Turner (no photograph)," *Individuals Active in Civil Disturbances*, vol. 2. Department of Public Safety, State of Alabama, ADAH; "WATS Report," Feb 3, 1965, SNCC Archives.

44 "King Taking Vote issue to Johnson," *Alabama Journal*, Feb 6, 1965, 1.

45 "Special Report," Feb 4, 1965, SNCC Archives; "Perry Co. School Boycott Continues," *Selma Times-Journal*, Feb 9, 1965, 2; "Negroes Kneel-in on Marion Square," *Montgomery Advertiser*, Feb 11, 1965, 2; "Marion Quiet," *Alabama Journal*, Feb 12, 1965, 2; "No Trouble Reported in Marion Marching," *Montgomery Advertiser*, Feb 16, 1965, 2.

46 John Herbers, "2 Inquires Open on Racial Clash in Alabama Town," *New York Times*, Feb 20, 1965,1; Fager, *Selma 1965*, 72–74; Raines, *My Soul Is Rested*, 206–207; John Fleming, "Who Killed Jimmy Lee Jackson?" *Sojourners Magazine*, Apr 2005, 20–24. In 2010, as a result of cold-case charges brought by Perry County's first Black district attorney, Fowler pled guilty to manslaughter for Jackson's death and received a six-month sentence; he died in 2015.

47 Raines, *My Soul Is Rested*, 206.

48 Carter, *The Politics of Rage*, 244; "Legislators to Probe Marion Riot," *Alabama Journal*, Mar 1, 1965, 13; "Alabama Senate Endorses Perry Work of Patrol," *Selma Times-Journal*, Feb 24, 1965, 1; S.J.R. 5, *Alabama Acts, 1965*, 30–31; Fager, *Selma 1965*, 80.

49 Raines, *My Soul Is Rested*, 213; Roy Reed, "Alabama Victim Called a Martyr: Dr. King and Others Speak at Marion Funeral," *New York Times*, Mar 4, 1965, 23.

50 Young, *The Civil Rights Movement and the Transformation of America*, 354–356; Fager, *Selma 1965*, 92–98.

51 Raines, *My Soul Is Rested*, 206.

52 Jimmy Breslin, "At End of Line—One Man's Story," *Boston Globe*, Mar 23, 1965; "A Fighter for the Vote, Albert Turner," *New York Times*, Mar 26, 1965, 23.

53 "Letter from Selma," *New Yorker*, April 10, 1965, accessed at https://www.newyorker.com/magazine/1965/04/10/letter-from-selma.

54 "Our God Is Marching On" in King, *I Have a Dream*, 122–123.

55 Roy Reed, "Alabama March By Negroes Fails: Camden Mayor and Officers Halt 200 at City Limits," *New York Times*, Mar 6, 1965, 10; Fager, *Selma 1965*, 84; *United States v. Logue*, 9 Race Rel. L. Rep. 770 (1964), 771–772. The Fifth Circuit Court

overturned Thomas's opinion on April 1, 1965. See *United States v. Logue*, 344 F. 2d 290 (1965).

56 Roy Reed, "Alabama March By Negroes Fails: Camden Mayor and Officers Halt 200 at City Limits," *New York Times*, Mar 6, 1965, 10; "Specialist in Voter Registration Says Voucher Rule Not Too Harsh," *Montgomery Advertiser*, Mar 4, 1965, 2.

57 "First Negro Registered in Lowndes," *Anniston Star*, Mar 17, 1965, 28.

58 "Court Hears Voter Test Arguments," *Montgomery Advertiser*, Mar 9, 1965, 2; Compliant and Brief in Opposition to Motion to Strike, to Dismiss, and to Drop Defendants as Parties," *United States v. Baggett*, Landsberg Papers.

59 Brief in Opposition *United States v. Baggett*, Landsberg Papers; "Court Hears Voter test Arguments," *Montgomery Advertiser*, Mar 9, 1965, 2.

60 Martha Witt Smith, "Doar Would Oust All Officeholders in Alabama," quoted in *Congressional Record*, House of Representatives, March 17, 1965, 5306.

61 Rex Thomas, "Rate of Registration Rejection at Selma Is Put at 3 of 4 Negroes," *Washington Post*, Mar 16, 1965, A-12.

62 "Government Asks Ruling on Referee," *Alabama Journal*, Mar 8, 1965, 11; "Perry Told to Speed Up Registration," *Alabama Journal*, Mar 16, 1965,11; "Board Doing More Than Court Requires," *Alabama Journal*, Mar 17, 1965, 26; Martha Witt Smith, "Voter Registration Situation in Alabama," quoted in *Congressional Record*, House of Representatives, March 17, 1965, 5305. Perry County registrar John Blackburn was removed from office according to reports because the county's "tense racial situation" had a "deteriorating effect on Blackburn's health," although it is not clear what, if any occurrence was related beyond Blackburn being contradicted in open court by local Black residents. See "Perry County Registrar Is Replaced," *Montgomery Advertiser*, Mar 2, 1965, 16.

63 "New Vote Requirements Endorsed," *Montgomery Advertiser*, Mar 18, 1965, 3.

64 "Wallace Gives Registrars Extra Time in 5 Counties," *Montgomery Advertiser*, Mar 17, 1965, 1.

65 "Action By State Governor," Feb 20, 1965, 10 Race Rel. L. Rep. 217 (1965); "Partial Text of Wallace Interview," *Minneapolis Star*, Mar 15, 1965, 3.

66 "New Vote Requirements Endorsed," *Montgomery Advertiser*, Mar 18, 1965, 3.

67 *Acts of Alabama*, 1965, Special Session, 112.

68 Ibid., 64–69, 113–115, 203–204, 289.

69 "Students, Faculty Fail Voter Tests," *Los Angeles* Times, Mar 26, 1965, 4; "Alabama's Voter Test 'a Failure,'" *Times* (San Mateo, California), Mar 18, 1965, 27; "Walter Winchell," *Wilkes-Barre Times Leader, Evening News* (Pennsylvania), Mar 27, 1965, 2.

70 "Alabama's Literacy Test Outrageous," *Pittsburgh Courier*, Apr 10, 1965, 10; "Art Buchwald's Column: Alabama Literacy Test," *Minneapolis Star*, Mar 19, 1965, 4.

71 "House Acts to Ease Voter Restrictions," *Huntsville Mirror*, Apr 10, 1965, 1; "Legislature May be Called on Vote Laws," *Alabama Journal*, Apr 6, 1965, 1; "Two Bills to Relax Voter Law," *Anniston Star*, Apr 9, 1965, 1; *Alabama Official and Statistical Register, 1963*, 412–413.

72 "Partial Text of Wallace Interview," *Minneapolis Star*, Mar 15, 1965, 3; "Wallace and

Wilkins Smiles, Shake Hands, Swap Verbal Blows," *Anniston* Star, Apr 4, 1965, 1; *Hearings before the Committee on Commerce, United States Senate, Eighty-eighth Congress*, 479.

73 "Selma Marchers Set to Defy Jail Threat," *New York Daily News*, Mar 15, 1965, 62.

74 Martha Witt Smith, "Voter Registration Situation in Alabama," quoted in *Congressional Record*, House of Representatives, March 17, 1965, 5306. Smith's estimates of Black voter registration in 1965 as 115,000 are higher than the 92,117, the number reported by the U.S. Civil Rights Commission for Black registration in 1964. Regardless, Smith's data on levels of education among Black adults in Alabama accurately reflected Census data as of 1960.

75 See Bureau of the Census, *Census of Population, 1960*, Vol. 1, Part 1, United States Summary, 1–260. The 1960 Census for Alabama and New York reports "white" and "non-white" statistics. Here and elsewhere "non-white" data is used as "black" persons by Smith and in the author's calculations.

76 Author calculations from data in Bureau of the Census, *Census of Population, 1960*, Vol. 1, Part 2, Alabama, 2–196 thru 2–201, 2–220 thru 2–224.

77 "New York Qualification Plan Set for Registering," *Montgomery Advertiser*, Apr 9, 1965, 1; "State House Group Okays Voting Bill," *Anniston Star,*, Apr 2, 1965, 1; "Committee OKs State Voting Bill; Senate Move Due," *Anniston* Star, Apr 14, 1965, 1; "Vote Bill Success Doubtful," *Montgomery Advertiser,* Apr 14, 1965, 1; "Vote Bill Is Approved by Senate," *Montgomery Advertiser*, Apr 23, 1965, 1; "Session Ends; Eases Literacy Rule on Voting," *Montgomery Advertiser*. May 1, 1965, 1; Act 296, *Acts of Alabama*, 1965, Special Session, 396–398.

Notes to Chapter 6

1 "Johnson Reveals Alert to Troops in Selma Crisis," *New York Times*. Mar 13, 1965, 1.

2 "Alabamians Call Criticism Unfair," *New York Times,* Mar 18, 1965, 21; *Congressional Record*, House of Representatives, March 17, 1965, 5298–5300, 5303, 5308.

3 *Congressional Record*, House of Representatives, March 17, 1965, 5301–5302, 5304–5307.

4 Ibid., 5308–5309.

5 *Hearings Before Subcommittee No. 5*, Committee on the Judiciary, House of Representatives, Eight-Ninth Congress, First Session, on H.R. 6400, Serial No. 2, 583–591, 657–660 (quote at 658), 756–760.

6 *Congressional Record*, U.S. Senate, March 8, 1965, 4335. The *Congressional Record* is filled with similar condemnations and expressions of shock and outrage from March 8, 1965 (4311) through March 23, 1965 (4311–5516).

7 *Hearings Before Subcommittee No. 5 on H.R. 6400*, 2, 25, 30–32, 135–256. Also, see Census Bureau, *1960 Population of Voting Age and Votes Cast for President, 1964 and 1960, for States and Counties*, Current Population Reports: Technical Studies, Series P-23, No. 14, April 21, 1965.

8 *Hearings Before Subcommittee No. 5 on H.R. 6400*, 12–17, 570–574. See also "The Vote and the Constitution," *New York Times,* Mar 29, 1965; Alexander M. Bickel,

"The Voting Rights Cases," *Supreme Court Review* 1966 (1966): 79–102; Archibald Cox, "Constitutionality of the Proposed Voting Rights Act of 1965," *Houston Law Review* 3:1 (1965–1966); Warren T. Christopher, "The Constitutionality of the Voting Rights Act of 1965," 18 *Stanford Law Review*, 1 (1965–1966).

9 *Hearings Before the Committee on the Judiciary*, United States Senate, Eight-Ninth Congress, First Session on S.1564 (1965), 729–737.

10 Ibid., 774.

11 "What we believe and where we stand . . ." [ad], *Montgomery Advertiser*, Apr 15, 1965, 17; Permaloff and Grafton, *Political Power in Alabama*, 215–116.

12 "State Business Groups Are Lauded by Johnson," *Montgomery Advertiser*, Apr 22, 1965, 1.

13 "Blount: We Don't Face Up," *Montgomery Advertiser*, Apr 22, 1965, 1. Blount's speech drew praiseworthy coverage from CBS' legendary Walter Cronkite in his daily radio commentary. The newsman expressed hope that the speech indicated in Alabama a trend where "courage can be just as contagious as fear." "CRONKITE- Friday, April 28, 1965," *Dimension* (typed transcript), via email from Cleophus Thomas Jr., Jan. 22, 2022.

14 "Red Blount Urges Support for Legislature on Voting," *Montgomery Advertiser* May 5, 1965, 10.

15 "Gilchrist 'Takes Shots' at Governor," *Alabama Journal*, May 5, 1965, 1; "Racial Policies of Wallace Under Attack for Second Day," *Montgomery Advertiser*, May 7, 1965, 23; "What Fast Industrial Growth?" *Alabama Journal*, Apr 19, 1965, 4; "Hunstvillians 'Not Serious on Secession,'" *Montgomery Advertiser*, Mar 17, 1965, 2.

16 "Alabama Voter Laws Criticized By Von Braun," *Alabama Journal*, Apr 13, 1965, 16.

17 "'Ala. Vote Laws Like Berlin Wall'" *Akron Beacon Journal* (Akron, Ohio), Apr 13, 1965, 29; "Dr. Von Braun's Hyperbole," *Alabama Journal*, Apr 16, 1965, 4; "Von Braun Takes Blast At State," *Selma Times-Journal*, Apr 15, 1965, 6. Von Braun did speak privately to the board of directors of the Alabama Chamber of Commerce in late May about the risk of Huntsville losing federal contracts in the space program due to "obstructionism and defiance," but he did not take up the issues publicly again. See Ben A. Franklin, "Von Braun Fights Alabama Racism," *New York Times*, Jun 14, 1965, 39.

18 "History in Alabama: Negroes, Solons Hold Parleys," *Chicago Daily Defender*, May 26, 1965, 3; "King Hails Conferences with Alabama Legislators," *Afro-American*, Jun 5, 1965, 14; "Legislature Will Attend Prison Fete," *Montgomery Advertiser*, May 25, 1965, 1.

19 "No Future Divided Says Businessman," *Selma Times-Journal*, Jun 22, 1965, 2; Carter, *The Politics of Rage*, 129–130 ("bullshit" quote); Oral History Interview with George A. LeMaistre by Allen J. Going, April 29, 1985, interview A-0358, (#4007) in the Southern Oral History Program Collection, Southern Historical Collection, Wilson Library, University of North Carolina at Chapel Hill.

20 Landsberg, *Free at Last to Vote*, 141; *United States v. Scarborough*, 348 F. 2d 168 (1965-, 171. Upon Thomas's retirement in 1971, Tigger Burke wrote to the Judge that they would soon be able to go "coon-hunting" together. It was a provocative

choice of words, inadvertent or deliberate. "Coon hunting" had been a longstanding, night-time sport in the Black Belt, but it also was a slang term for randomly finding a Black person to injure or kill. Also, white Southerners of various ranks began referring to Dr. Martin Luther King Jr. as "Martin Luther Coon," a practice that has persisted into modern day. See "Body of Hunter, Missing 4 Weeks, Found Under Tree," *Greensboro Watchman*, Dec 6, 1956, 1; "The White Supremacist's Badge of Honor," *Journal of Blacks in Higher Education*, No. 15 (Spring, 1997), 72; "Man Arrested Here, Disorderly Charge," *Selma Times-Journal*, Jan 19, 1965, 5; Suitts, "Voting Rights, the Supreme Court, and the Persistence of Southern History." Whatever his essential character, Judge Thomas was a man who was duplicitous regularly in his court opinions and occasionally in his personal life. See Suitts, *Hugo Black of Alabama*, 14.

21 "Alabama Eases Test for Voting," *Birmingham News*, Jul 22, 1965, 1; "Newer Literacy Test Effected," *Selma Times*-Journal, Jul 22, 1965, 6.

22 "Alabama Has New, Simpler Voting Test, *The Austin Statesman,* Jul 22, 1965, A16; "Registration Rules Eased in Alabama," *Baltimore Sun*, Jul 23, 1965, 5; Joseph R. L. Sterne, "Dixie Backing Helps House Pass Vote Bill: 23 Southerners Lend Support," *Baltimore Sun,* Jul 10, 1965, 1; Lawson, *Black Ballots*, 321 (Johnson quote).

23 "Registrar Asks Wait," *Anniston Star*, Aug 7, 1965, 1; "Registrars Advised to Wait," *Alabama* Journal, August 7, 1965.

24 "Boards Pledge to Proceed without Bias," *Alabama Journal*, Aug 10, 1965, 1; "5 Registrar Board Asking Purge of All Voter Rolls," *Montgomery Advertiser*, Aug 10, 1965, 3.

25 "Vote Act Challenged," *Afro-American,* Sep 25, 1965, 1; "It's Pretty Tough, Listing Illiterates," and "Federal Registrars In 4 Alabama Areas," *Anniston Star*, Aug 10, 1965, 1 (Mizell quote); "8 Counties Fight Voting Rights Act," *Afro-American,* Aug 21, 1965, 14 (Mizell quote).

26 "State Planning Suits on Protests, Vote Bill," and "Two More States Join Court Test of Voter Bill," *Selma Times-Journal*, Aug 13, 1965, 1, 12; Landsberg, *Free at Last to Vote*, n.185 227; Ashmore, *Carry It On*, 92 (Wallace quote). In fashioning his nonracial argument for an eighth-grade schooling as a needed test for military service and voting, Wallace relied on Martha Witt Smith's claim that practically all Negroes without an eighth-grade education failed to pass the "mental test." See *Congressional Record*, House of Representatives, March 17, 1965, 5306. In this instance, Smith appears to have manufactured the facts she wanted. During the draft of World War II, a detailed study included records from an enlistment station in the Deep South for three months of 1943 showing that approximately four out of five Negroes who were rejected had less than a 7th grade education. (Also, more than one-third of the whites who were rejected had less than a 7th grade education.) Of course, this data shows the educational attainment of those rejected—not how many of all Black applicants with only a 7th grade education were rejected. That was Smith's claim. It appears that 26 percent of all African Americans tested for military service in the summer of 1943 were rejected for failure to meet minimum standards on the "mental test." A Presidential Task Force in 1963 found that the military had high rejection rates, but its data provided no support for an assertion that virtually all Black applicants with less than an eighth-grade education in Alabama failed the "mental test." Slightly more

than 41 percent of all persons tested in 1962 in Alabama for military service failed the "mental test." In 1960. Alabama's median educational attainment for white adults was 10.2 years of schooling and for Black adults 6.9 years. See *The Black and White of Rejections for Military Service: A Study of Rejections of Selective Service Registrants, by Race, on Account of Educational and Mental Deficiencies*, The American Teachers Association, Montgomery, Alabama, August 1944, 6, 22; *One-Third of a Nation: A Report on Young Men Found Unqualified for Military Service*, President's Task Force on Manpower Conservation, Washington, January 1, 1964.

27 Bob Ingram, "2nd Term Campaign Opened?" *Montgomery Advertiser*, Sep 10, 1965, 1; "Message of Governor George C. Wallace to Joint Session of the Alabama Legislature at Second Special Session, September 9, 1965," *Acts of Alabama*, Special Session, 1965, 4.

28 "Message of Governor George C. Wallace . . .," *Acts of Alabama*, Second Special Session, 1965, 4–7.

29 Ibid., 7 [emphasis added].

30 Ibid., 8 [emphasis added].

31 Ibid., 8–11.

32 Ibid., 11.

33 "Mixmaster Reapportionment," *Alabama Journal*, Sep 20, 1965, 4; Act 48 and Act 49, *Acts of Alabama*, 1965, Special Session, 69, 70–71; *Sims v. Baggett*, 247 F. Supp. 96 (1965), 107; Act 410, *Acts of Alabama*, Special Session, 1965, 599. Act 221 passed in the 1961 session had made an exception for counties of 500,000 population.

34 Judith Helms, "Slim Chance of Alabama Negroes Voting Twice," *Alabama Journal*, Sep 10, 1965, 13.

35 Ibid.; "Wallace Fears Some Voters May Cast Multiple Ballots," *Montgomery Advertiser*, Sep 10, 1965, 2; "Voters' Hands Inked," *Montgomery Advertiser*, Sep 21, 1965, 2; Act 105, *Acts of Alabama*, Special Session, 1965, 142–144. The two sponsors were Senator Clayton Carson from Marshall County, with a Black voting age population of less than three percent, and Senator Bob Wilson of Walker County, with a Black voting age population below 10 percent.

36 "Voter Hearings in Camden Held 'Disappointing'," *Selma Times-Journal*, Sep 24, 1965, 1; Michael S. Lottman, "Governor Hampers Registration, Blasts Supreme Court, Congress," *Southern Courier*, Sep 18–19, 1965, 1; "Wallace Gets Injunction to Ban U.S. Voting List," *Montgomery Advertiser*, Sep 12, 1965, 1 (Wallace quote).

37 "Message of Governor George C. Wallace to Joint Session of the Alabama Legislature at Third Special Session, September 9, 1965," *Acts of Alabama*, 1965, Special Session, 199; "Wallace Ask Amendment," *Montgomery Advertiser*, Oct 1, 1965, 1.

38 "Message of Governor George C. Wallace . . . *Acts of Alabama*, Third Special Session, 200–201, 205.

39 "Judge Hare Rules Rights Act Unconstitutional," *Selma Times-Journal*, Oct 19, 1965, 1

40 Carter, *The Politics of Rage*, 267–271; Permaloff and Grafton, *Political Power in Alabama*, 228–230; "Judge Hare Rules Rights Act Unconstitutional," *Selma Times-Journal*, Oct 19, 1965, 1; "Federal Officials Sign Up 225 More," *Montgomery Advertiser*,

Oct 8, 1965, 1.

41 "Negroes Seek Federal Registrars," *Montgomery Advertiser*, Aug 17, 1965, 13; "Negroes Bypass Local Board for Vote Processing," *Selma Times-Journal*, Aug 16, 1965, 1; Watters and Cleghorn, *Climbing Jacob's Ladder*, 263; Francis X. Walter, "Activities Since Oct. 1," *Selma Inter-Religious Project Newsletter*, Dec. 6, 1965.

42 See *Southern Justice: An Indictment* (Atlanta: Southern Regional Council and American Civil Liberties Union, Oct 18, 1965) in Operation Southern Justice: Memoranda and Reports, 1965, Southern Regional Office Files, ACLU Papers; "Violence Stalks the South," *Southern Courier*, Aug 28–29, 1965; "Justice In South Held as Inadequate," *New York Times*, Oct 18, 1965, 25.

43 "The November Amendment Election," *Montgomery Advertiser*, Nov 6, 1965, 4.

44 "Alabamians Vote Next Tuesday on Space, Salaries, and Literacy," *Southern Courier*, Nov 27–28, 1965, 1.

45 *Alabama Official and Statistical Register, 1967*, 687–688, 707–709. Act 288, *Acts of Alabama*, 1965, 396–398. In Montgomery, the smallest margins of support for the Amendment were in the predominantly Black precincts. See "Apathy Marks Voting," *Montgomery Advertiser*, Dec 1, 1965, 1. Also while the NAACP-led state coordinating association for voter registration had the amendment on its agenda for discussion on October 30, apparently it undertook no campaign to rally voters one way or another during November. The NAACP scheduled a voter registration drive after the November 30—not before. See "PA Leaders to Meet Here Oct. 31," *Huntsville Mirror*, Oct 23, 1965, 6 and "Dec. 6–8 Designated Voter Emphasis Days," *Huntsville Mirror*, Nov 27, 1965, 4.

46 John Corry, "Wallace Ponders a New Strategy for Retaining His Power in Alabama," *New York Times*, Oct 31, 1965, 63; "Wallace Slates Monday Speech," *Selma Times-Journal*, Nov 28, 1965. 1; "Dallas County Annual meeting and Barbecue" [ad], *Selma Times-Journal*, Nov 28, 1965, 10; "Wallace Alerts Section to Economic Boon," *Selma Times*-Journal, Nov 30, 1965, 1 (quote). For the growing connection of the civil rights leaders with the antiwar efforts during 1965–1966, see "King, Pope on Peace Team?" *Alabama Journal*, Aug 13, 1965, 13; Garrow, *Bearing the Cross*, 429–430, 437–439; Branch, *Parting the Waters*, 611–612.

47 Ashmore, *Carry It On*, 93; "School Children Urged to Get Out the Vote," *Montgomery Advertiser*, Jan 21, 1966, 1.

48 "School Children Urged to Get Out the Vote," *Montgomery Advertiser*, Jan 21, 1966, 1; "Vote Leaflet Within Law, Says Howell," *Montgomery Advertiser*, Jan 22, 1966, 8.

49 Harold W. Stanley, *Voter Mobilization and the Politics of Race: The South and Universal Suffrage, 1952–1984* (Westport, CN: Praeger, 1987), 70.

50 Ibid., 71.

51 South Carolina v. Katzenbach, Oral Argument, January 17, 1966 at https://www.oyez.org/cases/1965/22_orig (quotes); "Supreme Court to Hear Mizell and Flowers," *Alabama Journal*, Jan 17, 1966, 1; "The South Has Its Say Before Court," *Montgomery Advertiser*, Jan 18, 1966, 1. The transcript of the argument shows Mizell referring to "illiterate citizen, Negro or otherwise" but anyone listening to the audio recording will hear Mizell say 'nigra," not "Negro." Even this pronunciation was less offensive than

the term he used on other occasions.

52 "Democrats Change Emblem," *Montgomery Advertiser*, Jan 23, 1966, 1.

53 "State Demos Strike 'White Supremacy' Motto," *Anniston Star*, Jan 23, 1966, 1.

54 "Democrats Change Emblem," *Montgomery Advertiser*, Jan 23, 1966, 1.

55 Ashmore, *Carry It On*, 93; "Federal Examiners Moving Into County," *Birmingham News*, Jan 23, 1966, 1; "Jefferson to Demand Registrar Investigation," *Montgomery Advertiser*, Jan 24, 1966, 2; "'Hometown' Registrars Still Signing Them Up," *Birmingham News*, Jan 24, 1966, 1; "Examiners' 'Registering' Denial Hit," *Birmingham Post-Herald*, Jan 25, 1966, 1.

56 Ashmore, *Carry It On*, 93.

57 Francis X. Walter, "Much of My Time Since December," *Selma Inter-Religious Project Newsletter*, Feb 1966; "Lowndes Negro Tent City Set Up," *Alabama Journal*, Jan 1, 1966, 7; Hasan Jeffries, *Bloody Lowndes: Civil Rights and Black Power in Alabama's Black Belt* (New York: New York University Press, 2009), 105–110.

58 Ashmore, *Carry It On*, 150–151, 198–199.

59 *Political Participation*, United States Commission on Civil Rights, May 1968, 43–44.

60 Jeffries, *Bloody Lowndes*, 81–102 (Carmichael quote, 102); Watters and Cleghorn, *Climbing Jacob's Ladder*, 264.

61 W. C. Patton, "The NAACP Sumer Projects-1965," (undated), Register and Vote Folder, NAACP Office Files, NAACP Papers.

Notes to Chapter 7

1 Rex Thomas, "Lurleen Entering Governor's Race," *Selma Times-Journal*, Feb 24, 1966, 1.

2 Frederick, *Stand Up for Alabama*, 166.

3 John Hayman, *Bitter Harvest: Richmond Flowers and the Civil Rights Revolution* (Montgomery: BlackBelt Press, 1996), 185.

4 Carter, *The Politics of Rage*, 276; Frederick, *Stand Up for Alabama*, 165–166.

5 Bob Ingram, "Rousing Rally Starts Wallace Drive," *Montgomery Advertiser*, Mar 19, 1966, 1; Frederick, *Stand Up for Alabama*, 177.

6 "Political Fever [photograph]," *Selma Times-Journal*, Mar 27, 1966. 8; "Candidates," *Selma Times-Journal*, Mar 28, 1966, 2; Carter, *The Politics of Rage*, 281–284.

7 Gene Roberts, "Negro Vote Tempers Racism by Alabama Foes," *New York Times*, Apr 17, 1966, 63; Carter, *The Politics of Rage*, 283; Lesher, *George Wallace*, 364.

8 Frederick, *Stand Up for Alabama*, 168.

9 Faulkenbury, *Poll Power*, 96–97; "New Voter Drive Opened in South," *New York Times*, Feb 18, 1966, 20; Ashmore, *Carry It On*, 129 (Turner quote).

10 Watters and Cleghorn, *Climbing Jacob's Ladder*, 246; Vernon E. Jordan Jr. and Marvin Walls, Voter *Registration in the South: Summer, 1966*, Voter Education Project Southern Regional Council, undated, Alabama, 1–4, in author's possession. Every politician in Alabama who could count knew the potential of these numbers because four years earlier Wallace won his runoff by fewer than 72,000 votes.

11 Rex Thomas, "Negroes Exercising New Voting Muscles," *Montgomery Advertiser*, Mar 3, 1966, 3; "Confederation of Alabama Political Organizations," Newsletter, 1966," SCLC Records.

12 Francis X. Walter, ""ONE LORD, ONE FAITH, ONE BAPTISM, ONE MAN, ONE VOTE" *Selma Inter-Religious Project Newsletter*, Mar 31, 1966.

13 *United States v. State of Alabama*, 252 F. Supp. 95 (1966), 100.

14 *South Carolina v. Katzenbach*, 383 US 301 (1966), 308.

15 "U.S. Advising State on Vote Procedures," *Alabama Journal*, Apr 26, 1966, 11; *Harper et al. v. Virginia Board of Elections* et al. 383 U.S. 663 (1966), 666.

16 Gene Roberts, "Negro Vote Tempers Racism by Alabama Foes," *New York Times*, Apr 17, 1966, 63; Frederick, *Stand Up for Alabama*, 173–177; "Folsom," *Montgomery Advertiser*, Apr 3, 1966, 2; Carl Elliott Sr. and Michael D'Orso, *The Cost of Courage: The Journey of an American Congressman* (New York: Doubleday, 1992), 276; Jack Nelson, "Flowers Wins New Backing From Negroes," *Los Angeles Times*, Apr 18, 1966, 14; "Think! Alabama! Think! Patterson Successfully Defended Your Constitutional Rights!" [ad], *The Anniston Star*, Apr 22, 1966, 9. Patterson's "Think!" ads also were on the radio.

17 Stuart X. Stephenson, "Negroes Bidding for Perry County Offices," *Montgomery Advertiser*, Apr 15, 1966, 14; Nicholas von Hoffman, "Alabama Negroes Exult In Long-Denied Vote," *Washington Post*, May 4, 1966, A-1.

18 James K. Batten, "A Black Belt Revolution," *Tallahassee Democrat*, May 1, 1966, 12D.

19 Ibid.

20 Nicholas von Hoffman, "Alabama Negroes Exult In Long-Denied Vote," *Washington Post*, May 4, 1966, A-1.

21 Ibid.

22 Author computations from data in *Alabama Official and Statistical Register, 1967*, 557–559; Gene Roberts, "Wife of Wallace Nominated for Alabama Governor; Turnout of Negro Voters Heavy," *New York Times*, May 4, 1966, 1.

23 Roy Reed, "Split Negro Vote in Alabama Eases White Fears of Whites," *New York Times*, May 5, 1966, 1; Ashmore, *Carry It On*, 181,183; Francis X. Walter, "The May 3rd Primary In Alabama," *Selma Inter-Religious Project Newsletter*, May 16, 1966; *Alabama Official and Statistical Register, 1967*, 576–587; Gene Roberts, "Negroes in Alabama Explain 'Defections'" *New York Times*, May 8, 1966, 1 (Jenkins quote).

24 "Katzenbach and Rights Leaders Laud Negro Voting in Alabama: Impact Is Weighed CORE Evaluation" *New York Times*, May 5, 1966. 30.

25 "County Dems Change Poll Method, Hopes of Negro Candidates Wane," *Alabama Journal*, Mar 2, 1966, 1; "Barbour Primary Hearing Is Scheduled for June 30," *Montgomery Advertiser*, May 27, 1966, 1.

26 "Howell See No Voting Trouble," *Alabama Journal*, Apr 28, 1966, 27.

27 Ashmore, *Carry It On*, 92; "Handbook," compiled by Martha Witt Smith, Alabama Correspondence, 1965–1971, Southern Regional Office Files, ACLU Papers. Alabama voters approved a state constitutional amendment in July 1939 allowing counties to opt to use voting machines and the legislature enacted regulations for voting

machines, including the 3-minute rule, in August 1939. See "Coffee, Clarke Fail to Line Up," *Birmingham News*, Jul 21, 1939, 1 and Act 292, *Acts of Alabama, 1939*, 543–548. The two limits on voting time were incorporated into the 1940 code of laws. See Title 17, sec. 105 and sec. 176, *Code of Alabama, 1940*. As a member of the Madison County Board of Registrars since 1949, Smith had first-hand knowledge of these rules and knew that in the past in north Alabama the time limits had not often, if ever, been applied. See "Better Be on Their Toes," *Huntsville Times*, Apr 23, 1954, 4.

28 *Political Participation*, United States Commission on Civil Rights, May 1968, 101–104.

29 "Long Lines Await Chance to Vote," *Alabama Journal*, May 3, 1966, 1; John Beecher, "Sword in the Heart of Dixie," *The Nation*, May 23, 1966, 612; "Dr. King, SCLC Join Fight on Alabama Voting Results," *The Chicago Defender*, May 7, 1966, 1.

30 "Tan Voters Underwent Hardships: Many Waited In Lines for Hours; Some Didn't Wait," *New Journal and Guide*, May 14, 1966, 9; Francis X. Walter, "The May 3rd Primary in Alabama," *Selma Inter-Religious Project Newsletter*, May 16, 1966.

31 Beecher, "Sword in the Heart of Dixie," 612–613; "Dr. King Hurls Fraud Charges in Wake of Alabama Election." *Philadelphia Tribune*, May 10, 1966, 1; Nicholas Von Hoffman, "Alabama Black Belt: 'The Marchin' Niggers Fought Me All the Way . . .,'" *Washington Post*; May 8, 1966, A-1; *Political Participation*, United States Commission on Civil Rights, May, 1968, 67–72, 87–89; statements and complaints in Alabama, 1966 file, Southern Regional Office Files, ACLU Papers.

32 *Political Participation*, United States Commission on Civil Rights, 96–97; Nicholas Von Hoffman, "Alabama Black Belt: 'The Marchin' Niggers Fought Me All the Way . . .," *Washington Post*; May 8, 1966, A-1; John Beecher, "Sword in the Heart of Dixie," 612–613.

33 Jack Nelson, "U.S. Examiners Unable to Watch All Balloting," *Los Angeles Times*, May 8, 1966, 4; "3 Counties Due Watch at Election," *Anniston Star*, May 28, 1966, 2; "Negroes Say Illegal White Ballots Cast," *Alabama Journal*, May 28, 1966, 9; " *Political Participation*, United States Commission on Civil Rights, 76–78; "U.S. Protects Dallas Ballots," *Alabama Journal*, May 6, 1966, 1.

34 Jack Nelson, "Smiling, Unafraid in Sunday Finest, They Came to Vote," *Los Angeles Times*, May 4, 1966, 1.

35 Nicholas Von Hoffman, "Alabama Black Belt: 'The Marchin' Niggers Fought Me All the Way . . .," *Washington Post*; May 8, 1966, A-1.

36 "Voting Machine Proposal Meets with Approval," *Selma Times-Journal*, May 15, 1966, 1. Due to the dispute over the voting in the Sheriff Jim Clark election, Selma's city government was considering a change from paper ballots to voting machines within the city limits.

37 Author computations from voting returns of May 3rd primary. Election returns are found in *Alabama Official and Statistical Register, 1967*, 557–559 (governor's race) and 570–587 (legislative races); *Montgomery Advertiser*, May 6, 1966, 24–25 (county returns) and *Selma Inter-Religious Project Newsletter*, May 16, 1966 (Greene County returns).

38 In most elections the top of the ballot with statewide races usually gets more votes

than the bottom of the ballot where local races are listed, but this election was special and different. In 1966, in the Black Belt, most Black voters marked their ballots according to sample ballots that listed all the competitive races. In the era before ever-present political adverting and electronic media, local Black and white candidates were far more visible and engaged voters far more often than statewide candidates, none of whom were African American in 1966. In Addition, most white voters in the Black Belt feared the election of local Black candidates as much and probably more than the loss of their candidate for governor. Under these unique circumstances, lower voting at the bottom of the ticket cannot be attributed primarily to the customary reasons.

39 See coverage of election in Gene Roberts, "Negroes in Alabama Explain 'Defections'" *New York Times,* May 8, 1966,1; Ray Jenkins, "Alabama Vote Poses Paradox: Attitude Changed Pattern Traced," *Christian Science Monitor,* May 6, 1966, 3; "Sheriff Wins with Negro Help," *Alabama Journal,* May 5, 1966, 37; Nicholas Von Hoffman, "Alabama Black Belt: 'The Marchin' Niggers Fought Me All the Way . . .," *Washington Post*; May 8, 1966, A-1; "Katzenbach and Rights Leaders Laud Negro Voting in Alabama: Impact Is Weighed CORE Evaluation," *New York Times,* May 5, 1966, 30 (Katzenbach quote).

40 Jack Nelson, "Smiling, Unafraid in Sunday Finest, They Came to Vote," *Los Angeles Times,* May 4, 1966, 1.

41 "Dismissal of Voting Rights Suit Denied," *Selma Times-Journal,* May 17, 1966, 1 (Mizell quote on statehood); "Vote Case," *Montgomery Advertiser,* May 18, 1966, 2; "Contest," *Selma Times-Journal,* May 18, 1966, 2; "Suit," *Selma Times-Journal,* May 19, 1966, 2; Gene Roberts, "U.S. Role Upheld in Selma Voting," *New York Times,* May 18, 1966, 24 (Mizell quote).

42 "Judge Delays Ruling in Dallas Vote Case," *Montgomery Advertiser,* May 19, 1966, 1.

43 "Court Ban Asked on Poll Watchers," *Montgomery Advertiser,* May 27, 1966, 1.

44 *United States v. Executive Committee of Democratic Party of Dallas Co., Ala.*, 254 F. Supp. 537 (1966), 541; *United States v. Executive Committee of Democratic Party of Greene Dallas Co., Ala.*, 254 F. Supp. 543 (1966), 547.

45 "Negroes Say Illegal White Ballots Cast," *Alabama Journal,* May 28, 1966, 9; NAACP Wins Indefinite Delay of Greene County Elections," *Afro-American,* Nov 5, 1966, 13.

46 "4 Negroes Victors In Alabama Runoff," *Atlanta Constitution,* Jun 1, 1966, 1; Jack Nelson, "Four Negroes Win Nomination in Ala.," *Los Angeles Times,* Jun 1, 1966, 1; *Alabama Official and Statistical Register, 1967,* 574, 583, 607, 617.

47 "For Immediate Release," June 2, 1966, Records of the Public Relations Department, May-June 1966, SCLC Records.

48 "CORE Anti-Viet Nam Resolution Fails at White House," B*oston Globe,* Jun 3, 1966, 25.

49 "III-B" edits in 'freedom elections" draft and handwritten notes on "Perry," in Alabama files, Jan 01, 1966-Jan 31, 1966, Student Nonviolent Coordinating Committee press releases, SNCC Papers. The Lowndes Freedom Party had a black panther as its emblem, but the Wilcox convention chose a black bulldog as its symbol. Greene County's Black leaders resolved SNCC-SCLC differences by having Democratic Black

candidates also become the nominees of their county's freedom party convention.

50 *Political Participation,* United States Commission on Civil Rights, 225–227; *Reynolds v. Sims*, 377 US 533 (1964); *Alabama Official and Statistical Register, 1967*, 579–581.

51 *Political Participation,* United States Commission on Civil Rights, 225–227; *Alabama Official and Statistical Register, 1967*, 585–596; John Beecher, "Sword in the Heart of Dixie," 613.

52 Fred Gray and the NAACP LDF did successfully challenge the last–minute decision of the Barbour County Democratic Executive Committee's change from electing members by precinct to the county at large. Judge Frank Johnson found that, although the Committee kept no minutes and had no discussion before adopting the change, the clear effect was "to turn Negro majorities into minorities in certain political areas, thus, as a practical matter, eliminating the possibility of a Negro candidate winning a place on the Executive Committee." Given the facts and the County's history of opposition to Black registration, Johnson found that "an inference of discriminatory intent compelling." *Smith v. Paris*, 257 F. Supp. 901 (1966). It was the first reported "racial vote dilution case brought in the modem era" in the courts. See Pamela S. Karlan, "The Alabama Foundations of the Law of Democracy," *Alabama Law Review*, 67, no. 2 (2015), 428.

53 *Reynolds v. Sims*, 377 US 533 (1964), 577; *Fortson v. Dorsey*, 379 US 433 (1965), 438–439. When Frank Mizell spoke openly in 1962 at the state Democratic Executive Committee about the need for numbered posts to cancel Black voters' choice of a candidates in Committee elections, he also referred to the recent state law providing for numbered posts in state and local government elections. He said, "it has occurred to a great many people, including the legislature of Alabama, that there should be numbered places." But that statement alone was hardly a "smoking gun" for the legislature's intent in 1966 since Mizell was not a sponsor of the bill or an elected legislator. The methods and case law for finding discriminatory intent also matured over time. Twenty years later, Mizell's statements helped historians build the case that dismantled most at-large local election in Alabama. See Peyton McCrary and J. Gerald Herbert, "Keeping the Courts Honest: The Role of Historians as Expert Witnesses in Southern Voting Rights Cases," *Southern University Law Review*, 16, no. 1 (1989), 120–121.

54 Civil rights attorneys considered ways of proving discriminatory intent in the 1965 litigation of *Sims v. Baggett* (247 F. Supp. 96, 1965) and filed suit even before the 1970 Census was released to created single member districts in Jefferson, Mobile, and Montgomery counties, but the federal court demurred in *Nixon v. Brewer* (49 F.R.D. 122. 1970) and took up the question in a later case, *Sims v. Amos* (336 F. Supp. 924, 1972). See "Brief on Motion for Preliminary Injunction," in Nixon v. Brewer (No. 3017-N, Briefs and Other Court Documents, 1969–1970, and handwritten letter to Chuck Morgan from Morris Dees, undated, in Sims v. Baggett: Miscellaneous file, 1971, Southern Regional Office Files, ACLU Papers.

55 "Memorandum of the United States as Amicus Curiae" in Sims v. Baggett Pleadings file, 1965, Southern Regional Office Files, ACLU Papers. As if hedging on the issue was not enough, the Department memorandum dropped a footnote stating, "We might feel differently if we had the close knowledge of the three counties."

56 Section 11 (b) of the Voting Right Act of 1965 provided: "No person, whether acting

under color of law or otherwise, shall intimidate, threaten, or coerce, or attempt to intimidate, threaten, or coerce any person for voting or attempting to vote, or intimidate, threaten, or coerce, or attempt to intimidate, threaten, or coerce any person for urging or aiding any person to vote or attempt to vote.." Today it is found in the United States Code at 52 USC §10307(b).

57 *Moses v. Kennedy*, 219 F. Supp. 762 (1963).

58 *United States v. Harvey*, 250 F. Supp. 219 (1966), 237.

59 "U.S. Court Suit Charges Intimidation in Lowndes," *Montgomery Advertiser,* Jan 18, 1966, 2; "Judge Refuses Injunction Against Lowndes Evictions," *Montgomery Advertiser,* Jun 16, 1966, 1.

60 "Judge Refuses Injunction Against Lowndes Evictions," *Montgomery Advertiser,* Jun 16, 1966, 1. *Miles v. Dixon* is an unreported case, which often meant Judge Johnson made a decision or order without an extended analysis of facts and law in the opinion. The *Advertiser* quotes Johnson's order as stating the plaintiffs' attorneys presented no evidence of intimidation. Johnson also charged the plaintiffs' attorneys with court costs in the case because most plaintiffs denied they had authorized such a lawsuit and no evidence was presented that they had been pressured to say so. The complaint filed in the case made specific factual allegations that specific persons were evicted because they registered to vote, but the attorneys were unable prove motive. See "Complaint," Miles v. Dixon, files on court cases, Jan 01, 1965–Dec 31, 1966, SNCC Papers. See Jeffries, *Bloody Lowndes,* 109–110 and Francis X. Walter, "Much of My Time Since December," *Selma Inter-Religious Project Newsletter*, Feb 1966. See Walter's newsletter for examples of the eviction letters that capture the evasive language and some of the "Southern way of life" in the Black Belt's racial hierarchy.

61 Gavin Wright, *Old South, New South: Revolutions in the Southern Economy Since the Civil War* (New York: Basic Books, 1986), 244–245; "Market Flooded by Beef Imports Says Speaker," *Selma Times-Journal,* Feb 2, 1964, 20; "Everyone Shares Value of State's Pulp Mills," *Selma Times-Journal,* Apr 26, 1966, 4.

62 "Economics, Not Politics Cited as Eviction Cause," *Montgomery Advertiser*. Jan 2, 1966, 39.

63 *McGill v. Ryals*, 253 F. Supp. 374 (1966), 374–375.

64 Ibid., 376.

65 Francis X. Walter, "Mr. Albert Turner's Letter," *Selma Inter-Religious Project Newsletter*, July 22, 1966; Susan Youngblood Ashmore, *Carry It On,* 198–200.

66 Transcript, White House Conference on Civil Rights, Committee NO. XI, Washington, DC, Afternoon session, June 2, 1966, in White House Conference on Civil Rights, Apr 01, 1966–May 31, 1966, SCLC Papers. The transcript shows Turner's pronouncing the Governor's name as "Wa-lace" but Turner used the expression "Wall-ass" in later years, including in conversations with the author. "He has called us enough dirty words to earn it," Turner once explained.

67 Transcript, White House Conference on Civil Rights, June 2, 1966, SCLC Papers.

NOTES TO CHAPTER 8

1 *United States v. State of Alabama*, 252 F. Supp. 95 (1966).

2 Section 10 of the Voting Rights Act of 1965. The Justice Department and the White House supported this section as an alternative to a proposal to outlaw the poll tax in the language of the Act. The Department was uncertain Congress had such powers to ban the poll tax in state as well as federal elections and the Johnson White House thought an outright ban would lose Republican votes for the Act. See Garrow, *Protest at Selma*, 123–126, n56–57 282–283. The four remaining poll tax states were Alabama, Mississippi, Texas, and Virginia. The first lawsuit was filed against Mississippi the day after President Johnson signed the Act and against Alabama and the other two states three days later on August 10.

3 "Summary of Plaintiffs Case," and "Summaries of Depositions Taken at the Instance of the Plaintiff, Volume I and Volume III," Civil Action No. 2255-N, United States v. State of Alabama, Civil Rights Litigation Clearinghouse.

4 "Summary of the Deposition of Albert Turner" in "Summaries of Depositions Taken at the Instance of the Plaintiff, Volume III," United States v. State of Alabama, Civil Rights Litigation Clearinghouse; *Turner v. Spencer*, 261 F. Supp. 542 (1966).

5 Ibid.

6 "Plaintiff's Trial Brief," Civil Action No. 2255-N, United States v. State of Alabama, Civil Rights Litigation Clearinghouse.

7 *United States v. State of Alabama*, 252 F. Supp. 95 (1966), 99–104.

8 Ibid.

9 Ibid.

10 Virginia Foster Durr and Hollinger F. Barnard, ed., *Outside the Magic Circle: The Autobiography of Virginia Foster Durr* (Tuscaloosa: University of Alabama Press, 1985), 304–307; Bass, *Unlikely Heroes*, 69–74. For more on the diverse role Rives played as a lawyer and politico in Montgomery, see "Gantt Sentenced on Rights Count," *Alabama Journal*, Nov 5, 1949, 1 and "Montgomery Hospital Vote Slated Jan 31," *Montgomery Advertiser*, Dec 20, 1949, 1.

11 "Sledge-Gewin," *Greensboro Watchman*, Dec 10, 1936, 5; "Meeting of the Hale County Historical Society," *Greensboro Watchman*, Jun 2, 1938, 4; "Walter Pettus Gewin," *Alabama Official and Statistical Register, 1939*, 262–264, 288; "McGowin," *Birmingham News*, Feb 24, 1939, 1; "Solons Help in Good Government Fight," *Birmingham News*, Feb 20, 1939, 7; "House Defeats One of Dixon's Pet Measures," *Huntsville Times*, Jul 28, 1939, 1; "Bar Association Held Wednesday," *Union-Banner* (Clanton), Jun 22, 1939, 1.

12 "Gewin Announces for State Committee," *Greensboro Watchman*, Feb 26, 1942, 1; "Chauncey Sparks Leads in Hale by Four to One," *Greensboro Watchman*, May 14, 1942, 1. The State Democratic Executive Committee endorsed the Boswell Amendment on January 12, 1946. See "To the Voters of Alabama From State Democratic Executive Committee" [ad], *Our Southern Home* (Livingston), Sep 26, 1946, 1.

13 Fred Taylor, "Judgeship Scramble," *Birmingham News*, Nov 14, 1950, 10; "Soil Conservation," *Greensboro Watchman*, Sep 19, 1946, 5; "Mrs. Burke Hostess," *Greensboro*

Watchman, Oct 16, 1941, 5; "Walter P. Gewin to Make Home in Tuscaloosa," *Greensboro Watchman*, Thu, Sep 6, 1951, 1; Hamilton, *The Bench and the Ballot*, 104–106, 239–240; Bass, *Unlikely Heroes*, 158–159.

14 "It's Now Judge Gewin," *Greensboro Watchman*, Oct 26, 1961, 4.

15 Suitts, *Hugo Black of Alabama*, 15.

16 Anne Emanuel, *Elbert Parr Tuttle: Chief Jurist of the Civil Rights Revolution* (Athens: University of Georgia Press, 2011), 260–261.

17 In 1964, for example, Gewin joined a three-judge opinion holding the public accommodations section of the 1964 Civil Rights Act unconstitutional. The per curium opinion declared, "If Congress has the naked power to do what it has attempted in title II of this act, there is no facet of human behavior which it may not control . . . and rights of the individual to liberty and property are in dire peril." *McClung v. Katzenbach*, 233 F. Supp. 815 (1964), 825. The opinion was overturned by the U.S. Supreme Court in *Katzenbach v. McClung*, 379 US 294 (1964). Also, in *United States v. Jefferson County Board of Education*, 380 F.2d 385 (1967), 406–409, Gewin objected to the courts ordering "compulsory integration." Compare his opinions with the arguments of Southern segregationists who developed the school plans to overturn *Brown v. Board of Education*. See Steve Suitts, *Overturning Brown*, 20–23. Jack Bass suggests that 1968 marked a "turning point" in Gewin's circuit court opinion upholding Judge Frank Johnson's dissent and finding that an amusement park was covered by the 1964 Civil Rights Act. See Bass, *Unlikely Heroes*, 159–160. The case was *Miller v. Amusement Enterprises, Inc.*, 394 F. 2d 342 (1968).

18 Sikora, *The Judge*, 78; Jack Bass, *Taming the Storm: The Life and Times of Judge Frank M. Johnson, J., and the South's Fight Over Civil Rights* (New York: Doubleday, 1993), 8,18; Clayton J. Butler, *True Blue: White Unionists in the Deep South During the Civil War and Reconstruction* (Baton Rouge: Louisiana State University Press, 2022), 12–14; Donald D. Dodd and Wynelle S. Dodd, *Winston: An Antebellum and Civil War History of a Hill County of North Alabama* (Birmingham: Oxford Press, 1972), 75–100; Webb, *Two-Party Politics*, 111–112, 147–148; McMillan, *Constitutional Development in Alabama*, 223–224.

19 Calculated by author from data in Horace Mann Bond, *Negro Education in Alabama: A Study of Cotton and Steel* (New York: Atheneum, 1969), 238.

20 "Under the New Constitution . . .," *New Decatur Advertiser*, Nov 1, 1901, 2.

21 "Sex, General Nativity, and Color," *Census of Population, 1900*, 529; Dodd and Dodd, *Winston*, 17–19; Moore, *History of Alabama*, 690.

22 *Official Proceedings of the Constitutional Convention of the State of Alabama*, vol. 3, 3333.

23 Bunche, *The Political Status of the Negro*, 282–283.

24 Calculations by the author based on data from "Sex, General Nativity, and Color," *Census of Population, 1900*, 529, and information in *Official Proceedings of the Constitutional Convention of the State of Alabama*, vol. 1, 101–103, and vol. 4, 5071–5073. Also see McMillan, *Constitutional Development in Alabama, 267.* The committee on representation was also stacked with Black Belt and Big Mule delegates, as noted by McMillan, *Constitutional Development in Alabama*, 306–307. The Black Belt leaders

had attempted in earlier years to hold a constitutional convention, but only if they controlled a majority of delegates. They did so in the 1901 convention. See Kousser, *The Shaping of Southern Politics, 132–133, 168–169.* Sheldon Hackney identified the "bosses," the early signs of the Black Belt and Big Mule alliance and the "planters," largely other delegates from the majority Black counties. See Hackney, *Populism to Progressivism*, 210–213.

25 Frank B. Williams, "The Poll Tax as a Suffrage Requirement in the South," *Journal of Southern History*, Vol. 18, No. 4 (Nov. 1952), 490–493; *Official Proceedings of the Constitutional Convention of the State of Alabama,* vol. 1, 346, 1257–1266; McMillan, *Constitutional Development in Alabama*, 280–282.

26 *Official Proceedings of the Constitutional Convention of the State of Alabama,* vol. 1I, 2808–2811. Sheldon Hackney's vote tallies at the convention documents that most "agrarians" or insurgents were supportive of compromises on the poll tax, they unanimously favored lowering the age for poll tax exemptions and, unlike the other delegates, overwhelmingly oppose the suffrage section that included the poll tax, as well as the education and property qualification for voting. See Hackney, *Populism to Progressivism,* 357–358.

27 *Official Proceedings of the Constitutional Convention of the State of Alabama,* vol. III, 3331–3333, 3356–3431.

28 *United States v. McLeod*, 229 F. Supp. 383 (1964); "Saluting Senior Selmians," *Selma Times-Journal*, May 10, 1959, 1; "Judge Reese Dies During Night Here, "*Selma Times-Journal*, Jun 26, 1969, 1; "Edward T. Graham," *Montgomery Advertiser*, Jun 20, 1911, 1; "Haleyville Got Its Name As Result of Bargain for Suit of Clothes," *Birmingham News*, Jan 11, 1925, 56; Frank Sikora, *The Judge*, 61; "Post Offices and Postmasters of Winston County," accessed at https://www.freestateofwinston.org/postoffices.htm.

29 "To Pick Registrars," *Montgomery Advertiser*, Dec 4, 1901, 5; "State Registrars," *Montgomery Advertiser*. Dec 11, 1901, 9; "Hewitt, Lewis, and Bondurant," *Birmingham News,* Dec 12, 1901, 2; "Montgomery Registrars," *Montgomery Advertiser*, Dec 18, 1901, 6; "Registrars for Walker Appointed," *Daily Mountain Eagle*, Dec 18, 1901, 1.

30 "Coosa's Vote Cut Down," *Gadsden Times-News*, Feb 21, 1902, 1; "Republicans to Speak," *Montgomery Advertiser*, Oct 17, 1902, 5; "Poll Tax," *Anniston Star*, Mar 12, 1902, 1; "White Voters Pay Poll Tax," *Weekly Advertiser*, Feb 7, 1902, 8; "Sumter Eliminates Negro," *Gadsden Times-News*, Feb 11, 1902, 1.

31 "White Voters Pay Poll Tax," *Weekly Advertiser*, Feb 7, 1902, 8; "Gov. Johnston's Poll Tax," *Marion Times-Standard*, Aug 7, 1902, 1.

32 "Alabama Happenings," *Birmingham News*, Feb 5, 1902, 4; "Those White Men . . ." *Birmingham News*, Feb 24, 1902, 4; "No Cause for Fear," *Birmingham News,* Sep 6, 1902, 10; "Voting Strength of Dallas," *Birmingham News*, Feb 3, 1902, 12; "Thirteen Hundred Negroes Disfranchise Themselves," *Birmingham News,* Feb 12, 1902, 7.

33 "From the Alabamian," *New Decatur Advertiser*, Mar 14, 1902, 6; "Editor- Alabamian," *Alabamian,* Mar 7, 1902, 1. See "The Passing of Fonville," *Pine Belt News* (Brewton), Sep 27, 1906, 4 for political background of J. C. Fonville.

34 "66,000 Disfranchised," *Alabamian,* Mar 14, 1902, 4; "The Poll Tax Return . . .," *Alabamian,* Apr 18, 1902, 1; "The Ratification Papers . . .," *Alabamian,* Mar 28, 1902, 4.

35 Hackney, *Populism to Progressivism*, 207–208.

36 "No Cause for Fear," *Birmingham News*, Sep 6, 1902, 10. Author calculations based on election returns found in *Alabama Official and Statistical Register*, 1903, 141, 218–219, and in "Results of Democratic Primary as Declared by State Committee," *Montgomery Advertiser*, Sep 4, 1902, 5. It is possible, but unlikely, that poor whites were disqualified from voting by failing to meet the new constitutional qualifications to vote—instead of their failing to pay a poll tax; however, the poll tax payments were required in 1902 before registrars began accepting and reviewing applications. Poor whites who lacked necessary education or property qualifications to vote were also the most likely to fail to pay a poll tax. So, the tax, more than the voter qualification, was the more likely cause for the declines. In addition, it appears from newspaper reports in 1902 that registrars did not exclude very many white voters, and the Republican and independent newspapers identified the poll tax, not the registrars' review of qualifications to vote, as the main culprit for excluding poor whites and insurgents.

37 Kousser, *The Shaping of Southern Politics*, 76–77; Hackney, *Populism to Progressivism*, 232–234. In 1902, the Democratic party also restricted voting in its August primary to only those voters who had cast a Democratic ballot in the last two elections. The restriction certainly aided Jelks in the primary.

38 "Giles Loses Two Suits," *Montgomery Advertiser*, Oct 14, 1902, 3; Louis R. Harlan, *Booker T. Washington: The Wizard of Tuskegee, 1901–1915* (New York: Oxford University Press, 1983), 244–247; *Giles v. Teasley*, 136 Ala. 164 (1902), *Giles v. Teasley*, 136 Ala. 228 (1902), *Giles v. Harris*, 189 US 475 (1903), *Giles v. Teasley*, 193 US 146 (1904); "The Giles Case," *Birmingham News*, Apr 28, 1903, 4.

39 *Giles v. Harris*, 189 US 475 (1903), 487–488.

40 Orville Vernon Burton and Armand Derfner, *Justice Deferred: Race and the Supreme Court* (Cambridge, MA: Belknap Press, 2021), 102; *Gomillion v. Lightfoot*, 364 U.S. 339 (1960); The Supreme Court did strike down the "grandfather clause" in state constitutions as well as explicit laws banning Black voters from participation. See *Guinn v. United States*, 238 US 347 (1915), *Nixon v. Herndon*, 273 US 536 (1927), and *Lane v. Wilson*, 307 US 268 (1939). But, when the Court was asked to protect constitutional rights that would involve supervising the conduct of state officials in assuring those rights, as in the 1946 case of *Colegrove v. Green*, the Court decided the "issue to be of a peculiarly political nature" barring "judicial determination." (328 US 549, 552). Joined by Justice William O. Douglas, Justice Hugo Black's dissent in *Colegrove* argued, "What is involved here is the right to vote . . . It has always been the rule that where a federally protected right has been invaded the federal courts will provide the remedy to rectify the wrong done." After *Gomillion*, the Court moved to do just that in a range of cases involving the right to vote, beginning with reapportionment, without again hiding behind the "political question." For the Court's discussion in conference along these lines, see Bernard Schwartz, *Super Chief: Earl Warren and His Supreme Court—A Judicial Biography* (New York: New York University Press, 1983), 377–378, 416.

41 "The Poll Tax Feature . . ." *Montgomery Advertiser*, Sep 2, 1903, 2; *Acts of Alabama*, 1903, 42–43, 394–395; "Pay Your Poll Tax," *Roanoke Leader*, Nov 4, 1903, 2.

42 "Vagrancy Law," *Birmingham News*, Sep 2, 1903, 1; Act 229, *Acts of Alabama*, 1903,

244–245; section 5628, Chapter 199, *Code of Alabama, 1897,* vol. 2, 508; section 4218, Chapter 5, *Code of Alabama, 1876,* 899. A second offense of vagrancy, if it occurred within six month of the first, could involve a fine of up to $100 and up to six months in jail or hard labor. A $500 fine in 1903 would be the equivalent in value in 2020 to a fine of $15,000 in real wages or $37,500 in purchasing power.

43 "A Terse Truth," *Birmingham News,* Dec 12, 1903, 4; "Idlers Must Move On," *Marion Times-Standard,* Oct 1, 1903, 1; "A Good Law," *Birmingham News,* Sep 19, 1903, 4.

44 Mayfield, *Constitutions of 1875 and 1901,* 225. The 1901 Constitution allowed for voting rights to be restored if a convict was granted a pardon (see Section 124); however, the Alabama attorney general in 1914 issued an opinion stating that a person who had his political rights restored would have to pay a poll tax that included $1.50 for each year he was in prison and disfranchised. See *1912 Alabama Attorney General Reports and Opinions* 47 (1912–1914), 222.

45 "Judge Osceola Kyle Announces His Platform," *Decatur Weekly News,* Jul 28, 1906, 4; "The Need of a Compulsory Poll Tax Law," *Lamar Democrat,* Oct 31, 1906, 1; "Work for the Legislature," *Evergreen Courant,* Jul 25, 1906, 4; "Non-Voters in Alabama," *Birmingham Age-Herald,* Jun 8, 1906, 4; "Poll Tax Disfranchisement," *Birmingham Age-Herald,* Sep 5, 1906, 4; "Wholesale Disfranchisement," *Birmingham Age-Herald,* Oct 8, 1906, 4; "Alabama's Light Vote," *Birmingham Age-Herald,* Sep 6, 1906, 4.

46 "Bowie Discusses Poll Tax Matter," *Birmingham Age-Herald,* Sep 16, 1906, 15.

47 "Poll-Tax Disfranchisement," *Fort Payne Journal,* Sep 5, 1906, 10; "Alabama's Light Vote," *Daily Mountain Eagle* (Jasper), Sep 12, 1906, 7; "Congressman Bowie on Poll Tax," *Progressive Age* (Scottsboro), Sep 20, 1906, 1; "Bowie on Poll Tax," *Marion Times-Standard,* Sep 27, 1906, 4; "Hon. J. S. Bowie . . ." *Montgomery Advertiser,* Sep 25, 1906, 4; "Poll Tax Disfranchisement," *Montgomery Advertiser,* Sep 28, 1906, 4; "Poll Tax Disfranchisement," *Prattville Progress,* Oct 12, 1906, 6.

48 Jefferson Cowrie, *Freedom's Dominion: A Saga of White Resistance to Federal Power* (New York: Basic Books, 2022), 178–181, 200-201, 208; "Message of B. B. Comer," *Acts of Alabama,* 1907, 60–63.

49 "To the Voters of Franklin County," *Franklin County Times,* Oct 18, 1906, 3; "Mr. Brown's Platform," *Franklin County Times,* Nov 1, 1906, 3. Brown lost to the Democrat, Benjamin Harris Smith.

50 *Alabama Official and Statistical Register, 1907,* 91; "The Man on the Corner," *Banner* (Clanton), Aug 7, 1902, 1; "The Confederate Veterans met here . . ." *Citizen-Examiner* (Hayneville), May 7, 1903, 2; "Thornsby Democratic Club," *Banner,* Feb 4, 1904, 4; "A New Law Firm . . ." *Banner,* Jun 18, 1903, 1; "Clanton Municipal Election," *Banner,* Jan 14, 1904, 1; "J. Osmond Middleton Has Been Appointed . . ." *Banner,* Jan 21, 1904, 5.

51 "Republican-Populist Primary," *Banner,* Aug 9, 1906, 4; "We notice an interesting article in the Birmingham Republican . . ." *Banner,* Oct 1, 1908, 4; *Alabama Official and Statistical Register, 1907,* 258; "National Committeeman Charles H. Scott . . ." *Birmingham Times,* Sep 6, 1907, 5. It is not clear why Middleton switched parties. After his marriage in 1910, his father-in-law was an erstwhile Populist who earlier served as an elected county official, but there is no public record available about the reasons for switch in 1906. See letter to the editor about father-in-law J. W. Littlejohn

in *Banner*, Mar 8, 1900, 1.

52 Paul McWhorter Pruitt Jr., "Joseph C. Manning, Alabama Populist: A Rebel Against the Solid South," PhD diss. (College of William and Mary, 1980), 32–266; "Liberty or Death: The Struggle in Alabama Has Begun," *People Party Advocate* (Clay County), Feb 9, 1894, 4.

53 Pruitt, "Joseph C. Manning, Alabama Populist," 360–371. See also Joseph C. Manning, *Rise and Reign of the Bourbon Oligarchy* (Birmingham: Roberts and Sons, 1904) and Joseph C. Manning, "The Federal Sovereignty Right of The United States Citizen," *The Voice of the Negro*, vol. 3, (Jan 1906), 132–134.

54 "Joe Manning," *Montgomery Advertiser*, May 10, 1907, 4 (reprinting *Boston Post*'s dispatch). This dispatch is confirmed in general terms and themes in A. Remington, "Boston Letter," *Zion's Herald*, vol. 85, no. 20 (May 15, 1907), 621.

55 "Mr. Middleton's Denial," *Banner*, May 23, 1907, 4 (quoting the *Boston Advertiser* and Clayton's Republican newspaper, *Union*).

56 "Negro Union Formed," *Baltimore Sun*, May 10, 1907, 14. About 60 years later, writer James Baldwin attempted to educate white Americans with a similar insight. See James Baldwin and François Bondy, "The Negro Problem," *Transition*, 1997, no. 75/76, 82–86.

57 "Two Young Alabamians . . ." *Banner*, May 16, 1907, 4; "Exchange Shots," *Roanoke Leader*, May 29, 1907, 2.

58 A. Remington, "Boston Letter," *Zion's Herald*, vol. 85, no. 20 (May 15, 1907), 621; Pruitt, "Joseph C. Manning, Alabama Populist," 386, 414–418.

59 "Joe Manning," *Montgomery Advertiser*, May 10, 1907, 4; "Two Young Alabamians . . ." *Banner*, May 16, 1907, 4; letter to editor from Howard Roper, *Banner*, Aug 1, 1907, 4; "Stump's Hill," *Banner*, May 23, 1907, 8.

60 "Hon. J. O. Middleton vs. Advertiser," *Birmingham Times*, Jun 7, 1907, 4; "The Southern American . . ." *Birmingham Times*, Aug 30, 1907, 4; "Mr. Middleton's Denial," *Banner*, May 23, 1907, 4.

61 "Hon. J. O. Middleton vs. Advertiser," *Birmingham Times*, Jun 7, 1907, 4; *Alabama Official and Statistical Register, 1909*, 269.

62 "Well Known Republican Here," *Birmingham Age-Herald*, Mar 27, 1908, 4; "Rep. Middleton, Republican, Is after Someone's Scalp," *Montgomery Times*, Aug 13, 1909, 8 (reprinting article from *Memphis Commercial*). The "revenue only" reference harkened Manning's oft-stated complaint about other Republicans who pursued federal patronage not democratic principles. For example, Manning wrote to other Republicans: "Rise up above this petty delegate getting, patronage manipulating, state chairman squabbling, until this small politics shall become lost in the great and the supreme issue. Stop this 'lily-white' nonsense . . . Recognise [sic] this vital force of the immovable truth . . . You can't have one law for the white man and another for the Negro in our form of government." See Ray Standard Baker, *Following the Color Line: An Account of Negro Citizenship in the American Democracy* (New York: Doubleday, Page, and Company, 1908), 264.

63 "The Fourth District Republican Convention . . ." *Union-Banner*, Aug 11, 1910, 4; "Judge Middleton's Retirement," *Alabama Journal*, Feb 27, 1956, 4; "Judge J.

Osmond Middleton," *Alabama Journal*, Jun 15, 1961, 4; Pruitt, "Joseph C. Manning, Alabama Populist," 386, 400–401. Middleton remained an active speaker for the Republicans, especially in Chilton County, ("Schedule of Republican Speaking," *Union-Banner*, Oct 22, 1942, 1) but said he had no time or money to be a Republican candidate ("Explanation from J. O. Middleton," *Union-Ba*nner, Jan 25, 1940, 1). His views on race and racism appear to have altered over time. In 1929, as Assistant U.S Attorney, he went out of his way to try to find aid for a penniless Black family who had been victims of illegal peonage. See Reba Ann Page, "'Wringing Their Bread from the Sweat of Other Men's Faces'—The Persistent Use of Forced Labor in the Postbellum South," PhD diss. (University of Nevada, Reno, 2017), 205–206. But, in 1936, he apparently spoke publicly about the "negro problem" arising at the Democratic National Convention ("Republican Rally Saturday Was Above All Fond Expectations," *Union-Banner*, Jul 2, 1936, 1) when President Franklin Roosevelt's political chief, James Farley, arranged for an African American minister to start the convention with an invocation of prayer for the first time in its history ("Carolina Group Walks Out Over Negro Question," *Montgomery Advertiser*, Jun 25, 1936; "Byrnes Asked to Fight for South," *Greenville News*, Jun 25, 1936, 1). Middleton also supported publicly Democratic Governor John Patterson when he ran as a strong segregationist in 1956, although Middleton's support could have been, in part, for personal reasons ("The Democratic Committee of Chilton County . . ." *Union-Banner*, Jul 30, 1959, 1).

64 James Benson Sellers, *The Prohibition Movement in Alabama, 1702 to 1943* (Chapel Hill: University of North Carolina Press, 1943), 149–156; "Hot Times Ahead for Birmingham," *Birmingham News*, Apr 19, 1910, 16; "Mobilian for Selma's Son," *Selma Times-Journal*, Mar 23, 1910, 3; "Col Murphee for Mallory," *Florence Herald*, Apr 7, 1910, 1 (quote). Mallory was also a former chairman of the state Democratic Executive Committee.

65 "Emmet O'Neal and Senator Johnston Speak to Large Crowd at Greenville," *Montgomery Advertiser*, Nov 1, 1910, 7. Also, see "Should J. O. Thompson Win, Booker T. Would Rule, Says Stallings," *Birmingham News*, Nov 2, 1910, 12. The state Republican platform called for changing the poll tax's cumulative feature. See *Alabama Official and Statistical Register, 1911*, 328. The platform was also circulated during the campaign by Republican newspapers ("Platform Adopted by the Progressive Republicans Alabama," *Birmingham Times*, Nov 4, 1910, 5).

66 Suitts, *Hugo Black of Alabama*, 116–121; the Prohibition referendum in 1909 lost by a wide margin (72,272 to 49,093), but the Prohibitionists were not defeated. They had earlier established Prohibition in Alabama through an act of the legislature and continued to fight politically to maintain the law. See Sellers, *The Prohibition Movement in Alabama*, 147–148.

67 "O'Neal's Majority Goes Over 13,000; Seed Is Nominated," *Montgomery Advertiser*, May 7, 1910, 1.

68 *Alabama Official and Statistical Register, 1915*, 401, 405; *Alabama Official and Statistical Register, 1913*, 294.

69 "Senator Beasley Would Change Poll Tax Laws," *Montgomery Advertiser*, Mar 11, 1911, 6; *Alabama Official and Statistical Register, 1911*, 106; "Jenkins Would Change

Suffrage Restrictions," *Montgomery Advertiser*, Feb 21, 1911, 7; *Alabama Official and Statistical Register, 1911*, 100; "Much Expected of Representative Jenkins," *Fairhope Courier*, Jan 13, 1911, 4.

70 "Leave Well Enough Alone," *Montgomery Advertiser*, Feb 25, 1911, 4; "Occasionally the Watchman . . ." *Greensboro Watchman*, Mar 2, 1911, 4. There remained expressions of support for change in the poll tax in some north Alabama newspapers. See "We Favor a Change . . .," *Marion County News*, Mar 2, 1911, 4, and "Senator Beasley's Poll Tax Qualification for Voters," *Daily Mountain Eagle*, Mar 22, 1911, 6.

71 *1910 Alabama Attorney General Reports and Opinions* 13 (1910–1912), 232–233; *1912 Alabama Attorney General Reports and Opinions* 47 (1912–1914), 222.

72 *Shepherd v. Sartain*, 185 Ala. 439 (1913), 452–459.

73 "Personals," *Emancipator*, Dec 15, 1917, 3; "Notice to Qualified Voter," *Emancipator*, Dec 8, 1917, 3. The white newspapers also kept up the concept. See "Alabama Voters Voluntarily Disfranchise Themselves," *Tuscaloosa News*, Mar 11, 1917, 12.

74 The 1901 Constitution exempted those persons who were exempt from paying the old poll tax under the laws of the 1875 Constitution, which included those in active service of the state's National Guard. See *1900 Alabama Attorney General Reports and Opinions* 149 (1900–1902), 215.

75 "Poll Tax Must Be Paid by Soldiers of National Army," *Montgomery Advertiser*, Dec 7, 1917, 12; *Shepherd v. Sartain*, 185 Ala. 439 (1913), 455.

76 "Fewer Alabama Citizens Pay Poll Tax in Past Year," *Montgomery Advertiser*, Mar 8, 1918, 3. Also, see "Alabama Voter Out of State Must Pay Poll Tax Is Opinion," *Montgomery Advertiser*, Feb 26, 1918, 3.

77 "Pay the Soldier's Poll Tax," *Wilcox Progressive Era*, Oct 31, 1918, 2.

78 Moore, *History of Alabama, 760.* The first mandatory registration for the military draft in WWI included men between ages of 21 and 30. The last registration included men from age 18 through 45. Only about 14 percent of the men who registered for the draft in Alabama were accepted for induction. The remainder failed to meet the military's health and intelligence tests or were exempt due to economic or family hardships. Alabama apparently had the highest rate of rejection among the states during the first part of 1918. See Robert Saunders Jr., "World War I: Catalyst for Social Change in Alabama," in Martin T. Olliff (ed.), T*he Great War in the Heart of Dixie: Alabama During World War I* (Tuscaloosa: University of Alabama Press, 2008), 1987.

79 *Journal of the House of Representatives,* 1919, vol. 1, 126–127, 209, 449, 711, 766; *Journal of the Senate 1919,* vol. 1, 262, 501, 660.

80 *Alabama Official and Statistical Register,* 1919, 136; Paul McWhorter Pruitt Jr., "Thomas Goode Jones," Encyclopedia of Alabama; William Warren Rogers, "Governor's Election of 1892," Encyclopedia of Alabama; William Warren Rogers, *The One-Gallused Rebellion,* 221–227, 272–292. A biography of Governor Jones suggests that some of the Black votes that historians have concluded were fraudulently counted for him in Black Belt counties may have been valid, although probably not enough to legitimate the election, and that Jones did not orchestrate the fraud himself. See Brent J. Aucoin, *Thomas Goode Jones: Race, Politics, and Justice in the New* South (Tuscaloosa: University of Alabama Press, 2016), 63–69.

81 *Official Proceedings of the Constitutional Convention of the State of Alabama,* vol. 1, 113; Walter B. Jones, "Constitutional Convention of 1901 and Poll Taxes," *Alabama Lawyer*, vol. 4, no. 1 (1943): 4; Aucoin, *Thomas Goode Jones*, 108–110, 116–119. Aucoin also recounts that Governor Jones argued at the convention for provisions holding sheriffs accountable for lynchings and against punitive measures relating to Black education (103–107, 111–114).

82 *Alabama Official and Statistical Register, 1919,* 136; "Judge Henry D. Clayton . . ." *Huntsville Weekly Democrat*, Jun 10, 1914, 2; "Walter B. Jones Announces Candidacy for Legislature; Oppose Amendment," *Montgomery Times*, Jun 4, 1918, 5. Clayton was a reform Democrat who supported the Populist insurgents in the 1890 but switched to support Jones in his bid for Governor. See Aucoin, *Thomas Goode Jones,* 58.

83 "War Stamps Report Shows Fine Progress in Campaign Here," *Montgomery Advertiser,* Mar 27, 1918, 2; "Large Crowd Hears Officer of Modern Woodmen Lecture," *Montgomery Advertiser,* Jul 14, 1918, 8; "Walter B. Jones Makes Answer to Innuendoes of Political Enemies," *Montgomery Advertiser,* Aug 2, 1918, 7.

84 "Class A—Or Nothing," *Montgomery Advertiser*, Aug 3, 1918, 4; "Walter B. Jones," *Montgomery Advertiser,* Aug 11, 1918, 13; "Representation of Montgomery," *Montgomery Advertiser*, Aug 12, 1918, 4; "Primary Vote in Montgomery County," *Montgomery Advertiser,* Aug 15, 1918, 3.

85 "Alabama National Guard, Co, 'A' 2nd. Infantry, Jones, Walter B.," Jan. 2, 1914 examination and oath of enlistment card; "Alabama National Guard, Co, Jones, Walter B., 'A' 2nd. Infantry," muster in roll, July 1, 1916, card; "roster, drill and report," 1914–1916; "Registration Card, Walter Burgwyn Jones," Jun 5, 1917, accessed at www.ancestry.com. In his published statement, after detailing his attempts to enlist, Jones admitted he asked the draft board for a deferment as an officer of the U.S. courts while implying he did so because he knew he would be turned down for enlistment—an act seemingly out of character for a person going to no ends to join. Also, neither Jones's statement nor any news coverage includes the name of any person who corroborated Jones's explanation or any documents supporting his claims. There is also no mention of exactly what was his physical disability. The only other person mentioned in the article was R. E. Steiner, an old friend of Governor Jones and adjutant general of the National Guard.

86 "Roberson Doesn't Carry a Ward . . ." *Montgomery Advertiser*, May 20, 1919, 1; "County Politics—The Slate" [ad], *Montgomery Advertiser,* Apr 28, 1920, 8; "Judge-Nominee Thanks Friends for Their Support," *Montgomery Advertiser,* May 16, 1920, 11; "Ex-Soldiers to Meet Saturday," *Daily Mountain Eagle*, Jun 25, 1919, 1; "The American Legion: What Will It Do in Alabama," *Anniston Star,* Oct 15, 1919, 4. Unable to join the American Legion, Jones did join the American Protective League and apparently became its assistant chief in Montgomery in late 1918. See "Badge Record- Application for Enrollment in the American Protective League" for Walter B. Jones accessed at www.ancestry.com. For a brief understanding of its work in Alabama, see Suitts, *Hugo Black of Alabama*, 234–237.

87 "Walter B. Jones Lodges Formal Complaint Over Act of Legislature," *Montgomery Advertiser,* Jan 15, 1919, 2; "Suffrage Amendment Is Attacked," *Montgomery*

Advertiser, Jul 12, 1919, 1.

88 "Taxing Machinery Restored to Bill," *Birmingham News*, Aug 21, 1919, 20; *Journal of the House of Representatives,* 1919, vol. 2, 1481–1483.

89 "Jones Makes Statement on Poll Tax Bill," *Montgomery Advertiser,* Aug 27, 1919, 1; "Soldiers Poll Tax," *Montgomery Advertiser,* Aug 24, 1919, 4.

90 "Strong Interviews Given by Heroes to Advertiser," *Montgomery Advertiser*, Aug 27, 1919, 1; "Soldiers' Poll Tax," *Montgomery Advertiser,* Aug 25, 1919, 4.

91 "The Soldier and His Poll Tax," *Montgomery Advertiser,* Aug 23, 1919, 4; "Removing the Soldiers' Disabilities: The Mistake of the Legislature," *Birmingham News*, Aug 27, 1919, 8; "Some More Political Graves," *Selma Times-Journal,* Aug 27, 1919, 4.

92 *Journal of the House of Representatives,* 1919, vol. 2, 1805–1807, 1839–1840.

93 *Journal of the Senate,* 1919, vol. 2, 1826, 2174–2175.

94 *Alabama Official and Statistical Register, 1923*, 344; "Tax Exemption Act for World War Men Leads," *Montgomery Advertiser*, Dec 30, 1919, 1.

95 "New Ruling Made on Poll Tax Measure," *Montgomery Advertiser,* Jan 19, 1920, 8; *1916 Alabama Attorney General Reports and Opinions* 27 (1916–1922), 452–453.

96 *Cornelius v. Pruet,* 85 So. 430 (1920); *Johnson v. Craft*, 87 So. 375 (1921); *Hooper v. State ex rel. Fox*, 89 So. 593 (1921); "Ex-Soldiers Who Failed to Pay Poll Tax Can't Vote," *Montgomery Times*, Jun 30, 1921, 1.

97 "Veterans Regret Kilby's Decision, *Birmingham News,* Aug 21, 1921, 22; *Journal of the House of Representatives,* 1921, 53–55, 133–135; *Alabama Official and Statistical Register, 1923*, 502.

98 "Big Majority Is Given Both Amendments," *Montgomery Advertiser*, Feb 14, 1922, 3.

99 For proper language in prior recent acts setting an election date for a proposed constitutional amendment, see *Acts of Alabama,* 1915, 107–108, 211, 289, 337–338. For the proper language in acts passed in the 1919 session, see *Acts of Alabama,* 1919, 727–729, 908–909; 1011–1012. The relevant provision of the Constitution of 1901 is Section 284.

100 "Morgan Campaign," *Birmingham News*, Jan 8, 1900, 3; "They Are Here," *Tuscaloosa Weekly Times,* Jan 13, 1897, 2; *Journal of the Proceedings of the Constitutional Convention, 1901,* 70, 263.

101 "Jones Club," *Livingston Journal,* Jul 22, 1892, 4; "Walter B. Jones Is Candidate for City Commission," *Montgomery Advertiser*, Mar 6, 1919, 1.

Notes to Chapter 9

1 *Alabama Official and Statistical Registers, 1919*, 95; 1903, 42.

2 *Alabama Official and Statistical Registers, 1903,* 42; *1915,* 135; *1919,* 95; *1935,* 146; "In the Sixth," *Montgomery Advertiser*, Sep 2, 1896, 3.

3 "Historic Resources of Gainesville, Alabama," National Register of Historic Places, Inventory Nomination Form, National Park Service, Sep 5, 1985; "Gainesville, Alabama," accessed at https://www.ruralswalabama.org/towns/gainesville; "Brown, Jeremiah H," in Owen, *History of Alabama,* vol. 3, 231–232; Tom Blake, "Large

Slaveholders of 1860 and African American Surname Matches of 1870," accessed at https://freepages.rootsweb.com/~ajac/genealogy/; John A. Wyeth, *That Devil Forrest: The Life of Lieutenant-General Nathan Bedford Forrest* (Charleston: Arcadia Press, 2017) 307–309.

4 Allen W. Trelease, *White Terror: The Ku Klux Klan Conspiracy and Southern Reconstruction* (New York: Harper and Row, 1971), 120–121, 246–252, 271–272; Michael W. Fitzgerald, *Reconstruction in Alabama: From Civil War to Redemption in the Cotton South* (Baton Rouge: Louisiana State University Press, 2017), 303; Jonathan M Wiener, *Social Origins of the New South: Alabama, 1860–1885* (Baton Rouge: Louisiana State University Press, 1978), 61.

5 "Hon. John A. Rogers," *Sumter County Journal*, Jan 2, 1930; "Sine Die," *Birmingham News*, Sep 11, 1895, 7; "A Telegram . . ." *Our Southern Home*, Aug 13, 1896, 3; "In the Constitutional Convention," *Our Southern Home*, Jul 31, 1901, 4. In arguing for the constitutional authority of the state to finance internal improvements, Rogers stated at the 1901 Constitutional Convention, "This is not dangerous legislation, except to greedy corporations." See McMillan, *Constitutional Development in Alabama*, 328.

6 "Views of Hon. J. A. Rogers," *Sumter County Sun*, Jan 19, 1899, 3.

7 "County of Sumter for Good Roads," *Birmingham News*, Jul 28, 1903, 9; "Sumter Campaign for Good Roads," *Birmingham News*, Aug 12, 1903, 8; "A New Enterprise . . .," *Anniston Star*, Mar 27, 1903; "John A. Rogers Against . . ." *Montgomery Advertiser*, Sep 8, 1903, 7; "Books Open in Demopolis," *Birmingham News*, Jun 20, 1903, 27; "The Bigbee Work to Be Pushed," *Birmingham News*, Jul 6, 1903, 3; "Sumter Is for Rogers for Delegate to St. Louis," *Birmingham News*, Apr 27, 1904, 11.

8 "Hon. John A. Rogers Withdraws from the Race for Railroad Commissioner," *Wilcox Progressive Era*, May 3, 1906, 6.

9 "Southern Development Company" [ad], *Gainesville Times*, Feb 3, 1910, 5; "John A. Rogers on the Cotton Crop," *Tuscaloosa News*, Dec 28, 1911, 1; "Oratory Flowed in Walker Saturday," *Daily Mountain Eagle*, Mar 16, 1910, 1; "Senator Moody Closes Campaign in Home City," *Tuscaloosa News*, Mar 31, 1912, 1; "Kolb Gets Great Reception from Crowds at Park," *Birmingham News*, Sep 2, 1913, 13; "Rogers Will Not Succeed Hobson," *Sumter County Sun*, Feb 20, 1913, 2; "Report of Highway Board Made by Sen. Spragins," *Huntsville Times*, Oct 10, 1912, 1; "Good Roads," *Marion County News*, Nov 10, 1915, 1; "Upholding Governor Henderson's Bond Issues," *Andalusia Star*, May 4, 1915, 2.

10 David Holt, "Review of the Legislature," *Tuscaloosa News*, Sep 28, 1919, 5. Also, see "John A. Rogers Is Dead at 75," *Montgomery Advertiser*, Sep 23, 1936. 7.

11 *Journal of the Senate*, 1919, vol. 1, 660; Alabama Official and Statistical Register, 1923, 115.

12 *Journal of the Senate*, 1919, vol. 1, 913, 969–971, 1007–1009. Other proposed amendments failed to pass.

13 *Journal of the House of Representatives*, 1919, vol. 2, 1663–1664.

14 *Journal of the House of Representatives*, 1919, vol. I, 868–875.

15 *Journal of the Senate*, 1919, vol. 2, 2086–2095, 2168–2169; 2263–2264; *Journal of*

the House of Representatives, 1919, vol. 2, 2576–2586; "Defeat of Orr Bill Cripples Highway Building Program," *Montgomery Advertiser,* Sep 21, 1919, 2.

16 "Craft Highway Bill Passed by House at Session Thursday," *Montgomery Advertiser,* Sep 26, 1919, 5; *Journal of the Senate,* 1919, vol. 2, 2240–2241; Act 527, *Acts of Alabama,* 1919, 787–791.

17 "Appointments to State Board," *Our Southern Home,* Oct 22, 1919, 4; Martin T. Olliff, "Getting Farmers—and Tourists—'Out of the Mud,'" in Glenn Feldman (ed.), *Nation Within a Nation: The American South and the Federal Government* (Tallahassee: University Press of Florida, 2014), 245–247; "Senator Rogers on Good Roads," *Franklin County Times,* Nov 27, 1919, 1; "State Landslide for Roads: May Be 60,000 Majority," *Birmingham News,* Feb 17, 1920, 1.

18 "Chairman Rogers Says Square Deal in Road Bond Money," *Our Southern Home,* Apr 14, 1920, 1; "Chairman Rogers Explains Road Bond Amendment," *Greenville Advocate,* Feb 2, 1921, 3; *Journal of the House of Representatives,* 1920, special session, 17, 82, 266–291; *Journal of the Senate,* 1920, special session, 275, 285, 327, 344, 401.

19 "$25,000,000 Good Roads Amendment Attacked," *Montgomery Advertiser,* Dec 23, 1920. 1; Section 284, 1901 Alabama Constitution; Section 2, Act 527, *Acts of Alabama,* 1919, 788.

20 Olliff, "Getting Farmers—and Tourists—'Out of the Mud,'" 247; "Road Bond Measure," *Union Springs Herald,* Dec 30, 1920, 4; "State Demurs to Road Injunction," *Montgomery Advertiser,* Dec 25, 1920, 14.

21 "Sp. Court Kills Road Bond Law," *Selma Times-Journal,* Feb 3, 1921, 1; *Johnson v. Craft,* 87 So. 375 (1921), 385.

22 *Johnson v. Craft,* 87 So. 375 (1921), 391. The controversy is reviewed succinctly in McMillan, *Constitutional Development in Alabama,* 256–259.

23 *Johnson v. Craft,* 87 So. 375 (1921), 388–389, 392.

24 *Alabama Official and Statistical Registers, 1923,* 504. The proposed amendment received 46 percent of slightly more than 75,000 votes cast. This also was the election in which voters rejected additional voter qualifications for "good character" and understanding the "obligations of citizenship" advanced by Black Belt Senator Robert B. Evins.

25 *Hooper v. State ex rel. Fox,* 89 So. 593 (1921); "Senator Rogers Talks Good Roads," *Montgomery Advertiser,* Mar 27, 1921, 3.

26 *Journal of the Senate,* 1921, special session, 40, 59, 69–71, 81, 107–118; "Original Highway Bill to Stand with Very Little Chance," *Montgomery Advertiser,* Oct 13, 1921. 1.

27 "Report 'Bloc' Broken Is Propaganda, Says Chief of Tax League," *Montgomery Advertiser,* Oct 14, 1921, 1; "Fight Against Tax Adjuster Expected to Be Renewed in House When Good Roads Bill Is Brought Up," *Montgomery Advertiser,* Oct 16, 1921, 1; "Table of Valuation and Taxation," *Annual Report of Auditor, State of Alabama, Fiscal Year 1922,* 34–35.

28 *Journal of the House of Representatives, 1921, special session,* 156, 278–293; David Holt, "Good Roads Act Now Complete," *Birmingham News,* Oct 26, 1921, 22; David Holt, "Elections on Amendments Voted Will be Held on January 30, 1922," *Birmingham*

News, Oct 30, 1921, 8. The bill eliminating the tax adjuster failed in the senate, and Senator Rogers broke from the Black Belt support for the repeal. Rogers stood by Governor Kilby as a leader of "iron will and invincible courage." See "Measure to Abolish State Tax Adjuster Defeated in Senate," *Montgomery Advertiser,* Oct 21, 1921, 2.

29 Olliff, "Getting Farmers—and Tourists—'Out of the Mud,'" 252; "Senator Rogers on the Good Roads Bond," *Montgomery Advertiser,* Jan 13, 1922, 4.

30 "Senator Rogers on the Good Roads Bond," *Montgomery Advertiser,* Jan 13, 1922, 4; *Twelfth Annual Report of State Highway Commission of Alabama, 1922–1923,* 21, 23; "Big Majority Given Both Amendments," *Montgomery Advertiser,* Tue, Feb 14, 1922, 3. The soldiers' exemption from the poll tax was the other amendment that passed.

31 "Jefferson County Board of Revenue Protests Gas Tax," *Tuscaloosa News,* Feb 1, 1923, 1.

32 *Journal of the House of Representatives,* 1923, vol. 1, 404–409; "Centralization of Power Is Given Jolt in House; Income Derived from Gasoline Tax Will Go to Counties," *Montgomery Advertiser,* Feb 1, 1923, 1

33 *Journal of the House of Representatives,* 1923, vol. 1, 509–512, 520.

34 Representative Long joined Representative A. M. Tunstall of Greensboro, the Black Belt dean of the lower chamber, and a north Alabama sponsor of the Roberts-backed bill as appointed house members. The senate members on the conference committee included a Black Belt legislator, a railroad attorney from Tuscaloosa County and W. C. Tunstall of Anniston, a native of Greensboro and Representative Tunstall's brother.

35 "Bitter Opposition Develops on Conference Committee Decision to Ask Split in Gas Tax Fund," *Montgomery Advertiser,* Feb 8, 1923, 1; "House Concurs in Conference Report on Gasoline Tax Bill," *Montgomery Advertiser,* Feb 9, 1923, 1. *Journal of the House of Representatives,* 1923, vol.1, 548–552.

36 "News from the State Capital," *Southern Democrat,* Aug 2, 1923, 2; "Gas Tax Money Should be Used to Maintain Roads," *Huntsville News,* Aug 9, 1923, 1; "Approved with Slight Change in Upper House," *Montgomery Advertiser,* Aug 17,1923, 1; "Appropriations to Occupy Time of Legislature," *Montgomery Advertiser,* Aug 19, 1923, 1; "One Cent Tax Explained to Voters," *Greenville Advocate,* August 29, 1923, 1; *Acts of Alabama,* 1923, 152–200 (section 83 pertaining to the gas tax).

37 Act 358, *Acts of Alabama,* 1923, 370–381; Martin T. Olliff, *Getting Out of the Mud: The Alabama Good Roads Movement and Highway Administration, 1898–1928* (Tuscaloosa: University of Alabama Press, 2017), 161–162; "Governor Names Freeman Suttle," *Selma Times-Journal,* Sep 28, 1923, 1.

38 *Annual Report of the Treasurer, State of Alabama, 1920,* 31; *Annual Report of the Treasurer, 1924,* 86; *Annual Report of the Treasurer, 1925,* 19; Olliff, *Getting Out of the Mud,* 157; "Brandon Calls for Concerted Plan on Road Bond Issue," *Montgomery Advertiser,* Nov 15, 1924, 1; "Bond Issue Still Sought," *Choctaw Advocate,* Dec 17, 1924, 1.

39 "Bond Issue Still Sought," *Choctaw Advocate,* Dec 17, 1924, 1.

40 "State Road Official Seeks to Oust Keller," *Montgomery Advertiser,* Aug 29, 1923, 1; "Highway Engineer W. S. Keller Dies," *Selma Times-Journal,* Sep 9, 1925, 1.

41 "Confidence in Keller Voted by Selma Chamber," *Selma Times-Journal*, Sep 4, 1923, 2.

42 "Keller Received Exoneration at Hands of Board," *Montgomery Advertiser*, Sep 11, 1923, 1. The legislature did not alter the scope of the relevant prohibition against conflicts of interest when it passed the new highway commission bill after Heller and his staff were cleared of wrong-doing. It did, however, make a violation of the law a felony instead of a misdemeanor offense, as it was earlier. See Section 11½ of Act 358, *Acts of Alabama*, 1923, 375.

43 Olliff, *Getting Out of the Mud*, 163–168; "Injunction Expected Against Highway Body," *Birmingham News*, Mar 2, 1924, 1; "Injunction Halts Proposed Building Gainesville Detour," *Montgomery Advertiser*, Mar 30, 1924. For an understanding of Wilkinson's checkered role, including his role in passage of the Boswell Amendment, see Feldman, *From Demagogue to Dixiecrat*, 123–140.

44 "Alabama Highway Commission Seeks to Dissolve Writ," *Montgomery Advertiser*, Apr 17, 1924, 1; "Judge Considering Road Controversy," *Birmingham News*, Apr 29, 1924, 6; "Rogers to Let Road Controversy Drop," *Birmingham News*, May 11, 1924, 30; *Bouchelle v. State Highway Commission*, 211 Ala. 474, 100 So. 884 (1924), 480. Wilkinson released the earlier federal report showing that the Gainesville detour would cost 60 percent more than the Boligee route and serve fewer residents. See "Gainesville Route for New Road Not Favored in Report," *Tuscaloosa News*, Apr 4, 1924, 1.

45 *Bouchelle v. State Highway Commission*, 211 Ala. 474, 100 So. 884 (1924) 480.

46 "Rogers to Let Road Controversy Drop," *Birmingham News*, May 11, 1924; "Statement from Mr. Rogers," *Our Southern Home*, May 14, 1924,1.

47 "For the Glory of Dallas and Adjoining Counties," *Montgomery Advertiser*, Jul 11, 1926; "Answer to Age-Herald Article of November 26th, in Regard to Eutaw-Gainesville Road," *Birmingham News*, Nov 29, 1925, 17; "Brandon Is Defiant on Criticism on State's Highway Policy," *Sumter County Journal*, Dec 11, 1925, 1; "Someone Has Summed Up . . ." *Coosa River News*, May 28, 1926, 2.

48 "Montgomery Journal," *Onlooker* (Foley), Apr 29, 1926, 4.

49 "Col. B. Graves for Governor" [ad], *Cleburne News*, Jul 8, 1926, 3.

50 *Alabama Official and Statistical Register, 1927*, 41, 49–50; Act 5, *Acts of Alabama*, 1927, 794–797; "Examiner's Report Lauds Work of State Highway Commission," *Montgomery Advertiser*, Dec 12, 1926, 3; *Examination of the Highway Department of Alabama, July 1922 to September 30, 1926*, 29.

51 "Long, Underwood, Gorgas, Tutwiler New Bridge Names," *Montgomery Advertiser*. Oct 27, 1929, 29.

52 "Where Was Black in 1928 and 1930?" [ad], *Montgomery Advertiser*, Jun 2, 1932, 3; "Make Up of New Senate," *Decatur Daily*, Jun 15, 1934, 6; "Graves Leader Breaking Down Opposition," *Anniston Star*, Mar 16, 1936, 1; "State Senator John A. Rogers . . .," *Southern Home*, Sep 30, 1936, 6.

53 "John A. Rogers Is Dead at 75," *Montgomery Advertiser*, Sep 23, 1936, 1; "John A. Rogers Sumter County Died Tuesday," *Pickens County Herald and West Alabamian*, Sep 24, 1936, 1; "The Long Roll for a Passing South," *Birmingham News*, Sep 23,

1936, 6; "J. A. Rogers Dies at 75," *Abbeville Herald*, Sep 24, 1936, 1.

54 See, for example, *Journal of the Proceedings of the Constitutional Convention, 1901*, 70, 263, 374–376. Three other bills proposing constitutional amendments with the correct method for setting the election were enacted by the legislature in its 1919 session; two originated in the senate and were reviewed by Rogers's constitutional revisions committee and one of the two was sponsored by Senator Craft. See *Acts of Alabama*, 1919, Act 495, 727–729; Act 656, 908–909; Act 699, 1011–1012.

55 *Journal of the Senate*, 1919, vol. 1, 1010. There were five other legislators in the 1919 session who were also members of the 1901 Constitutional Convention that considered and adopted the provision prohibiting the governor from any role in amending the state constitution. Four of the five were also Black Belt legislators: Sen, Joseph Norwood of Lowndes; Sen. John Miller of Wilcox; Rep. John Lee Long of Butler; and Sen. Boswell Waddell of Russell. The fifth was Sen. A. H. Carmichael of Colbert, who also represented Franklin and Marion counties in north Alabama. Only Sen. Miller of Wilcox voted on the motion for a correct form of election and he joined Rogers. Senator Carmichael was not present for any votes on the Craft bill, including the motion in question. See *Alabama Official and Statistical Registers, 1919*, 91–104, 11–146; *Journal of the Senate*, 1919, vol. 1 1007–1011.

56 "Political Potpourri," *Crenshaw County News* (Luverne), Jun 3, 1926, 1. The description of Rogers is from A. G. Patterson, who served with Rogers as a member of the highway commission from 1919 through 1923 and who in 1926 was president of the Alabama Public Service Commission and a candidate for governor.

57 Kenneth W. Holman, "Alabama's State Debt, 1920–1965," *Mississippi Quarterly*, fall, 1979, vol. 32, no. 4, n. 1 627, 630; *Annual Report of the Treasurer 1919*, 8; "The $25,000,000 Bond Issue for Roads," *Abbeville Herald*, Jul 17, 1919, 2.

58 *Banking and Monetary Statistics, 1914–1941*(Washington, DC: Federal Reserve System, Nov 1943), 468; "Chairman Rogers Explains Road Bond Amendment," *Greenville Advocate*, Feb 2, 1921, 3.

59 "Petition to Force Bond Commission Refused by Judge," *Birmingham News*, June 14, 1920, 1; *Weakley, et al., v. Henry County Treasurer*, 204 Al. 463, 86 So. 46 (1920).

60 Gov. Kilby authorized spending $2,000 for retaining a Boston law firm that, in league with David Weakley of the Alabama Bonding Company, searched for grounds upon which to annul the road bond amendment at the same time Rogers and the state highway department were still trying to sell bonds. The first road bonds were sold in November and December 1920 and amounted to only $96,000. They were bought by local Alabama financial institutions in two counties interested in local road construction. See Olliff, "Getting Farmers—and Tourists—'Out of the Mud,'" 247, 259 n. 58; "Road Bonds Are State-Aid Fund," *Montgomery Times*, December 3, 1920, 1.

61 See Olliff, *Getting Out of the Mud*, 166–168; "Ironing Out Road Dispute in Perry over Building," *Montgomery Times*, Apr 25, 1924, 7. Of course, there were also road disputes in other sections of Alabama. See, for example, "Gadsden Club to Hear Road Dispute," *Birmingham News*, Jan 6, 1924, 38.

62 This perception in the Black Belt was likely furthered by the fact that the state's chief Highway Engineer, W. S. Keller, had strong ties to Dallas County planters and businessmen. John Rogers certainly encouraged this impression on occasion, including in

1925 when he proposed the highway commission retain the state treasurer, a Selma native and the uncle of State Senator J. B. Ellis, to supervise the highway department's books. The proposal included paying George W. Ellis a retainer of $100 per month, but the retainer was disallowed when Alabama Attorney General Harwell Davis of Birmingham ruled it would be illegal. See Olliff, *Getting Out of the Mud,* 184; "Rules Necessitates Employment Title," *Montgomery Advertiser,* Feb 11, 1925, 2.

63 *Journal of the Senate,* 1915, 2297, 2839; "State System of Trunk Highways Mapped Out," *Montgomery Advertiser,* Sep 1, 1915, 10.

64 "State System of Trunk Highways Mapped Out," *Montgomery Advertiser,* Sep 1, 1915, 10.

65 *Acts of Alabama,* 1915, 365 (identified as trunk road 7). Rep. Sumner was a member of the conference committee that recommended the removal of his own amendment, a fact that makes the committee's recommendation all the more remarkable. The sponsor of the Governor's road bill, Senator J. T. Denson of Eutaw represented Greene County and may have opposed the re-routing of trunk road 7. After Denson's bill passed, Sumner pursued efforts to build a road connecting his land in Boligee to the road connecting Eutaw and Demopolis, the largest town in Marengo County. See "Hon. M. T. Sumner of Boligee," *Greene County Democrat,* Jun 30, 1916, 4; "Hon. M. T. Sumner of Boligee," *Greene County Democrat,* Aug 17, 1917, 4.

66 *Annual Report of State Highway Commission of Alabama, 1924–1925,* 18, 82,134; *Annual Report of State Highway Commission of Alabama, 1923–1924,* 19–23, 28.

67 "Exhibit 'T-2' Total State Funds" column in *Examination of the Highway Department of Alabama, July 1922 to September 30, 1926,* 280–283. Sumter ranked 4th among the 67 counties in the expenditure of both state and federal funds for roads during this period. The federally designated highways required Alabama to spend state funds on those highways in order to receive matching funds for state-designated roads. Therefore, Rogers had less influence in directing those combined state and federal funds.

68 Author's computations from data in *Annual Report of the Treasurer* from 1922 through 1926 and from "Total Exhibit T" column in Exhibit 'T-2,' Ibid.

69 "Brandon Is Defiant of Criticism on the State's Highway Policy," *Sumter County Journal,* Dec 11, 1925, 1.

70 "Those Who Hold the Belief. . .," *Our Southern Home,* July 14, 1926, 4.

71 "Allison and Rogers Address the Citizens of York and Vicinity," *Sumter County Journal,* Jul 9, 1926, 1.

Notes to Chapter 10

1 "John A. Rogers Is Dead at 75," *Montgomery Advertiser,* Sep 23, 1936, 1. Rogers was one of a few who has served on the board of trustees of both Auburn University and the University of Alabama.

2 *Alabama Official and Statistical Register, 1915,* 135.

3 "For the Independent," *Independent* (Gainesville), Jul 11, 1857, 1; "Superintendent of Schools," *Independent,* Mar 19, 1864, 2; "For Superintendent of Schools," *Livingston Journal,* Apr 14, 1866, 4; "Appointment," *Livingston Journal,* Oct15, 1868, 3; Walter

L. Fleming, *Civil War and Reconstruction in Alabama* (New York: Columbia University Press, 1905), 460; "A Card," *Livingston Journal*, Feb 17, 1871, 3; "To Whom It May Concern," *Livingston Journal*, May 19, 1871, 3; "Another Old and Respectable Citizen of Sumter, Gone," *Livingston Journal*, Apr 5, 1872, 5.

4 Bond, *Negro Education in Alabama*, 96.

5 Ibid., 90–94.

6 Ibid., 96–97. As Bond writes, the school reports in these years were mostly political polemics.

7 Ibid., 98–101. Bond notes that in 1870 school reports on the number of students in Black Belt counties exceeded the Census counts of school-age students. It appears that one strategy for more school funds was to exaggerate the number of enrolled students.

8 Ibid., 102.

9 "Schedule 1, Township 23, Sumter County, Alabama," U.S. Census of 1870 (manuscript), p 4; "List of Licensees," *Livingston Journal*, Jan 10, 1873, 3; *Report of Superintendent of Instruction, Scholastic Year, 1874*, 4–5; *State Auditor Report*, 1873, 65–66; Stephen B. Weeks, *History of Public Education in Alabama*, U.S. Bureau of Education, Bulletin 12, 1915, 101–102; W. E. Burghardt DuBois and Augustus Graville Dill, *The Common School and the Negro American*, Atlanta University Publications, No. 16, 1911, 69.

10 Bond, *Negro Education in Alabama*, 98.

11 *Alabama Official and Statistical Register, 1903*, 42 ("Mr. Rogers attended public schools and also a private school . . .); "The Address of Chas. Cooke, Esq.," *Livingston Journal*, Jun 30, 1876; "Report of the General Agent," January 21, 1868, *Proceedings of the Trustees of the Peabody Education Fund*, (Boston: John Wilson and Son, circa 1869), 76–77; (1875); 209–213 (1870); 256–258 (1871); 310–214 (1872); 376–378 (1873); 422–423 (1874). See also "The Grand Jury of Hale County," *Livingston Journal*, Nov 27, 1974, 2.

12 *An Educational Study of Alabama*, Bureau of Education, Department of Interior, Bulletin 1919, 41, 44–45; *Journal of the Constitutional Convention of the State of Alabama, 1875*, 172.

13 Bond, *Negro Education in Alabama*,102; McMillan, *Constitutional Development in Alabama*, 217.

14 Section 9, Act 14, *Acts of Alabama*, 1875–1876, 98–100. Both the *Code of Alabama, 1876* and the *Acts of Alabama* erroneously identify the enactment as H.B. 392 when in fact it was passed by the legislature as H.B. 397. Perhaps due to this confusion, Bond misidentified the first law segregating poll taxes as occurring in Act 9, *Acts of Alabama*, 1874–1875, 56–61. See Bond, *Negro Education in Alabama*,149, no. 7, 329.

15 *Acts of the Board of Education, State of Alabama, 1875*, 8–13; *Code of Alabama, 1876*, sec. 952, 376, sec. 1136, 391(where the words "applied exclusively" were added to assure local segregated poll taxes were used only for the schools of the poll tax payer's race).

16 *Code of Alabama, 1876*, sec. 1145, 393, sec. 907, 369.

17 *Annual Report of the Superintendent of Education*, 1886, Table II, 85; "To Hon. J, M. Mitchell, Foreman of Grand Jury, August Term, 1866," *Livingston Journal*, Sep

23, 1886, 3. The State Superintendent's report also included data purportedly showing that in Sumter and other Black Belt counties African American teachers were being paid on average more than white teachers and African American children were attending school for more days than white students. Yet, using reported data on average attendance by race and reported total salaries by race, it appears that in Sumter white teachers were paid almost one and a half times more per student than African American teachers. See data for comparisons and computations in *Annual Report of the Superintendent of Education, 1886*, 81–88, 96–98.

18 Suitts, *Hugo Black of Alabama*, 44–45, 49; "Moulton Advertiser," *Weekly Advertiser*, Jan 12, 1888, 4; "Of Interest to Farmers," *Clay County Watchman*, Nov 15, 1888, 2.

19 *Journal of the House of Representatives*, 1890–1891, 1092; "Special Order," *Weekly Advertiser*, Feb 5, 1891, 7.

20 Special Order," *Weekly Advertiser*, Feb 5, 1891, 7; *Journal of the House of Representatives*, 1890–1891, 562. The vote was 66 to 0. Thirty-three members or one-third of House did not vote on the bill. It's likely that most of the non-voting members did not vote because they were not in the chamber in order to vote. The prior vote on a different issue passed 55 to 0.

21 *Journal of the Senate*, 1890–1891, 521, 564.

22 Ibid., 569–570. The Senator from Marengo County in the Black Belt voted against the motion to remove the exemptions. Perhaps he may have seen no problem with allowing north Alabama counties to have exemptions, More likely, he voted with north Alabama counties in the event they prevailed on the vote so that he could have the vote retaken at a later time. By the rules of order, on only those who vote in favor of a motion have a right to have the vote reconsidered.

23 *Journal of the Senate*, 1890–1891, 564, 570; "Legislature," *Birmingham News*, Feb 10, 1891, 4.

24 "Opinion," *Selma Times and Messenger*, Jan 19, 1868, 1.

25 "Sunday School Organized," *Weekly Advertiser*, Dec 8, 1899, 6; "The Retrospect," *Daily News*, Jun 2, 1890, 5; "We Are Glad to See," *Sumter County Sun*, Mar 13, 1890, 2; "Maj. J. G. Harris for Superintendent of Education," *Livingston Journal*, Jan 31, 1890; 5; "Maj. J. G. Harris," *Livingston Journal*, Mar 28, 1890, 5.

26 "County Convention," *Sumter County Sun*, May 22, 1890, 2; "Democratic County Convention," *Livingston Journal*, May 23, 1890, 4.

27 Thomas McAdory Owen, *History of Alabama and Dictionary of Alabama Biography*, vol. 4, (Chicago: S. J. Clarke Publishing, 1921), 1171; "The Attorney General," *Montgomery Advertiser*, Mar 19, 1889, 7. One of Martin's sons, W. L. Martin Jr., followed him as an Alabama Attorney General from 1915 to 1919 and later was appointed Montgomery Circuit Court judge, only to lose an election for that post to Walter B. Jones. See Chapter 8. Martin's second son, Thomas, became the president of the Alabama Power Company.

28 *Annual Report of the Superintendent of Education, 1891*, 196.

29 See Steve Suitts, *Overturning Brown*, 20–21, 35, 37, 40, 91.

30 *Annual Report of the Superintendent of Education, 1891*, 173–176; Louis R. Harlan, Stuart B. Kaufman, and Raymond W. Smock (eds.), *Booker T. Washington Papers*

Volume 3: 1889–95 (Champaign, IL: University of Illinois Press, 1974), 262.

31 "Report of the Grand Jury," *Livingston Journal*, Apr 25, 1890, 4; "Superintendent's Report," *Livingston Journal*, Apr 22, 1892, 5. This pattern of equal amounts of funding between the races for educating an unequal numbers of school-age children apparently held through 1893. See "Co. Supt. of Education," *Sumter County Sun*, Apr 27, 1893, 2.

32 Joseph Columbus Manning, *From Five to Twenty-five* (New York: T. A, Hebbons, 1929), 40.

33 The data for the comparison from 1881 to 1898 are found in *Report of Superintendent of Education, 1881*, 25–27; *Biennial Report of the Superintendent of Education, 1896–1897 and 1897–1898*, 250–252, 268–270, 277–280, 282–283, 297–301.

34 Weeks, *History of Public Education in Alabama*, 143.

35 Ibid., 143–144; *Official Proceedings of the Constitutional Convention*, vol. 2, 1605–1606; *Biennial Report of the Superintendent of Education, 1905–1906*. 4–5.

36 "Governor Jones!" *Montgomery Advertiser*, Dec 2, 1890, 1; Aucoin, *Thomas Goode Jones*, 30–32. Jones echoed the popular white sentiment but did not agree with it. But others did. See Allen Johnston Going, *Bourbon Democracy in Alabama*, 1874–1890 (University, AL: University of Alabama Press, 1951), 157. For illiteracy gains, see *U.S. Census, 1870*, Table X, 401; *U.S. Census, 1900*, Table 84, 470.

37 *Official Proceedings of the Constitutional Convention*, vol. 1, 102; McMillan, *Constitutional Development in Alabama*, 320.

38 *Booker T. Washington Papers, Volume 6: 1901–1902*, 117–118, 129–133; "Memorial by Negroes," *Montgomery Advertiser*, May 29, 1901, 11. William Councill, president of the Alabama A & M College, sent an earlier, separate petition in which he asked the Convention to reject segregating school funds by race. See "Letter from Councill," *Montgomery Advertiser*, May 21, 1901, 3.

39 "Is Going Slow," *Birmingham News*, Jun 1, 1901, 19; "By Mr. Murphree," *Montgomery Advertiser*, May 29, 1901, 10; "Delegates in Caucus," *Montgomery Advertiser*, June 19,1901, 8; *Official Proceedings of the Constitutional Convention*, vol. 2, 2033–2038.

40 *Official Proceedings of the Constitutional Convention*, vol. 2, 2033–2038; Bond, *Negro Education in Alabama*, 179–180, 183–184.

41 *Official Proceedings of the Constitutional Convention*, vol. 4, 4163, with emphasis added.

42 Ibid., 4165.

43 *Alabama Official and Statistical Register*, 1903, 36, 4. For Rogers's advocacy of limiting the legislature to meeting only every four years, see debate in "Official Report of Proceedings of the Constitutional Convention of Alabama," *Montgomery Advertiser*, Jul 17, 1901, 11.

44 *Journal of the Senate*, 1903, 957–958; Section 4, S. 210, *Acts of Alabama*, 1903, 290.

45 "Gainesville," *Our Southern Home*, Oct 18, 1900, 1; calculations made from "Schedule No. 1, Township 23, Sumter County, Alabama, Gainesville Town," U.S. Census of 1900 (manuscript); Table 8, "Population of Incorporated Cities, Towns, Villages, and Boroughs in 1900, With Population for 1890," *Statistics of Population Census of 1900*, 438. Rogers raised this issue at the constitutional convention during debate on

the state education fund: "There are some beats in the Black Belt that have not enough school children . . .," "Official Report of Proceedings of the Constitutional Convention of Alabama," *Montgomery Advertiser,* Jul 6, 1901, 10.

46 Robert Volney Riser II, "Prelude to the Movement: Disfranchisement in Alabama's 1901 Constitution and the Anti-Disfranchisement Cases," PhD diss. (University of Alabama, 2005), 425–427, 445–479, 507; 208–209; Bond, "Negro Education: A Debate in the Alabama Constitutional Convention of 1901," *Journal of Negro Education*, Apr 1932, 57.

47 *Biennial Report of the Department of Education, 1902–1903,* 132–134; *Biennial Report of the Department of Education, 1905–1906,* 182–186, 202–204.

48 *Biennial Report of the Department of Education, 1902–1903,* 52–53.

49 Author's computations and estimates taken from data in *Biennial Report of the Department of Education, 1902–1903,* 141–150.

50 For a discussion of the 1901 constitutional convention as an exercise in the "white man's burden," see R. Volney Riser, "The Burdens of Being White: Empire and Disfranchisement," *Alabama Law Review*, vol. 53: 1, 2001.

51 "Minutes of Meeting, *Morning Mercury*, Jul 20, 1905, 5; "Hon. James Jefferson Mayfield," Moore, *History of Alabama and Her People,* vol. II, 109–110; *Report of James J. Mayfield, Code Commissioner of Alabama, 1907,* 43. See *Code of Alabama, 1907,* vol. I, 765, for the old Code's missing section 3608 between new sec. 1669 and sec. 1670. Mayfield labored over the education laws more than any other part of the Code and remained dissatisfied with his task of reconciling all of Alabama's education laws. See *Report of James J. Mayfield,* 38. His Code was approved by resolution of the Alabama Legislature. It would not be the only time Mayfield used his powers as Code Commissioner to revise Alabama laws. In 1923, a couple of years before he ran for U.S. Senate in an anti-Klan campaign, Mayfield indexed the Code to refer to lynchings and mob violence as "Ku Klux Prohibited," although no law made mention of the Ku Klux Klan. See Suitts, *Hugo Black of Alabama,* 503; *Code of Alabama, 1923,* vol. II, 867.

52 *Annual Report of the Superintendent of Education, 1891,* 174–179; *Biennial Report of the Department of Education, 1906–1908,* 126–129, 162–165. In 1890, expenditures for Black children who regularly attended school—the average number in daily attendance—was slightly higher—26 cents per child higher—than the average expenditures for the white schoolchildren in daily attendance.

53 Calculations of author from data in *Biennial Report of the Department of Education, 1906–1908,* 130–133, 162–165. I chose to calculate per pupil expenditures (PPE) by using the number of average student attendance instead of student enrollment as the divisor for two primary reasons. First, state law required no less than 95 percent its school funds to be spent for teachers. The costs of a building, overhead and operating costs of a school had to be funded by parents, donors, the community, or special appropriations from local governments. Therefore, the standing costs for schooling that might be required today to assure that all enrolled students were educated were not covered by state funds. Second, as noted in the text, there was a strong incentive for local white leaders to suppress the number of Black children who actually attended a school regularly.

54 *Annual Report of the Department of Education, 1910,* 11.

55 Theodore Rosengarten, *All God's Dangers: The Life of Nate Shaw* (New York: Alfred A. Knopf, 1975), 216–217.

56 *Biennial Report of the Department of Education, 1906–1908, 133.*

57 Author's calculations from data in *Biennial Report of the Department of Education, 1906–1908,* 130–133, 162–165.

58 "A.T. & N. Railroad Is Building Rapidly," *Gainesville Times*, Oct.28, 1909, 4; "Panola Is to Be the New Town . . .," *Sumter County Sun*, Apr 1, 1909; "Fair Oaks," *Gainesville Times*, Apr 16, 1099, 5; "Panola Our New Town of North-Western Sumter," *Gainesville Times*, Apr 23, 1909, 1; "Cochrane's Roads to Be Connected in Near Future," *Tuscaloosa News*, May 12, 1911, 1.

59 Nicholas Lemann, *The Promised Land: The Great Black Migration and How It Changed America* (New York, Vintage Books, 1991), 17–18; Isabel Wilkerson, *The Warmth of Other Suns: The Epic Story of America's Great Migration* (New York: Random House, 2010), 527–538; *Population 1910*, U.S. Census, vol. 2, Alabama-Montana, 59.

60 Dennis S. Nordin, *The New Deal's Black Congressman: A Life of Arthur Wergs Mitchell* (Columbia, MO: University of Missouri Press, 1997), 9; "New Incorporation," *Birmingham News*, Sep 12, 1907, 10.

61 "Negroes Eager for Schooling in West Alabama Community: The Principals Story," General-Clippings, Nov. 11, 1898–Jan 12, 1913, Arthur W. Mitchell Papers, Black Freedom Struggle in the 20th Century, Part 2, ProQuest/History Vault; Dennis S. Nordin, *The New Deal's Black Congressman,* 11; "A Deserving Negro," *Sumter County Sun*, Nov 3, 1910, 4.

62 "Resolutions," *Sumter County Sun*, Nov. 19, 1908, 4.

63 "A Negro Against Franchise," *Baltimore Sun*, Nov 4, 1905, 14.

64 "An Interesting Article from Colored Educator," *Gainesville Times*, Feb 17, 1910, 1.

65 "Has Plan to Get Value of Cotton," *Eutaw Whig and Observer,* Aug 22, 1912, 1.

66 Monroe N. Work, *Industrial Work: Tuskegee Graduates and Former Students During the Year 1910* (Tuskegee: Institute Press, 1911), 51. A copy of the letter is also found in Michell's papers and included in his promotional materials such as pamphlet, "The Struggles of the Negro for Self Improvement," General-Clippings, Nov. 11, 1898–Jan 12, 1913, Mitchell Papers.

67 "A Deserving Negro," *Sumter County Sun*, Nov 3, 1910, 4.

68 General-Clippings, Nov. 11, 1898–Jan 12, 1913, Mitchell Papers.

69 Nordin, *The New Deal's Black Congressman*, 9.

70 "Notice" [ad], *Sumter Enterprise*, July 23, 1908, 2. Similarly ads were published until 1911. See, for example, "Notice," *Sumter Enterprise,* Feb 4, 1909, Jan 13, 1910, Jul 6, 1911. The Black newspaper in which Rogers advertised referred to Rogers as "the colored peoples friend to education and selling them homes . . .," *Sumter Enterprise,* Jan 12, 1911, 1. No person was listed in Sumter County in the Census of 1900 or 1910 by the name of "John A. Rodgers." Rogers's name was sometimes misspelled as "Rodgers" in published reports. See "Senate," *Montgomery Advertiser*, Oct 9, 1902, 4; "Masters John and Maxie Rodgers, sons of Hon. Jno. A. Rodgers . . .," *Pickens County Herald and West Alabamian*, Jun 11, 1902, 1; "To Wipe Out Cattle Tick," *Huntsville Times*, Apr 12, 1911, 6.

71 "The Poor Man Is the Man We Want to Help" [ad], *Sumter Enterprise,* Jan 13, 1910, 1, Apr 7, 1910,1; "Southern Development Company" [ad], *Gainesville Times*, Dec 23, 1909, 8; "Notice to Farmers" [ad]" *Gainesville Times,* Dec 2, 1909, 4.

72 "The Struggles of the Negro for Self Improvement," General-Clippings, Nov. 11, 1898–Jan 12, 1913, Mitchell Papers; "Geiger Moving to the Front," *Gainesville Times*, Aug 26, 1909, 1; "North Sumter's Prospective City," *Gainesville Times*, Sep 30, 1909, 1.

73 Nordin, *The New Deal's Black Congressman*, 12, 14; "Working for Funds," *Springfield Union,* undated clipping, "The West Alabama Normal and Industrial Institute . . .," General-Clippings, Nov. 11, 1898–Jan 12, 1913, Mitchell Papers; *Sumter County Sun,* Nov 9, 1911, 5; Mitchell's stationery shows Pinson as a reference and the Bank of Geiger as the school's treasurer. See General-Clippings, Nov. 11, 1898– Jan 12, 1913, Mitchell Papers.

74 "Geiger, Alabama" [ad], *Montgomery Advertiser*, Feb 1, 1911, 12; "Sensational Land Distribution" [ad]" *Atlanta Constitution*, May 17, 1911, 5; "For Sale – Farm Land in 'Black Belt of Alabama'" [ad], *Chicago Tribune*, Mar 30, 1913, 10; "Farm Land for Sale" [ad], *Raleigh News and Observer*, Jul 19, 1914, 7.

75 "$100 Per Contract, Cash or Credit Geiger" [ad], *Birmingham News*, Apr 18, 1911, 17.

76 Undated newspaper clippings, General-Clippings, 1914–September 5, 1919, Mitchell Papers. Most of the articles came from northern newspapers covering Mitchell's fundraising speeches after the Panola school fire.

77 Ibid.; "Negroes Eager for Schooling in West Alabama Community: The Principals Story," General-Clippings, Nov. 11, 1898–Jan 12, 1913, Mitchell Papers.

78 Nordin, *The New Deal's Black Congressman*, 17–19; "Another Worthy Southern School," *Boston Evening Post*, undated, and West Alabama Agricultural and Industrial Institute stationery, General-Clippings, 1914–September 5, 1919, Mitchell Papers. Nordin finds that Mitchell blackmailed Washington into endorsing him and his school. It also appears Mitchell manufactured an endorsement from Washington in a brochure that added a Washington quotation into an article reprinted from the *Christian Science Monitor*. Compare brochure "Negroes Eager for Schooling in West Alabama Community: The Principals Story," General-Clippings, Nov. 11, 1898 -Jan 12, 1913," in Mitchell Papers with news article "Negroes Eager for Schooling in West Alabama Community," *Christian Science Monitor*, Apr 2, 1912, 7. Also, Mitchell misspelled Gov. O'Neal's name as "O'Neil" on his Institute's letterhead.

79 "White Mob Lynched Negro on Suspicion; Afterwards Converted to Cause of Negro Education," General-Clippings, Nov. 11, 1898 -Jan 12, 1913, Mitchell Papers.

80 Project HAL: Historical American Lynching Data Collection Project, accessed at http://people.uncw.edu; George M. Fredrickson, *The Black Image in the White Mind: The Debate on Afro-American Character and Destiny, 1817–1914* (New York: Harper & Row, 1971), 256–282.

81 "Awful Tragedy at Bellamy," *Brewton Standard*, Sep 16,1909, 1; "Woman Killed by Negro," *Gainesville Times*, Sep 30, 1909, 2.

82 "A. W, Mitchell Seeks to Better Blackbelt Conditions," *Springfield Union*, undated,

General-Clippings, Nov. 11, 1898 -Jan 12, 1913, Mitchell Papers.

83 "Meritorious Work," undated, and "Negroes Eager for Schooling in West Alabama Community: The Principals Story," General-Clippings, Nov. 11, 1898–Jan 12, 1913, Mitchell Papers.

84 "Another Worthy Southern School," *Boston Evening Post*, undated, General-Clippings, 1914- September 5, 1919, Mitchell Papers; "A. W. Mitchell Seeks to Better Blackbelt Conditions," *Springfield Union*, undated, and "White Mob Lynched Negro on Suspicion; Afterwards Converted to Cause of Negro Education," General-Clippings, Nov. 11, 1898–Jan 12, 1913," Mitchell Papers.

85 "A Deserving Negro," *Sumter County Sun*, Nov 3, 1910, 4; "Negroes Eager for Schooling in West Alabama Community: The Principals Story," General-Clippings, Nov. 11, 1898–Jan 12, 1913, Mitchell Papers.

86 See *Annual Reports of the Department of Education, 1908–1912*; "Township 23, Sumter County, Alabama, Gainesville Town," 1910 U.S. Census (manuscript).

87 "Board of Education and District Trustees," *Our Southern Home*, Aug 21, 1912, 1. John Rogers apparently served illegally as sole trustee in Swilley's Bend, a school district in a sparse, virtually all-Black area where he owned most, if not all of the property about five miles south of his home. Rogers was likely the only "freeholder" in the area, although the law required a trustee to a qualified voter in the school district. See Roger's land purchase in "The *Messenger* Says . . ." *Livingston Journal*, Mar 8, 1888, 5.

88 *Code of Alabama, 1907*, vol. I, sec. 1755, 761.

89 "A Deserving Negro," *Sumter County Sun*, Nov 3, 1910, 4.

90 "Geiger Solving Problem of Getting White Farmers," *Montgomery Advertiser*, Jun 17, 1912, 10.

91 Author's Computation from data in *Annual Report of the Department of Education*, 1911; not all Black Belt towns in 1911 avoided establishing public schools for Black children, although it was the preferred pattern for towns in Sumter County, where only Livingston, the site of a white teachers college, had a Black public school.

92 Mitchell's public account of Pinson's offer was that the planter gave him a "right to sell 2600 acres" adjoining the 450 acres set aside for Mitchell's school campus. See "Meritorious Work," undated, General-Clippings, Nov. 11, 1898–Jan 12, 1913, Mitchell Papers. Also, editors of Sumter County's Black newspaper, *The Sumter Enterprise*, were agents for two real estate companies and advertised to its Black readers, "To be somebody you must own something other than a mule . . ." See "Remember the Editor Is Agent . . ." *Sumter Enterprise*, Oct 19, 1911, 1.

93 "For John H. Pinson," *Our Southern Home*, Mar 22, 1916, 8; "Geiger Gurgles," *Our Southern Home*, Apr 2, 1913, 1.

94 "Board of Education and District Trustees," *Our Southern Home*, Aug 21, 1912, 1; *Annual Report of the Department of Education*, 1913, 42; "What Can Be Done with a Black Belt Plantation," *Our Southern Home*, Aug 9, 1911, 8; *Annual Report of the Department of Education, 1914*, 212, 340.

95 Mitchell to William J, Edwards, Nov 13, 1914, correspondence file, 1934–1935, Claude A. Burnett Papers: The Associated Negro Press, 1918–1967, ProQuest/History Vault.

96 Nordin, *The New Deal's Black Congressman*, 22–23.

97 Ibid., 26–27, 30–33, 67. A state court in Choctaw County ruled in favor of Mitchell in his dispute with the Black school's trustees. Both DePriest and Mitchel were born in Alabama and were children of the Great Migration.

98 *Annual Report of the Department of Education, 1913,* 34, 44–47, 163, 171, 175.

99 "Soldiers Realize Need of Education if They Are to Fight Educated Germans," *Montgomery Advertiser,* Dec 25, 1917, 5; "'Where Is This Berlin?' Asks Illiterate Alabama Soldier in Training for Great War," *Montgomery Advertiser,* Apr 14, 1918, 25.

100 *A Comparative Study of the Public School Systems in Alabama and Other Typical States and an Exhibition of Educational Conditions in the Sixty-Seven Counties of Alabama, 1916,* Alabama Department of Education, 8, 10,14, 18, 20, and 23.

101 *Negro Education,* Bureau of Education, U.S. Department of the Interior, Bulletin, 1916, no. 38, vol. 2, 1917, 28–29.

102 "Walter Jones Lodges Formal Protest Over Act of the Legislature," *Montgomery Advertiser,* Jan 15, 1919, 2.

103 *An Educational Study of Alabama, 1919,* 9–11, 18–21, 80–123, 284, 493–495. The state senator from the Black Belt's Wilcox County attempted unsuccessfully to remake the independent commission into a legislative recess committee, which would not have met until after the legislative session. See S. 89, *Journal of the Senate,* 1919, vol. 1, 205–206.

104 *An Educational Study of Alabama, 1919,* 84, 176–204.

105 Ibid., 179.

106 Author's calculations from data in Table 95, *An Educational Study of Alabama, 1919,* 502.

107 *An Educational Study of Alabama, 1919,* 499.

108 Ibid., 500.

109 "Education Commission Files Report with Kilby," *Montgomery Advertiser,* Jun 29, 1919, sec 2, 2. It is likely that the state's newspapers, especially its weeklies, did not see the federal Bureau's accompanying report. The *Montgomery Advertiser* appears to be the only newspaper that provided more than a passing reference to the Bureau's report and its coverage left out any mention of the Black Belt. See "U.S. Bureau of Education Points Out Needs of Schools," *Montgomery Advertiser,* Jul 13, 1919, 12.

110 "More Illiteracy in State Now Than in 1840 Says Special Educational Commission Report," *Birmingham News,* Jun 29, 1919, 20.

111 Ibid.; "Education Commission Files Report with Kilby," *Montgomery Advertiser,* Jun 29, 1919, sec. 2, 2. The *Advertiser* story quoted the Commission report with capitalized letters for the words "more revenue."

112 "$1,000,000 for the Public Schools of State Recommended," *Montgomery Advertiser,* June 24, 1919, 1; "Education Commission Files Report with Kilby," *Montgomery Advertiser,* Jun 29, 1919, sec 2, 2. The Commission and Bureau also analyzed and made recommendations concerning higher education that were less dramatic and controversial.

113 "More Illiteracy in State Now Than in 1840 Says Special Educational Commission

Report," *Birmingham News,* Jun 29, 1919, 20.

114 In the legislative 1919 session, six of the seven members of the Senate Constitution and Constitutional Revision and Amendments Committee were from majority-Black counties. For members of senate committees, see *Alabama Official and Statistical Register, 1919,* 83.

115 "Budget Body Bill Passes by Senate," *Birmingham News,* Feb 5, 1919, 12; "Budget Bill Passes," *Montgomery Advertiser,* Feb 6, 1919, 1; S. 74, *Acts of Alabama,* 1919, 33–37; Black Belt leaders may have also helped to transform the purposes of the budget commission, which Gov. Kilby promised in his campaign would improve tax assessments so that "the rich and the poor should pay alike." See "Kilby Would Abolish Local Tax Boards of Assessment" [ad], *Birmingham News,* Aug 9, 1918, 2. By January 1919, when 5 of 11 members in the Senate Finance and Taxation Committee were from Black Belt counties, the budget commission became only the means to advance or prevent spending, including education spending. See "State Budget Commission Bill Still in Hands of Committee," *Montgomery Advertiser,* Jan 26, 1919, 6.

116 "Finance Committee About Through," *Montgomery Advertiser,* Jun 29, 1919, 2; *Alabama Official and Statistical Register, 1919,* 141–142. Long also was a former tax collector in Sumter County. Black Belt leaders also extracted changes in Kilby's proposal for increasing property tax assessments—a controversial bill much "discussed and cussed." To garner enough south Alabama votes for passage, Kilby accepted a lower rate of assessment and Senate amendments requiring property assessments to be undertaken by a local county resident and permitting locally elected county commissions to hear any appeals by property owners. These changes, in effect, meant that Black Belt planters and others could continue the common rural practice of allowing large property owners to set the taxable value of their own lands. See "Revenue Bill Disposed of the House Take Up Heavy Calendar" and "Kilby Will Recommend Amendments to Revenue Bill Passed on Friday," *Montgomery Advertiser*, Sep 6, 1919, 7; Karl A. Bosworth, *Black Belt County: Rural Government in the Cotton Country of Alabama* (University of Alabama: Bureau of Public Administration, 1941), 40–42.

117 *Journal of the Senate,* 1919, vol. 2, 1833, 2122–2123; *Alabama Official and Statistical Register, 1919,* 92. A similar bill was introduced in the House by a north Alabama representative from DeKalb County, but it was never reported out of committee. See "Immense Calendar Face House Solons," *Montgomery Advertiser,* Sep 3, 1919, 10. It is, of course, unclear if the sponsors intended to include all children or just all white children to be granted equal education.

118 *Annual Report of the State Treasurer, 1919–1920,* 11–13.

119 "In the Constitutional Convention . . ." *Our Southern Home,* Jul 31, 1901, 4; *Official Proceedings of the Constitutional Convention,* vol. 2, 1738–1739.

120 Robert L. Cvornyek, "Convict Labor in the Alabama Coal Mines, 1874–1928," PhD diss. (Columbia University, 1993), 286–290, 310–315; *Journal of the House of Representatives,* 1915, 1616; Elizabeth Boner Clark, "The Abolition of the Convict Lease System in Alabama," Master's thesis (University of Alabama, 1949), 8–22; 51–70.

121 *Journal of the House of Representatives,* 1919, vol. 1, 849–850, 853.

122 Ibid., 860–865.

123 Ibid., 876, 880. A draft of the minority statement can be found in Roger's family papers. See "Report of the Minority Members of Recess Committee on Roads and Convicts," Families- Rogers John A., Sumter County Historical Society Collection, Julia Tutwiler Library, University of West Alabama.

124 *Journal of the House of Representatives,* 1919, vol. 1, 879.

125 Clark, "The Abolition of the Convict Lease System in Alabama," 78–79.

126 Ibid., 77–80; *Journal of the Senate,* 1919, vol. 2, 1415, 2060; *Journal of the House of Representatives,* 1919, vol. 2, 2124–2127; *Acts of Alabama,* 1919, 522–523. Senator J. B. Ellis of Dallas County took up leadership for defending convict leasing in the 1923 session and the issue continued hanging fire until after the election of Governor Bibb Graves. See Brenton K. Fisk to E. D. Banks, Jul 7, 1923, Convict Lease, 1913–1935. Alabama League of Women Voters Papers, ADAH.

127 Gilbert, "The First Administration of Governor Bibb Graves," 42; authors computations from data in annual reports of the State Treasurer, State Auditor, and Superintendent of Education / Department of Education for the years 1903 -1924. The 2020 amount was based on consumer price index (CPI) changes for each of those years.

128 Author's computations based on average school attendance from data in *Annual Report of the Superintendent of Education, 1933,* 26–37, 64–64, 110–111, 138–139. In his statistical atlas, Charles S. Johnson calculated per pupil expenditures (PPE) by race on the basis of enrollment instead of attendance for Southern counties for 1930. He computed $44.84 PPE for white students and $4.19 for Negro students in Sumter. In Alabama, he calculated average white PPE as $27.43 and Negro PPE as $8.31. See Charles S. Johnson, *Statistical Atlas of Southern Counties: Listing and Analysis of Socio-Economic Indices of 1104 Southern Counties* (Chapel Hill: University of North Carolina Press, 1941), 43, 53. The difference in findings results from the differences in PPE based on attendance instead of enrollment and on the year of measurement. It likely that in Depression years Black PPE suffered in Sumter.

129 Compare data in *Annual Report of the Superintendent of Education, 1933,* 88–90 and *State Auditor Report, 1933,* 59–60. The tax rate for schools in 1933 was 3 mil.

130 Nordin, *The New Deal's Black Congressman,* 79–80; "Mitchell, Negro Solon, Visits Alabama," *Birmingham News,* Nov 12, 1934, 2.

131 Virginia Pounds Brown and Laurella Owens, *Toting the Lead Row: Ruby Pickens Tartt, Alabama Folklorist* (University, AL: University of Alabama Press, 1981), 140–142.

132 "Single Primary Center of Fight," *Tuscaloosa News,* Jun 28, 1927, 1; J. Mills Thornton III, "Alabama Politics, J. Thomas Heflin, and the Expulsion Movement of 1928," *Alabama Review,* Apr 1968, 91–92. Max Rogers also attacked Governor Graves and Senators Hugo Black in 1927 as leaders of a Klan-run state government and reportedly called them "scalawags." "Says Klan Runs Alabama," *New York Times,* Sep 19, 1927, 12.

133 "Will Books, 1828–1938," Probate Court (Sumter County, Alabama, accessed at ancestry.com; Barnes Rogers to A. H. Woodward, May 8, 1945, Woodward Family Papers, Special Collections, University of Alabama Libraries.

134 Francis X. Walter, *From Preaching to Meddling: A White Minister in the Civil Rights Movement* (Montgomery: NewSouth Books, 2021), 64–69; "Beat Number 14

(Gainesville)," *Sumter County Journal,* Apr 4, 1940, 6; Table 28, Characteristics of the Population, Alabama, *U.S. Census, 1940*; Gainesville Beat," U.S. Census, 1940 (manuscript); "Mack Fields New Gainesville Mayor," *Sumter County Journal,* Sep 28, 1961, 1. The manuscript Census of 1940 suggests that at least 20 or more whites listed on the voter rolls for the Gainesville precinct in 1940 lived outside the town's boundaries.

135 Ashmore, *Carry It On,* 202; "Sumter Farmers Lose Their Homes . . . 'Don't Know Where We're Going,'" *Southern Courier,* May 20–21, 1967, 4.

136 Ibid.; "'I'm Glad to Be Out,'" *Southern Courier,* Feb. 3–4, 1968.

137 *Hearing before the United States Commission on Civil Rights,* Hearing held in Montgomery, Alabama, April 27–May 2, 1968, 94–104; "Washington, D.C.," *Southern Courier,* May 18–19, 1968; Ashmore, *Carry It On,* 209, 233. Barnes Rogers could not easily claim a lack of familiarity with the Department of Agriculture's regulations since he had sat on the local committee that administered the program. See "Plan to Be Made for Election of ASC Committeemen," *Sumter County Journal,* Jul 12, 1962, 1.

138 "Table 1—Desegregation Statistics," Trial Brief of the United States, *Lee v. Macon County Board of Education,* Civil Action No. 604 E, Civil Rights Litigation Clearinghouse; Suitts, *Overturning Brown,* 26–29; Act 383, *Acts of Alabama,* 1961, 398. While making no mention of race, the local laws permitting local school bords to dismiss teachers in such manner were adopted only in eight Black Belt counties. See *Alabama State Teachers Ass'n v. Lowndes County Bd. of Ed.,* 289 F. Supp. 300 (1968).

139 "Judges Say Order to Make Sumter Schools All-Negro," *Alabama Journal,* Jun 12, 1970, 1; "'Terminal' Phase of Desegregation Just Ahead for Alabama Schools," *Montgomery Advertiser,* Aug 9, 1970, 34; "Bob Hawkins," *Selma Times-Journal,* Sep 9, 1970, 4; Joshua Phillip Adams, " Social Capital, School Desegregation and Education in West Alabama's Black Belt," Master's thesis (Auburn University, 2005), 68–86; *Lynch v. Alabama,* 568 F. Supp. 2d 1329 (2008).

140 *Knight v. State of Alabama,* 900 F. Supp. 272 (1995). The civil rights attorneys in *Knight* attempted to litigate the issues of Alabama's tax structure for school financing as a part of their original case but were rebuffed and required to file a separate action. See *Knight v. Alabama,* 476 F. 3d 1219 (2007), cert. denied 551 U.S. 1146 (2007).

141 "Memorandum of Opinion [unpublished]," *Lynch v. Alabama,* Civil Action No. 08-S-450-NE, U.S. District Court, Northern District of Alabama. The plaintiffs' attorneys were three of Alabama's accomplished civil rights and voting rights lawyers: James Blacksher, Larry Menefee, and Edward Still.

142 Ibid., 639–640. *Also, see* Norrell, *Reaping the Whirlwind,* 79–80.

143 "Memorandum of Opinion [unpublished]," *Lynch v. Alabama,* 640–682, 753–769. Also, while dropping the assessed rate of Alabama agricultural, forestry, and residential property, the 1978 amendment also permitted these property owners to use a different measurement of value—"current use" instead of fair market value. In effect, this permitted large landowners of farmland and forests to claim a much lower taxable value as well as a much lower tax rate. See "Memorandum of Opinion [unpublished]," Lynch v. Alabama, 177–187.

144 Ibid., 694–714, 758–761. Judge Smith wrote of the Black Belt leaders: "While taking advantage of such political influence may demonstrate greed or power lust, it is not necessarily tantamount to a racially discriminatory intent . . ." (761).

145 In 1966, after court-ordered reapportionment, both Pruitt and Manley represented House District 27, which included Sumter, Marengo, and Perry counties. It was the first legislative election since the end of Reconstruction in which Black candidates were on the ballot in those counties. Pruitt defeated Albert Turner. See *Alabama Official and Statistical Register, 1967,* 650.

146 "Memorandum of Opinion [unpublished]," *Lynch v. Alabama,* 798.

147 Antonia Noori Farzan, "Sumter County, Ala., Just Got Its First Integrated School. Yes, in 2018," *Washington Post,* Aug 15, 2018. The school enrolled 35 percent of the county's public schoolchildren in 2021. Data from U.S. Department of Education, National Center for Education Statistics, Common Core of Data (CCD), "Public Elementary/Secondary School Universe Survey," 2021–22 v.1a.

148 Sumter County Alabama, 2020–Public GIS. Accessed at https://www.alabamagis.com/sumter/. Also see *Estate of Rogers v. Commissioner,* 79 T.C.M. 1891 (2000), a federal tax case which includes information concerning contract prices for land leased by Barnes Rogers and others in the Rogers family since the 1950s.

Notes to Chapter 11

1 "Union Men to Wear Poll Tax Buttons," *Montgomery Advertiser,* Jan 8, 1919, 8; "Central Labor Union Meeting," *Albany-Decatur Daily,* Dec 6, 1921, 1; *Alabama Official and Statistical Register, 1919,* 406–407; *State Auditor Report, 1920,* 68–69. The comparative data in this section is taken from *State Auditor Reports,* which reported the number of poll taxpayers for both current year and prior, unpaid years in most years after 1901 for three decades.

2 Thomas, *The New Woman in Alabama,* 207; "Alabama Women Will Get to Vote," *Fairhope Courier,* Oct 8, 1920, 1; *Alabama Official and Statistical Register, 1919,* 406–407; *Alabama Official and Statistical Register, 1923,* 355–356; "The Registering of Women Voters," *Montgomery Advertiser,* Oct 28, 1920, 4.

3 *1916 Alabama Attorney General Reports and Opinions* 27 (1916–1922), 675–676; "Registrar for Butler Named," *Greenville Advocate,* Oct 8, 1920, 1; *Cornelius v. Pruet,* 85 So. 430 (April 10, 1920); *Alabama Official and Statistical Register, 1935,* 574–575. The Alabama Supreme Court rejected arguments that women were exempt for paying poll taxes to vote in 1921. See *Graves v. Eubanks,* 87 So. 587 (1921). The population of Alabama's eligible white voters (21 years and over) increased by more than 166,000 persons from the 1920 Census to the 1930 Census.

4 *State Auditor Report, 1920,* 68–69; *State Auditor Report, 1921,* 80–81; "Women Continue to Lead in Poll Tax Race," *Montgomery Advertiser,* Jan 28, 1921, 7; "Alabama Women, Pay Your Poll Tax Now," *Cherokee Harmonizer,* Jan 20, 1921, 2; "Notice! Notice!" *Marion County News.* Feb 23, 1921, 1. The increase of poll taxpayers paying only for the year 1921 (not payments for unpaid back years) increased by more than 50,000. Most of these were likely women voters.

5 *Acts of Alabama,* 1921, 4–5; "Big Majority Given Both Amendments," *Montgomery*

Advertiser, Feb 14, 1922, 3. The veterans' participation In the 1922 Democratic primary for governor was probably dampened, even though they were not required to pay a poll tax, because of widespread confusion over requirements that they qualify as a voters in a prior, separate procedure and produce their military discharge papers to acquire an exemption certificate in advance of voting. See "Ex-Soldiers Asked to Show Service Papers," *Luverne Journal and The Crenshaw County News*, Mar 2, 1922, 6; "Notice to Voters," *Boaz Leader*, Mar 16, 1922, 6; "Ex-Servicemen Must Apply for Tax Exemption," *The Onlooker* (Foley), Apr 13, 1922, 1

6 *Alabama Official and Statistical Register, 1923*, 149; Suitts, *Hugo Black of Alabama*, 449–453, 477–479. During Holcombe's trial the Black Belt leader of the house, A. M. Tunstall, was the first witness to testify to Holcombe's good character and reputation. See "Bribe Conference Never Held, Three Witnesses Swear," *Birmingham News*, May 15, 1924, 2.

7 *Journal of the House of Representatives*, 1923, vol. 2, 1604–1606; *Journal of the Senate*, 1923, vol. 2, 1988–1989.

8 *Alabama Official and Statistical Register, 1927*, 346–347; *State Auditor Report, 1924*, 88–89. In the following year, the number of poll taxpayers dropped by 40,000 poll taxpayers. See *State Auditor Report, 1925*, 96–97.

9 Mark Ellis, *Race, War, and Surveillance : African Americans and the United States Government during World War I* (Bloomington: Indiana University Press, 2001), 208; Chad L. Williams, *Torchbearers of Democracy: African American Soldiers and the Era of the First World War*, (Chapel Hill: University of North Carolina Press, 2010), 231, 238–239, 196; Alsobrook, "A Call to Arms for African Americans," 90; Vincent Mikkelsen, "Coming from Battle to Face a War: The Lynching of Black Soldiers in the World War Era," PhD diss. (Florida State University, 2008), 67.

10 Mikkelsen, "Coming from Battle to Face a Wart," 99–102.

11 "National Association Protests Against Lynching," *Philadelphia Tribune*, Jan 4, 1919, 7; Mikkelsen, "Coming from Battle to Face a War," 103.

12 See. for example, "Negro Soldier Taken from Jail; Lynched," *Montgomery Advertiser*, Dec 17, 1918, 9.

13 "Hickman, Ky.," *Selma Times-Journal*, Dec 18, 1918, 4.

14 Mikkelsen, "Coming from Battle to Face a War," 139, 162; Rosengarten, *All God's Dangers*, 161; Williams, *Torchbearers of Democracy*, 241–243.

15 Williams, *Torchbearers of Democracy*, 237; "Three Negroes Are Lynched in Montgomery," *Gadsden Daily Times-News*, Sep 30, 1919, 1; "McCord Orders Special Jury to Probe Lynchings," *Birmingham News*, Sep 30, 1919, 1; "Three Negroes Lynched in Montgomery in 12 Hours," *Tuscaloosa News*, Sep 30, 1919, 1.

16 Suitts, *Hugo Black of Alabama*, 260–262. Vincent Mikkelsen lists those African American soldiers lynched after the War. All listed were in the southern states. See Mikkelsen, "Coming from Battle to Face a Warr," 213.

17 "Colored Registration," *Birmingham News*, Jan 14, 1920, 8.

18 "Recognition of Good Negroes: A petition and a Suggestion," *Birmingham News*, Jan 14, 1920, 8. The *News* apparently held the letter to the editor so that both the letter and the News comments on it could run on the same day.

19 "Alabama Voting Law Explained; Soldier Plan and New Law Discussed—Poll Tax Necessary," *Birmingham Reporter*, Jan 17, 1920. 1; C. J. Adams to National Association for the Advancement of Colored People, Feb 4 1920, John Shillady, Secretary, to C. J. Adams, Feb 9, 1920, Voting, Feb -July, 1920, NAACP Papers; "White Veterans Meet Here on June 29," *Huntsville Times*, Jun 6, 1919, 4; "Dixie Delegates of Legion Confer," *Birmingham News*, Oct 1, 1919, 16; "A Negro Ex-Soldier Makes an Appeal," *Birmingham News*, Jan 1, 1920, 8.

20 "Negro Lynched in Florala," *Troy Messenger*, Jan 21, 1920, 6; "He Went to France, Then to H–," *Choctaw Advocate*, Jan 21, 1920, 1; Williams, *Torchbearers of Democracy*, 244–245; Mikkelsen, "Coming from Battle to Face a War," 174–178; "Riot Spirit Ended in Florida Towns," *Birmingham News*, Nov 4, 1920, 26; Carlee Hoffman and Claire Strom, "A Perfect Storm: The Ocoee Riot of 1920," *Florida Historical Quarterly*, Summer 2014, Vol. 93, No. 1 (Summer 2014), 25–43.

21 Williams, *Torchbearers of Democracy*, 245.

22 "Bonus Opposition Gaining Strength," *Birmingham News*, Feb 1, 1922, 17; "Liles Speaks to Women for S. P. M'Donald," *Anniston Star*, Apr 6, 1921, 8.

23 "Pell City Offer May Get Hospital," *Birmingham News*, Jul 16, 1921, 6; "Local Contractor Secures Contract at Tuskegee," *Montgomery Advertiser*, Mar 14, 1925, 4; Jennifer Keene, "The Long Journey Home: African American World War I Veterans and Veterans' Policies," in Stephen R. Ortiz (ed.), *Veterans Policies, Veterans Politics: New Perspectives on Veterans in the Modern United States* (Gainesville: University Press of Florida, 2015), 161–163; *Acts of Alabama*, 1915, 98.

24 "Veterans Are Carrying On in the Carter N. Brown Legion," *Press-Forum Weekly* (Mobile), Feb 4, 1922, 1; "Colored War Veterans Are Organizing," *Birmingham Reporter*, Mar 11, 1922, 1; "Negroes of Ex-Soldiers of War Will Meet," *Birmingham News*, Dec 22, 1923, 14; "New Corporations," *Montgomery Advertiser*, Mar 7, 1923, 3.

25 Timothy Percy Patterson to President Calvin Coolidge, Oct. 16, 1923, U.S. Department of Justice, Class 72 (Elections and Political Activity) Litigation Case Files and Enclosures, 1919–1980, U.S. Department of Justice, National Archives; "Timothy P. Patterson," Registration Card # 167, Lamar County, Miss, June 5, 1917, accessed at Ancestry.com; "Timothy P. Patterson," U.S. Army Transport Service Arriving and Departing Passenger Lists, 1910–1939, accessed at ancestry.com.

26 Lula Murry to President Calvin Coolidge, Oct. 17, 1923, Justice Department, National Archives; "Murry, Lula," *Birmingham City Directory, 1925*, 958; "Murry, Jim / Murry, Lula." Enumeration District 75, Sheet 5, Birmingham City, 1920 U.S. Census (manuscript).

27 Liette Gidlow, "The Sequel: The Fifteenth Amendment, the Nineteenth Amendment, and Southern Black Women's Struggle to Vote," *Journal of the Gilded Age and Progressive Era*, 17 (2018), 443–444.

28 Suitts, *Hugo Black of Alabama*, 366–367.

29 Ibid., 307–317, 327–332; "To All White Servicemen," *Weekly Herald* (Wetumpka), Mar 30, 1922, 7; "No Negro Shall Vote in Primary Says Committee," *Montgomery Times*, Jul 29, 1922, 2.

30 "Klansmen Parade in Tuskegee," *LaFayette Sun*, Jul 5, 1923, 8; "White People of Ala. Won't Stand Negro Personnel," *Birmingham Reporter*, Jul 21, 1923, 1; Suitts, *Hugo Black of Alabama*, 433.

31 "To Address Negroes," *Birmingham News*, Nov 1, 1924, 12; *The World War Veterans' Act: 1924 with Amendments Prior to July 3, 1926*, accessed at https://archive.org/details/worldwarveterans00unit/mode/2up; Oscar W. Adams, "What Negroes Are Doing," *Birmingham News*, Nov 9, 1924, 48; "Merriweather, Jerry S.," *Birmingham City Directory, 1925*, 908.

32 "Negro Veteran to Speak," *Birmingham News*, Jun 21, 1925, 44.

33 "Negroes Organize Non-Partisan Body," *Birmingham News*, Sep 20, 1925, 16; "A League for Negro Voters," *Birmingham Reporter*, Sep 26, 1925, 4; "Negro Political League Holds Interesting Meeting," *Birmingham Reporter*, Oct 10, 1925, 1; "1,735 Register," *Birmingham News*. Jul 17, 1925, 17; Gidlow, "The Sequel," 444.

34 "Voting Books Open," *Birmingham News*, Jan 17, 1926, 1; "The Ex-Soldiers Cooperative Association, Inc.," *Birmingham News*, Jan 17, 1926, 27; "Brandon Declines Plea of Negroes," *Birmingham News*, Jan 21, 1926, 6. The petition is dated January 11, 1926.

35 "Birmingham Woman Held in Registration Dispute; Dept. Of Justice on Hand," *Pittsburgh Courier*, Jan 30, 1926, 8; "Delegation of Negro Women Start Row over Registration in Jefferson County Court House; One Arrested," *The Times* (Montgomery), Jan 19, 1926, 2.

36 "Negress Facing Vagrancy Charge," *Birmingham News*, Jan 20, 1926, 22; "Woman's Color Causes Assault," "Mrs. Little Refuses to Leave Registrar's Office," *Birmingham Reporter*, Jan 23, 1926, 1. See *Alabama Code*, 1941, Title 15, Sec. 408–412 for "security to keep the peace."

37 "Negro Women Attempt to Register at B'gham," *Selma Times-Journal*. Jan 19, 1926, 7; "Negro Woman, Demanding Vote, Placed in Jail," *Birmingham News*, Jan 18, 1926, 1.

38 "Delegation of Negro Women Start Row over Registration in Jefferson County Court House; One Arrested," *The Times* (Montgomery), Jan 19, 1926, 2.

39 Gidlow, "The Sequel,"444; Liette Gidlow, "Resistance after Ratification: The Nineteenth Amendment, African American Women, and the Problem of Female Disfranchisement after 1920," *Women and Social Movements in the U.S., 1600–2000*, Mar 2017, 21, available at https://alexanderstreet.com.

40 "Negro Servicemen Appeal to Brandon over Registration," *Albany-Decatur Daily*. Jan 20, 1926, 1; "; "The Ex-Soldiers Cooperative Association, Inc.," *Birmingham News*, Jan 21, 1926, 25; "The Ex-Soldiers Cooperative Association, Inc.," *Birmingham Reporter*, Jan 30, 1926, 2; "The Ex-Soldiers Cooperative Association, Inc.," *Montgomery Advertiser*, Jan 24, 1926, 11; "Brandon Declines Plea of Negroes," *Birmingham News*, Jan 21, 1926, 6; "Negroes Appeal to Chief Executive," *Montgomery Advertiser*, Jan 21, 1926, 1.

41 Gidlow, "The Sequel," 444; *Congressional Record*, 69th Congress, Feb 13, 1926, 3959.

42 Gidlow, "Resistance after Ratification," 22; Gidlow, "The Sequel," 444–445. For a understanding of Kennamer, see "Republicans to Contest," *Guntersville Advertiser*,

Nov 23, 1920, 1; "Democrats Smile at G.O.P. Row," *Birmingham News,* Jun 11, 1922, 8; Steve Suitts, *Hugo Black of Alabama,* 474–475; "Federal Judge Kennamer Dies of a Heart Attack Here at Home," *Alabama Journal,* Jun 3, 1955, 1. Kennamer was succeeded on the federal bench by Frank M. Johnson.

43 "Case Is Passed," *Birmingham News,* Jan 27, 1926, 2; Charles A. J. McPherson to Weldon Johnson, Mar 4, 1926, Branch Files, Birmingham, 1920–1926, NAACP Papers; "Little, Terrel," *Birmingham City Directory, 1928,* 702; "Register and Vote," *Birmingham Reporter,* Jan 23, 1926, 4; "The Opportunity for Registration Now," *Birmingham Reporter,* Mar 6, 1926, 4.

44 Incorporation Record 741–188, Ex-Soldiers Progressive Ass'n., Inc., Alabama Secretary of State, December 26, 1926; "Incorporations," *Birmingham New,* Jan 31, 1927, 17; "Ohio Bell Jailed on Fraud Charges," *Birmingham News,* Jan 17, 1928, 20; "Lacey Sentenced to Term in Pen," *Birmingham News,* Mar 14, 1928, 14.

45 Quoted in "Ohio Bell Goes to Federal Prison Atlanta," *Luverne Journal and The Crenshaw County News,* Mar 14, 1928, 1.

46 Author's calculations based on data in *State Auditor Report 1923,* 88–89; *State Auditor Report 1926,* 84–85; and *Alabama Official and Statistical Register, 1927,* 345–346, 362–363. The annual reporting of the year of the poll payers is inconsistent during this time. Often, but not always, the year of the report indicates those who paid poll taxes for the following year's election. The author relied on the proven historical pattern in which poll tax payments dropped notably in off years, when state and federal elections were not held, in order to determine the election year for which the reported poll tax was applied.

47 The Alabama Department Archives and History compiled during 2017–2018 Alabama's WWI personnel, totaling nearly 110,000 persons. Most are white since the state's African American men were not allowed to enlist voluntarily. Therefore, when the number of Black inducted soldiers (25,974) is taken from this total of military personnel, the balance of 83,666 is closest to the actual numbers of white ex-soldiers eligible for a poll tax exemption. See "Gov. Charles Henderson's Message to the Legislature," *Journal of the House of Representatives,* 1919, vol. 1, 18, and "Alabama World War I Service Records," accessed at https://digital.archives.alabama.gov/digital/collection/p17217coll3.

48 Samuel L. Webb, "Hugo Black, Bibb Graves, and the Ku Klux Klan: A Revisionist View of the 1926 Alabama Democratic Primary," *Alabama Review,* vol. 57, 4, Oct 2004, 272–273. Also, see Suitts, *Hugo Black of Alabama,* 513–518. Bibb Graves certainly engaged in political duplicity when it served him. For example, in his 1926 campaign he attacked the Black Belt for providing "a nine month's free school to the negroes" while "white children in white counties" received only six month's schools. Graves surely knew it was the Black Belt planters' white children—not Black children—who enjoyed nine month school terms. See "Bibb Graves, The Man for Governor" [ad], *Southern Aegis,* Aug 5, 1926, 3.

49 Suitts, *Hugo Black of Alabama,* 491, 497; William Edward Gilbert, "The First Administration of Governor Bibb Graves, 1927–1930," Master's thesis (University of Alabama, 1953), 5–7; "White Veterans Meet Here on June 29," *Huntsville Times,* Jun 6, 1919, 4.

50 Lorraine Gates Schuyler, *The Weight of Their Votes: Southern Women and Political Leverage in the 1920s* (Chapel Hill: University of North Carolina Press, 2006), 67; Gilbert, "The First Administration of Governor Bibb Graves," 15, 25–39. 53–65, 74–84; "Message of the Governor," *Journal of the House of Representatives,* 1927, vol. 1, 24.

51 *Davis v. Teague,* 220 Ala. 309, 125 So. 51 (1929); "St. Clair Clerk, Republican, Ordered Ousted," *Dothan Eagle,* Nov 7, 1929, 6.

52 Section 45 of Act 494, *Acts of Alabama,* 1927, 566–597; "Guardsmen Exempt from Poll Tax," *Montgomery Advertiser* Oct 10, 1930, 10; *1928 Alabama Attorney General Reports and Opinions* (1928–1930), 731–732, reiterating the opinion in *1900 Alabama Attorney General Reports and Opinions* (1900–1902), 215. "Township trustees"—once confined to only "freeholders"—also continued to enjoy an exemption due to the grandfathering provision of the 1901 Constitution. See *1902 Alabama Attorney General Reports and Opinions* (1902–1906), 154.

53 *1928 Alabama Attorney General Reports and Opinions* (1928–1930), 732–733.

54 *Journal of the House of Representatives,* 1932, vol. 1, 239–241, 805–907; *Journal of the House of Representatives,* 1933, 459–460; Glenn Feldman, "Benjamin Meek Miller (1931–35)," Encyclopedia of Alabama.

55 "Poll Tax Laws to Be Revised, M'Cord Pledges," *Huntsville Times,* Jan 28, 1934, 1.

56 Paul W. Terry and Verner M. Sims, *They Live on the Land: Life in an Open-Country Southern Community* (University, Ala.: Bureau of Educational Research, University of Alabama, 1940), 75.

57 "Graves against Sales Tax, for Referendum," *Anniston Star,* Feb 1, 1934, 1; "Plan for Schools Outlined by Dixon," *Birmingham News,* Apr 19, 1934, 19; "I Now Promise," *Onlooker* (Foley), Apr 26, 1934, 3; "McPhaul for Representative," *Fairhope Courier,* Apr 5, 1934, 4; "J. H. Johnson Issues Statement to Voters of Dale County," *Southern Star,* Apr 18, 1934, 1.

58 William A. Nunnelley, *Bull Connor* (Tuscaloosa: University of Alabama Press, 1991), 10–13; "Poll Taxes," *Anniston Star,* Feb 5, 1935, 1. Connor was born and raised in Dallas County in the Black Belt.

59 Ralph Hurst, "Politics," *Birmingham News,* May 10, 1935, 2.

60 "Legislators Resting After Stormy Week," *Birmingham News,* Jun 8, 1935, 2. Twenty five of the 37 votes against the bill were from Black Belt representatives; others were primarily from Big Mule allies, although a few north Alabama representative voted against the bill, especially Democrats who represented counties where Republicans remained a competitive force in local elections. For those voting "nay," see "See Your Legislators" [reprint of *Birmingham Post* editorial], *Union-Banner,* Aug 15, 1935, 3.

61 "Graves Routs Poll Tax Reform Foes," *Phenix-Girard Journal,* Aug 9, 1935. 1; *Journal of the Senate,* 1935, vol. 2, 1499.

62 "Poll Tax Bill Causes Brisk House Debate," *Huntsville Times,* Aug 15, 1935, 1; "Reapportionment Bill Beaten 6–37," *Anniston Star,* Aug 16, 1935, 1. It is quite possible Black Belt legislators did some vote-trading that saved the poll tax bill but defeated Graves's reapportionment bill.

63 "Connor Poll Tax Bill Holds Main Spot at Capitol," *Dothan Eagle,* Sep 5, 1935, 1;

"Poll Tax Bill Is Voted Out of Committee," *Troy Messenger,* Sep 5, 1935, 1; "Poll Tax Relief Killed in Senate by Narrow Vote," *Montgomery Advertiser,* Sep 11, 1935, 1; "Security Bills to Gov. Graves," *Huntsville Times,* Sep 11, 1935, 8; *Journal of the Senate,* 1935, vol. 2, 1892–1894, 2199–2201. One senators present also "paired" his vote with one senator who was absent.

64 Authors calculations based on the vote at *Journal of the Senate,* 1935, vol. 2, 2200–2201, and information in *Alabama Official and Statistical Register, 1935,* 125–126, 139–157.

65 "Amendment on Poll Tax Is Lost Today," *Decatur Daily,* Mar 31, 1936, 1; *Journal of the House of Representatives,* 1936, 746–751, 817–820, 1026–132. It is likely that the bill would have failed in the senate again in committee or on the floor, even if it had passed the house.

66 "A Grave Objection to Poll Tax 'Reform,'" *Montgomery Advertiser,* Apr 10, 1936, 4.

67 Campaign Rides on Same Issues as Close Nears," *Birmingham News,* Jun 6, 1936, 2.

68 Patricia Sullivan, *Days of Hope: Race and Democracy in the New Deal Era* (Chapel Hill: University of North Carolina Press, 1996), 60.

69 *Breedlove v. Suttles,* 302 US 277 (1937), 283.

70 "Court Upholds Government Trust Busting," *Anniston Star,* Dec 6, 1937, 1; Tindall, *The Emergence of the New South,* 641; Sullivan, *Days of Hope,* 62. Florida eliminated its poll tax in 1937.

71 "Women Bade Carry Gospel of New Deal," *Montgomery Advertiser,* Apr 5, 1938, 1; "Noted Women Leaders Visit City," *Birmingham News,* Oct 26, 1938, 2.

72 "Women Gather in Party Rally," *Huntsville Times,* Oct 26, 1938, 2.

73 "South's Power in Party Menaced," *Birmingham News,* Oct 27, 1938, 9; Sarah Wilkerson-Freeman, "The Second Battle for Woman Suffrage: Alabama White Women, the Poll Tax, and V. O. Key's Master Narrative of Southern Politics," *Journal of Southern History,* vol. 68, no. 2 (May 2002), 341, 343. Evans also noted that in 1936 the Democratic Party decided that its convention would no longer require presidential candidates to receive a ⅔ vote of delegates to win the nomination—a rule that the South had used to block unacceptable candidates in the past.

74 "South's Power in Party Waning, Claim," *Montgomery Advertiser,* Oct 27, 1938, 3.

75 John Egerton, *Speak Now Against the Day: The Generation Before the Civil Rights Movement in the South* (New York: Alfred A Knopf, 1994), 181–188; "Birmian Found in Road Ditch, Badly Beaten," *Anniston Star,* Sep 24, 1936, 1; Thomas A. Krueger, *And Promises to Keep: The Southern Conference for Human Welfare, 1938–1948* (Nashville: Vanderbilt University Press, 1967), 16–17.

76 Krueger, *And Promises to Keep,* 21–23; "Mrs. Roosevelt Has a Busy Day," *Birmingham News,* Nov 22, 1938, 12.

77 Egerton, *Speak Now Against the Day,* 193.

78 *Report of Proceedings of the Southern Conference for Human Welfare,* Birmingham, Alabama, November 20 -23, 1938, 28.

79 Krueger, *And Promises to Keep,* 37–38; Sullivan, *Days of Hope,* 100.

80 Linda Reed, *Simple Decency & Common Sense: The Southern Conference Movement,*

1938–1963 (Bloomington: Indiana University Press, 1991), 65–66.

81 Durr, *Outside the Magic Circle*, 114–115, 119–120; Sullivan, *Days of Hope*, 110–119.

82 "Dixon 'Peckerwood Clubs' Answer to Governor Graves," *Anniston Star*, Mar 26, 1938, 1; "Chauncey Sparks Upsets Dope-Sheet by Coming in Second Ahead of Goode," *Cullman Banner*, May 6, 1938, 1; "Runner Up Give Pledge to Work with New Regime," *Birmingham News*, May 10, 1938, 1. The term 'peckerwood" was often used to described "white trash." See, for example, C. Eric Lincoln, *Coming Through Fire*, (Durham: Duke University Press, 1996), 20.

83 "Dixon to Fight for Six Changes in State Laws," *Anniston Star*, Mar 12, 1939, 1; "A Proclamation by the Governor," *Journal of the Senate*, 1939, 3–4; "South Seeks to Kill Poll Tax System," *Chicago Defender*, May 27, 1939, 22; H. 41, *Journal of the House of Representatives*, 1939, vol. 2, 91–93, 159–160.

84 William Vernon Holloway and Charles W. Smith Jr., *Government and Politics in Alabama* (University, Alabama: University Supply Store, 1941), 120.

85 Holloway and Smith, *Government and Politics*, 120–121; Ralph J. Bunche, The Political Status of the Negro, 337.

86 Holloway and Smith, *Government and Politics*, 121; "Let Poll Tax Alone, Insist Alabamians," *Montgomery Advertiser*, Mar 7, 1940 "'National Unity' Need of Hour, Graves Asserts," *Montgomery Advertiser*, Mar 30, 1940, 7.

87 *Poll Taxes: Hearings before a Subcommittee of the Committee on the Judiciary*, United States Senate, Seventy-seventh Congress, second session, on S. 1280, 1942.

88 "Dixon Upholds Poll Tax Law," *Alabama Journal*, Aug 29, 1942, 2; Molly Guptill Manning, "Fighting to Lose the Vote: How the Soldier Voting Acts of 1942 and 1944 Disenfranchised America's Armed Forces, "*N.Y.U.J. Legis. & Pub. Pol'y*, vol. 19, 2016, 353–354; Sullivan, *Days of Hope*, 116–117.

89 Sullivan, *Days of Hope*, n. 24, 286; *Alabama Official and Statistical Register, 1947*, 745; "Apostate No. 2," *Greensboro Watchman*, Oct 22, 1942, 4.

90 Grafton and Permaloff, *Big Mules and Branchheads* 27–33; "Sparks Record Shows He Is Agin' Everything," *Franklin County Times*, Apr 30, 1942, 9; "State Press Predicts CHAUNCEY SPARKS WILL BE ELECTED GOVERNOR BY OVERWHELMING VOTE" [ad], *Union Springs Herald*, Apr 23, 1942, 5.

91 *Journal of the House of Representatives*, 1942–1943, Regular Session, 1943, 8–21, 351–355; *Journal of the Senate*, 1943, 29–30, 35, 203–204, 219, 229–230, 543–544, 705–706; *Acts of Alabama*, 1943, H. 1, 199–201.

92 *Journal of the Senate*, 1943, 586–588, 618; "Senate Approves Bill Freeing Servicemen of Poll Tax Payments, *Birmingham News*, Jun 23, 1943, 7; "Legislators Hit at New Deal in 2 Resolutions," *Montgomery Advertiser*, Jun 4, 1943, 1; "Legislature Asks Party to Desist," *Southern Watchman*, Jun 12, 1943, 6; "States' Rights," *Our Southern Home*, Jun 17, 1943, 4.

93 "Legislators Hit at New Deal in 2 Resolutions," *Montgomery Advertiser*, Jun 4, 1943, 1; "Manasco Scores 'Communists' Behind Anti-Poll Tax Bill," *Troy Messenger*, May 24, 1943, 1; *Alabama Official and Statistical Register, 1947*, 792–793.

94 "Manasco and the Communists," *Cullman Tribune*, Jun 3, 1943, 6.

95 "Worse Than Jackass Braying," *Fayette County Times*, May 27, 1943, 4.

96 "The Poll Tax," *Decatur Daily*, Jun 4, 1943, 4. In 1942, a brouhaha broke out over Roosevelt's Farm Security Administration including payment of a farmer's poll tax in computing the amount of funds he might need to continue to operate. See "FDR Says FSA Not Paying for Poll Tax, " *Huntsville Times*, Feb 13, 1942, 1.

97 "Poll Tax Fight to Echo Here in Legislature," *Montgomery Advertiser*, Nov 15, 1942, 1.

98 *Smith v. Allwright*, 321 U.S. 649 (1944).

99 Hamilton, *The Bench and the Ballot*, 124; "When Will the South Wake Up?" *Southern Watchman*, Apr 8, 1944, 1; "The Ultimate Insanity," *Selma Times-Journal*, Apr 7, 1944, 4.

100 "Alabama to Hold White Primary—McCorvey," *Montgomery Advertiser*, Apr 4, 1944, 1.

101 Author's calculation from voting returns in *Alabama Official and Statistical Register, 1947*, 526–538.

102 *Alabama Official and Statistical Register, 1947*, 429, 538; Frederic D. Ogden, *The Poll Tax in the South* (University: University of Alabama Press, 1958), 185–188.

103 "Voters to Air Poll Tax Views with Legislators from County," *Birmingham News*, Feb 15, 1945. 1; Hamilton, *The Bench and the Ballot*, 130; "Three State Congressmen Advocate Poll Tax Repeal," *The Birmingham News*, Feb 18, 1945, 13; "Folsom Says Poll Tax in Alabama Is Doomed," *Huntsville Times*. Feb 16, 1945, 2.

104 "State May Repeal Poll Tax if Left Alone to Decide," *Birmingham News*, Feb 18, 1945, 13; *Journal of the House of Representatives*, 1945, 26–26.

105 *Journal of the House of Representatives*, 1945, 55, 47; *Alabama Official and Statistical Register, 1943*, 272 (Charles Norman of Union Springs became house speaker in the 1945 session after the death of George Miller); "Poll Tax Outlook," *Birmingham News*, May 13, 1945, 17.

106 *Journal of the House of Representatives*, 1945, 325–328; "Eliminating Poll Tax Measure Killed in House," *Birmingham News*, May 16, 1945, 1. In a last ditch effort, the sponsor attempted to substitute his bill with an exemption for the wives and widows of wartime servicemen, but the speaker ruled the substitute out of order.

107 "Agitation Stalls Poll Tax Repeal, " *Dothan Eagle*, Feb 18, 1945, 1; "Bravo, Mr. McCorvey!" *LaFayette Sun*, May 23, 1945, 2; "House Passes Bill to Use Income Tax for State Services," *Union Springs Herald*, May 24, 1945, 1. Norman was the publisher of the *Union Springs Herald*. Representative Boswell whose interim committee refused to recommend a change in the poll tax made the same argument about "attempt in Washington." See "State Election Laws May Change, Give Primaries to Parties," *Birmingham News*, Sep 7, 1944, 4.

108 "Alabama Rebukes the Anti-Poll Tax Crowd," *Southern Watchman*, May 19, 1945, 1.

109 "Chairman McCorvey's Letter," *Southern Watchman*, May 19, 1945, 7.

110 *Smith v. Allwright*, 321 U.S. 649 (1944); *Nixon v. Herndon*, 273 US 536 (1927); *Nixon v. Condon*, 286 U.S. 73 (1932). The *Smith* opinion overruled another case that had given segregationists' refuge, *Grovey v. Townsend*, 295 US 45(1935), but President Roosevelt's appointment to the Supreme Court, beginning with Hugo Black of Alabama, changed its membership and, in this case, its line of rulings.

111 *Smith v. Allwright*, 321 U.S. 649 (1944), 664–663, 662.

112 "Chairman McCorvey's Letter," *Southern Watchman*, May 19, 1945, 7; Barnard, *Dixiecrats and Democrats*, 60, 99; "Letter Written on Boswell Amendment," *Shelby County Reporter*, Oct 24, 1946, 1. Appropriately, Black Belt leader Walter Givhan sponsored the 1965 state senate resolution mourning McCorvey's death and the state's loss of an exemplar of "Southern traditions" and "high principles." See *Acts of Alabama*, 1965, 2nd special session, 50–51.

113 Walter, *From Preaching to Meddling*, 72. The occurrence may have taken place in the summer of 1946 instead of 1945.

NOTES TO CHAPTER 12

1 "Big Jim Folsom to Wipe Out Poll Tax," *Weekly Review* (Birmingham), Apr 20, 1946, 1; Grafton and Permaloff, *Big Mules and Branchheads*, 60–69.

2 Grafton and Permaloff, *Big Mules and Branchheads*, 75.

3 "3,000 Ignore Rebuffs of Alabama Poll Bosses; Register for Primaries," *Chicago Defender*, Oct 28, 1939, 2; Charles V. Hamilton, *Minority Politics in Black Belt Alabama* (New York : McGraw-Hill, 1962), 1–2.

4 "Big Jim Folsom to Wipe Out Poll Tax," *Weekly Review* (Birmingham), Apr 20, 1946, 1.

5 Grafton and Permaloff, *Big Mules and Branchheads*, 81–87, 102; author's calculations from biographical and other information in *Alabama Official and Statistical Register, 1943*, 227–335, and *Alabama Official and Statistical Register, 1947*, 167–245. The turnovers in both chambers in 1947 (56 percent in the house and 74 percent in the senate) were larger than all others recorded from 1901–1943 by the state's premiere scholar of the Alabama legislature, Hallie Farmer. See Farmer, *The Legislative Process in Alabama*, 302–304.

6 *Journal of the House of Representatives*, 1947, vol. 1, 665; "Poll Tax Bill Finds Folsom for It—But," *Montgomery Advertiser*, Jul 22, 1947, 1; "Chloroform Blacks Out Poll Tax Bill," *Montgomery Advertiser*, Jul 24, 1947, 1; "Anti-Poll Tax Bill Passes House, Goes to Senate," *Birmingham News*, Jul 21, 1947, 1. The South's members prevented the bill from passing in the U.S. Senate.

7 *Journal of the House of Representatives*, 1949, vol. 1, 11.

8 *Journal of the House of Representatives*, 1949, vol. 1, 29,59; *Alabama Official and Statistical Register, 1947*, 197; Allen Rankin, "Rankin File," *Alabama Journal*, May 25, 1949, 3.

9 *Journal of the House of Representatives*, 1949, vol. 1, 287–291; "Rankin File," *Alabama Journal*, May 25, 1949, 3. Also, eight representatives who did not vote on the bill's fate were able to help defeat it without a record of voting "no" since passage of a proposed constitutional amendment required 60 percent of the total 105 house membership. Wallace did introduce a bill to exempt all veterans who had honorably served in the military, (not just those serving in wartime) from paying a poll tax. See "State Senate Refuses to Urge Cut," *Birmingham News*, May 17, 1949, 19.

10 "Here's How I Stand! Gordon Persons" [ad], *Decatur Daily*, Apr 11, 1950, 12; "States' Righter Eugene (Bull) Connor . . ." *Birmingham News*, Apr 16, 1950, 14.

11 "1951 Session Opens Here Tuesday," *Montgomery Advertiser*, Apr 29, 1951, 2; Ogden, *The Poll Tax in the South*, 231; "'Straight Down the Middle,'" *Montgomery Advertiser*, May 14, 1950, 16.

12 *Acts of Alabama*, 1951, 558–559; "Administration Wins First Test in Tax Battle," *Alabama Journal*, Jun 19, 1951,1; *Journal of the Senate*, 1951, vol. 2, 1084; *Alabama Official and Statistical Register, 1951*, 615 (election returns) and 219–235, 246–284 (for veteran status mentioned in legislators' biographies). Several bills with veteran benefits were introduced and passed by the legislature in 1951. See index listing in *Journal of the House of Representatives*, 1951, vol. 2, 2927.

13 *Journal of the House of Representatives*, 1951, vol. 2, 1868–1872. The house voted to change the limit on back poll taxes from two years to four years before failing to provide enough votes for passage.

14 G. C. Long Jr., "Little Opposition as Poll Tax Bill Is Okehed (sic)," *Montgomery Advertiser*, Jul 18, 1951, 1; "House Group Kills Bill to Limit Back Payments on Poll Tax," *Montgomery Advertiser*, Aug 3, 1951, 6; "Little Opposition Voiced," *Montgomery Advertiser*, Jul 18, 1951, 2.

15 Wilkerson-Freeman, "The Second Battle for Women's Suffrage," 355–359; Ogden, *The Poll Tax in the South*, 231–233; Carolyn Hinshaw Edwards, *Hallie Farmer: Crusader for Legislative Reform in Alabama* (Strode Publishers: Huntsville, Alabama, 1979), 11–13, 35–41; "Alabama's Poll Tax, Barrier to Female Voting," *Montgomery Advertiser*, May 8, 1949, 19.

16 "Voter League Hears Solons on Poll Tax," *Anniston Star*, Nov 26, 1952, 1; "Let the People Vote," *Birmingham News*, Apr 11, 1953, 4; "Women Voters Lay Final Plans to Get Poll Tax Repealed," *Decatur Daily*, Apr 30, 1953, 20; "Elmore County Legislators Go on Record as Favoring Poll Tax Abolishment at Meeting Here," *Wetumpka Herald*, Apr 2, 1953, 1; Edwards, *Hallie Farmer*, 37; "Poll Tax History to Be Discussed," *Alabama Journal*, Apr 14, 1953, 5; "Anti-Poll Tax Groups to Hear Attorney Here," *Montgomery Advertiser*. Apr 25, 1953, 5; "Poll Tax Death Would Cause No Upheaval, Attorney Tells Women Voters League," *Montgomery Advertiser*, Apr 16, 1953, 10.

17 "Poll Tax Repeal in 1953 Has a Head of Steam," *Dothan Eagle*, Apr 7, 1953, 4; "The Poll Tax Wallflower Again," *Montgomery Advertiser*, May 7, 1953, 4; "Poll Tax," *Sumter County Journal*, May 7, 1953, 2; "Poll Tax Should Be Abolished," *Monroe Journal*, Apr 9, 1953, 2; "Political Activities of the CIO," *Monroe Journal*, May 25, 1944, 2; Joseph Crespino, *Atticus Finch: The Biography: Harper Lee, Her Father, and the Making of an American Icon* (New York, Basic Books, 2018), 45–46.

18 "Mrs. Lois R. Green Is League Speaker," *Florence Herald*, Apr 23, 1953, 12; "Poll Tax Repeal Fight Is Shaped," *Alabama Journal*, Apr 25, 1953, 5; "BPW Clubs Will Place Emphasis on Politics," *Birmingham News*, Apr 12, 1953, 57; "Women's League Draws Applause," *Huntsville Times*, Apr 30, 1953, 12; "Women Voter Lay Final Plans to Get Poll Tax Repealed," *Decatur Daily*, Apr 30, 1953, 20; "Leaders Plan Strategy in Fight to Repeal Poll Tax," *Birmingham News*, Apr 5, 1953, 26.

19 "Legislative Closeups," *Montgomery Advertiser*, May 6, 1953, 1; "Mrs. Boyd H. Leyburn," *Montgomery Advertiser*, May 7, 1953, 36; "House Legislative Committee Okays Bill to Abolish State Poll Tax Law," *Montgomery Advertiser*, May 7, 1953, 1; "Legislature," *Alabama Journal*, May 11, 1953, 2.

20 *Journal of the House of Representatives,* 1953, 96–98; "Poll Tax Bill Draws Fire of Two Groups," *Opelika Daily News*, May 13, 1953, 1.

21 *Alabama Official and Statistical Register, 1951,* 206; "Poll Tax Bill," *Montgomery Advertiser,* May 14, 1953, 2.

22 "Poll Tax Bill," *Montgomery Advertiser,* May 14, 1953, 2; "Allen Rules Out Poll Tax Repeal," *Huntsville Times,* May 15, 1953, 2. Senator William James of Cullman was appointed by the state Democratic Executive Committee in a close vote to replace the late Senator Ben Faunt, representing north Alabama counties, including two (Blount and Winston) that continued to have Republican voters. Both James and Hollis—the two north Alabama senators voting to hold the bill—had districts where Democrats continued to worry about the poll tax enfranchising more Republicans.

23 *Journal of the Senate,* 1953, 139–140. Mobile Senator Thomas Johnston, a "states' righter" and Big Mule anti-labor attorney, also tried to recommit the bill arguing unsuccessfully that it should have been considered by the taxation committee.

24 Richard Kluger, *Simple Justice* (New York: Alfred A, Knopf, 1976), 650–652, 667; "Solons Face Crucial Issue of Segregation In Schools," *Montgomery Advertiser*, May 3, 1953, 1.

25 "Timing on Poll Tax Repeal May be Bad," *Huntsville Times*, Apr 14, 1953, 4.

26 "New Registrar Board Chosen for Madison," *Huntsville Times,* Jul 21, 1949, 1; Martha Witt Smith, "Madison Vote Purge Proves Lengthy Task" [AP wire story], *Selma Times-Journal,* Jun 19, 1950, 1; "Curb on Registration of New Voters Plea," *Selma Times-Journal,* Jan 26, 1954. 1; "Women's Voters League Picks Taxation Study," *Huntsville Times*, Apr 16, 1953, 10. Smith's husband was also at this time the *Huntsville Times'* business manager.

27 *Journal of the House of Representatives, 1953,* 411–413, 508–508.

28 *Journal of the House of Representatives,* 1953, 779–780.

29 "Conferees Urge Vote in 1954 in Poll Tax Cut," *Alabama Journal,* Jun 5, 1953, 1; *Journal of the House of Representatives,* 1953, 423–427; *Journal of the Senate,1953,* 429–430; *Acts of Alabama,* 1953, Act 109, S. 6, 159–160. To add to the arcane nature of the proceedings, much of the conference committee deliberations were about Rep. Hawkins's bill (H.B. 64) that quickly passed in the house in its first days of the session and was passed by the senate with the same amendment attached to S.B. 6. See *Journal of the Senate,*1953, 155–157. But the senate bill was essentially substituted for the identical Hawkins's house bill and approved by both chambers as the enacted law. Several senate sponsors, who favored only reducing the back payment of poll taxes were added to the enacted bill after passage by senate resolution. It is possible that this after-the-fact credit-taking assisted in the senate in accepting earlier the house's date for the referendum.

30 Ogden, *The Poll Tax in the South,* 231–234; "Poll Tax," *Birmingham News,* Dec 16, 1953, 2; "GOP Leader Is for Poll Curb," *Decatur Daily,* Nov 1, 1953, 2; "Dixon on Record Against Two-Year Poll Tax Plan," *Birmingham News,* Oct 15, 1953, 44.

31 Fred Taylor, "Battle over Two-Year Poll Tax Amendment Becomes Intense," *Birmingham News,* Nov 1, 1953, 8; "Bullock Demo Committee Opposes Poll Tax Plan," *Alabama Journal, Nov* 26, 1953, 32; Ogden, *The Poll Tax in the South,*235; Fred Taylor,

"Battle to Limit Poll Tax Hears More Shots Fired," *Birmingham News*, Oct 30, 1953, 18.

32 "Who Will Control" [ad], *Birmingham News*, Dec 14, 1953, 6 "NAACP" [ad], *Birmingham News*, Dec 9, 1953, 4; "Administration Seeks End to Segregation in Schools," *Montgomery Advertiser*, Dec 9, 1953, 1.

33 "Why Many Skilled Workers Are Voting 'NO' on the Poll Tax Amendment (No. 1)" [ad], *Birmingham News*, Dec 10, 1953, 8; "Jefferson County Demos Oppose Poll Tax Rollback," *Alabama Journal*, Nov 3, 1953, 17; Fred Taylor, "Demo Committee Blasted for Opposing Tax Reform," *Birmingham News*, Dec 10, 1953, 28; "Sponsors of State Poll Tax Amendment Move into High Gear for Tuesday's Vote," *Montgomery Advertiser*, Dec 9, 1953, 1.

34 *Alabama Official and Statistical Register, 1951*, 540–542. The author's calculations about county patterns are taken from this source. Also, see Ogden, *The Poll Tax in the South*, 236, for similar observations.

35 "The Twenty Yard Line," *Cullman Tribune*, Jun 18, 1953, 6.

36 "People Forum: Note of Appreciation," *Huntsville Times*, Jan 7, 1954, 4.

37 Edwards, *Hallie Farmer*, 41, 79.

38 "Patton Raps Boswell Amendment," *Weekly Review* (Birmingham), Oct 25, 1947, 1; "Negroes Plan Test Cases," *Decatur Daily*, Feb 2, 1948, 3; "Thousands of Negroes Seek Primary Vote," *Selma Times-Journal*, Sep 25, 1949, 17; Robin D. G. Kelley, *Hammer and Hoe: Alabama Communists during the Great Depression* (Chapel Hill: University of North Carolina Press, 1990), 182–183; Oral history interview with Arthur Shores by Jack Bass, July 17, 1974, Southern Oral History Program Collection, University of North Carolina at Chapel Hill; "Negroes File Petition for Right to Vote," *Huntsville Times*, Jun 25, 1939, 12; "Judge Bars Action on Negro Vote," *Southern Home* (Livingston), Jul 6, 1939, 1.

39 Scott C. F. Kennedy, "Vote, People, Vote! W. C. Patton, the NAACP, and the Birmingham Black Community," Master's thesis (University of Alabama, Birmingham, 2012), 306. The Encyclopedia of Alabama provides a useful, summary biography of each of these men, except for C. G. Gomillion, who told the author later in his life that he preferred "C. G."—not "Charles." See Norrell, *Reaping the Whirlwind*, 31–42 for his background.

40 Kelly Spring, "Ruby Hurley," National Women's History Museum, 2017; Patton to Gloster B. Current, Aug 1, 1950, Patton to Walter White, May 31, 1951, Patton telegram to Walter White, Nov 19, 1951, Utillus R. Phillips to Gloster B. Current, Jan 23, 1951, "NAACP Announces New S.E. Regional Office" [press release], Mar 20, 1952, Establishment of SE Regional Office, 1949–1953, Branch Files, NAACP Papers. For the reader's convenient understanding, Hurley's exact title of "Regional Secretary" is called "regional director," as it was renamed in later years.

41 Vernon Jordan with Annette Gordon-Reed, *Vernon Can Read!* (New York: Public Affairs, 2001), 147; Gloster B. Current to Rev. J. M. Hinton, Oct 1, 1951, Walter White to Utillus R. Phillips, Jul 13, 1951, Establishment of SE Regional Office, 1949–1953, Branch Files, NAACP Papers.

42 "'We Are Going Out for a Full Loaf,' NAACP Speaker Says," *Montgomery Advertiser*,

Jun 4, 1951, 5.

43 Raines, *My Soul Is Rested*, 139; "Alabama Demos Urged to Change Ballot Emblem," *Alabama Citizen*, Jun 28, 1952, 1. The Birmingham ordinance was codified in 1930 and also prohibited interracial playing of cards, dice, and dominos. See Murray, *States' Laws on Race and Color*, 615–616.

44 "When Will Christians Speak Out for Decency?" *Birmingham News*, Sep 28, 1953, 12. Also see "Byrnes Declared Unfit for World Order," *Birmingham News*, Aug 9, 1953, 32.

45 "NAACP Vows to Halt Relocation Project," *Huntsville Mirror*, Aug 15, 1953, 1.

46 "NAACP Leader Training Ends," *Birmingham News*, Feb 22, 1953, 16; "NAACP Pledges No Compromise with Jimcrow [sic]," *Alabama Tribune*, Feb 13, 1953, 1; "Resolutions" and "Southeastern Regional Leadership Training Conference Closes" [press release], Southeast Regional Office Reports, 1953–54, Branch Files, NAACP Papers.

47 "More Negroes Are Registered," *Decatur Daily*, Nov 8, 1953, 2; "Negro Group Asked to Back Poll Tax Bill," *Opelika Daily News*, Nov 9, 1952, 2.

48 "National Baptist Officials to Meet Here," *Birmingham News*, Dec 27, 1953, 15.

49 "Payment of Poll Tax Urged By State Leader," *Alabama Citizen*, Dec 26, 1953, 1; "Be Prepared, Pay Your Poll Tax Before February 1" [ad], *Huntsville Mirror*, Jan 9, 1954, 7; "Statewide Drive to Add New Voters to Continue until April 19," *Alabama Tribune*, Feb 5, 1954, 1; "3 Million Voters," *Alabama Citizen*, Feb 20, 1954, 8; "Campaign for State Elections Gets Underway," *Huntsville Mirror*, Mar 6, 1954, 1.

50 Annual Report from the NAACP Southeast Regional Office [1953], Memoranda to Gloster B. Current from Ruby Hurley, Jan 24, 1954, Apr 29, 1954, Southeast Regional Office Reports, 1953–54, Branch Files, NAACP Papers; "Nine Negroes Seek Offices in Elections," *Montgomery Advertiser*, Mar 14, 1954, 20; "Negro Balance of Power Out," *Decatur Daily*, Apr 8, 1954, 17; "The Registration Picture in Alabama," Voting Rights, General Files, 1956–1965, NAACP Papers.

51 "Thousands Added as Voters Since Poll Tax Curbed," *Selma Times-Journal*, Apr 7, 1954, 11; "Appendices A–F in Support of Plaintiff's Brief," Civil Action No. 2255-N, United States v. State of Alabama, Civil Rights Litigation Clearinghouse (1954 had the state's largest poll tax receipts since 1902); "Re-elect State Senator Albert Boutwell" [ad], *Birmingham News*, Apr 26, 1954, 1.

52 Author's calculations from election returns at *Alabama Official and Statistical Register, 1955*, 548–549; "Magic City Votes for Segregation," *Selma Times-Journal*, Jun 2, 1954, 1. There was a runoff for state superintendent of education in which both candidates campaigned on keeping segregation. See, for example, "See and Hear Dr. D. P. Culp" [ad], *Birmingham News*, May 25, 1954, 25; "Austin Meadows to Fight to Keep State Segregation," *Alexander City Outlook*, Jun 1, 1954, 3.

53 "Segregation Script," *Alabama Citizen*, Jul 31, 1954, 2; "State Leaders," *Alabama Journal*, May 18, 1954, 2.

54 "NAACP Condemns Anti-Semitic Leaflets," Feb 11, [1954], Southeast Regional Correspondence, 1954, Branch Files, NAACP Papers. See Raines, *My Soul Is Rested*, 139, 147 for Hurley's daily experience and impression of white attitudes. The reference to

Ashmore derives from his conversation in 1983 with the author about his editorial strategies to encourage compliance with *Brown* despite his own pessimistic opinion about the community response.

55 Hurley to Fellow Workers, Jun 7, 1954, Southeast Regional Correspondence, 1954, Branch Files, NAACP Papers.

56 "Committee to Draft Statement of Negro Needs," *Alabama Citizen*, May 15, 1954, 1. For reference to the founding of the Alabama Coordinating Committee, see "The Registration Picture in Alabama," NAACP Papers.

57 "NAACP to File 38 Petitions," *Alabama Journal*, Sep 25, 1954, 1; "Segregation Ban Sought by Naacp [sic]," *Selma Times-Journal*, Nov 14, 1954, 1; McMillen, 43. Patton's internal report on voter registration for 1954 estimated only about 50,000 registered Black voters. See "The Registration Picture in Alabama," NAACP Papers.

58 "Thousands Watch New Governor In," *Alabama Citizen*, Jan 22, 1955; Jo Ann Robinson, "Folsom Promises A Brighter Future for All Alabamians," *Huntsville Mirror*, Jan 22, 1955.

59 "2500 at 'Bama State Ball for Folsom," *Alabama Tribune*, Jan 1955, 1; Bill Martin, "Alabama's New Governor Says He Means Everybody When He Says 'Y'all Come,'" *Afro-American*, Jan 29, 1955, 1.

60 Jo Ann Robinson, "Folsom Promises A Brighter Future for All Alabamians," *Huntsville Mirror*, Jan 22, 1955.

61 Ibid.1

62 Gwendolyn M. Patton, "Madison Family Collection," H. Councill Trenholm State Community College Archives, https://www.trenholmstate.edu; "Of Men and Maids," *New York Age*, Mar 19, 1955, 14; "New Garment Factory Opens in Montgomery," *Huntsville Mirror*, Dec 4, 1954, 1; "Register Now" [ad], *Huntsville Mirror*, Jan 1, 1955, 2.

63 Raines, *My Soul Is Rested*, 140; "Report for the September Meeting of the Board," Aug 18, 1955, and "Report for the January Meeting of the Board," Dec 28, 1955, Southeast Regional Office Reports, 1955, NAACP Papers.

64 Hurley to Dear Friend, Oct 15, 1954, Southeast Regional Office Correspondence, 1954, Branch Files, NAACP Papers.

65 "NAACP Charges Fight Looming to Oust Group in Mississippi," *Montgomery Advertiser*, Sep 4, 1954, 10; Hurley to Members of the Regional Advisory Board, Nov 30, 1954, Southeast Regional Office Correspondence, 1954, Branch Files, NAACP Papers; Hurley to Medgar W. Evers. Nov 29, 1954, Mississippi State Conference, 1954–55, Branch Files, NAACP Papers. Evers had been a very active local chair of the Mount Bayou branch of the NAACP before his hire as the first full-time state director.

66 Hurley to Roy, Aug 30, 1954. Southeast Regional Office Correspondence, 1954, Branch Files, NAACP Papers.

67 Charles M. Payne, *I've Got the Light of Freedom* (Berkley: University of California Press, 1995), 36–41.

68 John Dittmer, *Local People: The Struggle for Civil Rights in Mississippi* (Urbana: University of Illinois Press, 1994), 46–56; Raines, *My Soul Is Rested*, 141.

69 Raines, *My Soul Is Rested*, 141–143.

70 Mileage calculated by author from Hurley's staff reports found in Southeast Regional Office Reports, 1955, NAACP Papers; "NAACP Cancels Tour of Till's Mother," *Birmingham News,* Nov 8, 1955, 5; Report for the October Meeting of the Board, Sep 30, 1955, Southeast Regional Office Reports, 1955, NAACP Papers; Raines, *My Soul Is Rested,* 145. Hurley maintained this practice throughout her career and imposed it on her field staff whenever they joined her for meetings. See Jordan, *Vernon Can Read!,* 148–151.

71 "Program . . . November 11, 12, 13, 1955" and other documents in Alabama State Conference, 1953–55, NAACP Papers.

72 "NAACP," *Decatur Daily,* Oct 13, 1955, 2.

73 "Negroes to Ask Integration in Macon County," *Birmingham News,* Jul 17, 1955, 1.

74 Report for the May Meeting of the Board, Apr 28, 1955, Southeast Regional Office Reports, 1955, NAACP Papers; "Two Selma, Ala. Policemen Held in Connection with Arson, Shooting," *Atlanta Daily World,* Oct 21, 1955, 1; "Dallas County Grand Jury Clears 5 of Arson Charges," *Montgomery Advertiser,* Nov 16, 1955, 1.

75 Patton to Roy Wilkins et. al., Oct 31, 1955, Reprisals, Alabama, 1955, NAACP Papers. See *Acts of Alabama,* 1955, 548–550.

76 "B'ham NAACP, 8 Others Named in $100,000 Suit Filed by Former Lawman," *Alabama Citizen,* Oct 1, 1955, 1; Complaint, Lynch v. NAACP et al., and The Selma Alabama Report, Reprisals, Alabama, 1955, NAACP Papers.

77 "Statement from the Annual Meeting of the Southeast Advisory Board, National Association for the Advancement of Colored People," Dec 11, 1955, Southeast Regional Office Reports, 1955, NAACP Papers.

78 "Pupil-Faculty," *Decatur Daily,* Feb 14, 1956, 2; "Folsom Attacks," *Alabama Citizen,* Feb 18, 1956, 8. Folsom not only failed to take actions to avoid or contain the riots, he escaped Montgomery for a fishing trip in the Gulf of Mexico. The governor was increasingly under frequent attack for failing to actively support the white resistance movement, for allowing the capital city to be hampered by a bus boycott, and for treating African American Congressman Adam Clayton Powell as a social equal during Powell's visit to the Governor's Mansion while failing to roll out the red carpet for Mississippi's segregationist Senator James Eastland's visit to Montgomery to speak to the White Citizens' Council. See "Governor Pledges to Halt Mob Rule," *Montgomery Advertiser,* Feb 11, 1956, 1.

79 See Jo Ann Gibson Robinson, *The Montgomery Bus Boycott and the Women Who Started It* (Knoxville: University of Tennessee Press, 1987).

80 Raines, *My Soul Is Rested,* 144–45.

81 "NAACP Outlawed in Alabama" [photograph], *Alabama Journal,* Jun 1, 1956, 1; "Injunction Against NAACP" [photograph], *Huntsville Times,* Jun 1, 1956, 1. Patterson's staged filing in the circuit clerk's office required Jones's cooperation and approval. Otherwise, the Judge would have prevented it or reprimanded Patterson after the fact for using his court in a publicity stunt.

82 "Jones Grants Writ on Patterson Plea," *Alabama Journal,* Jun 1, 1956, 1; *State of Alabama ex rel. John Patterson, Attorney General v. National Association for the Advancement of Colored People,* 1 Race Rel. L. Rep. (1956), 707–709.

83 "Institution Within an Institution," *Montgomery Advertiser*, Jun 2, 1963, 12; "In Memoriam: Judge Walter B. Jones," *Alabama Lawyer* 24, no. 4 (October 1963), 332–334; Walter B. Jones, "Alabama's Economic Loss Due to Reconstruction," *Alabama Lawyer* 14, no. 2 (April 1953): 147–155.

84 Walter B. Jones, "Constitutional Convention of 1901 and Poll Taxes," *Alabama Lawyer*, 4, no. 1 (1943), 18–19; "Held in Negro Vote Case," *New York Times*, Apr 10, 1944, in Voting, Alabama, Madison, Arthur, 1944, Legal Files, NAACP Papers; Walter B. Jones, "Montgomery Bus Segregation Case," *Alabama Lawyer*,17, no. 3 (July1956), 239.

85 Trest, *Nobody But the People*, 148,155, 187.

86 William L. Taylor to Robert L. Carter, Feb 27, 1957, and Petition for Writ of Certiorari to the Supreme Court of Alabama, NAACP v. State of Alabama, October 1956 Term, U.S. Supreme Court, NAACP v. Alabama, Sep 1956–July 1957, Case Files, NAACP Papers; *State of Alabama ex rel. John Patterson, Attorney General v. National Association for the Advancement of Colored People*, 1 Race Rel. L. Rep. (1956), 917–919.

87 Mabel Spenser to Gloster Current, Jul 30, 1956, Sep 19, 1956, and Ruby Hurley, "Greetings from the West Coast" [newsletter], July 1956, Southeast Regional Office Reports, 1956, NAACP Papers; Raines, *My Soul Is Rested*, 145–147.

88 Raines, *My Soul Is Rested*, 147; Gary M. Pomerantz, *Where Peachtree Meets Sweet Auburn: A Saga of Race and Family* (New York: Penguin Books, 1997), 216. Also, see "Ruby Hurley at 70; Civil Rights Leader," *New York Times*, Aug 15, 1980, B-15; "Registration Group to Hear Detroit Negro Representative," *Montgomery Advertiser*, Oct 21, 1957, 5; Kennedy, "Vote, People, Vote!," 104–106.

89 See *Louisiana ex rel. Gremillion v. NAACP*, 366 US 293 (1961); *Harrison v. NAACP*, 360 US 167 (1959); *Bates v. Little Rock*, 361 US 516 (1960).

90 For an illuminating summary of the legal filings in this case and others used against the NAACP in the South, see Burton and Derfner, *Justice Deferred*, 203–207.

91 Walter B. Jones, "I Speak for the White Race," *Alabama Lawyer* 18, no. 2 (April 1957), 203.

92 "Courts Question NAACP Operations," *Huntsville Mirror*, Dec 30, 1961, 1.

93 *Ex parte National Association for Advancement of Colored People*, 91 So. 2d 214 (1956); 91 So. 2d 221(1956); 109 So. 2d 138 (1959); 109 So. 2d 140 (1959); 122 So.2d 396 (1960); *National Association for Advancement of Colored People v. State*, 150 So.2d 677 (1963); *NAACP v. Alabama ex rel. Patterson*, 357 US 449 (1958); 360 US 240 (1959); *NAACP v. Alabama ex rel. Flowers*, 377 US 288 (1964), 304.

94 Jordan, *Vernon Can Read!*, 147; author's conversation with Ruby Hurley at the offices of the Southern Regional Council, Oct. 1977. The choice of language by whites in describing African Americans often served as a casual measure by civil rights leaders of a white person's or white community's views on race. See, for example, Andrew Young's remarks in Burton and Derfner, *Justice Deferred*, 238.

NOTES TO CHAPTER 13

1 Carter, *The Politics of Rage*, 90–91; Trest, *Nobody But the People*, 218–219; "John Patterson 'Kicks Off' with Speech at Birthplace," *Phenix Citizen*, Feb 13, 1958, 1.

2 "Patterson Renews Blast at Folsom," *Centreville Press*, Apr 24, 1958, 9; "Patterson Hits at NAACP During Weekend Tour," *Alexander City Outlook*, Apr 22, 1958, 12.

3 "It's Time to Clean House in ALABAMA" [ad], *Decatur Daily*, May 2, 1958, 12; "John Patterson Will be a Great Governor" [ad], *Huntsville Times*, May 5, 1958, 10; "NAACP Launches Voter Drive Against John Patterson" [ad], *Atmore Advance*, May 1, 1958, 28; *Clarke County Democrat*, May 1, 1958, 2; *Evergreen Courant*, May 1, 1958, 4.

4 "Comments about People and Things," *Centreville Press*, Apr 24, 1958, 9; "Patterson Spoke at Courthouse Friday," *Union-Banner*, May 1, 1958, 19.

5 Carter, *The Politics of Rage*, 95; "Jimmy Faulkner, Alabama Next Governor" [ad], *Luverne Journal and News*, Apr 16, 1958, 9; "Dignified Segregation Vowed by Wallace in Telecast Here," *Montgomery Advertiser*, Mar 8, 1958, 7. The Ku Klux Klan publicly endorsed Patterson.

6 "Vote for north Alabama's Best Candidate for Governor" [ad], *Decatur Daily*, May 4, 1958, 14; "Shorty Price Speaks Whole Night Through," *Dothan Eagle*, May 4, 1958, 24; "The Daily Chooses a Fighter," *Decatur Daily*, Apr 27, 1958, 4; "A. W. Todd is the Man, Give Todd the Nod" [ad], *Sand Mountain Reporter*, Apr 29, 1958. 7.

7 *Journal of the House of Representatives, 1955*, 16, 612, 640; *Journal of the Senate, 1955*, 1752; *Acts of Alabama*, 1953, 837–838; Proposed Amendment No. 6, *Alabama Official and Statistical Register, 1955*, 603–604; "Poll Tax Revision Gathers Scant Support, *Montgomery Advertiser*, May 26, 1957, 3; "Hawkins Assails Efforts to Reenact Poll Tax Feature," *Birmingham News*, May 19, 1957, 24.

8 "Hawkins Vows to End Reign of Black Belt," *Montgomery Advertiser*, Feb 28, 1958, 1.

9 "Hawkins Hits Black Belt's Domination," *Montgomery Advertiser*, Mar 8, 1958, 7.

10 Morgan, *One Man, One Voice*, 11, 13; Chuck Morgan's conversation with the author, Jun 1987; "Alabama Editors Are Saying," *Montgomery Advertiser*, Mar 25, 1958, 4; "Faulkner Opens 'Victory March,'" *Birmingham News*, Apr 30, 1958, 4; "Harrison Lashes at Big Promises," *Selma Times-Journal*, Apr 6, 1958, 23; "A Fair Share for All of Alabama," *Decatur Daily*, May 5, 1958, 18; "North Alabama's Candidate for Governor . . . George Hawkins" [ad], *Cullman Tribune*, Apr 24, 1958, 7; *Moulton Advertiser*, May 1, 1958, 8.

11 Authors calculations from election returns in *Alabama Official and Statistical Register, 1959*, 592–593.

12 Frederick, *Stand Up for Alabama*, 19.

13 "Judge Jones Old Hand at State Inaugurations," *Montgomery Advertiser*, Jan 20, 1959, 14 (earlier, Jones administered the oath of office to Governor Persons after the chief justice became incapacitated); "Mahoney—'As I See It,'" *Alabama Journal*, Oct 15, 1962, 4; "First Official Act" [photo], *Alabama Journal*, Jan 20, 1959, 1; "Walter B. Jones Becomes Senior Judge in Alabama," *Montgomery Advertiser*, Jan 22, 1959, 5; "Jury Board Gets Set Up for Spring Trip; Seeks Names for Box," *Alabama Journal*,

Jan 23, 1959, 13; "Veterans Publish Patriotic Record of Judge Walter B. Jones" [ad], *Montgomery Advertiser*, May 3, 1958, 11; "Contempt Case Going Ahead; Delay Refused," *Alabama Journal*, Jun 20, 1958, 1.

14 Samantha Barbas, *Actual Malice: Civil Rights and Freedom of the Press in New York Times v. Sullivan* (Oakland: University of California Press, 2023), 105; "Convalescent Soldiers Guests at Jonesboro," *Montgomery Advertiser*, Jun 25, 1944, 20; "Young Cadets Left Mark at Jonesboro, Including Crosses," *Dothan Eagle*, Sep 19, 1946, 10; "Jonesboro, Here We Come," *Sylacauga Advance*, Aug 4, 1960, 12.

15 Trest, *Nobody But the People*, 349, 393–394; "Feds Move to Toss Out Probe Ban," *Montgomery Advertiser*, Jun 14, 1960, 1; *State of Alabama v. Rogers*, 187 F. Supp. 848 (1960); Rex Thomas, "Legal Bludgeon Found for Out of State Newspapers," *Decatur Daily*, Sep 25, 1960, 22; "N.Y. Times Libel Trial Jury Named," *Birmingham News*, Nov 1, 1960, 1; *New York Times Co. v. Sullivan*, 144 So. 2d 25 (1962); *New York Times Co. v. Sullivan*, 376 US 254 (1964).

16 Walter B. Jones, "Judge Jones on Court Room Segregation," *Alabama Lawyer*, 22, no. 2 (April 1961), 190–192.

17 "'Freedom Riders' in State Barred by Court Order," *Montgomery Advertiser*, May 20, 1961, 1; Trest, *Nobody But the People*, 339–341; Durr, *Outside the Magic Circle*, 298; Raines, *My Soul Is Rested*, 339–341, n. 144; *Lewis v. The Greyhound Corporation*, 199 F. Supp. 210 (1961); *United States v. U.S. Klans, Knights of Ku Klux Klan, Inc.*, 194 F. Supp. 897 (1961). Judge Johnson issued an order restraining the Klan from any involvement with the Freedom Riders. He also ordered the Freedom Riders to stop for the time being from testing the desegregation laws in Alabama.

18 "Units Asks Restoration of Cumulative Poll Tax," *Montgomery Advertiser*, Mar 27, 1959, 1; "Revival of Old Poll Tax Measure Has Little Chance, Hawkins Says," *Anniston Star*, Mar 29, 1959, 1; *Journal of the Senate*, 1959, 722; "Cumulative Poll Tax Asked Again," *Atlanta Journal and the Atlanta Constitution*, Sep 27, 1959, E5; "The Poll Tax Proposal," *Enterprise Ledger*, Apr 9, 1959, 4.

19 "Court Questions NAACP Operations," *Huntsville Mirror*, Dec 30, 1961, 1; "Citizenship Observance Gets Support," *Huntsville Mirror*, Nov 29, 1958, 1; "Registration Group to Hear Detroit Negro Representative," *Montgomery Advertiser*, Oct 21, 1957, 5.

20 "Vote Bill Success Doubtful," *Montgomery Advertiser*, Apr 14, 1965, 1; "Committee Oks State Voting Bill; Senate Due Move," *Anniston Star*, Apr 14, 1965, 1; "Voter Bill Is Approved by Senate," *Montgomery Advertiser*, Apr 23, 1965, 1; "Two Voter Registration Bills Unanimously Passed by Senate," *Montgomery Advertiser*, Apr 30, 1965, 1.

21 "States Study, Seeks to Answer Poll Tax Suits," *Anniston Star*, Aug 11, 1965, 1.

22 "Hearing Brings Outcries, But No Ruling," *Montgomery Advertiser*, Dec 21, 1965, 1.

23 See Daniel Webster Hollis III, *An Alabama Newspaper Tradition: Grover C. Hall and the Hall Family* (University, Alabama: University of Alabama Press, 1983), 92–110, 119–128.

24 Grover Hall Jr., "The Poll Tax Carcass," *Montgomery Advertiser*, Mar 4, 1965, 4. All subsequent quotations of Hall are from this editorial. The earlier editorial was "A Secondary Reform," *Montgomery Advertiser*, Mar 2, 1951.

25 See the 1953 amendment 1 and its voting returns in *Alabama Official and Statistical Register, 1955,* 534–535, 540–542. Macon County was the one Black Belt county to support amendment 1. It also had almost as many Black registered voters in 1953 as there were whites who were eligible to vote. It is likely that virtually all of Macon's Black voters and a minority of its white voters constituted the county's majority who supported the amendment.

NOTES TO CHAPTER 14

1 Charles Morgan Jr., "Vote Law Will Rip 'Cotton Curtain,'" *Southern Courier,* Aug 13, 1965, 2.

2 James W. Silver, *Mississippi: The Closed Society* (New York: Harcourt, Brace, and World, 1966), 22.

3 "The Triangular Tie-Up," *Selma Times-Journal,* Dec 13, 1938, 4, reprinting the editorial of the *Tuscaloosa News*; "'Do Something!' Mizell Urges in Parley Bid," *Montgomery Advertiser.* Feb 29, 1948, 1

4 "Sparks Deplores Racial Meddlers," *Huntsville Times,* May 4, 1944, 13. Emphasis added.

5 Alexander P. Lamis, "Partisan Politics," in Janes W. Ely and Bradley G. Bond (eds.), *The New Encyclopedia of Southern Culture*: Volume 10: Law and Politics (Chapel Hill: University of North Carolina Press, 2008), 236–41.

6 "The Afternoon," *Dothan Eagle,* May 1, 1946, 4.

7 "WBRC BELIEVES . . ." *Birmingham News,* Apr 8, 1947, 8.

8 Dan T. Carter, *Unmasking the Klansman: The Double Life of Asa and Forrest Carter* (Athens: NewSouth Books, 2023), 65–66, 145; Eric Vaillancourt, "Rock 'n' Roll in the 1950s: Rockin' for Civil Rights," Master's thesis (SUNY-Rockport, 2011), 43–44; "Segregationists Would Ban All Rock, Roll Hits," *Billboard,* Apr 7, 1956, 68; James K. Hutsell, "While We Are Off the Subject," *Alabama Journal.* Apr 5, 1956, 4.

9 McWhorter, *Carry Me Home,* 360.

10 "The Lie Loses in Alabama," *Daily Mountain Eagle,* 20, 1954.

11 Walter Spearman and Sylvan Meyer, *Racial Crisis and the Press* (Atlanta: Southern Regional Council, 1960), 37.

12 Gene L. Howard, *Patterson for Alabama: The Life and Career of John Patterson* (Tuscaloosa: University of Alabama Press, 2008), 115.

13 "TV Schedules," *Birmingham News,* May 27, 1958, 5; "TV Program Schedule," *Progressive Age* (Scottsboro), Feb 12, 1959, 7; "TV Schedules," *Birmingham News,* Mar 1, 1960, 8; "Foghorn Leghorn," https://en.wikipedia.org/wiki/Foghorn_Leghorn; "Negroes Take Bus Ride for Cameras," *Birmingham News,* Dec 28, 1956, 14; "Screaming on Cue," *Montgomery Advertiser,* Dec 11, 1960, 14; Aniko Bodroghkozy, *Equal Time: Television and the Civil Rights Movement* (Champaign, IL: University of Illinois Press, 2012), 63–64.

14 Gene Roberts and Hank Klibanoff, *The Race Beat: The Press, the Civil Rights Struggle, and the Awakening of a Nation* (New York: Random House, 2006), 244–253. The Alabama Press Association condemned the state's failure to "provide protection to

the citizens and news media personnel." See "Press Group Resolution Hits Racial Violence in Alabama," *Montgomery Advertiser*, May 22, 1961, 1.

15 Anthony Lewis, *Make No Law: The Sullivan Case and the First Amendment* (New York: Random House, 1991), 7, 9–11, 20–26.

16 Ibid., 27–33.

17 Ibid., 36–37; Roberts and Klibanoff, *The Race Beat*, 229–240, 251–255. According to Lewis, national media had been sued for as much a $300 million by the time the U.S. Supreme Court issued the opinion of *New York Times Co. v. Sullivan*, 376 U.S. 254 (1964).

18 "Governor Asserts State Unable to Protect Mixers," *Selma Times-Journal*, May 16, 1961, 1.

19 See, for example, Carter, *The Politics of Rage*, 121–124.

20 Roberts and Klibanoff, *The Race Beat*, 316–322; McWhorter, *Carry Me Home*, 371–376; "Fire Hoses, Police Dogs Used to Halt Downtown Negro Demonstrations," *Birmingham News*, May 3, 1963, 2.

21 "Police Squirt Negro Mob at B'ham" *Huntsville Times*, May 6, 1963, 1; "Negro Attacks Police Dog," *Huntsville Times*, May 4, 1963, 7; "Police Dogs Assist Birmingham Officers Against Demonstrators," *Montgomery Advertiser*, May 4, 1963, 16; "Police Dogs Break Riot in St. Louis," *Birmingham News*, May 4, 1963, 2; "Close-Quarters Actions Force Use of Dogs," *Selma Times-Journal*, May 9, 1963, 1; "Use of Police Dogs Widespread," *Birmingham News*, May 14, 1963, 14. Likely because of its city editor, Ray Jenkins, the *Alabama Journal* ran on page 8 a graphic photograph of police dog ripping at the shirt of a Black youth and a Black youth being hosed down by firemen with the caption, "Hoses with up to 100 pounds of pressure used . . ." See *Alabama Journal*, May 4, 1963, 8.

22 Roberts and Klibanoff, *The Race Beat*, 315.

23 "Blame Laid, to Negroes, not Whites," *Montgomery Advertiser*, May 9, 1963, 1; "Governor Talks Tough," *Daily Northwest Alabamian*, May 8, 1963, 1.

24 McWhorter, *Carry Me Home*, 462.

25 "The Phenix City Story!" [ad], *Birmingham News*, Sep 15, 1955, 30; "Strickland to Speak," *Montgomery Advertiser*, May 27, 1965, 40; *Biennial Report to the Alabama Legislature by the Alabama Legislative Commission to Preserve the Peace*, undated [circa 1965], *Wallace v. Brewer*, Clippings, 1964–1969, Southern Regional Office Files, ACLU Papers.

26 "The 1964 Civil Rights Bill . . . Its Pattern . . . Its Architects," *Alabama Legislative Commission to Preserve the Peace*, ACLU Papers.

27 *Biennial Report to the Alabama Legislature by the Alabama Legislative Commission to Preserve the Peace*, 12–13, ACLU Papers.

28 "'Pains and Shame'—Why Bloody Tuesday Remains Less Known," *Tuscaloosa News*, Jun 6, 2021, A1; Tommy Stevenson, "Old Files Show City's Role in Civil Rights Era," *Tuscaloosa News*, Apr 26, 2011.

29 King, *I Have a Dream*, 105.

30 "Integration Acceptance Flouted by Governor before Large Crowd," *Selma*

Times-Journal, Aug 30, 1963, 1.

31 See "Communists in Civil Rights," *Alabama Legislative Commission to Preserve the Peace,* ACLU Papers.

32 "Injunction Insult, Says Wallace," *Birmingham News,* Sep 25, 1963, 1; McWhorter, *Carry Me Home,* 519–532. 534.

33 Morgan, *A Time to Speak,* 10–14.

34 Frank Holeman, "Capitol Stuff on Tour," *New York Daily News.* Sep 22, 1963, 66; "Birmingham Not 'Dead,' Seibels Says," *Montgomery Advertiser,* Nov 21, 1963, 2.

35 "Bright Young Birmingham Man," *Greensboro Watchman,* Oct 3, 1963, 4.

36 Roberts and Klibanoff, *The Race Beat,* 353–364; John Dittmer, *Local People,* 239–247.

37 Simon Wendt, "God, Gandhi, and Guns: The African American Freedom Struggle in Tuscaloosa, Alabama, 1964–1965," *Journal of African American History,* vol. 89, no. 1 (Winter 2004), 36–37, 44–45; "Number Arrested in Tuscaloosa Riot," *Florence Herald,* Jun 11, 1964, 2; "Eighteen Persons Hurt In Tuscaloosa Rioting by Negroes, Policemen," *Anniston Star,* Jun 9, 1964, 1.

38 "Bill," *Anniston Star,* Sep 7, 1963, 2; "Strong Reaction Follows Address," *Montgomery Advertiser,* Aug 7, 1964, 1; "State TV to Carry Wallace's Speech Opening Session," *Alabama Journal,* Jul 25, 1966, 13; Bodroghkozy, *Equal Time,* 63–87; "Lay My Burden Down," *Selma Inter-Religious Project Newsletter,* Dec 16, 1966; ; Frederick, *Stand Up for Alabama,* 125; Reginald Stuart. "News and Blues: Minority Journalists in the South, Twenty-Five Years Later," *Southern Changes,* vol. 19, no. 2, 1997, 5–9; "All Negro TV Show Famous," *Montgomery Advertiser,* Jul 31, 1964, 31; "Gospel Time Performers" [photograph caption], *Montgomery Advertiser,* Dec 31, 1964, 13. Also, see William G. Thomas III, "Television News and the Civil Rights Struggle: The Views in Virginia and Mississippi." *Southern Spaces,* Nov 3, 2004.

39 Bodroghkozy, *Equal Time, 40.*

40 Allison Perlman, *Public Interests: Media Advocacy and Struggles over U.S. Television* (New Brunswick, NJ: Rutgers University Press, 2016), 46, 56–58.

41 "Editors Coming Monday to Tour Questioned Areas," *Selma Times-Journal,* Jun 6, 1965, 1; Travis Wolfe, "March Film Is Described as Accurate," *Montgomery Advertiser,* Dec 15, 1965, 22; "'Selma March' Film Shown to 1800," *Alabama Journal,* Dec 15, 1965, 17.

42 "Conservative Books" [ad], *Alabama Journal,* Sep 22, 1966, 5; "Large Crowd at Tanyard Cheers Sheriff Jim Clark," *Union Springs Herald,* Jul 29, 1965, 1; "Auburn Students Hear Speech by Jim Clark," *Alabama Journal,* Mar 4, 1966, 10; Martin A. Berger, *Seeing Through Race: A Reinterpretation of Civil Rights Photography* (Berkley: University of California Press, 2011), 118–119; "State Republicans Hail Barry's Win," *Montgomery Advertiser,* Jun 4, 1964, 1; "Want to Know the Real Story" [ad], *Selma Times-Journal,* Oct 7, 1965, 19; Mike McGrady, "Selma: Epilogue to a March," *Weekend with Newsday,* Oct 9, 1965, W-2; "U.S. Should Mean Equality, Tolerance," *Charlotte Observer,* Nov 26, 1965, 50. The author of *The True Selma Story,* 'Buck" Persons was also a relative of former Alabama governor Persons and author Truman Capote. See Don Noble, "Author Shares Details from Bay of Pigs Mission," *Tuscaloosa News,* Oct 12, 2008.

43 Allen Tullos, *Alabama Getaway: The Political Imaginary and the Heart of Dixie* (Athens: University of Georgia Press, 2011), 25.

44 Patricia Sullivan (ed.), *Freedom Writer: Virginia Foster Durr, Letters from the Civil Rights Years,* (New York; Routledge, 2003), 327.

45 Roberts and Klibanoff, *The Race Beat*, 407.

Notes to Chapter 15

1 Street and Lozano, "Introduction," *The Shadow of Selma,* 4. The pivotal role of "Bloody Sunday" was recognized in Alabama at the time the Voting Rights Act was passed. The *Alabama Journal* called it the "Wallace-Lingo Act" due to their decisions that unleashed the brutal attacks: "Mark it well: Alabama passed this law." See "Wallace-Lingo Act," *Alabama Journal,* Aug 9, 1965, 4.

2 "President Johnson's Special Message to the Congress: The American Promise," March 15, 1965, accessed at http://www.lbjlibrary.org/lyndon-baines-johnson/speeches-films/president-johnsons-special-message-to-the-congress-the-american-promise.

3 Garrow, *Protest at Selma*, 236. For Garrow's detailed analysis of the role of "Bloody Sunday" in shaping passage of the Act, see pages 133–178.

4 See Payne, *I've Got the Light of Freedom*, 236–284; Dittmer, *Local People*, 242–288.

5 Bodroghkozy, "Mediating Selma: 1965, 2015," *The Shadow of Selma,* 138–142; Mark Walmsley, "'They Couldn't Just Write It the Way It Wasn't Anymore': Mainstream Media Narratives and the 1965 Selma Campaign," *The Shadow of Selma,* 156–159, 163–164. Also, see in general Berger, *Seeing Through Race.*

6 Julian Bond, "History, Hope and Heroes," *Southern Changes*, vol. 15, no. 4, 1993, 7. Also, see Julian Bond, "Democracy Demands Memory," *Southern Changes*, vol. 19, no. 1, 1997, 3–4.

7 Armand Derfner, "Racial Discrimination and the Right to Vote," 26 *Vanderbilt Law Review*, vol. 26, 3.1973, 546–547.

8 Landsberg, *Free at Last to Vote*, 171.

9 Derfner, "Racial Discrimination and the Right to Vote," 549–550.

10 Landsberg, *Free at Last to Vote*, 172; Derfner, "Racial Discrimination and the Right to Vote," 561.

11 Bass, *Unlikely Heroes*, 15–22, 259–272; *Racial Discrimination in Southern Federal Courts* (Atlanta: Southern Regional Council, 1965); Fred P. Graham, "The Week in Law," *New York Times*, Apr 25, 1965, E-6.

12 *United States v. State of Alabama*, 252 F. Supp. 95 (1966); *Harper v. Virginia Board of Elections*, 383 U.S. 663 (1966); The Texas poll tax was also struck down before the Supreme Court acted in the Virginia case; see *United States v. State of Texas*, 252 F. Supp. 234 (1966); Memorandum to the President, "RE: Reasons Why the Department of Justice Has Favored the Mansfield-Dirksen Approach to Elimination of the Poll Tax," May 21, 1965, The White House Central Files, The Black Freedom Struggle in the 20th Century. Federal Government Records, Civil Rights During the Johnson Administration, 1963–1969, Part I, ProQuest/History Vault.

13 Landsberg, *Free at Last to Vote*, 189.

14 "Voting Rights Bill Called 'Punishment to Confederacy.'" *Boston Globe*, Jul 7, 1965, 10.

15 "Thurmond Blasts LBJ Bill: Says Negroes Can Vote Now," *Boston Globe*, Mar 22, 1965, 3; "King Called 'Godless, Racketeer' by Demo," *Austin Statesman*, Mar 18, 1965, A-24; Sam J. Ervin Jr., "Literacy Tests for Voters: A Case Study in Federalism," *Law and Contemporary Problems*, vol. 27, summer, 1962, 481–494; "An Immoral Law," *Wall Street Journal*, Mar 22, 1965, 14; *Hearings Before Subcommittee No. 5*, Committee on the Judiciary, House of Representatives on HR 6400, 30–32.

16 "House GOP's Own Voting-Rights Bill Bid Hits Barrier: Southern Democrats Back It," *Wall Street Journal*, Jul 8, 1965, 2; "Dixie Backing Helps House Pass Vote Bill," *Baltimore Sun*, Jul 10, 1965, 1.

17 "People Oppose Denial of Vote to Illiterates," *Washington Post*, Mar 19, 1965, A-2.

18 Tom Wicker, "President and Congress Shaping Voting Bill," *New York Times*, Mar 21, 1965, E-5.

19 "Senate and House Panels Stiffen Voting-Rights Bill," *New York Times*, Apr 10, 1965, 1; "Literacy Test Queries," *New York Times*, Apr 8, 1965, 38; "Dixie's Voting Barriers," *Los Angeles Sentinel*, Apr 8, 1965, A-6.

20 "Alabama Using New Voter Test; Negro Sees 'Just Another Trick,'" *New York Times*, Jul 23, 1965, 26; Roy Reed, "Negroes in Greensboro Expand Challenge to the White Minority," *New York Times*, Aug 2, 1965, 15.

21 "Alabamians Resentful Race Gains Go Unsung." *Los Angeles Times*, May 16, 1965, F-4; In the month following the signing of the Voting Rights Act, Gallup found that 90 percent of Americans answered "yes" to this question: "Do You Think People Who Have Quit School and Never Completed High School Should Be Permitted to Vote?" See Gallup Poll #714, Question 13, USGALLUP.714.Q12A, Gallup Organization, (Cornell University, Ithaca, NY: Roper Center for Public Opinion Research, 1965).

22 *Hearings Before Subcommittee No. 5*, Committee on the Judiciary, HR 6400 [1965], 51–52; "Voting Bill No Aid to Puerto Ricans," *New York Times*, Mar 20, 1965, 12; "Democratic Bill on Voting Passed by House, 333–85," *New York Times*, Jul 10, 1965, 1; "Conferees Reach Impasse on Voting Rights Measure," *Los Angeles Times*, Jul 28, 1965, 2; "Conferees Agree on Voting Rights," *New York Times*, Jul 30, 1965, 1. See Section 4E(1) and (2) of the Voting Rights Act of 1965.

23 Hearings before the Subcommittee on Constitutional Rights of the Committee on the Judiciary, United States Senate, Eighty-Seventh Congress [1962], 672–675; *Report of the President's Commission on Registration and Voting Participation*, November 1963, 39–40.

24 Hearings before the Subcommittee on Constitutional Rights of the Senate Judiciary Committee on S. 818, 2456, 2507, and Title IV of S. 2029, 91st Congress [1969, 1970], 399, 400–407.

25 Warren Weaver Jr., "Another Debt Is to the South," *New York Times* Jun 29, 1969, E-1; Hearings on S. 818, 2456, 2507, and Title IV of S. 2029, 182–191, 467 [quoted in testimony by representatives of the Association of the Bar of New York City]; "The South Finally Backs a Voting Bill," *Boston Globe*, Jul 13, 1969, 31; "Scott Disputing Nixon on Rights," *New York Times*, Jun 28, 1969, 12.

26 "Black Answer to Mitchell," *Los Angeles Times,* Jan 12, 1970, A-7.

27 George Gallup, "Wallace Still Thorn in Republican Side," *Orlando Sentinel,* Mar 22, 1970, 63; Russell Baker, "Observer: Elephants in Dixie," *New York Times,* Dec 16, 1969, 46.

28 Carter, *The Politics of Rage,* 382–383, 391–395.

29 "Geo. Wallace Won by Waging Dirtiest Campaign in History," *Philadelphia Tribune,* Jun 6, 1970, 1; Whitney Young, "Cabinet, White House Changes May Aid Plans for Needy," *Journal News,* Jun 24, 1970, 22.

30 "Senate Passes Extension of '65 Voting Act," *Washington Post,* Mar 14, 1970, A-1; "Wallace Recast in 1972 'Spoiler' Role," *Newsday,* Jun 6, 1970, 6; Kevin P. Phillips, "Wallace Victory Shows Nixon Gain," *Newsday,* Jun 15, 1970, 122.

31 *The Voting Rights Act: Summary and Text,* U.S. Commission on Civil Rights, Sep. 1971.

32 Howard A. Glickstein, "Mexican Americans Need Voter Safeguards, Too," *Los Angeles Times,* Apr 27, 1975, E-3; *Using the Voting Rights Act,* U.S. Commission on Civil Rights, Apr 1976.

33 *Extension of the Voting Rights Act of 1965,* Hearings before the Subcommittee on Constitutional Rights of the Senate Judiciary Committee on S. 407, S. 903, S. 1297, S. 1409 & S. 1443, 94th Congress, April 8, 9, 10, 22, 29, 30; May 1, 1975, (1975), 89–90, 100, 108.

34 "Democrats Support Voting Rights Act," *Baltimore Sun,* Jul 20, 1975, A-3; "Ford Signs Vote Rights Bill," *Chicago Defender,* Aug 7, 1975, 1, 4.

35 Peyton McCray, Jerome A. Gray, Edward Still, and Huey L. Perry, "Alabama," in Chandler Davidson and Bernard Grofman (eds.), *Quiet Revolution in the South: The Impact of the Voting Rights Act, 1965–1990* (Princeton, NJ: Princeton University Press, 1994, 38–65.

36 Stipulation, Harris v. Samuels, Civil Action No. 68–598, U.S. District Court, Northern District of Alabama, Southern Regional Office Files, ACLU Papers; *Harris v. Samuels,* 440 F. 2d 748 (1971); Richard Singer, "Student Power at the Polls," *Ohio State Law Journal,* vol. 31, no. 4, 1970, 705–706; "Madison Registration Hit," *Anniston Star,* Apr 3, 1974, 2; "Funds Asked by Peace Commission," *Alabama Journal,* Mar 14, 1969, 15.

37 *Broughton v. Brewer,* 298 F. Supp. 260 (1969). The case consolidated two lawsuits, one involving Black and white students at the University of Alabama, including the author, and another case involving young Black protestors claiming racially discriminatory employment by Mobile merchants. The Court's decision ended Alabama's long history of misuse of the state and local vagrancy statutes, especially in matters involving Black workers and Black protest. See Suitts, *Hugo Black of Alabama,* 235–236 and Risa Goluboff, *Vagrant Nation: Police Power, Constitutional Change, and the Making of the 1960s* (New York: Oxford University Press, 2016), 112–146, 251. In 1972, the U.S. Supreme Court struck down a Jacksonville, Florida, vagrancy ordinance in a challenge brought by an unrelated, interracial group of plaintiffs including one student. See *Papachristou v. Jacksonville,* 405 US 156 (1972). The section of Alabama's 1901 Constitution that used vague and petty crimes such as vagrancy for the purpose

of disfranchising Black voters and their political white allies was successful challenged in 1985. See *Underwood v. Hunter*, 730 F. 2d 614 (1984), affirmed in *Hunter v. Underwood*, 471 US 222 (1985).

38 "The Statistical Panjandrum," *Alabama Journal*, Feb 22, 1972, 4.

39 "3,000 Alabamians Protest Muslims," *Alabama Journal*, Nov 22, 1969, 1; "Fire Rips Dealership of Man Who Sold Land to St. Clair Black Muslims," *Birmingham Post Herald*, Dec 9, 1969,1; "U.S. Judge to Rule on St. Clair Case Today," *Montgomery Advertiser*, Dec 11, 1969, 2. In 1961, the legislature added Muslims to the state law requiring registration of Nazis, communists, and "communist front" organizations. See Act 890, *Acts of Alabama*, 1961, vol. 2, 1403–1404.

40 Stipulation, Harris v. Samuels, Civil Action No. 68–598, U.S. District Court, Northern District of Alabama, Southern Regional Office Files, ACLU Papers; "Auburn Students Line Up for Registration," *Anniston Star*, Apr 6, 1972, 6; "Voting Consultant Ordered to Cease Board Interference," *Anniston Star*, Apr 7, 1972, 8; "Registrars Sue to Force Court Vote Guides," *Birmingham Post Herald*, Jul 20, 1972, 1. The U.S. Supreme Court voided lengthy residency requirements for voting in *Dunn v. Blumstein*, 405 U.S. 330 (1972).

41 Amendment to Complaint, Wallace v. Brewer, U.S. District Court, Middle District of Alabama, Southern Regional Office Files, ACLU Papers.

42 Motion to Intervene, Nance v. Jackson, U.S. District Court, Middle District of Alabama, Southern Regional Office Files, ACLU Papers.

43 *Wallace v. Brewer*, 315 F. Supp. 431 (1970), 456.

44 *Nance v. Jackson*, 56 F.R.D. 463 (1972).

45 "State Sovereignty Commission Exempt from Public Disclosure," *Selma Times-Journal*, Jun 12, 1973, 2; "Sovereignty Panel's Budget Secret," *Anniston Star*, Jun 12, 1973, 1; "Secret Agency Deleted in Bill," *Anniston Star*, Aug 10, 1973, 16; "District 18 (Madison)," *Montgomery Advertiser*, Mar 3, 1974, 55; "Democratic Leader Dies," *Anniston Star*, Aug 16, 1975, 5.

46 "ACLU Suit Challenges State Peace Commission," *Montgomery Advertiser*, Sep 9, 1975, 15; "Suitts Welcomes Baxley's Offer to Join in Suit," *Alabama Journal*, Sep 9, 1975, 9; "City Attorney in ACLU Suit," *Montgomery Advertiser*, Oct 1, 1975, 36; "ACLU Motion Opposes Slowdown In Suit Against Peace Commission," *Montgomery Advertiser*, Oct 9, 1975, 17; "Judge Impounds Records, Orders Peace Panel to Cease Operations," *Alabama Journal*, Apr 28, 1976, 1; Bauer, "Domestic Anti-Communism in Alabama," 130–131. In a deposition in 1970, Strickland stated his agency kept "hundreds of files," but few were there in 1976. See "Brief of Attorney General McDonald Gallion," *Wallace v. Brewer*, Southern Regional Office Files, ACLU Papers. The author was the named plaintiff in the Peace Commission suit. See *Suitts v. Alabama Commission to Preserve the Peace*, C.A. No. 75–331-N, U.S. District Court, Middle District of Alabama, 1975 (unpublished).

47 *Congressional Records*, 91st Congress, June 17, 1970, 20199–20200; and 94th Congress, June 4, 1975, 16916–16917.

48 Carter, *The Politics of Rage*, 417; "New Voting Plan Readied for '74," *Anniston Star*, Oct 10, 1973, 28.

49 Jack Drake email to author, May 15, 2020; Kenneth Riech, "Ala. Democrats Act to Bring Blacks into State Committee," *Washington Post*, Feb 1, 1970, A-2.

50 "Former Director Claims Peace Probes Justified," *Montgomery Advertiser*, May 25, 1976, 1; Bauer, "Domestic Anti-Communism in Alabama," 133–135.

51 See *Sims v. Amos*, 365 F. Supp. 215 (1973); *Burton v. Hobbie*, 561 F. Supp. 1029 (1983).

52 "Wallace Capture 4th Term as Governor of Alabama," *New York Times*, Nov 3, 1982, A-22; Steve Suitts "Rendering Wallace," *Southern Changes*, vol. 17, no. 3–4, 1995, 2; Tullos, *Alabama Getaway*, 119–124, 126, 264.

53 Randall Williams, "In Wallace's Wake—New Demagoguery for the Eighties," *Southern Changes*, vol. 8, no. 3, 1986, 10–12; Tullos, *Alabama Getaway*, 21–23, 136–144; City of *Mobile v. Bolden*, 446 US 55 (1980); Reginald Stuart, "Voting Rights Backers Assail Reagan's Stand," *New York Times*, Nov 8, 1981, 22; *Voting Rights Act Extension*, Report of the Committee on the Judiciary, United States Senate, on S. 1992, 97th Congress, May 25, 1982.

54 Allen Tullos, "Crackdown in the Black Belt," *Southern Changes*, vol. 7, no. 1, 1985, 1–5.

55 Allen Tullos, "Crackdown in the Black Belt: Not-So-Simple Justice," *Southern Changes*, vol. 7, no. 2, 1985, 2–11; "Marion Three Cleared of Vote Fraud Charges," *Montgomery Advertiser*, Jul 6, 1985, 1; "Mistakes by Prosecution Aided Marion Three, Attorney Says," *Montgomery Advertiser*, Jul 7, 1985, 1; Randall Williams, "Crackdown in the Black Belt: On to Greene County," *Southern Changes*, vol. 7, no. 3, 1985, 2–5.

56 Steve Suitts, "States' Rights Resurgent: The Attack on the Voting Rights Act," *Southern Spaces*, Aug 29, 2013; James Blacksher and Lani Guinier, "Free at Last: Rejecting Equal Sovereignty and Restoring the Constitutional Right to Vote: Shelby County v. Holder," 8 *Harvard Law & Policy Review*. 39 (2014). In *Dred Scott v. Sandford*, 60 US 393 (1857), 527, the Chief Justice wrote: "the citizen of each State secures his equality through the equality of his State, by virtue of that great fundamental condition of the Union— the equality of the States."

57 Steve Suitts, "Voting Rights, the Supreme Court, and the Persistence of Southern History."

58 See Burton and Derfner, *Justice Deferred*, 268–273, 283–286; Alan G. Pike, "Voting Rights and Southern Legislatures Post-Shelby County v. Holder," *Southern Spaces*, July 10, 2013; Steve Suitts, "Undoing the Voting Rights Act," *Southern Spaces*, Jul 12, 2921.

59 "Alabama's Republican Secretary Of State Calls Voting A 'Privilege,'" *Huffington Post*, Nov. 3, 2016; Carol Anderson, *One Person, No Vote: How Voter Suppression Is Destroying Our Democracy* (New York: Bloomsbury Publishing, 2018), chapters 4 and 5; "Voting Laws Roundup: December 2021," Brennen Center for Justice.

60 Steve Suitts, "Undoing the Voting Rights Act." At least one scholar suggests that Arizona's own early efforts to advance white supremacy in that state might be explained by the fact that a large number of former Southerners served in the state legislature. See Mary Melcher, "'This Is Not Right': Rural Arizona Women Challenge Segregation and Ethnic Division, 1925–1950," *Frontiers: A Journal of Women Studies*, 20, no. 2

(1999): 198–199.

61 *Merrill v. Milligan*, 142 S. Ct. 879 (2022); Application Reply of Applicants John Merrill, Feb 2, 2022, 32 and Reply of Appellants/petitioners John H. Merrill, Alabama Secretary of State, 24, 2022, 41–42, SCOTUSblog, https://www.scotusblog.com. Also, see Linda Greenhouse, "John Roberts's Long Game: Is This the End of the Voting Rights Act?" *Atlantic*, Oct 2022; Merrill v. Milligan, No. 21-1086 and 21-1087, Supreme Court of the United States, June 8, 2023.

62 Freeman W, Pollard, "The Transition of Political Culture in Alabama," PhD diss. (Indiana University, 1981), 138.

63 See Dan T. Carter, *From George Wallace to Newt Gingrich: Race in the Conservative Counterrevolution, 1963–1994* (Baton Rouge: Louisiana State University Press, 1996); Joseph Crespino, *Strom Thurmond's America* (New York: Hill and Wang, 2012); Geoffrey Kabaservice, *Rule and Ruin: The Downfall of Moderation and the Destruction of the Republican Party, from Eisenhower to the Tea Party* (New York: Oxford University Press, 2012), 363–388; Doug McAdam and Karina Kloos, *Deeply Divided: Racial Politics and Social Movements in Post-War America* (New York: Oxford University Press, 2014), 2–29; Jason Morgan Ward, *Defending White Democracy: The Making of a Segregationist Movement and the Remaking of Racial Politics, 1936–1965* (Chapel Hill: University of North Carolina Press, 2011), 179–183.

64 See Heather Cox Richardson, *How the South Won the Civil War: Oligarchy, Democracy, and the Continuing Fight for the Soul of America* (New York: Oxford University Press, 2020); Dan T. Carter, "What Donald Trump Owes George Wallace," *New York Times*, Jan. 10, 2016, SR-6.

65 See Richard L. Hasen, "The Supreme Court Puts Democracy at Risk," *New York Times*, Jul 3, 2021, A-19; Ezra Klein, *Why We're Polarized* (New York: Avid Reader Press/Simon & Schuster, 2020); Philip Bump, "By 2040, Two-thirds of Americans will be Represented by 30 percent of the Senate," *Washington Post*, Nov. 28, 2017; Laura Bronner and Nathaniel Rakich, "Advantage, GOP: Why Democrats Have to Win Large Majorities in Order to Govern While Republicans Don't Need Majorities at All," FiveThirtyEight, Apr 29, 2021; Steven Levitsky and Daniel Ziblatt, "End Minority Rule," *New York Times*, Oct 25, 2020, SR-6.

66 Allen Tullos, "Selma Bridge: Always Under Construction," *Southern Spaces*, Jul 28, 2008.

Index

B

C

Y

Z